General History of Africa · V

Africa from the
Sixteenth to the Eighteenth Century

Abridged Edition

Unabridged Paperback Edition

The abridged edition of
THE UNESCO GENERAL HISTORY OF AFRICA
is published by the following publishers

In Ghana, Sierra Leone,
the Gambia and Cameroon by
F. Reimmer Book Services
P.O. Box CT3499
Cantonments – Accra, Ghana
In Kenya by
EAEP
P.O. Box 45314
Nairobi, Kenya
In Nigeria by
Heinemann Nigeria
P.O. Box 6205
Ibadan, Nigeria
In South Africa, Namibia, Botswana,
Lesotho and Swaziland by
David Philip Publishers
P.O. Box 23408
Claremont 7735, South Africa
In Tanzania by
Tanzania Publishing House
P.O. Box 2138
Dar es Salaam, Tanzania
In Uganda by
Fountain Publishers
P.O. Box 488
Kampala, Uganda
In Zambia by
UNZA Press
P.O. Box 32379
Lusaka, Zambia
In Zimbabwe,
Botswana, Swaziland and Malawi by
Baobab Books
P.O Box 1559
Harare, Zimbabwe
In the United States of America and Canada by
The University of California Press
2120 Berkeley Way
Berkeley, California 94720
And in the United Kingdom, Europe
and the rest of the world by
James Currey Publishers   and
73 Botley Road   UNESCO Publishing
Oxford OX2 0BS   7 Place de Fontenoy, 75700 Paris

International Scientific Committee for the Drafting of a General History of Africa (UNESCO)

General History of Africa · V

Africa from the
Sixteenth to the Eighteenth Century

EDITOR B. A. OGOT

Abridged Edition

JAMES CURREY • CALIFORNIA • UNESCO

First published 1999 by the
United Nations Educational, Scientific
and Cultural Organization
7 Place de Fontenoy, 75700 Paris

James Currey Ltd
73 Botley Road
Oxford OX2 0BS

and
University of California Press
2120 Berkeley
California 94720, United States of America

ISBN (UNESCO): 92-3-102497-3
ISBN (UC Press): 0-520-06700-2

British Library Cataloguing in Publication Data
UNESCO general history of Africa. – Abridged ed.
  Vol. 5: Africa from the sixteenth to the eighteenth century.
  1. Africa – History – To 1884
  I. Ogot, Bethwell A.   II. UNESCO.   III. General history of Africa
960.2'2

ISBN 0-85255-095-2

**Library of Congress Cataloging-in-Publication Data
is available on request from the Library of Congress**

Typeset in Monotype Bembo 11/11 pt by Long House, Cumbria, UK,
and printed in Britain by Villiers Publications, London N3

Contents

Preface

AMADOU-MAHTAR M'BOW
Former Director-General of UNESCO (1974–87)

For a long time, all kinds of myths and prejudices concealed the true history of Africa from the world at large. African societies were looked upon as societies that could have no history. In spite of important work done by such pioneers as Leo Frobenius, Maurice Delafosse and Arturo Labriola, as early as the first decades of this century, a great many non-African experts could not rid themselves of certain preconceptions and argued that the lack of written sources and documents made it impossible to engage in any scientific study of such societies.

Although the *Iliad* and *Odyssey* were rightly regarded as essential sources for the history of ancient Greece, African oral tradition, the collective memory of peoples which holds the thread of many events marking their lives, was rejected as worthless. In writing the history of a large part of Africa, the only sources used were from outside the continent, and the final product gave a picture not so much of the paths actually taken by the African peoples as of those that the authors thought they must have taken. Since the European Middle Ages were often used as a yardstick, modes of production, social relations and political institutions were visualized only by reference to the European past.

In fact, there was a refusal to see Africans as the creators of original cultures which flowered and survived over the centuries in patterns of their own making and which historians are unable to grasp unless they forgo their prejudices and rethink their approach.

Furthermore, the continent of Africa was hardly ever looked upon as a historical entity. On the contrary, emphasis was laid on everything likely to lend credence to the idea that a split had existed, from time immemorial, between a 'white Africa' and a 'black Africa', each unaware of the other's existence. The Sahara was often presented as an impenetrable space preventing any intermingling of ethnic groups and peoples or any exchange of goods, beliefs, customs and ideas between the societies that had grown up on either side of the desert. Hermetic frontiers were drawn between the civilizations of Ancient Egypt and Nubia and those of the peoples south of the Sahara.

It is true that the history of Africa north of the Sahara has been more closely linked with that of the Mediterranean basin than has the history of sub-Saharan

Africa, but it is now widely recognized that the various civilizations of the African continent, for all their differing languages and cultures, represent, to a greater or lesser degree, the historical offshoots of a set of peoples and societies united by bonds centuries old.

Another phenomenon that did great disservice to the objective study of the African past was the appearance, with the slave trade and colonization, of racial stereotypes that bred contempt and lack of understanding and became so deep-rooted that they distorted even the basic concepts of historiography. From the time when the notions of 'white' and 'black' were used as generic labels by the colonialists, who were regarded as superior, the colonized Africans had to struggle against both economic and psychological enslavement. Africans were identifiable by the colour of their skin, they had become a kind of merchandise, they were earmarked for hard labour and eventually in the minds of those dominating them, they came to symbolize an imaginary and allegedly inferior 'Negro' race. This pattern of spurious identification relegated the history of the African peoples in many minds to the rank of ethno-history, in which appreciation of the historical and cultural facts was bound to be warped.

The situation has changed significantly since the end of the Second World War and in particular since the African countries became independent and began to take an active part in the life of the international community and in the mutual exchanges that are its *raison d'être*. An increasing number of historians has endeavoured to tackle the study of Africa with a more rigorous, objective and open-minded outlook by using – with all due precautions – actual African sources. In exercising their right to take the historical initiative, Africans themselves have felt a deep-seated need to re-establish the historical authenticity of their societies on solid foundations.

In this context, the importance of the eight-volume *General History of Africa*, which Unesco is publishing, speaks for itself.

The experts from many countries working on this project began by laying down the theoretical and methodological basis for the *History*. They have been at pains to call in question the over-simplifications arising from a linear and restrictive conception of world history and to re-establish the true facts wherever necessary and possible. They have endeavoured to highlight the historical data that give a clearer picture of the evolution of the different peoples of Africa in their specific socio-cultural setting.

To tackle this huge task, made all the more complex and difficult by the vast range of sources and the fact that documents were widely scattered, Unesco has had to proceed by stages. The first stage, from 1965 to 1969, was devoted to gathering documentation and planning the work. Operational assignments were conducted in the field and included campaigns to collect oral traditions, the creation of regional documentation centres for oral traditions, the collection of unpublished manuscripts in Arabic and Ajami (African languages written in Arabic script), the compilation of archival inventories and the preparation of the *Guide to the Sources of the History of Africa*, culled from the archives and libraries of the countries of Europe and later published in eleven volumes. In addition, meetings were organized to enable experts from Africa and other continents to discuss questions of methodology and lay down the broad lines for the project after careful examination of the available sources.

The second stage, which lasted from 1969 to 1971, was devoted to shaping the *History* and linking its different parts. The purpose of the international meetings of experts held in Paris in 1969 and Addis Ababa in 1970 was to study and define the problems involved in drafting and publishing the *History*: presentation in eight volumes, the principal edition in English, French and Arabic, translation into African languages such as Kiswahili, Hausa, Fulfulde, Yoruba or Lingala, prospective versions in German, Russian, Portuguese, Spanish and Chinese, as well as abridged editions designed for a wide African and international public.[1]

The third stage has involved actual drafting and publication. This began with the appointment of the 39-member International Scientific Committee, two-thirds African and one-third non-African, which assumes intellectual responsibility for the *History*.

The method used is interdisciplinary and is based on a multifaceted approach and a wide variety of sources. The first among these is archaeology, which holds many of the keys to the history of African cultures and civilizations. Thanks to archaeology, it is now acknowledged that Africa was very probably the cradle of mankind and the scene – in the Neolithic period – of one of the first technological revolutions in history. Archaeology has also shown that Egypt was the setting for one of the most brilliant ancient civilizations of the world. But another very important source is oral tradition, which, after being long despised, has now emerged as an invaluable instrument for discovering the history of Africa, making it possible to follow the movements of its different peoples in both space and time, to understand the African vision of the world from the inside and to grasp the original features of the values on which the cultures and institutions of the continent are based.

We are indebted to the International Scientific Committee in charge of this *General History of Africa*, and to its Rapporteur and the editors and authors of the various volumes and chapters, for having shed a new light on the African past in its authentic and all-encompassing form and for having avoided any dogmatism in the study of essential issues. Among these issues we might cite: the slave trade, that 'endlessly bleeding wound', which was responsible for one of the cruellest mass deportations in the history of mankind, which sapped the African continent of its life-blood while contributing significantly to the economic and commercial expansion of Europe; colonization, with all the effects it had on population, economics, psychology and culture; relations between Africa south of the Sahara and the Arab world; and, finally, the process

1 At the time of going to press Volume I has been published in English, French, Arabic, Spanish, Portuguese, Chinese, Italian and Korean; Volume II in English, French, Arabic, Spanish, Portuguese, Chinese, Italian and Korean; Volume III in English, French, Arabic and Spanish; Volume IV in English, French, Arabic, Spanish and Chinese; Volume V in English and Arabic; Volume VI in English, French and Arabic; Volume VII in English, French, Arabic, Spanish, Portuguese and Chinese; Volume VIII in English and French.

of decolonization and nation-building which mobilized the intelligence and passion of people still alive and sometimes still active today. All these issues have been broached with a concern for honesty and rigour which is not the least of the *History*'s merits. By taking stock of our knowledge of Africa, putting forward a variety of viewpoints on African cultures and offering a new reading of history, the *History* has the signal advantage of showing up the light and shade and of openly portraying the differences of opinion that may exist between scholars.

By demonstrating the inadequacy of the methodological approaches which have long been used in research on Africa, this *History* calls for a new and careful study of the twofold problem areas of historiography and cultural identity, which are united by links of reciprocity. Like any historical work of value, the *History* paves the way for a great deal of further research on a variety of topics.

It is for this reason that the International Scientific Committee, in close collaboration with Unesco, decided to embark on additional studies in an attempt to go deeper into a number of issues that will permit a clearer understanding of certain aspects of the African past. The findings being published in the series *Unesco Studies and Documents – General History of Africa*[2] will prove a useful supplement to the *History,* as will the works planned on aspects of national or subregional history.

The *General History* sheds light both on the historical unity of Africa and on its relations with the other continents, particularly the Americas and the Caribbean. For a long time, the creative manifestations of the descendants of Africans in the Americas were lumped together by some historians as a heterogeneous collection of 'Africanisms'. Needless to say, this is not the attitude of the authors of the *History*, in which the resistance of the slaves shipped to America, the constant and massive participation of the descendants of Africans in the struggles for the initial independence of America and in national liberation movements, are rightly perceived for what they were: vigorous assertions of identity, which helped forge the universal concept of mankind. Although the phenomenon may vary in different places, it is now quite clear that ways of feeling, thinking, dreaming and acting in certain nations of the western hemisphere have been marked by their African heritage. The cultural inheritance of Africa is visible every where, from the southern United States to northern Brazil, across the Caribbean and on the Pacific seaboard. In certain places it even underpins the cultural identity of some of the most important elements of the population.

---

2. The following twelve volumes have already been published in this series: *The peopling of ancient Egypt and the deciphering of Meroitic script; The African slave trade from the fifteenth to the nineteenth century; Historical relations across the Indian Ocean; The historiography of Southern Africa; The decolonization of Africa, Southern Africa and the Horn of Africa; African ethnonyms and toponyms; Historical and socio-cultural relations between black Africa and the Arab world from 1935 to the present; The methodology of contemporary African history; Africa and the Second World War; The educational process and historiography in Africa; Libya Antiqua; The role of African Student Movements in the political and social evolution of Africa from 1900–1975.*

The *History* also clearly brings out Africa's relations with southern Asia across the Indian Ocean and the African contributions to other civilizations through mutual exchanges.

I am convinced that the efforts of the peoples of Africa to conquer or strengthen their independence, secure their development and assert their cultural characteristics must be rooted in historical awareness renewed, keenly felt and taken up by each succeeding generation. My own background, the experience I gained as a teacher and as chairman, from the early days of independence, of the first commission set up to reform history and geography curricula in some of the countries of West and Central Africa, taught me how necessary it was for the education of young people and for the information of the public at large to have a history book produced by scholars with inside knowledge of the problems and hopes of Africa and with the ability to apprehend the continent in its entirety.

For all these reasons, Unesco's goal will be to ensure that this *General History of Africa* is widely disseminated in a large number of languages and is used as a basis for producing children's books, school textbooks and radio and television programmes. Young people, whether schoolchildren or students, and adults in Africa and elsewhere will thus be able to form a truer picture of the African continent's past and the factors that explain it, as well as a fairer understanding of its cultural heritage and its contribution to the general progress of mankind. The *History* should thus contribute to improved international co-operation and stronger solidarity among peoples in their aspirations to justice, progress and peace. This is, at least, my most cherished hope.

It remains for me to express my deep gratitude to the members of the International Scientific Committee, the Rapporteur, the different volume editors, the authors and all those who have collaborated in this tremendous undertaking. The work they have accomplished and the contribution they have made plainly go to show how people from different backgrounds, but all imbued with the same spirit of goodwill and enthusiasm in the service of universal truth, can, within the international framework provided by Unesco, bring to fruition a project of considerable scientific and cultural import. My thanks also go to the organizations and governments whose generosity has made it possible for Unesco to publish this *History* in different languages and thus ensure that it will have the worldwide impact it deserves and thereby serve the international community as a whole.

Description of the Project

B. A. OGOT[1]
Former President, International Scientific Committee for the Drafting of a General History of Africa (1978–83)

The General Conference of Unesco at its 16th Session instructed the Director-General to undertake the drafting of a *General History of Africa*. The enormous task of implementing the project was entrusted to an International Scientific Committee which was established by the Executive Board in 1970. This Committee, under the Statutes adopted by the Executive Board of Unesco in 1971, is composed of thirty-nine members (two-thirds of whom are African and one-third non-African) serving in their personal capacity and appointed by the Director-General of Unesco for the duration of the Committee's mandate. The first task of the Committee was to define the principal characteristics of the work. These were defined at the first session of the Committee as follows:

(a) Although aiming at the highest possible scientific level, the *History* does not seek to be exhaustive and is a work of synthesis avoiding dogmatism. In many respects, it is a statement of problems showing the present state of knowledge and the main trends in research, and it does not hesitate to show divergencies of views where these exist. In this way, it prepares the ground for future work.

(b) Africa is considered in this work as a totality. The aim is to show the historical relationships between the various parts of the continent, too frequently subdivided in works published to date. Africa's historical connections with the other continents receive due attention, these connections being analysed in terms of mutual exchanges and multilateral influences, bringing out, in its appropriate light, Africa's contribution to the history of mankind.

(c) The *General History of Africa* is, in particular, a history of ideas and civilizations, societies and institutions. It is based on a wide variety of sources, including oral tradition and art forms.

(d) The *History* is viewed essentially from the inside. Although a scholarly work, it is also, in large measure, a faithful reflection of the way in which African authors view their own civilization. While prepared in an international framework and drawing to the full on the present stock of scientific knowledge, it should also be

---

1. During the Sixth Plenary Session of the International Scientific Commitee for the Drafting of the General History of Africa (Brazzaville, August 1983), an election of the new Bureau was held and Professor Ogot was replaced by Professor Albert Adu Boahen.

a vitally important element in the recognition of the African heritage and should bring out the factors making for unity in the continent. This effort to view things from within is the novel feature of the project and should, in addition to its scientific quality, give it great topical significance. By showing the true face of Africa, the *History* could, in an era absorbed in economic and technical struggles, offer a particular conception of human values.

The Committee has decided to present the work covering over 3 million years of African history in eight volumes, each containing about eight hundred pages of text with illustrations, photographs, maps and line drawings.

A chief editor, assisted if necessary by one or two assistant editors, is responsible for the preparation of each volume. The editors are elected by the Committee either from among its members or from outside by a two-thirds majority. They are responsible for preparing the volumes in accordance with the decisions and plans adopted by the Committee. On scientific matters, they are accountable to the Committee or, between two sessions of the Committee, to its Bureau for the contents of the volumes, the final version of the texts, the illustrations and, in general, for all scientific and technical aspects of the *History*. The Bureau ultimately approves the final manuscript. When it considers the manuscript ready for publication, it transmits it to the Director-General of Unesco. Thus the Committee, or the Bureau between Committee sessions, remains fully in charge of the project.

Each volume consists of some 30 chapters. Each chapter is the work of a principal author assisted, if necessary, by one or two collaborators. The authors are selected by the Committee on the basis of their curricula vitae. Preference is given to African authors, provided they have requisite qualifications. Special effort is also made to ensure, as far as possible, that all regions of the continent, as well as other regions having historical or cultural ties with Africa, are equitably represented among the authors.

When the editor of a volume has approved texts of chapters, they are then sent to all members of the Committee for criticism. In addition, the text of the volume editor is submitted for examination to a Reading Committee, set up within the International Scientific Committee on the basis of the members' fields of competence. The Reading Committee analyses the chapters from the standpoint of both substance and form. The Bureau then gives final approval to the manuscripts.

Such a seemingly long and involved procedure has proved necessary, since it provides the best possible guarantee of the scientific objectivity of the *General History of Africa*. There have, in fact, been instances when the Bureau has rejected manuscripts or insisted on major revisions or even reassigned the drafting of a chapter to another author. Occasionally, specialists in a particular period of history or in a particular question are consulted to put the finishing touches to a volume.

The work will be published first in a hard-cover edition in English, French and Arabic, and later in paperback editions in the same languages. An abridged version in English will serve as a basis for translation into African languages. The Committee has chosen Kiswahili and Hausa as the first African languages into which the work will be translated.

Also, every effort will be made to ensure publication of the *General History of Africa* in other languages of wide international currency such as Chinese, Portugese, Russian German, Italian, Spanish, Japanese.

It is thus evident that this is a gigantic task which constitutes an immense challenge to African historians and to the scholarly community at large, as well as to Unesco under whose auspices the work is being done. For the writing of a continental history of Africa, covering the last three million years, using the highest canons of scholarship and involving, as it must do, scholars drawn from diverse countries, cultures, ideologies and historical traditions, is surely a complex undertaking. It constitutes a continental, international and interdisciplinary project of great proportions.

In conclusion, I would like to underline the significance of this work for Africa and for the world. At a time when the peoples of Africa are striving towards unity and greater co-operation in shaping their individual destinies, a proper understanding of Africa's past, with an awareness of common ties among Africans and between Africa and other continents, should not only be a major contribution towards mutual understanding among the people of the earth, but also a source of knowledge of a cultural heritage that belongs to all mankind.

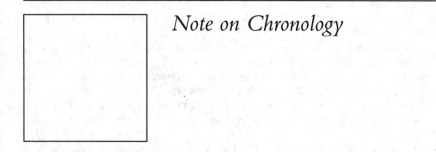

Note on Chronology

It has been agreed to adopt the following method for writing dates. With regard to prehistory, dates may be written in two different ways.

One way is by reference to the present era, that is, dates BP (before present), the reference year being +1950; all dates are negative in relation to + 1950.

The other way is by reference to the beginning of the Christian era. Dates are represented in relation to the Christian era by a simple + or − sign before the date. When referring to centuries, the terms BC and AD are replaced by 'before the Christian era' and 'of the Christian era'.

Some examples are as follows:
(i)   2300 BP = −350
(ii)   2900 BC = −2900
         AD 1800   = +1800
(iii)   Fifth century BC = Fifth century before the Christian era
         Third century AD = Third century of the Christian era.

Members of the International Scientific Committee for the Drafting of a General History of Africa

The dates cited below refer to dates of membership.

Professor J. F. Ade Ajayi
(Nigeria), from 1971
Editor Volume VI

Professor F. A. Albuquerque Mourão
(Brazil), from 1975

Professor D. Birmingham
(UK), from 1985

Professor A. A. Boahen
(Ghana), from 1971
Editor Volume VII

The late H. E. Boubou Hama
(Niger), 1971–8 (resigned 1978);
deceased 1982

Dr (Mrs) Mutumba M. Bull
(Zambia), from 1971

The late Professor D. Chanaiwa
(Zimbabwe), from 1975;
deceased 1993

Professor P. D. Curtin
(USA), from 1975

The late Professor J. Devisse
(France), from 1971;
deceased 1996

Professor M. Difuila
(Angola), from 1978

The late Professor Cheikh Anta Diop
(Senegal), 1971–86; deceased 1986

Professor H. Djait
(Tunisia), from 1975

The late H. E. M. El Fasi
(Morocco), from 1971; deceased 1991
Editor Volume III

Professor J. D. Fage
(UK), 1971–81 (resigned)

The late Professor J. L. Franco
(Cuba), from 1971; deceased 1989

The late Mr M. H. I. Galaal
(Somalia), 1971–81; deceased 1981

Professor Dr V. L. Grottanelli
(Italy), from 1971

The late Professor E. Haberland
(Germany), from 1971; deceased

Dr Aklilu Habte
(Ethiopia), from 1971

The late H. E. A. Hampâté Bâ
(Mali), 1971–8 (resigned); deceased
1991

Dr I. S. El-Hareir
(Libya), from 1978

Dr I. Hrbek
(Czech Republic), from 1971;
deceased 1993
Assistant Editor Volume III

Dr (Mrs) A. Jones
(Liberia), from 1971

The late Abbé Alexis Kagame
(Rwanda), 1971–81; deceased 1981

Professor I. N. Kimambo
(Tanzania), from 1971

Professor J. Ki-Zerbo
(Burkina Faso), from 1971
Editor Volume I

Mr D. Laya
(Niger), from 1979

Dr A. Letnev
(USSR), from 1971

The late Dr G. Mokhtar
(Egypt), from 1971
Editor Volume II; deceased 1998

Professor P. Mutibwa
(Uganda), from 1975

Professor L. D. Ngcongco
(Botswana), from 1971

Professor D. T. Niane
(Guinea), from 1971
Editor Volume IV

Professor T. Obenga
(People's Republic of the Congo),
from 1975

Professor Bethwell A. Ogot
(Kenya), from 1971
Editor Volume V

Professor C. Ravoajanahary
(Madagascar), from 1971

The late Professor W. Rodney
(Guyana), 1979–80; deceased 1980

The late Professor M. Shibeika
(Sudan), 1971–80; deceased 1980

Professor Y. A. Talib
(Singapore), from 1975

The late Professor A. Teixeira da Mot
(Portugal), 1978–82; deceased 1982

Mgr T. Tshibangu
(Zaire), from 1971

Professor J. Vansina
(Belgium), from 1971

The late Rt Hon. Dr E. Williams
(Trinidad and Tobago), 1976–8
(resigned 1978); deceased 1980

Professor A. A. Mazrui
(Kenya)
Editor Volume VIII,
not a member of the Committee

Professor C. Wondji
(Côte d'Ivoire)
Assistant Editor Volume VIII,
not a member of the Committee

*Secretariat of the International
Scientific Committee*
C. Wondji
Sector for Culture
Director, 'Chargé de mission'
Head of History Projects
1, rue Miollis
75015 Paris

Biographies of the authors who contributed to the main edition

The abridged version was prepared from the texts of the main version written by the following authors:

CHAPTER 1   M. Malowist (Poland): specialist in the economic and social history of the Late Middle Ages and early modern times; author of various publications and articles on the subject; former Professor of History, University of Warsaw; former member of Clare Hall, Cambridge and visiting member of the Institute for Advanced Study, Princeton; deceased.

CHAPTER 2   P. Diagne (Senegal): Doctor of Political and Economic Science; economist and linguist; author of several works on African political power and on modern Wolof grammar; currently Professor and consultant.

CHAPTER 3   J. Vansina (Belgium): specialist in African history; author of numerous works and articles on pre-colonial history of Africa; Professor of History and Anthropology, University of Wisconsin.

CHAPTER 4   J. E. Inikori (Nigeria): specialist in economic history; author of various publications and articles on the subject; Professor and Head of Department, Ahmadu Bello University, Zaria.

CHAPTER 5   J. E. Harris (USA): specialist in African diaspora; author of various publications and articles on the subject; currently Professor at Howard Univer sity, Washington DC.

CHAPTER 6   R. Vesely (Czechoslovakia): specialist in history of Egypt, diplomatics, economic problems of Arab lands in the Middle Ages; author of several works on history and diplomatic studies of the medieval period of Arab (especially Egyptian) and Islamic countries; lecturer for Arab and Islamic lands and their history at the Philosophical Faculty of Charles University, Department of Oriental and African Studies, Prague.

CHAPTER 7   Y. F. Hasan (Sudan): specialist in the history of the Sudan; author of various works on the subject; formerly Professor of History, University of Khartoum and Director of the Sudan Research Unit, University of Khartoum; at present Vice-Chancellor, University of Khartoum.

B. A. Ogot (Kenya): specialist in African history, pioneer in the techniques of oral history; author of many publications on East African history; former Director of the International Louis Leakey Memorial Institute; former Deputy Vice-Chancellor, University of Nairobi; Professor of History, Kenyatta University, Nairobi.

CHAPTER 8   M. El Fasi (Morocco): author of a number of works (in Arabic and French) dealing with linguistic history and literary criticism; former Vice-Chancellor of the Ḳarāwiyyīn University, Fez.

CHAPTER 9   M. H. Cherif (Tunisia): specialist in North-African social and political history; author of several articles on North-African history; University Professor and Dean, Faculté des sciences humaines et sociales, Tunis.

CHAPTER 10   B. Barry (Senegal): Doctor in History; author of numerous works on Waalo, Senegambia and Futa Jallon; former Secretary-General of the Association des historiens africains; now teacher at the Faculty of Arts, Université Cheikh Anta Diop, Dakar.

CHAPTER 11   M. Abitbol (Israel): specialist in Nigerian Sudan; author of works on the history of the Sudan; Senior researcher at the Hebrew University of Jerusalem.

CHAPTER 12   M. Izard (France): specialist in the pre-colonial history of the Mossi kingdoms (Burkina Faso); anthropologist and historian; author of numerous publications and articles, especially on the ancient kingdom of Yatenga; Senior Researcher at the Centre national de la recherche scientifique (Laboratory of Social Anthropology), Paris.

J. Ki-Zerbo (Burkina Faso): specialist in the methodology of African history; author of a number of works dealing with Black Africa and its history; Professor of History, University of Dakar.

CHAPTER 13   C. Wondji (Côte d'Ivoire): specialist in the modern and contemporary history of Africa, author of numerous works on African cultures and the history of Côte d'Ivoire; formerly Head of the Department of History, Faculté des lettres de l'Université nationale de Côte d'Ivoire (Abidjan) and Deputy Director of the Institut d'art et d'archéologie, University of Abidjan; at present Councillor at the Permanent Delegation of Côte d'Ivoire at UNESCO, Paris.

CHAPTER 14 A. A. Boahen (Ghana): specialist in West African history; author of numerous publications and articles on African history; former Professor and Head of the Department of History, and now Emeritus Professor, University of Ghana.

CHAPTER 15 E. J. Alagoa (Nigeria): specialist in African history and historiography; author of various studies of the Ijo, the techniques and methodology of oral tradition and archaeology; Professor of History, University of Port Harcourt.

CHAPTER 16 D. Laya (Niger): specialist in West African cultures; sociologist; author of works on the subject; Director of the Centre d'études linguistiques et historiques par tradition orale (CELHTO), Niamey.

CHAPTER 17 B. Barkindo (Nigeria): specialist in state formation and inter-state relations in the Chad basin; author of numerous works on the subject; Reader in History, Bayero University, Kano.

CHAPTER 18 E. M'Bokolo (Zaire): specialist in the history of Black Africa; author of numerous works on the subject; Senior Researcher at the Ecole des hautes études en Sciences sociales (EHESS); lecturer at the Institut d'etudes politiques (IEP), Paris; producer at Radio France Internationale.

CHAPTER 19 J. Vansina.
T. Obenga (People's Republic of Congo): specialist in African languages; author of a number of articles on African history and of works on Africa in the ancient world; formerly Professor at the Faculty of Letters of Marien N'Gouabi University, Brazzaville; at present Director-General of the Centre international des civilisations bantu (CICIBA), Libreville.

CHAPTER 20 Ndaywel è Nziem (Zaire): specialist in the history of Central Africa; author of works on the subject; teaches History at the University of Kinshasa and at the Institut pedagogique national; Director General of the Bibliothèque nationale du Zaire.

CHAPTER 21 K. M. Phiri (Malawi): specialist in the history of Malawi, and of Central and Southern Africa; formerly lecturer and senior lecturer in History, University of Malawi; at present Associate Professor in History, University of Malawi.
O. J. M. Kalinga (Malawi): specialist in the history of the Lake Malawi region; author of works on the subject; Professor of History, National University of Lesotho.
H. H. K. Bhila (Zimbabwe): specialist in the history of South-Eastern Africa; author of works on Southern Africa; former Chairman of the Department of History, University of Zimbabwe; at present Deputy Secretary to Parliament of Zimbabwe.

CHAPTER 22 H. H. K. Bhila.

CHAPTER 23 D. Denoon (UK): specialist in Southern and East Africa; author of works on the subject; formerly visiting lecturer at the University of Ibadan; currently Professor at the Australian National University, Canberra.

CHAPTER 24 E. Haberland (Germany): specialist in pre-colonial Ethiopia and West Africa; author of works on Ethiopia, Director of the Frobenius Institute. Frankfurt; Professor of the Chair of Ethnology and African history, University of Frankfurt; Director, Centre of African Studies in Frankfurt.

CHAPTER 25 A. I. Salim (Kenya): specialist in East African history; author of many articles on the Swahili-speaking peoples; Professor and currently Chairman, Department of History, University of Nairobi.

CHAPTER 26 J. B. Webster (Canada): specialist in pre-colonial history, with special attention to climate; author of works on Acholi and Iteso history as well as *Chronology, Migration and Drought in Interlacustrine Africa;* formerly Professor and Head of History at Makerere and the University of Malawi; now Professor of African history, Dalhousie University.
B. A. Ogot.
J. P. Chrétien (France): specialist in the history of Burundi; author of numerous works on the Great Lakes kingdoms and German East Africa; Senior Researcher at the Centre de recherches africaines (CRA), University of Paris I.

CHAPTER 27 W. R. Ochieng' (Kenya): specialist in the history of Kenya; author of numerous works on the subject; formerly Senior Lecturer in Kenyan history, Kenyatta University College, Nairobi; currently at Moi University, Eldoret, Kenya.

CHAPTER 28 R. K. Kent (USA): specialist in the history of Madagascar; author of numerous works on the subject; Professor of African History, University of California, Berkeley.

CHAPTER 29 B. A. Ogot.

1

The struggle for international trade and its implications for Africa

Introduction

In 1500 the geo-political map of the world revealed the existence of a number of major, relatively autonomous regions: the Far East, the Middle East, Europe and finally Africa, with its Mediterranean, Red Sea and Indian Ocean seaboards which were opening up to growing trade with the orient.

The period from 1500 to 1800 was to witness the establishment of a new Atlantic-oriented geo-economic system, with its triangular trading pattern linking Africa to Europe and the Americas. With the opening up of the Atlantic trade, Europe – particularly Western Europe – gained ascendancy over the Americas and African societies.

In most European countries, the period from 1450 to 1630 saw considerable economic, political and cultural expansion. Expansion overseas reached into vast territories bordering the Atlantic and even as far as the Pacific coastline. From the beginning the African coast was one such area, but the situation in North Africa differed from that in the sub-Saharan regions. The Mediterranean was the scene of bitter rivalry between, on the one hand, Spain, Portugal, France and Muslim North Africa and, on the other, the Ottoman empire which was becoming ever more influential. In 1517 the Ottomans conquered Egypt. Subsequently they subjugated a large part of the Arabian peninsula and gradually established their rule over Tripoli, Tunis and Algiers. In Morocco, however, the Portuguese managed to dominate a large part of the coast as far as Agadir and Safi, while the Castilians established bases in Tlemcen and Oran.

These conquests gave the Portuguese control of some long-established and important gold- and slave-trade routes from Western Sudan through the Sahara and the Maghrib to the Mediterranean. The Europeans diverted part of this trade previously sent to the Muslim world to their own benefit, thus reducing the amount of gold reaching the Maghrib. This might explain the conquest of the Niger bend by the Moroccans in 1591, which enabled the latter to gain control of a number of gold- and slave-trade routes running from West Africa to the Maghrib and Egypt. The famous campaign of Djudar Pasha, himself a renegade of Iberian background, is a typical example

1

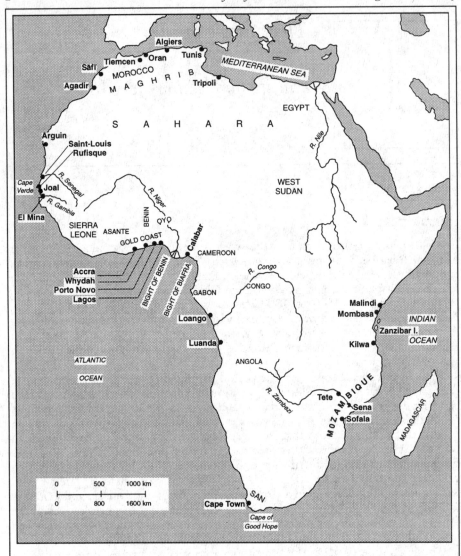

1.1 *Africa: the main points of European trade contact from the sixteenth to the eighteenth century*

of the great conquests so characteristic of the sixteenth century.

Throughout the fifteenth and the early sixteenth centuries the Portuguese established numerous trading posts on the West African coast and made the coastal population and its rulers participants in trade with the Europeans. After 1481–2 the fort at El Mina became the busiest trading post on the Gold Coast. In East Africa the Portuguese used different methods: they crushed the defences of Sofala, Mombasa and other coastal towns, installed garrisons there and raised taxes for the king of Portugal. At the same time, they tried to take over the trade in gold, ivory and metals between the coast, its hinterland and India.

In the early sixteenth century the trade at El Mina, at the mouth of the River Gambia, in Sierra Leone and in Sofala brought large profits mainly from the purchase of gold at low prices and, to a lesser extent, from the trade in slaves supplied from the hinterland. This trade initially brought Portugal great profit. The considerable inflow of African gold made it possible for John II and his successor, Manuel, to mint the *cruzado* – a high-value gold coin – and, more importantly, to expand the fleet and strengthen colonial and state administration. This latter measure opened opportunities for the aristocracy and gentry to obtain numerous prestigious and profitable offices. Trade with Africa, and subsequently with India, accelerated the development of the Portuguese trader class which had still been relatively weak in the fifteenth century. Thus Portugal might be thought to have entered upon a path of lasting economic and political expansion. However, its backward and sluggish socio-economic structure prevented this from happening. Overseas expansion necessitated large financial outlays, and the purchase of gold and slaves depended on supplying Africa with large quantities of iron, brass and copper goods, cheap textiles, silver, foodstuffs and salt. These goods were not produced in Portugal but had to be bought from foreign traders or in Bruges and, later, from the major European trade centres of the time. Furthermore, expansion of the fleet depended on the import of timber, mainly from the Baltic countries. Portugal was unable to develop its own production because of its small population and the severe competition from abroad, notably in industrial goods.

Europe's economic boom triggered a gradual rise in prices from the 1470s. During the second half of the sixteenth century this rise became enormous, affecting both agricultural products and industrial goods. The relationship between the rise in prices and the increase in Portugal's profits from overseas trade seems not to have benefited Portugal. The high expenditure associated with overseas expansion was profitable only when it was possible to buy cheap and sell dear. To do this, however, meant limiting or even excluding European competitors, and that required a strong fleet. That was a costly enterprise. By the 1470s Portugal was already engaged in armed conflict with Castile, which it eliminated from West Africa, thanks to the temporary supremacy of the Portuguese fleet and to diplomatic manoeuvres. The discovery and conquest of America turned Castile's attention away from Africa but this did not happen with other European countries which were more economically advanced than Portugal and thus more of a threat.

The Portuguese rulers, John II and Manuel, were compelled to seek support for their colonial activities among the big financiers of Italy and Germany. The King of Portugal's accounts, in Bruges and subsequently in Antwerp, revealed that the crown was heavily dependent on the major firms such as those of the Frescobaldi, the Affaitati and the Fuggers. In the first stage of expansion, the Portuguese rulers managed to monopolize the import of gold from Africa and, to a large extent, the slave trade – or at least its indirect profits.

In the mid-1520s the Portuguese encountered their first difficulties in acquiring gold, even in the region of El Mina. It seems that they were by then already unable to supply enough goods in exchange and were facing competition from their European rivals who were better placed because they did not have to import the goods they supplied to the Africans. In addition, France, England and Holland were not yet burdened with an overdeveloped administration regulating overseas trade. Their traders had the wherewithal to buy greater quantities and sell more cheaply.

The slave trade

Portugal was initially attracted to Black Africa by its gold, which had previously been exported to the Islamic countries. However, they soon discovered a second African product attractive to Europeans, namely slaves. Slaves had been exported to the Arab countries for many years from much of the continent, particularly Sudan. In the fifteenth and sixteenth centuries the Portuguese benefited from this tradition and were making regular purchases of slaves from West Africa, particularly Senegambia, which was a long-established economic partner of the Maghrib. They successfully applied the trade methods used in Senegambia, and, realizing that co-operation with local rulers and traders was the key to success, successfully got them involved in the slave trade.

The Portuguese soon abandoned any moral objections to the slave trade, believing, as did many Europeans, that it enabled blacks to attain salvation. As non-Christians remaining in their own countries, they would have been damned. It should, however, be added that black slaves appeared in Europe at a time when the trade in white slaves from the Black Sea area was almost at an end, and that from this time slave and Negro became interchangeable terms.

Throughout the fifteenth and the beginning of the sixteenth centuries the main market for 'black merchandise' was Europe, particularly Spain and the countries subject to Spanish rule, and, to a certain extent, islands in the Atlantic such as Madeira, the Canaries, the Cape Verde Islands and the island of St Thomas. The main incentive for the slave trade in these islands was the introduction of the cultivation of sugar cane and cotton. Slavery could not develop to any great extent in Europe because there was no economic reason for it. According to P. D. Curtin, the number of slaves taken from Africa by Europeans between 1451 and 1600 amounted to 274,900. Of these Europe and the Atlantic islands took about 149,000, Spanish America about 75,000 and Brazil about 50,000. These figures are characteristic of the early period of the Atlantic slave trade, before the great development of the plantation system in the New World, which sparked off a heavy demand for black labour.

The first Africans in America were brought there by the conquistadores who were their masters. They came mostly from Senegambia and either had first been brought to Europe or had been born there. They were called *ladinos* in America because they knew Spanish and Portuguese and had been at least partly influenced by the civilization of the Iberian countries. They were highly thought of, contrary to the *bozales*, who had been brought directly from Africa and were thus carriers of a very different culture.

In the fifteenth century the Portuguese had become increasingly interested in the slave trade and, in the following century, they began to seek territories that could supply them with large numbers of slaves. This was the basis for Portuguese penetration in the Congo which began in the early sixteenth century, and their subsequent conquest of Angola. The settlers on the island of St Thomas were also seeking supplies of slaves, not only for their own plantations, but also to sell to the Spanish colonies in America and also, from the end of the sixteenth century, to Portuguese Brazil. The size of Brazil's black population then was only a few thousand but the following century saw an increase in this number to 400,000–450,000 following the development of sugar-cane plantations.

The conquest of America created great problems for the Castilian crown which had to supply slaves to the colonists. However, the Royal Treasury found an abundant source of revenue in the system of licences granted to traders importing slaves for the colonists, especially as the price of the licence rose as the demand for slaves grew. Among the first to obtain licences were aristocrats close to the throne, and also big capitalists, probably because of their proposals for settlement and mining in Venezuela. Naturally, the potential slave traders sought to eliminate the costly offices of the Portuguese. For that, they had to overcome the obstacles set up by the Portuguese in Africa, while in America they had to resort to contraband as the Castilian crown permitted only those to whom it had granted licences to import slaves. But the Spanish colonists in America were permanently short of labour and were therefore willing to deal with smugglers, who unloaded their cargoes in illegal harbours.

Thus, all seemed to favour increased exports of Africans to America, although the slave trade only really boomed with the establishment of the great sugar-cane plantations. It transpired quite quickly that in Spanish America and subsequently in Brazil the Indian population could not stand the steady hard work on the plantations, whereas Africans had all the required qualities.

Thus from the early 1500s, but more particularly from 1550, Africa played a major though undesirable role as a supplier of labour and of some gold to a flourishing world economy.

But the Portuguese position was constantly deteriorating. In Morocco, they suffered severe blows from the Sa'ādī sharīfs' holy war against the infidels. In 1541 they lost Agadir and soon after were compelled through financial difficulties to give up almost all their Moroccan ports. The year 1560 witnessed the first bankruptcy of the Portuguese crown. The cost of a colonial empire, while bringing enormous profits to part of the aristocracy, the bourgeoisie and some traders, had emptied the Royal Treasury and laid an ever-increasing burden on much of the population.

Arrival of new European powers

From the 1520s the French, and from the 1550s the English, became dangerous rivals to the Portuguese in Africa; and from the late sixteenth century the Dutch were even more dangerous. Initially only individual French traders or trading companies were active. Neither the French king nor the English crown was directly involved in trade with Africa. Francis I even unsuccessfully tried to stop his subjects from making expeditions to Africa so as not to jeopardize his relations with Portugal at a time when France was in open conflict with the Spanish Habsburgs. The French presence was particularly strong in the area of Cape Verde and Senegal. The French often looted Portuguese ships at sea as they were returning from Africa with a cargo of gold or from India with goods from the Orient. By the last quarter of the sixteenth century the position of the French in Senegambia was very strong, particularly in such centres as Gorée, Portudal, Joal and Rufisque (Rio Fresco) in Wolof country. The French brought textiles from Normandy and Brittany, spirits, metal goods and firearms. The arms trade seems to have swung the balance in favour of France, as the Portuguese crown long and stubbornly prohibited the export of firearms to Africa, despite the eagerness of the local rulers to obtain them. The French bought gold and ivory, and also malaguetta pepper, hides and palm oil. The slave trade was not yet of any interest to them. By the mid-sixteenth century the French were dangerous rivals to the Portuguese on the Pepper and Gold Coasts, as they exported more goods to Africa than the Portuguese, harming them particularly in the region of El Mina. Eventually they drove the Portuguese out of the estuary of the Senegal and the Gambia, only to be pushed out in turn by the English at the end of the sixteenth century.

English expansion in Africa in the sixteenth century was similar to that of the French. They began by establishing solid economic relations with Morocco, after the departure of the Portuguese in 1541. Between 1550 and 1565 English trading companies sent several expeditions, reports of which have survived. They explored the coasts of West Africa as far as the Gulf of Benin where they bought gold, hides and a few slaves. Portuguese accounts show that by the end of the sixteenth century the English were in contact with the population of the Gold Coast, but were little interested in the slave trade. By the end of the century their position was very strong on the fringes of Senegambia, from where they had ousted both the Portuguese and the French. In 1588 the first English company for trading with Guinea was established mainly by merchants from London and Exeter. There is no evidence that this company developed to any great extent. Possibly, at the end of the sixteenth century, the English found that looting Castilian ships on the waters of the Atlantic was more profitable than trading with Africa.

It was at exactly this time that the Dutch made their appearance on the coast of the African continent. They were at war with Spain and treated Portugal, which was then ruled by Philip II, as an enemy. The huge capital amassed by their traders and the strength of their fleet made it possible for them to expand in India and Africa. Between 1593 and 1607 some 200 ships set out for Africa from Holland. In 1594 and 1595 the Dutch came to Gorée, and a few years later they reached Benin, where they bought cotton goods and cowrie shells which they traded for gold and silver on the Gold Coast. In 1611 they built Fort Nassau (Mouri) on the Gold Coast, their first fortified trading post on the West African coast. They also developed trade with the Accra region. They exported copper and tin ware, cheap textiles, spirits, weapons, various adornments, things in everyday use and even spectacles which enjoyed varying popularity. They also imported sugar from the island of St Thomas and transported the semi-finished product to their refineries in Amsterdam.

By 1617 the Dutch were so strong in Senegambia that they were a dominant force on the island of Gorée and had supplanted not only the Portuguese but also the English and French in Joal, Portudal and Rufisque. They retained this strong position for over 50 years. At the same time their ships visited the coasts of the Congo and Angola. The Dutch, like the English and the French, were initially little interested in the slave trade. But things changed at the beginning of the sixteenth century when the Dutch began to purchase slaves in El Mina, Accra, Arda and Benin and also Calabar, Gabon and Cameroon. These slaves were sold in exchange for sugar to planters on the island of St Thomas, or transported to Brazil. The conquest of Angola in 1641 was closely associated with the labour needs of the Dutch in Brazil. Though the Dutch lost north-eastern Brazil and were driven out of Angola in 1648, the close association of the two territories, based on the slave trade, continued until the nineteenth century.

Throughout this period, East Africa was of little interest to Europeans. The Portuguese, who held Sofala and politically controlled the other coastal towns, did not penetrate into the interior. The volume of gold reaching the coast from the hinterland was already declining in the mid-sixteenth century. This reduction in supplies of gold may partly explain the decline of such towns as Kilwa, Mombasa and Malindi, which, prior to the arrival of the Portuguese, had been active in supplying gold and other goods to traders from India and Arabia. The coastal inhabitants vainly attempted to persuade the Turks from the Arab Peninsula to intervene against the Portuguese. The territorial expansion of the *Imāmate* of Oman along the East African coast and islands at the end of the seventeenth century brought about some changes, confining the Portuguese to Mozambique alone, but it was not till the late eighteenth and the nineteenth centuries that marked changes occurred.

At the southern tip of Africa the first signs of European expansion appeared in the seventeenth century, when the Dutch East India Company encouraged the settlement of Dutch (and German) peasants, who became known as Boers. The pressure of the Boers who reduced the San to slavery or drove them out of their lands was a bad omen for the indigenous population.

1.2 *Negro slaves washing for diamonds in Brazil (©The Wilberforce Museum, Hull)*

Africa as a reservoir of labour

P. D. Curtin estimates that between 1541 and 1600, 274,900 blacks were carried to Europe and America. Over the next few years, the number rose to 1,341,100 to reach 6 million in the eighteenth century, almost 2 million of them being exported to Brazil. In the eighteenth century the export of black labour to the English and French West Indies increased enormously and exports to Cuba also grew. Africa, which had initially been seen by Europeans as a rich source of gold, now became a reservoir of labour for the many European estates in America, particularly the rapidly developing sugar-cane plantations. The import of black labour to north-eastern Brazil, which had been very heavy at the time of Portuguese rule, increased yet further with the Dutch occupation. The situation changed only when the Dutch were driven out of Brazil and began to apply their sugar-refining techniques in the islands in the Caribbean, whose new plantations became serious rivals of the Brazilian ones.

In the English colonies in the Caribbean, slave imports rose from 263,700 in the seventeenth century to 1,401,300 in the eighteenth century. The situation was similar in the islands occupied by France, with San Domingo importing almost 790,000 slaves in the eighteenth century. The cultivation of sugar cane was also started in Cuba, creating a similar need for labour. Dutch Surinam, the English and French plantations in Central America and the northern part of South America also absorbed great numbers of black slaves. In North America the tobacco plantations in Virginia and the rice plantations in Maryland also helped to expand the slave trade. In the nineteenth century the development of cotton plantations would transform the south of the United States into a vast area whose economy rested on slavery.

The demand for black labour presented Western Europe with an unprecedented task at a time when radical economic and political changes were taking place. In the second half of the seventeenth century the decline of Spain and Portugal became increasingly evident. Holland, then at the peak of its power, began to be ousted by France and England whose economies were developing rapidly. From the end of the seventeenth century these two countries were exercising ever-increasing influence in Africa, while the Spaniards and even the Dutch were playing no more than marginal roles. Meanwhile, Portuguese success in Angola allowed them to retain an advantageous position in the slave trade.

In the seventeenth century, Holland, England, and later France and other countries set up companies for trading with Africa and transporting slaves to America. The companies obtained from their respective governments monopoly rights for trading with Africa, which enabled them to control prices. In return, they were obliged to maintain the old forts and build new ones to protect the European trading posts on the coast of Africa. The number of European forts increased all through the seventeenth and eighteenth centuries, particularly on the Gold Coast and nearby.

Meanwhile, whites in Africa were at loggerheads among themselves. The traders and trading companies sought to secure for themselves control of the best situated trading posts on the African coast. Each of the different rival European groups was backed by its government. The great powers could not be uninterested in Africa, since great stakes were involved. Even less powerful countries such as Sweden, Denmark and Prussia tried to involve themselves in African affairs.

The trading companies did not, however, have the success expected of them. The first two English companies were not particularly active. The Royal African Company, founded in 1672, controlled a large part of Africa's external trade passing through the West African coast in the last quarter of the seventeenth century, but its policy was challenged by American planters and many English traders. After 1689 its privileges were gradually curbed and it lost its monopoly.

An era of free trade with Africa had already begun a few years earlier in England. The Liverpool merchants were the most powerful. Their remarkable success in the eighteenth century was made possible by the rapid industrial development of the Midlands, particularly of metals in Birmingham and textiles in Manchester, which enabled them to supply Africa, cheaply, with knives, weapons and other metal goods, as well as textiles. The English traders exchanged these goods on the coast of Africa for slaves whom they carried to America to sell to the planters in the colonies.

During the eighteenth century, England became the leading trading country on the African coast. Its influence was felt from Senegal to the boundaries of Cameroon. Though England had to hand over its outposts in Senegal to France in 1799, its position in the Gambia and Sierra Leone had become stronger. It also occupied a leading position in the Gold Coast's slave trade which had been growing since the seventeenth century. But the English were not the only Europeans involved. Holland and France were increasingly active on the Slave Coast, in Senegal, in the region of Cameroon and in Loango.

Attempts at settlement began in Angola, where a few Europeans went to settle. Along the coast from Cape Verde to the Congo, however, European activity was limited to trade. The trading posts and factories founded by the Europeans (such as Saint-Louis in 1626) were scattered along the coast, close to convenient bays and, usually, African towns. El Mina, Accra, Whydah, Porto Novo, Badagri and both Old and New Calabar – all famous in the eighteenth century – were meeting places where blacks supplied whites with slaves in return for European goods. African rulers generally reserved for themselves priority in trading with Europeans, but black traders also played an important role. Even in Angola the Portuguese captured only a few slaves themselves, leaving it to local agents to buy or kidnap slaves in the interior.

It is difficult to know the territorial extent of the slave trade in Africa. The coastal regions were not the only ones to suffer. As early as the sixteenth century there were reports of the long journeys slaves had had to make from their places of origin to the ports where they would be embarked. In the eighteenth century, when the export of Africans became large-scale, the main suppliers were the rulers of powerful countries such as Asante or Dahomey or the traders of Calabar. The old African states such as Benin or Ọyọ, were much less involved. The Congo, which entered a period of complete disintegration in the eighteenth century, was never an important supplier of slaves.

The Europeans were not yet ready to undertake the conquest of Africa, mostly because they found the climate hard to bear and they were helpless in the face of tropical diseases. The early Europeans, the Brazilians and the North Americans who first made an appearance on the African continent preferred to win the friendship of African rulers by supplying them generously with whatever goods they wanted. A community of interests united those dealing in slaves, that is African rulers, dignitaries and traders. It should be mentioned that the movement for the abolition of slavery, started in the second half of the eighteenth century, was strongly resisted in England not only by West Indian planters but by merchants in the metropolis. It later became clear that the kings of Asante and Dahomey were also firmly opposed to the abolition of the slave trade.

It was only in the eighteenth century that European slave-traders appeared on the eastern coast of Africa. The great distance from there to the American markets made the transport of Africans to the colonies in the New World much more difficult, though not impossible. According to Curtin, the number of slaves brought to the Americas from central and south-eastern Africa between 1711 and 1810 was about 810,100, or 24 per cent of the total number of slaves imported. In East Africa slave exports to Arabia, carried on by subjects of the *Imām* of Oman, increased during the eighteenth century. But it was in the nineteenth century that these regions suffered the incursions of Arab slave dealers.

In North Africa the expedition to the Lower Niger in 1591 seems to have had no lasting effect on Morocco. The conquerors quickly made themselves independent of their metropolis and their descendants, the Arma, set up small, short-lived states. There is no evidence of any important changes having taken place in trade between Morocco and the Niger bend. The slave trade seems to have been considerable since, at the end of the seventeenth century, the sultans of Morocco possessed an army composed of slaves which, for a certain period, also exerted a strong influence on the country's politics.

Conclusion

The following can be said of Africa's external contacts from the sixteenth to the eighteenth century:

(1) They mostly occurred on the west coast of Africa and in its hinterland.
(2) Initially, the Europeans were interested in African gold but, from the second half of the sixteenth century, the slave trade became more important. It helped to ensure the economic development of much of America and the Caribbean, and also accelerated the accumulation of capital in Europe (especially in England) and in Africa.

(3) At this time, European expansion in Africa was proto-colonial but largely commercial. Exchange between the two parties was unequal, since the whites were selling cheap goods in exchange for huge numbers of slave labourers. Thus, although they did not try to conquer the continent, they inflicted great demographic damage on Africa.

(4) Africa's role as a market for many European industrial goods in the sixteenth and seventeenth centuries has probably been underestimated.

(5) The advantages accruing to Africa from these contacts were limited to the introduction of maize and manioc cultivation. That in no way compensates for the huge demographic losses, let alone the sufferings imposed on countless human beings abducted from their country and carried to far-off lands to toil on plantations.

2 — African political, economic and social structures during this period

Largely as a result of internal factors such as demography and ecology or under the impact of external forces such as the slave trade, Christianity, Islam and capitalism, African social, economic and political structures were continuously transformed between 1500 and 1800.

New social structures

Islam and Christianity

In the religious area, European and Middle Eastern philosophies and religions began to impinge, with Christianity and Islam becoming political forces in areas where they had previously been unknown.

Any ground gained by Christianity in the coastal areas of East Africa was lost with the assassination of Father Gonçalo da Silveira, a Portuguese priest who had been trying to bring the Mwene Mutapa under Christian influence in 1560. Islam, on the other hand, made gains with the conquests of Aḥmad Grañ (1531–35) in Ethiopia and those of the *mai* of Borno and the *askiyas* of Songhay in the Sahara and Western Sudan.

The transition from captive to slave societies

The second important change was the replacement in most of Africa of the black African *jonya* system by the European and Middle Eastern slave-owning system.

The *jonya* (from the Mande word *jon* meaning 'captive') was found mainly in Western Sudan and the Niger–Chad region. A *jon* was not transferable; he owned the bulk of what he produced, was part of a lineage and belonged to a socio-political category that was part of the ruling class. *Jonya* played a considerable role in the states and empires of Ghana, Takrūr, Mali, Kānem-Borno, Asante, Yoruba and Mutapa. The élite of the royal slaves belonged to the ruling class; they exercised some power, made fortunes and could themselves own slaves.

Oriental and Western slavery, on the other hand, in both its ancient and its

13

colonial form, made slaves beings with practically no rights who could be bought and sold as chattels.

With the setting up of Muslim states or emirates, which progressively took over the whole of Western Sudan in the course of the eighteenth century, Muslim law and tradition were established in the region and the slave-owning system replaced the *jonya*. The *jonya* did, however, survive amongst the traditional aristocracy of Western Sudan and the Niger–Chad region which had experienced little Muslim influence. Until the colonial conquest, *jonya* continued to retain some influence in the Wolof, Serer, Hausa, Kanēmbu and Yoruba states.

The spread of feudal structures

The third change was the spread of feudal structures in either pure or distorted forms among the agrarian civilizations of Africa.

Feudalism as a political structure, a mode of production or a socio-economic system entailed not only ties of fealty and suzerainty but an opportunity to speculate and to make a profit out of the means of production. Landed property was a key feature of the European and oriental feudal systems which took root in the predominantly agrarian civilizations of Africa. Their influence was to be seen wherever land tenure or control over a territory led to duties, taxes and rents.

But before the advent of Islamic law or the Western-inspired *mailo* (land system), land was not a source of income in black Africa. Those who appropriated or passed on a plot of land or a hunting, fishing or food-gathering area worked on the basis of simple user rights which entailed neither lucrative speculation nor the possibility of sale. The sub-Saharan agrarian societies had given rise to *lamana*, a land tenure system which precluded land-renting, tenant farming and share-cropping. The form of economy peculiar to black Africa entailed above all production for consumption. People produced what they needed, but did not own the means of production.

Interaction between the different social structures gave rise to hybrid, heterogeneous societies. From the sixteenth to the eighteenth century, African society contained marginal areas of debased feudalism mixed with *lamana*. Feudalism held sway where there was production for exchange and the *lamana* system had been either done away with or modified.

In Egypt, the Turkish *beylik* system helped to foster the feudal system. The rural aristocracy was protected, as in the Middle Ages in Europe, by *odjaks* (Turkish fortresses and garrisons). Great local chiefs ruled an '*arsh* (ethnic area) and the *dwars* (tented camps) according to a hierarchical system. In the Sahel and the Mauritanian Sahara, religious families and *djuad* (warrior chiefs) took over and vassalized confederations of smaller communities under the cloak of religious brotherhood or by right of conquest.

The chief Turkish and native dignitaries in the Maghrib were often granted large estates. As in Egypt, economic activity was in the hands of the *beylik* which monopolized manufacturing industry and controlled the cereal, oil, salt and textile trades as well as trade routes. The guilds of craftsmen and merchants were under its supervision.

In the rest of North Africa and northern Ethiopia, the feudal system developed differently because of ecological conditions which in some areas made land ownership less concentrated. The great beylical estates of the Maghrib extended over a wide area, and gave rise to the widespread distribution of *azel* (fiefs) worked by the *khammāsat* (tenant farming) system on a one-fifth basis. At the regional level, the pattern was still one of *milk* (small family holdings) and *'arsh* (community holdings) but always within the speculative feudal super-structure.

In Egypt and the rest of North Africa, several centuries of Graeco-Roman rule had already prepared the ground for the transition to feudalism, the *iḳṭā'* system of the Mamluks. South of the Sahara, the transition to feudalism took place under outside influence.

In northern Ethiopia, for instance, there emerged a landed gentry which created large estates, because the Ethiopian nobility subverted the principles of ambilineal descent and equal partible inheritance, thereby creating among themselves transgenerational 'families'. Political power was gradually concentrated in the hands of land owners, and this accumulation of landed property and political power led to greater class differentiation in northern Ethiopia.

This semi-feudal regime was extended by Christian northern Ethiopians to the southern areas where the *ketema* (garrison towns) were established with a *neftenia* (landed élite) colonizing the *gasha* (occupied lands). The *gabar* (peasants) who worked the lands for the benefit of the landed élite were more or less serfs or, at least, tributaries obliged to pay the *gabir* or *siso* depending on whether they were share-croppers or tenant farmers.

In the Great Lakes region, especially in the southern area which comprises much of present-day north-western Tanzania, Burundi, Rwanda and Uvira in north-eastern Zaire, the institutions of clientship constituted a semi-feudal bond which regulated relations between pastoralists and agriculturalists. It was a sort of contract between the donor (pastoralist), who provided cattle, and the recipient (agriculturalist), who put his services and those of his family and future generations at the disposal of the donor and his heirs. These contracts varied from society to society and changed over the years.

The main factors contributing to the adoption of the Ottoman feudal socio-economic system were the spread of the Muslim emirate with the advent of the *askiyas* in Western Sudan, the expansion of the empire of the Islamized *mai* of Borno and the introduction of Ḳur'ānic law as a result of conversion and the *djihāds*. In Songhay the *askiyas* kept part of the traditional socio-economic structure.

In the emirates the Muslim law of the *djihāds* was adopted, thus implanting more firmly semi-feudal socio-economic structures. The *almamia* of Futa Toro, Futa Jallon and the Sokoto caliphate were simply copied from Ottoman land tenure and taxation systems.

The new legal system established under the emirates introduced feudal-type land speculation. The *njoldi* (symbolic payments attaching to the master of the land), *kawngal* (fishing grounds), *yial* (hunting grounds), *hore kosam* (grazing land) and *gobbi* (mines) were transformed into annual dues payable to those in power, and collected under state supervision. The office of tax-collector became negotiable for a fee, as did most of the official posts within the system. Share-cropping, tenant farming and land rental became the rule. In the Islamized areas the many landless peasants, dispossessed by conquest or the new legal system, became serfs and vassals subject to the Ottoman system.

Thus, from the sixteenth century onwards, socio-economic structures from different backgrounds were therefore combining. The result was the emergence of a new social order in which feudal structures were superimposed on the African *lamana*. In Western Sudan and Northern Nigeria, which were becoming Islamized, the Muslim institution of the emirate replaced the *mansaya* or was superimposed on it. In the Gulf of Guinea and Central and East Africa, where Christian rulers appeared, the influence of the Christian feudal monarchy became increasingly apparent.

Architectural and artistic developments

There were some important architectural and artistic achievements. The men who built the towns in the Nile valley, the Maghrib and the Sudan and on the coast, and erected Yoruba palaces, the edifice known today as the Zimbabwe ruins, the houses, palaces and mosques of the East African coast and the *tata* (forts) surrounding the Hausa cities were at once architects, masons, decorators and town planners. The round or pyramidal huts made of stone or clay and the storey houses of the Jolla were in the same architectural tradition as the Koutoubia of Marrakesh, the tomb of the *askiyas* in Gao and that of the caliphs in Cairo.

After the sixteenth century new advances in architecture continued to be made, perhaps mainly in Western Sudan and Nigeria, but the towns of North Africa and the Nile valley declined. The *askiyas*, however, who carried on the tradition in West Africa, were great builders, like their Moroccan contemporary, Abū'l-ʿAbbās al-Manṣūr, whose accession to power coincided with a vogue for big public works. The architectural traditions of the Sahel and the Islamic world increasingly spread southwards. The Sudanese architectural style, of which the mosques at Sankore and Jenne were the prototypes, spread from the sixteenth century.

In Ethiopia, the Gondar period (*c.* 1632–*c.* 1750) witnessed the development of new architectural styles promoted by the court. In Gondar and in other towns, the imperial families erected huge and beautiful palaces, castles, churches and libraries with elaborate interior decorations. In the Swahili-speaking coastal regions of East Africa there were major architectural innovations in the period between 1700 and 1850, both in the patterns and in the design of houses. These architectural developments were accompanied by great productivity in related fields such as wood-carving and furniture-making.

New economic structures

Major economic structures developed during this period: the caste system, which replaced the guild or corporation system; the predatory economy, mainly in North and East Africa; and the trading-post or entrepôt economy, mainly in Central and West Africa.

A craft economy and a caste-and-guild society

Medieval urban civilization had contributed to the division of labour through the development of crafts and manufacturing activities. But in the sixteenth century this development was uneven, with different tendencies showing themselves in different social contexts.

In the civilizations of Western Sudan, the Niger–Chad region and the Sahara, for instance, crafts and manufacturing activities developed on the basis of more or less closed castes, organized on a lineage basis. Under the growing influence of the civilizations of Takrūr and the Sahara, the caste system tended to crystallize, notably in southern Senegal, Mande territory and Hausaland. The Mande *nyamankala* (caste system) long raised the status of blacksmithing until the Takrūri occupied the area after *djihāds*. Metalworkers were held in high esteem among the Fon and the Yoruba, but there, too, the impact of immigrants from Takrūr and the Sahara was to upset the prevailing order. In Songhay, the *askiyas* were already governing a society in which the caste system had taken root and developed.

The Torodo revolution at the end of the eighteenth century accentuated the caste system in Takrūr by deepening class divisions. The Sebbe peasants, the Subalbe fishermen and even the Buruure nomadic herdsmen were progressively reduced in status. They were not identified with the *benangatoobe* (including cobblers, blacksmiths or griots) and were segregated from the *nangatoobe* (higher caste). The Torodo marabout élite came to despise the defeated aristocracies and to monopolize high office. The Torodo *marabout* élite came to despise the defeated aristocracies and to monopolize high office. In the Negro–Berber societies of the Sahara, religious, ethnic and racial divisions gradually crystallized into hierarchies of castes.

A major aspect of the organization of industry or crafts at the time was the degree of state control. In Mediterranean civilizations, there was generally a state monopoly in a number of activities, such as weaving, shipbuilding, the development of arsenals, refining and foreign trade, but the states in black Africa seldom exercised such control, even with the expansion of the armaments industry.

This period was marked by the contrast between the versatility of country-dwellers and the marked specialization of townsmen. State industries developed, with arsenals for weapons and even the building of river- and ocean-going fleets, both in Western Sudan and on the West Atlantic coast and also in the Mediterranean and Indian Ocean countries.

The multiplicity of wars sometimes lent fresh impetus to metalworking. In the sixteenth century Sonni 'Alī reorganized the Songhay arsenals, setting yearly production targets for the workshops. Egypt became skilled in metallurgy and began to produce Damascus steel. The Mande blacksmiths, organized on a caste basis, exported their techniques to the new towns that had sprung up as a result of the Atlantic trade. The precious-metal industry in Egypt and North Africa continued to be supplied with gold from Nubia, Sofala and Western Sudan. Craftsmen working in gold and silver stimulated trade in the sūks (markets) of towns in the Maghrib, Egypt and Western Sudan. Berber and Wolof jewellers were outstanding for their gold and filigree jewellery work. The Swahili also manufactured beautiful jewellery and other silver and gold items. Ceramics gave rise to industries, pottery (like basketry) remaining a female preserve. The glass industry continued to develop, spreading throughout Yoruba country, Nupe, Hausaland, Egypt and the Maghrib. Among the Shona in the southern Zambezi region, mining was widespread, and the gold and copper mines sustained the economies of the region up to the eighteenth century.

Leather-working flourished most in Nigeria, where stock-breeding provided ample raw materials. From the sixteenth to the eighteenth century, basketry and weaving assumed an important place among the industries of the Niger-Chad region. The manufacture of paper, which had replaced papyrus, developed chiefly in Egypt under the influence of Samarkand. The Sudan did not lag far behind and gradually began to turn out manuscripts, with Kānem producing Ḳur'āns that were sold throughout the Muslim world. Trades associated with the food industry, which had grown up in the Middle Ages in towns in the north and in Western Sudan, also became established in Nigerian cities. In the textile area, the growing of cotton and the weaving of cotton cloth were well established in the Zimbabwean highlands and the Zambezi valley by the sixteenth century. The Swahili city-states were also famous for their fabrics. In Central Africa the raphia cloths of Kongo were renowned from the fifteenth to the nineteenth centuries.

The predatory economy

Prior to the sixteenth century, long-distance trade had played a major role in the economy of Africa. This had encouraged high productivity and had led to the rise of urban civilizations and the forging of strong links between town and country. Between 1500 and 1800, however, the predatory economy, a consequence of Spanish and Portuguese expansion, was introduced and became established.

Between 1495 and 1523 Spain and Portugal had gradually extended their sway over the Maghrib. When the Portuguese occupied Azemmūr, in 1513, the Arab-Berbers and the Sublime Porte decided to oppose European aggression and the corsairs, sailing under the Ottoman flag, helped to redress the balance of power. In 1514 one of the Barbarossa brothers, Abū Yusuf, recaptured Djidjelli and Algiers, and his brother Khāyr al-Dīn consolidated the reconquest. Tunisia and Algeria came under Ottoman sovereignty once again and remained so, at least nominally, until the nineteenth century, despite Charles V of Spain's expeditions. In 1551 Sinan Pasha occupied Tripoli in the name of the Sublime Porte and then Tunis in 1574. In the mid-1500s, Morocco asserted its independence after reconquering Agadir, Sāfi and Azemmūr from Portugal.

Despite their clashes with the European powers, the North African states continued to preserve their freedom but their progress was impeded in the sixteenth century by the breakdown of the world economic order. Henceforth, the ports of the Maghrib and the rest of North Africa lived mainly by piracy and on tributes and duties, rather than by trade or new industries. The ports of Salé (Morocco), Algiers, Tunis and Tripoli had the protection of the privateer fleet which, in the seventeenth century, enjoyed its golden age in the Mediterranean. The corsairs spread terror, and throughout the eighteenth century, too, there was continual instability in the western Mediterranean. The Ottoman regencies of Algiers and Tunis were almost constantly at war with one or other European power and this situation inevitably hurt mercantile capitalism and the merchant class.

It is against this background that the Moroccan expedition against Songhay in Western Sudan should be seen. The Moroccan ruler, Abū 'l'Abbās al-Manṣūr, endeavoured after the conquest of Songhay in 1591 to re-open the gold and slave routes. In 1593 the capture of Timbuktu made it possible to bring 1,200 slaves across the Sahara, but the expedition, led by Djūdar Pasha, only hastened the downfall of this trade. That was the end of what had been the greatest empire in Western Sudan in the sixteenth century.

Tripolitania and Egypt suffered less from the consequences of the decline of trade in the Sahara and maintained their traditional trans-Saharan routes. The Sublime Porte, which was established in Egypt and Tripoli, signed an alliance with Kānem-Borno and was thus able to maintain the flow of north-south trade – vital for its own supplies – until the nineteenth century.

The predatory economy certainly contributed to the slow-down of economic and technological growth in the southern Mediterranean, but socio-economic and political structures also played a part in the stagnation of that area and its hinterland.

All the countries of the Nile and East Africa, as well as those in the Niger-Chad region and Western Sudan were affected in varying degrees. In the western Indian Ocean, for example, the years 1680 to 1720 became known as 'the period of the pirates'. Countries in direct contact with the new European hegemonies were physically disrupted by the predatory economy, although their decline was also due to their inability to put new life into a socio-economic structure increasingly influenced by a backward East. They were also handicapped by their inability to establish power relationships that would have enabled them to escape the inequality of the trading system as it existed during the period.

The decline of the countryside:
poverty and insecurity among the peasantry

The predatory economy caused trade between town and country to stagnate and therefore affected the relationship between them. Previously, their activities and produce had been complementary. Towns had broken the vicious circle of subsistence farming, deepened the division of labour and contained the seeds of the new society. It was urban industries and crafts that had stimulated large-scale agriculture, stock-breeding, fishing and hunting. They had also been responsible for the planting of sugar and cotton on an industrial scale and the growing of dye and perfume plants. Hydraulic installations, roads and stock-breeding for wool, milk and meat all owed their development to the towns.

The sixteenth century brought disruption and crisis to that world. Urban depopulation brought about decline in the rural economy, leading to wide-spread poverty among the peasants and the reversion to bush of large tracts of arable land. Increasingly insecure, people in the rural areas sought refuge in the depths of the forests where, cut off from the consumer culture of the towns, they withdrew more and more into family or village subsistence farming. Exchange of produce and barter were the main forms of trade.

The slave trade brought about new upheavals. Depleted of able-bodied men, the rural economy declined. In some areas, peoples subject to continual harassment reverted to a nomadic economy of hunting and gathering with many leaving the savannah region for the forest.

The warrior aristocracy diverted a great deal of peasant manpower to its own benefit, which had disastrous demographic consequences for the rural areas. The ruling élites gave up farming and relied instead on raiding using the services of the freemen and slaves they had captured. Peasants suffered most in Western Sudan and the Niger–Chad region.

The oppression of the African peasantry by the rural and urban élites increased with the tightening of the fiscal screw. Under Turkish Muslim law taxation could be increased in non-Islamized lands. Muslims were made to pay not only the *zakāt* (the only tax to which a Muslim was liable) but also the *kharādj*. As the black market in taxation rights in Muslim countries became widespread, so the burden of taxation grew even heavier.

In such a situation the leaders of the *djihāds* and the Christian messianic movements found it easy to enlist the mass support of the peasantry. Religious leaders promised equality once order was restored. They blamed the traditional aristocracies and the Europeans for all the disruption and social injustice.

From the seventeenth century, the peasantry's political role increased. Peasant revolts swept the continent like a religious revolution, thus paving the way for resistance to colonial conquest. These revolts were not the work of captives or slaves but of the largest and most exploited class, the small peasants.

The countries of the Nile and the Indian Ocean

The impact of the predatory economy on the countries of the Nile Valley and those bordering the Indian Ocean was equally disastrous. The East African ports had been known for their trading activities since the eleventh century, and were in direct contact with Arabia, Persia, India, China and the Mediterranean. The Portuguese invasion marked the beginning of the collapse of this urban commercial civilization. In 1502 Kilwa and Zanzibar were placed under tribute by Portugal. In 1505 Francesco d'Almeida sacked Kilwa and Mombasa and then built Fort Santiago at Kilwa. He prohibited all trade between the towns and the merchants left them for Malindi and the Comoro Islands. Lamu and Pate were occupied.

With the exceptions of Luanda and Mozambique, none of the stations set up by the Portuguese and later by the Dutch, English and French was as big as an average town in Western Sudan, or even the Swahili and East African ports of the tenth to sixteenth centuries.

The entrepôt or trading-post economy

While the predatory economy became widespread in the areas bordering the Mediterranean, the Nile and the Indian Ocean, the entrepôt or trading-post economy prevailed along the Atlantic seaboard. The new maritime entrepôt towns were fortresses before becoming centres of commercial civilization – scenes of violence and spoliation.

On the Guinea and equatorial coasts, the Portuguese, who had established the entrepôt economy in the sixteenth century, looted more than they bought. They had little to offer economically: apart from wine and iron bars, their goods were imported. They exchanged them for gold, slaves, leather, gum, ivory, amber, yellow civet, cowries, cotton and salt. In the Gulf of Guinea, the Portuguese bought goods from the Akan and resold them on the Nigerian coast or in Kongo or Angola. In Senegambia, they took up residence in the ports and became successful merchants. In the seventeenth century, when European industry began to produce textiles and hardware, the economic decline of the towns accelerated.

The trading posts contributed nothing to local prosperity. Before 1800, Albreda, Cacheu, Santiago de Cape Verde, El Mina, Ketu, Calabar and San Salvador were the most important trading posts and all had fewer than 5,000 inhabitants. Apart from the Europeans, most of the inhabitants of the trading posts were *laptos* (local interpreters). The trading-post economy rested on the Atlantic slave trade. At the height of this trade none of the trading posts provided a market for local products or promoted the commercial and industrial activities of the indigenous population. The slave-trade trading post was above all an instrument of depopulation.

The direct and indirect contribution of the trading-post economy to world prosperity, however, was considerable. After the discovery of the American mines, the trading posts supplied a substantial part of the gold and silver of the world. Moreover, the bulk of the labour force which developed the American continent originated from them. In a word, they kept world trade going. They were the fountainhead of industry, finance, and European and international capitalism. France's trade, for instance, saw tremendous growth in the course of the eighteenth century.

By getting a firm foothold in the economic network, the European navigators interrupted the normal pattern of inter-African trade and established their own monopoly of middlemen operating from the trading posts. Africans no longer traded between Saint-Louis and Portendick, Grand Lahou and El Mina, Angola and Kongo or Sofala and Kilwa.

The Portuguese network was used by other maritime powers from the sixteenth century onwards. The abundant sources of information on trade in the entrepôt forts and the seasonal trading stations from the time of the Portuguese until the arrival of the Dutch, French and English tell a story of violence and continual conflict. The Atlantic and Indian Ocean trading posts were destroyed and rebuilt and changed hands several times in the course of the struggle by the European, Ottoman and Omani maritime powers against the stubborn resistance of local rulers, who levied duties or *curva*.

Finally, the technological innovations that revolutionized Europe had little impact. The African economy suffered most from competition from European industry and business. By cornering the ports the European traders paralyzed the links between the coast and the interior. Thus the European states that annexed coastal areas demarcated Portuguese, Dutch, French and English spheres of influence even before the colonial conquest and, in so doing, determined the development and political geography of these areas in the eighteenth century. From the Moroccan expansionist drive against Songhay to the shifting fortunes of the internecine wars in Western Sudan, most of the upheavals on the African political scene originated in the process of disruption set off by the European powers in the sixteenth century.

New political structures

The African political scene had already reached a degree of balance and stability in the period between the twelfth and sixteenth centuries. In the sixteenth century, Mediterranean Africa constituted a sub-system within the Arab-Ottoman empire, with Morocco, Ifrikiya and Tripolitania making up part of it. Egypt was an entity on its own. The Nile area, consisting of Nubia and Ethiopia, stretched south to the state of Bunyoro-Kita in the area of the Great Lakes, the Swahili city-states and the area south of the Zambezi dominated in the late sixteenth century by the state of Mutapa. Southern Africa as yet had few state structures. In Central Africa one system was dominated by the Kongo and Tio kingdoms, another by the Luba kingdom. But the peoples in the forests were not organized into states. Western Sudan and the Niger-Chad region adjoined each other, with every-changing borders.

The development of the political map was to reflect external pressures and their repercussions. New states emerged: either because they were better armed, such as Kānem-Borno, or because they had more outlets to the sea, such as Kayor in Senegambia, Dahomey in the Gulf of Guinea, Angola in Central Africa or the kingdom of Changamire south of the Zambezi.

The character of the African state itself altered. Huge areas without rulers or sovereigns hitherto peopled by farmers, nomadic herdsmen and hunters were conquered and turned into states with centralized structures. The village structures of the Bantu and the Kabyles and Berbers of the Sahara were

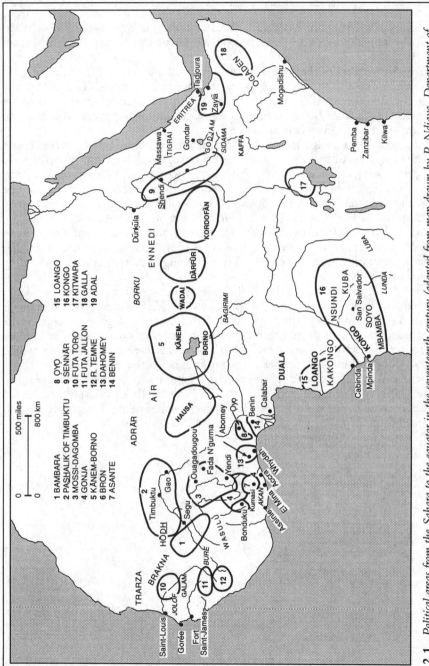

2.1 *Political areas from the Sahara to the equator in the seventeenth century (adapted from map drawn by P. Ndiaye, Department of Geography, University of Dakar)*

1 BAMBARA
2 PASHALIK OF TIMBUKTU
3 MOSSI-DAGOMBA
4 GONJA
5 KÂNEM-BORNO
6 BRON
7 ASANTE

8 OYO
9 SENNAR
10 FUTA TORO
11 FUTA JALLON
12 R. TEMNE
13 DAHOMEY
14 BENIN

15 LOANGO
16 KONGO
17 KITWARA
18 GALLA
19 ADAL

replaced by the Maghribi Ma<u>kh</u>zen, the autocratic *mansaya* or *farinya* of black Africa, the feudalism of the Ottoman beylikates or the system of the Muslim emirates.

From the sixteenth century onwards, political life centred increasingly on the coastal areas, the privateering ports and the trading posts. The aristocracy collected tithes there; African governments equipped themselves with revenue departments to collect taxes on foreign trade. Many treaties were concluded in an attempt to codify this taxation system.

Morocco, Tunisia, Algeria and Tripolitania signed many trade agreements and short-lived treaties of friendship with the Europeans and even the Americans. In 1780 a war between Morocco and Spain was ended by the Treaty of Aranjuez, which redefined their borders and codified their trade relations. At about the same time, Algeria, and then Morocco, compelled the United States to pay ransom to the pirates to secure the freeing of some of their nationals.

It took wars, the destruction of trading posts and prohibitions on trade to persuade the European powers to pay taxes. But these more or less regular sources of income were the cause of wars among the aristocracies and ruling classes throughout the continent.

Political entities were predominantly areas in which a balance had been achieved and which had developed in relation to their domestic circumstances. They varied in size and in the stability of their borders and governments. Some were confederations of states and others unitary states or chiefdoms with limited jurisdiction. Sometimes they were a clan, or an independent *lamana* in which the first occupants lived a completely autonomous existence.

The instability introduced by the predatory and trading-post economies thus set the pattern, from the sixteenth to the eighteenth century, for states or economies which could no longer base their development on a consistent and organized foundation.

3

Population movements and the emergence of new socio-political forms in Africa

The nature of population mobility

One of the main ways in which the history of pre-colonial Africa differs from the history of Europe and most of Asia is in population mobility, especially the mobility of farmers. African farmers in tropical and subtropical regions were more mobile than farmers in Europe or Asia because they practised extensive agriculture and could not cultivate the same land year after year. They were thus not tied to definite plots of land. It was the same with herdsmen, although their techniques of coping with the environment were more comparable with those of the pastoralists of central Asia and the transhumance practised in Europe. This population mobility is a basic characteristic to be considered in any study or reconstruction of Africa's past.

This volume gives evidence of many migrations, from the *trekboere* at the Cape to those of the Somali and Oromo in the Horn of Africa, the Ngbandi of Ubangi, the Jaga in Central Africa, the Tuareg in the Niger bend, the Mane in Sierra Leone, the Fulbe all over West Africa and all the peoples of Madagascar. These migrations were not any more typical of the period between 1500 and 1800 than of any other period; but by the late sixteenth century Portuguese travellers speculated that these migrations were all related, being for them characteristic of barbaric tribesmen, a stereotype to be found in African history right down to recent years. This conception is not only derogatory; it also makes it impossible to understand what really happened.

The word 'migration' means the movement of a population from one area to settle in another. Migration is thus a concept expressing a change in the relationship that exists between people, space and time. In this general sense, it is better to speak of population movement. Such movements may occur because the ratio of people to resources alters or because people try to reorganize their space and its resources on a relatively large scale. In Africa the main large-scale spatial organizations were states and trading networks.

Africans stressed the importance of migrations in their oral traditions. Many traditions that seek to explain the origin of the world refer to founder peoples or individuals who came from elsewhere – a place of genesis. Other myths assert that people emerged from the soil and were thus the owners of the land. The first hypothesis was adopted by European scholars who were confirming their preconceived ideas. They had an image of constant invasions during which the peoples of Africa were pushing one another around like billiard balls, with each conquest setting off a new wave of refugees who would go off to seek haven elsewhere, or perhaps would themselves drive out other peoples.

Despite appearances, the notion that Africans were forever on the move is a baseless stereotype. In a crucial article, P. E. H. Hair documented the remarkable 'stability' of all the coastal languages from Senegal to Cameroon, and this observation can be extended to most of the farming societies of Africa after the sixteenth century.

Like the concept of 'migration', the concept of 'stability' refers to a relationship among people, time and space; it expresses an absence of change. But both concepts are relative. Given a large enough area, such as the area stretching east and north of the White Nile, the movement of peoples, such as that of the Jie, for example, becomes stability, a mere adaptation of people to the soil and the climate. At the other extreme, the removal of a village 10 kilometres away can be described as a 'migration'. It is the same with time: only by looking over long periods of time is it possible to see the 'migrations' of some peoples who move slowly over several centuries (like that of the Bantu, for example, which may have gone on for 2 thousand years).

We must first examine the usual movements brought about by the quest for a livelihood so as better to understand the unusual, abnormal movements and see how the different population movements actually arise. We can then turn to the kinds of evidence of these unusual movements and take a look at the major population movements in Africa between 1500 and 1800.

Mobility and land use

As there are four main ways to exploit the environment for food production – hunting and gathering, herding, agriculture and fishing – so there are four main patterns of usual movement associated with these activities.

Hunters and gatherers roam a territory which is fairly stable as long as the population density is adapted to the requirements of the way of life. They live in camps and move about frequently inside the territory, like the Ituri pygmies and the Kung San in Botswana. They have to do this to follow game and find sufficient quantities of plants on which to feed. Their movements vary according to the season. The mobility is high, yet such populations can sometimes exploit the same territory for a very long time.

Herders too are mobile. Their animals need water, grass and salt and the availability of these commodities varies with the seasons. In the Sahara, for instance, nomads usually live near the edge of the desert or major oases during the dry season and go deep into the desert when the rains come. These movements are known as transhumance and they often followed the same route year after year. Such movements could involve enormous distances for camel herders such as the Rigeibat of the western Sahara. Often, complex reciprocal movements occurred between nomads herding different kinds of stock, according to the various requirements of camels, goats, cattle and sheep. Moreover, the nomads also cultivated a few crops and exchanged food with specialized hunters or gatherers where they existed – as did the eighteenth-century *trekboere* in South Africa. Thus the natural resources were exploited in various complementary ways by groups who coexisted, each with its own mobility over the same area. Herding, however, was more susceptible than hunting and gathering to climatic variations, especially to short-term ones.

Farmers were also mobile because they practised shifting agriculture, leaving fallow the land they had farmed the previous year. Villages had to move when the fields became too far away from people's homes. In recent times this occurred every ten years on average. The best lands were those that were fertilized both by irrigation and an annual deposit of silt. On such lands there could be stable cropping which led to a settled population pattern. But, apart from Egypt and the belt of wet rice cultivation on the western coast of Guinea, areas of permanent cultivation were very rare in Africa, for lack of efficient methods of intensive fertilization.

Most villages moved then, but so long as the population density remained low, they followed a more or less circular pattern within a given territory. The mobility of villages was not dependent on the state of the soils alone. In many regions, for instance throughout the tropical rainforest of Central Africa, farmers also practised hunting and trapping, with some gathering too. Thus, among the Nzabi of Gabon, for example, the siting of the village could be dictated as much by the needs of trappers as of farmers. The greatest menace to this way of life was climatic variation, especially irregular rainfall patterns. Famines were possible even close to the equator, despite its being a well-watered area. To have no rain after planting was a disaster but so was continuous rain that prevented planting. Droughts were more common in areas close to deserts, but no region was entirely safe from them.

In short, for farmers as for herders or gatherers there was a maximum population density and an optimum population density which varied with the environment – the nature of the soil, rainfall, topography, the availability of supplementary food resources, the state of technology and the arrangements for the sharing or distribution of resources.

Fishermen were settled people and rarely moved their villages. Yet seasonal variations in the levels of rivers could force them to undertake long expeditions. They would then settle in camps on sandbars as on the Zaire or the Kasai, sometimes hundreds of kilometres from the villages where they had left their families. Permanent settlement was likeliest among fishermen operating on the coast or on the shores of large lakes. Because they had boats they had a cheap means of transport, which turned many into traders acting also as middlemen among different groups settled on land.

It goes without saying that peoples who moved regularly could do so for other than economic reasons. The departure of a group could be precipitated by a rise in mortality or conflicts with other groups or the need for self-defence. There was also much individual mobility. Women would often marry into another village; sons would go to live with their mother's kin. Slaves, pawnbrokers, traders and pilgrims, reputed medicine men and hunters would often be on the move. The stereotype that some African ethnic groups had hardly any contact with the outside world is as false as the opposite one of perpetual wandering.

It should be stressed that the distinction between usual and unusual movements was much more tenuous in the case of individuals, even though the resulting population movements could in total be spectacular. The slave trade after 1660 could be seen as an everyday movement of people. Yet the transport of slaves to America was by far the largest population movement that Africa has ever experienced.

Urbanization also represents population movements. By the beginning of the fourteenth century, the population of the city of Zimbabwe could have been 10,000, which means that there must earlier have been migration to the city. When cultivated land became exhausted, the inhabitants abandoned the city and moved back to the villages. Their dispersal represents an equally important population movement. But, urbanization and the slave trade apart, there is little information about the movements of individuals and even families. We shall only know more about them when we know how much population densities varied decade by decade and area by area. But such individual movements did exist and they could be enough to have a marked impact on population density.

Typology of unusual population movements

Unusual population movements by communities fall into two major categories – drift and migration. Drift is gradual, slow movement while migration is a sudden movement. In addition, drift does not necessarily mean abandonment of the original settlement, although it may eventually, whereas migration ordinarily means abandoning the territory of origin. These two categories of population movement can be subdivided into several types. Drift is called expansion when it enlarges the territory of a group and diaspora when it is discontinuous and new distinct settlements result. On the other hand, there is mass migration, band migration (generally a band of pillaging warriors) and élite migration when it involves tiny groups whose arrival precipitates major changes in the host society.

The historical importance and scale of a population movement depend on the number of people involved, the distance travelled, the duration of the movement, its causes and its consequences. All these factors need to be taken into account in each case, but they cannot be used as a basis for classification because they are too variable in meaning. Thus it is the characteristics of the movement itself that we shall now examine for each of the five migration types set out above.

Expansion

Expansion has occurred countless times because of the natural mobility of most

African populations, and its character differs according to the way of life of the society being examined. Shifting agriculture becomes expansion when drift occurs primarily in one direction rather than in a haphazard or circular pattern. The expansion may last a very long time and yet the population will always appear to be settled.

In the forest, Mongo expansion southward from the great bend of the Zaire began long before the sixteenth century and was still in progress at the end of the nineteenth century in most of the area between the Zaire in the west and the Lomami in the east. This expansion caused a flow from nuclei of higher population density around the equator and 1° south, to the river valleys and the fringes of the forest.

Expansion could easily be accelerated either by increasing the distances travelled during each move or by moving more frequently. Such expansion then became a matter of precise intentions, often a pull factor. Thus, in just half a century, the Nzabi of Gabon/Congo moved from their lands in the east of the great Ogowe bend to the south-west so as to be closer to the trade routes and be able to exploit new mineral resources. The Fang of the Upper Comoe reached the Gabon estuary in a mere twenty years and then continued for another forty years towards the Ogowe delta. They never abandoned their usual way of life, villages would move one after the other, each one leap-frogging past the one that had preceded it.

Expansion by pastoralists followed a different pattern. The most common was for members of a younger generation to leave the pole of transhumance of the group and settle with their stock in fresh pastures. The Maasai advanced in this way in the seventeenth and eighteenth centuries until all suitable lands were occupied. Another example is that of the *trekboere* of South Africa. Second-generation European settlers established themselves near the Cape from about 1680 onwards. From the start, the herders complained about overpopulation, despite the fact that the population was sparse. Taking some of the stock, members of the younger generation would go off and settle elsewhere. Until about 1780 this expansion continued into areas occupied mainly by other herders (Khoi groups) whom the *trekboere* would replace. But then they came up against a frontier of much better watered land occupied by Xhosa farmers and herders.

Even hunter-gatherers could show drift. This may be the explanation for the presence of Baka hunters in eastern Cameroon. These pygmies speak Ubangian languages, but live further west than farmers belonging to the same language group. The reason for this probably lies in a movement from the upper valley of the Sanga which gradually expanded the area in which the Baka hunted further west.

Large expansion movements are indicative of new population distribution. One of the deepest and longest trends in the history of Africa has been the inexorable advance of people in larger and larger numbers setting out to con-quer new areas and mould their environment to their way of life rather than be determined by it. Thus the expansion of the Igbo east of the lower Niger resulted in a complete transformation of the forest landscape and a marked population increase. Such expansions into sparsely populated areas had the effect of raising population density over the continent as a whole as population increased.

Expansion movements must have occurred from an early date in Africa. Hunters and gatherers were the first to extend the areas over which they operated, followed by populations that were exploiting their environment in a more intensive way. In some cases long-term deterioration of resources due to climatic change led to expansion, the most spectacular case being the desiccation of the Sahara which gradually forced the farmers of Mauritania southward.

A people that was expanding did not necessarily drive out the other peoples it met with on its way. Often a mixing of populations occurred, with the indigenous adopting the culture of the newcomers, as in the case of the Fang; or a new society and culture might emerge from such a fusion. Thus the Mongo expansion southward gave rise to various peoples, including the famous Kuba. When there was no fusion, the indigenous peoples would gradually abandon their territory. It appears that it hardly ever happened that a people driven out of its territory invaded a neighbouring territory. Expansions produced few refugees given the low population densities involved.

Diaspora

A diaspora is a discontinuous population movement which leads to the creation of new settlements separated from the parent settlement. All diasporas are linked to trade or pilgrimage, except perhaps that of the Fulbe herders all over West Africa.

The most typical diasporas grew out of trade. The Phoenician, Greek and Arab settlements along the coastal areas of the Horn and the East African littoral, the European forts and the colony of Cape Town were all founded by overseas traders. River trade and fishing played a major role in the history of diasporas. For instance, between 1750 and 1850 the inhabitants of a large village at the mouth of the Ubangi founded trading posts and settlements all along the Zaire as far as the mouth of the Kasai; they mixed with other peoples and founded a new ethnic group, the Bobangi. In East Africa the Swahili and their culture spread in a similar way, from the coasts of Somalia and Kenya to the island of Ibo off Mozambique and the Comoros. Diasporas also followed overland routes. Mande traders formed Jahanka diasporas from the Upper Niger to the coast of Senegal and Joola (Dyola) settlements from the Upper Niger to the Akan coast.

Other diasporas were due to the yearly *hadj* to Mecca. When, for one reason or another, pilgrims could not continue on their way, they would settle where they had had to stop. This is how the Takrūri, from West Africa, came to settle in Sudan in the nineteenth century. Similarly, most of the *marabtin bilbaraka* in Barka were descended from pilgrims from North Africa.

Diaspora peoples typically maintained contact with their home countries, either through trade or because they lived close to pilgrim routes. In some cases, however, they gradually moved apart. For instance, by the fifteenth century the inhabitants of Sofala no longer had special links with the Lamu archipelago or the Bajun islands in the Swahili heartland. Even the European colonies tended to become removed from their home countries and formed trading relations with other colonies. Thus the colonists at Cape Town were closer to the Netherlands East Indies with Batavia as its capital than they were to the Netherlands.

Diasporas are highly visible population movements. They are a sign of the existence of long-distance communication networks and flourish with the development of trade routes. They attest to the success of man's control over space.

Mass migration

A mass migration occurs when a whole people – men, women and children – leave their homeland with all their belongings to travel long distances for a year or more. The greatest invasion of North Africa was that of the Banū Hilāl and the Banū Sulaym from 1052 onwards which has been tentatively linked to recurrent droughts in Arabia. It continued until about 1500 when it reached Mauritania. It changed the cultural map of all northern Africa which became fully Arabized.

True mass migrations are dramatic but they are rather rare. In the period between 1500 and 1800 the only real mass migration was that of the Oromo which precipitated other population movements. In the nineteenth century there were only the Nguni migrations which convulsed Africa from the Cape to Nyanza.

Mass migrations were difficult undertakings. The movement called for new forms of social and political organization, often of a military kind. Migrants would often resort to raiding and pillaging. Other peoples, disrupted by their passage, would often join them, gradually increasing their numbers. Migrations could lead to serious clashes and create refugees and set off secondary migrations or rapid expansions. Even when the initial migration was fairly rapid, the population movements that it set off could last for a century and more. Thus the Oromo migration began perhaps in the 1530s, but stability did not return to the regions affected until about 1700.

This description applies to the most extreme cases. Earlier, when documentation is scant, it is often difficult to distinguish between mass migrations and quick but massive expansions, especially by pastoralists. Thus the expansion of the Luo is often understood as a mass migration. It involved whole populations and precipitated numerous secondary movements, and brought turmoil to a vast area, mainly east of the White Nile. But the movement of the Luo went on for a very long time, perhaps half a millennium, and what evidence there is points to drift rather than mass migration, as the Luo usually moved with their flocks and stopped to raise crops. Parts of the Oromo migration show the same characteristics. These examples show that a mass migration is sometimes more like a massive expansion and that drift may also occur at such times. Its distinctive features remain the productive capacities and the militarized structure of a vast people on the move.

Mass migrations are usually attributed to cataclysmic causes, for example a sudden change in climate with ensuing famine and epidemics. Sometimes, however, they are not due to natural disasters. The Vandal migration, for example, is linked to other migrations and to the fall of the Roman empire. Relative over-population is advanced as a cause for the migration of the Banū Hilāl, the Oromo and the *mfecane* but so far there is little proof of this. Population pressure may well be involved in all mass migrations, but it is inadequate by itself as a complete explanation.

Band migrations

Migrations by bands, always armed, involves a relatively small number of people, mostly young men, constituting but a fraction of a population. The usual process was for bands of warriors to strike out to conquer new lands, sometimes, but not always, under a single leader. In some cases, such as that of the Jaga and the Zimba, for instance, the bands finished up disintegrating after defeat; in others, such as that of the Mane, the Tyokosi and the Imbangala, they succeeded in establishing chiefdoms or kingdoms.

Bands could cause serious destruction but because their migrations were smaller in scale and shorter than mass migrations, they caused less turbulence. In most cases they arose from pull factors, but push factors were also sometimes important, for example when the expansion of the *trekboere* drove the Korana and Gonaqua to migrate to the Orange and Caledon rivers. Band migrations were sometimes the consequence of the formation of a state or an expansion of trade from which the migrants wished to reap profits, as in the case of the Jaga.

The Imbangala case is an instructive example. Bands formed near the Kwango river, perhaps following changes within the expanding Lunda state. These bands mixed with marginal people of Ovimbundu and Mbundu polities. The Imbangala engaged in pillage for several years as allies of the Portuguese who were carving out a colony in Angola. By about 1620 they settled near the Kwango, just out of reach of the Portuguese. Their migration resulted in the formation of a state, the kingdom of Kasanje, which became the premier entrepôt for the processing of slaves exported from inner Africa on the route to Luanda. The Imbangala case therefore amounts to a reorganization of socio-political structures and trade, nothing more.

Élite migration

Élite migration is a favourite subject of oral traditions about the founding of states. The first king is a foreigner, often a hunter; he comes from elsewhere, alone or with a few companions; and while the population movement involved is insignificant, the socio-cultural results are vast.

Some of these stories may well be wholly fictitious and do no more than reflect the idea that the king had to be a foreigner because he is a being apart, enveloped in an aura of sacredness and mystery. Others, however, are better founded. Thus a Kuba tale tells of how an exiled Bushoong, Shyaam a Mbul a Ngoong, returned home from the west and formed a kingdom out of antagonistic chiefdoms. It has been shown that linguistic influences from the west entered the Kuba area and then radiated outwards from the court, which supports the notion of cultural domination. It is, however, unlikely that such an effect was obtained from the arrival of one person, and even less from the return of an exile.

In a study of population movements élite migrations can be ignored, but for a study of the development of socio-cultural formations, especially states, they can be of considerable importance.

Documenting population movements

The major sources documenting the history of population movements in Africa are oral, linguistic, archaeological and written. But using them is difficult and requires great care.

Oral tradition cannot record long-term expansion because daily life is so little disturbed by it and the movement so slow that the population is hardly aware of it. No oral tradition can encompass a mass migration because the scale of events is too large; it can only record episodes in it. Moreover, oral traditions tend to confuse mass migrations with band migrations which, being more localized but equally striking, remain in the folk memory. People often remember a diaspora because the inhabitants of a village know from which village their ancestors came. Finally, élite migrations are often remembered in detail. The movements of the ruling family of Mangbetu, for example, are told almost two centuries before their kingdom was founded.

But if the researcher does not take into account the fact that traditions express ideologies and cosmologies, he may fall into error. If a people believes that everything comes from a single place, it will obviously believe too that a migration brought it from that original place to where it lives now. The existence of a paradise implies that of an original migration.

Ideology is also responsible for such themes of origin as the foreign hunter becoming king. This theme is to be found among the Igala of the lower Niger, the kingdoms of the southern savannah and the Great Lakes region, the Shambaa kingdom in Tanzania and the Fipa state between lakes Tanganyika and Rukwa. All these stories reflect not the migration of an élite but the ideology of a state. But a state may indeed have been founded by a foreigner or a small group of foreigners. These stories thus need to be checked by other means, taking account of their precise symbolic meaning and their ideological worth.

Another error often made in the interpretation of traditions is taking the part for the whole. The traditions of origin of the Kamba, the Meru and the Gikuyu in Kenya seem in each case to have elevated the story of one small portion of the population into that of the whole population.

In general, the more stereotypical themes oral traditions contain (and they are to be found even in clan, lineage, village or family histories) the more suspect those traditions are.

Recourse is often had to linguistics, but the facts of language are also difficult to interpret. The general rule is that, when speakers of two languages mix, those in the majority end up imposing their language on the minority. That is why migration or massive expansion generally leads to the spread of the language of the migrating population. When, conversely, as a result of a diaspora or a band migration, a small number of newcomers is brought into contact with greater numbers of indigenous people, it is the newcomers' language that disappears. Most of the apparent exceptions to this rule are not in fact so. A population retains its language in a diaspora when it is reasonably compact and retains relations with its original home. Migrant bands also maintain their language when they do not mix with other peoples: this was the case with the Tyokosi and Mende of Sierra Leone, as opposed to the Imbangala bands who abandoned their language because it had disappeared from their home country.

But there are genuine exceptions to the rule of linguistic assimilation by the more numerous population, which can be traced to the prestige that some minority languages had. Ndebele and Kololo survived in Zimbabwe and Zambia less because they were the languages of conquerors than because, shortly after the conquest, they began to be committed to writing and taught in school. Otherwise, they would have been absorbed by the majority languages, Shona and Luyi.

A second basic rule is that the language absorbed always leaves traces in the language that absorbs it, in the form of loan words, expressions (calques), personal and place names or peculiarities of morphology and syntax. Study of such traces can provide information on the relations among populations.

Linguistics even makes it possible to distinguish the various population movements that occurred. Diasporas are the easiest to detect because they result in long-lasting multi-lingualism and sometimes the formation of creoles. Afrikaans is a creole, as is shown by the major changes in its morphology and even its syntax, as well as the lexical contributions from Malay, Portuguese, Bantu and Khoi or San. Bobangi is a creole from several closely related Bantu languages. Diaspora languages are characterized by simplified grammar and multiple-origin vocabulary. Expansions give rise to far fewer linguistic borrowings. They result in languages being distributed over a wider area than the region directly affected by the movement, which is fairly congruent with the supposed kinship ties among the populations. In mass migrations, on the other hand, this distribution only weakly reflects kinship ties. Mass migrations often produce mixes between more than two languages. The Langi are unlikely to have been involved in a mass migration because their language, Luo, has only been influenced by a single language, Karimojong. When a migrant band is large enough, it imposes its language on the region where it settles and leaves traces in the regions through which it passes, provided that these languages are not too close to its own.

But the main difficulty with the use of linguistics is that unless loans are studied in detail using the 'words and things' (*Worter und Sache*) method, it is not possible to know whether they ought not to be attributed to other causes than population movements such as trade relations, the influence of a state where the language is spoken by the ruling family or the prestige of a religious language. Such a study would be arduous but might yield valuable results.

Archaeology has often been called to help assert the existence of expansions or migrations when similar or identical elements of material culture (objects) or identical customs (such as funerary urns) have been found in different places. But archaeologists today are moving away from this theory of 'migrationism', with the recognition that independent invention occurs more frequently than was previously thought and items could have been diffused by many other means than migrations.

Nevertheless, in many cases population movements seem to have been the source of a great deal of diffusion. When it is observed that a new pottery style, markedly different from previous ones, has spread uniformly in different areas, it is reasonable to suspect diffusion. Thus archaeology does indeed seem to confirm the existence of a population movement, called *kutama*, from south-east Africa to Zimbabwe around 1000. There are many other unfortunately doubtful cases.

Some authors still use ethnographic distributions as evidence of migrations. This once fashionable approach is now completely discredited. Thus, to argue that simply because the Fang had crossbows like other peoples in the Ubangi region, they must have migrated from there, is clearly unreasonable. Ethnographic characteristics can spread without population movement. Their similarities may be due to chance or independent invention. They prove nothing if they are not accompanied by linguistic similarities.

The major population movements 1500–1800

Only two parts of Africa were subject during this period to major redistributions of population and the ensuing creation of new societies and cultures. This was, on the one hand, the Horn area south of the Abbay or Upper Blue Nile, including most of what is now Somalia and northern Kenya, and, on the other, the area to the east of the White Nile, north of lake Nyanza and south of the Sobat. There were several population movements in this area. The most spectacular was the migration of the Oromo into Ethiopia in about 1535. By 1700 a large part of Ethiopia was under Oromo control. The Christians and Muslims had completely lost power in the south-west; the Somali and Oromo were locked in competition for good lands as far as the Tana and smaller sedentary populations had been driven out of Shungwaya, a coastal area just north of the Somali–Kenyan border. These groups, ancestors of the Miji-Kenda, settled in large fortified villages (*kaya*) behind the major port towns of Kenya.

Further west, population movements had begun much earlier, perhaps about 1000, with the migration of the Luo along the White Nile. A large number of groups were on the move, notably the so-called Karamojong group, the Turkana, further east, and the Maasai and southern Nilotes. All these peoples, except the Luo, were primarily pastoralists, like the Oromo and Somali. All were seeking 'empty' lands – lands with a relatively low population density. Their movements were heavily dependent on natural conditions. Thus, the Luo needed well-watered lands, while the camel-rearing nomads, the Somali and southern Oromo, could live in dry areas. It is rare for a population to change its way of life. In some cases, as expansions came to an end, armed conflicts occurred between populations with the same type of economy. Thus, the Kenya Luo wrested lands from their neighbours in the eighteenth century and various Maasai groups fought over land in the nineteenth century. Clearly population pressures were involved here.

These population movements were in effect the story of the colonization of marginal lands, at least until the eighteenth century. The best-watered lands, along the Nile, were first occupied by farmers who also kept cattle. They repelled the newcomers who were seeking to extend their ranges as their numbers increased. This mobility highlights the stability that prevailed everywhere else on the continent, where man had mastered space.

It has been suggested that drought played a major role in these population movements in north-east Africa, but it is no more adequate to explain the mobility of populations than is the collapse of the powerful Ethiopian empire. The fundamental causes are to be found rather in the tensions between the areas where population density was relatively high, as in the Oromo heartland and perhaps the Ethiopian highlands, and, on the other hand, less populous areas such as northern Uganda and Kenya and the Rift Valleys in Kenya and Tanzania. By 1700 these latter regions had been occupied by new groups with economies and societies that permitted higher densities.

Elsewhere, population movements were occurring on a much more modest scale. In southernmost Africa the *trekboere* were colonizing the Karroo veld by ousting or killing its pastoral occupants, while in Namibia both the Herero and the Namib were expanding at the expense of the original San and Dama. The fringes of the Kalahari were being settled as were the arid lands of northern Uganda and northern Kenya. But in the south-east a major area of dis-equilibrium was building up as population growth was outstripping resources. The first signs of instability, perhaps, were the movements of the Tonga northwards into south-eastern Zimbabwe and the band migrations of raiders in Zimbabwe itself.

In the rainforest of Central Africa and in the savannahs of what is now the Central African Republic, mass population movements were under way, but slowly, maintaining a reasonable balance between their number and the available resources. The drift of Mongo groups south led to the formation of the Kuba kingdom and the powerful chiefdoms north of the lower Kasai. Between the Zaire and the Ubangi some higher densities built up – but in patches. It was still possible for a people such as the Ngbandi in the Ubangi valley to drift southward, beyond the river. But by the eighteenth century there were signs of relative overpopulation and the second half of the century saw the birth of a new people, the Zande. They expanded rapidly eastward towards the Nile, creating a series of chiefdoms. In the western part of the rainforest of Central Africa constant migration by drift was taking the populations settled at the confluence of the Mbam and the Sanaga into less populated areas in the south and also perhaps to the west.

Most of the small population movements occurred around states being formed or collapsing. In West Africa the decline of the Mali empire seems to have caused the Soso (Susu), the Baga and the Nalu to leave Futa Jallon and the Mane to migrate in bands to Liberia and Sierra Leone. The development of the Mossi states may well have been connected to the northward movement of the Dogon who settled on the Bandiagara scarp and to the foundation, further south, of Gonja by Mande bands. The formation of the Asante state led to expansion in the west by Baule and Agni groups.

In Central Africa fewer such movements are known. The expansion of the Lunda empire first, then of the Yaka kingdom on the Kwango precipitated the migration of armed bands. The ones in southern Lunda and the one that founded the Kazembe kingdom are the best known. In Malawi a spectacular rise of armed bands occurred as a byproduct of the creation of the Maravi and Lunda states in about 1600. In Zimbabwe small movements of expansion and raiding cannot be confidently associated with the development or decline of states. Some population movements had more to do with the colonization of sparsely settled lands in the south. Madagascar is perhaps the prime example of population movements related to the emergence of kingdoms and chiefdoms: the Maroserana migrations are a good example of this. By 1500 the population of the island was still very mobile, and there were still empty lands. By 1800 most of the island was organized into states of various sorts. During the process of state formation space had been tamed. On the mainland state formation was limited to part of central Tanzania, southern Tanzania and northern Mozambique.

The impressive further development of trade routes south of the Sahara led to the creation of new diasporas and the strengthening of older ones. From west to east the Jahanka, Joola, Yarse, Hausa, Bobangi, Vili, Hungaan, Bisa, Yao and Swahili diasporas are the best known. To these must be added the European ones: the French on the Senegalese coast, the Portuguese in Luanda and Mozambique and the Dutch at the Cape greatly influenced the African mainland in this period. Both European and African diasporas played a growing role in the slave trade as trade routes developed. Peoples living near such major routes sometimes moved closer to them and sometimes fled from them. Thus the Itsekiri expanded to the nearby coast in order to gain a foothold on the sea route to Benin and many inhabitants of Gabon drifted slowly toward the delta of the Ogowe in order to trade there. But the population that was living between the Kwongo and the Kasai seems to have fled the traders and raiders and many in Zimbabwe seem to have moved away from the turbulence created by the Portuguese *feiras*. But all these population movements were small-scale. They represent no more than dynamic readjustments to a reorganization of space in the light of new developments in trade and socio-political relations.

Conclusion

Space had been tamed in most of Africa long before 1500 and population density was sufficiently low for processes of expansion to settle the problems arising from excessive pressure on the land. The main exception was eastern Africa, from the Horn to the Zambezi, excluding the Great Lakes area but including Madagascar. The northern half of this area saw mass migration, new forms of settlement and the rapid expansion of herding groups. In the southern half and on Madagascar a new social organization, associated with the formation of kingdoms and chiefdoms, helped to stabilize settlement and make for more intensive land use.

Population growth cannot have had serious consequences for Africa during this period since it was easily compensated for by population movements. Only here and there do we see the emergence of new technologies making possible better land use and, in turn, higher population densities. The lower Casamance, Igbo country, the Cameroon grasslands, the mountains of the Great Lakes area, along the western Rift with their systems of irrigation and intensive cultivation of bananas, the Kukuya plateau with its novel forms of fertilization or the valley of the Upper Zambezi were and still are exceptions in western and Central Africa. Without going into detail here about why population growth was not greater, we must at least mention that large numbers of Africans left the continent as a result of the trans–Atlantic slave trade.

Outside eastern Africa, population mobility was affected most by the rise and fall of states and by the extension of trading networks. Despite the collapse of some of the larger states in the Sahel in West Africa, the percentage of areas controlled by states was higher in 1800 than it had been in 1500.

An extensive network of trade routes and settlements existed in North and West Africa long before the sixteenth century. There were also a few trade routes in Central Africa, but they only developed in the seventeenth and eighteenth centuries, linking the Atlantic to the Indian Ocean. The spread of trading networks made it possible to exploit resources on a larger scale just as, politically, states controlled larger areas than chiefdoms and village confederations. By linking Africa to other continents, trade routes drew it into the hierarchical organization of the world, that is a system which, from 1500 onwards, was increasingly dominated by Europe.

These three centuries must be seen as a portion of a much longer evolution. Compared with the previous half-millennium, the population of Africa experienced much more stability and the mastery of space was much greater.

But we still know little about population movements. Historical demography and the history of technology are only in their infancy in Africa. We need more data and we particularly need to replace vague notions such as 'migration' by more refined analyses. We shall then be better placed to chronicle a fundamental theme in African history: the slow, gradual colonization of the continent by its inhabitants.

Africa in world history: the export slave trade from Africa and the emergence of an Atlantic economic order

Introduction

While in Graeco-Roman times the slave trade was a known fact in the area around the Mediterranean, the export of slaves in significant quantities from black Africa to the outside world dates from the ninth century. This trade mainly served the area around the Mediterranean (including southern Europe), the Middle East and parts of Asia, and went on for several centuries, lasting even into the early twentieth century. However, the numbers exported annually to this area were never very great. With the opening up of the New World to European exploitation, following the voyage of Christopher Columbus in 1492, a much more extensive slave trade from Africa, involving far larger numbers of people, was added to the older trade: this was the trans-Atlantic slave trade which lasted from the sixteenth century to the mid-nineteenth century. The place of this trade in world history has hitherto not been properly demonstrated.

It must first be noted that trading in slaves is not something that has only occurred in Africa. The world has known chattel slavery and large-scale trade in slaves since the days of the Roman empire. Historical records amply show that all the races of the world have at one time or another sold their own people into slavery in distant lands. For many centuries ethnic groups in eastern and central Europe (particularly the Slavs from whose name the word slave is derived) supplied slaves to the Middle East and North Africa.

Yet, from the point of view of world history, the export slave trade from Africa, particularly the trans-Atlantic trade, is unique in terms of its sheer size, its geographical extent and its economics.

The difficulty of determining its exact place in world history is tied up with the problem of the historical origins of the contemporary world economic order. The controversy over this issue arises from a number of factors: first, the tyranny of differing paradigms conditioning the thought patterns of different scholars; second, the intrusion of political influences into scholarly explanations; and third, inadequate information at the disposal of many scholars.

In this chapter, an attempt will be made to analyse the consequences of the slave trade from Africa in the context of the evolution of the world economic

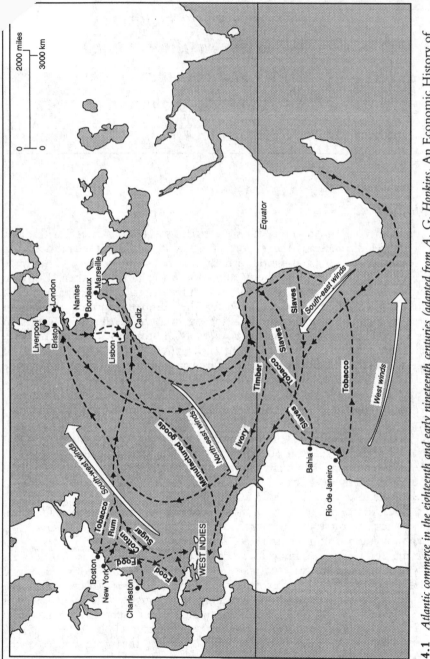

4.1 *Atlantic commerce in the eighteenth and early nineteenth centuries (adapted from A. G. Hopkins, An Economic History of West Africa, London, Longman, 1973. Map reproduced by kind permission of Longman Group UK Ltd)*

order from the sixteenth century. An economic order may be defined as a system of economic relations embracing several countries, simultaneously allocating functions and distributing rewards among them through the mechanism of a trading network. The development of such a system of international economic relations entails the evolution of economic, social and political structures in the various member countries which make it possible for the operation of the system to be maintained entirely by the forces of the market. Once it has reached that point, any important modification of the system can only arise from a deliberate political action, occasioned possibly by a change of regime in one or more countries within the system.

The starting-point here is the notion that an economic order linking together a vast area comprising diverse regions of the world emerged in the Atlantic zone in the nineteenth century. These regions were Western Europe, North America, Latin America, the Caribbean and Africa. The core of this order was Western Europe and later North America, while Latin America, the Caribbean and Africa formed the periphery, with economic, social and political structures to match. The extension of the Atlantic economic order to Asia and the rest of Europe in the nineteenth and twentieth centuries produced the modern world economic order which has since undergone only minor changes. The regions comprising the core and peripheral areas of the nineteenth-century Atlantic economic order have retained their positions ever since, even within the wider order.

This chapter intends to show that the slave trade from Africa was a key factor in the development of the nineteenth-century Atlantic economic order. To develop this argument, efforts will be made to bring out, on the one hand, the role of the African slave trade and slavery in America in the capitalist transformation of Western Europe and North America and, on the other, the role of the same factors in the emergence of dependency structures in Latin America, the Caribbean and Africa by the mid-nineteenth century.

Methodology

Scholars often use differing conceptual frameworks which make them view the same social facts differently. This explains much of the controversy surrounding underdevelopment and dependency. On the one hand, there is an undifferentiated view of all social change as leading to economic and social development. On the other, especially among scholars within the dependency and underdevelopment tradition, social change is differentiated: a distinction is made between two directions of social change, one leading to economic development and the other to underdevelopment and dependency. Both are change, however, and can therefore be studied historically.

Looking at the historical processes leading to the present state of national economies, the undifferentiated view of social change proves incapable of offering a satisfactory explanation. Social change has been taking place in all societies over the centuries. If all social change leads ultimately to economic development, then surely most economies in the world should by now be developed. Yet, by any accepted definition of 'economic development', only a few economies in the world today are developed. The vast majority can only hope to become so by taking very drastic measures such as those taken by China. It follows that the social change which led these economies over the centuries to their present situation is something other than a process of development. It is a historical process which some analysts describe as a process of underdevelopment and dependency.

The approach of underdevelopment and dependency theorists needs closer examination. Social change entails economic, social and political structuring. Some mixture of economic, social and political structures produces economic development, but others create obstacles to development. Analytically, therefore, three types of economies can be distinguished: undeveloped, developed and underdeveloped.

A developed economy should be taken to mean an economy with strong internal structural and sectoral linkages, supported by advanced technology and social and political structures that make self-sustained growth possible. An underdeveloped and dependent economy is an economy that is structurally and sectorally disarticulated by certain internal structures arising from previous international relationships which make it extremely difficult for advanced technology to take root, giving rise to a situation where the economy's expansion or contraction depends entirely on the external sector. Finally, an undeveloped economy is one that possesses neither the structures of development nor those of underdevelopment and hence is still free to move in either of the two directions depending on the opportunities that arise.

Thus, to understand the global effects of the process through which the international economy was created, we need to examine the kinds of economic, social and political structures to which that process gave rise in the different economies it embraced. For that, it will be useful to use a fundamental hypothesis provided by underdevelopment and dependency theorists, which is that, during the mercantilist epoch, the capitalist transformation of what became the core countries of the world economy produced at the same time a consolidation and further extension of pre-capitalist social formations in areas that became the periphery. If this was indeed the case, then the development of the core countries led to both underdevelopment and dependency structures in the periphery. This chapter is organized around this hypothesis in order to test it against the historical evidence.

The volume of the slave trade from Africa

To make a fair assessment of the role of the slave trade from Africa in world history, it is important to establish as accurate an estimate as possible of the volume of the trade over the centuries. In this regard, considerable progress has been made with respect to the most important branch of this trade, the trans-Atlantic slave trade, starting from estimates published by P.D. Curtin in 1969. Since 1976 other specialists (J. E. Inikori, C. A. Palmer, E. Vila Vilar, L. B. Rout

Jr., D. Eltis and R. Stein) have published the results of detailed research centred on different portions of these estimates.

Although this research work is not yet complete, all the results go to show that Curtin's global figures for the Atlantic slave trade were much too low and require a 40 per cent upward revision. Curtin's global estimate of 11 million slaves exported thus rises to 15.4 million.

For the trade across the Sahara, the Red Sea and the Indian Ocean, the existing estimates are less firmly founded. Raymond Mauny computed 10 million slaves for the period 1400–1900 and Ralph Austen arrived at a total of 6,856,000 for the period 1500–1890, 3,956,000 for the trans-Saharan trade and 2,900,000 for the trade across the Red Sea and the Indian Ocean. Taking Austen's estimates, which seem more securely based, then some 22 million people were exported from black Africa to the rest of the world between 1500 and 1890.

The capitalist transformation of Western Europe and North America in the era of the slave trade and slavery

When Christopher Columbus arrived in the Caribbean in 1492, the West European economies were by definition undeveloped. Subsistence agriculture and self-employed handicraft manufacturing were still the dominant economic activities of the working population employed. Social and political structures were such that extra-economic coercion still dominated the distribution of the social product.

However, some major changes had been occurring in Western Europe in the previous three or four centuries. The growth of population and its regional redistribution during the Middle Ages stimulated the development of inter-regional and international trade. Major innovations had been introduced in the organization of land and labour and these changes were accompanied by some changes in social structures. The conditions were thus prepared which enabled the economies of Western Europe to seize the opportunities offered by the emergence of the Atlantic system.

Of course, not all the economies of Western Europe underwent changes to the same degree in the late Middle Ages. In particular, England experienced the most remarkable changes as a result of the combined effects of the wool trade and population expansion. These marked differences from country to country in the level of change explain the differing rates of capitalist transformation of the countries of Western Europe between the sixteenth and nineteenth centuries.

In order to analyse the impact of the evolving Atlantic system on the economies of Western Europe, two periods are distinguishable: 1500–1650 and 1650–1820.

During the first period, the economies and societies of the Atlantic region were not yet structured in a way that enabled market forces to maintain fully the operation of a single economic system that could allocate functions and

rewards among member countries. In consequence, Western Europe
..s military superiority to command resources from other economies and
..eties in the region.

The most important resources that came to Western Europe from the rest of
the Atlantic area during this period were silver and gold. These came mainly
from Spanish America (the Spanish colonies in the New World), the gold trade
from West Africa having declined as the slave trade took hold. From Spain, the
silver and gold from the New World were distributed throughout Western
Europe, accelerating the process of commercialization of economic activities.
The interaction between the rapidly increasing quantities of money in circulation and population growth produced what is known in European history as the
price revolution of the sixteenth century.

The import of American bullion also gave a fillip to the growth of international trade within Europe. In Spain, only Spanish nationals and Spanish
ships were allowed to carry goods to and from Spanish America, and trade was
restricted to only two ports in the whole of Europe, Cadiz and Seville. Yet, all
sorts of underground arrangements enabled merchants from other European
countries to participate in this trade with Spanish America.

Thus, in the sixteenth century, Spain became the centre of a large-scale international trade dominated by Holland, France and England. The silver and gold
from Spanish America left Spain within months of their arrival and, injected into
the major economies of the region, fuelled their transformation processes. As A.
Christelow wrote: 'Spain kept the cow and the rest of Europe drank the milk',
and this continued all through the seventeenth and into the eighteenth century.

In the second period, 1650–1820, the structuring of the economies and
societies of the Atlantic area reached its climax and the process of capitalist transformation in Western Europe came to depend on the Atlantic system. The role
of the latter system in the economic development of Western Europe can only
be fully appreciated when viewed against the background of the general crisis
of the seventeenth century in Western Europe.

Imports of American bullion reached their peak in the 1590s and then
declined, and population growth slowed down. The situation was worsened by
the policy of economic nationalism adopted by a number of West European
countries during the seventeenth century. As a result of the tariff walls erected by
France, England and other countries to protect home industries, the economic
situation degenerated into a general crisis and inter-regional trade collapsed. The
process of capitalist transformation was stopped in its tracks in some countries,
while a reverse process occurred in others, with Italy being the worst hit.

The nature and origin of the seventeenth-century crisis show clearly that for
the capitalist transformation process to be completed, the region needed much
greater economic opportunities than Europe alone could offer.

The changes that occurred in the structuring of the economies and societies
of the non-European areas of the Atlantic between 1650 and 1820 offered both
immense opportunities and challenges, which would completely alter the
economic situation in Western Europe. In the New World, the production of

precious metals continued to be important, but the key element in the structuring of the economies and societies of the region was the growth of large-scale plantation agriculture. In mainland North America, the products were chiefly tobacco and cotton, but in Latin America and the Caribbean, sugar was king. The scale of operation of the new economy necessitated a complete repopulation of the New World.

A great volume of trade was organized around the shipping of goods from Africa and the Americas, slaves from Africa to the Americas and agricultural produce and precious metals from the Americas to Western Europe. Since the colony-owning Western European countries restricted the movement of goods, their control of the distribution of American commodities in Europe became a major factor in the growth of intra-European trade in the seventeenth and eighteenth centuries. The main beneficiaries of these developments were England, France and Holland. According to F. Crouzet, a French economic historian, 'the eighteenth century can truly be called the Atlantic stage of European development'.

The new economic opportunities brought about by the expansion of the Atlantic system increased employment and stimulated population growth all over Western Europe after the seventeenth-century decline. The growth of domestic markets in England, France and Holland, combined with the growth of exports, provided the demand pressures that provoked the inventions and technological innovations of the eighteenth-century and nineteenth-century industrial revolutions in Western Europe. In this way, the phenomenal expansion of commodity production, trade, finance and shipping which occurred in the Atlantic area between 1650 and 1820 enabled the countries of Western Europe to overcome the crisis of the seventeenth century, break the shackles of traditional economic and social structures and complete the process of capitalist transformation. The first country to succeed in doing this was England.

That part of the New World that in 1783 became the United States of America, but which in the seventeenth century and until 1776 was made up of colonies, nevertheless played a considerable role in this expansion even in this early period. When Columbus arrived in the Americas, these territories were probably among the most economically undeveloped. Population density was very low and the territories were dominated by subsistence activities which continued long after their settlement by European colonists.

The involvement of these territories in the Atlantic system in the years immediately preceding the Declaration of Independence considerably altered the situation. The total annual value of the Atlantic trade of British North America during these years was £8.4 million. With a total population of 2.2 million in 1770, that represents £3.80 per head of population. The magnitude of involvement in the Atlantic system stimulated the growth of the domestic market and production for market exchange, as it encouraged specialization, raised per capita income and influenced the rate of migration into the area.

As the British North American colonies moved gradually from subsistence activities to market production under the impact of the Atlantic system, three economic regions comprising the southern, middle and northern (mainly New England) colonies became distinguishable. The combination of rich natural resources and cheap African slave labour encouraged the southern colonies to expand plantation agriculture, first rice and tobacco, then cotton. The middle colonies took to foodstuffs production on family farms. The northern colonies were relatively poor in natural resources for agriculture but were endowed with deep natural harbours and forest resources for shipbuilding and this encouraged early specialization in trade and shipping. In this way, the south produced practically all the plantation commodities that were exported to Europe, while the north produced the bulk of the invisible exports (shipping, merchants, services, insurance etc.) and the middle colonies produced foodstuffs for export and some export services.

These differing forms of involvement in the Atlantic system produced differing economic and social structures. In the middle and northern colonies, production was based on free white labour, property ownership was widely spread and incomes were quite evenly distributed. In the southern colonies, the predominance of plantation agriculture dependent on African slave labour produced a population with a large proportion of slaves, a high concentration of property ownership and an extremely uneven distribution of income. Of the 697,000 slaves in the United States in 1790, 642,000 were in the southern states, where they accounted for 36 per cent of the total population. While the structures in the middle and northern colonies encouraged the growth of a home market for mass consumer goods, the structures in the south restricted the growth of that kind of domestic market and encouraged the import of foreign luxury goods. In this way, while the foundation for self-sustained economic growth was laid in the middle and northern colonies during the colonial period, dependency structures were built up in the south.

After the achievement of independence, the economy of the southern states continued to depend on African slave labour, to whom they owed the phenomenal expansion of their cotton production between 1790 and 1860. In consequence, the economic and social structures of the colonial period were maintained.

However, the politically independent United States government adopted economic measures which gradually turned the south from dependency on Europe to dependency on the northern states. With government protection, the ship-owners and merchants of the north-eastern states took over the shipping of southern cotton to Europe and the import of European manufactures for southern planters and their slaves. At the same time, the expansion of cotton production in the south provided a growing food market which stimulated the growth of commercial food production in the west and the flow of immigrants. The creation of a vast domestic market encouraged the growth of import-substitution industries in the north-east. In this way, the United States took advantage of its political independence at the right moment to manipulate the forces operating in the Atlantic area to the benefit of its economy, aided by the favourable structures that developed in the middle and southern colonies during the colonial period. The dependency structures of the southern states thus acted as essential conditions for the capitalist transformation of the northern and western states.

The evolution of underdevelopment structures in Latin America and the Caribbean

By our definition, the countries of Latin America and the Caribbean were un-developed economies when Columbus arrived in the area. Three main factors were responsible for this general absence of development: population, geography and isolation from the rest of the world.

Estimates of the population of all the Americas in 1492 vary enormously, from 8.5 million to 112 million. The more recent research of the Berkeley School, however, indicates that a range of between 50 million and 100 million is more plausible. Relative to the large geographical extent of the Americas, even the highest figure is small. Moreover, it was broadly concentrated in three areas: Central America, comprising the kingdoms of the Aztecs and the Mayas; the Inca empire of ancient Peru; and the Caribbean island of Hispaniola, now made up of Haiti and the Dominican Republic. The rest of the New World was very sparsely populated.

The low population density had adverse effects on the development of trade and the division of labour. Areas with high population densities were difficult of access because of the topography, and this limited intra-American trade. In addition, the Americas remained isolated from the rest of the world until 1492 and, as a result, their rich natural resources had little commercial value and there-fore made little or no contribution to population and trade. This explains why, by 1492, the ancient civilizations of Central and South America had reached a high level of cultural development but were not at all developed economically.

The trading opportunities opened up by the arrival of Europeans came under conditions which led to the evolution of structures of underdevelopment rather than development. First, the West European countries forcefully seized control of the natural resources of Latin America and the Caribbean. The Indian population, humiliated and demoralized, then overworked and decimated by the unfamiliar diseases brought by the Europeans, collapsed all over the region. Thus, the population of central Mexico, estimated at between 18.8 million and 26.3 million before the European conquest, fell to 6.3 million in 1548 and 1.9 million in 1580. By 1605, it was down to only 1.1 million.

The virtual annihilation of the Indian population had two major consequences. The first was the massive import of African slave labour, intended to replace it, and the other was the take-over by European colonists of agricultural land that was turned into large estates (*hacienda* or *fazenda*). Both developments provided trading opportunities that stimulated the capitalist transformation of Western Europe and North America, while at the same time producing underdevelopment and dependency in Latin America and the Caribbean.

4.2 *Negro slaves cutting sugar cane on a plantation in the West Indies, c.1833* (The Saturday Magazine, 1833, © The Mary Evans Picture Library)

The magnitude of contraband slave imports into Spanish America in the sixteenth and seventeenth centuries makes it almost impossible to quantify the contribution of African slave labour to the production of precious metals in this region during this period. However, a census taken in Spanish America by the clergy in 1796 shows that there were 679,842 people of African origin in Mexico and 539,628 in Peru. In Brazil, production of sugar for export in these centuries depended entirely on African slave labour and, when the gold boom occurred in the eighteenth century, actual production still practically depended on their labour. This is borne out by the ethnic composition of the Brazilian population in the eighteenth and nineteenth centuries. In 1798 people of African origin made up 61.2 per cent of the total population of Brazil and in 1872, 58 per cent. The slave populations were concentrated in the six provinces that produced gold and agricultural products for export: Bahia, Pernambuco, Rio de Janeiro, São Paulo, Minas Gerais and Rio Grande do Sul.

In the Caribbean, from the second half of the seventeenth century, the large-scale import of African slaves and the expansion of plantation agriculture precipitated the demise of subsistence agriculture while production for export grew rapidly. The ethnic composition was also profoundly altered. Thus, to take the combined population of Barbados, Jamaica and the Leeward Islands, the slave population increased from 40.5 per cent in 1660 to 80.2 per cent in 1713. Similarly, the population of African origin in the French West Indies grew from about 52 per cent of the total population in the late seventeenth century to about 88 per cent in 1780.

It was this massive transplantation of African labour into Latin America, the Caribbean and the southern territories of North America that produced the phenomenal expansion of commodity production and trade in the Atlantic area between the sixteenth and nineteenth centuries, but it was far from having the same effects in these countries as in Western Europe and North America. Because the population in Latin America and the Caribbean included a high proportion of slaves, the vast majority of the people earned far too little for a domestic consumer goods market to develop. Lacking an outlet locally, the profits from mining and plantation agriculture thus went for the purchase of manufactured articles imported from Europe or were repatriated to Europe to finance investment and consumption there. This situation was aggravated by colonial laws which restricted the establishment of industries in Latin America and the Caribbean.

The lack of industrial development gave rise to disarticulated economies in Latin America and the Caribbean, with the mining and agricultural sectors being closely linked to the economies of Western Europe and also, later, to the economy of the United States. Associated with this development was the emergence of economic empires closely tied to importing and exporting, the only activities in which the mining magnates and agrarian oligarchies of Latin America and the Caribbean saw any interest. The prosperous merchant class also became enmeshed in importing and exporting. Even after the major countries of Latin America won political independence in the nineteenth century, governments continued to favour the production of primary commodities for the export and import of manufactured goods. In addition, the industrial revolutions in Western Europe and the United States in the nineteenth century reduced production costs, which meant that the prices of manufactured goods traded in the Atlantic area were so low that the newly independent countries of Latin America were unable to establish competitive national manufacturing industries for the domestic market. Thus, by the mid-nineteenth century, the economies and societies of Latin America and the Caribbean had become so structured that underdevelopment and dependency had become entrenched.

The laying of the foundations of dependency structures in Africa

The available data show that African societies were going through major processes of transformation when the Europeans arrived in the late fifteenth century. Recent archaeological findings, such as the remains of Igbo-Ukwu, indicate that a high level of social and economic transformation had already been attained in a number of places by that time. However, the process had hardly begun and economic and social structures still conformed basically to our definition of undevelopment. The total population relative to the available agricultural land was still very small and, in addition, was scattered over the huge continent, with groups separated from one another by long distances and difficult terrain. The presence of a massive desert between black Africa and the Mediterranean and the Middle East (the centres of international commerce for many centuries) limited black Africa's trade with the rest of the world to commodities with very high value but relatively low transport costs – gold and slaves.

The establishment of seaborne commerce between Africa and Western Europe from the second half of the fifteenth century seemed at first to offer the kind of possibilities that black Africa needed for rapid social and economic transformation. The gold trade expanded. Trade in agricultural commodities, such as pepper, was initiated and some stimulus was even given to African cloth producers as the Portuguese and the Dutch participated in the distribution of African cloths to different parts of the African coast.

These early developments, however, were short-lived. When the vast resources of the Americas became accessible to Western Europe, the role of Africa in the Atlantic economic system was altered. The population which Africa needed to build up in order to provide the internal conditions necessary for a complete structural transformation of its economies and societies was transferred massively to the Americas. The conditions created over a period of three centuries by this massive transfer of population discouraged the development of commodity production in Africa and laid the foundations for dependency structures there.

The first loss inflicted by this forced migration was the elimination of population growth and the depopulation of large areas of the continent. It was estimated above that some 22 million people were exported from black Africa to the rest of the world between 1500 and 1890.

In order to determine how far these exports reduced the reproductive

4.3 *Slaves being loaded on to a European slaving ship (©The Hulton-Deutsch Collection, London)*

of the populations of black Africa, an analysis is needed of the age and
_position of the exported population, because it is the number of females
of chi_d-bearing age that is important.

In the case of the trade across the Sahara and the Red Sea, young and
attractive females predominated because of the demand for concubines. It is
generally believed that the sex ratio was two females to one male. For the trans-
Atlantic trade, recent research now provides data with which to show sex ratios
for 404,705 Africans imported into various New World territories during the
seventeenth, eighteenth and nineteenth centuries, that is, about 3 per cent of
total exports to the Americas. Overall, females made up 32.9 per cent of the
sample.

An examination of data for the trans-Atlantic trade shows consistent
variations of the sex ratios according to the regions of Africa from which the
slaves came. The Nigerian area, from the Bight of Benin to the Bight of Biafra,
exported the largest proportion of females, ranging from two-fifths to one-half of
total exports. However, the other major exporting area, the Congo–Angola area,
regularly exported a larger proportion of males than the general average. This
regional variation is very important in assessing the demographic impact of slave
exports at the micro-regional level.

For the whole of black Africa, the evidence analysed shows that the number
of females exported annually was of a magnitude that must have drastically
reduced the region's reproductive capacity. Considering the additional population losses caused by exports to the Americas (mortality between the time of
capture and the time of final export) and the 6.9 million blacks exported to the
rest of the world, the evidence indicates that the population of black Africa
declined absolutely, at least between 1650 and 1850. As for the areas of origin of
the large numbers exported through the Bight of Benin, the Bight of Biafra and
Congo–Angola, they must have suffered serious depopulation.

Again, because the enslavement of the bulk of the exported population was
achieved largely through force, the export slave trade had a serious distorting
impact on African social and political structures. Indeed, a number of contemporary observers say as much. In 1730 an officer of the Dutch West India
Company observed that the Gold Coast had become virtually a pure Slave
Coast and that, since the introduction of firearms by the Europeans, the kings
and princes had engaged in terrible wars against one another with the aim of
taking prisoners who were immediately resold as slaves. Later in the eighteenth
century, an African observer, Olaudah Equiano, wrote:

> From what I can recollect of these battles, they appear to have been irruptions of one
> little state or district on the other, to obtain prisoners or booty. Perhaps they were
> incited to this by those traders who brought the European goods I mentioned
> amongst us. Such a mode of obtaining slaves in Africa is common; and I believe
> more are procured this way, and by kidnapping, than any other.

These observations show the strong link that existed between the export slave
trade and the frequency of wars in Africa during the period.

One major distortion was the creation of military aristocracies that became so politically influential that they determined the direction of state policy in virtually all major African states of the period. The existence of a large export market for captives made them see war as a means of acquiring prisoners to be sold rather than more territories whose natural and human resources could be integrated and exploited. This had two negative effects on these states: on their size, which remained limited, and on their internal political stability, which remained extremely fragile.

In several African societies, the existence of these military aristocracies, combined with the prevailing economic conditions, also stimulated the growth of the slave mode of production. Large sections of the populations of major African societies came to be held by individuals who, as either merchants or government functionaries, were connected directly or indirectly with the export slave trade. Given the shortage of human resources relative to the available cultivable land, the structures that had been established remained even after the suppression of the external demand for slaves.

The overall consequences of these historical processes covering a period of more than three centuries was to alter the direction of the economic process in Africa away from development and towards underdevelopment and dependency. The expansion of the slave mode of production in large areas of Africa had the effect of limiting the development of domestic markets and market production. Moreover, the Atlantic slave trade in various ways obstructed the development of commodity trade with Europe that would have stimulated the growth of intra-African trade and production for the market. Hence, by the middle of the nineteenth century, subsistence production of foodstuffs remained dominant in African economies. This virtually eliminated any capital accumulation in agriculture and, therefore, any increase in productivity in food-crop farming for the domestic market. The low productivity of African foodstuffs farmers today is the legacy of three centuries of history, whose negative features were made worse by the economic impact of colonialism in the twentieth century.

The low level of the division of labour and the limited size of the domestic markets were unfavourable to the development of manufacturing beyond the handicraft stage. The development of manufacturing was further hampered by the uncontrolled import of European and oriental manufactures in exchange for captives. Thus, with limited domestic markets, non-capitalized agricultural and industrial sectors and small-scale states dominated by merchants and warriors depending on a slave mode of production, the foundation was firmly laid for Africa to become dependent on the industrialized economies of the Atlantic area. And, starting in the late nineteenth century, the full edifice was completed by colonial rule.

Conclusion

The evidence and analysis can now be summarized. When Christopher Columbus arrived in the Americas, the economies of the Atlantic area were all,

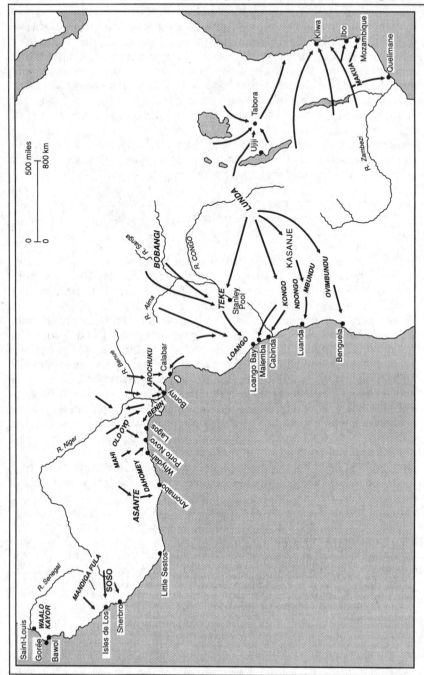

4.4 Sources of the Atlantic slave trade from Africa in the eighteenth and nineteenth centuries (after J. E. Inikori)

by definition, undeveloped. In Europe as in Africa and the Americas, manufacturing was at the handicraft stage and was part and parcel of agriculture, the overwhelmingly dominant sector. Pre-capitalist modes of production were everywhere dominant. By the mid-nineteenth century enormous gaps had opened up between the economies of the various regions of the Atlantic area. On the one hand, mechanized industries were concentrated around the fringes of the Atlantic in north-western Europe and the north-eastern USA. On the other, the greater part of the Atlantic area was dominated by primary commodities: commercial foodstuffs production and plantation agriculture in the western and southern USA; plantation agriculture in the Caribbean; mining, large-scale livestock raising and plantation agriculture in Latin America; and subsistence farming and part-time gathering of wild products for export in Africa (the export of slaves having been halted). The economies and societies of the Atlantic area had become structured into a single economic system ruled by market forces. Barring deliberate political action in one or more member states to alter these structures radically, the situation was bound to be self-perpetuating.

The facts clearly show that this situation derived ultimately from the export of slaves from Africa. The industrial revolution in England in the eighteenth and early nineteenth centuries and in the north-eastern USA in the nineteenth century could not have occurred without the phenomenal expansion of commodity production and trade in the Atlantic area from the sixteenth to the nineteenth century. There is no doubt whatsoever that it was African slave labour provided by the slave trade from Africa that made this phenomenal expansion possible.

While this expansion stimulated the growth of free wage labour to become the dominant form of economic activity in north-western Europe and the north-eastern USA, in the rest of the Atlantic area the slave mode of production expanded. In Latin America, the Caribbean and the southern USA, its expansion provided the conditions for unequal development that facilitated the rapid development of capitalism in north-western Europe and the north-eastern USA. The historical process that produced capitalism in these areas along the fringes of the Atlantic produced at the same time a consolidation and an extension of pre-capitalist modes of production in Africa, Latin America, the Caribbean and the southern USA.

It is important to note that at the time the Atlantic economic order was being constructed, Western Europe could not establish with Asia a firm trading link based on the exchange of what each produced. Europe had little to offer apart from the gold and silver of the Americas. By the nineteenth century, however, Western Europe and North America were able to integrate the economies of Asia firmly into the Atlantic economic order, as Asians found it difficult to resist the products of their mechanized industry, notably textiles from English and North American mills.

In this way, with the help of colonial rule, the Atlantic economic order was extended to the rest of the world, producing the twentieth-century world economic order, which was originally constructed with the sweat and blood of Africans.

5

The African diaspora in the Old and New Worlds

Europe and the Americas

Lack of documentation makes it difficult to know exactly when Africans first arrived in Iberia or the rest of Europe. However, it is likely that some Africans from north and south of the Sahara made their way into the Iberian Peninsula in ancient times when trans-Saharan trade flourished.

Africans also took part in the Muslim campaign in Iberia in 711, and the ensuing centuries of Muslim-Christian warfare saw Africans fighting as soldiers and serving as slaves. Indeed, as early as the thirteenth century, Moorish merchants were selling slaves from sub-Saharan Africa at fairs at Guimarães in northern Portugal.

The Portuguese capture of Ceuta in 1415 opened up the era of European penetration into Africa. Africans were taken to Lisbon from 1441, and this was the prelude to the slave trade which continued into modern times. Indeed, between 1450 and 1500 Portugal imported an estimated 700–900 African slaves annually. In 1468 the Portuguese crown initiated the famous *asiento* (monopoly) over the trade in slaves south of the Senegal river.

The papal bulls of Nicholas V (1454) and Calixtus III (1456), which presented Portuguese expansion into Africa as a crusade to Christianize the continent, gave a degree of justification to the enslavement of Africans. This argument was further supported by the biblical myth of Ham, the son of Noah, whose descendants were said to be cursed and condemned to slavery.

In Spain and Portugal black slaves worked in mines, on farms, in construction, as soldiers, guards, domestics, messengers, stevedores and factory labourers; women were concubines. Those who were not slaves were invariably to be found doing the most menial and arduous tasks.

The sale and use of slaves were primarily urban phenomena, as African labour largely came in through ports and cities, chiefly Barcelona, Cadiz, Seville and Valencia in Spain, and Lisbon in Portugal. Urban life provided numerous opportunities for slaves to escape and, in some cases, to purchase their freedom. The 'free' blacks congregated and sought to cultivate a community spirit and defend their interests. Religious brotherhoods were organized in Barcelona in

1455, in Valencia in 1472 and Seville in 1475. These organizations sponsored recreational activities, raised money to free other slaves and bought burial plots, as blacks had generally to be buried in separate areas.

Some free blacks achieved distinction in Spanish society. Cristóbal de Meneses became a prominent Dominican priest; Juán de Pareja and Sebastián Gómez were both painters; Leonardo Ortez became a lawyer; in 1475 Juán de Valladolid was appointed supervisor over the blacks in Seville. More remarkable still is the case of Juán Latino, a black scholar, who received two degrees at the University of Granada and taught there.

There was no official policy for the slave trade to the New World until 1518 when Charles I of Portugal proclaimed the *Asiento do Negroes* which had the effect of intensifying competition in the trade in African slaves. Although under Spanish rule, Portugal established a virtual monopoly of the slave trade for itself by 1600, making contracts with the Spanish, the Dutch and the French. In 1713, following the War of the Spanish Succession, this monopoly went to England, which then became the biggest slave-dealer in the world.

Yet the number of Africans living in England itself was growing all the time. In 1556 Elizabeth I observed that there were too many 'blackamoors' in England and that they should be returned to Africa. From the eighteenth century, West Indian planters adopted the habit of bringing their African domestics with them when they came on home visits. Military and naval officers and captains of slave vessels did the same. Gradually ownership of black slaves came to be seen as a mark of social distinction. Newspapers in London, Bristol, Liverpool and elsewhere offered slaves for sale and carried advertisements to secure the return of runaways. In England slave-hunters became past masters at capturing Africans who enjoyed no legal protection. Many of them were identified by the marks that had been burnt into their skins by slave-owners. The psychological effects of this control by whites over blacks cannot be overestimated. The process of dehumanizing the African was well under way by the eighteenth century.

But the question arose of knowing the status of Africans living in England. Some English people thought that conversion to Christianity should bring freedom and the rights of civilized men. Granville Sharp was one of those who fought for the abolition of slavery. He defended the case of African slaves before the courts, notably in 1772, that of James Summerset, who had run away and been recaptured. Lord Mansfield, who ruled on the case, did not abolish slavery but did rule that a slave-master could not legally compel a slave to accompany him abroad – a decision that signalled the beginning of the erosion of slavery in England.

In France, people began to pay attention to the African presence in the fifteenth century. This was the period when French sailors frequented various parts of the West African coast, bringing back Africans to France, first as evidence of their voyages and later for sale as slaves.

The development of slavery in France was not originally intended. Indeed, a royal court in 1571 proclaimed that: 'France, mother of freedom, admits of no

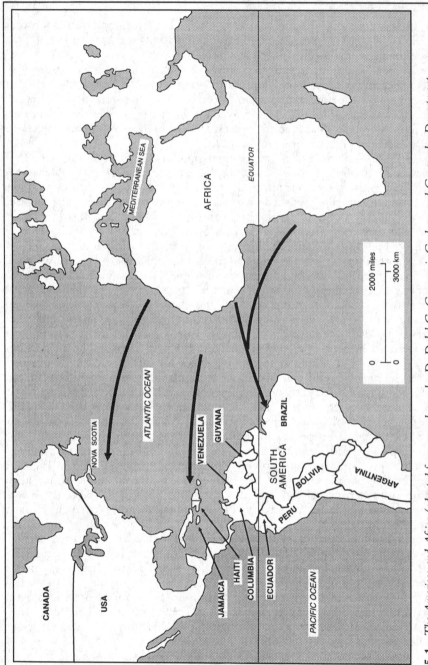

5.1 *The Americas and Africa (adapted from map drawn by Dr Dulal C. Goswami, Geology and Geography Department, Howard University, Washington DC)*

slave.' However, practices varied from case to case: some Africans were enslaved while others remained nominally free in a hostile environment. Several observers noted the African presence in such cities as Angers, Lyon, Orléans, Nantes and Paris. They were active as servants, domestics and even as pages in noble households. Others were soldiers, such as those in the Saxe-Volontaires Regiment which was made up of people from Guinea, Congo and Madagascar; they won acclaim in several battles in Europe in the eighteenth century. The most distinguished black in the French military was General Alexandre Davy Dumas (1762–1806), born of a French father and an African mother, whose son and grandson won fame in the world of the arts.

From the end of the seventeenth century, Africans were arriving in France in significant numbers and, during the eighteenth, royal policy permitted French slave-owners in the Americas to bring their slaves to France.

Much less has been written about the African presence in other parts of Europe. It is known, however, that a number of Africans, especially Ethiopian envoys and pilgrims, visited Europe during the late Middle Ages and other Africans were living in Venice, the Vatican and neighbouring cities. Venetians were both slave-traders and slave-owners. Although most slaves seem to have been of European and Asian origin, some were Africans. Documentation is too scanty to give a picture of the lives of Africans in Venice and neighbouring areas. Some reports assert that they became absorbed into local families, which would explain their virtual disappearance by the late eighteenth century. All had to be baptized, and that may have helped to alleviate their lot.

The most dramatic effects of the African diaspora occurred on the other side of the Atlantic Ocean, in the Americas. For most of the fifteenth century the slave trade remained limited to the Caribbean and Central and South America. It was associated with the development of Portuguese plantations in Brazil and Dutch ones in the Guyanas. The sixteenth-century phase of the trade coincided with African participation in the exploration of the Americas. Two hundred Africans accompanied Alvarado's expedition to Quito, and others joined Pizarro's expedition to Peru. The best known of them was Estevanico, who played an important part in the Spanish exploration of New Mexico and Arizona. Africans also participated in the French expeditions to Canada and in the conquest of the Mississippi valley.

In 1619 a Dutch vessel brought 20 'negars' to Jamestown as indentured servants. This introduction of African labour initiated a demand for black workers and various practices were introduced to restrict their freedom. This culminated in the official establishment of slavery in the English North American colonies in 1660 and, by the end of the century, Africans were legally relegated to the position of slaves, property to be disposed of as their masters saw fit without regard to the fact that they were human beings.

Meanwhile, England and Spain were fighting for dominance in the Caribbean. The sugar plantations demanded a big labour force and large numbers of slaves were imported from the Gold Coast, Angola, Congo, Nigeria, Dahomey and, by the 1690s, Madagascar.

By the last decades of the seventeenth century, the English and the French had secured their dominance in the Caribbean and slavery developed in Jamaica and Barbados, providing a model for North America. In addition, the Caribbean 'seasoning' centres, where African slaves were 'broken in', came into being. The rebellions of these 'seasoned' slaves also served as models for slave resistance in North America.

Areas with a high density of black slaves, such as British Guyana, Jamaica, Brazil and San Domingo (Haiti), were the areas which experienced the most frequent and most serious conspiracies and revolts. The first was the Maroon War which broke out in Jamaica in 1725, when bands of slaves fled into the mountains and established their own communities there. Guyana suffered several serious revolts during the eighteenth century. In the 1740s black resistance led the Dutch to sign a treaty of friendship with the Coromante leader Adoe. The 1760s were marked by the great rebellion of 1763–4 by Africans and creoles led by Cuffy.

But it was in Brazil that the African armed struggle reached unprecedented proportions and lasted longest, at least in the seventeenth century. In the state of Palmares, an autonomous community of Africans estimated to number 20,000, chiefly Bantu from the Congo–Angola region, survived from 1605 to 1695. They sought to model their society on that of their homeland and resisted both the Dutch and the Portuguese before being finally overcome in 1695.

These freedom struggles illustrate the awakening of African nationalism among the slaves in the Caribbean and Latin America. In these struggles African religions such as *obeah* and *vodum* were powerful organizing tools. Islam played a similar role, especially in Bahia where it helped to bring the Hausa and Yoruba together.

In North America too, during the same period, Africans fomented plots and launched several insurrections. Most plantations were situated far away from terrain suitable to rebellious activity, such as the mountains of Jamaica or the jungles of Guyana. But many slaves from the southern colonies of North America fled to live among the Indians with whom they later raided neighbouring plantations. Insurrections also occurred in Virginia and Maryland in the early eighteenth century as soon as it became clear that the indentured system was going to be replaced by life enslavement.

In 1730 slave conspiracies were uncovered in the three colonies of Virginia, Carolina and Louisiana. In 1731 a mutiny broke out on board a slave ship lying off Rhode Island and, four years later, slaves on board the slaver *Dolphin* destroyed themselves and their captors. The most serious revolt was in 1739 in South Carolina, just as Cudjoe was holding off the British army in the mountains of Jamaica. It is known as Cato's Rebellion.

Similar troubles occurred in the northern colonies of North America, where there were fewer than 3,000 Africans among almost six times as many whites and there were no plantations. In 1712 a group led by a Gold Coast African attempted to burn down New York City. A similar attempt was made in

Boston in 1723. In 1741 Africans again attempted to burn down New York, and this incident was widely publicized. By 1772 it was being suggested in the American colonies that all free blacks be deported to Africa or the West Indies, they being regarded as the instigators of resistance. Hanging and brutal treatment were meted out to those caught engaging in revolutionary activities.

Between 1750 and 1775 events that would decide the fate of Africans were moving to a climax in both North America and the Caribbean. As British supremacy was becoming more and more firmly established, the anti-slavery movement began to take off in Britain. In 1772 Lord Mansfield made his famous decision that it was illegal to hold an individual in slavery within the British Isles. In the American colonies a movement was developing among whites in favour of political independence from the British crown.

In 1776 the North American colonies proclaimed their Declaration of Independence. Literate Africans, whether slave or free, joined Europeans in claiming the right to freedom. Some fought side by side with whites against the British. A group of coloured volunteers came from the French colony of San Domingo to support the colonists who were fighting the British at Savannah in Georgia. In North America, the struggle for freedom had begun: the Europeans were seeking freedom from British rule, while the Africans wanted freedom from both the British and the American colonists.

The Africans in the American diaspora were an integral part of a world dominated by European powers where powerful economic and intellectual forces were reshaping political and social structures. Faced with these forces, Africans were divided: some were convinced that salvation lay in the assimilation of European values; others sought to assert their Africanness and were ready to risk their lives in protest and resistance against European repression.

The Sierra Leone experiment reflected the convictions of the former group. In London there was a sizeable black community and the abolitionists had the idea of resettling liberated Africans in Africa so that they might found there a society based on free labour which would spread Christianity, develop a Western-style economy and contribute to the abolition of slavery. Thus, in 1787, over 400 liberated Africans were sent from England and settled in Sierra Leone. This was the first attempt to repatriate former African slaves. It inspired a self-financed effort by Africans organized under the leadership of Paul Cuffee, in the United States, with the aim of reuniting blacks wanting to return to Africa. Paul Cuffee's efforts resulted in the repatriation of 38 blacks to Africa in 1814, and his example was to inspire future generations.

While the Europeans in the USA were establishing institutions as expressions of their culture and their independence, the Africans also established a number of institutions. Although they had little on which to base their ethnic identity, since they were forbidden to speak African languages or practise their religions, they began calling themselves 'Africans'. In 1787 an African Methodist minister in the United States, Richard Allen, in protest against the segregation policy in his own church, broke away and formed the Free African Society, which had both religious and social objectives. Africans adopted the same approach in other parts of the United States. At the same time, a Barbadian-born preacher, Prince Hall, who had been initiated as a Mason by some British soldiers during the American War of Independence, tried to secure the right to found a lodge for free black men. The Masons of the Scottish Right granted him the charter to organize an African lodge of which he became the grand master. This was the first Western-style fraternal organization among black men. The lodges and religious organizations were to be Afro-Americans' most powerful institutions in the nineteenth century, since they bound blacks together nationally.

While these organizations identified themselves with African traditions and culture, they were also carriers of Western values such as thrift, puritan theology, personal advancement through work, and education and concern for the less fortunate. Such was the motivation of George Liele, for example, who founded Baptist churches in the United States and Jamaica in the late eighteenth century. These pioneering innovations among American blacks would later help provide the basis for an evolving community identity in the United States, the Caribbean and Africa.

Most Afro-American leaders of this period were self-educated. Phyllis Wheatley, born in Africa around 1753, became a renowned poet; Gustavus Vassa, born in Benin in 1745 and taken to America and later England, was active in the anti-slavery movement and wrote his memoirs (*The Interesting Narrative of the Life of Olaudah Equiano, or Gustavus Vassa*). Benjamin Banneker, nicknamed 'the Ethiopian', became a noted mathematician and astronomer.

Africans living in Europe also contributed to the struggle for freedom and human dignity. After studying at the Universities of Halle and Wittenberg, Anton Azmo returned to help his compatriots in the Gold Coast; Ottobah Cagoano, who was freed by the Mansfield decision, wrote *Thoughts and Sentiments on the Evil and Wicked Traffic of the Slavery and Commerce of the Human Species*. Ignatius Sancho's posthumously published letters confirm him as an important spokesman for Africans abroad. In Europe, as in the United States, African protestors found allies among the whites, such as the Paris-based Société des Amis des Noirs.

It was in America, however, that the freedom struggle took on a real international dimension with the events on the island of San Domingo.

When a revolution broke out in France in 1789 to the cry of 'Liberty! Equality! Fraternity!', the movement shook the French colony of San Domingo, covered with prosperous sugar plantations, where half a million slaves and 24,000 free persons of colour lived under the domination of 32,000 French settlers, known for the cruelty with which they treated their slaves. The free African population demanded full equality with the whites. Then, in 1791, the great mass of blacks began to stir under the leadership of an illiterate fieldhand, Boukman, who bound his followers with voodoo ritual and African-style secret oaths to rise against their masters. The revolutionary government in Paris dispatched an army to restore order. It was at this point that a quite remarkable figure appeared on the political scene, a literate, Christian slave, born in the diaspora of an African father – Toussaint, who took the name L'Ouverture.

5.2 *Toussaint L'Ouverture of Haiti (The Moorland-Springarn Research Center, Howard University, Washington DC)*

Toussaint called for guerrilla action to support his small army and, within five years, had defeated Napoleon's forces, with assistance from yellow fever. He restored order and prosperity to Haiti and was acclaimed throughout the world for his military ability, administrative skills, humanity and statesmanship. Haiti and Toussaint L'Ouverture became symbols that gave inspiration to blacks aspiring to freedom and even independence in other parts of the Americas and the Caribbean.

At the beginning of the nineteenth century, a black preacher, Gabriel Prosser, organized a march on Richmond, in Virginia, at the head of a thousand slaves. They hoped to use this demonstration to secure their freedom, but the governor called out the militia. Many Africans, including Prosser, were arrested and executed; but the example of Haiti remained very much alive.

With the nineteenth century, a new era dawned for Africans living in Europe and the Americas. It is true that the various legal systems in both Europe and America did not grant blacks either equality or real freedom, but there were instances of greater flexibility. They learned to read and write, even where the laws forbade it; there were inter-racial marriages, despite the fact that they were repugnant to most people; and travel facilitated the development of networks. Nevertheless, Africans in the diaspora realized that their deprived status stemmed from the fact that they belonged to a different race and a different culture, whence their efforts to save their racial brothers and their heritage. This psychological unity continued to prevail, and indeed became a source of strength among the African peoples culminating in the pan-African movement of the nineteenth and twentieth centuries.

Africans in the diaspora, however, could not escape the influence of the environment to which they had been transplanted nor several centuries of inculcation with Euro-American culture. Their language and life-style changed, and so did their values and goals. Africans in the diaspora in Europe and America thus became cultural intermediaries between indigenous Africans and Euro-Americans.

Asia

While the forced migration of Africans to Europe and the Americas is a relatively recent chapter in world history, the trade in slaves to Asia constitutes a much older historical phenomenon. The *Periplus of the Erythraean Sea*, written in *c*.50, refers to slaves taken from the Horn of Africa and it seems likely that trade between peoples on both sides of the Red Sea goes back to prehistoric times.

From the seventh century, that is with the birth of Islam, a kind of cultural unity evolved throughout the Indian Ocean and Red Sea area. Several coastal towns in East Africa became Islamized and Muslims increasingly dominated trade, including the slave trade.

For many centuries Turkey and neighbouring countries were the major entrepôts for slaves from Tripoli and Benghazi, and also a transit zone for the

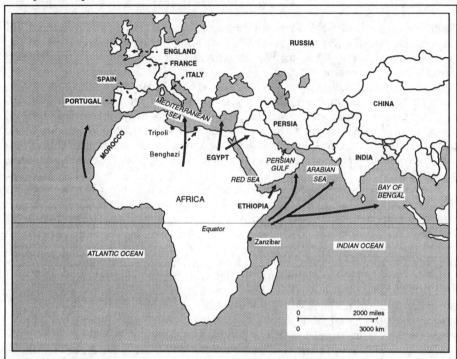

5.3 *Africa, Europe and Asia (adapted from map drawn by Dr Dulal C. Goswami, Geology and Geography Department, Howard University, Washington DC)*

inland traffic. The purchase in Constantinople in 1696 of several African boys for Emperor Peter the Great of Russia deserves mention since one of them was Abram Petrovich Hannibal, the great-grandfather of Aleksander Pushkin. Hannibal appears to have been born in Ethiopia where he was captured by Turks. How many other African slaves arrived in Russia and neighbouring areas via Turkey is not known, but the numbers were probably small. Since slavery was abolished in Russia during the first quarter of the eighteenth century, Africans in that country were probably servants rather than slaves.

Most slaves imported into Asia were children, and the majority were girls. From the East African ports, slaves were normally taken to the Arabian port of Mocha on the Red Sea. From there many were sent on to Hodeida, Jeddah, Mecca and other entrepôts in Arabia. Others were shipped to Persian Gulf ports. Indian ports such as Bombay, Goa, Surat, Karikal, Pondicherry and Calcutta usually received their shipments from Mocha or the Persian Gulf, but some came directly from East Africa.

In Arabia, Oman held the key position in the naval and commercial strategy of the Middle East. Its capital, Muscat, commanded the approach to the Persian Gulf, through which large numbers of African slaves were transported. Omani

Arabs captured the East African ports of Kilwa and Zanzibar in 1784 and 1785 respectively; from then on they claimed sovereignty over several parts of the coast and procured slaves to harvest cloves and coconuts on Arab-owned plantations in the region.

In Yemen and Hadramawt, black people of Ethiopian origin had been living since ancient times. In Aden, these blacks formed a group comparable with the caste of 'untouchables' in India. In several other parts of southern Arabia, black slaves from Africa served in the armies of local sultans; they were also to be found as concubines and domestic servants, eunuchs, crewmen, stevedores and agricultural labourers working in the salt marshes and sugar and date plantations.

Africans were scattered on many Indian Ocean islands. The Dutch procured slaves in East Africa and Madagascar and took them to Indonesia. The French and the British settled East Africans as slaves on the Mascarene Islands of Bourbon and Mauritius. The expansion of the slave trade in the nineteenth century favoured the development of African communities in those islands, but, even before this period, there had emerged a community of creoles whose influence would be felt all through the nineteenth and twentieth centuries.

There were far more African slaves in South Asia than in other parts of Asia, probably because trade with Africa was older and busier. The Muslims controlled the west coast of India and Indians had settled in East Africa. There were many African slaves in India as early as the thirteenth century.

The second half of the fifteenth century witnessed the assertion of an African presence in one part of northern India, Bengal. Africans had migrated there from the coastal region of Calcutta, the area of Dakha and several inland regions. The ruler of Bengal, Rukn-ud-dīn-Barbak (1459–74), used to promote loyal Africans to responsible military and administrative posts. On the death of Barbak in 1486, Shāhzāda, eunuch commander of the palace guards, seized power and assumed the title of Barbak Shah. He was murdered and replaced by another African, who had remained loyal to the former ruler. Africans remained in power until 1493 and made their mark during this short period.

In Gujarat Africans served in the army from at least the thirteenth century and possibly earlier. In 1537 the city of Aḥmadābād was employing as many as 5,000 Africans in government service. Several of these Africans in Gujarat distinguished themselves during the sixteenth century. Some were important military commanders: Ikhtiyar-ul-Mulk, for example, organized an army of some 20,000 men to challenge the troops of the Mughul Emperor Akbar. Ikhtiyar was defeated, but he won Akbar's respect.

An African, a former slave, Shaykh Sayyid al-Ḥabshī Sultani, served as a soldier in Jhujhar Khān's army. When he retired, he purchased some land, made the pilgrimage to Mecca and then worked his lands, which enabled him to feed hundreds of poor people daily. He founded a library which attracted many scholars. In 1573 Sayyid (Saʿīd) constructed a mosque in Aḥmadābād famous for its simple design: a roof of arches and beautiful arched perforated windows with exquisite tracery and floral patterns.

Another African, Sīdī Bashīr, built a noted mosque in Aḥmadābād, which is unique in that it possesses two 'shaking' minarets. When one minaret is shaken, the vibration is carried to the other.

Not far from Gujarat is Janjira Island which, in ancient times, was part of the prosperous commercial activity of north-western India, including what is today Bombay, and the Konkan coast. If local traditions are to be believed, the *Siddis* of Janjira descended from Africans who arrived from Gujarat in 1489.

From the 1530s the Portuguese developed political and economic control over parts of the west coast of India, especially the Konkan coast where many African slaves were imported. Most of these slaves came from Mozambique and the Portuguese used them in trading, on farms or as domestics. Some were trained as priests and teachers for religious schools, especially in Goa, which became Portugal's headquarters for its East African and Asian colonies.

Throughout this period, Janjira Island retained its autonomy. By the seventeenth century the *Siddis*, who comprised the bulk of the Muslims on the island, had become its principal land owners. A council of elders of the major *Siddi* leaders chose a *nawab* who acted as temporal and spiritual ruler. Having established their political base, the Janjira *Siddis* expanded their power over the north-western coast thanks to their naval power. In 1616 they formed an alliance with Mālik Ambar, a *Ḥabshī* king of the Deccan, in central India. Both forces fought the Mughuls for many years.

During the seventeenth century, the British East India Company made repeated efforts to negotiate an alliance with the *Siddis*, who ruled over the Konkan coast. The *Siddis* continued to exercise independent power in the area, and it was not until 1759 that the British were able to curb their power. Janjira was only brought under direct British control in the nineteenth century.

The Janjira *Siddis* played a considerable role in Indian history. There can be no doubt that their religion (Islam) and their maritime and military skills were major assets for them. It is of great importance that this small group of African migrants had such an impact on the policies and actions of Great Britain, Portugal and the Netherlands, as well as on local Indian states.

Africans also settled along parts of the Malabar coast during the seventeenth and eighteenth centuries. These were black Jews, descendants of African slaves, who had left Cochin and Kerala in southern India, to come and settle on that coast. Most became domestics and intermarried with local inhabitants and other Jews. The Portuguese were responsible for settling African slaves along parts of the Malabar coast, especially around Goa, which became one of its head-quarters in the sixteenth century.

The Italian scholar and traveller, Pietro della Valle, reported that blacks from East and West Africa (Guineans and Mozambicans) were sent by sea to the Portuguese territories. The Portuguese made their black slaves domestics, bearers and guards for their escorts. The women were often taken as mistresses.

Another part of India, the Deccan, witnessed a dramatic rise to power, that of the African Mālik Ambar, an Ethiopian who had been sold several times as a slave before reaching India. Ambar's historical significance lies in the fact that

5.4 *Mālik Ambar, an African king in India in the seventeenth century*
(The Ross-Coomaraswamy Collection, courtesy of the Museum of Fine Arts, Boston, MA)

he became the commander of a powerful army fighting under the banner of the king of Aḥmadnagār and resisted several attacks by the Mughuls, thus preventing the Mughul rulers from conquering the Deccan in his lifetime. He ruled supreme over the area around Aḥmadnagār, where several thousand Africans lived, from 1602 to 1626. He founded towns, constructed canals and irrigation schemes, stimulated trade with Asia and Europe and attracted scholars and poets to his court.

Mālik Ambar's activities confirm two significant points: first, that individual Africans played influential roles in Indian history; and second, that Africans managed to win support and respect from Indians while retaining a sense of their own identity.

Conclusion

The history of African people has been so much influenced by perceptions stemming from the slave trade that it is necessary to emphasize that Africans of their own volition migrated between continents, as merchants, clerics, seamen, adventurers and so on. This presence of free blacks abroad deserves further study to provide a more rounded and realistic picture of world civilization.

It was, however, the intercontinental slave trade which, more than anything else, established a world black presence. It was the nature of this trade and its consequences which, especially in the Americas and the Caribbean, caused Africans to organize freedom struggles. This process began at the beginning of the modern era and took a quite different turn when in around 1800 Toussaint L'Ouverture emerged as the international symbol of black liberation. The liberation process continued, despite colonial rule, and may indeed be the greatest historical consequence of the African diaspora.

The Ottoman conquest of Egypt

At the beginning of the sixteenth century a new Islamic great power entered the history of Africa and Arabia: the Ottoman empire, which had come into being in Asia Minor and the Balkan peninsula and went on to subjugate a large part of the Arab countries in West Asia and North Africa.

It was in 1516 that Mamluk sultanates in Syria and Egypt collapsed under the attack by the Ottoman army. Egyptian–Ottoman relations had been strained since the 1480s, but in 1514, following Sultan Selim I's first successful campaign to put an end to the power of Persia, the rulers of Egypt took a firm stand against the Ottomans. Selim decided to break the Mamluk–Safavid coalition once and for all.

In August 1516 the Ottoman army routed the Mamluk troops north of Halab; it owed its victory largely to its technical superiority but it was also helped by betrayal by a pro-Ottoman faction in the Mamluk camp. Sultan Selim occupied Damascus without encountering much resistance and took all of Syria and Palestine as far as the Sinai Desert. But the Sultan's advisors and the Mamluk *amīrs* who had gone over to the Ottoman side persuaded Selim to crown his campaign with the conquest of Egypt. Selim came within sight of Cairo without much difficulty and routed the Mamluk troops in a short battle in January 1517. That marked the end of the Mamluk sultanate.

Military superiority was not the only reason for the Ottoman victory over the Mamluks. The main reason lay in the differences in the economic and political situations of the two states. In Europe and Asia Minor the Ottoman empire dominated territories that were economically advanced, and had mines and raw materials as well as production centres connected to international trade. The Mamluk states, on the other hand, had almost no mineral resources and depended virtually exclusively on agriculture and the international transit trade, whose main branch, the trade in eastern spices, had fallen into the hands of the Portuguese. Imports of precious metals from Africa were also declining. For many years the Mamluks had been trying to compensate for this loss of profit by drawing on their economic reserves, confiscating land and increasing taxes, measures which had intensified the indigenous inhabitants' hatred of the foreign caste of Mamluk exploiters.

6.1 *Sultan Selim I, conqueror of Egypt (© The Hulton-Deutsch Collection, London)*

Selim's victory had far-reaching consequences for West Asia and North Africa. The conquest of Egypt in particular impelled the Ottoman empire to control the Mediterranean sea routes and attempt the conquest of other Arab countries in North Africa.

The territories conquered from the Mamluks included regions of great economic, political and strategic importance. Egypt was particularly important because of its intensive agriculture, its large population and its location on the Red Sea. In addition, the prestige of the Ottoman sultans was enhanced by the fact that they became guardians of the two holy cities of Islam, Mecca and Medina.

Before leaving Egypt in September 1517, Selim placed Khāyr Bey, the Mamluk defector, at the head of the province of Egypt. He governed Egypt more as the sultan's vassal than as a provincial administrator and remained in office until his death in 1522. He retained his Mamluk title *Malik al-umarā* (King of the Commanders) and conducted his court according to Mamluk ceremonial. He surrounded himself with former Mamluk dignitaries willing to serve the new regime, entrusting them with administrative tasks and also political and military assignments. The organization of justice continued to be based on the system of four Chief Judges, one for each School of Law. Selim left Khāyr Bey to control the province's income, and the regular presents sent by Khāyr Bey to Istanbul were expressions of his personal allegiance to the Sultan rather than obligatory deliveries to the state treasury.

Khāyr Bey worked hard to secure his control of the province's resources. He abolished the *iḳṭaʿ* (extant feudal tenures) and incorporated them into the state property, their former holders being allotted fixed wages paid from the provincial treasury. He caused a complete cadastral survey to be made and revised the land tenure system, which enabled him to discharge the task entrusted to him of supplying the two holy cities of Hidjaz with corn.

Khāyr Bey's powers, however, were not unlimited. Sultan Selim had left a strong body of troops in Egypt to consolidate Ottoman authority and, if necessary, deter any attempt by the Mamluks to seize back power. These troops were made up of two infantry corps (one of Janissaries and one of Azabs) and two cavalry ones. In order to maintain his authority over these somewhat undisciplined units, Khāyr Bey formed his own cavalry corps, recruited from among former as well as new Mamluks.

When Khāyr Bey died in 1522, the process of incorporating the city of Cairo was well under way, while the state of which it had been the centre had been reduced, after centuries of independence, to the rank of a mere Ottoman province.

Ottoman administration and conflicts within the ruling class

The beginning of the new period was marked by a revolt against Ottoman supremacy, launched by the new vice-regent, Aḥmad Paṣha, in 1524. He proclaimed himself Sultan of Egypt and started minting his own coins. He

6.2 *The Janissaries, as portrayed in a sixteenth-century Turkish miniature*
(Topkapi Museum, Istanbul, H1524, p. 271A, © Sonia Halliday Photographs)

managed to win the support of a few Arab groups and took the citadel of Cairo, but was subsequently driven out of the city after being betrayed by the Bedouin chiefs who had initially supported him.

In the light of these events, it became obvious that the Istanbul government had to clarify the precise status of Egypt within the Ottoman empire. This was done by issuing an edict, the *Ķānūn Nāme*, which regulated the political, military, civil and economic life of Egypt. By the terms of this edict, the vice-regent, the *wālī*, who had always held the rank of *pasha*, was accorded certain privileges based on customs in use at the court in Istanbul. As his seat he was given the Cairo citadel, the seat of the former sultans, and he was entitled to his own personal guard, called the *mūteferriķas*, like the Istanbul sultan's own personal guard.

The *Ķānūn Nāme* adopted a number of Mamluk administrative customs in the area of financial and civil administration. Egypt was divided into fourteen districts each headed by a *kāshif* whose task it was to maintain the irrigation system in good working order and levy taxes from the farmers. The region south of Asyut was left under the Arab *shaykhs* of the Hawwāra group who had gained control of the area after 1517. The *Ķānūn Nāme* also enacted the creation of the *odjaks*, imperial troops introduced into Egypt by Sultan Selim I. In reward for their loyalty during the revolt, the Janissaries became the main prop of the Sultan's power. Their commander, the *agha*, was one of the most prominent members of the council of state and, in addition, the mint producing Egyptian currency was situated in the area of their barracks inside the citadel.

All the troops stationed in Egypt received regular pay; the highest dignitaries, including the vice-regent, the Chief Judge and 24 other senior figures with the title of *sandjak bey*, also received salaries, *sāliyāne*, paid out of the Egyptian treasury.

These salaries were paid out of the land tax, taxes and duties levied on productive activities in the towns and cities and the head tax to which followers of religions other than Islam were liable. The land tax was levied by the administrators of each region and the taxes on urban residents by tax collectors, *kāshifs* or *emīns*, who were paid a fixed annual salary. The Arab *shaykhs* in the region south of Asyut could, in accordance with the *iltizam* system described below, raise the tax in their respective areas and retain what it produced, provided that they guaranteed agricultural work and paid a fixed percentage of their receipts to the Egyptian treasury.

From 1525 the surplus remaining after covering expenses was sent each year to Istanbul instead of Hidjāz. The regular remittance of this treasure (the *hazine*) was one of the vice-regent's most important tasks. Egypt also fulfilled its obligations to Mecca and Medina.

The *Ķānūn Nāme* also made it legal to levy duties on individual holdings of tax-farms known as *iltizams*. At first this system only applied to agricultural holdings, but in the course of the sixteenth century it spread more widely, as the *odjaks* and their officers grew more powerful, at the expense of the representatives of Ottoman rule. In such conditions, tax collectors found themselves reduced to being mere officials with no direct influence on tax collection or any other aspect of fiscal policy.

Towards the end of the sixteenth century two levels of political power crystallized. One consisted of those officially holding power, appointed by Istanbul, headed by the vice-regent, and the other consisted of the *odjaks* and their officers, and the *sandjak* beys and their Mamluks. Although unofficial, this group had both economic and military power, and from the late sixteenth century onwards its significance in Egypt's political life became more and more apparent.

Ottoman influence in north-east Africa

Throughout the sixteenth century Egypt played an important role in the expansionist policy of the Ottoman empire. Because of its geographical position it formed a natural link between the Mediterranean Sea and the Indian Ocean, with the trade route bringing eastern goods to Europe passing through the Red Sea and Egypt itself. By 1517, the trade with the east was in the hands of the Portuguese. Once Egypt had been subjugated, therefore, the Ottomans faced the task of eliminating the Portuguese from the Indian Ocean or at least hindering their penetration into the Red Sea. The occasion to intervene was provided when the ruler of Gujarat solicited Sultan Sulaymān for help against the Portuguese who had occupied the port of Diu. Sulaymān Pasha, the vice-regent of Egypt, was entrusted with the campaign. On his way to Diu, in 1538, he seized Aden, in Yemen, and established Ottoman rule there. Although he failed to dislodge the Portuguese from Diu, Sulaymān Pasha landed in Upper Egypt and, after reaching Aswan, continued his march along the Nile as far as northern Nubia.

It was difficult to maintain authority in this area of Upper Egypt dominated by the Hawwāra *shaykhs*. In the middle of the sixteenth century Ottoman supremacy had to be re-established there. An expedition headed by the former vice-regent of Yemen, Ozdemir Pasha, reoccupied Ibrim, Aswan and Say and a new province, Berberistan, was created and placed under the authority of a *kāshif* directly subordinate to the vice-regent in Cairo.

In 1557 Ozdemir Pasha took Massawa on the Red Sea as well as Zaylā', opposite Aden, and he conquered part of the inland region ruled by the king of Ethiopia. Massawa became the centre of Habesh, another Ottoman province in Africa, which played an important role in the Ottoman defence of the Red Sea against the Portuguese. The creation of these Red Sea posts was important to the continuation of the transit trade in which coffee had taken the place of the traditional spices from the east. Because of the new popularity of coffee, Egypt reaped considerable profits from this transit trade.

The period from 1517 to the 1580s marked the zenith of Ottoman power in Egypt. No symptoms of Istanbul's decline had yet appeared; on the contrary, its power was even further consolidated. In 1583 the province of Upper Egypt was created, and the Hawwāra chiefs were replaced as administrators by an official sent from Cairo.

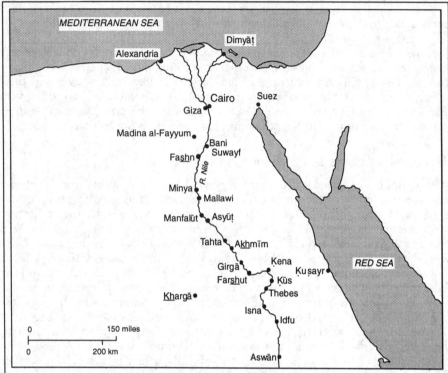

6.3 *Middle and Upper Egypt (al-Saïd) (adapted from ʿAbd al-Rahim ʿAbd al-Rahman and Wataru Miki,* Village in Ottoman Egypt and Tokugawa Japan – A Comparative Study, Institute for the Study of Languages and Cultures of Asia and Africa, *Tokyo, p. (ii) – (map published by kind permission of Professor Wataru Miki, Keio University, Tokyo))*

Traditionally, Upper Egypt had occupied a distinctive place within the political organization of the Nile valley states. It was different from the rest of Egypt in its geography, its social systems, its politics, and its ethnic and religious particularities. On numerous occasions it had been the refuge of movements directed against lawfully constituted authority. It commanded trade routes and the traffic along the Nile. The Ottomans' interest in this territory was demonstrated in the special status it was accorded within the province of Egypt. Thus, the administrator of Upper Egypt, like the administrator of all Egypt, had the title of vice-regent and his political importance was emphasized by the considerable number of troops at his disposal.

Internal military conflicts

The period of peace that followed the suppression of Aḥmad Paṣha's rebellion in 1524 lasted some 60 years. In the 1580s, as a result of its socio-economic dependence on the Ottoman empire, Egypt began to experience the first economic difficulties, which sparked fierce conflicts within the ruling military caste.

Between 1598 and 1609 a number of revolts broke out, led by the *spahi* cavalry corps, who were badly hit by inflation. The subsequent years saw the growth in importance of the 24 *sandjak beys* who came to form a group in some ways comparable to the great *amīrs* of the old Mamluk sultanate. Their high rank entitled them to hold the most senior political offices. Until about 1620 they held the office of *Serdar*, commander of the troops operating within or beyond Egypt's borders. They had command of the units escorting the Egyptian *hazine* sent to Istanbul and of the troops entrusted with protecting the pilgrim caravans travelling to Mecca. At the beginning of the seventeenth century one of them was chosen as *Ḳā'im Maḳam* (acting vice-regent).

Their first significant political coup was the removal in 1631 of vice-regent Mūsā Paṣha and his replacement by their *Ḳā'im Maḳam*. Despite the protests of the vice-regent, the Sublime Porte endorsed their decision, thereby creating a precedent that would be repeated several times in the years to come. The *beys* and the *odjaḳs* had got rid of Mūsa Paṣha because he had tried to put an end to the increasingly common practice of soldiers illegally taxing the urban residents in the form of alleged protection money, himāye. Originally this had been caution money protecting cities from looting, but it had become a means by which the soldiers enriched themselves by exploiting the urban populations.

Mūsā Paṣha was replaced by Riḍwān Bey al-Fāḳārī who was vice-regent until his death in 1656. He was the leader of the Fāḳārīya, political group which was opposed by the Ḳāsīmīya. These two groups consisted of *beys* and their Mamluk retinues and they sought followers among the nomads and the urban dwellers. Their struggle also involved the *odjaḳs*, the Janissaries supporting the Fāḳārīya and the Azabs the Ḳāsīmīya, with the result that by the end of the seventeenth century Egyptian society was completely divided.

Riḍwān Bey secured his position by obtaining from the Sultan a decree appointing him life commander of the pilgrim caravan while his ally 'Alī Bey was appointed life vice-regent of Upper Egypt. The Fāḳārīya was thus well-placed politically, with its two leading figures firmly entrenched at the top of the hierarchy. After Riḍwān Bey's death, however, disagreements within the Fāḳārīya led to the collapse of the party.

The Ḳāsīmīya succeeded in gaining, briefly, the offices previously held by the Fāḳārīya *beys*, but in 1662 the head of the Ḳāsīmīya was assassinated on the orders of the vice-regent.

Yet in 1661 the Sublime Porte had managed to suspend all non-military personnel in the seven *odjaḳs* and impose a 20 per cent increase in the *multazims'* payments from their benefices to cover the treasury deficit caused by inflation. Despite the discontent, the Istanbul court decided to introduce further measures. In 1670 the vice-regent, Ḳara Ibrāhīm Paṣha, was instructed to carry out fiscal reform in Egypt with the help of the army. After a radical rearrangement of the budget and four years of negotiations with the interested parties, he doubled the sum of the treasury. The principles of this reform became the basis for solving fiscal problems all through the period from this time until 1798. But the results achieved were short-lived because the decision to weaken the influence of the *odjaks* had come too late. The weakening of the *pasha*'s position during the first half of the seventeenth century and the elimination of the *beys*' parties in the 1660s had enabled the *odjaks* to seize the benefices arising from exploitation of the urban population. The *beys*, meanwhile, continued to exploit the rural population.

Between 1670 and 1750, political life became even more complicated. It was marked not only by dissensions among the *odjaks* but also by conflicts generated by party affiliation, with some supporting the Fakāriya and others the Ḳāsimiya. The most contentious issues were the two main elements of political and economic power: the benefices held and their redistribution on the one hand, and on the other illegal takings. The most strife-ridden *odjak* was that of the Janissaries which controlled the most lucrative benefices.

For almost 20 years the main protagonist in the struggle within the Janissaries' *odjak* was the Janissary Bashodabashi Küchük Meḥmed. He had been expelled from Egypt in 1680 and when he returned he won the support of the *Agha* who introduced him to the Fakāriya. With the help of the leader of this party, Küchük Meḥmed succeeded in ridding the Janissaries' *odjak* of its Kasimi commanders and securing his own domination of it from 1692. Shortly after, he secured approval by the top officials of all seven *odjaks* of his decision to abolish some of the protection charges and all the other illegal charges demanded by the Janissaries and the Azabs. The main reason for this new course was the fear of a repetition of the riots of 1678 which had been caused by inflation and a sharp rise in the price of corn.

During the summer of 1694, tension within the Janissaries' *odjak* reached a critical level. At the same time, a low flood of the River Nile caused a sudden rise in corn prices. True to his political principles, Küchük Meḥmed moved against speculators, fixing wheat prices and excluding middlemen from its distribution. These measures brought the Janissary opposition and the Azabs who controlled the grain stores together and Küchük Meḥmed was assassinated. Once again the *odjaks* had access to their lost benefices along with the freedom to determine food prices. The subsequent rapid escalation in the prices of basic commodities caused a famine in 1695. It was only the abundant floods of 1697 that put an end to this difficult period.

Since 1688 the state of crisis had been aggravated by the continuous erosion of the value of the currency and, by 1692, the situation had reached a critical point. The provincial administration tried to compensate for the shortfall in the *hazine* by an increase of 4 per cent in deliveries from the *iltizams*, but Istanbul demanded that the *hazine* be delivered in undepreciated currency, a demand which aroused strong opposition among the *odjaks* who were deriving huge profits from the devaluation, as were their merchant clients. It was their opposition that wrecked the attempt at financial reform and change in the tax system prepared by the financial expert Yāsīf al-Yahūdī in 1697.

In the early 1700s a new wave of price rises occurred, resulting from an influx of valueless currency from other parts of the Ottoman empire. It was decided that depreciated coins could only be used for their metal weight and that silver coins of a higher fineness (*fidda diwani*) would be minted to replace them. This decree helped to slow down the decline of the Egyptian currency but the serious problem of protection charges remained unresolved, with the *odjaks* quite unwilling to abandon them. So tension persisted, threatening to erupt into a new crisis.

The crisis finally broke in about 1710, caused initially by the growth in coffee exports. These earned the wholesalers and their Janissary protectors profits that the other *odjaks* found intolerable. The dispute led to a serious clash within the Janissaries' *odjak* in which the *beys* also participated.

The man at the centre of the affair was Bashodabashi Ifrandj Aḥmad, who was in favour of the Janissaries involving themselves in economic activities. He was expelled from the *odjak* in 1707 but was readmitted with the backing of the Fakārīya and his position appeared secure. But a decree from Istanbul dealt the Janissaries a serious blow: the decree put an end to all abuses and the patronage relations between military protectors and non-military personnel. In addition, the mint was to be moved from the Janissaries' barracks to a new building. At the end of 1710 the crisis was further aggravated by a split between the two leading Fakārīya *beys*. The delicate balance of power was disturbed and the crisis degenerated into an armed conflict in which the *beys* were openly engaged. In June 1711 the resistance of the Janissaries who were holding out in the citadel collapsed, the Fakārīya *beys* fled Egypt and Ifrandj Aḥmad was executed.

The effect of these events was to weaken the influence of the Janissaries and the other *odjaks*, exhausted by 20 years of endless struggle. A new period now began in which the *beys* once again took the limelight on the Egyptian political scene.

Despite the economic and political crises of its final decades, the *odjaks'* period of rule had witnessed great economic and social change in Egypt. Agricultural production had increased as had trade in Egyptian goods, and the transit trade, especially in coffee, contributed to general prosperity. The healthy state of the economy was accompanied by rapid population growth. There was, it is true, an ongoing problem of depreciation of the currency, aggravated by Ottoman defeats in Europe, but Egypt was not overly affected by these wars in which *odjak* participation was negligible. Under these conditions, the social character of the *odjaks* had gradually changed. The soldiers had begun to integrate with the local people, mostly through marriage; their discipline declined and their military ability was no longer what it had been.

After 1711 the struggle for power continued both between political groups and within each of them. In 1714 leading figures in the ruling Ḳāsimīya killed Ḳāytās Bey and seized supreme authority (*riyāsa*). But in 1718 the Mamluks of Abū Shanab formed an opposition group, the Shanabīya, which in co-operation with the Fakārīya *beys* regained power.

The never-ending struggles among the *beys* gave the vice-regents an opportunity, after 1720, to strengthen their authority. The vice-regent, Bakir Pasha, took advantage of the rivalry among the three leaders of the Fakārīya to try to divert both the lawful and the illicit taxes collected by the *odjaks* into the state treasury. To break their resistance, he had all three leaders assassinated. But the new leadership of the Egyptian military caste, represented by 'Uthman Bey and the Janissary Kāhya Ibrāhīm Kazdoghlu, took the side of the *odjaks*. The opposition was reinforced by representatives of the *ulamā*, the religious brotherhoods.

With Ibrāhīm Kazdoghlu at the head of the Janissaries' *odjak*, the Kazdughlīya, a strong Fakārīya faction which had previously remained in the background, came to the fore. From 1743, after he had forced 'Uthman Bey to leave the country, Ibrāhīm Kāhya became the sole leader of the country's military and the Kazdughlīya ruled as the sole party until 1798.

Ibrāhīm Kāhya joined forces with Ridwān, the Kāhya of the Azabs. This duumvirate ruled undisturbed for the years after 1744. Ridwān Kāhya indulged his passion for building, while Ibrāhīm Kāhya turned Egypt into his personal domain, using every means to enrich himself and building up a strong retinue of Mamluks. Yet, despite the seeming stability of the duumvirate, symptoms were developing which heralded the collapse of the socio-economic structures on which the power of the military rested.

The underlying unrest became apparent soon after the death of Ibrāhīm Kāhya in 1754. Ridwān Kāhya perished in a Janissary revolt precipitated by his decision to impose a new tax on coffee. The *odjaks* were showing their determination to protect their much eroded privileges, but they were also expressing their hostility towards the Mamluks who, promoted to *beys* and *odjak* officers, were now assuming political and economic power. This shift in power from the *odjaks* to the Mamluk *beys* was reinforced after 1760, and the *odjaks* degenerated into mere reserves for Mamluk retinues whose members were allowed to hold the rank of officer.

Cultural development

The extinction of the sovereign Mamluk sultanate and the transformation of Egypt into a province of the Ottoman empire had cultural repercussions. Cultural activity in Ottoman Egypt as it developed bore very distinctly the imprint of the new social, economic and national relations. Egypt's new political position also affected education and the role of Arabic as the medium of cultural expression.

After the fall of the Mamluk sultanate, Cairo ceased to be the spiritual centre of the Sunnite world, which it had been since 1261. Although Al-Azhar remained one of the most prestigious schools for students from Arab countries even after 1517, those who wanted to achieve success in public life found themselves increasingly forced to attend schools in Istanbul.

The incorporation of Egypt and other Arab countries into the Ottoman empire, in whose public and cultural life Ottoman–Turkish occupied a leading position, marked a significant step in the decline of Arabic as mediator of Arab-Islamic culture. The loss of political independence by countries with an Arab population naturally signified the end of the use of Arabic as the language of state administration.

As in all the Arab provinces of the Ottoman empire, the culture of Egypt fell under strong Ottoman-Turkish political, social and cultural pressure. It nevertheless retained a certain character of its own which was to become the starting-point and regulator of the Arab national awakening in the nineteenth and twentieth centuries. This special character was retained by Egyptian Arabic literature of the sixteenth, seventeenth and eighteenth centuries but it contributed nothing new in the classical genres, although it did bring about a new orientation of literary production. Writings in the Arabic language were directed at readers from the middle strata of the urban population, hence the strong popular character of the genres and language of that literature.

This trend was particularly pronounced in poetry. As the Dervish orders became more widespread, mystic ṣūfi poetry became popular through works marked by the influence of Ibn al-Fārid, who sang the praises of the Prophet Muḥammad. Satire was also introduced during this period, a remarkable example being *Hazz al-kuhūf* (Shaking the Peasants' Heads) by al-Shirbīnī (1787), in which the author ridiculed the stupidity of the peasants and the narrow-mindedness of the 'ulamā'. The language of this work is the Arabic dialect of Egypt. Another noted poet was Ḥasan al-Badrī al-Ḥidjāzī (died 1719) who, in addition to a collection of poems on religious themes, wrote a collection of satires on contemporary society. Apart from this poetry addressed to a wide public, formalistic poetry appeared with a tendency to self-conceited eccentricity, whose representative in Egypt was Abdullāh al-Idkāwī (died 1770).

Narrative folk prose was enriched by a novel on the conquest of Egypt by Selim I, in which the hero is the last Mamluk Sultan, Tūmān Bey. Scientific literature, however, continued to decline. The period from the sixteenth to the eighteenth century simply continued the previously existing state of affairs, marked by a lack of originality in the processing of knowledge and sterile commentaries on the writings of the great figures of the past. Historiography had better possibilities, but it suffered from a lack of patrons. Apart from the works of Ibn Iyās, which although ending in 1522 are considered to be part of Mamluk historiography, most works were of poor quality, especially in their methodology. Only a few books from this period are lengthy chronicles containing well-organized materials. Usually, they are but dry chronological lists of sultans, vice-regents and Chief Judges, or short summaries of the history of Egypt. The closing decades of the eighteenth century are described in an important work written in the nineteenth century, the chronicle by al-Djabarti.

A popular genre was treatises on pilgrim routes to Mecca and Medina, as well as writings on places of pilgrimage and the tombs of outstanding figures, especially those of scholars and shaykh saints.

The veneration of saints was associated with the advance of the Dervish orders and the growing interest in mystics. The most popular order was the Aḥmadīya, founded by Aḥmad al-Badawī (died 1276), whose tomb in Tanta was the centre of a special cult. Among the influential orders, mention should be made of the Ḳādirīyya, the Rifāīya and the Nakshbandīya. The Dervish orders were headed by a representative of the descendants of the Prophet (*nakīb al-ashrāf*), a *shaykh* from the al-Bakrī family which derived its origins from the first Caliph Abū Bakr. These orders were associated with certain social strata and their solid organization gave their leaders significant political power. The orders also had a cultural role as they contributed to the education of people by passing on to them a written literature, mostly poetry. Mystic poetry was cultivated by a number of poets, such as the pleiad of members of the al-Bakrī family, ʿAbdullāh al-Shaʿrāwī, Aḥmad al-Dardīr and others.

Throughout the eighteenth century Egypt had no printing press, although from 1729 Turkish and Arabic books were being printed in Istanbul. Copying by hand continued to be the only way of increasing the number of copies of literary works.

Cairo and other Muslim cities are still adorned today by numerous architectural monuments built during the Ottoman period. Most of them are buildings serving religious or educational purposes which were financed by gifts from vice-regents, senior *odjak* officers, *beys* and even Ottoman sultans or other members of the dynasty. These buildings contain a number of specifically Egyptian elements, both in their architectural conception and decoration. The imported elements are chiefly represented by the *manāra* (minaret), the faience wall decoration and the flowers painted on the ceiling and walls. The ample size and comfort of surviving private houses reflect the well-being of city-dwellers. They are a testimony to the changes under way in Egyptian society and the growing importance of traders, the nucleus of the future bourgeois class.

Economic decline and attempts to achieve independence

After the deaths of Ibrāhīm Bey and Riḍwān Kāhya, fierce fighting broke out among the Kazdughlīya. For a brief period, a number of *beys*, all of them former Mamluks of Ibrāhīm Kāhya, followed one another at its head. The previously rarely used honorific title of *Shaykh al-Balad* began to be conferred in 1756. In 1760 ʿAlī Bey, known as *al-Djinn* (the demon), became the new *Shaykh al-Balad* and soon revealed himself to be an extraordinarily ambitious and energetic man. He secured his position in Egypt and, through his contacts with the Sublime Porte, succeeded in persuading Istanbul that he was the only man capable of putting Egypt to rights. In exchange for permission to retain all the property confiscated from his adversaries, he pledged to pay Istanbul the debt accumulated on the *hazine* over the past ten years, amounting to 91 million paras, and to pay the sum of 50 million paras raised by the sale of confiscated beneficies. The harshness of his measures against land owners and the politically influential triggered the formation of an opposition headed by Ṣāliḥ Bey who left for Upper Egypt in 1765 to join forces with Shaykh Humām, the leader of the Hawwāra Arabs, who was already harbouring many of ʿAlī Bey's enemies.

Aware of the threat represented by this group which was firmly in control of Upper Egypt, 'Alī Bey attempted to destroy it through a military campaign but he failed and was forced to flee to Syria in 1766. But the following year 'Alī Bey returned to Egypt with the support of the Sublime Porte; he reconciled himself with Ṣāliḥ Bey and rid himself of his opponents who had formed a duumvirate in his absence.

As soon as 'Alī Bey had fulfilled his promise to the Sublime Porte to pay off the deficit, he radically shifted policy. In 1768 he deposed the vice-regent and appointed himself to the post. By adding the office of titular head of the Egyptian administration to his political power as *Shaykh al-Balad* he became the real ruler of Egypt and his subordination to the sultan was merely formal. 'Alī Bey did not go so far as to declare himself an independent sovereign, but he usurped the right to mint coins of his own and had his name proclaimed during Friday prayers. He endeavoured to consolidate his economic and political power by strengthening the army and developing agriculture and trade. He also opened commercial negotiations with leading European powers.

In 1770 his office enabled him to become involved in the succession dispute among the Hashemite *amīrs* in Mecca. The settlement of the succession by an Egyptian intervention and the replacement of the Ottoman vice-regent in Jeddah by an Egyptian *bey* marked a gain for 'Alī Bey at the expense of the Sultan's supremacy in Ḥidjāz. Stimulated by this success, 'Alī Bey began to cherish the idea of unifying under his rule, but within the framework of the Ottoman empire, the areas that had once formed the territory of the Mamluk sultanate: Egypt, Ḥidjāz and Syria.

'Alī Bey decided to extend his grip to Syria as soon as favourable circumstances arose in 1770. The Ottoman navy had just been destroyed by the Russian fleet and the vice-regent of Damascus was facing problems with the revolt of Shaykh Zāhir 'Umar. 'Alī Bey sent troops to help the latter and the two armies, reinforced by further units under the command of Muḥammad Bey Abu'l-Dahab, defeated the government forces and occupied Damascus. Despite these initial successes, the two *beys* gave up their adventure and, assuring the sultan of their loyalty, returned to Cairo with their army at the end of 1771. In 1772, following desertion by his allies, 'Alī Bey's power collapsed and he had to hand over office to Muḥammad Bey. With the support of his allies in Syria and Palestine, 'Alī Bey made a fruitless attempt to return and died soon after in captivity.

Although 'Alī Bey was inspired by Egypt's past, some features of his ambitious career foreshadowed his ultimate failure. He was also ill-served by the system of Mamluk houses and the fickleness of their allegiance.

While he was in power, symptoms appeared of an economic crisis which continued, with varying intensity, until the nineteenth century. Prompted by the need to increase the receipts from the feudal rent, 'Alī Bey first inflicted his harsh fiscal policy on the rural areas. It was undoubtedly one of the main causes of the impoverishment of the farmers and their fleeing to the towns, which however were unable to provide them with the means to make a decent living,

6.4 *ʿAlī Bey, vice-regent of Egypt (© The Mansell Collection, London)*

as more and more craftsmen and traders there were also subject to high taxes. This general impoverishment grew worse as the years passed and was aggravated by a series of epidemics.

In the person of the new *Shaykh al-Balad*, the Porte hoped that they had at last found a man that would be wholly committed to them. In 1775 Muḥammad Bey dispatched over 130 million paras as the annual payment and, in the same year, he sent an expedition against Shaykh Zāhir al-'Umar on the Sultan's orders. But he was killed during the siege of Akka and that was the end of Egypt's involvement in Syria. The Porte actively exploited the power struggle which broke out among members of the Mamluk elite after Muḥammad Bey's death. It was ready to support whoever promised to send the largest portion of the tax levied from the new benefice holders but had no intention of intervening directly in Egyptian affairs.

In the struggle for power, which lasted almost ten years, the main protagonists were three Ḳazdughlīya *beys*, Ismā'īl Bey, Murād Bey and Ibrāhīm Bey. The first phase of the struggle saw the latter two succeed in forcing Ismā'īl Bey and his followers to leave Egypt. This was followed by a prolonged fight between the two victors, as Ibrāhīm, although officially recognized as *Shaykh al-Balad*, was prevented by Murād from being fully master of the situation. This rivalry gave the Porte the chance to manipulate the adversaries with the aim of increasing to the maximum the sum of the annual *hazine*. But it was not able to make full use of the opportunity as the two men gradually gained control of the whole administration of the province, seizing all the financial resources which they used for their own purposes.

When the two rivals were reconciled, the Sublime Porte, considering that its interests were endangered, decided to re-establish direct control over Egypt through military intervention. In July 1786 an Ottoman expeditionary force landed at Alexandria under the command of Ḥasan Pasha. It dispersed the Mamluk troops but Murād Bey and Ibrāhīm Bey retreated into Upper Egypt with what remained of their forces. To restore the Sultan's authority, Ḥasan had to break the military power of the two usurpers and remould the Mamluk elements that had remained loyal. He sought to do this by creating a new set of *beys* and garrison commanders appointed from among the various Mamluk households. Given that the main aim of the punitive expedition was to restore regular delivery of the *hazine*, Ḥasan Pasha prepared a number of decrees to ensure that the province of Egypt complied with its obligations to the Porte and the holy cities. But before he could implement these laws, he was sent elsewhere on a military mission.

The military intervention in Egypt did not have the expected results. The virtual division of Egypt into a lower part, ruled by the Sultan's representative, and an upper part, dominated by the two rebels, came to be accepted as a reality. Despite the changes brought about by Ḥasan Pasha among the holders of titles and offices, and notably the appointment of Ismā'īl Bey as the new *Shaykh al-Balad*, the Mamluk regime remained intact and with it all the conditions for a resurgence of the old problems.

The political crisis was seriously aggravated after 1783 by economic difficulties such as poor harvests, famines, price increases and currency devaluations. An unusually severe epidemic broke out in 1791, which claimed the lives of loyal *beys*, notably Ismā'il Bey. Murād Bey and Ibrāhīm Bey were thus able to return to Cairo in the summer of the same year without encountering any resistance and re-establish their authority over the whole of Egypt.

The Porte consented to their rule on condition that they fulfilled all their obligations. In 1792 the two *beys* signed an agreement stipulating the total sum to be paid and the method of payment but they kept it reluctantly and only in part. Their return to power signified the return of the harsh, exploitative regime that Egypt had experienced before Ḥasan Pasha's expedition and its consequences for the economy were even more disastrous. The country had been disrupted by the political anarchy of the previous ten years and the never-ending plundering of its resources and reserves. The critical state of the economy was a reflection of the political oppression to which the whole of society was subjected by a small élite made up of the Mamluk *beys* and their retinues. But the central government lacked the strength required to eliminate them and Egyptian society was not yet ready to do so itself. But the ousting of the Mamluks would not be long in coming. The first impulse was given by the totally unexpected arrival in 1798 on the Egyptian coast of the French military expedition under the command of Napoleon Bonaparte.

Conclusion

During the historical period from the fall of the Mamluk sultan in 1517 to the French expedition of 1798, the development of Egyptian society was determined by its own inner dynamics. Unlike the European parts of the Ottoman empire, Egypt remained on the fringes of political developments and its socio-economic development did not reach the stage where the bourgeoisie made its appearance as a new social class. Socially, therefore, it remained at the stage traditionally known as feudalism.

The incorporation of Egypt into the Ottoman empire was, however, a significant gain for the empire in that it enhanced its economic potential and political strength. But relations between the central government and the province of Egypt were often strained and the gradual decline of the Ottoman empire led to clashes and crises which led to the emergence of decentralizing forces.

The growth of separatist forces in Egypt in the late eighteenth century was not an isolated phenomenon in the Arab countries of the Ottoman empire. But in the case of Egypt they were not accompanied by the ambition to get rid of the last vestiges of subjection to the Ottoman sultan.

Ḥasan Pasha's expedition in 1787 revealed the military inadequacy of the Mamluk regime and its vulnerability to an attack by a stronger enemy as Napoleon's expedition was to demonstrate. Moreover, by trying to destroy decentralizing forces and reassert ties between the province and the central

6.5 *The mosque of Muḥammad Bey Abū'l-Dahab, 1188/1774 (Institute of Egyptology, Charles University, Prague)*

government, the Ottoman expedition foreshadowed the efforts that the Ottoman state would make in the course of the nineteenth century.

Egypt's increasing interest in territories beyond its borders and its efforts to enter into independent commercial relations with other regions show that it had broken out of its centuries-long isolation. That isolation was ended when France embarked on its colonial expansion in the eastern Mediterranean. In the increasingly problematical context of the Eastern Question, Egypt was to become a country of major importance on the chessboard of world politics.

The Sudan, 1500–1800

Introduction

The history of the Sudan in the period under discussion was characterized by population movements both into and out of the Sudan. In the north, the slow penetration of large numbers of Muslim Arabs, well under way by the beginning of our period, led to the integration of the region into the larger pan-Islamic world. The process of cultural and ethnic assimilation was a two-way process: it led, on the one hand, to the Arabization and Islamization of large numbers of Sudanese peoples and, on the other, to the integration of Arab immigrants.

The influence of Islam and Arabic culture on the Southern Sudan was negligible. The expansionist energies of the Nilotes from the south succeeded in arresting the southward march of the Arabs as well as the spread of Islam. Indeed the Nilotes, especially the Shilluk and the Jieng, posed a serious threat to the northern Muslim states until the end of the period.

This chapter will deal primarily with the establishment and expansion of the two Muslim savannah states (the Fundj and Fūr sultanates), their relations with each other and their interaction with non-Muslim African societies which were also in the process of formation from diverse linguistic and cultural groups. It will also attempt to show that the expansion of Islam constitutes an important factor in the history of the Sudan during this period.

The southward process of Arabization and Islamization was halted where the rivers divide (the Baḥr al-Ghazāl and the Baḥr al-'Arab), thus creating a sort of cultural frontier between the northern Sudan and the southern Sudan which has deeply coloured the interpretation of Sudanese history.

From the southern Sudanese viewpoint, relations between the two regions have been marked essentially by the incursions and economic exploitation by the Fundj in the Upper Nile and later by the Fūr in the Baḥr al-Ghazāl region. But from the northern viewpoint political, economic and social changes have generally been explained by the arrival of Muslim immigrants, the 'wise strangers' from the north or east. Today, the north is presented as Arab and Muslim, and the south as African (or negroid) and 'pagan' (or 'animist'). Thus the frontier that separates them becomes increasingly defined in religious and ethnic terms.

The historical reality was of course more complex than this. First, the frontier between these two regions was constantly shifting and not always southward or westward.

Second, the frontier was a vast area which, around the Upper Nile, for instance, stretched over several hundred kilometres. The same was true for the western area. Furthermore, within the frontier itself, cultural, ethnic and social transformations were taking place all the time, with people becoming Arabs, Fūr, Fundj, Shilluk, Naath or Jieng according to political and economic circumstances.

Third, within the northern Muslim sultanates themselves the process of ethnic change was a complex phenomenon. To begin with, the word Arab, which had strong cultural connotations, was progressively emptied of its ethnic significance, as in the case of the Bakkāra Arabs who lived along the frontier. Furthermore, by the eighteenth century, each sultanate was divided into a number of chiefdoms most of which were plural societies. The social formations within these sultanates were further complicated by the factor of slavery. Many slaves brought from the south formed an important part of the sultans' army, while others were completely assimilated into their new societies.

Finally, with the exception of the people who had come from the central and western *Bilād al-Sūdān* (such as the Takrūr and the Fulbe) and the Rashayida from Arabia, no new ethnic groups emerged in the Sudan in the nineteenth or twentieth centuries, and major population movements were practically over by about 1800.

The ʿAbdallābi state

During the second half of the fifteenth century, a confederacy of Arab *kabīlas* led by their chief ʿAbdallāh, nicknamed Djammāʿ (the Gatherer), succeeded in conquering the kingdom of "Alwa". The conquest of Soba was an indication of the supremacy of the Arabs and marked the beginning of Arab influence in the eastern *Bilād al-Sūdān*. ʿAbdallah Djammāʿ and his descendants, the ʿAbdallābi, established the seat of their government at Kerri, north of Soba, on the Nile. Kerri was easy of access for the Buṭanā Arabs whose support was essential to the ʿAbdallabi. It also made it possible to monitor movements along the Nile valley and across it on the western bank.

The extent of the new state is not easy to determine. The ʿAbdallābi hegemony seems to have extended over the Arabs in northern Djazira, the Buṭana, east of the Nile, and possibly some of the Bedja groups. The independent ʿAbdallābi state did not last long enough to develop its own institutions. By the beginning of the sixteenth century it had to face a powerful enemy, the Fundj, who were cattle nomads migrating down the Blue Nile. The two migratory forces clashed, probably over possession of grazing land north of the Djazīra. At Arbadjī, in 1504, the Fundj defeated the ʿAbdallābi and reduced their king to the status of a vassal. The ʿAbdallābi continued to rule the northern part of the Fundj sultanate as feudatories until the Turco-Egyptian conquest in 1820.

The Fundj sultanate

The origin of the Fundj has given rise to many contradictory hypotheses. Their kingdom is known in Sudanese traditions as *al-Sultana al-Zarka* (the Blue Sultanate). David Reubeni, a Jewish adventurer who went there in 1522–3, described their monarch as a black Muslim who ruled over a nation of blacks and whites, referring to the indigenous population and the Arabs respectively. Local traditions attribute an Arab ancestry to the Fundj, and say that they are descendants of an Umayyad refugee who came via Ethiopia and who allegedly married an indigenous princess. He is described as a 'blessed man' who brought new customs.

It is not clear at what date the Fundj dynasty began to claim an Umayyad descent but it seems that the Fundj were rapidly Islamized. Like other convert peoples living on the fringes of Muslim societies, the Fundj wanted to be regarded as Arabs, hoping thereby to enhance their moral authority over their Arab subjects.

Having asserted their suzerainty over the ʿAbdāllabi territories, the Fundj ruled their domains from Sennār which became their seat of government. The ʿAbdāllabi shaykh became a vassal of the Fundj and bore the title of *Māndjil* or *Māndjuluk* which the Fundj monarchs bestowed on their principal vassals.

In an attempt to shake off Fundj domination, Shaykh Adjīb I, who came to power in the middle of the sixteenth century, challenged the Fundj, defeated them and drove them into Ethiopia. In the reign of Dakīn (1568/9–1585/6) the Fundj recovered their former supremacy but they had to concede Adjīb I's right to appoint judges in his domains. Dakīn's policy of reorganizing the kingdom and introducing new regulations appears to have upset the delicate balance between the two sides and driven Adjīb into open rebellion. In 1611–12, a Fundj army inflicted a crushing defeat on the ʿAbdāllabi in a battle in which Adjib I was killed. A settlement between the Arabs and the Fundj was negotiated which restored the status quo. Thus, the descendants of Adjīb, with the title of *wad ʿAdjīb*, continued to rule directly the territories as far north as Hadjar al-ʿAsal and indirectly over the ethnic groups living in the Nile valley as far as the border of Ottoman Nubia. This settlement gave the sultanate a fairly long period of stability. However, in about the middle of the seventeenth century, the Shaykīyya chieftaincy revolted against the ʿAbdāllabi hegemony and asserted its independence from the Fundj sultanate.

The extension of the Fundj sultanate

The extension of Fundj authority as far as lower Nubia seems to have been viewed with suspicion by the Ottomans, who had conquered Egypt in 1517. In the reign of Sulaymān the Magnificent (1520–66) they sent a naval expedition under Ozdemir Pasha into the Indian Ocean against the Portuguese, who were threatening the Red Sea lanes; as he was returning, Ozdemir was instructed to put an end to the Fundj 'rebellion' in Nubia where two rival factions were fighting one another. Ozdemir captured the strategic fortresses of Ibrim and Dirr on the border and built a fortress at Say which marked the southern limit of Ottoman Egypt. The new province, known as Berberistan, was administered by the Ottomans.

Ozdemir Pasha was later entrusted with the task of conquering Habesistān (Abyssinia). After detailed preparations in Egypt, the expedition started up the Nile. At Aswan, Ozdemir lost control of an undisciplined army and had to call off the campaign. There it was understood that the expedition had not been directed against Habesistān but against Fundjistān (the land of the Fundj). The Egyptian frontier was finally consolidated at Hannik in 1622 after some fighting between the 'Abdallābi and the Fundj.

Ozdemir is also credited with establishing a base at Sawākin against the Portuguese and above all the Ethiopians. Sawākin came under Ottoman suzerainty and Massawa was annexed in 1557. The coastal strip between the two ports constituted the province of Habesh. Once the Portuguese threat had been removed, Sawākin once again became the main commercial outlet of the Fundj sultanate. Relations between the Ottoman governor and the Fundj were at first unfriendly and deteriorated into armed confrontations in 1571. However, because of the extensive commercial relations that had developed between the two sides, tension declined and Sawākin took on an importance which it retained until the beginning of the twentieth century.

By the beginning of the seventeenth century, the Fundj had apparently consolidated their position at Sennār. The territories they ruled directly extended from Arbadjī to the south of Fazūghlī. The expansion of their power to the west into Kordofān had been initiated by Sultan 'Abd al-Kadīr in about 1554. The increasing pressure of the Nilotic peoples on the White Nile at the expense of Sennār seems to have led to a confrontation between the Fundj and the Shilluk. Sultan Bādī II Abū Dikn (1644/5–1718) established a bridgehead and a Fundj garrison at Alays, on the river. From that strategic position the Fundj were able to monitor movements across the river and check the Shilluk, who appear to have entered into an alliance with them.

The Fundj then penetrated the Nūba mountains, one of the principal sources of slaves. The Islamized kingdom of Takali was reduced to the status of a tributary. Likewise, the Fundj extended their rule over the northern hills of al-Dāyr and Kordofān. The numerous prisoners captured among the non-Muslim 'hill-Nūba' were settled in villages around Sennār. They formed a slave guard to protect the sultan. The establishment of a slave army dependent on the ruler was viewed with concern by the traditional warriors, the Fundj aristocracy, and they revolted in the reign of Bādī III (the Red, 1692–1716).

A new crisis was precipitated during the reign of Bādī IV Abū Shullūkh (1721–62), the last effective Fundj monarch. In the first half of his reign, Bādī IV left the affairs of state to his minister Dōka, but when Dōka died, Bādī banished the *ahl al-uṣūl* (members of the old lineage and rank) and began to rule arbitrarily. To rid himself of the Fundj notables who were opposing him, he sent them on a campaign against the Musabbaʿāt who had encroached on Fundj land in Kordofān. After a number of setbacks, the Fundj army, under the command of Muḥammad Abū Likaylik, won a decisive victory in 1747. Abū Likaylik remained viceroy of Kordofān for 14 years.

The record of relations between the Fundj and the Ethiopians is one of numerous border disputes, but that did not prevent positive co-operation and economic interdependence between the two countries. To the Christians of Ethiopia, Sennār was for many years their sole outlet to the outside world and trade routes remained open even when relations between Sennār and Gondar were strained.

Yet the Fundj waged two wars against Ethiopia. The first broke out at the beginning of the seventeenth century. Relations between the Fundj sultan and the Ethiopian emperor had deteriorated when the latter granted political asylum to the deposed sultan ʿAbd al-Ḳādir and made him a governor. Frontier incidents escalated during 1618 and 1619 when large numbers of troops were involved in clashes. The fact that the two rulers were fighting this war far from their capitals meant that it did not represent a serious threat to either of them. It ended in favour of Ethiopia.

In the following century, a second war began with incursions into the Ḳalābāt-Dindera region. In March 1744 Iyasu II advanced at the head of a large Ethiopian army against Sennār. The two armies fought a pitched battle on the banks of the Dindera, in which the Ethiopians were routed. The Fundj victory was celebrated by Bādī IV and his subjects with religious fervour. This was echoed as far away as Istanbul and the Ottoman Caliph was said to have been pleased with the victory of Islam.

The progress of Islam

The Fundj-ʿAbdallābi sultanate gave the country a measure of unity and stability that facilitated the spread of Islam. This was the work of Muslim scholars whom the rulers encouraged to come and settle in the country. Before this, Islam had been spread by two groups – traders and nomadic Arabs. Among the first group, trade and proselytization had always gone hand in hand on the margin of Islamic societies. The second group, although not well versed in doctrine, played a major role in the spread of Islam notably through their inter-marriage with indigenous Sudanese people. Islamization was the normal concomitant of Arabization.

The early Fundj period witnessed a rise in the number of Muslim teachers. Some came from Egypt, Ḥidjāz, Yemen and the Maghrib but most of them were born in the country and some had studied in Cairo or other holy places. On his return from Cairo in the middle of the sixteenth century Maḥmūd al-ʿAraki, the first Sudanese Muslim scholar, established 17 schools on the White Nile. In about 1570, Ibrāhīm al-Būlād ibn Djābir was the first to base his teaching on two Māliki textbooks: the *Risāla* by Ibn Abī Zayd al-Ḳayrawānī, and the *Mukhtasar* by Khalīl ibn Isḥāḳ. This teaching helped to establish the predominance of the Māliki rite in the region.

The first trained Muslim scholars were primarily concerned with teaching Muslim law, the sharī'a and its application. Their efforts to transmit orthodox teaching and raise the level of religious life encountered serious difficulties in a vast, isolated and backward country. Before orthodox Islam took root there, a more popular and less exacting type of Islam had been introduced.

Most of the *sūfī tañḳas* (religious orders) came from Ḥidjāz. The first, and probably the most popular, was the Ḳādirīyya. It was introduced into the Sudan by Tādj al-Dīn al-Bahārī of Baghdad, who came from Mecca in 1577 and stayed in the Djazīra for seven years, initiating many prominent Sudanese into the Ḳādirīyya order. Another order, the Shadhiliyya, was introduced into the Sudan by a member of the Dja'aliyyūn clan who had studied in Ḥidjāz.

When *Ṣūfism* began to spread in the Fundj kingdom, it had already lost much of its importance in the Muslim world and had become tainted with some unorthodox practices. People believed that *baraka* (divine blessing) emanated from holy men and that such men acted as intermediaries between man and God, hence the emphasis on the cult of saints. *Ṣūfī* teachers were generally granted land or were exempted from paying taxes and some of them wielded considerable political influence, such as Idrīs wad al-Akbār and the Madjadhīb. Rulers and their subjects came to revere them even more than they did jurists.

The jurists, faced with the gratifying position attained by their rivals, sought to combine the teaching of law with *ṣūfī* authority. This development was clearly reflected in local usage in the seventeenth century when the title *fakī* (a corruption of *fakīh,* a jurist) was applied indiscriminately to jurists and mystics. The *fakī* established numerous religious centres and gave a degree of stability to the fluid and heterogenous Fundj society. Their missionary zeal was not confined to the Fundj kingdom but radiated as far as Kordofān, Dārfūr and Borno.

Trade and state

Major trade routes crossed the Fūr and Fundj sultanates linking them to Egypt and the Red Sea. They played an important role in strengthening cultural and economic links with the outside world. The Fūr and Fundj sultans, like most rulers in the Sudanic belt, encouraged long-distance trade. Slaves, gold, ostrich feathers and other African products were exchanged for fine cotton textiles, weapons, jewellery and other luxury items. Besides the customs duties they collected on goods passing through, the sultans needed luxury objects to maintain their prestige and reward their loyal supporters.

External trade ran along two main axes, one west-east and the other south-north. The first connected Borno-Wadai with Sennār, through Kobbie and Kordofān. From Sennār it went on to Ḳoz Radjad and Sawākin either directly or through Shandī. Through this route, known as the Sudan Road, the Eastern Sudan was laid open to cultural influences from the Western Sudan and North Africa. The Sudan Road was taken by indigenous Muslim scholars and pilgrims who could not afford the cost of crossing the desert through Egypt with the

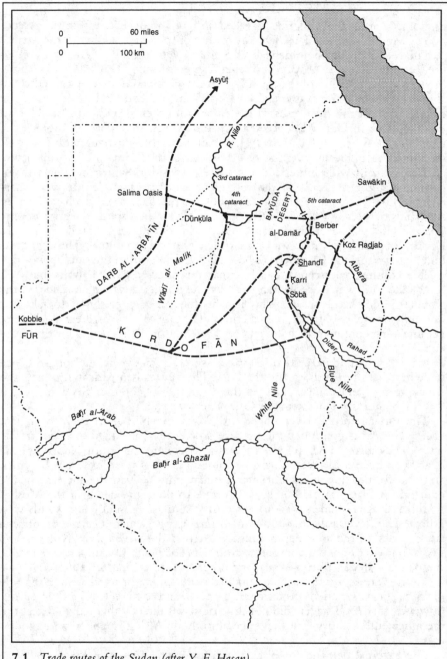

7.1 *Trade routes of the Sudan (after Y. F. Hasan)*

caravans. Most of these pilgrims travelled on foot and benefited from the protection of Muslim peoples. They lived by charity or sold asses, books or other items.

The second route commenced at Sennār, went through Kerrī and crossed the Bayūda desert to Asyūt in Upper Egypt through Dūnḳūla and Salima. However, the uprising of the Shayḳīyya in the eighteenth century caused chaos along this route and it was abandoned in favour of a route which followed the eastern bank of the river, crossed the Atbara and then went across the Nubian desert to Isna in Upper Egypt. At the Salima Oasis, the Nile route joined the *Darb al-'Arba'in* (Forty-Day Road), the main artery of Fūr trade with Egypt. It started from Kobbie and went to Asyūt by way of the Salima and Khardja oases.

Thanks to its wide hinterland and strategic position Sennār became a major commercial centre. Most of the foreigners who came to Sennār were merchants and a few were craftsmen. The bulk of the trade seems to have been in the hands of Sudanese *Djallāba* (traders). Thanks to their spirit of enterprise, the *Djallāba* also played an important role in the development of Fur trade. In Dārfūr, long-distance trade was more or less under state control. Through these trading caravans, the Fūr sultanate became better known to the outside world.

The commercial ascendancy of Sennār was affected by the rivalry between Fundj and Fūr over Kordofān and also by the Shilluk raids which rendered the Kobbie–Sennār road unsafe. This is why the caravans preferred to take the northerly route by Shandī, which, in the course of the eighteenth century, became a big commercial centre and replaced Sennār as the market for Ethiopian and Fūr trade.

In the east, the Hadāriba of Sawākin were also active in the long-distance trade between the Red Sea and the Nile. They purchased African products and slaves from Shandī and exchanged them for Indian goods at Sawākin, which was the biggest slave market after Cairo and Massawa.

The movement of slaves northward down the Nile goes back to ancient times. The Arabs continued the practice when they concluded the *baḳt* (treaty) with the Nubians. Four hundred slaves a year were sent from Nubia and the Arab world came to favour them as domestics. They were excellent bowmen and also formed highly sought-after combat units. Given the increase in the demand for black slaves, Nubia was unable to meet the needs of the Muslim world and Arab traders had to tap other sources in south and south-west Nubia. The slave trade thus took on an importance which it retained until the last decades of the nineteenth century. At first the slaves were Nubians and Bēdja, but later they were imported from Kordofān and Dārfūr and, eventually, the Bahr al-Ghazāl, Borno-Wadai and other areas in central *Bilād al-Sūdān*.

Slaves were acquired through conquest, kidnapping or purchase and the role of Arab dealers varied in different periods and different places. It seems, however, that Arab traders did not procure slaves directly themselves (except in the nineteenth century) but they relied mostly on African suppliers and middlemen.

The external demand for black slaves for armies shrank in the time of the Ayyubids (1172–1251) who replaced their black troops with white ones. The

Mamluks (1251–1517) pursued the same policy and, so long as they ruled, the army was almost exclusively made up of white slaves. However, the demand for black slaves continued in other regions, particularly in the new Fundj and Fūr sultanates where such slaves formed the core of the army. In the nineteenth century Muḥammad ʿAlī Pasha, viceroy of Egypt, began to recruit black slaves for a modern army and throughout the nineteenth century the Egyptian army included a significant number of Sudanese soldiers.

The decline of the Fundj sultanate

The commercial decay of Sennār was accompanied by political decline. With the increase in the repressive measures taken by Bādī IV, some members of the Fundj aristocracy, who had accompanied Abū Likaylik to Kordofān, induced the general to depose the sultan, which was done in 1762. The success of the revolt of Abū Likaylik was an important landmark in the history of the sultanate. Shaykh Muḥammad Abū Likaylik and his successors, the *wazirs,* became the effective hereditary rulers or regents of the kingdom until its downfall. The Fundj sultans were no more than puppets in their hands.

On the death of Abū Likaylik in 1776–7, the Fundj kings conspired with the provincial governors, particularly the ʿAbdallābi, to oust their regents. The last 50 years of the Fundj sultanate were punctuated by intrigues, revolts and civil wars among rival factions.

In the north, the authority of the ʿAbdallābi chiefs over the Nile valley was also in decline: the Saʿdāb of Shandī and the Madjādhīb of al-Damār became virtually autonomous. The Shaykīyya warriors, who dominated the Dūnkūla region, were being constantly harassed by the Mamluks of Egypt. In the west, the Fundj, harassed by the Fūr sultanate, were ultimately driven out of Kordofān. When the Turco-Egyptian forces approached Sennār in 1821, the sultanate was too feeble to muster any resistance.

The Fūr sultanate

The Fūr sultanate was one of the Islamic kingdoms in the savannah belt of the eastern *Bilād al-Sūdān.* To the west, it was separated from the sultanate of Wadai by small independent kingdoms whose allegiance was divided between the two sultanates. To the east, the plains of Kordofān, which stretched between the Fūr sultanate and the Fundj kingdom, were the source of dispute between the two states. The Libyan Desert to the north and the Bahr al-ʿArab to the south formed natural borders to the state. The central region, dominated by Djabal Marra, the cradle of the Fūr sultanate, was the meeting place of a number of trade routes, which were sources of economic prosperity, human migrations and cultural influences.

The origins of the Fūr sultanate are obscure but, according to oral tradition, the Fūr state was preceded by two indigenous dynasties: the Dādjū and the Tundjūr. The Dādjū kingdom flourished during the thirteenth and fourteenth centuries, but at the beginning of the fifteenth century the Dādjū lost control of the trade and the Tundjūr succeeded them. It was probably during the reign of the Tundjūr that the influence of Islam was first felt. It resulted from the many commercial contacts with the Muslim world and the gradual penetration of Arab immigrants. However, the proper Islamization of the region only began with the establishment of the Fūr sultanate in the early seventeenth century.

The sultanate owed its name to the Fūr, a Sudanese people who lived around Djabal Marra, and who, for reasons unknown, left their mountain home and settled in the savannah. The Kayra sultanate flourished from about 1640 to 1874. It was restored in 1898 and was finally annexed to the Anglo-Egyptian Sudan. Sulaymān Solongdungu was probably the founder of the dynasty (*c.* 1640–60). He is remembered as a conqueror who drove out the Tundjur and annexed the area around Djabal Marra.

The policy of expansion and consolidation started by Sulaymān was continued by his successors who advanced to the north and north-west. Aḥmad Bukr b. Mūsā (*c.* 1682–1722) annexed the strategic state of Dār Kimr. This expansion brought the Kayra dynasty into contact with the Zaghāwa whose territories became a source of conflict between the sultanates of Wadai and Dārfūr. Wadai was forced to pay the Kayra sultanate the tribute that it had formerly paid to the Tundjūr kings. When Sultan Yaʿḳūb refused to pay the tribute and invaded Dārfūr, Bukr eventually drove him out.

Until the end of the eighteenth century the political history of Dārfūr was dominated by the struggle between two factions of the Kayra dynasty: the sultans who sought to centralize power in their own hands and other princes who wanted to strengthen the powers of the dynasty as a whole. Conflict broke out when Sultan Bukr sought to ensure that each of his sons should succeed him in turn. He had a hundred children, five of whom ascended the Fūr throne. His first successor, Muḥammad Dawra, began by eliminating or banishing his brothers and named his son as his successor. When ʿUmar Lel came to power, he was met with hostility from his uncles, the sons of Bukr. Sulaymān ibn Aḥmad Bukr vainly sought the support of first the Musabbaʿāt and then the sultan of Wadai. However, his action provoked ʿUmar Lel to invade Wadai, about the middle of the eighteenth century. After heavy fighting, the Sultan of Wadai, Muḥammad Djawda, defeated the Fūr army and captured the sultan.

The conflict continued during the reign of the sixth sultan, Abūʾl-Ḳāsim ben Aḥmad Bukr. To consolidate his position, he fought his brothers and recruited slave troops rather than the traditional ethnic levies, which offended many title-holders. Indeed, it produced tensions similar to those that developed in the Fundj kingdom during the reign of Bādī IV.

During the battle against the Wadai forces, Abūʾl-Ḳāsim was deserted by the traditional war chiefs and the ethnic levies. He was left alone with his slave army and lost the battle. The old Fūr nobility and the traditional warriors proclaimed a new sultan, Muḥammad Tayrāb ibn Aḥmad Bukr, who followed the example of his predecessors and created a standing slave army, the *Kurkwā* (spearmen). One of them, Muḥammad Kurra, a eunuch, became one of Tayrāb's masters of the royal grooms. He later played an even more important role.

Having failed to expand westward against his enemy, the sultan of Wadai, Tayrāb, concluded a treaty with him which remained effective for a hundred years. He then turned eastward against the Musabba'āt who were attempting to establish a strong state in Kordofān. Tayrāb may also have had economic objectives, such as controlling the trade routes and the sources of slaves and gold in southern Kordofān. His immediate objective was probably to drive his brothers and other nobles out of Dārfūr so as to enable his son to succeed him. At the head of a large army, Tayrāb attacked Hāshim, Sultan of Kordofān. The latter, deserted by his army, took refuge in the Fundj kingdom, while Kordofān remained in the hands of the Fūr until the Turco-Egyptian conquest.

Tayrāb's death was followed by a bitter struggle over the succession. Finally, Ahmad Bukr's youngest son, 'Abd al-Rahmān, emerged victorious from the civil war thanks to the support of Muhammad Kurra. The new sultan rewarded Muhammad Kurra with the position of Ab Shaykh, a rank that gave him great authority. From 1790 to 1804 Muhammad Kurra was the strongest man in the state.

'Abd al-Rahmān marked his victory by building a new royal residence (fāshir) at Khor Tandalti, east of Djabal Marra, in 1741/2. Until then the Fūr sultans had had no fixed capital. The growth of a permanent capital at al-Fāshir and the consolidation of the centralizing forces and Islamizing influences made the reign of 'Abd al-Rahmān the apogee of the Kayra sultanate. There were increasing contacts with the outside world through trade and the arrival of religious teachers. 'Abd al-Rahmān exchanged presents with the Ottoman sultan, who bestowed on him the honorific title of al-Rashīd (the Just). He also corresponded with Bonaparte in 1799 during the French occupation of Egypt.

The adoption of Islam in Dārfūr was probably a much slower process than in the Fundj kingdom. It speeded up in the eighteenth century, but African religious rituals and practices coexisted with Islam at the Kayra court for some time. The propagation of Islam was encouraged by Ahmad Bukr who built mosques and schools while Muhammad Tayrāb obtained religious books from Egypt and Tunisia. 'Abd al-Rahmān al-Rashīd, himself a Muslim scholar, encouraged jurists and mystics from other countries to come and settle in his sultanate. Among these was the Tunisian Arab 'Umar al-Tunisi, later followed by his son Muhammad, whose account of Dārfūr is one of the main sources for the history of the country. Other scholars came from Egypt, Hidjāz, the Nilotic Sudan and western Bilād al-Sūdān. To attract them to his country, the sultan offered religious teachers lands through the hakura (tax exemption) system, as was the case in the Fundj kingdom.

By the end of the eighteenth century the sultan and his immediate associates, who had no ethnic affiliations, had gone a long way in developing external trade and adopting Islamic institutions to govern the country. This state of affairs helped to alter the ethnic structure of the state and weaken old religious practices. The emergence of a new class of merchants, jurists and mystics was instrumental in bringing this change about. However, the Kayra dynasty, despite its Arab lineage, had its roots among the Fūr. Although Arabic was used in diplomacy and trade, Fūr remained the language of the court.

On the death of 'Abd al-Raḥmān in 1801/02, his son Muḥammad al-Faḍl succeeded him with the help of Muḥammad Kurra. But the new sultan soon fell out with this man whom he had made his chief minister and killed him. Muḥammad al-Faḍl reigned for 40 years, during which the state began to decline.

The Southern Sudan

Despite the existence of serious anthropological works by eminent scholars, historical research on Southern Sudan is still in its infancy. The same applies to archaeological investigations and historical linguistic research. From the meagre evidence, however, certain broad outlines are beginning to emerge. From linguistic evidence, for example, it is becoming increasingly clear that Nilotic cultures and probably Central Sudanic ones have their roots in Southern Sudan.

Much of Southern Sudan and northern Uganda was probably occupied by peoples speaking Central Sudanic languages until the last decades of the last millennium when the area began to be colonized by Eastern and Western Nilotic speakers. Indeed, one of the major historical themes during our period is the progressive Niloticization of the peoples of Southern Sudan. Today the region is mostly occupied by Nilotes, with only the Moru and the Madi who live to the west of the White Nile remaining to remind us of the former presence of Central Sudanic speakers.

Recently, Roland Oliver attempted a synthesis of Iron Age archaeological evidence for the prehistory of this region which tends to confirm the linguistic picture. He envisaged two centres of Iron Age cultures, one to the east of the Nile swamps in the Sudan–Ethiopian borderlands and the other on the ironstone plateau of the Nile–Congo watershed. These two cultures, one Nilotic and the other Bantu, were separated by Central Sudanic cultures. The Nilotics moved southwards into the Bantu regions and, as a result of that meeting, the Bantu-speakers began to practise intensive pastoralism.

Regarding the Sudan, Oliver identified two Iron Age periods among the Nilotes. In Western Equatorial and Baḥr al-Ghazāl provinces the first period is associated with Iron Age pastoralists, the Luel, who kept humpless cattle and built artificial mounds in order to protect themselves from flooding during the rainy season.

The beginning of the Later Iron Age of the Nilotes seems to have coincided with the appearance of humped cattle on the Baḥr al-Ghazāl and the full development of transhumance. Humped cattle probably spread southwards with the Baḳḳāra Arabs following the fall of the kingdom of Dūnḳūla. Thus the Arab penetration of Northern and Central Sudan in the thirteenth and four-teenth centuries not only coincided with but might have triggered the Western Nilotic migrations.

The rapid expansion of the Western and Eastern Nilotes southward and east-ward may therefore be linked with the appearance of intensive cattle-herding combined with cereal agriculture. This combination provided a means of food production well suited to drier areas which enabled the Nilotes to occupy many areas previously avoided by Bantu-speakers.

The Shilluk kingdom

In Southern Sudan, the Shilluk constitute the largest component of the Northern Luo group, the others being the Luo of Bahr al-Ghazāl and the Anywa who straddle the Sudan–Ethiopia border. The Shilluk initially settled near Malakal in the early sixteenth century, after driving out the Fundj who lived in the area at the confluence of the Nile and the Sobat. This region controls access to Lake No, giving it great strategic importance. This small group of Luo-speakers incorporated Fundj, Nuba and other elements. All these groups, with different cultures and economic traditions, combined in the crucible of history to form what became the Shilluk nation from the second half of the seventeenth century.

During this formative century, the Shilluk established a mixed economy based on cattle-herding and cereal agriculture. They were essentially sedentary and did not practise transhumance; they lived in a string of villages along the western bank of the Nile between Muomo and Tonga.

Frontiers and socio-economic interdependence

By the beginning of the seventeenth century, the west bank of the Nile was already overpopulated and the Shilluk began to expand into two frontier areas. Northwards, they attempted to take possession of the White Nile valley between Muomo and Alays. The area was unsuitable for agriculture but provided abundant game, fish and honey. From the reign of Odak Ocollo (*c.*1600–35) to 1861, the Shilluk dominated this region, which the Muslim peoples called 'Bahr Scheluk'.

The second frontier area was the region between the Nile and the Nuba Mountains. Tradition dwells so much on Shilluk–Nūba activities in this area that it must have been important for both peoples before it was occupied by the Bakkāra Arabs in the second half of the nineteenth century.

We learn from Shilluk traditions that, during the reign of Odak Ocollo the Shilluk supported Dārfūr in its struggle with the Fundj sultanate for the control of the White Nile trade. With the capitulation of Takali, the Fundj and the Shilluk were left confronting each other along the White Nile, exhausted after three decades of warfare.

From about 1630 the Jieng, another Jii-speaking people, invaded southern Fundj. Throughout the seventeenth and eighteenth centuries, they expanded into southern Djazīra, which gradually altered the balance of power in the region. The presence of the Jieng represented such a threat that the Shilluk and the Fundj joined forces against them. They succeeded in preventing them from expanding northwards and westwards and even forced them eastwards towards the Ethiopian border.

The alliance with the Fundj marked the beginning of a socio-economic interdependence that the Shilluk established with different groups at different times (Fundj, *Djallāba*, Baḳḳāra Arabs, Arab freebooters, European traders and Mahdists), usually to exploit the Jieng. The fact that the Shilluk combined time and again with these various groups to exploit a related Jii-speaking people shows that such socio-economic alliances were untainted by any racial or ethnic ideology. Racial ideology in Southern Sudan was a post-Mahdiyya-period phenomenon.

The development of political and social institutions

During the second half of the seventeenth century, political developments occurred which significantly affected the socio-economic development of Shillukland. Despite its diversity, the population acquired a sense of national unity and a more centralized administration was established under the king (*reth*). A royal monopoly of economic resources as well as of local and long-distance trade was gradually established.

Three names are associated with these developments in Shilluk history: Abudhok, queen and daughter of Reth Bwoc, and one of the many powerful women in Shilluk history; her half-brother Dhokoth; and Tugo, the latter's son. Reth Dhokoth (*c.* 1670–1690) is famous for having made raids down the Nile and westwards into the Nuba Mountains. The great famine of 1684 (*Umm Laham* in Arabic) was probably responsible for making many Shilluk move north to raid or settle in 'Baḥr Scheluk'. Dhokoth's raids were extremely successful and brought back many captives.

Reth Dhokoth's military and economic successes were largely responsible for the centralization of royal power which was completed by his son Togo (*c.* 1690–1710). Togo founded the village of Fashoda which became the permanent residence of the reth. He also instituted the elaborate installation ceremony for a Shilluk reth. His fame spread rapidly both within and outside the kingdom.

By the beginning of the eighteenth century, the Fundj empire was disintegrating and, as the power of the Fundj declined, that of the Shilluk increased. The end of the century saw the total collapse of the Fundj sultanate, which enabled the Shilluk to strengthen their control of the White Nile. The English traveller, W. G. Browne, who stayed in Dārfūr for four years (1793–6), reported that the Shilluk were in complete control of the river at Alays where they provided a ferry service enabling caravan traders moving between Sennār and al-'Obeyd to cross the Nile.

The decline of Shilluk power

During the reign of Reth Nyakwaa (*c.* 1780–1820) the Jieng migrated en masse across the River Sobat and the Shilluk, who for a century and a half had been in complete control of the White Nile area from Lake No to Alays, had to accept the presence of other Jii-speakers. But more was to come. A year after the death of Nyakwaa, the armies of Muḥammad 'Alī Pasha, Viceroy of Egypt, invaded Sudan, put an end to the Fundj administration and installed Turco-

Egyptian rule. A clash with the Shilluk was inevitable. From 1821, despite sustained Shilluk resistance, the Shilluk frontier steadily retreated southwards before the gradual encroachment of the Arabs and the Turco-Egyptian regime.

In order to dominate the White Nile, the Shilluk had to control the navigable waterways. They possessed a large number of vessels and were fine oarsmen. For their raids or military expeditions groups of 30 or 40 canoes travelled together and constituted a considerable military force in the region. But a Turco-Egyptian government shipyard was established at Mandjara in 1826 and that put an end to Shilluk naval supremacy on the White Nile.

The peoples of the Baḥr al-Ghazāl

The country south of the Baḥr al-Ghazāl and west of a line from Meshra al-Rek to the point where the boundaries of modern Sudan, Zaire and Uganda meet, was occupied by peoples belonging to two major language families: the Ubangian (Niger-Congo) and the Central Sudanic (Sahara-Nile). Central Sudanic speakers had been settled there since very early times; they settled along waterways and lived by farming cereal crops, keeping cattle and hunting. Ubangian speakers arrived from the west (Central African Republic) and settled mostly to the west of the Central Sudanic speaking communities or in between, which is understandable given the very light settlement of peoples in the area. Ubangians were farmers who first based their economy on yams but later shifted to producing cereal crops or bananas, depending on the local environment. They did not keep cattle, which implies substantially different attitudes towards wealth, and especially bride-wealth, from those of the Central Sudanic people.

We know very little about the life of these people before 1800 because nineteenth-century developments led to the break-up of their communities. Furthermore, no oral tradition could be found about what happened before 1800. The only genealogies that go back further (to between 1650 and 1705) are those of the ruling families of three Bongo clans. They merely tell us that the people were already settled in the Wau-Tonj area in the eighteenth century. By 1800 slave-traders from Dārfūr were already active in Dār Fertīt and Dār Banda while the Zande were beginning to conquer the areas further south.

All that can be said for the period covered by this chapter is that Dārfūr began to exercise informal control over Dār Fertīt well before 1800 and demanded tribute from the inhabitants of the Hofrat-en-Nahas region, while Arab or Fūr families established themselves as leaders over small groups in the area of Raga. More research is needed throughout this area where it may still be possible to gather data on ways of life, trade and possible population movements before 1800.

Morocco

In Volume IV it was shown that the fifteenth century was marked by Spanish and Portuguese offensives against North Africa, particularly against Morocco. Since 1415 – the year in which the Portuguese took Ceuta – they had seized many coastal places on the Atlantic littoral, making them bases for raids into the Moroccan hinterland. All these events aroused firm resistance. The *zāwiya* *Shaykhs* and religious brotherhoods encouraged this spirit, using it to prepare the population to fight the invaders.

Some of the *sharīfs* of Darʿa, led by Abū ʿAbd Allāh, known as al-Ḳāʿim bi-ʿAmr Allāh (he who rises at the command of God) appointed themselves to fight the infidels and drive them from the forts they were occupying in the country. Al-Ḳāʿim bi-ʿAmr Allāh's proclamation in 1511 marked the beginning of the Saʿādī dynasty. Their struggle lasted some 40 years, and was directed partly against the Portuguese and partly against the Waṭṭāsid kings.

In southern Morocco, the Portuguese invaders were before long safe only in their forts and, consequently, Portuguese colonization declined at an increasing pace. The Portuguese were also threatened from the north by the fighters of Salé who continually harried them and drove them out of Maʾmurā, at the mouth of the Sebū river.

During this period, the struggle between the new dynasty of the Saʿādī and the old Waṭṭāsid-Marinid dynasty did terrible damage to Morocco. Fortunately, after an indecisive battle between the Waṭṭāsid sultan Aḥmad and the *sharīf* Aḥmad al-Aʿradj at Tadla in 1527, a treaty was concluded which gave the Saʿādī the Sūs and Marlakesh and left the rest of the country in the hands of the sultan, with Fez remaining the capital. These provisions gave Morocco 12 years of peace, during which the Saʿādī organized their forces and concentrated on the struggle against the Portuguese.

The first major event was the capture of Agadir, which the Saʿādī sultan, with the help of a powerful artillery, succeeded in taking after a six-month siege. The capture of Agadir led to the immediate evacuation of the towns of Sāfī and Azemmūr by the Portuguese in 1542. These successes made Muḥammad al-Shaykh the hero of national liberation and brought him considerable prestige throughout the country. He could now resume his struggle against the

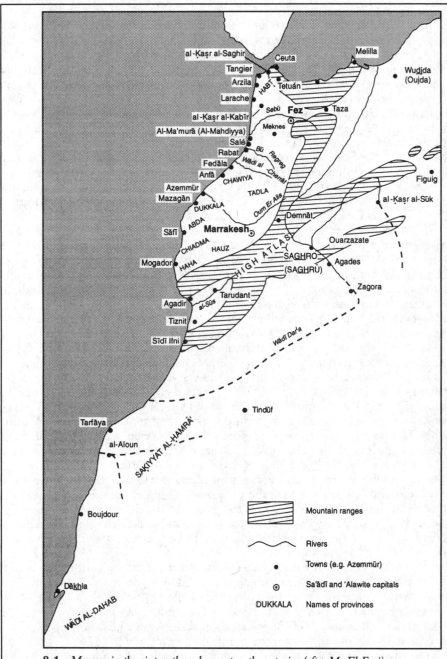

8.1 *Morocco in the sixteenth and seventeenth centuries (after M. El Fasi)*

Wattāsids and attempt to reconquer the north of Morocco which they were still governing under the terms of the Treaty of Tadla.

After defeating his brother and rival, Aḥmad al-Aʿradj Muḥammad al-Shaykh, now the sole leader of the Saʿādī, decided to deal with the Wattāsids once and for all and set out to occupy Fez, possession of which would give him supreme power in Morocco. The struggle between the old and the new dynasties lasted some ten years and ended with Muḥammad al-Shaykh's entry into Fez on 13 September 1554. But the sultan was concerned about the threat to his country from the Turks in Algiers. In his view, the only real danger to Morocco came from the Ottoman empire, which had subjugated all the eastern and western Arab countries. To safeguard his country from a Turkish invasion, he therefore decided to force the Ottomans out of Africa Two sons of the Saʿādī sultan, ʿAbdallāh and ʿAbd al-Raḥmān, had already taken Tlemcen in 1550, but the Turks had retaken it in 1552.

To carry through his grand design of conquering Algeria, Muḥammad al-Shaykh sought an alliance with Spain. Talks were arranged with the Spanish governor of Oran and the two sides agreed to mount an expedition against Algiers. Two thousand Spanish cavalry paid by the sultan were to join this Moroccan-led operation. The Turks got wind of these preparations and the Sublime Porte sent reinforcements to attack Oran, then occupied by Spain. However, the Turkish fleet which was to have blockaded the Spanish fleet by sea was recalled to fight the Christian fleet of Andrea Doria that was threatening the Bosphorus. The sultan could now turn to the conquest of Algeria. He began by laying siege to Tlemcen and succeeded in capturing it.

In 1557 Sultan Muḥammad al-Shaykh was assassinated by an officer of his own guard who was in the pay of the Ottoman government. But this made no difference to the determination of the Saʿādī to press on with clearing Morocco of all foreign occupants and defending it against all incursions, even a Muslim one. The new Caliph, Abu Muḥammad ʿAbdallāh, who was proclaimed sultan after the murder of his father, followed the policy laid down by his predecessor. He was known as al-Ghālib Billāh (victor through the strength of God). He set out to rebuild the army, obtain the most modern weapons and organize a vast psychological campaign among the people with the help of the *zāwiyas* and the leaders of the brotherhoods. When al-Ghālib Billāh felt himself strong enough, he laid seige to Mazagān with a strong artillary force. Although his attempt failed, it showed the Portuguese that they had to reckon with a genuine new power.

The sultan felt that the Portuguese threat to the interior of Morocco was now averted and he turned to developing his kingdom's prosperity. He encouraged trade with European states, especially France. Al-Ghālib Billāh was one of the greatest builders of the Saʿādī dynasty. He constructed a great mosque in Marrakesh and restored the Almohad mosque in Agadir Casbah. His reign was on the whole calm and prosperous and he died peacefully in 1574.

His succession proved more difficult. Transgressing the long-established rule whereby the family's eldest male had a prior right to succeed over the eldest son of the late ruler, Muḥammad, the son of al-Ghālib Billāh, was proclaimed sultan. The new sultan took the title of al-Mutawakkil, but is still known by the nickname of al-Maslukha. Mawlāy ʿAbd al-Mālik, the eldest of the Saʿādī princes and uncle to al-Maslukha considered that the throne was rightfully his. When al-Ghālib Billāh's son was proclaimed sultan of Fez, he took refuge first in Sidjilmāsa, then in Algiers and eventually in Constantinople. He entered the Ottoman army and took part in the reconquest of Tunis, where he displayed great courage. On his return to Constantinople, he found the Caliph disposed to help him regain the throne of his ancestors. With the small army made available to him, Mawlāy ʿAbd al-Mālik arrived in Morocco where he met with no opposition, since the people were all on his side. Al-Mutawakkil was abandoned by his army and forced to flee, and Mawlāy ʿAbd al-Mālik entered Fez on 31 March 1576, where he was enthusiastically welcomed by the population.

Al-Mutawakkil escaped towards the south and succeeded in retaking Marrakesh. He was again defeated but managed to escape northwards and asked the governor of Vélez de la Gomera to grant him refuge in his town. His request was granted, with the permission of King Philip II, on condition that he be accompanied by only a few members of his family.

Mawlāy ʿAbd al-Mālik, once freed – at least for the time being – from his nephew, began to reorganize the state and rebuild his army, and he made his brother Mawlāy Aḥmad Caliph in Fez. To replenish the treasury, he did not want to levy fresh taxes and sought other methods. He expanded the navy, had new ships built and repaired the older ones. This policy stimulated many different crafts and increased trade with the rest of the world, especially with Europe, and had beneficial effects in all fields.

The battle of the three kings

In the sixteenth century, Portugal had a powerful empire which embraced vast territories in America, Asia and Africa. At the time when the dethroned Saʿādī Sultan al-Mutawakkil took refuge at Vélez de la Gomera, this empire was ruled by the young King Don Sebastiān, who dreamed of conquering Morocco, and from there the whole of the Maghrib, and then pushing on eastward to deliver Christ's tomb from Muslim hands. In his search for help to regain the Saʿādī throne, al-Mutawakkil had turned in vain to the king of Spain; he now contacted Don Sebastián, who jumped at this opportunity to embark on the expedition of which he had always dreamed and for which he had Portuguese public opinion on his side.

When Mawlāy ʿAbd al-Mālik was informed of the preparations being made by the young king, he endeavoured to dissuade him from his rash adventure. He wrote Don Sebastián a letter which is unique in the history of diplomacy, not only for its substance but for its sincerity, to convince him to give up his expedition. The French archives possess the Italian translation of this document which has been published in Count Henry de Castries' *Sources inédites de l'histoire du Maroc*. In that letter Sultan Mawlāy ʿAbd al-Mālik also displayed diplomatic skill, making it clear that the real aggressor in the Mediterranean region was in fact the king of Portugal.

However, Don Sebastián continued to prepare for war and landed at Arzila (Asila). Mawlāy ʿAbd al-Mālik, who understood the king of Portugal's sense of honour, wrote to him again asking him not to attack defenceless people and to wait for him where he was to join him in battle. Members of Don Sebastián's entourage, especially Muḥammad al-Maslukh, advised him not to comply because it was a trap. On the contrary, he should make haste to attack and occupy Larache and al-Ḳaṣr al-Kabīr. But Don Sebastián decided not to move from Arzila, where he remained for 19 days until the eve of the battle.

The Saʿādī forces set out from Marrakesh northwards and were continually joined by large numbers of volunteers. In addition, the sultan had requested his brother, the Caliph at Fez, to get to al-Ḳaṣr al-Kabīr before him with the contingents from Fez and its region, in particular the elite corps of young archers (the Rima). When the Saʿādī army arrived at al-Ḳaṣr al-Kabīr, Mawlāy Aḥmad was already there and Mawlāy ʿAbd al-Mālik charged the archers – once Don Sebastián had crossed the Wādī al-Makhāzin – to destroy the bridge across the river so as to prevent the Portuguese from making their way to the sea once they had been defeated.

The 'battle of the three kings', known among Arab historians as the battle of Wādī al-Makhāzin and among Spanish and Portuguese historians as the battle of Alcazarquivir, was fought on 4 August 1578.

The day of the battle

On the Monday morning, at the end of the month of Djumada II in the year 986 of the Hegira (4 August 1578), the opposing camps prepared for battle. It was an historic day, the culmination of long centuries of conflicts between Muslims and Christians which had begun in Spain and then spread to Morocco.

The opposing forces prepared to attack, each employing its own tactics. The Christian army was drawn up on the field of battle in a square, with a corps of legionaries in front; the German troops held the right flank and the Spanish and Italian ones the left. The cavalry advanced on each wing. There was also a body of supporters of Muḥammad 'the Flayed'. The Moroccan army was deployed in the form of a crescent, from within which Sultan Mawlāy ʿAbd al-Mālik, who was ill, directed the battle from a litter. The cavalry manned the tips of the crescent, with the infantry and artillery in the centre.

After the dawn prayer, the order was given to open fire. The mercenaries flung themselves on the Muslims' left flank, taking them by surprise. Sultan ʿAbd al-Mālik then rose from his litter to urge his men on. He succumbed from his efforts but, before he died, he gave orders for his death to be concealed, since the battle had barely begun. As the battle raged, many men fell on both sides. The Christians fell back and then fled towards the bridge which they found destroyed. Many then tried to swim across the river, but were carried away by the current and drowned.

Don Sebastián stood firm, displaying enormous courage, until he fell on the field of battle. Muḥammad 'the Flayed' drowned in the river as he attempted to flee. His body was fished out and brought to Aḥmad al-Manṣūr, who was proclaimed king after the victory (which gave him his name, al-Manṣūr, the Victorious).

The losses on both sides were heavy and tradition has it that there were nearly 14,000 Christian prisoners. Negotiations were entered into for the ransom of Don Sebastián's body, but al-Manṣūr was too proud to accept any offer, especially as the ransoms for the prisoners had yielded him sums which some historians gave as the origin of his nickname of al-Dhahabī (the Golden). He therefore returned the king's body without any payment of any kind.

The consequences of the battle of the three kings

This decisive battle had major consequences which for many centuries set their mark not only on Islam and Morocco, but also on Portugal and Europe. The victory imparted fresh vitality to the Saʿādī dynasty and brought Morocco peace and prosperity.

Morocco experienced an economic boom, especially in the sugar industry. In the arts, encouraged by the Saʿādī dynasty and the newly enriched bourgeoisie, architecture developed and achieved considerable refinement. The Moroccans' newly recovered stability and their feelings of pride produced a wealth of art, poetry and literature.

The battle also had major repercussions internationally. There was a substantial decline in Portuguese influence in the Muslim world, particularly in the Gulf countries. The battle finally put an end to the threat from crusaders to the countries of the East. The Saʿādī victory also strengthened the power of the Ottoman empire, and Europeans are right to consider this Moroccan victory as a victory of all Muslims.

But this victory also resulted in the Ottomans abandoning any idea of conquering Morocco, which remained the only Arab country outside Turkish influence. The Arabic language was thus able to retain its purity and authenticity in Morocco.

Saʿādī expansion in the sixteenth century

Al-Manṣūr reigned for a quarter of a century and devoted himself to consolidating the power of the Saʿādī dynasty and developing his kingdom in every possible way.

After the victory of Wādī al-Makhāzin, he set out to liberate the towns that were still in the hands of Europeans: Arzila (Asila), Tangier, Ceuta and Mazagān. He succeeded in driving the occupiers out of Arzila (1589), but Tangier was not liberated until the following century. Ceuta passed into the hands of King Philip II of Spain, who had inherited the kingdom of Portugal. Along with Melilla and three other *presidios* it remains a Spanish dependency to this day.

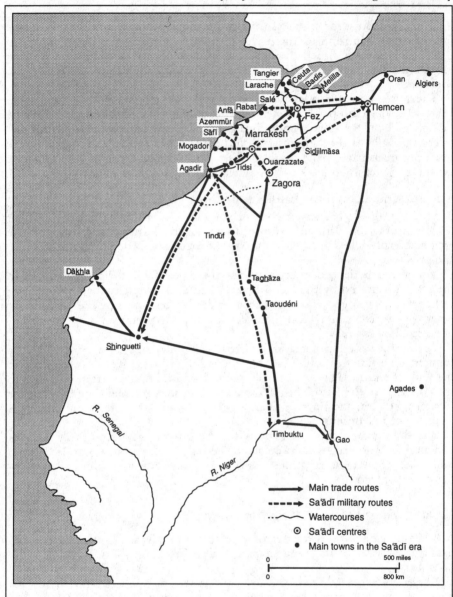

8.2 *The empire of Aḥmad Al-Manṣūr, 'the Golden' (1578-1603) (after M. El Fasi)*

Al-Manṣūr's success encouraged him to look beyond Morocco's traditional boundaries with a view to restoring the situation as it was at the time of the Almoravids and unifying Islam. In the case of the expedition to the Sudan, the real motive was most likely the expansionism common to all great powers.

Before embarking on this campaign Al-Manṣūr convened a council of war at which he set out his plans. In his *Histoire du Maroc*, H. Terrasse writes that 'Almost everyone was against the venture, because it was too risky and *above all* because it would mean waging war against other Muslims'. The *'ulamā'*, the true representatives of the people, also took this view. But Al-Manṣūr overrode this advice,' and decided on his own to undertake the Sudanese expedition. There is no need to describe this expedition in detail here, since all works on the history of Morocco deal with it.

Al-Manṣūr's death in 1603 was followed by a period of instability as a power struggle broke out among his successors who engaged in endless internecine strife which drenched Morocco in blood for half a century. In all parts of the country, adherents of religious brotherhoods rose in the name of patriotism to restore peace and fight against the Portuguese and the Spaniards who had taken advantage of the weakness of the last rulers of the Saʿādī dynasty to blockade the coasts of Morocco.

The most famous of these war leaders was certainly Abū ʿAbdallāh Muḥammad al-ʿAyyāshī of Salé, who fought successfully against the Portuguese at Mazagān. He managed temporarily to pacify the areas under his control, in particular the town of Fez. Despite all his successes he never laid claim to supreme power, since he was a true saint. He was assassinated on the orders of his enemies, the Moriscos of Rabat, in 1641.

In 1636-7, for the first time in the history of the Middle Atlas, the grandson of a *shaykh* universally renowned for his learning and holiness declared himself sultan of the whole of Morocco. This pretender's name was Muḥammad ibn M'Ḥammad ibn Abū Bakr al-Dalāl. His grandfather had founded a *zāwiya* in the Middle Atlas which had become almost as prestigious a centre of Islamic studies as Ḳarāwiyyīn University in Fez. The success of this university-cum-monastery encouraged in him ambitions for power, all the more so as the weakness of the last members of the Saʿādī dynasty left the way open for him.

Following al-Manṣūr's death, ten of his descendants competed for power for a little over half a century. Two of them managed to reign for more than 20 years, with interruptions when their brothers or cousins took power only to lose it subsequently – to say nothing of the claimants from among the heads of the *zāwiyas* and other adventurers. All these claimants to the throne of Morocco made themselves out to be saviours of the unity of the country and champions of stable governmnet.

Mention should be made of the revolt of the Shbanāte who established a short-lived period of rule in Marrakesh after killing the last Saʿādī sultan. The Shbanāte were a faction of the Aʿrāb (Arab nomads) who had been driven out of Cairo by the Fatimids and invaded the Maghrib in successive waves, destroying everything in their path. In the twelfth century they had been brought into

Morocco by the Almohad Ya'kub al-Manṣūr. They ultimately settled on the fertile plains of the Atlantic coast, and it was they who were responsible for the real Arabization of Morocco. In 1658–9 a caid of the Shbanāte by the name of Abd al-Karīm ibn Abū Bakr al-Shbāni and known as Karrūm al-Ḥadjdj rose up in Marrakesh against Sultan Aḥmad, known as Mawlāy al-'Abbās. He put him to death and declared himself sultan and occupied the royal palace. This reign lasted some ten years and was marked by Karrum al-Ḥadjdj's extortion, injustice and cruelty. Even his followers and supporters sought to get rid of him and he was killed by one of those close to him. His son Abū Bakr ibn 'Abd al-Karīm was proclaimed sultan and reigned for a time until his death, 40 days before the 'Alawite sultan Mawlāy al-Rashīd reached Marrakesh.

The early sultans of the 'Alawite dynasty

The honour of setting up a strong, lasting and beneficent government was to fall to the Sharifian dynasty of the 'Alawites, who have reigned over Morocco for three and a half centuries. The 'Alawites are a family whose descent from the Prophet has been scientifically established by leading Moroccan scholars.

The descendants of this family, created by al-Ḥasan ad-Dakhil, formed a religious aristocracy which acquired great prestige among all the peoples of the Tafilālet. Al-Ḥasan's great grandson, Mawlāy al-Sharīf, became very famous. He had nine sons, one of them being Mawlāy al-Sharīf whom the Filali proclaimed sultan. At this time Morocco was divided among the Dilawiyya of the Middle Atlas, who occupied Fez, Ibn Hassūn, who reigned over the Sūs and the High Atlas, and al-Khaḍr Ghaylān, who was ravaging the north-west.

In the Tafilālet itself, a family was occupying a fortress, Tabousamt, in opposition to the 'Alawite *sharīfs*. There was fighting between the two sides and, after various incidents, Mawlāy al-Sharīf in favour of his son Mawlāy M'hammad, who was enthroned as king of Morocco in 1640. This was the beginning of the 'Alawite dynasty.

Mawlāy al-Rashīd was not willing to acknowledge his brother Mawlāy M'hammad and left the Tafilālet. He began by wandering in the towns and the *ḳabīlas* in the south and the north, he went to the Todgha valley, to Demnat, to the *zāwiya* of Dila and to Fez. Mawlāy M'hammad raised an army and marched on the Dar'a, which was occupied by Abū Hassūn. He fought the latter and drove him out of the area. He then marched on the *zāwiya* of Dila and gave battle against the Dilāwīyya, but was defeated. He then went and laid siege to Fez which he succeeded in occupying in 1650. But he failed to establish himself there and headed for eastern Morocco, occupied the town of Udjda and advanced towards Tlemcen. The whole of western Algeria was invaded by his troops. After signing an agreement with the Turks who governed Algeria, Mawlāy M'hammad returned to Udjda.

Mawlāy al-Rashīd, pursuing his plan to ascend the throne of Morocco, came and established himself at Tāzā. He now had the money and the men to pursue his plans and take power. Having conquered the whole of the Tāzā area, he declared himself sultan. When his brother Mawlāy Mḥammad learned about these happenings he came to meet him to put a stop to his doings but he was killed at the beginning of the battle. This was in 1664, a year which saw the beginning of the conquest of Morocco.

Mawlāy al-Rashīd then went to the Tafilālet, the cradle of the family, where one of his deceased brother's sons had risen up against him. He fled on Mawlāy al-Rashīd's arrival and the new sultan was able to enter his native town peacefully. After two vain attempts to occupy Fez, he finally entered the town in triumph in 1666. The taking of this capital, without which no government can maintain itself in Morocco, marked the definitive establishment of the 'Alawite dynasty.

Mawlāy al-Rashīd first set about organizing the administration. He distributed money to the 'ulamā' and made them his privy councillors. He appointed the scholar Hamdūn al-Mazwār al Kāḍī of the capital. All these actions won him the devotion of the Fāsīs. He spent two years pacifying the whole of northern Morocco, and, at the end of 1668, he prepared to reduce the zāwiya of Dila which still constituted the only authority in the Middle Atlas area He met the troops of Muḥammad al-Hadjdj al-Dilā'ī in the plain of Fāsīs and inflicted an overwhelming defeat on them. He then entered the zāwiya with his troops, treated the occupants humanely and did not shed one drop of blood. This happened at the beginning of 1668.

After this victory, it only remained for Mawlāy al-Rashīd to crush the last pockets of resistance in southern Morocco. He first liberated Marrakesh from the Shbanāte, and then went on to attack the Samlālīyūn who had established their power in the Sūs; he took Tarūdant and the fortress of Ighīl. By 1670 the whole of Morocco was pacified and 'Alawite power finally established. A year and a half later, Mawlāy al-Rashīd met his death in a riding accident.

The story of the last rulers of the Sa'adi dynasty is largely one of events, as the strife that then prevailed and the instability of government did not allow arts and letters to flourish It was only under Mawlāy al-Rashīd that Morocco resumed its cultural traditions and its social and economic achievements.

Mawlāy al-Rashīd built the biggest madrasa (college) in Fez, and another in Marrakesh. He was also responsible for the construction of the bridge over the Wādī Sebū 15 kilometres east of Fez.

On the economic side, he lent traders considerable sums to develop their businesses and thus create prosperity for all. He took an interest in the water problem, especially in the desert areas, and had many wells dug in the eastern deserts, particularly in the Dar'a, through which caravans of traders and pilgrim caravans passed on their way to Mecca.

By and large, the reign of Mawlāy al-Rashīd was marked by remarkable progress in all domains and by peace and prosperity.

The reign of Mawlāy Ismā'īl

Mawlāy Ismā'īl completed the task begun by his two brothers, that of unifying

Morocco by putting it under a single throne. He strengthened the basis of the state and saw to it that Muslim law was extended to all parts of Morocco, in order to give the country religious as well as political unity.

He was extremely interested in matters relating to religion and proselytization on its behalf, and he even wrote to Louis XIV of France and James II of England inviting them to embrace Islam. He strictly observed the precepts of Muslim law and led an austere life. Christian historians have described him as cruel, violent and despotic. This false image of Mawlāy Ismāʿīl derives from the stories told by European prisoners who had naturally been treated m accordance with the fashion of the time – that is with retaliatory violence.

Ambassadors from the sultan were sent to all European capitals and, in neturn, delegations from the European states came to seek his friendship. He was thoroughly conversant with what was happening in France and England, through his intelligence agents, and showed perspicacity in politics.

He came to the throne on 16 April 1672. The notables of the towns and *kabīlas* came to swear allegiance to him, except for those from Marrakesh, where his nephew Ahmad ibn Muhriz had hastened to have himself proclaimed sultan. Mawlāy Ismāʿīl was obliged to march against his nephew and fight him and the *kabīlas* in the Hauz who had joined cause with him. He defeated them, entered Marrakesh and forgave the inhabitants for their lack of haste in swearing allegiance to him. His nephew who had fled after his defeat started plotting again, urging the people of Fez to revolt.

Mawlāy Ismāʿīl marched against him and forced him to flee a second time into the Sahara. He laid siege to Fez and secured its surrender, but later decided to make Meknes his capital. He gave orders for palaces, houses, walls, stables, warehouses and other large buildings to be put up there. He had gardens and ponds laid out, to such good effect that Meknes came to rival Versailles.

Ahmad ibn Muhriz tried a third time to revolt against his uncle. He succeeded in occupying Marrakesh in 1674 and fortified himself there. His uncle laid siege to the town for nearly two years, at the end of which time ibn Muhriz fled to the Sūs. Mawlāy Ismāʿīl then made his entry into Marrakesh and this time he gave orders for those who had supported ibn Muhriz to be punished.

One of the domestic political events of Mawlāy Ismāʿīl's reign was the revolt by three of his brothers, Mawlāy al Harran, Mawlāy Hāshām and Mawlāy Ahmad, which broke out at the end of Ramadān in 1678–9. The rebels were supported by the Aït ʿAttā *kabīla*. The sultan marched against them at the head of an imposing army and the three defeated brothers fled into the Sahara. Meanwhile, after suffering various up and downs, ibn Muhriz joined forces with his uncle al-Harran. When Mawlāy Ismāʿīl learned that they were occupying the town of Tarūdant in 1684–5, he laid siege to the town; during the siege ibn Muhriz was killed. The royal army took Tarūdant by storm and al-Harran fled into the Sahara. From that date, 1687, on, there was no further challenge to Mawlāy Ismāʿīl's rule.

8.3 *Sultan Mawlay Ismāʿīl (Muḥammad V Mausoleum, Rabat, courtesy of the Curator)*

Mawlāy Ismāʿīl's campaigns to recover the Moroccan towns occupied by the Europeans

After consolidating the achievements of his two predecessors, Mawlāy Ismāʿīl completed the unification of Morocco by liquidating Christian colonization.

The retaking of al-Mahdiyya

Al-Mahdiyya, which was then called al-Ma'murā, was one of the biggest ports in Morocco. Pirates of various nations attempted to occupy it. Taking advantage of the Moroccans' weakness as a result of the quarrels among al-Manṣūr's sons, the Spaniards occupied al-Mahdiyya in 1614 and held it until Mawlāy Ismāʿīl decided to drive them out. He marched on the town, laid siege to it, cut off its water supply and occupied it in 1681, taking all the Spaniards there prisoner.

The retaking of Tangier

Tangier had come under English rule after one of their kings had married a Portuguese princess. Mawlāy al-Rashīd had attempted to return this town to Morocco but died without having been able to do so. Mawlāy Ismāʿīl deputed one of his greatest generals, ʿAlī ibn ʿAbdallāh al-Rīfī to lay siege to it. Historians agree that the English evacuated Tangier without a fight after demolishing the towers and fortifications but opinions are divided on the reasons for that evacuation. Moroccan historians say that the English did so because of the severity of the siege that they were suffering. European historians attribute it to reasons of domestic politics. Nevertheless, they acknowledge the difficulty the English were having in repelling Moroccan attacks. Be that as it may, the Moroccan army entered Tangier in February 1684.

The retaking of Larache

The town of Larache had not been forcibly occupied by the Spanish enemy but had been ceded to King Philip III of Spain by Muḥammad Shaykh in return for help in regaining the throne of Morocco which his two brothers were fighting him for. The bargain was struck in 1610 and Larache remained under Spanish rule for 80 years. Mawlāy Ismāʿīl sent a powerful army against Larache, and besieged the Spaniards there for over five months. The retaking of Larache, which took place in November 1689, gave the Moroccans enormous joy, on a par with the grief they had felt at its loss.

The retaking of Arzila

The port of Arzila had fallen into the hands of the Portuguese at the beginning of the reign of the Banū Waṭṭās. After being recovered by the early Saʿadī kings it was retaken by the Portuguese and eventually came into the possession of the Spaniards. When General ibn Ḥaddu had finished with Larache he received orders to go and lay siege to Arzila. When the besieged inhabitants, worn out, sued for their lives, the request was granted subject to the sultan's approval but, fearing the worst, they fled by night in their ships. The Moroccans entered Arzila in 1691.

The armies of Mawlāy Ismā'īl

The Wadāya militia
The Moroccan kings raised their armies either from the *kabīlas* of their own clan or from allied *kabīlas*. This was so until the advent of the Sa'ādī dynasty who recruited their soldiers from the *kabīlas* of Beduin Arabs introduced into Morocco in the time of al-Manṣūr the Almohad who had settled in the south of the country. The Sa'ādī dynasty raised a militia known as the 'Wādaya militia', which was dispersed on their decline. During his stay in Marrakesh, Mawlāy Ismā'īl had the idea of reassembling them and making them into soldiers. These new recruits were taken to Meknes, the capital, where they were joined with Shbanāte and Zirāra. Their numbers having grown, Mawlāy Ismā'īl divided them into two groups: one was sent to Fez, and the other stayed at Riyāḍ in Meknes.

The Bawākhir militia
Mawlāy Ismā'īl was fully aware that the strength of a nation depends on its military power, but he feared the acquisition of excessive authority by soldiers and their leaders. That is why he decided to establish a militia composed of slaves.

One of the secretaries of the Makhzen, named Muhammad ibn al-Kāsim 'Alīlīsh, whose father had been secretary to the Sa'ādī ruler al-Manṣūr, told Mawlāy Ismā'īl that the king once had a militia of black slaves, adding that he possessed the register in which their names were recorded. Mawlāy Ismā'īl entrusted 'Alīlīsh with the task of tracing these men, of whom there were still many in the Marrakesh area, and enrolling them, whether they were slave or free. Public opinion was shocked, especially the '*ulamā*' repositories of Islamic law, which forbids the exploitation of free men. This issue gave rise to a long controversy between the king and the '*ulamā*' of Fez and to a voluminous correspondence, part of which still exists. These are the famous letters from Mawlāy Ismā'īl to Shaykh al-Islām al-Fāsī.

Mawlāy Ismā'īl was convinced that he was acting in accordance with Muslim law in this matter which he regarded as best for Morocco and Islam and he relied on the assertions of 'Alīlīsh that these men, or at any rate their fathers, had already been slaves in the time of the Sa'ādī. The earliest letter from the correspondence between Mawlāy Ismā'īl and Sīdī M'hammad ibn 'Abd al Kādir al-Fāsī that has survived is dated July 1693. In this letter, the ruler asks Sīdī M'hammad to study 'Alīlīsh's arguments and to state whether the reduction of free men to slavery was in accordance with the law. The scholar no doubt answered that the law did not allow free men to be reduced to slavery, as the sultan's letters show growing irritation.

Firmly decided to organize the army of the Bawākhir, the ruler wrote to the

S͟h͟ayk͟h͟ al-Islām in December 1698 that he had freed all the slaves that he had enrolled in his militia and that he held them in mortmain to defend the territory of Islam. We do not know what Sīdī M'ḥammad's reply was; he died in 1703 and Mawlāy Ismāʿīl continued to ask the *ʿulamā* of Fez for their agreement. The affair had all sorts of ups and downs until 1708–9, when the king finally forced them to approve the *Dīwān al-ʿAbīd* (Register of Slaves).

That is how the Bawāk͟h͟ir militia came to be formed, and it greatly helped in maintaining peace and security in the unified country. Mawlāy Ismāʿīl had established forts and citadels (*kaṣabas*) in all parts of Morocco, and they were garrisoned by these soldiers. Thanks to this powerful militia, Mawlāy Ismāʿīl was able to restore Morocco's strength and prestige in the eyes of the great nations of the day.

Mawlāy Ismāʿīl appoints his sons viceroy in the various parts of Morocco

This selection caused Mawlāy Ismāʿīl serious problems as he had 500 sons and as many daughters. Hence he could not satisfy them all. In these circumstances, he would have done better to have adopted from the outset the solution he finally arrived at.

In 1699–1700 he divided the provinces among his sons as follows: Mawlāy Aḥmad (nicknamed al-D͟h͟ahabi) was sent to Tadla with 300 black soldiers: Mawlāy ʿAbd al-Mālik was sent to the Darʿa at the head of 1,000 horsemen; Muḥammad al-ʿAlem to the Sūs with 3,000 horsemen; and Mawlāy al-Maʿmūn al-Kābir to Sid͟jilmāsa. The last-named set up his base at Tizīmī, but died two years later and was replaced by Mawlāy Yūsuf in 1701-2. Mawlāy Zaydān was sent to eastern Morocco, where he launched expeditions against the Turks, once even sacking the *amīr* ʿUt͟hman Bey's palace in Mascara. His father removed him from office, in view of the pact between himself and the Ottoman Caliph, and replaced him with Mawlāy Hāfiḍ.

Those of Mawlāy Ismāʿīl's elder sons who did not receive viceroyships felt slighted. Some of them tried to occupy provinces by force, such as Mawlāy Abū Naṣr, who attacked his brother Mawlāy ʿAbd al-Mālik and seized the Darʿa. The sultan had to send his son Mawlāy S͟h͟arīf to recover the province and then assigned it to him. Mawlāy Muḥammad al-ʿAlem rose up in the Sūs, had himself proclaimed sultan and marched on Marrakesh, which he occupied. Mawlāy Ismāʿīl sent his son Mawlāy Zaydān against him, and he fought the rebel for two years. Having seen the unfortunate consequences of this experiment and the squabbles amongst his sons, Mawlāy Ismāʿīl decided to send to the Tafilālet all his sons who had attained the age of puberty. He set each of them up in a house, gave them a number of palm trees and a plot to farm along with slaves to help them in their work. It was a wise solution for the ruler had too many sons for them all to lead a princely life in Meknes or other towns in Morocco. In 1717–18 he removed all his sons from office except Mawlāy Aḥmad al-D͟h͟ahabī, governor of Tadla, who had succeeded in his task since, in 20 years, there had not been a single uprising in his province.

Following this measure the country had peace and quiet and the Moroccans contributed to increasing the country's wealth by developing trade and agriculture. Mawlāy Ismāʿīl had a very long reign. He died on 21 March 1727, after being on the throne for 57 years.

Mawlāy Ismāʿīl's successors

After Mawlāy Ismāʿīl's death his many sons, who already during his lifetime had fought for power in the regions, rose up to win supreme power. For decades none of the claimants was successful in maintaining a strong and lasting government. The first of them, Mawlāy ʿAbdallāh, was enthroned and deposed several times.

Towards the end of the eighteenth century a great king, Sīdī Muḥammad ibn ʿAbdallāh or Muḥammad III, came to the throne of Morocco. He restored order, strengthened the power of the monarchy and made Morocco a country respected by all nations. His primary interest was in the development of trade and he saw to the modernization of the ports, in particular the port of Mogador, which has since that time been called Essaouira. He also took an interest in the Karāwiyyīn of Fez for which he drew up a whole programme of reforms.

As far as religion is concerned, he believed in the original purity of Islam, which rejects maraboutism or the veneration of saints. Nevertheless, as he was on excellent terms with the *sharīf* of Mecca, Sourour, he did not push too far in the direction of religious reforms that coincided too closely with the ideology of the Wahhābis, enemies of the *sharīfs* of Mecca. Nevertheless, the power of the brotherhoods declined considerably during his reign and that of his son, Mawlāy Sulaymān.

As regards foreign relations, he concluded numerous agreements with foreign countries. He recognized the independence of the United States of America, suggested to Louis XV that he abolish slavery and supported the Ottoman empire in its conflict with the Russian empire. In 1767 he expelled the Portuguese from Mazagān, but died suddenly while preparing to lay siege to Ceuta.

In conclusion, the reign of Muḥammad III can be said to have had a major stabilizing effect on the state and the power of the ʿAlawite dynasty. He loved peace and settled issues of domestic and foreign policy through negotiation and dialogue. He only went to war to liberate Mazagān. His wise and realistic policy was beneficial to the Moroccan people who, during the second half of the eighteenth century, enjoyed security and prosperity.

Algeria, Tunisia and Libya: the Ottomans and their heirs

The early sixteenth century was marked by a profound crisis which put an end to the old state structures in the Maghrib and the former balances implicit in them. Thanks to Ottoman intervention in Algiers, Tunis and Tripoli, this time of troubles was overcome and gave way to a new order which eventually brought some stability to the Maghrib until the early nineteenth century when a new structural crisis erupted, heralding colonial domination.

What was the underlying significance of this crisis? To what extent did the Ottomans help in re-establishing stability in the sixteenth century and how was it done? It is clear that the situation of Algiers was different from that of Tunis and that of Tunis from that of Tripoli. Similarly, the seventeenth century, a time of hesitations and experiments, was different from the eighteenth century, a period of relative stability.

The sixteenth-century crisis and the Ottoman solution in the Maghrib

The crisis which affected the entire Arab world at the time was a many-faceted one: it was an economic crisis, due in part to the abandonment of this part of the world as a major trade route, a social and political crisis consequent upon the weakening of the unifying forces in society, and a cultural crisis arising from an excessive attachment to the past. It was particularly dangerous because Europe was awakening economically, politically and culturally, as the Renaissance brought about new ideas, new ways of doing things and new technologies.

Only the Osmanli Turks, on the fringe of the Muslim world, managed to make some adaptation to the times. Limited though it was, this Ottoman reaction was nonetheless a solution for societies and states in full decline who were also exposed to outside threats as the Maghrib states were at the beginning of the sixteenth century.

The crisis in the Maghrib

By the late fifteenth century the Maghrib was in a state of severe crisis, marked by a dwindling population, the dislocation of the economy and society and incurable political weakness. The reasons for this state of affairs there was the

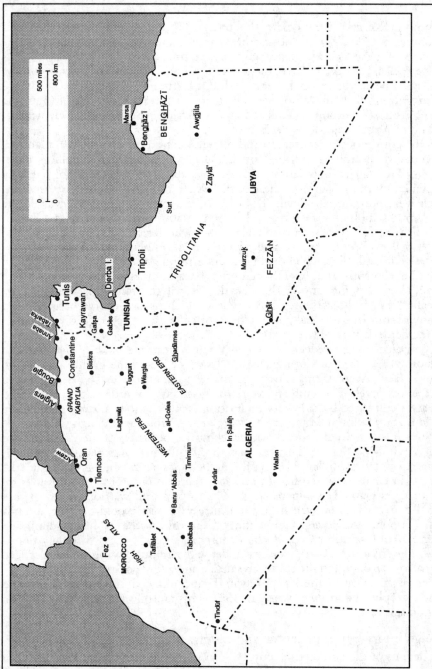

9.1 *Algeria, Tunisia and Libya from the sixteenth to the eighteenth century*

alarming proximity of the desert, the juxtaposition of diverse societies that did not always get along with one another, the weakness of the unifying elements of society and the lack of technological and cultural progress.

The Hilālian nomads have often been blamed for the decadence of the Maghrib. The accusation lacks subtlety, but it is true that through their activities and organization, their way of life and their warrior ethic, the *ḳabāʾil* (nomadic Arabic groups or groups assimilated to the Arabs) represented an element of weakness for the Maghrib as a whole.

In tbe course of the fourteenth and fifteenth centuries epidemics and famines had reduced the total population of the Maghrib to between 3 million and 6 million. This fall in population had led to a decrease in production, already threatened by the advance of the desert. In addition, the treasures of America, which were pouring into Seville from 1503–05 onwards, seriously devalued the Old World's monetary reserves and helped establish the power of those who owned them, first the Iberians and later those who seized them in the service of the New World economy, particularly the Dutch, English and French.

The gradual decline which had been undermining the towns of the Maghrib since the eleventh and twelfth centuries became a rapid decay in the late fifteenth century and during the first decades of the following century. Leo Africanus invariably attributed this poverty which he saw everywhere, both in the towns and in the areas under sedentary cultivation, to oppressive taxation and the depredations of the nomads.

The nomads were indeed freeing themselves from the yoke of the state and extending their control and their pastoral way of life to the greater part of the country. They were taking advantage of the vacuum created by depopulation and the low level of farming and were using violence in order simply to subsist. The areas cultivated by sedentary populations shrank as they advanced and there would be tiny fields in which cereals were grown protected by high walls.

It was in such circumstances that the centuries-old states of the Zayyānids (or Banū ʿAbd al-Wadids) in Tlemcen and the Ḥafṣids in Tunis began to founder. Their resources dwindled as a result of the disorganization of trade and the decrease in taxable commodities. In addition, there were the *iḳṭaʿ* (concessions) of land or taxes granted by inpecunious rulers to powerful warrior groups. Before long the towns far removed from the centre of power would become autonomous (Tripoli, Bougie and Constantine in the case of the Ḥafṣid kingdom) and the great confederations would reign supreme over the areas that they dominated. The *Bilād al-Makhzen* (country under state authority) was gradually reduced to a narrow area around the sultan's residence and a few pockets further away.

The domination of the Zayyānids in Tlemcen and the Ḥafṣids in Tunis was already deeply undermined when the Spaniards and the Ottomans set foot on their possessions.

Foreign intervention in central and eastern Maghrib

The designs of the conquerors must be seen in the light of the religious passions of the time: the crusading spirit of the Spaniards who had only just completed the *reconquista* of their land; and the defence of *Dār al-Islām*, combined with the ideal of *ghāzī* (conquest) of the Ottomans. Moreover, the coastal strongholds of the Maghrib were of undeniable strategic interest to the two protagonists. Finally, the Spanish offensive in the Maghrib came shortly after the first arrivals of precious metals from America which provided the Spaniards with the means of pursuing a vigorous expansionist policy.

The Spaniards in the central and eastern Maghrib

From 1505 to 1574 the kings of Spain repeatedly tried to secure firm footholds on the coasts of the Maghrib. One has only to recall the great expeditions of Pedro Navarro in 1505–11, Charles V in 1535–41 and finally those of Don John of Austria, who recaptured Tunis from the Turks in 1573. The results were limited, however, as the conquest of the interior of the Maghrib and the conversion of the indigenous inhabitants rapidly proved impossible. The Spaniards contented themselves with occupying a few *presidios* (towns) such as Oran and Tripoli and building a number of fortresses such as the Peñon at the entrance to Algiers or La Goulette in the outer harbour of Tunis.

This policy of limited occupation had to be supported by a constant quest for local allies. The most famous were the Ḥafṣid sultans who, from 1535 onwards, played a subtle balancing game between the Spaniards and the Ottomans. Similarly, the last Zayyānids of Tlemcen made on-and-off alliances with the Spaniards until the fall of their capital to the Turks and their final disappearance in 1551–4. In general, however, the religious and cultural barriers were such that no durable rapprochement between the Spaniards and the local rulers was possible and the Muslim Turks took advantage of the situation.

The Ottomans' fight against the Spaniards

The first Turks to wage war on the Christians in the Maghrib were the *Raʾīs* corsairs. They acted first on their own account although in agreement with the local rulers and aided by the local inhabitants. Such was the case of the Barbarossa brothers, ʿArrudj and Khayruddīn, between about 1500 and 1519. After the defeat and death of ʿArrudj and Khayruddīn appealed to the Ottoman sultan, whose suzerainity he acknowledged, and so the Maghribi *iyāla* (Regencies) came into being.

Thanks to the Janissaries and the weapons provided by Istanbul, Algeria was gradually subjugated by Khayruddīn and his successors, in particular Ṣālaḥ Raʾis (1552–6) and the all-powerful *beylerbey* of the '*odjaks* of the west', Killidj or ʿIldj ʿAlī (1568–87). For 40 years (1534–74), East Ifrīkiya was the scene of a long drawn-out struggle between the Spaniards and the Turks in which Ḥafṣid rulers and local leaders intervened actively, although not always to their advantage. The principal stages in the Turkish conquest of the eastern Maghrib were the taking of Tripoli in 1551, Kayrawān in 1557, Djerba in 1558 and, lastly, Tunis in 1569 and again in 1574. Thereafter the situation stabilized in favour of the Turks who remained masters of the central and eastern Maghrib, with the exception of the enclave of Oran, Marsa al-Kabīr and the small island of Tabarka.

The organization of the Ottoman Regencies
The '*odjaks* of the west', as the new African provinces were called, were never completely integrated into the Ottoman political and military system. There was no regular tribute and no direct administration by Istanbul. Initially under the authority of a single warlord, the *beylerbey* of Algiers, the three Maghribi Regencies were separated after the death of the all-powerful Killidj.

Each province was entrusted to a *pasha* appointed by Istanbul and assisted by a *dīwān* (council of senior Turkish officers). The militia of the Janissaries, numbering several thousand, was responsible for the defence of the country, maintained a minimum of order and played an active role in the raising of taxes and the running of the 'administration'. From the very start it was the mainstay of the new regime. The corsairs, who came from the Greek archipelago, Albania or neighbouring European countries, had all converted to Islam and were regarded as Turks; they were assimilated into the caste of conquerors and shared their privileged status.

The Makhzen (administration) fulfilled various simple functions: the raising of taxes to meet the cost of waging war and maintaining the corps of conquerors in the country, maintaining order and dispensing justice; and providing the postal service. A small staff of *khudja* (scribes) and accountants, a few highranking political and religious figures and, above all, soldiers of all ranks carried out these tasks. With time, the Makhzen had to recruit civilian and military auxilliaries within the country. In other respects, local institutions continued to govern society with the new masters intervening now and again.

Although slight and rudimentary, the new Ottoman organization gave the Maghrib what it needed most – the means of adapting to the modern world. It introduced an army that was disciplined and used firearms and a relatively centralized administration and by privateering it secured some of the money being circulated in the Mediterranean. The new regime was generally well received by the cities and also by the clergy, particularly the '*ulamā*' who favoured a strong central power. Opposed to the Turks were all those who had benefited from the freedom of the early eleventh century, the rural population which had its own social and war-making organizations and found in its new masters only harsh rule and burdensome exploitation. The Turks had to wage long wars to subjugate the interior of the country and impose a minimum of order there.

The Maghrib in the seventeenth century: in search of equilibrium

In the seventeenth century, Maghribi society, little changed by the Ottoman episode, gradually recovered from the crisis of the previous century. Its coastal cities and perhaps too its sedentary population even experienced a degree of development, but it remained susceptible to grave crises (epidemics, famines, civil wars) which shook it periodically. The Turkish ruling class underwent some internal changes as a result of the entry of new elements and also by its becoming to some extent rooted to the Maghrib. A number of problems arose concerning relations with Istanbul, and Barbary privateering, which enjoyed its golden age between 1600 and 1650. The Regencies grew further apart as their political development followed different lines.

Seventeenth-century Ottoman Maghribi society

Ottoman North Africa comprised a variety of socio-economic groups. The rural people were made up of sedentary or semi-sedentary farmers, nomadic shepherds, nomadic desert camel-herders and sedentary oasis dwellers. The urban population included principally the clergy and merchants, craftsmen, the *kulughli* (descendants of locally married Ottoman immigrants) and the military and civilian Ottoman ruling class.

The rural people belonged to various *kabīlas* which allied to form confederations (*saff*, pl. *sufuf*). These decided, on a case by case basis, whether to rebel or cooperate with the existing regime. Great blocks, subject to or allied to the Makhzen, stood in opposition to the *sība* (dissident blocks).

The seventeenth century stood out from previous centuries by a greater degree of spatial stability and a consequent reduction in turbulence, at least in the well-watered parts of the Maghrib.

While most of the countryside was Arabic-speaking, substantial Berber-speaking communities continued to survive that had taken refuge in the mountains, from the Djabal Nafūsa in Tripolitania to the Aurès and Grand Kabyila in the central Maghrib and the Atlas and Rīf mountains further west. They were distinguished from Arab communities by their elaborate defence system which enabled them to resist the Turks suceesfully and preserve various forms of Berber culture. They mostly preserved their autonomy, refusing, for example, to pay taxes.

The village areas, the southern oases, the wheat-producing regions under the control of the masters of the towns and the flat country of the towns were occupied by a society very different from that of the mountain areas in the hinterland. This society led a sedentary life, was open to the market and possessed a better defined *milk* (land ownership). It was influenced by the economy and culture of the towns, and values such as submission to authority spread more easily than in the mountain areas. Patrilineal kinship links there coexisted with hierarchical relationships, such as those linking the owner of the means of production to the *khammā* (one-fifth share-cropper) in the large cereal-producing areas. All these traits must have been accentuated during the seventeenth century with the advances in security, the consolidation of urban society and the establishment of relations with European trading states which stimulated the extension of export crops.

Thanks to their remoteness from the sea and the central authorities, and also to the continued existence of the caravan trade with black Africa and the East, the oases were home to better integrated societies and produced well-entrenched oligarchies or local dynasties, such as that of the Fāsī in the Fezzān.

The cities, for their part, made their presence felt throughout the Maghrib, whether it be the coastal capitals such as Algiers, Tunis and Tripoli or old centres such as Ḳayrawān, Constantine and Tlemcen. Trade and handicrafts took on renewed vigour from the first half of the seventeenth century. *'Ilm* (religious knowledge) slowly revived after the crisis of the previous century, stimulated by the relative material prosperity of the towns and the consequent increase in the number of *wakfs* (religious foundations). The Turkish authorities encouraged this revival, for reasons perhaps more secular than spiritual.

At the top of the political and social hierarchy was the ruling class, made up, in theory, of members of the Turkish army but open, in fact, to other categories. These were originally Christians who had converted to Islam and were called Turks despite their French, English, Corsican or Sardinian names. They introduced modern European technology, especially in military and maritime matters, and played a very active role not only in these areas but also in various administrative and political posts. In Tunisia and Tripolitania the Turks quickly gave their children by indigenous women (the *kuluġhli*) the responsibilities and privileges reserved for themselves. The Turks in Algiers were more exclusive and refused to do likewise, thus provoking a serious *kuluġhli* insurrection which ended in the defeat of the latter and their total exclusion, at least between about 1630 and 1680.

In short, in the seventeenth century the ruling class began to associate with the local élites in Tunis and Tripoli, while that in Algiers remained adamantly alien. The difference stemmed essentially from the strength or weakness of those élites: they were powerful in Tunis by virtue of their historic traditions and their activities and they were strong in Tripoli through large-scale trade, but in Algiers, a new town practically created by the Turks in the sixteenth century, they were but poorly established.

The political regimes in the Regencies in the seventeenth century

The three Regencies, in principle Ottoman provinces, became largely independent of Istanbul from the beginning of the seventeenth century but, apart from this common feature, they developed differently.

Developments were most rapid in Tunis. Soon stripped of any real power by senior militia officers in the *dīwān*, the Tunisian *pasha* was nevertheless retained as a symbol of Ottoman allegiance. However, in 1591, these senior officers had to yield their places in the *dīwān* to the representatives of the Janissaries. The military democracy thus installed did not last long: in 1598 a single Turkish leader, the *dey*, seized all powers and established an autocratic regime. In about 1630 a new authority emerged in the country, the *bey* or commander of the land troops. This office, held by a *mamlūk* (freed man) of Genoese origin, Murād, enabled its holder to conquer the hinterland at the expense of the large confederations, hitherto independent. The *bey* consolidated his position, concentrated power in his family (the Muradite dynasty) and adopted a veritable monarchical policy in keeping with the country's traditions. He won out over his rival, the *dey*, particularly during an armed conflict in 1673. But the Muradite triumph was short-lived. The crisis of the late seventeenth century, the weakening of the Turkish militia, the internecine strife among rival *beys* and the intrigues and interventions by Algiers brought this first experiment in semi-national monarchy to an end in 1702.

A similar development occurred in Tripoli, although a little later. A *dey* was appointed in 1603 and a policy analogous to that of the Muradites in Tunis was adopted between about 1630 and 1672, with the *bey* pre-eminent, especially in the time of Murād al-Malṭī (1679–86) and the *kulughli bey* AḥmadḲāramānlī in 1711. However, this evolution in the direction of a monarchical regime better integrated into the country was thwarted in Tripoli by a number of factors: interventions by Istanbul which was trying to regain real power in the country, the omnipotence of the Beduin confederations, the desire for autonomy on the part of the eastern province, Bengḫāzī and the southern province, Fezzān, and, finally, the meagreness of the country's resources. Power ultimately depended on a fragile balance between the Turks and urban notables, maritime and land interests, the towns and the great *kabīlas*, and the centre and the provinces.

The regime in Algiers preserved for longest its original character as a Turkish military province. There the *pasha* kept some of his prerogatives until 1659, when the *dīwān* and the *āgḫa* (senior officers of the militia) seized power. This was not for long, as a *dey*, representing first corsair captains then the Janissaries, succeeded in seizing power in 1671. But the *deys'* power remained precarious and most of them were deposed and killed in revolts by the Janissaries. The Algiers regime was thus a military regime which became more democratic during the seventeenth century but only to the benefit of the Turkish caste, in the absence of a strong group of indigenous notables.

In general, whatever its attitude to local élites, the regime in the Regencies remained close to Istanbul. Their policy towards rural communities was very harsh and sought to put the maximum pressure on their subjects. From the seventeenth century, however, the ruling class began to use alliances with certain local forces to impose their domination at least in Tunis. But, for most of the time, force continued to prevail over any other policy.

External revenue: privateering and trade

Some colonial historiography improperly reduced the modern history of the Magrib to the history of privateering equated with piracy. But privateering, quite different from piracy, involved only a tiny minority in Maghribi society and, during the latter part of the seventeenth century, had to contend with the mercantile interests of the great European states and their local allies.

Maghribi privateering in the seventeenth century

A legacy of the great struggles fought by the Ottomans against their Christian enemies in the sixteenth century, privateering became the prerogative of the Turkish Regencies in the Maghrib once Turkey had made peace with the Spaniards in the Mediterranean and the Ottoman provinces in the west had acquired freedom of action. It was practised primarily by Turks, Albanians and converted Christians, for their own account, and remained a monopoly of a fraction of the Ottoman ruling class. Its aims and purposes were many: as a holy war *par excellence*, it helped to justify Turkish conquest and power in the Regencies and it brought in enormous profits from the ransoming of slaves and the capture of Christian ships. It was an extremely lucrative activity for the privateers and corsairs who engaged in it, for the states that took a not insignificant share of the profits and indirectly for the whole population of the corsair ports.

Its importance varied greatly from one period to another. Beginning its history in the Regencies in the 1580s, it reached its zenith as a result of the European wars of the first half of the seventeenth century. The Regencies were able to build up substantial fleets, based principally at Algiers and Tunis. The second half of the century saw an irreversible decline of Maghribi privateering consequent upon the increasing fire-power of the European fleets and the mercantile advances of the big Christian powers. From the 1680s onwards France and England compelled the Regencies to respect their shipping and their trade and privateering continued only against nationals of the small Christian powers. From then on it was only in exceptional circumstances, such as European wars (particularly those of the late eighteenth and early nineteenth centuries), that Maghribi privateering could really regain its freedom of action, and even then only temporarily.

Progress in trade between Europe and the Maghrib in the seventeenth century
Privateering never completely eclipsed peaceful dealings and it began its decline and yielded to trade in the second half of the seventeenth century. This change would seem to be due, in the first p]ace, to the influence of the major European states that eventually imposed their views on the rulers of the Maghrib. These latter were split between a military faction and a civilian one, favourable to trade and prevailing over its rival, mainly in Tunis. Such were the circumstances in which trade links with Europe were strengthened on new bases.

The traditional transit trade was in decline, except for the trans-Sabaran links through Tripolitania and pilgrim caravans between southem Morocco and Mecca which crossed the Algerian and Tunisian oases, Tripolitania and Egypt. What now became predominant, in both quantity and value, was the maritime trade imposed by the European states.

The products exported to Europe came from the Maghribi countryside. There was an increasing demand for cereals, in particular, in the southern provinces of westem Europe. To meet this demand and improve their finances, the Maghribi states intervened strongly in this export trade. Exports of craft products were of secondary importance and were mainly to other Muslim countries, such as the *chechia* (red woollen bonnets) from Tunis, luxury textile products and worked leather.

Besides the luxury products for the use of a small élite, imports included the means of controlling the country such as weapons, coins, paper and a number of products for the use of local craftsmen such as wools and dye-stuffs.

Without doubt the main beneficiaries of these trading relationships were the European states and their merchants and carriers. The main aim of the great

9.2 *View of the city and port of Algiers, by the eighteenth-century French engraver F. A. Aveline (© Bibliothèque nationale, Paris)*

9.3 *View of the city and port of Tripoli, by the eighteenth-century French engraver F. A. Aveline (© Bibliothèque nationale, Paris)*

naval expeditions of the 1670s and 1680s was to reduce privateering and put European trade on a convenient, reliable and profitable basis. This was the beginning of the policy of unequal treaties.

Paradoxically, these treaties were mostly accepted by the Maghribi authorities, not only out of fear of European fire-power but also out of self-interest, as they derived substantial profits from sea-borne trade and could use them to acquire European products and weapons. Moreover, some social groups associated with European trade also stood to gain by it, as did olive-growers in the Sahel and the owners of the large estates where cereals were grown.

The eighteenth century: achievement or respite?

Historians traditionally see the Ottoman eighteenth century as a period of crisis and accelerating decline. How far is this true for the Regencies or '*sandjaks* of the west'?

Maghribi societies in the eighteenth century

Unlike during the previous century, the Maghrib did not undergo any fundamental changes. Yet some progress can be seen, such as the spread of cereal-growing on large estates and the extension of the valuable prickly pear well beyond the areas of Andalusian settlement where it was first introduced.

But the means of production remained unchanged and social structures retained their distinctive features, whether inherited from a remote past or a recent one. The only noteworthy changes were those brought about by public service or the growth of trade with Europe. Thus the power of certain families of local notables at the head of rural communities, in certain religious offices and in administrative or venal offices was consolidated. There are well-known examples of the rise of certain *kulughli* families in the Algerian *beyliks* and of Algerian Jewish families who played a leading role m relations between Algiers and Europe in the late eighteenth and early nineteenth centuries. In Tunis, large-scale *lizma* (farming of provinces) enabled some families to acquire wealth and power.

The Tunisian state in the eighteenth century

In the eighteenth century it was the best-consolidated and best-integrated state. It was still a province of the Ottoman empire, ruled by a *veli* (governor) appointed by Istanbul; the Turkish caste continued to dominate both politically and socially but in reality, Turkish suzerainty was becoming increasingly notional. The *bey* of Tunis enoyed complete autonomy, the Turkish ruling class, which had completely absorbed the *kulughli*, became more and more open to local notables, and the Janissary militia was restricted to a strictly military role. Lastly the effects of the policy of force were attenuated by the *beys*' practice of making alliances with local notables, especially religious leaders, won over to the dynasty by a whole host of advantages.

Taking advantage of the invasion of the Tunisian countryside by Turkish troops from Algiers in 1705, a *kuluġhli* officer, Ḥusayn b. 'Alī, had himself proclaimed a *bey*, led the resistance against the invader, and took advantage of his victory to found a lasting semi-monarchical dynasty. Restricting the Turks to purely military roles and their representatives, the *pasha* and the *dey*, to an honorary role, he relied on the *kuluġhli*, the Andalusians and the local notables and managed to achieve a relatively high degree of centralization. But contradictions accumulated between the attempts at centralization and the mostly segmentary nature of rural society, between the removal of the Turks from political life and the Regency's status as an Ottoman province and between the subsistence economy and the large-scale trade in which the *beylik* was involved. In 1728 the *bey*'s nephew, 'Alī Bashā, revolted. The country split immediately between the supporters of the revolt (the *bāshiya* or pashists) and those loyal to the reigning *bey* (the *ḥusayniya* or husseinists). The crisis dragged on until 1762 with numerous twists and turns.

The Regency then once again experienced peace until just after 1815. This was the time of 'Alī Bey (1759–82) and Ḥammūda Pasha (1782–1814), a relatively prosperous period despite the terrible plague of 1785 and the famines of 1777–8 and 1804. Revenue from external sources rose considerably as a result of the strengthening of trade links with Europe, the strong European demand for food products during the revolutionary and Napoleonic Wars (1792–1814) and lastly the resumption of corsair activity taking advantage of those wars. This enabled the state to lighten the tax burden or at least not increase it, thus lessening political tensions.

In addition, the *bey* of Tunis triumphed in wars against foreigners at Venice (1784–92), Tripoli (1793–4) and above all Algiers whose domination was ended in 1807.

This period of equilibrium and success which Tunis enjoyed for over half a century ended just after 1815, with the resumption of European expansion in new circumstances heralding colonial imperialism.

The Regency of Algiers in the eighteenth century

Of the three regencies in the Maghrib, Algiers retained an alien military ruling class longest. Yet it still underwent some changes.

Although privateering had greatly declined, it was still practised selectively against certain Christian countries such as Spain. To safeguard their merchant ships, the Scandinavian countries and a number of Italian states, such as Venice, agreed to pay tribute to Algiers. At the same time trade developed with the major European trading states of France and England which mostly bought cereals.

Warfare against neighbouring states paid the ruling class in Algiers handsomely. Interventions in Tunis in favour of pretenders in 1735 and 1756 resulted in considerable booty and a disguised tribute paid by Tunis from 1756 to 1807.

Domestically, taxes continued to be raised through the *mah'alla* (armed expedition) for the benefit of the Turkish caste, which excluded the *kuluġhli* from the militia and higher state offices. This policy aroused a great deal of opposition: numerous Kabyle insurrections, popular uprisings in Oran led by religious brotherhoods, and revolts in Constantine at the beginning of the nineteenth century led by local feudal leaders.

Since the late seventeenth century there had been an increasing trend for a single leader, the *dey*, to monopolize power. He was increasingly supported by a small body of Turkish dignitaries from amongst whom he was chosen. As a result, the Algerian regime became more stable and effective. Between 1710 and 1798 the *deys* remained longer in office, with Muḥammad b. 'Uthmān ruling from 1766 to 1791.

In the provinces the changes were even more marked as the *beys* of Constantine, Titteri and the west, with only a small number of Janissaries, were forced to rely on local notables and leaders. There were even *kulughli beys* who had blood ties to the leading indigenous families.

These changes were felt, although belatedly, in the capital itself. With the support of the *kulughli* and the Zwawa, Dey 'Alī Khōdja got rid of what remaiined of the Janissary militia, as had the *beys* of Tunis and Tripoli a century earlier. A nationalization of the Algerian regime could then have been enacted, but the French conquest put an end to a trend which had possibly begun too late.

The Regency of Tripoli in the eighteenth century

As in Tunis at the beginning of the century, in 1711 a *kulughli* officer, Aḥmad Kāramānlī, seized power in Tripoli and founded a dynasty of *beys* which was to rule until 1835. The success of this family is due to several factors: first, there was the length of the reigns of Aḥmad, 'Alī and Yūsuf; second, there was the existence of multiple alliances between the *kulughli* and the leading families of Tripolitania; third, there was the size of the *beys'* revenues from external sources. There were the direct and indirect revenues from privateering revived after 1711 and again between 1794 and 1805, and there were also the revenues from the large-scale trans-Saharan trade across the Fezzān and the Mediterranean trade with Leghorn and the Levant.

Yet the Regency of Tripoli experienced serious problems. First, there were natural disasters such as the famine of 1767–8 and the plague of 1785. Next, there was the fact that the country's population was split into two great confederations whose rivalry was the source of revolts and civil wars, like that of 1791–3, which pitted different members of the Kāramānlī family against one another. Finally, Istanbul did not give up its attempts to regain real power in Tripoli. In 1793 a Turkish officer, 'Alī Burghūl, entered Tripoli and drove the Kāramānlīs out. When he extended his action to Djerba, in Tunisian territory, he was driven out by the *bey* of Tunis, who restored Yūsuf Kāramānlī. But in 1835 the Ottomans landed at Tripoli and the Porte resumed direct control over Libya.

The final source of difficulties for the Regency, and not the least of them, lay in Christian attempts to reduce privateering. Just starting out on the international stage, the United States made war on Tripoli from 1801 to 1805.

The war ended with a compromise peace. After 1815, it was the Europeans who eliminated privateering and opened the country to their trade on terms that suited them. They repeatedly demanded compensation of the Tripolitanian regime for anything and everything. With its financial resources exhausted, the Tripolitanian state found itself paralysed, and, to make matters worse, undermined by revolts that it was quite unable to put down. It was easy prey for the Ottoman empire which re-established itself there in 1835 to rule for a long time.

Conclusion

In the sixeenth century the Maghrib expenenced a serious crisis, the fundamental cause of which was its failure to adapt to the age of firearms, centralizing monarchies and the treasures of America. The Ottomans provided the countries of the central and eastern Maghrib with a solution by setting up modern military and administrative systems there, capable of ensuring external defence and the minimum of order necessary for common survival. But, at the sarne time, they imposed an iron rule along with harsh exploitation of resources, which contributed to the stagnation of the indigenous societies.

Rapidly becoming independent of Istanbul (without ever renouncing official allegiance to the mother city), the '*odjaks* of the west' gradually separated into individual states which were inclined to be mutually antagonistic. There were no fewer than ten wars between the regimes of Tunis and Algiers between 1600 and 1800. These states developed along somewhat different lines: whereas the Ottoman ruling class gradually opened up to the *kulughli* and local notables in Tunis and Tripoli, in Algiers it was uncompromisingly exclusionary. The result was the emergence of semi-national monarchies in the eighteenth century in the first two countries and the continuance in Algiers of a regime strongly influenced by its conquering foreign origins. This separate and different development of the three Regencies (later accentuated by the diversity of their colonial situations) was to determine the partition of the Maghrib into separate states down to the present day.

The history of the Ottoman Maghrib was also determined by its relations with Christian Europe. The latter supplied many of the instruments of modernity which enabled the states and ruling classes to exercise their hegemony over the local populations. They also supplied men who brought new technologies and ideas. Relations with Europe were thus vital to the ruling classes of the Maghrib. First came relations of war, with privateering, then relations of peace, mainly commercial. The chief beneficiary of these commercial relations was European capitalism, but the states of the Maghrib and their local allies also benefited, at least so long as they were able to defend their interests against their European protagonists until about 1815. That date clearly marks the end of one period and the beginning of another – that of exclusive domination by Europe.

Senegambia from the sixteenth to the eighteenth century: evolution of the Wolof, Sereer and Tukuloor

Introduction

Senegambia, which comprises the basins of the Senegal and Gambia rivers, lies between the Sahara and the forest. Until the fifteenth century it remained a dependency of the states of the Sudan and the Sahara but its opening up on its Atlantic side with the arrival of the Portuguese gave it its full geopolitical importance as an avenue for the penetration of Europe's economic and political domination and as an outlet for the products of the Western Sudan.

From the fifteenth century the Portuguese trade in gold, ivory, leather and slaves diverted the trade routes from the interior towards the coast and, in the course of the sixteenth century, precipitated the break-up of the Jolof confederacy and the rise of the Denyanke kingdom in the Senegal valley and the kingdom of Kaabu in the Southern Rivers.

During the seventeenth century the division of the coast into Dutch, French, English and Portuguese spheres of influence coincided with the development of the slave trade which remained throughout the eighteenth century the corner-stone of the Atlantic trade. The Atlantic slave trade brought violence and strengthened the warlike and arbitrary character of the *ceddo* (warlord) regimes, exemplified by the reigns of the *damel-teen* of Kayor and Bawol and the *satigi* of Futa Toro. In the face of *ceddo* violence, Islam formed the sole bulwark against the arbitrary rule of the aristocracy. At the end of the seventeenth century the adherents of Islam took up arms in the *Marabout* War. Their defeat was followed by the success of the three glorious revolutions in Bundu, Futa Jallon and Futa Toro during the eighteenth century. The opposition between the Muslim theocracies and the *ceddo* regimes thus forms the background to the history of Senegambia suffering the consequences of the Atlantic trade.

The Portuguese monopoly and re-drawing of the political map in the sixteenth century

Senegambia is the sector of the African coast most open to the west. Long a dependency of the Sudan and the Sahara, in the sixteenth century it was

134

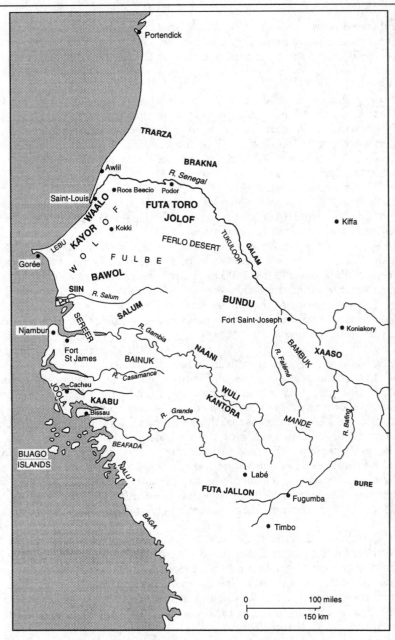

10.1 *Senegambia from the sixteenth to the eighteenth century*

subjected to the influence of the Atlantic with the arrival of the Portuguese, whose trade gave rise to profound changes and, in particular, the re-drawing of the political map of Senegambia as early as the middle of the sixteenth century.

The Portuguese trade

Senegambia, a dependency of Mali, was soon dominated along the River Gambia by the Mande Juula (Dyula) who, through a series of stages, linked the Niger bend to the kola, iron and indigo trade from the forest areas. The Mande conquerors thus founded the kingdom of Kaabu south of the River Gambia which, in the name of Mali, came to dominate all southern and part of northern Senegambia.

The succession crisis that followed the *mansa* Sulaymān's death in 1360 facilitated the creation of the Jolof confederacy whose ruler, Njaajan Njaay, extended his rule over all of northern Senegambia between the Senegal and Gambia rivers. Jolof's hegemony was soon undermined, however, and finally broke up in the middle of the sixteenth century following the invasion led by Koly Tengella who left the Malian Sahel with many Fulbe to settle in the highlands of Futa Jallon. After 1490 the many companions of Koly or his son headed north and founded the Denyanke dynasty of Futa Toro in the Senegal valley.

The appearance of the Denyanke kingdom coincided with the arrival of the Portuguese who were the first Europeans to explore the African coast. They established themselves at Arguin around 1445 with the aim of diverting towards the Atlantic the trade of the Sudan and Senegambia which, traditionally, had been directed northward across the Sahara.

The Portuguese, working out of the Cape Verde Islands, participated in the trade along the coast and at the mouths of the Senegal and Gambia rivers in the form of cabotage. They established themselves firmly in the Southern Rivers and in the Gambia because of the commercial importance of this region. The Portuguese trade in gold, ivory, hides, spices and also slaves was grafted on to the old inter-regional trade in kola nuts, salt, cotton goods, iron and indigo. The Portuguese were also soon heavily engaged in the major trading centre of Wuli at the starting-point of the caravans that linked the Gambia northward towards the upper Senegal and eastward towards the Niger bend, thus obliging Mali, then in decline, to turn increasingly towards the Atlantic to market its gold.

The Sudanese gold trade, which now overflowed in the fairs of Wuli and Kantora, was a major factor in detaching the Bambuk and Bure area from its links with the Niger bend and the Sahara and making it an integral part of Senegambia. Leather was Senegambia's second export item after gold. In addition there were ivory, wax and above all slaves for which Senegambia was the first and main source of exports by sea to Europe in the sixteenth century and, later, to the New World.

Moreover, from the start, on the basis of the slave trade, the Portuguese developed a plantation economy in the Cape Verde Islands which enabled them to produce sugar, cotton and indigo. The *lançados* or *tangomãos* (the Afro-

Portuguese) gradually asserted themselves as the indispensable middlemen between European trade and Senegambia which by the second half of the sixteenth century was undergoing profound changes.

The re-drawing of the political map of the states of Senegambia in the second half of the sixteenth century

Despite its relatively minor importance, in the sixteenth century Portuguese trade brought about an economic and political crisis in the Southern Rivers and accelerated the break-up of the Jolof confederacy in northern Senegambia.

The crisis occurred earliest in the region between the River Casamance and the Rio Cacheu where numerous Cape-Verdean traders were operating. Here the Bainuk and Kasanga, who were highly skilled at weaving and dyeing, bought cotton from the Cape Verde Islands. The Bainuk also became prosperous through their agricultural produce, which was needed both by the European residents and for the provisioning of slave cargoes. The favourable position of the Bainuk provoked conflict with the *lançados* who, in 1570, exploiting the rivalry between the Bainuk and the Kasanga, sought help from the *mansa* Tamba, king of the Kasanga. The conflict only ended in about 1590, with the death of the *mansa* Tamba.

From the beginning, the slave trade began to upset the situation in the Southern Rivers in a more enduring way. The Mande, who specialized in large-scale slave-hunting, consolidated the power of Kaabu which thus came to control all the land between the River Gambia and Futa Jallon. Similarly, the inhabitants of the Bijago Islands organized themselves so as to participate actively in the hunt for slaves on the mainland. While the women devoted themselves to farming, fishing and house-building, the men made *almadies*, the famous boats that made up a veritable war fleet and enabled them to spread terror in the Southern Rivers. Thus the mosaic of peoples in this area were the first victims of the overseas slave trade. However, it was the minority groups in the Tenda area, the Bassari, the Koniagui and the Badyaranke, living between the highlands of Futa Jallon and the Southern Rivers, who were the main victims of the slave trade.

The political evolution of the Southern Rivers lineage states was blocked by the pressure of neighbouring peoples and by the violence engendered by the hunt for slaves which induced defensive and isolationist reactions. This blockage continued practically until the nineteenth century and the colonial conquest.

Kaabu became the dominant power in the region after the final decline of the empire of Mali. It controlled the Bainuk and Beafada trading network to its own advantage and also seized the Mande principalities along the River Gambia. The Maane and the Saana, who formed the ruling Naanco dynasty in Kansala, strengthened their warlike character and from the beginning symbolized the rule of the *ceddos*, who dominated political life in Senegambia during the era of the overseas slave trade.

The sixteenth and seventeenth centuries marked the apogee of the kingdom of Kaabu which replaced Mali throughout the Southern Rivers until the triumph of the theocratic revolution in Futa Jallon at the beginning of the eighteenth century. The expansion of Kaabu coincided with the development of the overseas slave trade and with the takeover by Europeans of trade in the Southern Rivers. The initiative in this inter-regional trade, so vital for the whole of Senegambia, passed from the indigenous peoples to the Portuguese who turned the Beafada, Bainuk and above all the Mande and the Bijago into mere slave-hunters or brokers in the Atlantic trade towards the interior.

Northern Senegambia between the Gambia and Senegal rivers also underwent a far-reaching and lasting re-drawing of its political map in the course of the second half of the sixteenth century.

The Jolof confederacy, already shaken by the massive invasion led by Koly Tengella, broke up completely under the impact of the Portuguese trade which favoured the coastal provinces. Thus, Amari Ngoone, the *damel* of Kayor, after his victory over the Buurba Jolof, declared the independence of the Kayor and became its first *damel*. His example was followed by the provinces of Waalo, at the mouth of the Senegal river, and Bawol in the south-west. Jolof was thus much reduced in size, deprived of direct relations with the Atlantic trade and cut off too from the trans-Saharan trade by the powerful Denyanke kingdom of Futa Toro.

The *ceddo* monarchies that emerged from the break-up of Jolof introduced violence not only into relations among the states of Senegambia but also into political and social relations within each state. The same process also gave birth to the kingdoms of Siin and Salum, both of which finally freed themselves from the Jolof empire during the sixteenth century.

At one point Amari Ngoone tried to impose his hegemony by annexing Bawol and part of Waalo. He took the title of *damel-teen*, thus inaugurating a long series of short-lived unions between the kingdom of Kayor and the kingdom of Bawol. But the duel between Kayor and Bawol soon prevented the *damel* from achieving his ambition of unifying the former provinces of the Jolof confederacy under his rule.

This setback, however, favoured the rise to power of the Denyanke kingdom of Futa Toro. The *satigi* took advantage of the break-up of Jolof to extend his domination over most of northern Senegambia. The Denyanke dynasty thus reached its apogee at the beginning of the seventeenth century during the reign of Samba Lamu. Futa Toro now controlled both the trade between the Sudan and the Sahara and the European sea-borne trade.

The partition of the Senegambian coast and Muslim reaction in the seventeenth century

At the beginning of the seventeenth century the Portuguese monopoly on the coast of Africa was successfully challenged by the arrival one after the other of the Dutch, the English and the French. The European powers engaged in sharp competition, creating spheres of influence in Senegambia jealously protected by fortified trading posts along the coast.

These trading posts served above all as entrepôts for the slave trade which, by the second half of the seventeenth century, had become the main activity of the European powers. The slave trade, with its corollary of manhunts, engendered violence in relations between states and the militarization of power and promoted the advance of militant Islam. Thus, by the end of the seventeenth ccntury, a widespread *marabout*-led movement had developed which sought to unify the states of the Senegal valley to fight the noxious effects of the overseas slave trade.

The trading posts and the partition of the coast

The re-drawing of the political map went hand-in-hand with the recrudescence of violence between states and the development of the slave trade. It also coincided with the arrival of the Dutch, the French and the English, whose presence on the Senegambian coast was consolidated during the second half of the seventeenth century.

In 1621 the Dutch established themselves on Gorée, followed in 1659 by the French at Saint-Louis at the mouth of the River Senegal, while the English built Fort St James on the estuary of the Gambia in 1651. The Portuguese were thus progressively eliminated from northern Senegambia but retained, in addition to their permanent base in the Cape Verde Islands, the trading posts at Cacheu and Bissau. But they were already being forced to share the rich market of the Southern Rivers with the new European powers.

The fort at Saint-Louis enabled the French to control all trade along the River Senegal between February and May, and the building of Fort St Joseph in Gajaaga at the end of the seventeenth century ensured a French monopoly as far as the upper Senegal at the gateway to the Sudan trade.

Gorée Island, which held the monopoly of trade along the *petite côte*, was first occupied by the Dutch, then taken by the Portuguese in 1629 and 1645, re-taken by the English in 1667 and finally by the French in 1677. Thus, from Gorée, the French traded with Kayor at the factory at Rufisque, with Bawol at the factory at Portudal and with Siin at the factory at Joal. Further south, they encountered competition from the Portuguese and above all from the English. Fort St James controlled all the trade along the Gambia as far as the Barakunda Falls. Each Mande principality along this river, which is navigable all year round, was a potential port for the dominant English trade.

Senegambia was thus enclosed all along its seaboard by a series of fortified trading posts whose main function was to divert the region's trade towards the ocean. These permanent structures were designed to protect each sphere of influence against competition from other European powers and prevent the states of Senegambia from uniting against the monopoly of European trade.

The massive presence of the Dutch, the French and the English, following that of the Portuguese in Senegambia, was closely linked with the emergence of colonial mercantilism. In their fever to accumulate money wealth, the

Atlantic powers threw themselves into the conquest of the markets of Africa, Asia and the New World.

Each of the European powers had companies which had been granted a monopoly of seaborne trade: the Dutch West India Company, set up in 1625, the French West India Company, set up in 1664, and the Royal African Company, set up by the English in 1672. These companies symbolized the rise of nation-states in Europe and reflected the competition among these powers for the conquest of markets.

The Dutch, who had been the first to upset the Portuguese monopoly, were eliminated from the Senegambian coast by the English and the French in 1677, except for Arguin and Portendick, where they remained until the first half of the eighteenth century. Senegambia then remained divided between the French sphere of influence from Saint-Louis to Gorée and the English sphere of influence in the Gambia, where the French and the English vied for the Southern Rivers with the Portuguese. Possession of the Gambia was of vital importance because of its proximity to Europe at a time when the development of the plantations was accelerating and tripling the demand for slaves bound for the French and English West Indies between 1651 and 1700.

Saint-Louis, Gorée, St James, Cacheu and Bissau were transformed into entrepôts where slaves brought from the interior down to the coast awaited slave ships to take them to the New World. Senegambia was important in the early days of the slave trade, in the sixteenth and seventeenth centuries, as the great markets of the Gulf of Guinea and Angola were only opened up later.

It is not possible to give a quantitative estimate of exports from Senegambia but it is certain that the Atlantic slave trade engendered a profound political and social crisis. This crisis in turn provoked a widespread *marabout*-led movement in the Senegal valley a few years after the building of the fort at Saint-Louis.

The Marabout *War*

After the reorganization of states during the sixteenth century under the impact of Portuguese trade, Senegambia, in the first half of the seventeenth century, experienced an acute crisis, which was particularly manifest in northern Senegambia.

The *marabout* movement, led in the name of Islam by the Moorish *marabout* Nāsir al-Dīn, was well aware of the effects of the European presence in Senegambia, for it started in the south of present-day Mauritania where Berber society was suffering an acute economic crisis as a result of the decline of the trans-Saharan trade, which had accelerated since the establishment of the French at Saint-Louis in 1659.

The island of Saint-Louis, by virtue of its strategic position at the mouth of the Senegal, was drawing the valley's trade towards the Atlantic, thus breaking up the age-old complementary relationship between the nomadic Berbers of Chamana and the sedentary agriculturalists living along the river. The trading monopoly of Saint-Louis thus deprived the Moors not only of the slave labour that had been used for centuries, but also of the cereals from the valley which acted as a granary for the countries of the Sahel north of the Senegal river. This economic crisis exacerbated the political and social antagonism between the Hasaniyya warriors of Arab origin, the Banū Maghfar, and the Sanhādja *marabouts* of Berber origin.

Berber society was caught in a vice between the southward movement of the Hasaniyya Arab warriors and the monopoly of Saint-Louis which was diverting the trade of the Senegal valley to its own benefit. Nāṣir al-Dīn raised a religious movement, based on puritanical Islam, to save Berber society from disintegration. This movement attempted to regulate political and social life according to the teachings of the *sharī'a* (Islamic law) in its purest orthodox form, by putting an end to the arbitrary power of the Hasiniyya warriors and establishing a Muslim theocracy.

The proclamation of a *djihād* in the kingdoms of the river valley was motivated by both economic and religious considerations, to reconquer the trade in grain and slaves and to convert the peoples and purify the practice of Islam. In 1677 the success of the holy war in Waalo, Futa Toro, Kayor and Jolof was greatly assisted by the state of crisis in northern Senegambia as a result of the slave trade.

Nāṣir al-Dīn's movement was initially opposed to the continuance of the overseas slave trade and strongly condemned the tyranny of kings participating in the hunt for slaves. This opposition in no way signified a desire to suppress domestic slavery or the small-scale trade in slaves, an age-old practice which, in the framework of the trans-Saharan trade, had never precipitated such a crisis as had the Atlantic slave trade.

Islam, which served as an excuse for the *marabout* movement, was changing its character. From being the religion of a minority caste of merchants and courtiers in the royal courts, it was becoming a popular resistance movement against the arbitrary power of the ruling aristocracies and against the noxious effects of the Atlantic trade. With the connivance of indigenous Muslims and popular support, it swept away one after the other the ruling aristocracies in Futa Toro, Waalo, Kayor and Jolof without meeting any great resistance. After the defeat of the four kingdoms, Nāṣir al-Dīn replaced the fallen aristocracies with religious leaders who espoused his cause. This marked the triumph in all of northern Senegambia of Muslim theocracies, with specific features in each of the kingdoms.

In Futa Toro the victory of the *marabouts* was swift and marked by massive and violent popular participation in the overthrow of the rule of the *satigi*. In Waalo the *brak*, Fara Kumba Mbodji, put up strong resistance but died in battle and the *marabout* party installed a puppet *brak*, Yerim Kode, a member of the royal family who accepted the conditions of the theocratic system set up by Nāṣir al-Dīn.

In Kayor the *marabout* movement was greatly assisted by the political crisis within the aristocracy. Oral tradition supplies many details about how the movement, led by the *xaadi*, espoused the cause of the *linger*, Yaasin Bubu, who had been removed from office by the new *damel*. Yaasin Bubu converted to Islam, bringing with her part of the *garmi* (ruling class) and its clients. She married the *marabout* Njaay Sall who, after various twists and turns, proclaimed himself viceroy.

But the death of Nāṣir al-Dīn in 1674, killed in battle against the Hasaniyya warriors in Mauritania, precipitated the decline of the *marabout* movement. This decline enabled the French at Saint-Louis to intervene directly to give their support to the fallen aristocracies in Futa Toro, Waalo, Kayor and Jolof. The French at Saint-Louis wanted to prevent the consolidation of a vast political grouping which, under cover of Islam, might be able to dictate to them their terms of trade. They also wanted to resume the trade in slaves which was so vital for the plantations in the New World.

In the framework of their own interests, the French put their support behind the *brak* of Waalo, Yerim Kode, who immediately deserted the *marabout* movement and played a key role in the annihilation of the movement in Futa Toro, Jolof and Kayor. Thus, by 1677 the *marabout* movement had been almost wiped out and the old aristocracies had recovered their former prerogatives. The failure of this first popular resistance to the overseas slave trade and the arbitrary power of established authority had lasting consequences for the development of the kingdoms of Senegambia.

In Mauritania, the movement's original home, the defeat of the Berber *marabouts* ensured the survival of the political power of the Hasaniyya warriors who founded the emirates of Trarza and Brakna. In the eighteenth century, when the development of the gum trade enabled them to participate profitably in the Atlantic trade, these emirates kept up constant military pressure on the states on the left bank of the Senegal. The *Marabout* War – known as the Tubenan movement in European sources and <u>Sh</u>urbuba in the Berber chronicles – had more lasting consequences than the Almoravid movement which had started in the same area in the eleventh century.

The Chamama Berbers, attracted by the Atlantic trade towards the Senegal valley, participated increasingly in the political, economic and religious history of Senegambia. While the emirates of Trarza and Brakna participated in the widespread violence in relations among states in the Senegal valley, the *zwawiya marabouts* continued to forge close links with the established *marabout* parties in the kingdoms of Senegambia, thus participating in the Islamic opposition to the military powers.

This long *Marabout* War gave rise to a series of famines all over the region and above all to the repression of the Muslims. Their defeat, with the complicity of the aristocrats who were the only Africans to benefit from the Atlantic trade, ensured the continued commercial expansion of Saint-Louis. Political disintegration proceeded apace as a result of internal crises and wars among the various kingdoms over who should supply the slave trade. The use of firearms became widespread, and autocratic and military governments came to power in all the kingdoms. Islam now formed the chief focus of opposition to the ruling regimes throughout Senegambia.

From this time many *marabout* families began to leave the coastal areas and the Senegal valley and take refuge inland, notably in Bundu and Futa Jallon, where they endeavoured to consolidate the autonomy of the Muslim communities. The Muslim revolutions at the beginning of the eighteenth century marked the triumph of militant Islam.

The impact of the overseas slave trade: ceddo rule and Muslim revolutions in the eighteenth century

The Atlantic trade, and particularly the slave trade, accentuated the crisis in the states of Senegambia throughout the eighteenth century. In an atmosphere of widespread violence, the *ceddo* aristocracies strengthened their warlike character and imposed centralized monarchical rule. In reaction against the arbitrary rule of the aristocracy, Muslim communities formed enclaves within the states or organized revolutions as in Bundu, Futa Jallon and Futa Toro.

The strengthening of ceddo rule and political crises

The Wolof kingdoms of Kayor, Bawol and Waalo and the Sereer kingdoms of Siin and Salum experienced the same strengthening of monarchical power. Kayor in the reign of Lat Sukaabe Fall (1695–1720) was the supreme example of the evolution of the *ceddo* regime towards autocracy. Lat Sukaabe Fall took advantage of the unrest in Kayor to bring together the two crowns of Bawol and Kayor under the title of *damel-teen*. He enforced a royal monopoly over the sale of slaves and the purchase of firearms and strengthened monarchical rule by eliminating the Dorobe and Gelowar royal branches to the benefit of his own *meen* (maternal family), the Geej.

Aware of the danger that the *marabout* movement represented, he introduced institutional reform to ensure integration of the *marabouts* into the political system. He appointed *serin lamb* (holders of new titles) who became agents of the central government responsible for the defence of the frontiers and soon adopted the military ways of the ruling *ceddo* party. Conversely, the *serin jakk* rejected any compromise with the rulers and, while devoting themselves to religious activities and teaching, continued to focus the discontent of the peasant masses.

Lat Sukaabe Fall's reign marks the final advent of the warlords in the Wolof and Sereer kingdoms. Lat Sukaabe Fall imposed himself through his skill at settling internal political disputes to his own advantage and also because of the royal monopoly on arms imports. As ruler of both Kayor and Bawol he could now dictate his terms to the trading posts at Gorée and the factories at Rufisque and Portudal, which considerably harmed French commercial interests. On the death of Lat Sukaabe Fall, the French took advantage of the succession crisis to prevent the reunification of Kayor and Bawol under the authority of a single ruler.

In Waalo too, the French at Saint-Louis intervened in the succession crisis among the three royal families – the Tejek, the Loggar and the Joos. This interventionism came at a time when the economic situation was changing owing to the growing importance of the gum trade. The French wanted to attract this trade to factories on the Senegal river as they were facing competition from the Dutch and the English in the factories at Arguin and Portendick on the Mauritanian coast. The first gum war between 1717 and 1727 had lasting consequences, particularly on the development of the kingdom of Waalo.

After the failure of de la Rigaudière's expedition in 1723 to recapture the Mauritanian factories from the Dutch, Brué, the officer in charge at Saint-Louis, sought an alliance with the *beecio*, Malixuri, *kangam* (provincial chief) of Roos beecio. The aim of this alliance was to induce Alichandora, the *amīr* of Trarza, to give back the fort at Arguin to the French and also to act as a counterweight to the enmity shown by the *brak* of Waalo and the *damel* of Kayor. In 1724, supported by Saint-Louis, Malixuri rebelled against Yerim Mbanik, *brak* of Waalo. But, after the failure of mediation between Saint-Louis and Alichandora, he lost the company's support and was defeated by the *brak* Yerim Mbanik. By 1734 the latter, who had a good army, had become one of the most powerful kings in the region. This enabled his successors, his two brothers, Njaag Aram Bakar (1733–57) and above all Naatago (1756–66), to exercise hegemony over the neighbouring kingdoms, particularly Kayor, which had been undermined by famine and seven years of civil war.

The policy of hegemony pursued by Waalo was ended by the English who occupied Saint Louis from 1758 onwards. The *brak*, Naatago Aram, who now controlled access to trade on the Senegal repeatedly demanded an increase in the dues and the price of slaves. In 1764 he twice blockaded Saint-Louis's trade. The English reacted by giving assistance to the *damel* of Kayor, Makoddu Kumba Jaaring, who succeeded in recovering most of the territory annexed from him by Waalo.

The English governor, O'Hara, took advantage of Naatago Aram's death finally to break the power of Waalo. His chief concern was to get as many slaves as possible out of the region for his own plantations in the West Indies and he supplied arms to the Moors who overran all the Senegal river area. In 1775, in the kingdom of Waalo alone, the English took more than 8,000 slaves in less than six months. The over-supply of slaves on the market was such that in the streets of Saint-Louis a slave was being sold for one piece of cloth.

This tremendous drain of manpower coincided with the beginning of a long civil war lasting almost 29 years, during which two royal families, the Loggar and the Joos, tried to recover the power which the Tejek family had monopolized since the early eighteenth century. But Waalo was feeling pressure from the Trarza Moors who were intervening regularly in the succession disputes and completely destroying the power of the kingdom, which was henceforth incapable of pursuing an independent policy.

The Sereer kingdoms of Siin and Salum underwent a development similar to that of the Wolof kingdoms. But whereas Siin, being small, tried to close itself off from external influences, Salum, being larger, with a cosmopolitan population and an advantageous commercial position on the River Salum, participated in the slave trade and expanded toward the Gambia.

Futa Toro, under Denyanke rule since Koly Tengella, experienced a situation identical to that of the Wolof kingdoms. The lack of detailed rules for succession to the office of *satigi* encouraged war among various claimants. In 1716 Bubakar Sire called on the Moroccans for help, thus giving them the opportunity to interfere in the affairs of Futa Toro which from then on was forced to pay the *muudal horma* (tax payable in grain). In addition, Futa Toro took part in the struggle between Alichandora, *amīr* of Trarza, and Brakna.

In 1720 Alichandora, driven out by his powerful neighbours, the Ulad Dellim, sought the help of the sultan of Morocco. But the Moroccan troops, the Ormans, subsequently acted quite independently and put all the countries along the Senegal river to fire and sword. They ended up splitting into two factions, one of which allied with Trarza and the other with Brakna. Alichandora, defeated in 1722 by the faction allied with Brakna, took refuge with the *beecio*, Malixuri, in Waalo. From this time onwards the Ormans intervened actively in the numerous succession crises in Futa Toro during the first half of the eighteenth century. From 1721 to 1724 there was total confusion, until the legendary Samba Gelaajo Jeegi seized power in 1725 with the help of the Ormans of Gaidy and the commander of Fort St Joseph.

Samba Gelaajo Jeegi (ruled 1725–31) is the prototype of the warlord whose exploits still fuel the legendary tales of the griots of Futa Toro. He was the *ceddo* leader par excellence, who, with his army of *sebbe* equipped with firearms, waged 45 battles during his reign to the sound of *bawdi peyya yiyan* (blood drums) and *dadde yiyan* (war songs/blood songs).

The saga of Samba Gelaajo Jeegi is magnificently evoked in the two versions published by Amadou Ly and Amadou Abel Sy. The *ceddo* epic is still marvellously sung by the *sebbe* in their war songs, *gumbala* and *lenngi*. The *gumbala*, a hymn to dash and courage, is the epic song of death in which the *ceddo* assumes his destiny as a warrior, his faithfulness to his ancestors and to the ethic of his caste. The *lenngi*, sung solely by *sebbe* women at weddings or circumcisions, are heroic songs summoning up contempt for death and the protection of honour. But the saga of Samba Gelaajo Jeegi is unfortunately evoked out of its true historical context which was dominated by the violence of the overseas slave trade.

Two factors were responsible for this state of permanent violence. First, Morocco, with its army of Ornans, intended to control the Moorish emirates tied into the Atlantic trade circuit. Second, the French trading post at Saint-Louis was active throughout the Senegal valley, with the aim of extracting as many slaves as possible from the region. Samba Gelaajo Jeegi first allied with the Moors but later sought a rapprochement with the French at Saint-Louis to shake off the Moroccan yoke. In 1725 he asked the company for firearms and also to build a port in his capital at Jowol. He even tried to protect French interests against pillaging by the Moors. It was perhaps this alliance that enabled him to reign uninterruptedly from 1725 to 1731 despite the claims of his two rivals, Bubu Musa and Konko Bubu Musa.

However, Konko Bubu Musa seized power with the help of the *tunka* of

Gajaaga. After an exile in Bundu, Samba reconquered power between 1738 and 1741 but he remained a prisoner of his Orman and Moorish allies and died in obscure circumstances. According to tradition, he died at the treacherous hand of his wife suborned by his enemies during his second exile in Bundu.

In 1752 the new *satigi* Sube Njaay, was in turn driven out by Yaye Hoola and his warriors who ravaged Bundu with the help of Xaaso and the Ormans. Futa Toro seemed to be at its nadir, as the *satigis* followed one another in bewildering succession to the sole profit of the Moors who dominated the country. The conditions were now ripe for the success of the Muslim revolution in 1776.

Gajaaga, on the upper river, had also been integrated into the Atlantic trade circuit since the end of the seventeenth century. But despite the dynamism of Soninke traders who were the main suppliers of the Niger bend in salt and European goods and of western Senegambia in cotton goods, Gajaaga suffered the same political and social crises linked to the slave trade and the invasion by the Ormans. The political crisis began in about 1700 with the struggle between the *tunka* Naame of Maxanna and his cousin, Maxan of Tamboukane, and was extended in 1730 by the war between Gey and Kammera. Tensions multiplied and led to a series of civil wars between 1744 and 1745 which finally destroyed the unity of the Soninke confederacy.

Little is known about the development of the kingdom of Kaabu which dominated southern Senegambia until the victory of the Muslim revolution in Futa Jallon. But the power of Kaabu was based on trade in slaves. In about 1738 the *mansa* of Kaabu was delivering 600 slaves a year to the Portuguese alone, while the Southern Rivers, under Kaabunke control, were exporting thousands of slaves. Kaabu strengthened its hold over the coastal provinces while also raiding its inland neighbours, the Bajaranke, Fulakunda, Koniagui and Bassari. With Biram Mansa, who died in about 1705, Kaabu seemed to be at the height of its power under the leadership of the Nanco aristocracy. But here too, dissension among the three royal lineages, Sama, Pacana and Jimara, was the source of numerous civil wars. This situation explains the success of the holy wars later led from Futa Jallon and Bundu and the internal Muslim revolutions against the Soninke state of Kaabu.

Muslim revolutions in the eighteenth century

The military defeat of the *marabout* movement led by Nāsir al-Dīn in the second half of the seventeenth century was followed by the spread of underground action by Islam against *ceddo* rule and the disastrous effects of the overseas slave trade.

Within the states controlled by the powerful military aristocracies, the Muslim communities strengthened themselves under the leadership of influential *marabout* families. Linked to one another through a long chain of religious, political and economic ties, they embarked either on creating new states or seizing power where they were through violence and the proclamation of a holy war.

Thus, at the end of the seventeenth century, Maalik Sy founded the Muslim theocracy of Bundu which was followed, at the beginning of the eighteenth century, by the Muslim revolution in Futa Jallon under the leadership of Karamokho Alfa. The second half of the eighteenth century saw the triumph of the Torodo *marabout* party led by Sulayman Baal in Futa Toro, the stronghold of the Denyanke regime. These three successes demonstrate the continuity and solidarity of the *marabout* movement throughout Senegambia.

The Muslim revolution in Bundu

The repression directed against the *marabout* after the defeat of Nāṣir al-Dīn led to the mass departure of Muslims from Futa Toro to Bundu where Maalik Sy founded the first Muslim theocracy on the borders of Senegambia in about 1690.

Maalik Sy was one of that group of Muslims who had received their religious education in Pir or Kokki in Kayor, which had close connections with the Berber *zāwiyas*. After travelling through Senegambia he finally settled on the borders of Gajaaga with the permission of the *tunka* of Ciaabu who granted him a piece of land. Maalik Sy, settled in this cosmopolitan area, took advantage of the weakness of Gajaaga to declare a holy war. His religious prestige, and the military organization he forged with the help of Muslims, most of whom had come from Futa Toro, enabled him to create the theocratic state of Bundu.

Maalik Sy supported the Jaxanke *marabouts* whose commercial interests were constantly threatened by the pillaging of the Gajaaga aristocracy. He took the title of *almamy*, which is the Fulfulde version of al-Imām, which had earlier been adopted by Nāṣir al-Dīn. Although he did not take a direct part in the Marabout War, he achieved some of the political and religious objectives of the *marabout* party.

The Muslim revolution in Futa Jallon

The success of the Muslim revolution in Bundu was followed a few years later by a revolution in Futa Jallon. The fate of the mountainous massif of Futa Jallon, which over the centuries had become a place of refuge for the Jallonke, the Soso and the Fulbe, was transformed by Koly Tengella's invasion and, above all, the development of the Atlantic trade. This major crossing-point was economically revitalized by the existence of large herds of cattle belonging to Fulbe herdsmen who had been flooding into the area since the fifteenth century, drawn by the abundant grazing areas in the highlands, and had become the richest and most powerful group.

The Muslim revolution was not at all, as some have suggested, an ethnic war between Fulbe herdsmen and Jallonke settled farmers. Tradition clearly demonstrates the multi-ethnic character of this revolution, initially led by twelve Fulbe *marabouts* and ten Mande *marabouts*, who were certainly of Jaxanke origin. Conversely, the movement was confronted with opposition from the leaders of Kafu, who were Jallonke, and also from non-Muslim Fulbe, who lived in the bush with their cattle. The Muslim Fulbe, who wanted to abolish cattle taxes, formed an alliance with the Mande Juula or Jaxanke, whose trading way of life had always been associated with the practice of Islam, to create a vast political grouping capable of ensuring the security of the population threatened by the overseas slave trade. The *marabout* party was in fact consolidated by the participation of numerous Fulbe who could put their cattle wealth to profitable use in the framework of gradual sedentarization. The trade in cattle and hides gave them economic power while Islam gave them the ideology necessary for the construction of a new political and social order.

Thus, after the victory of the *marabout* party in the holy war against the various ruling Janonke aristocracies, the Muslim leaders created the Confederation of Futa Jallon under the leadership of Ibrahima Sambegu, known as Karamokho Alfa, the head of the Sediyanke lineage of the Barry family of Timbo, who took the title of *almamy*. The confederation was divided into nine *diwe* (sing. *diwal*) (provinces) whose heads bore the title of *alfa* and were appointed from among those who had contributed to the liberation of the country. From the beginning the power of the *almamy*, with his seat at Timbo, was limited by the wide autonomy granted to the heads of the provinces, and also by a council of elders acting as a parliament at Fugumba, the religious capital.

The Muslim theocracy in Futa Jallon was thus the outcome of a series of military campaigns between the *marabout* party and the leaders of Jallonke Kafu. After the famous battle of Talansan, which sealed the victory of the *marabout* party, the holy war was continued by the attempt to convert to Islam the non-Muslim populations of the Futa Jallon massif. The Muslims met opposition from the Fulbe herdsmen, who had been leading a nomadic way of life in the area for centuries and were hostile to Islam, which they saw as synonymous with sedentarization and political and economic control. All this explains why hostilities lasted so long and why the theocratic regime was so slow to consolidate itself during the first half of the eighteenth century.

On the death of Karamokho Alfa in about 1751, the *almamy*ship devolved on Ibrahima Sory, known as Sory Mawdo (Sory the Great). The religious leader of the *djihād* was thus followed by the commander of the army who involved Futa Jallon in an aggressive policy against neighbouring countries. As with the kingdom of Dahomey or the Asante confederacy, the evolution of Futa Jallon is incomprehensible outside the context of the overseas slave trade. These kingdoms, originally formed in reaction against the noxious consequences of the hunt for slaves, ended up participating in that trade. Islam then became just one ideology among many to maintain and consolidate the power of the ruling aristocracy.

Ibrahima Sory Mawdo, assisted by the leader of the Jallonke kingdom of Solimana, thus engaged in a series of wars against his neighbours to procure slaves and booty. But the alliance was defeated in 1762 by Konde Burama, king of Sankaran, who occupied Timbo. It took an outburst of national energy to stop Konde Burama's army at the gates of Fugumba and it was only in 1776 that Ibrahima Sory finally defeated the king of Sankaran. His victory consolidated his power and he imposed the authority of the military faction over the religious faction until his death in 1791.

The death of Sory Mawdo gave rise to much political confusion. It is from this time that the system of alternating rule dates between the two families of the Alfaya, descendants of Karamokho Alfa, and the Soriya, descendants of Ibrahima Sory Mawdo. This duality considerably weakened the central government, but despite the weakness inherent in the political system, the kingdom of Futa Jallon was able to preserve its independence until the colonial conquest and even to extend its frontiers. But the new regime lost its revolutionary character as the *marabout* party transformed itself into a religious and military aristocracy actively participating in the overseas slave trade. As elsewhere, the trade in slaves became a monopoly of the state which supervised the trade routes and organized caravans to the coast. Islam became a mere pretext for the hunt for slaves among the infidels on Futa Jallon's frontiers. Non-Muslims, captured in vast numbers, were either sold on the coast or simply kept in *runde* (slave villages). Situated between the Bambara states and the coast, Futa Jallon participated in raids or bought slaves for its domestic use and sold the surplus to obtain European goods and the salt needed for its pastoral economy. In the eighteenth and nineteenth centuries this trade introduced a large number of slaves from various areas into Futa Jallon: Bambara, Kisi, Jallonke, Fulbe, Bassari and Koniagui.

The internal history of Futa Jallon was marked by the formation of a hierarchical society based on Islam as the ideology of power. The Muslims had all the rights of free men while non-Muslims had servile status within the new society governed by the *sharī'a*. The predominance of the Fulfulde language and culture should not obscure the true dynamism of internal development which was marked by the existence of distinct social classes.

Beyond the basic distinction between *rimbe* (sing. *dimo*), free men, and *maccube*, slaves, within the dominant society of free men there was a hierarchical ranking reflecting relations of inequality and exploitation. Among the *rimbe* there were at the top the *las li* (the aristocracy of the sword and the lance and the aristocracy of the book and the pen), descendants of the great *marabout* families who had launched the holy war and monopolized power. Next there was the great mass of free men whose condition derived from their position in relation to the ruling class. Classed among lowest free men, the bush Fulbe, slow to convert to Islam, had their cattle as their only wealth and were subject to endless taxes and labour dues. But it was the development of domestic slavery, closely correlated with the Atlantic slave trade, that was the major feature of the evolution of Senegambian societies during the eighteenth century.

The practice of domestic slavery doubtless lay behind the cultural revolution in Futa Jallon where the *marabout* and political class, freed from agricultural work, could devote itself to teaching. The new regime set up many Ku'rānic schools throughout the country. A strong political and social organization henceforth based on the _shari'a_ and the prohibition of the sale of Muslims enabled Futa Jallon to avoid anarchy and depopulation. The theocratic state thus enjoyed a degree of stability.

The *marabouts* soon translated the Ku'rān (Qoran) into Fulfulde to facilitate the religious instruction of the masses. The outcome was not only a plentiful and rich literature in Fulfulde but also a deeper Islamization of the masses. Thus, the Islam of cities such as Timbuktu and Jenne became, through the Muslim revolution in Futa Jallon, a popular Islam which subsequently inspired the formation of a string of theocratic states throughout West Africa.

The Muslim revolution in Futa Toro
Islam triumphed in Futa Toro during the second half of the eighteenth century under the leadership of the Torodo *marabout* party led by Sulaymān Baal and 'Abd al-Kādir. Here, even more so than in Bundu and Futa Jallon, there is a clear line between the Torodo movement and Nāsir al-Dīn's movement in the late seventeenth century. At the same time, however, the Torodo movement, working closely with the Moorish *zāwiyas*, took much of its inspiration from the success of the *djihad* in Bundu and Futa Janon.

The succession crisis initiated in about 1716 by Bubakar Sire continued thoughout the eighteenth century, plunging Futa Toro into insecurity and civil wars. The situation worsened when the new English governor, O'Hara, facilitated the occupation of Futa Toro by the Brakna and Trarza Moors. In these circumstances the Torodo revolution was directed not only against the Denyanke regime but also against the domination by Brakna and the sale of Muslims as slaves. The Torodo party, led by Sulaymān Baal, was able at once to win a military victory against the Ulad 'Abdallāh at Mboya and thus put an end to the *muudul horma*. After establishing its authority in central Futa Toro, the Torodo party put an end to several centuries of Denyanke domination and, in July 1776, forbade all English trade with Galam in reaction to the ravages perpetrated by O'Hara to procure slaves.

The Torodo victo coincided with the death of its famous leader, Sulaymān Baal. His successor, 'Abd al-Kādir, once elected *almamy*, borrowed many ceremonial practices from Futa Jallon while maintaining some of the traditions of the Denyanke regime. He carried out a redistribution of *bayti* (vacant lands) while confirming the rights of the powerful Torodo families over most of central Futa Toro. The three 'Abe' families – the Bosseyabe, the Yirlabe and the Hebbyabe – provided most of the great *jaggorde* (the Council of Electors). Nevertheless, 'Abd al-Kādir consolidated the new regime and extended its religious influence beyond the frontiers of Futa Toro. His success gave rise to high hopes of change and increased the tension between the Muslim reformers and the *ceddo* ruling classes of Waalo, Jolof, Kayor and Bawol.

In 1786 the Torodo regime embarked on the conquest of Trarza where 'Abd al-Kādir wanted to impose his authority and the payment of tribute, as he had on Brakna. He defeated Trarza, whose *amir*, Ely Kowri, was killed in battle. After this victory, 'Abd al-Kādir rightly considered himself the Commander of the Faithful, the legitimate heir of Nāṣir al-Dīn. His ambition was thus to impose Islamic law on the rulers of Waalo, Jolof and Kayor and extend his rule over the upper river.

But in 1790 the new *damel* of Kayor, Amari Ngoone Ndeela, renounced the submission made by his predecessors to Futa Jallon and harshly suppressed all attempts at independence on the part of the reformers in the Muslim enclaves in the province of Njambur. 'Abd al-Ḳādir then organized a great military expedition with the purpose of colonizing Kayor. This expedition ended in the disaster of Bungoy where the great army was beaten through the scorched-earth tactic organized by Amari Ngoone Ndeela. Numerous Futanke were sold to the slavers and 'Abd al-Ḳādir was held prisoner in Kayor and later sent back to Futa Toro.

With the defeat at Bungoy, 'Abd al-Ḳādir's authority began to wane. He was now challenged in Futa Toro by two influential members of the *jaggorde*. The powerful Torode family of Thierno Molle, hostile to the religious strictness of the Muslim leader, obliged the *almamy* to leave his capital for Kobbilo, on his own lands, while the new unlettered princes, 'Alī Sīdi and 'Alī Dundu, imposed themselves as sole intermediaries between the central governent and the western and eastern provinces of Futa Toro.

The internal power struggle coincided with the development of hostilities between Futa Toro and the trading post at Saint-Louis, whose trade on the river was interrupted between 1801 and 1803. But in 1806 a new agreement confirming that of 1785 was signed between the two parties, as the stoppage of trade was hurting both parties.

'Abd al-Ḳādir then embarked on an expedition to the upper river to put down the ravages of the *almamy* Sega, at the expense of the *marabouts* of Bundu. He had Sega executed and appointed his own candidate, Ḥammādī Pate, thus precipitating an alliance between Ḥammādī Aissata, the unsuccessful but popular claimant of Bundu, and the king of Kaarta. Deposed by the *jaggorde*, 'Abd al-Ḳādir allied with Gajaaga and Xaaso but was killed in 1807 by the combined forces of Bundu and Kaarta with the connivance of the second generation Torodo party. His death opened the way for the triumph of the *jaggorde* who could henceforth impose an *almamy* devoted to their cause and retain a wide degree of autonomy in their respective chiefdoms. As in Bundu and Futa Jallon, the *marabout* party, initially made up of learned men, gave way to a political system in the hands of a warrior aristocracy with no religious learning.

'Abd al-Ḳādir's failure to impose Islam as the state ideology in the Wolof kingdoms was largely offset by the considerable progress made by indigenous *marabout* parties. Growing numbers of Muslims tried to challenge *ceddo* violence from within. In Kayor in particular, the defeat at Bungoy led to the departure of large numbers of Muslims from the province of Njambur for the Cape Verde peninsula where they helped to found a theocracy under the leadership of Jal Joop. From there they encouraged the Lebu opposition and Kayor separatist movement. After several years of resistance the *marabout* party won its independence, the first territorial breach in the kingdom of Kayor.

Conclusion

The evolution of Senegambia from the sixteenth to the eighteenth century was profoundly influenced by the impact of the Atlantic trade which made black Africa dependent on the dominating power of Europe. During this period the Jolof confederacy disintegrated and gave way to the kingdoms of Waalo, Kayor, Bawol, Siin and Salum, while the Denyanke kingdom became dominant in the Senegal valley. In the Southern Rivers, Portuguese trade ruined the inter-regional trade and facilitated the rise of the military power of Kaabu which took over from the declining empire of Mali.

The dominance of the slave trade in overseas exchanges resulted in the seventeenth century in the partition of the coast into spheres of influence and the building of fortified trading posts. The slave trade strengthened the violent character of the *ceddo* regimes which in turn gave rise to a widespread *marabout* movement hostile to the military aristocracies. After the failure of Nāṣir al-Dīn's movement (1673–7), the adherents of militant Islam organized themselves in Bundu, Futa Jallon and Futa Toro.

At the end of the eighteenth century, however, the theocratic states gradually lost their revolutionary character just when Europe was thinking of abolishing the slave trade whose role in the accumulation of finance capital was diminishing. Europe then tried to integrate Senegambia into the capitalist system as a direct periphery of the European centre for the supply of raw materials for industry. Senegambia, already ravaged by the profound crises of the era of the slavers, stood no chance of resisting the military conquest embarked on by Europe in the second half of the nineteenth century.

The end
of the Songhay empire

The collapse of the Songhay empire

Reasons for the Moroccan invasion

When Mawlāy Aḥmad al-Manṣūr acceded to the Saʿadī throne after the battle of Wādī al-Makhāzin, his victory over Portugal placed him among the great defenders of Islam, and the money paid him to ransom his Christian captives made him one of the most influential figures on the world scene.

As Caliph, *Imām* and Prince of the Faithful, his ambition was to bring all the Muslim peoples together in a 'single same way of thought' and to revive the tradition of the *djihād*. Thus the profits he planned to derive from the Saharan salt deposits at Taghāza would be devoted to replenishing the *Bayt al-Māl* (Treasury), and slaves won in the conquest of Songhay would be set to work in the navy that would go and attack the infidels.

But these lofty motives did not exclude far more tangible ones – the gold and slaves of the Sudan. Slaves were needed in the sugar industry in southern Morocco. As for Sudanese gold, supplies had dwindled rapidly since the rise of the Songhay empire in the Niger bend. In addition, trade between Morocco and the Sudan was still threatened: by the Portuguese, who in 1565 had tried to reach Timbuktu via Senegal, and by the Turks, some of whose moves suggested that they were seeking to extend their supply lines towards the southern Maghrib. Finally, the Saʿadīs' hopes focused on Taghāza faded as the Songhays developed the new salt deposits at Taghāza al-Ghizlān (Tauodéni).

In 1582 al-Manṣūr seized the oases of Tūwāt and Gurāra. This occupation of the oases was officially presented as a measure to restore order, but was really a first step towards the conquest of the Sudan. In 1583 the king of Borno, May Idrīs Alaōma, gave al-Manṣūr an unhoped-for opportunity to realize his ambitions. Fearing a Turkish advance into his territories from the Fezzān, he asked for al-Manṣūr help to fight the non-Muslim groups 'on the borders of the Sudan'. The Moroccan ruler agreed after extracting from the king of Borno a *bayʿa* (an act of allegiance) in due form. The following year a Moroccan expeditionary force entered the Atlantic Sahel in the direction of Senegal, but was obliged to turn back in circumstances which are not clear.

The order to attack the Songhay empire was almost given in 1586, but in view of the difficulties presented by the operation, al-Manṣūr gave himself a few years to equip his army, collect all possible intelligence on the *Askiya's* empire and finally convince his own leading citizens of the soundness of his plan.

Tondibi and the causes of Songhay's collapse

On 30 October 1590 an impressive Moroccan column set out from Marrakesh under the command of Djūdar Pasḥ. It crossed the High Atlas and went down the Dar'a valley to Ktawa, where it entered the Sahara. On 1 March 1591, after a forced march of 60 days, the Moroccan army reached the banks of the Niger, and eleven days later arrived at Tondibi, some 50 kilometres from Gao, the Songhay capital.

The *askiya* Isḥāḳ II belatedly mobilized his troops. He neverthless faced the invader with a considerable force but, against the Moroccans' guns, the Songhay troops were crushed after a day of heroic resistance. And so collapsed the last great Sahel empire whose rulers, absorbed in their domestic quarrels, had failed to recognize the extent of the Moroccan threat.

Since the fall of the great *askiya* Muḥammad al-Ḥadjdj in 1529, the court at Gao had been the scene of relentless struggles among various pretenders to the throne. Five years before the Moroccan invasion the Songhay empire was practically divided into two as a result of the rebellion of the *balama* al-Ṣadduḳ, whose headquarters were in Timbuktu. Isḥāḳ II put down the revolt, but did not have sufficient time to reunite the country.

Economically Songhay had for several decades been suffering from the adverse effects of Portuguese trade on the coast. In addition, the military reverses in Dendi, Borgu and Mossi country, together with the loss of Taghāza in 1585, exacerbated the economic and social difficulties.

Finally, the empire built up by Sonni 'Alī and the *askiya* Muḥammad stretched over a vast area but it lacked an ethnic and socio-cultural framework which would give it genuine unity. Paradoxically, the empire's centre of gravity was neither in Gao, the political capital, nor in the Songhay hinterland, but in conquered territory, at Timbuktu and Jenne.

The setting up of the Moroccan pashalik

In pursuit of the remains of the Songhay army, Djūdar Pasha marched on Gao, which had been deserted by irs inhabitants. Isḥāḳ II did not make any attempt at a counter-offensive and preferred to negotiate with Djūdar the conditions of his return to Morocco. The Moroccan *pasha*, disappointed at Gao's lamentable state and aware that his own men were in poor physical shape, was prepared to accept the *askiya's* suggestions, but al-Manṣūr was not. He recalled Djūdar and replaced him with the second-highest ranking officer in the Moroccan army, Maḥmūd b. Zarkun, who was given the task of conquering the whole of the Sudan.

11.1 *A Songhay village (H. Barth, Travels and Discoveries in Northern and Central Africa, Harper and Brothers, New York, 1857, © Royal Commonwealth Society Library, London)*

Maḥmūd Pasha set about destroying Songhay political power. He seized the traditional capital of Kukya, drove Isḥāk II from the country, laid a fatal trap for his appointed successor, Muḥammad-Gao, and then endeavoured to wipe out the last pockets of Songhay resistance in Dendi (1592–4). Zarkun then returned to Timbuktu to destroy the educated classes as a political force: dozens of *'ulamā'* were slain or sent into exile in Morocco.

Maḥmūd b. Zarkan was killed in 1594 in an ambush laid by Songhay resistance, and the task of completing the occupation of the area was again entrusted to Djūdar. This quickly proved impossible in the face of the fierce opposition from Fulbe, Bambara and Manden grouped around the *mansa* Maḥmūd. A *modus vivendi* was established between the Moroccans installed in Jenne and the main peoples of the area who accepted, although 'only in words', the Moroccan occupation.

Al-Manṣūr's soldiers were forced to limit themselves to the effective occupation of a few river ports, where they installed *kaṣabas* (permanent garrisons). Most of them were on the river line from Jenne to Timbuktu, while on both banks of the Niger lay vast areas scarcely touched by Moroccan influence.

The *pashas* did not try to change the local administration. Whenever an indigenous chief was appointed he had to be approved by the *pasha* who also granted investiture to the *kāḍīs* and the *imāms* in the big towns as well as the Fulbe *ardos* and the Tuareg *amenokals*. The Moroccan representatives, like the *askiyas* before them, only rarely interfered in the choice of candidates.

The Moroccan garrisons were not closed on themselves: they were not living in enclaves or fortified camps. Al-Manṣūr believed the fruits of conquest would be short-lived if pacification were not followed by colonization of the country and its settlement by people from the Maghrib who might take permanent root there. Thus the Sudan saw the arrival of the Guish people from Sūs and the Haha along with Maʿkil and Djusham elements whom al-Manṣūr was anxious to get rid of. From 1599 onwards the legionaries of Christian origin who had come with Djūdar were sent back to Morocco.

Sudanese politics to the end of the eighteenth century

The post-imperial experience of the peoples of the Niger bend: general features

In the climate of uncertainty and insecurity resulting from the fall of the Songhay empire, political power was within the reach of any who could effectively defend and protect their peoples. The imposing states of the past were to be replaced by a mosaic of kingdoms and princedoms limited to an ethnic group, a clan, a town or even a string of large villages.

The political leader was first and foremost a warrior, influenced more by local tradition than the universe values transmitted by Muslim scholars. Islam, which had made such a brilliant contribution to the building of the Sudanese empires, now temporarily ceased to play an important political role, but it continued to be carried ever farther afield by Jula traders who travelled the trade routes from the Sahel to the forest.

Timbuktu, Jenne and the Arma

After 1618 Morocco stopped appointing the chief officials of the pashalik or sending military reinforcements and the last survivors of al-Manṣūr's army and the descendants, the Arma, were left to their fate. They remained legitimate masters of the Timbaktu area until the beginning of the nineteenth century.

Although its military power was much reduced, the *pasha* state proved remarkably durable and retained its structures virtually intact until the advent of Shaykhū Aḥmadu. And yet, before the foundation of the Fulbe empire of Macina, there were forces in the Niger bend capable of wiping out the remnants of the old Moroccan colony. There were the Bambara of Segu, the powerful Tuareg confederations of the Kel-Awllimiden and above all the Kel-Tadmekket who, despite their overwhelming victory over the Arma in 1737, never thought of seizing power in Timbuktu. Similarly, the Kunta only entered Timbuktu on the eve of its conquest by the Fulbe in 1825–6.

At first there seemed to have been no special rules governing appointment to the various offices in the pashalik, including that of *pasha* itself. But from the middle of the seventeenth century, when the first generation of locally-born Arma came to power, rules for the transmission of authority began to emerge, based on the rotation of the chief offices among the three great Divisions to which all the Arma belonged.

This system led to frequent interregnums and short 'reigns'. In addition, as the same individuals would be called to power more than once, a number of great families or lineages emerged, distinguished from the rest of Arma society by their political power and economic influence. There thus came into being a 'ruling class', described in the chronicles as a 'class of chiefs'.

Between 1646 and 1825, 145 *pashas* were appointed in Timbuktu. Most of them belonged to the three lineages of the Tazarkini Mubarak al-Dar'i and al-Zar'i. It was to this last lineage that the *pasha* Manṣur b. Mas'ūd al-Zar'i belonged: he seized power by force in 1716 and plunged Timbuktu into a reign of terror. In 1719 the people rose up and drove the *pasha* and his *leghas* (henchmen) from the town and restored the old Arma political system with its chronic instability.

In 1766 the Arma elected as *pasha* Ba-Haddū b. Abū-Bakr al-Dar'i, who performed the unusual feat of remaining in office for more than eight years, but, after his death, the town remained without a *pasha* for 18 years. In 1794, when the great Divisions agreed on a *pasha*, their choice, al-Muṣtafā al-Tazarkini, restored all the former offices of the pashalik. Under his successor, Abū Bakr b. Aḥmad al-Dar'i, the office of the *pasha* became hereditary and his two sons, Muḥammad and 'Uthmān, succeeded him. The *Ka'id* Uthmān was the last *pasha* of Timbuktu.

By the end of the seventeenth century the pashalik had begun to break down into a number of more or less autonomous units grouped around the great *ḳaṣabas* of Gao, Bamba, Timbuktu and Jenne. While continuing to recognize the authority of Timbuktu, each garrison elected its own leaders quite independently.

The garrison at Jenne was as independent as the other *ḳaṣabas*, except when a particularly enterprising *pasha* came to power in Timbuktu, as happened in 1767, when Ba-Haddū Pasha himself appointed a new governor of Jenne. The commercial links and political relations between Timbuktu and Jenne were never interrupted and the two *ḳaṣabas* repeatedly rendered services to each other.

But in 1796 the Scot Mungo Park was told in Segu that Jenne officially belonged to the Bambara kingdom though in fact it was governed by the 'Moors'. Should this be taken to indicate that the Bambara exercised a 'protectorate' over Jenne? Local sources tend rather to confirm René Caillie's assertion that Jenne lived 'alone and independent' until it was conquered by the Fulbe of Macina in 1818–19.

The Songhay of Dendi

After being driven out of Gao and losing two kings and dozens of members of the imperial family within a few months, the Songhay, led by the *askiya* Nuh, managed to halt the Moroccan advance in Dendi. Resorting to ambushes, they held off Zarkun's troops and he was killed in Bandiagara. His successor, Manṣūr b. ʿAbd al-Raḥmān Pasha (1595–6) made them pay dearly for their victory. Nuh, defeated and forced to leave some of people in the hands of the Moroccans, withdrew to Dendi while the Moroccans appointed an *askiya* for the Songhay who remained under their rule.

The Songhay of Dendi broke down into several kingdoms, although they did succeed in maintaining their unity until the middle of the seventeenth century. In 1630 they signed a peace treaty with the Moroccans who subsequently began to interfere in their internal affairs and arbitrate in their succession disputes. But they retained their freedom until the beginning of the nineteenth century, despite strong pressure from the Fulbe and Tuareg nomads from Liptako and Aïr.

The Bambara kingdoms of Segu and Kaarta

After the disintegration of the western marches of Songhay, the Bambara peasants along the Niger were dangerously exposed to Fulbe and Arma incursions. Divided into several *kafus* whose Marka and Muslim leaders maintained reasonably amicable relations with Jenne and Timbuktu, they appealed for protection to the traditional hunter confraternities or to clans specialized in warfare.

In the middle of the seventeenth century the Bambara revolted against their Marka leaders and it is probably at this time that the Kulibali clan made their mark; it would later found the kingdoms of Segu and Kaarta.

In Segu, Biton Kulibali (*c.* 1710–*c.* 1755) imposed his authority with the help of his *ton-dyon* (captives or former captives), but no sooner had he established his position than, around 1739, his kingdom was attacked by the Joola of Kong, who remained in the country until 1745. Biton Kulibali, now weakened, spent the rest of his life consolidating his kingdom by getting rid of competition from his Masa-si cousins who were settled to the north-west of

Segu in the region of Murdia. In 1753–4 he carried the war into their own territory, defeated them and captured their leader. Following this defeat the Masa-si, led by Sebamana, moved into Kaarta where they established their rule.

After Biton Kulibali's death, the kingdom of Segu went through a long period of anarchy which ended only in 1766 when a new dynasty rose to power founded by Ngolo Diarra. The excellent relations between him and the Azawad Kunta and their leader Shaykh al-Mukhtār, seems to have made him treat Timbuktu with circumspection.

Ngolo was succeeded by his son Monzon (c.1789–1808), who was the real organizer of the kingdom of Segu. Like Biton Kulibali, he had to deal with rivalry from the Masa-si, who seized Nyamina on the Niger, thus cutting one of Segu's main supply routes. Monzon's reply was terrible: after liberating Nyamina he moved on to Kaarta, sacked the capital, Guemu, and forced the Masa-si king to flee to Guidimakha. Monzon then attacked the Awlād M'Bark Moors in the Nioro region who had refused to help him in his war against Kaarta.

Monzon died in 1808, followed three years later by Shaykh al-Mukhtār. After the demise of these two leaders, the Niger bend experienced a time of troubles until the advent of Shaykhū Ahmadu, troubles for which the Fulbe and Tuareg forces were largely responsible.

Fulbe and Tuareg

One of the chief consequences of the collapse of the Songhay empire was social disorganization.

From the beginning of the seventeenth century the Saharan nomads were advancing towards the Niger valley and the lake area south of Timbuktu. In Macina the Fulbe achieved complete preponderance. The Fulbe withstood Moroccan attacks from Timbuktu and Jenne, preserving their independence, and stepping up their migration towards Futa Jallon in the west and Liptako and Hausa country in the east.

Also contemporary with the Moroccan occupation was the expansion of the Tuareg of Adrar – the Kel-Tadmekket and the Kel-Awllimiden. While the former remained in the background until the end of the seventeenth century, the latter soon brought their weight to bear on the eastern part of the Niger valley, especially between Gao and Dendi. Interfering in conflicts among Arma chiefs and pillaging the farming villages along the river, they became a scourge for Timbuktu. The eighteenth century was full of confrontations between the Tuareg and the Arma.

In May 1737 the *amenokal* Oghmor ag Alad overwhelmed the Arma forces at Toya, inflicting considerable losses. In 1770 the Tadmekket laid siege to Timbuktu, reducing the population to starvation, after a group of Arma had murdered their *amenokal* Habatīt. The town was only saved by the intervention of the shaykh of the Kunta, who managed to reconcile Bā-Haddū Pasha Habatīt's successor, *amenokal* Hammiyuk. An agreement was reached between the two parties in August 1771, but the Tuareg broke it and the *shaykh* withdrew his moral support from Hammiyuk and set up a rival, thus causing the Tadmekket to break up into two branches. At the same time he won the confidence of the Awllimiden who took advantage of the disunity among the Tadmekket to try and extend their rule over the Saharan nomads of the Timbuktu region.

The Awllimiden thus became the chief support of the Kunta who, as the Arma grew weaker, succeeded in filling the political vacuum left in the region and limiting the effects of the resulting anarchy. But until the founding of the Fulbe empire of Macina they took care not to assert any political rights in Timbuktu or to drive out the last vestiges of Arma power. Thus Kawa ag Amma, the powerful *amenokal* of the Kel-Awllimiden, followed the old custom and, in July 1796, went to Timbuktu to receive investiture at the hands of the *pasha*, Abū Bakr.

Western Sudan and the outside world

Despite Morocco's gradual withdrawal after the death of al-Manṣūr, the *pashas* of Timbuktu remained loyal to the last sultans of the Saʿadī dynasty. The Friday *khutba* (sermon) was recited every week in the name of the rulers in Marrakesh who took care to announce their accession to the throne to the *pashas* of Timbuktu and the heads of the garrisons in Gao and Jenne. When the ʿAlawite dynasty seized power the Arma renewed their allegiance to the Moroccan throne, first to Mawlāy al-Rashīd and then to Mawlāy Ismāʿīl.

But unlike the Saʿadīs, the ʿAlawites paid little attention to the Sahel regions along the Niger. Their policy was focused on Mauritania rather than the Sudan. Mawlāy Ismāʿīl supported the *amīr* of Traza and occasionally sent more or less regular troops, the Ormans, to the Senegal valley, where they terrorized the inhabitants until the 1720s. Once masters of Futa Toro, they brought strong pressure to bear on the inhabitants of the upper Senegal valley and the captives they took there went to swell the ranks of the famous black army formed by the sultan of Morocco.

With the coming to power of Sultan Sīdī Muḥammad (1757–90), Morocco's policy in the Sudan made a fresh start, with the revival of trade across the Sahara. Like the last Saʿadī rulers, the ʿAlawite sultan referred to himself as 'sovereign of Gao and Guinea' in his correspondence with European governments. This was not mere boastfulness, according to contemporary evidence. The fact is that the political evolution of Timbuktu in relation to Morocco is comparable in many respects to the evolution of the Barbary regencies in the seventeenth and eighteenth centuries, when Constantinople's sovereignty, though now nominal, continued to be significant.

Economic and social evolution

Natural calamities and human environment

By the end of the eighteenth century Western Sudan was no longer the dazzling and prosperous country of which al-Manṣūr had spoken in 1591.

The beginning of the seventeenth century brought a string of calamities (drought, food shortages, epidemics and famines) which destroyed harvests and decimated populations, exacerbating tensions between nomads and sedentary peoples. In 1639 there was famine in the Jenne region, the granary of the Niger Bend. From the central delta it spread all over the bend for four consecutive years. The resulting distress was probably the origin of the social movement that preceded the rise of the Bambara kingdom of Segu,

There were few years without crises in the eighteenth century. After a seven-year food shortage from 1711 to 1718, Western Sudan experienced one of its worst famines ever starting in 1738. It affected the whole of the Sahel and much of the Maghrib. In 1741 the scourge was combined with a plague epidemic. The effects of the famine began to fade after 1744 but plague remained endemic, breaking out now and again until 1796.

The land between Timbuktu, the Great Lakes and the Niger was the meeting-place of many ethnic groups, and for much of the year became a mosaic of peoples and a contact zone between two ways of life – pastoral and rural sedentary. But because good grazing land was also the best arable land, this contact often produced conflicts, all the more serious because there was no political force in the area strong enough to limit the incursions of herders at the expense of farmers' fields, and vice versa. The pressure was greatest at the end of the hot season, when the first rains brought the peasants out into the fields: any delay or disorder in the withdrawal of the nomads was enough to produce a serious threat to the harvest.

Local production and regional trade

In general, agriculture receded in the areas bordering the desert. But in some places occupation of land for agricultural purposes intensified, as is shown by the Bambara migrations in Bara, the beginnings of sedentarization among the Fulbe of Macina and the permanent settlement of some Tuareg groups around Timbuktu.

Furthermore, thanks to the incomparable advantages of the Niger as a means of communication and the extension of traditional trade networks, inter-regional trade flourished.

In Jenne, food production was supplemented by contributions from the surrounding region of San: groundnuts, flour from the baobab tree, shea, honey, dried onions, pimentos, beans and fonio. There were also cotton, indigo, senna for making soap, wool, wax, iron from Bendugu and, of course, the two main imports from the forest area, kola nuts and gold.

In the Timbuktu region the areas of cultivation were near Lakes Tele, Oro and Fati and along the backwaters. Wheat-growing spread after the arrival of the Moroccans in the Sudan but the Arma and the Maghribi merchants in the big towns were the only people who ate bread. Among the industrial crops produced were tobacco and gum arabic, collected in large quantities around Gundam and Lake Faguiban.

The commercial life of Timbuktu was underpinned by numerous craftsmen:

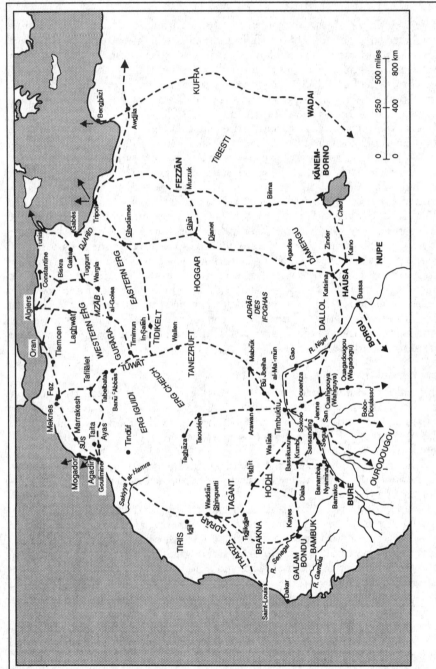

11.2 *Trans-Saharan routes in the sixteenth to eighteenth centuries (after M. Abitbol)*

salt-processors, weavers, tailors, tanners, goldsmiths and makers of agricultural implements and weapons. Each craft was the monopoly of an ethno-professional corporation: all dyers, for example, came from Sansanding while the Arma had the exclusive privilege of making shoes.

The eastern part of the Niger valley, suffering from a worsening climate and isolated from trade networks as a result of the decline of Gao, was the area that had suffered most since the days of the Songhay.

Trans-Saharan trade and the Atlantic trade

Despite political changes, the commercial organization of the Niger bend remained established on firm geographical economic and social foundations which survived both the Moroccan conquest and the intensification of European trade on the coast. Overcoming numerous political and military difficulties, trans-Saharan trade remained the main economic activity of vast areas of the Maghrib and the Sahel. What changed after the end of the fifteenth century was not the volume of trade but its economic significance in relation to the development possibilities of the countries involved.

Routes
After 1591 the route from Darʿa to Taghāza became the royal road for trade between Saʿadī Morocco and Western Sudan. But this was the first route to be affected by the disturbances which followed the death of al-Manṣūr. Merchants gradually abandoned Darʿa and Taghāza for Sūs and Tafilālet, where the local religious leaders wielded a beneficial influence. Thus, less than half a century after the Moroccan conquest the road network had almost reverted to what it had been before. The most lasting changes were those affecting the Sahel and Sudanese part of the network.

The Atlantic route The revival of this route was begun in the 1620s and continued by the ʿAlawites. The Tadjukant were masters of all caravan traffic between southern Morocco and Mauritanian Adrār. Furthermore, the dissemination in the western Sahara of religious doctrines such as those of the Ḳādirīyya and Tīdjānīyya brotherhoods led to a considerable movement of people and ideas between the religious centres of southern Morocco and those of the southern Sahara.

Caravans from Shinguetti or Waddān travelled to Saint-Louis in Senegal via Trarza, Galam via Brakna country and Hōdh along the Dhār track. From Hōdh, several tracks led towards the Bambura kingdoms of Kaarta and Segu.

Moorish caravans travelled as far as Segu, Banamba and even Nyamina, but most Bambara trade was transacted at Sansanding, the commercial centre of the kingdom of Segu.

The eastern route This group of roads started in Tafilālet and crossed Tūwāt, through which the great caravans of Moroccan pilgrims passed. At Timimun the road from Tūwāt to the Sudan connected with the tracks from central Maghrib. Further south, at In-Ṣalāḥ, was the junction with the track from

Ghadāmes, disputed by Tunis and Tripoli throughout the eighteenth century, which was the channel through which Sudanese goods flowed to both capitals. After Tidikelt the caravans skirted the western border of Ahnet and then, after the arduous crossing of Tanezruft, reached Azawad where there were Kunta encampments. The Kunta provided services, knowledge and *baraka* and were also the most effective protectors of the roads to Timbuktu.

On arrival in Timbuktu, the Maghribi merchants were looked after by *diatiguis*, who provided them with hospitality, transport and, if necessary, an armed guard. For many of them, the journey continued as goods from North Africa had to be taken on to Jenne.

The Jula network Jenne was linked by two main routes to the forest regions and the countries that produced gold and kola nuts. The first, to the south-west, went to Bure or Wurodugu, the second, to the south-east, to Kong and Asante.

Kong supplied Jenne with kola nuts and gold from Lobi and the Gold Coast. Both were carried by the same Jula traders who sold slabs of salt from Taoudéni to Buna The rest of their load would be made up of cotton goods and European products which were marketed around Kumasi.

Parallel to this route, the Mossi Yarse had established direct links between Timbuktu and Asante country, skirting Jenne and the inner delta.

Trade goods

Salt played a very small part in trade between the people of the Maghrib and those of the Sahel and the Sudan. From the beginning of the seventeenth century, towns along the Niger had access to the Saharan salt deposits by means of separate and independent routes: the Moorish and Tuareg *azalai* (large caravans).

The Sudan traditionally exported gold, slaves and ivory, but it also needed to dispose of a number of manufactured goods, such as cloth and jewellery, the proportion of which grew as the export of gold and slaves declined.

Although the amount of gold exported never again equalled the huge amounts taken out immediately after the Moroccan conquest, Sudanese gold formed part of the returning freight of all caravans coming from the Sudan. At the end of the seventeenth century there was an appreciable increase in the export of slaves after Mawlāy Ismāʿīl formed his ʿAbīd army and, in the second half of the eighteenth century, gum arabic played an important role in exports to Morocco. The opening of the port of Mogador provided Sudanese caravans with a new maritime outlet where, in addition to the articles already mentioned, they also sold large quantities of ivory and ostrich feathers.

Moroccan exports to Western Sudan were extremely varied, whether they were local products (cereals, Meknes tobacco, silk garments and religious works) or goods from the eastern Mediterranean (spices and silk) or from Europe (textiles, sugar, coffee, glassware and firearms).

In the central Maghrib, Sudanese trade was the chief source of activity for the provinces of Tūwāt, Mzāb, Sūf and Djarīd. It covered a wide range of goods, from indigo cloth and *turkedi* from Kano to kola nuts from Asante.

This trade, both varied and continuous, was very lucrative. In addition, the trans-Saharan trade was transporting not only merchandise, but also the ideas and values of a whole civilization.

Cultural and religious development

Islam in the Sudan on the eve of the *djihāds* of the nineteenth century

The period being examined is often described as one of decay and cultural stagnation, which is untrue if by that is meant a decline or regression of Islamic culture.

Through the continuous commerce across the Sahara, through the *zāwiyas* (sanctuaries), the brotherhoods and the *marabout* groups and through the highly organized networks of Jula traders, the influence of Islam continued to spread in varying degrees through all the peoples of the Niger valley.

René Caillié observed at the beginning of the nineteenth century that all the inhabitants of Timbuktu and Jenne were able to read and write Arabic. Furthermore, the *ta'rikhs*, the famous chronicles of Timbuktu, were all written between the seventeenth and nineteenth centuries.

Islam was no longer a purely urban phenomenon as it had been in the previous period. Propagated by Berber or Sudanese *marabout* groups, it now spread into the countryside and affected both Bambara peasants and Fulbe herders.

The emergence of *marabout* groups (*zuwaya* or *insilimen*) is one of the most striking aspects of the ethno-social stratification which occurred on the southern edge of the Sahara during the second half of the seventeenth century. Nomad society, from Senegal to Aïr, split into two distinct strata: 'warrior' groups and clerical groups. The latter enjoyed great religious prestige, and their *zāwiyas* attracted students as well as travelling merchants seeking protection. Many of these sanctuaries, established along trade routes, later became caravan stages. The *shaykhs* of the desert were to eclipse the urban *'ulamā'* and become the spiritual masters of most of the instigators of the *djihāds* of the eighteenth and nineteenth centuries.

The Islam of the *marabouts* was to a certain extent a continuation of the Almoravid tradition, and its militancy contrasted sharply with the tolerant syncretism which characterized the 'Black Islam' of the Sudanese towns and the Jula centres. Also, by quickly associating itself with brotherhoods and religious orders as universal as the Ḳādirīyya, the Islam of the *marabouts* offered its followers a framework which went beyond the traditional categories of identification, such as clans or ethnic groups.

It was a rallying point, a force for political and social emancipation, and as such it attracted all the Tukuloor of Futa Toro who were opposed to the Denyanke dynasty; it also attracted the Fulbe of Macina, who were shaking off the Bambara yoke, as well as the Fulbe and the farmers of Hausa country, who were struggling against the hegemony of various royal powers.

12

From the Niger to the Volta

The fall of the Gao empire in 1591 following the Moroccan invasion created a major political vacuum which other powers gradually began to fill. In the Niger bend and the upper reaches of the Voltas, four poles emerged during the seventeenth and eighteenth centuries: the Bambara kingdoms of Segu and Kaarta, the Mossi kingdoms, the kingdoms of Kong and Gwiriko and the Gulmanceba kingdoms. This took place against a backcloth of numerous ethnic groups with non-centralized authority. It has been said that power was 'tribalized' during this period. But this is inaccurate, as the traditions of Mali and Gao continued but in a context increasingly dominated by external factors and internal conflicts that shaped new political structures. In addition, certain socio-economic and religious factors, that were in no way 'tribal', influenced the reorganization processes and, at the end of the eighteenth century, precipitated the first cracks that heralded the upheavals of the nineteenth.

Peoples, chieftaincies and kingdoms

The Bambara kingdoms of Segu and Kaarta from the sixteenth to the nineteenth century

Political evolution

The origins of the Bambara kingdoms, while not ancient, are obscured by the diversity of the oral traditions and the chronicles. The order of succession of rulers is not always the same, nor is the length of reigns. This study, however, is more concerned with the organization and relations of force that moved these peoples from the sixteenth to the nineteenth century than with events.

A highly disputed issue relates to the peoples responsible for taking the historical initiative in the Bambara kingdoms. L. Tauxier is categorical on this point: 'In the final analysis', he writes, 'the Bambara were never capable by themselves of founding kingdoms: the kings of Segu and Kaarta were of Fulbe origin, those of Sikasso and Kong of Manden–Jula origin.' Although the

166

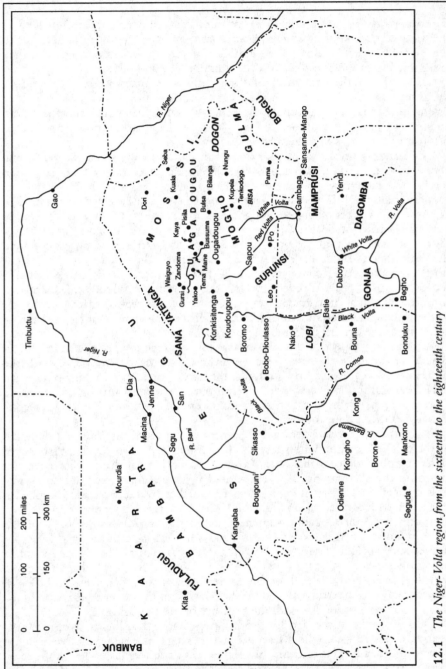

12.1 *The Niger-Volta region from the sixteenth to the eighteenth century*

Bambara's origins are certainly lost, contemporary movements are reflected in traditions that make it possible to assert that they have long been indigenous to the Niger bend. The Bozo were almost certainly there before them and they also mixed with the Soninke, Soso, Malinke, Fulbe and others.

The story of the migration of the eponymous ancestors of the Bambara dynasties contains the theme of the river crossing found in so many legends of origin in Africa. Two brothers, Baramangolo and Niangolo, pursued by an enemy and having no canoe, crossed the river thanks to an enormous *m'polio* fish (catfish) which saved them at the last minute.

The striking aspect of this story of origin is the rapid association that came about with the Soninke (Marka). The Soninke were traders who had been settled for centuries, sometimes as slave-dealers, and had little interest in soldiering although the Bambara newcomers made it almost a profession. One of the brothers, Baramangolo, sought asylum on the right bank of the Niger with the Buare of Segu. The Segu Buare, who were Soninke, gave him a district which, although separate, allowed the newly arrived Bambara to defend the entire Segu kingdom. Meanwhile, the other brother, Niangolo, built a *tata* (fort) at Baïko. After failing to take the fort by storm, the Marka eventually settled down to peaceful relations with the newcomers. Hence the Bambara's (no doubt gradual) movement from the status of refugees to that of protectors of their hosts and then to that of masters. This process stands out clearly in most accounts of the origins of Bambara power.

Another key aspect of this history was the strategic importance of the Niger where the bend of the river reaches farthest into the desert and towards the routes to North Africa. By unifying the two banks, the middle Niger had polarized political power for four centuries. It was difficult for power to be shared, which is why the two sister kingdoms of Segu and Kaarta were continually attacking one another.

It is difficult to relate the two legendary ancestors of the Bambara dynasties to the first leaders known historically. Regarding Segu, we are told that one of Baramangolo's descendants was Kaladian Kulibali. Kaladian, who does not appear in the oral traditions, is represented as having almost restored the greatness of Mali in the seventeenth century, notably by reconquering Timbuktu from the Moroccans. Meanwhile in Kaarta, on the left bank of the Niger, according to Nioro legend, Sunsan (*c.* 1635), the son of Niangolo, is said to have founded Sunsana, near Mourdia. His son, Massa (*c.* 1666), was a famous farmer and a prolific father who systematically married off his daughters not to princes he could not win over but to poor men on condition that they come and live with him and espouse his cause. Massa's son, Benefali (*c.* 1710–45), considerably extended the power of the Massasi using methods that combined the patriarchal farming life with the brutality of military raids.

Fulakoro, who succeeded his brother Benefali, was unable to avoid the first serious clash between the Massasi and the kings of Segu, who were more powerful because their territory was richer and its different peoples more complementary. The person he had to confront was Mamari Kulibali (1712–55), great-grandson of Baramangolo, the founder of the kingdom. Mamari, who was endowed with extraordinary strength, rapidly became the leader of a *ton* (an association of boys circumcised at the same time), hence his name, Biton or Tiguiton, and then a social and political leader outside the gerontocratic and religious institutions of the country.

He seized the chance to consolidate his domestic achievements with external successes, one against Kong and the other against the Massasi.

Mamari was only able to repel the first intervention by Kong through his coalition with the Macina Fulbe. The second attack was driven off with the aid of the Tyero Somono, using swarms of bees against the Kong cavalry.

Fulakoro was besieging Mourdia, which sent an appeal for help to Mamari. Mamari, who was only waiting for such a signal to intervene, defeated Fulakoro and took him prisoner, and once again the Massasi had to move westward. Mamari Kulibali conquered the whole of Bambara territory, including Beledugu. Macina and Jenne were placed under his authority and he had palaces built by a Jenne architect. Finally, in 1751, Mamari easily conquered Niani, the capital of declining Mali, whose ruler, Massa Maghan Keita, paid him tribute. The *pashas* of Timbuktu had to do likewise after Biton's fleet and cavalry had cleared the Niger bend of Tuareg exactions.

Biton's successors were rulers of no great stature and his son Denkoro (1755–57), an arrogant bloodthirsty man, who had seized the golden axe (the symbol of royal power), was executed by the war chiefs. The average length of reigns was less than three years. Only Ngolo Diarra (1766–90) reigned long enough to develop a serious policy. He put an end to the agitation by the *tondyon* chiefs who had become mercenaries, and restored a true monarchy. He abandoned Segu-Koro to settle up-river at Segu-Si-Koro. He strengthened the Bambara hold on both Macina and Timbuktu where civilian officials descended from the Moroccans, the Arma, were now to be watched over by Bambara war chiefs. His campaign against the Fulbe chief Sila Makan Yero took him even into Dogon country. When he was very old he went on an expedition against Yatenga which failed, and he died on the return journey, having created a new dynasty at Segu.

After Ngolo, internal conflict erupted again, and only Monson Diarra (1792–1808) made the power of Segu felt from San to Timbuktu and from the land of the Dogon to Kaarta.

But Kaarta was not yet finished. After Fulakoro's death in captivity, it had recovered through raids at the expense of Beledugu, Bambuk and Khassonke country. After Deniba Bo (1758–61), a great warrior – Sira Bo Kulibali (1761–80) – had established the royal residence at Guemu. He had seized half of Bakhunu while Ngolo Diarra was occupied in the north and east. He pillaged Kita, a large Malinke town in Fuladugu, and, taking advantage of a dispute between two Diawara clans, the Sagone and the Dabora, he drove the latter out while the Sagone were exempted from paying tribute but were obliged to provide a contingent of warriors in the event of war.

The socio-political organization of the Bambara kingdoms
The most striking feature of the Bambara's move towards a state form is the
novel formula they evolved for reconciling Bambara practices with the imperatives inherent in the life of large-scale multi-ethnic kingdoms. Starting from the
working of the ordinary basic association of the *ton*, they gradually forged the
machinery of a state, passing, in the space of a few decades, from 'clans to
empires'.

In the kingdom of Segu The starting-point was the *fla-n-ton* (peer association) led
by Mamari Kulibali. A *fla-n-ton* was an association of young men who had
undergone the rite of circumcision together.

The *ton-den* (association members) elected a *ton-tigui* (chief) who might
equally well be a house captive as a son of a notable. The prime characteristic
of the *fla-n-ton* was the absolute egalitarianism among people of all social backgrounds, which contrasts with the prevailing clan or gerontocratic hierarchy.
The *ton*'s aims were mutual assistance and the sharing of resources for
participation in social life.

Mamari Kulibali had to strengthen his group against the elders who opposed
his *ton* plan, using first their role as *faaya* (fathers) and the demands of farm
work. By killing the elders of Donkouna and Banankoro, Mamari at once
broke with gerontocratic authority and replaced it as *faa* (father) of the *ton-den*.
But, as the leader's successes mounted, many other association members had
joined the original group – insolvent debtors, pardoned condemned men,
prisoners who had broken parole and young adventurers. Such new recruits
were admitted with the status of *ton-dyon* (captives of the *ton*).

When the members of the association – which basically coincided with the
Bambara state's army – poured in, it was no longer a matter of *fla-n-ton* but of
foroba-dyon (captives of the big common field) or *furuba-dyon* (captives of the
Great Union), the first *ton-dyon* of which formed the aristocracy. This structure
was strengthened by the involvement of the *ton-dyon* in cults of which Mamari
was the grand master.

The end-result of this process of the personalization and accumulation of
power was the attribution of the title *faama* (lord holding supreme power) to
the leader of this politico-military machine. The confusion of this status with
that of patriarch of a family community was one of the system's serious
contradictions. Originally, property accumulated through contributions, raids
and war-takings had remained in the *foroba* (public treasury) and profited the
whole community. But eventually the *faama* had discretionary control of state
property. The ruler was indeed assisted by a consultative senate of 40 members
including warriors and holy men, but these notables had sworn fidelity to him
at secret rituals on an island in the River Niger and had sworn allegiance after
the investiture.

Another serious contradiction was the attempt by Mamari's successors to
settle the *foroba-dyon* as state serfs tied to farming, a move which precipitated a
serious resistance crisis among the warriors.

Except during the reigns of strong figures such as Mamari Kulibali and Ngolo Diarra, however, the egalitarian and almost anarchical spirit of the *fla-n-ton* never completely disappeared. It was this spirit that impelled the assembly of *ton-dyon* to eliminate Denkoro, Mamari's son, 'to change the seed'. However, the council of military leaders gradually supplanted the general meeting, itself becoming weakened as some of its members moved away from Segu as the kingdom expanded. To rekindle his troops' devotion to him, the *faama* still convened a general meeting at least once a year for the re-swearing of loyalty oaths, the performance of religious rites and the incorporation of young recruits.

SEGU'S ARMY At the time of the election, the royal insignia comprised the bow, the quiver and the golden axe, unequivocal symbols of the main activity of the state. Oral tradition records the feats of the *faama* of Segu's army, notably in the siege of towns. When the army was arrayed in battle order, the main mass – the *sofa* (grooms) – was in the centre, called *disi* (chest). This main body of troops was flanked right and left by *bolo* (arms) which were made up of *foroba-dyon* officered by *ton-dyon*. Behind the *disi* was a reserve corps of experienced *ton-dyon* called *ton-koro-bolo*.

Arms consisted of axes, arrows, lances and guns, the first of which, of blunderbuss type, seem to have come from Kong. The drums played an important role, either the great *tabala* drum associated with each ruler, which announced war, or the *dunuba* drum, which transmitted messages over considerable distances. The man responsible for inspiring this whole body was the *griot*, whose job it was to ensure that the men had the heart for battle.

The army was the main arena for people of different nationalities to rub shoulders. It contained men of every social, ethnic and geographical background. Young people were thus attracted, being assured – if they survived – of rapidly making their fortunes.

The overall organization of the territory, as in most African kingdoms, was concentric – from the original core along the River Niger, from the capital, Segu-Koro, to Kirango, to the territories annexed over the years, which stretched along the river from Kanbaga to Timbuktu. This main area of state activity by the kings of Segu was given the evocative name *too-daga* (millet paste pot). As a result of the increasing confusion of state property and personal wealth, the eldest sons of kings were generously provided for and their residences dotted the course of the Niger. In the outlying areas, it was almost a matter of delegated power, either to the indigenous chiefs or to governors appointed by Segu.

Particular use was made in the organization of the army and the kingdom of two communities – the Somono and the Fulbe. The River Niger was the kingdom's main artery, vital for the supply of fish, for civil transport and military logistics. The Somono fishermen were required to provide transport and supply fish, while the Fulbe were expected to raise the public herds. These two groups were backed by *foroba-dyon*, but there were also many *foroba-dyon* established as peasants on agricultural lands for the needs of the rulers of Segu.

In the kingdom of Kaarta The socio-political organization of the Massasi kingdom of Kaarta was similar to that of the kingdom of Segu. The royal succession did not pose problems among the Massasi, as they had firm control over the country through provincial governors and heads of army corps. Moreover, the *sofa* corps directly bound to the king was highly organized and all men in authority, all the corps of troops and the allies of the clan were members of the brotherhood that venerated the guardian spirit of the clan.

In short, the Massasi clan seems to have been more homogeneous than that of Segu because it was not initially locked into a pre-existing indigenous institution. It was formed and developed freely under the initiative of the Massasi family which always jealously kept its leadership for itself.

On the Central Volta Plateau: Mossi kingdoms from the sixteenth to the nineteenth century

Origins
The most important development on the Volta plateau during this period is undeniably the formation of the Mossi kingdoms, the earliest of which dates back to the twelfth century. Assuming, as most authors do, that the Na Gbewa and Na Nedega of Mossi traditions are the same person, through Naaba Rawa and Naaba Zungrana, the sons of Naaba Wedraogo, the Mossi dynasties are linked to the Mamprusi, Nanumba and Dagomba kingdoms. With Naaba Wubri, whose advent at the head of the future kingdom of Ouagadougou dates to about 1495, and Naaba Yadega, Naaba Wubri's agnatic grandson who founded the kingdom of Yatenga in about 1540, there began the process of organizing the political structures of the Mossi kingdoms.

Of the three kingdoms (Mamprusi, Nanumba, Dagomba) founded by Na Gbewa's descendants, only Dagomba was to play a major role, from the time of Na Nyaghse (1460–1500). Little is known about succeeding reigns from the early sixteenth to the mid-seventeenth century. Dynastic strife seems to have been the main feature. But in the second half of the sixteenth century a Manden chief (Naaba) established the kingdom of Gonja.

In the second half of the seventeenth century, the Gonja kings launched expeditions from their capital, Yagbum. One of these wars, against Dagomba, was successful and Gonja took Daboya, the centre of a salt-producing area. But in 1713, during the reign of Na Zangina, a convert to Islam, Dagomba held off a new invasion by Gonja. The peace that followed put an end to acts of aggression by Gonja which also harried the Nanumba kingdom.

In about 1740, however, a war of succession broke out between the newly designated Na Garba and a prince who had been an unsuccessful candidate for the throne. Taking advantage of the situation, in 1744 the Asante ruler, Opoku Ware, mounted an expedition against Yendi in support of the faction opposed to the new king. Na Garba was taken prisoner and only freed after undertaking to send to Kumasi an annual tribute of 2,000 prisoners. Dagomba's future was dogged by the aftermath of this treaty, which compelled it to engage in man-hunting and to be ever finding new sources of prisoners. By the end of the eighteenth century, Dagomba was no more than a channel for Asante influence which reached as far as the borders of Mogho (the name of the Mossi country).

The kingdom of Ouagadougou
Twenty-three successors to Naaba Wubri are known in central and southern Mogho between 1500 and 1800. Naaba Kumdumye, the son of Naaba Nyingnemdo who had established Mossi government over the old settlement of Ouagadougou, began his reign with a dynastic dispute which was to have serious consequences. Naaba Kumdumye had competed for the kingship with another candidate, Naaba Yadega, who, after he had been rejected, stole Naaba Wubri's regalia. With the insignia of royal legitimacy, Naaba Yadega made for Gursi and conquered the region which subsequently bore his name, Yatenga (from *Yatega-tenga*: the land of Yadega).

Naaba Kumdumye put his sons to rule in Yako and Tema, which were both later to become independent chiefdoms. By finding a place for princes whose loyalty was not above suspicion, the king was killing two birds with one stone: he was occupying the ground politically, and also keeping happy potential candidates for the throne. But it was through this process that several peripheral chiefdoms were transformed into kingdoms or independent principalities: initially loyal dynasties became less so as they became genealogically and territorially more distant from the royal line.

At the end of the sixteenth century, Naaba Kuda moved the royal residence to Sapone, which shows that the state apparatus was still poorly developed. He also placed his sons in such areas as Laale, Zorgo and Riziam.

Almost nothing is known of Ouagadougou until the reign of a Fulbe usurper, Naaba Moatiba (1729–37), a warlike man who is said to have died by poisoning. His name was erased from the official genealogy of the court.

The reign of Naaba Warga (1737–44) was short but full of new moves to strengthen the monarchy. He was a great legislator. According to Yamba Tiendrebeogo, he established the ritual announcement of *zabyuya* at the cere-monial investiture of chiefs. He organized the royal court, establishing two corps of servants, one made up of Mossi and the other of prisoners. He also institutionalized the royal *pogsyure* (*napogsyure*) system – a system of capitalization and distribution of women – to enable royal servants to have children. He is said to have codified customary law to the state in which it existed in the pre-colonial period.

In short, the end of the seventeenth century and the first half of the eighteenth century saw the final establishment of the Mossi political system both in Yatenga and in central and southern Mogho. However, after Naaba Zombre's long and peaceful reign (*c*. 1744–84) and that of Naaba Koom (*c*. 1784–91), who was the first to spread Muslim influence, the reign of Naaba

Saaga (1791–6) was marked by internal conflicts which heralded the upheavals of the nineteenth century.

The small kingdoms of Mogho

The small kingdoms and chiefdoms of southern Mogho are as yet little known. In the north and north-east, however, three kingdoms stand out: Bulsa, Busuma and Tatenga.

The principality of Bulsa probably dates back to the beginning of the sixteenth century with the installation of Naaba Namende, son and *kurita* of Naaba Wubri. The kingdom of Busuma absorbed one by one the chiefdoms that were still scattered in this area: Naamtenga (in the Luda region) at the beginning of the eighteenth century, then the chiefdom of Pisila, and finally Salmatenga (in the Kaya region). The neighbouring state of Tatenga, founded by one of Naaba Kuda's sons, dominated the region in the eighteenth century when a formidable and ambitious warrior, Naaba Manzi, came to power. However, Naaba Ruubo of Busuma succeeded in eliminating the terrible Manzi in battle. His son Wema had no choice but to take refuge in the farthest parts of the Riziam massif, which was later to lose more land to Yatenga during the nineteenth century.

Yatenga

The successors of Naaba Yadega, the founder of the kingdom, held sway over a limited area, gradually moving their royal residences northwards. The north, however, was occupied by the kingdom of Zandoma under the sway of Naaba Rawa's descendants. Naaba Lambwega's political and military activity consisted precisely in dismantling Naaba Rawa's inheritance, while in the east he incorporated the former Kurumba chieftaincies of Lurum.

In the late seventeenth and early eighteenth centuries, Naaba Lambwega's descendants tried to saturate the considerably enlarged area of the kingdom by establishing Mossi chieftaincies there, containing the Macina and Jelgoji Fulbe, and also by maintaining the internal territorial *status quo* in Mogho.

Naaba Kango

No sooner had Naaba Kango come to power in 1754 than he was faced with violent opposition from princes led by Naaba Wobgo and he was obliged to abdicate and go into exile with a handful of trusty followers. He reached Kong and then moved on to Segu, where he won the support of the Kulibali to regain his throne. In 1757 he returned to Yatenga at the head of an army of mercenaries and defeated Naaba Wogbo, who went into exile.

Naaba Kango began his reign with a spectacular gesture which marked a decisive break with the past: he refused to make the *ringu* (enthronement) journey, which alone gave the ruler of Yatenga the rank of *rima* (king). In about 1780 he founded the capital at Waiguyo, not far from the former royal seat at Biisigi. It was a new town around a vast palace built in the Malian style and bringing together his old comrades in exile. For the first time the inhabitants of a capital consisted exclusively of representatives of the state apparatus, the world of politics and members of the royal household, both prisoners and free. The name of the new capital, Waiguyo, is itself indicative of a whole programme: 'come and bow down and make your submission'. This demand was addressed first and foremost to all members of the royal lineage, royal *nakombse* (princes of the blood) who had supported the usurper Wogbo and who now had to be reduced to subjection. But, up to the time of colonization, the princes refused to acknowledge defeat.

To restore order, which had been seriously disturbed during the years of instability, Naaba Kango put down banditry mercilessly. The indiscipline of chiefs was also severely punished, as was all ostentatious munificence on their part.

Did the massacre of Bambara warriors precipitate an expedition by Segu against Yatenga? There is no reference to such an expedition in Mossi tradition, whereas there is in Bambara traditions. In any event, Naaba Kango, who intended to give royal prisoners a special place in the system of government, needed many more of them. Some were taken from among prisoners of war, but most were captured in raids.

When Naaba Kango died in 1787, he was buried in his capital and not in the royal cemetery. His death must have come as a relief to many, for he ruled without pity. The princes' resentment was so great that they had the only daughter of the dead king stifled to death; but the court aristocracy which had remained loyal were able to have one of his lifelong companions, Naaba Saagha (1797–1803), nominated to succeed him.

The socio-political structures of Mogho
By the Mossi kingdoms is meant not states comprising a homogeneous society the Mossi ethnic group – but composite socio-political formations resulting from conquest, by warriors called Mossi, of the White Volta basin. However, the process of intermarriage and slow infiltration by settlement carried out by Mossi peasants was certainly much more decisive than military conquest. Each time that an area was taken over, it was organized on the Mossi socio-political model.

In the case of Yatenga, at the end of the nineteenth century, the population comprised three distinct societies: Mossi society, Silmiga (Fulbe) society and Silmi–Mossi society. The first alone was subject to the authority of the king, the *Yatenga-Naaba*. The Fulbe or Silmiise had, as it were, the status of guests, on the basis of settlement contracts under which a broad strip of territory in the northern part of the country was reserved for them. The Fulbe had been settled in Yatenga since the seventeenth century and had established permanent villages there from which the transhumance of cattle was organized. It is perhaps misleading to speak of Silmi–Mossi society, but the sedentary small stock-breeders, quite numerous in the south-east of Yatenga, certainly fall into a separate category. Their compound name is a reminder that they were the offspring of mixed marriages (which anyway were forbidden) between Fulbe

12.2 *Mossi statuette commemorating a female ancestor, made of wood with a natural patina. Height: 47cm (H. Dubois, Brussels)*

men and Mossi women. Arriving from the chiefdom of Tema in the eighteenth century, they did not come under Mossi authority and eventually passed under the somewhat distant protection of the Fulbe politico-religious centre at Todiam in the east of the kingdom.

But what of Mossi society itself? Its internal cleavages were linked to the distinction made by the Mossi between the *naaba* (chief), the *naabiise* (chiefs' sons) and the *nakombse* (sons or descendants of sons of princes who had not become chiefs). Only chiefs' sons could become chiefs, and so, strictly speaking, except for the tiny minority of chiefs and chiefs' sons, all other Mossi who claimed to be descendants of Wedraogo could be regarded as *nakombse*. The *nakombse* belonging to the royal lineage were themselves divided into five branches, each consisting of one generation of princes. The royal lineage was apparently very early seen as having been of a constant generational depth (five generations), the entry of a new generation into the royal lineage entailing the exclusion of the oldest generation and its transfer to the *talse* group (commoners).

To the extent that they held village chieftaincies, the *nakombse* constituted a category of power-holders below the chiefs. There were two others: the *tasobnamba* (war chiefs), local notables of ancient stock, and the members of the king's household. In the case of court offices, the structure that prevailed at the top of the political hierarchy around the king was the same as that around each local chief. Three dignitaries assisted the chief, to which the royal court added a fourth, the *Bin-Naaba* or *Rasam-Naaba*, the chief of the royal prisoners.

Thus members of the royal lineage too deeply involved in the struggle for the throne could not serve the king. Lastly, the institutional holders of power were actually effectively divided into two sub-groups with opposing interests: the war chiefs and royal servants, on whom the king relied to govern, and the *nakombse*, against whom he governed. This division went deep among the Mossi as these men of lowly origin who held the great offices of state were at the same time the great electors who chose a new *Mogho-Naaba*. Internal conflicts have always punctuated the history of all the Mossi kingdoms and they are always about the transmission of power. Generally, there was rivalry between the ruling monarch's younger brothers and his sons.

In contrast to the world of government, to which the royal prisoners belonged, lay the world of the land. The people or sons of the land were, in theory, the descendants of the indigenous peoples, blacksmiths excepted. Deprived of all political power, they were responsible for the earth rituals, which concerned both the harvests and the social order and the perpetuation of the local group. The figure of the *naaba* was contrasted to that of the *tengsoba* (earth-priest), the holder of sacred power. This dualism was reflected cosmogonically in the divine couple of Naaba Wende, the King-God, and Napaga Tenga, the Queen-Land.

The definition of the category of people of the land changed substantially down the centuries because the true Mossi became absorbed into the category of indigenous peoples and used this status to become earth-priests. Alongside the earth-priest there was the *bugo* (fertility priest), an office that seems to have been of Dogon origin.

The political world and the world of the land were integrated into a system with the king as its central focus through the medium of great yearly rituals. The Yatenga Mossi, like the Kurumba, had an annual solar calendar divided into lunar months, the discrepancy between the lunar year and the solar year being compensated for by an intercalary month every three years. After the new year *filiiga* (thanksgiving festival) came the ceremonies of *napusum* (greeting the king) at which, in three separate ceremonies, the royal servants, the war chiefs and the *nakombse* paid homage to the king. The following period, from the second to the sixth month, was taken up with a great ceremonial cycle called *bega*, which involved the king and all the dignitaries of the land in sacrifices intended to ask for a good harvest. The feasts of the *bega* ended at the beginning of the rainy season. Ceremonial activity was resumed during the harvest season, with two festivals of first-fruits.

This highly complex religious-cum-political system gave cohesion to a state society which was made up of groups of varied origin, which had usually retained cultural features from their pre-state past, starting with their own socio-political stratification. Thus the division of society as a whole into four large functional groups – power-holders, people of the land, blacksmiths and craftsmen, and traders – turns up, with certain differences, among the Kurumba or Fulse.

All the ethnic groups were divided in two ways: into descent groups and local groups.

In this composite society, patrilineal and patrilocal, the Mossi term *budu* denotes any descent group that operates as the exogamous reference unit. With a history of its own, distinguished by the name of a founder and a place of foundation, a *budu* defined its identity by the existence of a *bud-kamsa* (head) and a *kiims'rogo* (ancestral shrine) along with having one or more *sonda* (collective names or mottoes).

The patrilineage existed territorially only at its first level of segmentation, the *zaka* (section). The section was divided in turn into *yiiya* (households), which were production and consumption units. The sections belonging to one lineage were generally scattered and hence came under several village units. In other words, a Mossi village contained parts of several lineages, and a lineage was dispersed in several villages.

Gulma and Borgu

For a long time, little was known of the history of the Gulma (or Gurma) bank of the Niger – the right bank downstream from the bend, but thanks to research carried out by the historian Georges Madiega we now have incomplete but scientifically sound information about northern Gulma.

The Dogon constitute one of the oldest populations of north Gulma. After them came the group called today the Tindamba (people of the earth) and the Woba from the south. North Gulma was also peopled by the Kurumba. In south Gulma the oldest inhabitants included the Tankamba, the Berba and, as in the north, Tindamba and Woba. The latter certainly occupied a huge area before being partially assimilated by the Gulmanceba and other peoples who set up states there.

On this substructure of early populations a foreign power superimposed itself, the Bemba or Buricimba, who later gave rise to the Gulmanceba states. Madiega has two major hypotheses: the first is that the ancestors of the Mamprusi passed through Gulma before the arrival of the Buricimba; the second is that first Gulmanceba dynasties were contemporary with the first Mossi dynasties. This would suggest that the beginning of Gulma's history as a state was probably in the fifteenth century. The figure of a historical-mythical ancestor called Jaba is associated with the birth of the Gulmanceba states. He does not seem to have been a great warrior, like Naaba Wedraogo in Mossi history, as the powers attributed to him have more to do with magic than with generalship. What seems certain is that the links suggested by the Mossi between Na Bawa's descendants and Jaba's are simply late reconstructions thought up at the court of the *Mogho-naaba* to justify the virtual amalgamation of Gulmanceba power and Mossi power during the colonial period. All the evidence suggests that, from the point of view of dynastic origins, the Mossi and Gulmanceba hegemonies must be treated separately.

Where did the Buricimba come from? There is at present no way of knowing which warlike migrations gave rise to the Gulmanceba empire. We know that the earliest Gulmanceba political centre was Lompotangu or Sangbantangu, south-east of Nungu. The Buricimba later moved to Kujuabongu, south of Pama. They were not the only founders of kingdoms in this area. The Jakpangu dynasty is of Berba origin, and the Gobnangu one of Hausa origin. There are also dynasties whose founders came from Yanga.

Buricimba expansion continued throughout the sixteenth and seventeenth centuries, and the apogee of Gulmanceba power can be put at about the middle of the eighteenth century. At that time the Gulmanceba held sway over an enormous, though no doubt sparsely populated, territory, bounded to the south by the Mamprusi kingdom and Borgu, to the east by Torodi and the last vestiges of the Songhay empire, to the north by the Sahel areas inhabited by Kurumba, Songhay and Fulbe, and to the west by the Mossi chiefdoms of Tuguri, Bulsa, Kupela and Tankudgo. In the middle of the eighteenth century two large kingdoms, Bilanga and Kuala, shared most of the territory of north Gulma between them, plus three minor states, Piala, Bongandini and Con.

The history of central and southern Gulma remains obscure. Among the eleven kingdoms in the south, the kingdom of Nungu was founded by Yendabri, a descendant of Jaba's, in the mid-eighteenth century. That was the time when southern Gulma was overrun by the Tyokosi, Manden mercenaries belonging to the Wattara group who had originally been in the service of the Mamprusi kings. Yendabri, the ruler of Nungu, took on the leadership of a coalition of kingdoms to drive the Tyokosi out of Gulma. Hard pressed by their enemies, the Tyokosi withdrew to their capital, Sansane-Mango, to which the allies laid siege. It is questionable whether the victorious Yendabri then took advantage of his success to strengthen his authority over the league he had formed. What is certain is that, in the eighteenth century, the Nunbado (the ruler of Nungu) became the leading ruler in Gulma. His royal seat became the main town of the land, largely because of the economic role of the Hausa traders there. It is difficult to interpret the relations Nunbado had with the Gulmanceba rulers. There does not seem to have been a Gulmanceba confederation, and the Nunbado's actual authority was no doubt just as territorially limited as that of the other kings, but he enjoyed exceptional moral and ritual prestige in that he came – belatedly – to be regarded as the direct heir of Lumpo and hence of his 'father', Jaba.

Borgu, south-east of Gulma, has a somewhat confused history, with several state-type formations, the earliest having apparently been Busa which reached its apogee in the sixteenth century and then declined. The other kingdoms, such as Nikki, are more or less direct offshoots of Busa.

The peoples with non-centralized authority
These peoples are described in this way for lack of a better term. They had come into being at a very early date and were settled in the upper Volta basin. Although these peoples did not dominate the political stage, their contribution to the history of Africa must not be overlooked, as they form the underlying human population on to which external contributions were biologically grafted.

The very term Moaga (pl. Mossi) means mixed. We cannot insist too strongly on the role of the Nioniosse, who existed at a very early date. The peoples of Yatenga themselves were not untouched by the contributions from the Manden peoples of the Niger bend. On the cultural and economic levels, the contribution of the indigenous peoples was a considerable one. We have seen the contribution of the Dogon in the area of political and religious organization and of the Kurumba to the system of dynastic rule in Yatenga.

The indigenous peoples, whether of Manden or Voltaic culture, were open to exchanges but refused to accept domination – a strategy that was highly successful until the colonial period.

Despite the absence of a centralized state, the Gurunsi and the Bwaba developed a marked individual personality. The Gurunsi, living withdrawn into family groups in remarkably designed huts, were fiercely opposed to any form of complex political hierarchy. In the east, however, there did exist a more organized structure under a canton chief with a court and a religious advisor responsible for the cult of his *kwara* (magical symbol). The Bwaba appear to have emerged as a specific entity between the tenth and fifteenth centuries. They did not recognize any political authority above the village level. The religion of *Do* formed a bond between those initiated in one village and those in neighbouring villages.

Near Yatenga were the northern Samo, whose concentrated settlements are marked by enormous grain stores. Their political organization consisted of reasonably stable confederations of dozens of villages around a few political centres corresponding to the *kafu* (Manden canton). Their system rested on both clan alliances and territorial coalitions. The Sana (Samo is the Manden name), hardened warriors and peasants fiercely attached to their freedom, never gave in to the pressures from Yatenga, which tried several times to overcome them.

As for the Bisa, who were related to the Sana and separated from them after a clan dispute, they were based in south-eastern Mogho. They, too, put up remarkable resistance despite mutual cultural exchanges and a tribute in captives at the end of the eighteenth century.

Kong and Gwiriko

Since the time of the Sudanic empires from the tenth to the fifteenth centuries, Jula traders, called Wangara, had been travelling the routes to the forest where gold and ivory were to be found. But, from the sixteenth century, a new factor arose along the Gulf of Guinea: the trade in slaves and firearms. This single event is enough to explain why groups of Jula – now traders, now soldiers, now Muslim missionaries – went further and further south into the savannah areas where the goods most demanded by the new dispensation were increasingly traded. It was Jula who helped to establish the great trading centre of Begho. The Begho route was soon linked to the one crossing present-day Côte d'Ivoire from Assinie to Bobo and Bamako through Yakasso. At the end of the sixteenth century the Gonja kingdom came into being and, at the end of the seventeenth century, after the destruction of Begho, Jula refugees fell back into the Abron kingdom and founded Bonduku.

A number of important circumstances gave a sharp push to the activities of the Jula from the seventeenth century onwards. First there was the fall of the empire of Gao and, second, the creation of the Asante empire which constituted a major centre for the supply of gold, arms, salt and manufactured goods. Third, there were the Voltaic savannah societies, which were quite densely populated and most of which had no centralized political authority, and therefore could supply the slaves and also the cattle and gold that the coastal areas wanted. It is thus easy to understand why the Dagomba should have organized the Kulango kingdom of Buna in Lorhon country on the same model as their own.

It was in this context that a new diaspora of settlements that were at once commercial, political, military and religious came into being on the initiative of the Jula. In the middle of the eighteenth century, armed bands that had come down from Segu – the Diarrasouba – brushed the Senufo aside and set up a Manden kingdom at Odienne.

The Senufo belong to the Voltaic group of language-speakers. They were settled in clans around Korogho, Seguela, Odienne and Kong. The fall of Mali seems to have opened up to them possibilities of territorial expansion northwards as far as Sikasso and Boungouni and southwards into the region of Bouaké, where they would be absorbed into the Baule block. In the east they gave rise to isolated groups before falling under Abron control. The Senufo were above all a peasant élite. They were egalitarian and independent-minded and they had only one large-scale social institution, the Poron, which had a religious character and also helped to regulate the social hierarchy. They had consummate artists who, since early times, had been producing some of the masterpieces of the Negro–African symbolist style. It was only in about the nineteenth century that the Senufo set themselves to building a few centralized kingdoms.

At the beginning of the eighteenth century the Manden added the famous centre of Kong to the chain of Jula settlements. It was there that Keita and Kulibali Mande, who had become Wattara, subdued the indigenous people. One of them, Sekou Wattara, eliminated the other Jula groups and reigned at Nafana and Kong, thanks to a powerful army. This military force enabled him to conquer part of western upper Volta as far as Dafina.

Subsequently, the Kong forces subdued Turka country and Folona, laid waste the Sikasso region and part of Minianka and Macina, and even got as far as Sofara, opposite Jenne on the River Bani. We have seen how this expedition was finally driven back by Biton Kulibali. After Sekou Wattara's death in 1740, the empire was profoundly disrupted. There was a split between the caste of non-Muslim Joola and Senufo warriors, the Sohondji, and the Salama Jula, who were traders and Muslims. Kong had indeed become a great centre of Islamic learning, but attempts to control Jenne show that the Wattara's grand design was above all economic: to control the trade routes linking the forest to the Niger bend over the greatest possible distance. After the failure of this ambitious project, the Jula groups fell back on more limited undertakings.

One of the boldest was the creation of the kingdom of Wiriko, founded by Famaghan Wattara, in a gold-rich area around the watershed of the Banafin (a tributary of the Niger), Comoe and Black Volta rivers. Famaghan Wattara seized Tiefo, Dafin and Bwamu (the land of the Bwaba) more or less permanently. His successors only managed to contain the revolts by peoples reduced to Jula domination by repeated repression. This domination was above all economic, even when it was made to appear as proselytism.

Economic life from the Niger to the basin of the Voltas

J B. Kietegha dates the period of high gold production from the Black Volta at the mid-eighteenth century, when the newcomers monopolized the extraction of the gold of Pura and introduced technological improvements.

Trade was busiest in the western and northern half of the area between the River Niger and the basin of the Voltas. But during the seventeenth and eighteenth centuries – even in the Mossi kingdoms and among the peoples with non-centralized authority, above the subsistence economy base – there gradually came into being a trading network which came to involve more and more professional traders.

In Mossi country, an area of near monoculture in millet on exhausted soils with irregular rainfall, shortages, even famines, were not uncommon. In addition to millet, the staple food, crops included maize, groundnuts, cowpeas, beans, sesame and some potherbs. Cotton, the main plant used in crafts, seems to have been grown for a long time. The Muslim Yarse have been associated with weaving since the beginning of Mossi history and strips of cotton cloth formed their cargo goods in the north–south caravan trade. The Marase (Songhay), who specialized in dyeing, used indigo. The main wild plants gathered were *nere* and shea nut.

In Lurum's pre-Mossi era (up to the fifteenth and sixteenth centuries) the Kurumba had among them Marase who engaged in the Saharan salt trade. After the formation of the northern Mossi states, including Yatenga, the Marase were supplanted by the Yarse, who in addition to the salt trade took up trade in kola nuts, which they bought on the northern fringes of Asante. The large markets of the kingdom, such as Yuba and Gursi, were the termini of the salt and kola caravans. The Yarse of Yatenga were a dynamic group of traders found not only at Timbuktu, but also in the valley of the Bani and throughout Macina. In Mossi country they lived in symbiosis and compromise with the leaders: in return for certain privileges, they undertook not to encourage any subversion, to sell to the *Naaba* as a matter of priority, to support him through appropriate rituals and even, on occasion, to act as intelligence agents.

While the accounting unit for the traders was the cowrie, other units were used in the caravan trade and there were various systems of equivalence between the cowrie, the cubit of cotton strip, the block of salt, slaves and horses.

Yatenga was one of the great metal-working areas of West Africa, and the blacksmiths combined metal-working with the export trade to central Mogho, which was poor in iron ore.

The slave trade, going on on every part of the coast of black Africa during this period, introduced into the mechanism of trade and socio-political relations a terrible logic from the moment firearms, slaves and political power were made part of the same equation. The greatest kings of the time participated in this slaving activity, fuelled by the host of local chiefs who, willy-nilly, embarked on this business to enter the political game.

We have seen how, in the Bambara system, the status of captive had been ingeniously institutionalized by turning to account the already existing institution of the *ton-den* (association member) to create the *ton-dyon* (captives of the community). A further step was taken with the *furuba-dyon* (crown slaves). These were prisoners of war grouped into contingents, each of which was defined by the *faama* who had formed it. After suffering the fate of any trade goods sold on the market, they saw their situation improve when they were purchased by a community. A woman, as soon as she produced a child, acquired the status of *woloso* (born in the house) and a man could acquire the same status as soon as his master had sufficient confidence in him. As soon as he reached the status of *woloso*, he became a caste member. He could no longer be put on sale, and had a right to property and to transmit his estate to his children.

It is true that the status of *woloso* was transferred to his descendants, even if, as happened at royal courts, a few caste men might rise to the highest positions. The mark persisted ineradicably in the collective mind. Thus, the great king

Ngolo Diarra's family was unable to eradicate the memory of the servile status of their ancestor, which provoked taunts from the Massasi of Kaarta.

Islam and traditional African religions

It used to be a commonplace to say that the Bambara and the Mossi had constituted strong barriers to the advance of Islam in West Africa. This is a simplistic assertion that needs revision. Islam, at work since the eighth century if not before, increased its influence in the great empires from the empire of Ghana to the empire of Gao. Naturally, there were obstacles and resistance. Even as late as the eighteenth century the Jelgoobe and Feroobe Fulbe were often followers of traditional religions. For a millennium, however, from the eighth to the nineteenth century, Islam continued to penetrate the whole of this region through numerous channels including traders, prayer-leaders and even violence.

The Bambara initially looked upon Islam syncretistically: its presence impelled them to stress once again the Supreme God, Maa Ngala. Having assimilated Islam in this way, the kings of Segu and Kaarta saw no obstacle to consulting the ministers of this great God through the persons of the *marabouts*, while remaining faithful to their own cults – of which they were practically *ex officio* the high priests – and to the magician.

Although they practised traditional rites, the Kulibali took part in Muslim religious festivals, at least by their presence, and offered lavish gifts to the Sarakolle *marabouts*. These syncretisms, which at the same time were developing with Christianity in Afro-American worship in Brazil, Haiti and Cuba, were one of the characteristics of the Negro–African religious spirit. Thus, if the appeals to the spirits failed to provide a clear and satisfactory response, the intervention of the *marabout* would then be sought and welcomed piously by the various Bambara kings.

What is certain is that Islam presented itself to the Bambara with institutions such as polygamy, divorce, repudiation and slavery that did not systematically challenge their own. Moreover, the *marabouts* did nothing that might put off Bambara neophytes. Thus at Dia, probably one of the oldest centres of Islam in the Western Sudan, teaching generally adapted itself to indigenous customs and gave plenty of attention to magic. The most numerous *marabouts* among the Bambara were the Marka, the Bozo and the Somono, who claimed to be in the line of Moorish or Fulbe Islam. Some ethnic groups, such as the Soninke, the Marka, the Fulbe and the Torobe, Islamized long before and enjoying religious toleration, acted as models and catalysts.

In short, this mutual tolerance was of great benefit to both parties: it associated the Muslim leaders with government and it used endogenous channels to win these peoples to the faith of the Ḳurʾān. It also contributed to the strengthening of the power of monarchs who, faced with the ethnic and social heterogeneity of their states, could not afford the luxury of religious discord. Such at least was the state of affairs before the dissimilar *djihāds* of Sekou Ahmadu Barry and al-Ḥādj dj ʿUmar.

In Mossi country, the beginning of Muslim influence at the court of Ouagadougou probably dates from the reign of Naaba Kom, son of Naaba Zombre (*c.* 1744–84). Islam spread into the Volta basin in the wake of Jula traders and warriors, along a north-south line in the west of the Volta area, along the Black Volta valley. The town of Bobo-Dioulasso was one of the main centres of Muslim proselytism.

The founders of Gonja were Muslim Manden. From Gonja, Islam moved into Dagomba country. Trading centres in these areas soon became religious centres, distinguished by the presence of *malams* (Muslim scholars). The first Dagomba king to be converted was Na Zangina, who reigned at the very beginning of the eighteenth century.

Islam penetrated Mamprusi country at roughly the same time. Gambaga, the main market, quickly became a Muslim centre. Thus it was from the south that Islam came to Mogho at the end of the eighteenth century, during the reign of Mogho-Naaba Zombre, who showed himself sympathetic to the Muslims. It was in the reign of Naaba Dulugu (*c.* 1796–1825) that the decisive step was taken. He formally converted and built the first mosque in Ouagadougou. This early Mossi Islam, like that which then prevailed in the Mamprusi and Dagomba kingdoms, was an aristocratic Islam, and for the Mogho-Naaba and the other chiefs and dignitaries its practice was in no way inconsistent with observance of the traditional religion. Far from trying to impose the new religion on his subjects, Naaba Dulugu seems to have been afraid that Islam might make too rapid progress in his kingdom.

Thus, in the Bambara kingdom as in Mogho, although there was a decided tolerance towards Islam, the traditional religion remained on its guard and sought compromise formulae. For the other two political centres, the empire of Kong and Gwiriko on the one hand, and the Gulmanceba kingdoms on the other, the general attitude was decidedly different. At Kong, as among the Bobo-Jula, the Islamic religion was both a reason to live and a way of life, such that their policy, imbued with a militant faith, foreshadowed the *djihāds* of the nineteenth century. Conversely, the Gulmanceba were resolute upholders of the traditional religion.

Conclusion

For the countries of the Niger bend and the upper Volta basin, the period from the sixteenth to the eighteenth century was unquestionably a state-building phase.

In accordance with an ancient tradition in the region, the Jula, Mossi, Gulmanceba and Bambara states were all multi-ethnic units. Even if the dominant ethnic group claimed certain privileges, it was itself the outcome and source of inter-ethnic mixing. The sometimes highly sophisticated political machinery was nevertheless vulnerable, mainly because of the almost total lack of a written form of administration.

Moreover, the states were undermined by internal contradictions. In the first place, the devolution of power often gave rise to serious difficulties. When Naaba Kumdumye of Ouagadougou found positions for the unsuccessful candidates for the chieftaincy, little did he suspect that his successor, Naaba Warga, would have to wage war on the descendants of those chiefs. This political difficulty was compounded by a social problem, for the princes excluded from power turned their animosity against the peasants, who were thus exploited mercilessly. Second, there was a formidable opposition between the royal entourage, made up of commoners, and the king's relatives, who were held in check by a series of measures the most striking of which was the policy of Naaba Kango of Waiguyo.

Furthermore, the question of religion must not be played down. It is true that, until the end of the eighteenth century, the Mossi and Bambara states succeeded in maintaining a *modus vivendi* based on tolerance, syncretism and an exchange of services. But there was a noteworthy difference between the Mossi and Bambara states, on the one hand, and the empire of Kong and the Gulmanceba kingdoms, on the other.

State-building in the region, however, fitted into an overall economic context which spelt ultimate doom for such political experiments. All these countries lay between the southern edge of the Sahara and the Atlantic coast, which was increasingly controlled by the Europeans, whose commercial policy reshaped commercial circuits and the structure and terms of trade to their advantage. Supply and demand were gradually disrupted. In the economic chain that each ruler attempted to control, the relative importance of the commodities used to win and maintain power (horses, arms and captives) constantly increased, with the consequent spectre of the slave trade.

By comparison with the African rulers along the coast, who were directly confronted by the Europeans and had no other choice but submission or war, these countries of the interior certainly enjoyed a respite and seemed to have their fate in their own hands. But that fate was in fact caught up in a process that was increasingly dependent on the outside world. The hegemonies of the region did not have enough time to establish a *de jure* state providing the stability and order mentioned by chroniclers in reference to the previous empires. Nevertheless, it has been demonstrated that, in difficult circumstances, people proved capable of building a state with their own African means.

The states and cultures of the Upper Guinea coast

Introduction

From the Casamance to Côte d'Ivoire inclusively, there stretches an enormous area of coasts and forests, inhabited by many and various peoples. This area is far bigger than the one historians normally call Upper Guinea. This chapter aims at sketching the outline of its development between 1500 and 1800.

The societies

By comparison with the big ethnic masses of the Sudan, where state-type societies predominate, this area is characterized by many small socio-cultural units organized on the basis of lineages, clans and villages. From the Casamance to the Tanoe, between the northern savannah and the southern coastline on the one hand, and between the mountain ranges of Futa Jallon and the Guinea Spine and the western and south-eastern coastline on the other, there are more than a hundred ethnic groups and sub-groups.

This multiplicity of human groups explains the many linguistic differences that characterize the cultural landscape. There are sometimes dialectal variants within a single language, which restricts mutual linguistic intelligibility within a single ethnic group,

Despite this diversity, there are wider linguistic entities. Three big language families share the area between the Casamance and the Tanoe. Within the family of Manden languages, the Southern Manden sub-group is predominant – Northern Manden only appearing in the form of the Manden spoken in the Gambia, Casamance, Guinea-Bissau, Sierra Leone and Liberia. South of the Manden languages, along the coastline from the Casamance to Liberia, the so-called West Atlantic languages are also divided into northern and southern groups and are extremely varied. Lastly, to the east and south-east, the so-called Kwa languages comprise the Kru-Bete and Akan languages, which show the same heterogeneity as the West Atlantic languages.

The difficulty of producing an historical synthesis

Tracing the development of the countries of the coast of West Africa from the

Casamance to Côte d'Ivoire between the fifteenth and nineteenth centuries is a difficult task for the historian.

The difficulties relate first to the sources themselves. After the fifteenth century, written European sources become more and more numerous and accurate as trade intensifies, but they are unevenly distributed by periods and regions: they are plentiful for Senegambia, the Rivers Coast and the sector from the Gold Coast to the Niger delta, but are less so for Liberia and Côte d'Ivoire. Although they reflect the prejudices of Europeans, they nevertheless give a good picture of the coastal area, including the geographical setting, economic activities, systems of government and habits and customs.

When these sources are inadequate or non-existent, they need to be supplemented by archaeology, oral tradition and other sources. While the archaeology of the dry Sudan-Sahel area is developing, that of the humid Guinea area is still in its infancy despite excavations in Casamance, Guinea-Conakry, Sierra Leone and Côte d'Ivoire. Research on oral tradition has made crucial progress in the Manden and Fulbe sectors but has not yet given its full measure elsewhere. Moreover, oral tradition rarely goes back beyond the seventeenth century. Lastly, apart from the relatively homogeneous Manden-speaking groups, historical linguistics in this area of amazing linguistic complexity is still at the planning stage.

There are also difficulties relating to the socio-political fragmentation typical of this region. Historians of the states that came into being as a result of the sharing out of colonies often give more space to the peoples of the Sudanic parts than to those of the coast. Moreover, no overall historical study of these coastal and forest peoples is possible without precise knowledge of each of their histories.

Our study will keep to historical reality as experienced by the peoples themselves, without losing sight of the flow of world history. The West African coast acted as the main link between the historical pressures of the Sudan and those of European trade; and down the centuries different parts of it became active, came to life again and settled down.

Population movements

The Manden movements

In the area between the Gambia and the rivers of Guinea and Sierra Leone, signs of the first Manden (Malinke) advance towards the Atlantic go back to the twelfth century. Oral traditions collected in the Gambia, Casamance and Guinea-Bissau mention Manden agricultural settlement in the late twelfth century. This peaceful peasant migration was followed by the conquering migration of the soldiers of Tirmaghan Traore, one of Sundiata's generals. The conquest of the Atlantic coastal areas gave Mali wide access to the sea by the late fifteenth century and it dominated the area between the Gambia and Sierra Leone.

However, it is misleading to see these movements purely as military conquests. A deeper analysis of this westward expansion suggests it may have been the consequence of certain factors inherent in Manden society. The practice of collateral succession made it difficult for sons of rulers to succeed their fathers. Many therefore set out westwards with their families to found their own states. Other members of Manden society, intent on exploiting trade with the West and finding areas for settlement, were actively involved in this westward expansion.

The peoples of the coastal belt and the hinterland in 1500

The peopling of the coasts and forest before the European voyages of the fifteenth and sixteenth centuries is one of the most obscure areas in West African history. Only a few written sources dealing with the Sudanese empires and the gold trade can give us some information on the peoples of Senegambia, the Southern Rivers and the Gold Coast. For the areas in between we can only guess the history on the strength of hasty notes by Portuguese travellers and the oral traditions of some peoples of the hinterland who claim 'to have always been there'.

The Southern Rivers between the Gambia and Cape Mount

Southern Senegambia – Casamance and Guinea-Bissau Three main groups occupied the estuaries and lower rivers when the Portuguese arrived: the Bainuk or Banhun, a people of Manden origin who had come from the east in the fourteenth century; the Joola, who had come from the south before the fifteenth century; and the Balante from the east, who had imposed themselves on the Bainuk before the fifteenth century. Behind these coastal groups there were the Manden who had arrived from the east in the twelfth and thirteenth centuries driving the other peoples westward towards the sea. After the Manden, Fulbe from Macina came in the fifteenth century.

Guinea-Conakry and Sierra Leone Archaeological discoveries at Yengema in Kono country, confirmed by linguistic research, have prompted C. Fyfe to suggest that the Windward Coast had long been inhabited, since the third millennium before the Christian era. The earliest inhabitants were probably the Limba of Sierra Leone. Next came the Temne and Baga, with their related languages. Lastly came the Kisi and Bullom, two related groups who split up, the former remaining in the interior and the latter going on to the sea.

At the end of the twelfth century, movements following the fall of Ghana and Sosso brought the Soso to Futa Jallon, where the Dyallonke, Baga, Nalu, Landuma and Tyapi were already. There followed a mingling of peoples which ended in some migratory movements to the west. The Nalu, Baga and Landuma–Tyapi settled on the coast and in the immediate hinterland. At the end of the fifteenth century the pressure of the Fulbe on the Soso–Dyallonke–Baga and Temne set off new migratory movements which enabled the Baga to spread southwards along the coast, thus bringing them into contact with the Bullom.

Cape Mount to the River Bandama: Liberia and western Côte d'Ivoire
This area was inhabited by the Kru, Kwa-speaking peoples, and this section of the coast was the area of the trade in malaguetta or fool's pepper. The hinterland was dominated by the high forest and the eastern heights of the Guinea Spine, which allowed only limited links with the world of the Sudanic savannahs.

The European voyagers of the late fifteenth century met peoples along this coast from Cape Mesurado to Cape Lahou. Historians think that these were part of a long-established Kru settlement. Archaeology and research in oral tradition also show that this region has been populated for a very long time. We must therefore suppose that the savannah north of the forest was occupied by Southern Manden groups. In the fifteenth century they had, no doubt, begun to thrust south into the forest under pressure from the Northern Manden from the upper Niger. This north–south drive must have brought many little groups of Kru to the seaward fringe of the forest.

Population movements from Sierra Leone to Côte d'Ivoire
In the sixteenth century new peoples came from the interior to join those already there. They were mainly Manden, driven by Mali's economic and political difficulties to move southward. This expansion to the forest fringes was the work not only of warriors but also of merchants.

The first of the Manden to move were the Kono-Vai, who came from the upper Niger and migrated towards the coast between 1500 and 1550. By the beginning of the seventeenth century, the Vai occupied the mouths of the Mano and Moa rivers, while their Kono relatives were in the immediate hinterland.

In the mid-sixteenth century, the Mane-Sumba, a group of Manden invaders from the upper Niger, also arrived on the coasts of Sierra Leone and Liberia. The Mane reached Cape Mount in 1545 and then moved northward, crushing the indigenous peoples and making an incursion into Futa Jallon by way of the Scarcies. They were driven back by the Soso, the allies of the Fulbe, and had to return to the coast, which they occupied from Liberia to the islands of Los, merging with the original inhabitants.

The precise composition of the groups that were involved in this migratory flow is not yet clear. What is certain is that this invasion had important consequences for all the peoples in this area – Southern Manden, Kru and West Atlantic – starting with the destruction of the famous kingdom of the Sapes and continuing with the building of a new political society under Manden rule. The peoples of this coast were reorganized into four kingdoms: Bullom, Loko, Bure and Sherbro. These peoples were then integrated socio-culturally. In the course of their conquest the Mane embarked on a process of miscegenation which led to the implantation of Manden influence in this region. Finally, the

Mane introduced military innovations which enhanced the fighting prowess of the coastal peoples. By the end of the sixteenth century the invaders seem to have become naturalized, and, by the beginning of the seventeenth century the original Mane had been completely absorbed.

In the sixteenth century a Southern Manden group, the Manden (Malinke) of the Camara clan from the upper Niger, settled in Liberia and western Côte d'Ivoire, causing not only the movement of the Kono and the Vai towards the coasts of Sierra Leone and Liberia but also that of the Toma, Guerze and related groups towards the forests of what are now the republics of Guinea and Liberia. At the same time the Diomande, brothers of the Camara, were moving eastward, settling at Touba (Côte d'Ivoire) and driving out the Dan-Toura. Advancing still further east, the Manden (Malinke) entered Worodugu and displaced the Guro south-eastward, towards the forest.

This thrust by the Southern Manden put pressure on the Kru, who moved deeper into the forest in the direction of the coast. By the middle of the sixteenth century the north–south movement of the Kru was probably already completed. In the Côte d'Ivoire sector the movements seem to have taken place later.

Population movements in the seventeenth and eighteenth centuries

The population movements of the seventeenth and eighteenth centuries affected the whole coastal and sub-coastal area and took the form of multi-directional migratory flows. The sector most affected was the area between Liberia and the River Tanoe. Warren L. d'Azevedo has suggested that these population movements were largely stimulated by the desire to control the slave trade which in turn led to conflicts and the formation of military and commercial alliances between and within ethnic groups.

From the Gambia to Sierra Leone

Casamance and Guinea-Bissau In the seventeenth and eighteenth centuries no new peoples appeared in this sector; but with the boom in the slave trade there was a mingling of peoples due in part to the devastating raids of the Manden, backed by the expansion of Kaabu, then at its peak. The Manden and their Kasanga vassals continually harassed the Bijago, Joola, Balante and Bainuk. To escape the pressure of the slave-traders, many peoples sought refuge in the inaccessible coastal swamps, abandoning to Manden control the rivers leading into the interior.

Guinea-Conakry and Sierra Leone The growing influence of the Atlantic trade on the peoples of the Sudanese zone and the expansion of Islam marked by the Fulbe revolution in Futa Jallon in the eighteenth century formed the backdrop to the population movements in this sector in the seventeenth and eighteenth centuries.

In the first third of the eighteenth century the Fulbe of the holy war set off the movement of the peoples of the Tyapi group towards the coasts of what is now the republic of Guinea. Rejecting the authority of the masters of the new religion, and having lost several hard-fought battles, such as that at Talansam fought by the Baga, the last groups left Futa Jallon for the coast.

Another major movement was the one that brought powerful waves of Soso-Dyallonke to the coast. Driven from Futa Jallon, the Soso moved slowly towards the coast which was already occupied by the Nalu and Baga. But the big wave started in 1760 when the Soso, under the leadership of Souba Toumane, invaded the Baga and set up the chieftaincy of Toumania in the immediate hinterland of the Kaloum peninsula. They welcomed their Dyallonke relatives, who had also been driven out of the mountains by the Fulbe, and, by the end of the eighteenth century, dominated the coast between the Rio Pongo and Sierra Leone.

However, the peoples of the Tenda group, on the north-western spurs of the Futa Jallon mountains, resisted the Muslim Fulbe. So did the Koniagui and Bassari who had escaped domination by the invaders since the fifteenth century.

Other prime movers of this population movement into Guinea and Sierra Leone were the Northern Manden, who caused the migrations of the Toma, Guerze and Manon into the forest zone of Guinea, the Mende into Sierra Leone and the Quoja into Sierra Leone and Liberia. A distinction must be made here between movements connected with the already long-established migratory movement of the Manden southward towards the sea and movements which stemmed from the expansion of Islam.

With the advent of the Muslim revolution in Futa Jallon, the Manden joined with the Fulbe to convert or subjugate the Soso, Baga, Bullom and Temne. Thus they occupied the Mellacorie in the eighteenth century, organized Muslim Manden chieftaincies and were represented all along the coast from the Island of Matacong to the Saint Paul river. At the end of the eighteenth century, resistance to Islamization broke out among the Soso and the West Atlantic peoples when the *almamy* of Futa Jallon sought to impose his authority over the whole area. Nevertheless, the society of the Guinea and Sierra Leone rivers was not to escape the influence of Futa Jallon, nor the political and cultural influence of the Manden trader-*marabouts*.

Liberia to the River Bandama

The migrations that helped to establish the peoples of this sector in the seventeenth and eighteenth centuries were primarily a continuation of the north–south movements that took place in the fifteenth and sixteenth centuries. They were also due to the upheavals in the Akan world during the seventeenth and eighteenth centuries, and to the various attractions and disadvantages of the situation on the coast at that time. The results were migratory flows in various directions which, in the forest, were sometimes decidedly circular in nature.

The Mande and the We The Quoja-Karou invasion of the coasts of Sierra Leone and Liberia shows that the Manden thrust was still pressurizing the forest and coastal peoples in the eighteenth century. The Northern Manden had continued their advance to the south and south-east and reached the Bandama River. Their movement intensified that of the Southern Manden; the Dan continued to move south-eastward and south-westward while the Guro and Gagu were heading towards the Bandama river and beyond.

This Southern Manden thrust affected the We, in particular the We of Touleplu in Côte d'Ivoire, who reached the forest in the mid-seventeenth century and the River Cavally later.

The Magwe-Kru C. Behrens thinks that the Kru moved into Liberia along the coast from east to west during the sixteenth century. After splitting into various groups, they occupied what is now Grand-Bassa County in the middle of the seventeenth century. As regards the Kru settlement of Côte d'Ivoire, it seems that a west–east movement followed the north–south one. Thus the Kru of Grand-Béréby came to Côte d'Ivoire from Liberia following the fragmentation of the Guerre groups (the We) from the north.

This great migratory wave led large groups of the Magwe from the Cavally basin in the west to the Sassandra basin and beyond to the Bandama River. It supplied population for the settlement of the area between the Sassandra and Bandama rivers until the end of the eighteenth century.

Political mutations and socio-economic changes

The establishment of sea routes: late fifteenth to early seventeenth centuries

Once open to traffic and trade, between the late fifteenth century and the early seventeenth century the coastal area became a magnet to the coastal and sub-coastal peoples and the Sudanese traders from the interior. The establishment of sea routes had begun before the arrival of the Portuguese caravels when Manden expansion linked the Central Sudan to the Atlantic coast, from Senegambia to the Gold Coast.

Internal actors leading to the establishment of sea routes
In the fourteenth and fifteenth centuries, with its expansion westward, Mali had created the conditions for the commercial expansion of the Manden into the coastal area. The Gambia and Casamance, having become western provinces of Mali, exchanged their agricultural produce and craft products for iron and other metals from the interior. The trading towns of Kantor ran this trade which used the waterways, particularly the Gambia and Casamance rivers, whose mouths were linked by a busy coastal trade. A different trade flowed from the River Niger to the forest, where the Joola exchanged salt, copper, cotton goods and fish for kola nuts and, sometimes, palm oil. The Joola brought goods from the Niger bend to El Mina, as they are reported at Begho in the first half of the fifteenth century.

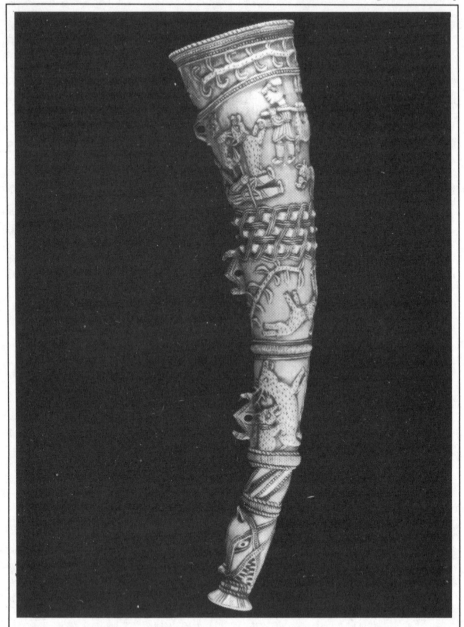

13.1 *Sixteenth-century carved ivory hunting-horn from Sherbro Island (Bullom), Sierra Leone. Height: 43 cm (© Luigi Pigorini Museum, Rome, photo: Rossini)*

The trading sphere of the Manden relied on a network of routes and market staging-posts with which the forest fringes were amply supplied and which the river valleys extended down to the coast.

External circumstances: the Portuguese explorations

The Portuguese were the first Europeans to explore the West African coast in the fifteenth century, once the development of the caravel had enabled them to round Cape Bojador in 1434. They landed on the island of Arguin in 1443 and established trading posts at various places along the coast, from Senegal to the Gold Coast, and explored the whole of the Gulf of Guinea. In search of gold and spices, they joined their emergent maritime empire to the Manden trading sphere, nurtured by the expansion of Mali.

Portuguese documents of the time provide lists of the goods which formed the cargo of returning caravels. They include rice, copal, civet, palm mats and sacks and carved ivory objects – mainly spoons, pedestal bowls and hunting-horns. Some of these items have been preserved and are to be found in the museums of three continents. The finest of them, which are the work of the Bullom of Sherbro Island, bear witness to the high artistic level reached by the coastal peoples before the arrival of the Europeans.

Throughout the sixteenth century, the Portuguese maintained maritime and commercial supremacy on the West African coast from Arguin to Angola. In Upper Guinea they travelled by river in search of the gold of the Sudan. In this area, which was then Mali's ocean gateway, they helped to improve the links between the Rivers Coast on the one hand and the upper Gambia, upper Senegal and upper Niger on the other.

In the sixteenth century, Joola inland trade routes led to coastal positions occupied by the Portuguese. The gold of the Sudan therefore reached Lisbon together with malaguetta pepper. In this way the European and Manden trading spheres became intertwined and the economic takeover of the Saharan traffic was under way.

European voyages and early trading

Portuguese supremacy, however, had to contend with French and English pirates operating on the Guinea coast from 1530 onwards. Later their difficulties were deepened by Dutch competition. Dutch ships began to ply to West Africa in the 1590s and a decade later the Netherlands was doing more trade with West Africa than most European nations put together. Dutch supremacy replaced Portuguese supremacy.

Nevertheless, by the end of the sixteenth century the Portuguese had completed the opening up of the Atlantic coast of West Africa to trade and inaugurated the strategy that was to prevail during the following centuries.

Early social formations and the 'Kingdom of the Sapes'

The West Atlantic civilization, which stretched from the Joola of Casamance to the Temne of Sierra Leone, was characterized by its adaptation to the ecological environment of the lowlands and stagnant waters. It consisted of swamp agriculture, the extraction of salt, paddy rice-growing and the use of waterways for transport and communications.

Organized into village societies without slaves or castes but with age-groups and work associations, the Joola had already reached the Iron Age when they came into contact with the Manden. They did not have any state structure but did have a unified civilization and culture. All authors accept that the caste system, patrilinear succession and state structures are institutions of foreign origin. Thus, under Manden influence brought about by the expansion of the Mali empire, the various peoples of the coast were organized into chieftaincies and principalities subject to the suzerainty of the *mandi-mansa*, the emperor of Mali.

In the fifteenth century the Portuguese observed the existence of these 'western provinces' but reported the presence to the south of the 'Kingdom of the Sapes'. Was this a large confederation comprising the Baga, Nalu, Landuma, Limba and Temne peoples, or was it a kingdom formed between Cape Verga and Cape Saint-Anne following the infiltration southward of the Tyapi-Landuma-Baga-Nalu under the leadership of Manden chiefs? Historians have divergent hypotheses on this question.

Kaabu: from emancipation to hegemony

Mali's expansion to the Atlantic along the Gambia basin had brought about the establishment, in the fifteenth century, of politico-military structures such as the little kingdoms of the Gambia, Casamance and Guinea-Bissau which formed the western marches of the Manden empire. Their rulers paid tribute to the *mansa* of Mali through his *farins* (governors). But by the sixteenth century it was the *farin* of Kaabu who was receiving the tribute from the Manden chiefs throughout the Gambia.

Lying between the middle Gambia, the Rio Grande and Futa Jallon, the Malian province of Kaabu controlled the trade of Kantor. In the sixteenth century Kaabu annexed the province of Sankola, south of the upper Casamance, and became a powerful province, although still a dependency of Mali. But the old Mali empire was weakening under attacks from Songhay, and most of its western provinces freed themselves from its sway, with the *farins* setting themselves up as independent kings; Kaabu did so in 1537.

After its emancipation, Kaabu unified all the countries between the Gambia, the upper Casamance and the upper Geba, and supplanted the *Mansa* of Mali in this region. It went on to extend its sway over the Kasanga, Balante, Joola and Beafada peoples. Its *farin* wielded authority over all southern Senegambia and controlled the trade of the region.

Atlantic trade and the peoples of the Southern Rivers

In Sierra Leone the Bullom, Temne and neighbouring groups played an active part in trade with the Portuguese. The Bullom, who traded sea salt for gold from Mali, now sold this gold to the Portuguese for cotton goods, copper bells

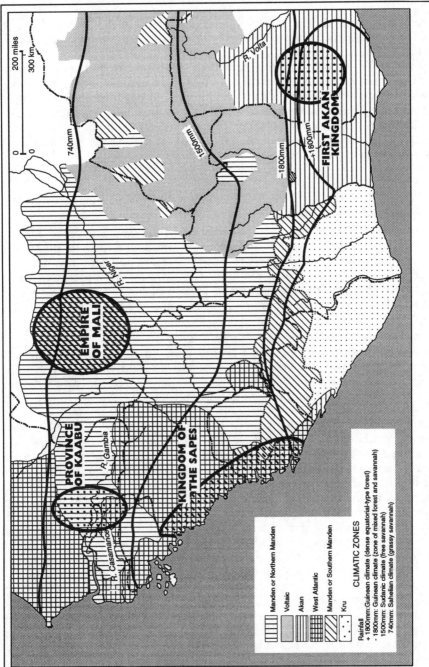

13.2 *The main states of West Africa, pre-sixteenth century (after C. Wondji)*

and various utensils. At the end of the sixteenth century the Temne, keen to profit from the maritime trade, reached the estuary of the Sierra Leone, thus splitting the Bullom into two.

By this time, not only had the Portuguese set up many trading settlements along the coasts of the Southern Rivers, but they had established numerous points of contact with the Manden in the middle and upper basins of the rivers. Links with the hinterland were thus intensified, as were north–south ones. The Cape-Verdeans traded directly with the region of the Sierra Leone rivers, selling their cotton on the way to the Bainuk and Kasanga, and handicraft articles from the coast reached as far as the Scarcies.

The coastal areas as a new West African trading front in the seventeenth and eighteenth centuries

By opening the West African coast to world trade, the great European explorations committed the countries of Guinea to an unprecedented process of historical development, with the expansion of trade, population movements from the interior to the coast and the appearance of new societies. These changes brought about the gradual marginalization of the Sudanese zone which, to survive, had to reactivate the routes leading to the forest and the sea.

The establishment and consolidation of European trade

The development of European trade on the West African coast was characterized by three features: the consolidation of this trade through the systematic organization of commercial exchanges, the increasing importance of the slave trade and the bitter competition among European nations.

In the seventeenth century, the Dutch perfected the organization of the world mercantilist system by creating chartered companies. The West India Company, established in 1621 and given a 24-year monopoly over trade with America and Africa, had a military and naval guarantee from the state and could pursue its commercial and colonial expansion in complete security. The Dutch redistributed in Europe the products that they imported from Asia, Africa and America, in particular a great quantity of gold and ivory, and thus made huge profits. They supplied slaves to the American colonies of the other European nations (Spain, Portugal, France and England) which, in 1641, acknowledged their trading monopoly over the whole of the Guinea coast.

However, after 1660, France and England embarked on a merciless struggle against the Dutch monopoly, equipping themselves with the same tools of power as their rival. The English created the Company of Royal Adventurers (1660) and later the Royal African Company (1664), while the French created the Compagnie française des Indes occidentales (1664) and later the Compagnie de Guinée (1685). Between 1640 and 1750, many forts and trading stations were built on the coasts of Africa but changed ownership continually according to the vicissitudes of war between the slave-trading nations.

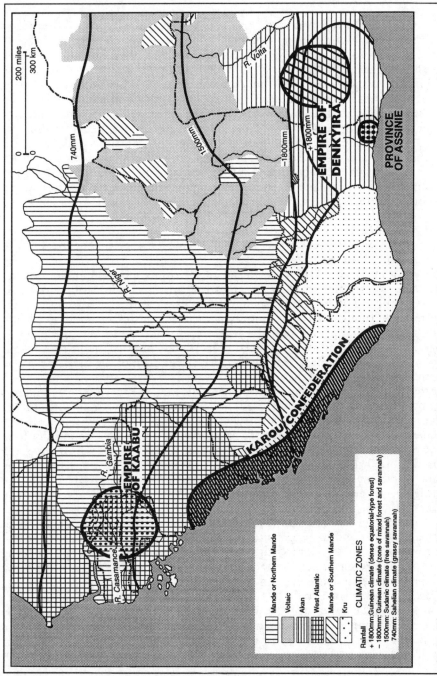

13.3   *The main states of West Africa in the seventeenth century (after C. Wondji)*

From the shelter of these forts and around the trading stations, the Europeans pursued the commercial exploitation of the Atlantic coastal area. From Gorée to Sherbro Island, in Sierra Leone, trade flourished but no French or English company could monopolize trade because of the many coastal islets and offshore islands where any ship that wanted to could anchor. This part of the coast was thus a happy hunting ground for slavers of all nations who were not associated with the big companies. The chartered companies did not bother with the Grain Coast or Côte d'Ivoire in the seventeenth and eighteenth centuries because malaguetta pepper was no longer prized on world markets, ivory was in decline and anchoring difficulties kept ships away from the coast. But by the beginning of the eighteenth century the growing demand for slaves in America was encouraging individual traders to take an interest in this sector.

Changes in the Sudan
In the Sudan, and particularly in the Manden world, the consequences of the Atlantic trade, dominated by the slave as merchandise, were various. At the socio-economic level, relations with the coast became more important and the slave trade was accompanied by the spread of firearms by Joola merchants. At the socio-cultural level, Islam having lost its sway with the fall of the great empires, the ruling class split into two rival factions. One, traditional and political, set itself up as a military aristocracy, while the other, made up of *marabouts* and merchants, advanced Islam and inspired politico-religious revolutions. Both sought to resolve the social crisis born of the break-up of the empires and the spread of the slave trade.

After the political fragmentation that followed the decline of the great empires, surrogate hegemonies tried to reconstruct the various parts of the hinterland. In the north and north-west the Grand Foul empire arose in the seventeenth century on the ruins of Songhay but later, in the second half of the eighteenth century, gave way to the empire of Kaarta. Along the Atlantic, the countries that had emerged from the dismemberment of Mali were unified by Kaabu in the seventeenth and eighteenth centuries, and then by Futa Jallon in the eighteenth and nineteenth centuries. Along the Niger, the recovery took place at the beginning of the eighteenth century under the aegis of the Bambara of Segu, under Biton Kulibali. But in the south, from the upper Niger to the Bandama and eastward into the Volta-Senufo area, the Joola increased their influence. In the eighteenth century they organized the empire of Kong to ensure movement along the trade routes from the middle Niger to the forest and the Gold Coast and they founded market towns.

Just as trans-Saharan trade had helped bring about Sudanese political hegemonies along the Sahel strip between the seventh and sixteenth centuries, so the intensification of European trade encouraged the emergence of political hegemonies on the coast and in the hinterland in the seventeenth and eighteenth centuries.

The sub-coastal hegemonies of the north-west: from Kaabu to Futa Jallon
In the seventeenth century Kaabu established itself as the great power in the Southern Rivers sector. Organized into twelve confederated Manden provinces, it was led by a supreme *mansa* supported by an aristocracy of soldier-officials and a standing cavalry corps. This kingdom, which had become an empire, controlled the trade of the Gambia valley and the Guinea rivers on which the European trading stations were situated.

In the second half of the eighteenth century the Fulbe Muslim confederation established itself, emerging out of the Muslim revolution that shook the Guinea-Sudan massif in about 1725-30. Situated at the confluence of the rivers that run down to the sea from the upper Niger area, Futa Jallon was to set itself up as a serious competitor to the Kaabu Manden and fight them until they collapsed in the nineteenth century.

The coastal hegemony of the Karou in Sierra Leone and Liberia
The history of the Karou has been written by O. Dapper. First there was the Quoja kingdom, around Cape Mount, which was conquered by the Karou and Folgia, peoples from the interior. The Karou leaders were essentially war-lords. Absolute monarchs, defenders of the kingdom, they succeeded one another from father to son. They put down revolts in the conquered provinces, repelled the attacks of neighbouring peoples and constantly defended the integrity of the empire. Yet they still remained allied to the Folgia and Manou of the interior, with whom they had relations of vassalage. A rising chain of vassalage led from the coast inland to the *Mandi-Mani* (the Lord of the Manou), the greatest suzerain in the whole region.

The function of Karou hegemony was to regulate trade between the coast and the interior. Their main economic base was trade with the Europeans, from which they made enormous profits as middlemen. The trading area that they dominated seems to have been indispensable to the operation of the mercantilist slave-trading system in the region in the seventeenth and eighteenth centuries.

European trade and the comprador *peoples of the coast*
The development of trade in the seventeenth and eighteenth centuries brought about the formation among the coastal peoples of merchant groups acting as middlemen between the European ships and the African societies of the interior. Such were the *mestizos* (half-castes) and Creoles of the rivers in Casamance, Guinea and Sierra Leone.

From the Portuguese lançados *to the* mestizos *and creoles of the rivers in Guinea and Sierra Leone*
Whether Afro-Portuguese descended from Portuguese settlers of the fifteenth and sixteenth centuries or Anglo-Africans descended from British traders in the seventeenth and eighteenth centuries, the mulatto groups made up a very special people whose influence on the historical development of the coast between the Gambia and Sierra Leone was decisive.

Lançados *and* Afro-Portuguese Many Portuguese expatriates populated the Southern Rivers and the Atlantic islands (especially Cape Verde) from the fifteenth century onwards. They included merchant adventurers and agents of the trading companies and were called *lançados*. Most of them were Portuguese, with a sprinkling of Greeks, Spaniards and even Indians. They recruited *grumetes* (African auxiliaries) and plied the valleys of the Senegal, the Gambia, the Casamance and the small rivers of Guinea. Many settled in the Cacheu and Geba sectors in what is now Guinea-Bissau.

The *lançados* soon laid the foundations of an Afro-Portuguese community: settled in villages and living close to black people, they took African wives or mistresses. But the flow of migrants slowed in the seventeenth century and the number of pure Portuguese fell below that of the mulattos. These *mestizos* became darker and darker until they could hardly be distinguished from pure Africans. By the end of the seventeenth century the Afro-Portuguese community thus comprised few whites and many blacks, but it was run by the *mestizos* who gave it its main socio-cultural features.

The *lançados* had produced a new socio-cultural group on the coasts of Africa. Speaking Portuguese, dressing in European style, living in houses with whitewashed walls, they nevertheless adopted such African customs as tattooing and ethnic markings. They practised a rather peculiar Catholicism in which the celebration of the Christian saints did not inhibit ancestor worship.

The *lançados* initially established ties of friendship with the peoples of the coast. Later, some of them became bound by kinship ties into the social, political and cultural life of the African peoples. Thus José Lopez de Moura, grandson of a Mane king of Sierra Leone, often took part in the political life of this sector. Others were simply Europeanized Africans.

This Afro-Portuguese group drew its strength from its function as a *comprador* class. Its members did no productive work but supplied goods for the European ships and carried on a seasonal trade related to the agricultural activities of the indigenous Africans. Some were even rich enough to do without the European ships. Among the great mulatto families, the Bibiana Vaz family became prominent in the Cacheu sector in the seventeenth century. José Lopez de Moura was the richest man in Sierra Leone in the first half of the eighteenth century.

There were many disagreements between these wealthy mulatto merchants, supporters of unrestricted trade, and the trading companies anxious to preserve their monopoly. The Afro-Portuguese merchants fiercely defended their freedom to trade along the coast. Thus, when the Royal African Company attempted to break the alliance between the African rulers and the mulattos and put an end to the latter's role as middlemen, there was a sharp reaction. Led by Lopez de Moura, the mulattos destroyed the English company's factory and it was never able to resume its activities in Sierra Leone.

From English merchant adventurers to the Anglo-Africans in Sierra Leone
Another mulatto group was the Anglo-Africans of Sierra Leone. By the end of

the eighteenth century they formed a group of nearly 12,000 people, among whom the Tuckers, Rogers, Corkers and Clevelands were the leading families. The Tuckers, Rogers and Caulkers (later Corkers) came from England in the seventeenth century and were initially involved in the trade of the English companies. They married African wives and penetrated indigenous society, where they were associated with the ruling class. As with the Afro-Portuguese, a cultural hybrid social group came into being in which a man such as James Cleveland, whose mother was a Kisi woman, could occupy a prominent position in the secret society of the Poro.

Thus, in the seventeenth and eighteenth centuries the Afro-Portuguese and the Anglo-Africans constituted a social group with specific economic functions, and provided a cultural milieu in which Europeans and Africans came together. But, conscious of their interests, they exploited the Africans from whom they extracted maximum profits and, although they rebelled against the rigid monopoly of the trading companies, they were none the less agents in the service of European mercantile capitalism.

Trade and peoples from the Grain Coast to the Tooth Coast
From Cape Mesurado to Cape Lahou, the development of European trade in the seventeenth and eighteenth centuries did not give rise to any dynamic merchant groups among the Kru peoples. Although poorly linked to the Sudanese hinterland, this coastal sector nevertheless boasted many villages built at the mouths of rivers and abounded in a great variety of products. The English and Dutch ships took on supplies of malaguetta pepper at the River Sestos, Cape Palmas and Cavally and slaves at Bassa, Drewin and Saint Andrew: ivory they bought everywhere.

Conclusion

Despite the difficulties inherent in drawing up an historical synthesis, it can be seen that between 1500 and 1800 the peoples and countries of this region broadly experienced the same development. From relative isolation they were gradually integrated into the circuits of a world market built up by the Europeans' Atlantic voyages since the great explorations. This integration was accompanied by population movements from the interior to the coast and by sharp social and political changes wherever the peoples tried to take advantage of the opportunities European trade offered them.

The states and cultures of the Lower Guinea coast

For the peoples of the Lower Guinea coast living in the area between Côte d'Ivoire and modern Benin, or between the Bandama and the Mono rivers, the period between 1500 and 1800 was probably one of the most revolutionary periods in their history. It witnessed, first and foremost, the completion of the migrations of these peoples and the formation of most of the ethno-linguistic groups that exist today. Second, it saw the intensification of the trading and cultural links between these peoples and those of western Sudan, the Sahara and the Maghrib and the new possibilities of links across the Atlantic – first with Europe and then with the Americas. Third, it saw the gradual centralization of states and the evolution of larger political entities. Finally, the period was one of social and cultural transformation.

Migrations and the formation of new ethno-linguistic groups

In 1500, most of the peoples were still living in their various places of origin and only a few of them had penetrated into some of the areas in which they live today. Their migratory movement occurred between 1500 and 1800, particularly in the seventeenth century and the early decades of the eighteenth. For economic, social and above all political reasons, the Akan, Ga-Adangbe and Ewe peoples began to scatter in small clan and lineage groups.

In the sixteenth century the Akan migrated first north and east into the present Kumasi, Mampong and Akyem areas, and then south and south-west into the Wassa, Igwira, Sanwi and Assini areas. In the seventeenth century, other Akan moved in various matrilineal clan groups north and north-west, and also south-west into Wassa and Sefwi and the Lagoon areas of Côte d'Ivoire. Between 1680 and 1730 there was a particularly large migration of Akan into the Nzima, Aowin, Sefwi, Ahafo and northern Bono areas and the Anyi and Baule areas of Côte d'Ivoire. By the mid-eighteenth century the Akan flow seems to have dried up.

The Ga continued their dispersion towards the coast, attracted by the presence of Europeans and the consequent economic opportunities that opened up. The Ga-Mashi, the Nungua and the Tema were the first to move in the sixteenth

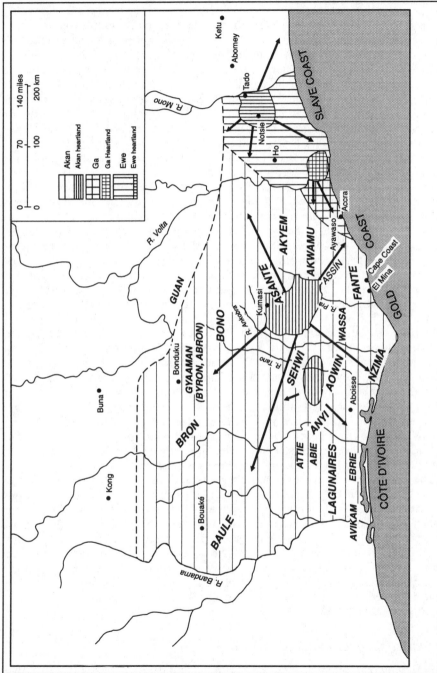

14.1 *The Akan, Ga and Ewe peoples (after A. A. Boahen)*

century, followed in the seventeenth by the Osu and Teshi peoples. Their kinspeople, the Adangbe, also began to spread out southwards and northwards into the Accra plain during the sixteenth and seventeenth centuries.

The most dramatic migrations, however, were those involving the Ewe. In the late sixteenth or early seventeenth century, to escape the tyrannical rule of their king, Agokoli, the Ewe left Notsie in two main groups, the southern Ewe and the northern or interior Ewe. The southern group moved towards the coast while the northern groups occupied the central and northern part of what is now the southern Volta Region. Sub-groups soon moved off to found other settlements, and this process of fission and diffusion went on throughout the seventeenth and eighteenth centuries.

These peoples did not only disperse and migrate; they also underwent ethno-linguistic changes. The Ewe and Ga-Adangbe, who moved into very sparsely populated areas, were able to maintain their ethnic and linguistic purity. Many of the Akan, however, migrated into areas quite densely populated by peoples speaking different languages. The mixture of these peoples and the incoming Akan gave rise to, among others, the Mbalo, Alladian, Ebrie, Eotile, Avikam, collectively known as the Lagunaires. Similarly, it was the mixture of the later Akan migrants and some of the pre-existing peoples that gave birth to the Anyi, Baule and Sefwi. The Akan therefore became divided into the two broad groups of today, the Eastern Akan and the Western Akan. Each of these groups became further divided: the Eastern Akan, divided into the Asante, Akuapem, Akyem, Akwamu, Bron, Wassa, Kwahu, Fante, Assin, Denkyira and Gomua, all speak the same language, Twi, while the Western Akan, divided into the Anyi, Baule, Nzima, Ahanta, Sanwi, Aowin and Sefwi speak mutually intelligible Akan dialects.

In the sixteenth century, the socio-political institutions of these groups in their new homes showed similarities as well as differences. The Ga-Adangbe and the Ewe lived in scattered independent settlements, in patrilineage and clan groups. In each group, each lineage had its own senior god whose priests were its leaders. However, by the end of the fifteenth century the Ga-Mashi had provided themselves with a king, who kept his court at Ayawaso.

The Akan lived in towns ruled by kings and queens and villages ruled by chiefs. Each town or village was made up of families belonging to the eight matrilineal clans into which they were all divided. Each family had an *abusuapanin* (head), and so did each clan. It appears that each family or clan had its own god or gods, as did each village, and that their priests wielded consider-able power. In other words, society had already become divided into three broad classes: a ruling aristocracy consisting of priests and kings, ordinary subjects and relatively small numbers of domestic slaves. This social set-up was greatly altered by the political and economic developments of the period between 1500 and 1800.

Economic changes in Lower Guinea

Far-reaching economic changes, both internal and external, took place in Lower

Guinea during this period. Internally, already-established econ⟋ continued and expanded. These included gathering, farming, li⟋ hunting, fishing, salt-making and gold-mining. The main item ⟋ gathered was kola nuts in the forest areas of the Gold Coast. These nuts formed the mainstay of trade between the Akan and northern and western Sudan.

The main crops were plantain, bananas, yams and rice. In the sixteenth and seventeenth centuries new crops introduced from Asia and the Americas by Europeans were added to these traditional ones, including maize, cassava, various types of yam, tomatoes, onions, aubergines, avocado pears, sweet potatoes, citrus fruits and groundnuts. The rapid adoption of these crops diversified the agricultural economy of the Guinea coast and thereby accelerated population growth.

Livestock-raising involved poultry, sheep, goats and pigs. Fishing was the main economic activity of the Ewe, Ga and other coastal peoples. Hunting was a universal pursuit.

Salt-making and gold-mining became increasingly important between 1500 and 1800. Nearly all salt was produced by the coastal inhabitants while gold-mining was the exclusive preserve of the inland forest peoples, especially the Akan. It was obtained either by panning the alluvial soils or by deep-mining (*nkoron*). Gold-mining was rigidly controlled by the state and formed the main source of income of the rulers. It reached its peak in the late seventeenth century and remained the exclusive monopoly of the Akan, despite European – particularly Dutch – efforts to participate in it directly.

Alongside these activities, trade developed, with slaves playing a growing role in it. A distinction needs to be made between internal and external trade. The Ewe, the Ga and the Akan had long been trading among themselves. Fish and salt produced by the Ewe, the Ga and the Fante and Adangbe pottery were exchanged for gold, chewing sticks (*tweapea*), ivory and iron and other metal goods produced by the Akan of the interior. Two branches of external trade developed: the older one with the savannah and western Sudan, and the other across the Atlantic with Europe and the Americas. The Ga, the Ewe and the Akan had already established trading links with the Guan and the Gur to the north, with the Hausa of northern Nigeria to the north-east and with the Manden of the Niger bend to the north-west in gold, kola nuts, textiles, slaves and salt. With the rise and expansion of Songhay in the fifteenth and sixteenth centuries, trade between the Akan and the Mande prospered and it was to control this trade effectively that the Joola established a number of trading posts or staging posts such as Bobo-Dioulasso, Kong, Bonduku, Buna and Begho between the Niger bend and the gold-producing countries in the south. The towns of Jenne and Begho, the main entrepôts of the trade to the north-west, became extremely wealthy during the sixteenth century, as is evident from both written and archaeological sources. In the north-western markets, the Akan exchanged mainly gold, kola nuts and, later, European imports for cloth, blankets, Turkish carpets, striped and blue silks, leather goods, ironware, brassware and salt.

The overthrow of Songhay in the late sixteenth century and the subsequent

.nsecurity were once thought to have destroyed trade along the north-west routes. But it has now been convincingly shown that trade did not decline and even increased in volume during the eighteenth century.

Trade between the Akan and Hausaland and Borno also continued. It was already of some importance by the beginning of the sixteenth century, as evidenced by the eye-witness account of Leo Africanus, who visited Songhay and Hausaland at that time. It grew in intensity in the seventeenth and eighteenth centuries with the growth of the Mole-Dagbane states of Mamprusi, Dagomba, Nanumba and Mossi and of the Hausa states. Towns such as Kano and Katsina, in Hausaland, and above all Salaga to the north of the Gold Coast were extremely prosperous.

The export of gold by the Akan to Hausaland seems to have ceased in the eighteenth century, probably because of strong European competition, but Akan kola continued to be the mainstay of trade with the north-east. Kola nuts were re-exported from Hausaland and Borno into the Sahara and to the Barbary states.

A far more important trading relationship, however, was also developing elsewhere – the trans-Atlantic trade between the Lower Guinea coast and Europe and the Americas. It started when the Portuguese dropped anchor off the coast of modern Ghana in 1471. They were followed in the sixteenth century by the French, the English and the Dutch and in the eighteenth by the Danes. Direct trade with the West Indies began in 1518 when the first cargo of slaves was sent there in a Spanish ship. Trade with the North American mainland began in 1619 when a Dutch frigate discharged the first cargo of West African slaves at Jamestown in the state of Virginia. Thus, by the midddle of the seventeenth century, the triangular trade linking the Guinea coast, Europe and the Americas was fully established.

The commodities sold to the Europeans varied from region to region and century to century. Until the late seventeenth century the Akan between the Bandama and the Ankobra rivers sold mainly ivory to the Europeans, while the Akan and the Ga living between the Ankobra and the Volta sold mostly gold. Throughout the sixteenth century there seems to have been little trade between the Ewe and the Europeans in the area between the Volta and the Mono rivers. It was not until the mid-seventeenth century that the Dutch and the Danes embarked on trade there, and the main commodity was slaves. It was as a result of this specialization that European traders divided the Lower Guinea coast into the Ivory Coast, the Gold Coast and the Slave Coast.

Until the end of the seventeenth century, the gold trade was by far the most important. It impelled every European nation to gain a footing on this coast, with the result that a huge number of forts and castles was built along the coast between the Ankobra and the Volta rivers.

Between 1650 and 1800, however, the export trade between the Ga and the Eastern Akan and Europe underwent a revolutionary change. Starting in the mid-seventeenth century, the Ga and the Akan exported slaves in such increasing numbers that by 1710 the trade in slaves exceeded that in gold. The number of slaves exported from the Gold Coast continued to grow throughout the first half

of the eighteenth century. According to K. Y. Daaku,
being exported annually by the late seventeenth century,
6,000–7,000 in the eighteenth century. According to P.
474,000 slaves was exported from the Gold Coast in the eig.
it is widely believed that Curtin underestimated the number
from West Africa by 7.3–18.4 per cent. The Ewe areas also
numbers of slaves, especially after 1730 when the Akwamu invadec   .n.

Why did the trade in slaves supersede the trade in gold on the   Coast?
There are three main answers to this question. The first is the great increase in
the demand for slaves following the introduction of sugar-cane plantations in
the West Indies and on the American mainland from the 1640s onwards. The
second is the enormous rise in the number of war-captives. The third reason is
that after the rise of the Denkyira, Akwamu and Asante empires, the vassal
states paid their tribute in the form of slave deliveries. It should be added that
the supply of slaves to the Europeans on the Gold Coast was the exclusive
preserve of the Africans themselves.

Imports into Lower Guinea also underwent revolutionary changes in both
volume and quality. In the late fifteenth century and throughout the sixteenth
centuries, the principal imports were articles of clothing mostly manufactured
not in Europe but in the Barbary states, Benin and Côte d'Ivoire. Fabrics from
Benin and Quaqua cloths from Côte d'Ivoire were very popular and they were
certainly still being imported in the seventeenth century, but by then the list of
imports had greatly lengthened. Pieter de Marees, writing in the early
seventeenth century, gives a detailed list of the goods brought by the Dutch
and concludes that the most sought-after wares were linen cloth, brass and
copper objects, basins, pots, knives and corals.

This list does not mention firearms, since the import of guns and gunpowder
only began in earnest in the 1640s, when the English and the interlopers started
selling arms on the coast. In 1660 the Dutch lifted their firearms export ban and
started exporting them in large quantities. The volume of firearms exports
continued to rise throughout the eighteenth century. They remained the item
most in demand on the Gold Coast and ended up becoming the mainstay of
English trade with West Africa.

The effects of economic developments

One of the first effects of the economic changes was the appearance of a complex network of major and minor trade routes. These first linked the peoples of
the area to one another, then linked them to the Mole-Dagbane and Hausa to
the north-east, the Manden to the north-west and the Barbary states and the
Muslim world across the Sahara. Finally the network spread across the Atlantic,
first to Europe and then to the Americas. At the centre of this network lay the
town of Kumasi.

A number of urban centres developed along these routes. These included
Kong, Bobo-Dioulasso, Buna, Begho and Bonduku to the north-west, Salaga,

...nd Sansanne-Mango in the north-east and Tiassalé, Sakasso, Yakasso, ...njabo, Kumasi, Kete-Krachi and Akwamufie to the south. These centres served as entrepôts, market centres and termini. Furthermore, the European presence accelerated the growth of the towns on the coast at the expense of the former capital towns immediately inland.

The effect of the new network established with Europe was the integration of the Lower Guinea coast into the larger economic area formed by the countries of western Europe and America on the one hand and the Manden-Hausa-Muslim world on the other. However, this latter link gradually weakened while the one with Europe and the Americas grew ever stronger.

The effect of this integration was the destruction or atrophy of economic and industrial development in Lower Guinea. The slave trade – the most inhuman of all trades – steadily replaced trade in natural products, depriving the region of needed manpower as well as of many of its artisans and artists. In addition, Europe exported cheap mass consumer goods, thereby killing most existing industries or seriously retarding their growth. In short, between 1500 and 1800 there was economic growth in Lower Guinea but without economic development. Moreover, since Europe controlled both imports and exports, it kept most of the profits. Herein lie the roots of the process of underdevelopment, aggravated in the nineteenth century by the abolition of the slave trade and the establishment of colonialism in Africa.

Political change on the Lower Guinea coast

Political change between 1500 and 1800 was even more radical than economic change. By 1500 the process of state formation had already begun and a number of states had emerged both on the coast and in the savannah regions. The Portuguese arrived to find the coastal states of Ahanta, Shama, Aguafo, Fetu, Asebu, Agona and Accra, and there were also the Mole-Dagbane states and the Akan state of Bono in the savannah belt. The process continued to gather momentum when the first Akan kingdom, Bono, emerged in the second half of the fifteenth century, and reached its peak through the lucrative trade between the Manden and the Akan.

During the sixteenth century, the Ga-Mashi, the Nungua and the Tema were joined on the Accra plain by the Labadi and the Osu, all of whom founded numerous settlements. Until the fourteenth century the Ga had priests as chiefs, but by the end of the following century secular kingship had evolved, probably borrowed from their Akan and Adangbe neighbours. At the beginning of the seventeenth century some Ga moved to the coast, attracted by the European presence, and they were followed by the La and the Osu. All the coastal towns that they founded recognized the suzerainty of the Ga *mantse* (king) and Ayawaso remained the kingdom's capital until 1680, when it was moved to the coast.

What seems to have happened among the Akan in the sixteenth century is the formation in the Pra-Ofin basin of a number of small communities and city-states or chiefdoms bound together not by allegiance to a common sovereign but by kinship, agnatic and clan ties. However, it appears from the oral traditions of Adansi that, in about 1550, there was a move towards centralization which led to the formation of the Adansi confederation of states and also precipitated the migration of some Akan peoples northwards and southwards where they founded chiefdoms, city-states and principalities.

This process of state formation seems to have accelerated between 1580 and 1630, as is demonstrated by a map of the states of the southern Gold Coast between the Tano and Volta rivers drawn by a Dutch cartographer in 1629. This map describes 38 states and kingdoms. All except Great Incassa and Incassa Igwira have been identified and still exist in the same areas.

The states founded by the Ga and the Akan who had migrated were probably small but were all similarly structured, with a single leader, chief or king with his queen. In the Adansi confederation, power rotated among the royal families of the various states. In the single states, the king was selected from the first family or clan to arrive in the area. He was advised by a council composed of family and clan heads. Each state had its own gods, for example rivers, lakes or rocks, and their priests wielded considerable influence in society.

Between 1630 and about 1670, two main political developments took place in the Ga and Adangbe areas: the consolidation of the states shown on the 1629 map and the emergence of new states. Oral sources show that kingdoms like Akwamu, Denkyira, Accra or Ga, Fante, Wassa and Adom greatly expanded their frontiers, largely through peaceful means. The Ga kingdom reached its greatest extent and the peak of its power under the king Okai Akwei (*c.* 1640–77).

During this period the Aduana state of Akwamu also became a strong kingdom while Denkyira broke away from the Adansi Confederation after a series of wars and firmly established itself at the confluence of the Ofin and the Pra. On the coast the Fante also extended their territory inland and European records frequently refer to wars between the Fante and the Etsi to the north.

The Denkyira–Adansi wars (1650–70) and the Bono wars had accelerated migration southwards and westwards into the forest, where older peoples such as the Adisi, the Ewotre, the Agwa, the Kompa and the Lagunaires lived. These new groups founded not only Aowin, near present-day Wassa Amanfi, but also the three Sefwi states in the south and states such as Assini, Abripiquem and Ankobra and a host of coastal towns. Situated in one of the richest gold-bearing areas and on the main trade route linking the northern markets with the coast, by the 1670s Aowin had grown into a rich and powerful kingdom.

The Denkyira-Adansi migrants who moved northwards founded the Oyoko states of Kumasi, Kokofu, Dwaben, Nsuta and, later, Bekwai and the Bretuo states of Mampong and Afigyaase, all within a 50-kilometre radius of Kumasi. Further north, others founded the Aduana state of Gyaaman or Abron.

The new states seem to have been organized on the same basis as the old ones. The Sefwi and Aowin states, for example, superimposed the sophisticated Akan clan system and the institutions of matrilineally elected kingship on the existing socio-political structure based on *asago* (warriors) grouped around living-quarters.

However, in the last 30 years of the seventeenth century a political revolution took place marked not by the emergence of new states but by the increasing centralization of existing ones. Aowin and Denkyira seem to have led the way in this shift. Aowin conquered the Sefwi states to the north and west and expanded far west to embrace such towns as Keteso, Yawu, Brako and Sikasso in what is now Côte d'Ivoire.

In the 1670s and 1680s the Agona rulers of Denkyira conquered all the Adansi states together with the pre-Asante states near Kumasi to the north and Assin and Twifo to the south. Between 1686 and 1690, Denkyira defeated Aowin, the Sefwi and Wassa states to the south-west and the coastal kingdoms of Adom and Fetu. By 1690, Denkyira dominated the south-western Gold Coast and parts of Côte d'Ivoire.

In the south-eastern regions, the Akwamu leaders were also embarking on expansionist wars. They first attacked the Ga kingdom, which they conquered in 1681. They then conquered the coastal kingdom of Agona to the west in 1689. In their final campaigns (1702–10), they conquered the Adangbe states to the east and Kwahu to the north and, crossing the Volta, subdued the Ewe states of Peki, Ho and Kpandu.

The Denkyira and Akwamu evolved similar machinery to administer their empires. Each was divided into two areas, the metropolitan area and the provincial area. The metropolitan area was centred on the capital, the seat of the *omanhene* (king), who reigned over the whole empire. Under him there was a series of officials or kings who performed certain functions at court. For politico-military purposes, each state was divided into wings, three in Denkyira and five in Akwamu. Each wing was headed by the king of a town or state in the metropolitan area or in the capital itself. He exercised political control over this wing in peacetime and became its *osafohene* (war-leader) in wartime. All the wing chiefs were members of the council that advised the *omanhene*. The provincial area consisted of all the conquered states now part of the empire. Each continued to be ruled by its own king but was placed directly under the control of the *omanhene* or a wing chief. Each state was expected to pay annual tribute and to fight in battle under its wing chief.

Many historians have seen the political history of the Gold Coast in the eighteenth century almost exclusively in terms of the rise of the Asante empire, but the course of political events was much more complex. First, other states came into being outside the Asante empire. Second, there was the revival, albeit short-lived, of Aowin and the overthrow of Denkyira and Akwamu by Akyem and Asante respectively. Third, there was the expansion of the Fante kingdom to its widest extent and, finally, the brilliant rise of the Asante empire.

The wholly new states that came into being in the eighteenth century were Nzima, the Aowin or Anyi states of Sanwi, Ndenye, Diabe, Moronou and Bettie and many Baule principalities. After being defeated by the Denkyira in the 1680s, the Aowin, or Anyi, left Anwianwia and, crossing the River Tano, recreated their kingdom around Enchi. They were still consolidating when in about 1715 the Asante attacked. Some then migrated westward where they founded the kingdom of Sanwi. Having established their capital at Krinjabo they quickly seized Assini, thus securing control of trade between the hinterland and the Aby lagoon.

North of Sanwi emerged the other Anyi states, Ndenye and Diabe, founded by the group of refugees from Anwianwia that moved north-westward. Until about 1715, the Anyi of Ndenye owed allegiance to Aowin, but a section of them refused to accept this and moved away to found the kingdom of Bettie. Some Anyi, the Monfwe, crossed the River Comoe to establish the kingdom of Moronou.

North-west of the Anyi, between the Comoe and Bandama rivers, there also arose, in the first half of the eighteenth century, a host of Baule principalities or chiefdoms. The oral traditions of the founders show that they arrived from the Gold Coast in two separate waves. The first brought the Alanguira Baule in about 1700. They had come from Denkyira after its defeat by the Asante, and settled in the area of the present-day canton of Agba. From there some moved west to live among the Guro and the Koro.

The second, much larger wave, the Assabu, came from Kumasi following a disputed succession that broke out after the death of Osei Tutu in 1717. According to their oral tradition, they were led by their queen Abla Poku, who sacrificed her son to the spirit of the River Comoe before they could cross it, whence their name *Baule* (the infant is dead). The group divided, but the bulk, still led by Abla Poku, crossed the Bandama and went and settled near Bouaké. Akwa Boni, who succeed Abla Poku, was able to impose his authority over the Baule, the Malinke and the Manden, who were occupying the Warebo region. After his death, however, the kingdom broke up into independent chiefdoms. Both waves of invaders soon mixed with the Guro, the Malinke, the Senufo and the Goli to form the modern Baule people.

The Nzima kingdom, which also emerged at this time, was the creation of three brothers who amalgamated under their rule the three existing states of Jomoro, Abripiquem and Ankobra through the fortune that they had acquired from trading with the Europeans. Known in the European records as Apollonia, this new state dominated the south-western corner of the Gold Coast throughout the eighteenth century.

Meanwhile, some of the older states, such as Bron, Sefwi-Wiawso, Aowin and Fante were extending their power and influence. Aowin, for example, appears to have regained its independence from Denkyira in the 1690s. Greatly strengthened by refugees fleeing the Asante–Denkyira wars, it came to dominate the Sefwi states and embarked on the conquest of the gold- and ivory-producing areas to the north. Aowin became so powerful that its warriors invaded Asante in 1718–19, sacked the capital, Kumasi, and returned home with booty and captives, including some members of the Asante royal family.

Also at the beginning of the eighteenth century, the state of Bron considerably enlarged its territory through conquest. The new Bron state was unique, being made up of Akan, Kulango, Nafana and Manden elements. The Akan invaders, who dominated the state politically, retained their clans, their matrilineal system of inheritance, their judicial system and aspects of their traditional religion. But they left untouched Kulango and Nafana social structures and political organization at the rural and village level. Finally, some adopted Islam, introduced by the Manden–Jula, who also greatly influenced the economic system of the kingdom.

It was also between 1700 and 1710 that the Akwamu extended their territorial empire across the River Volta. Partly in response to this Akwamu expansion and later that of Asante and Akyem, the Fante conquered their neighbouring coastal states, thereby gaining control of the coast from the mouth of the Pra to the Ga kingdom.

The political changes that occurred in the central forest regions between the Comoe and Volta rivers were even more dramatic. First there was the fall of the Denkyira empire in a series of wars between 1699 and 1701 waged by the young Asante confederation of states. This defeat was followed by the conquest of all Denkyira's former vassal states: the Sefwi states, Twifo and Wassa, then Aowin, Nzima, the Anyi state of Ndenye, Wenchi and Bono, and finally the Bron state and Gonja. By 1730 the whole of the area between the Comoe and Volta rivers was under Asante control.

Then there was the defeat of Akwamu by Akyem Abuakwa and its allies, the Ga, Kotoku and Agona. The Akwamu rulers were driven out of their lands across the Volta where they founded their present capital, Akwamufie. Thus, by 1733, the whole area between the Comoe and Volta rivers was partitioned among the Asante, the Akyem and the Fante.

The process of centralization was completed between 1731 and 1750 when the Asante conquered not only Akyem Kotoku and Akyem Abuakwa and the Ga state to the south, but also eastern Gonja and the Dagomba state to the north of the Volta river and the Krakye and Bassa states to the north-east. The Fante alone maintained their sovereign existence throughout the eighteenth century, partly through their own diplomatic skills and partly through the support of the British who wanted to stop the Asante gaining control over the whole coast.

The structure and government of the Asante empire were similar to those of the Akwamu and Denkyira empires. It was divided into two parts: metro-politan Asante and provincial Asante. Metropolitan Asante consisted of all the former states within a 50-kilometre radius of Kumasi. All recognized the *ohene* of the Kumasi state as their *asantehene* (paramount king). They were represented by their own king on the Asanteman Council, the governing body of the confederation and the entire empire. For politico-military reasons, metro-politan Asante was divided, like Akwamu, into five wings.

Provincial or Greater Asante consisted of all the states conquered and reduced to vassal status. These states had no direct representative on the Asanteman Council nor any direct access to the *asantehene*. Instead each state served the *asantehene* through an intermediary, who was one of the kings or one of the member states of the confederation or one of the wing chiefs of the Kumasi state. This system of provincial administration (*adamfo*) was liberal and the states were largely left alone so long as they paid their annual tribute and participated in any wars being fought by the Asante.

Thus a political revolution had taken place in the forest and coastal regions of Lower Guinea between 1670 and 1750. From the 38 states of the 1629 map had emerged the three great empires of Aowin, Denkyira and Akwamu, which by 1750 had merged into the single empire of Asante.

If these empires were able to come into being, it is because they had the means to buy arms and ammunition and also the necessary motivation to expand. Aowin, Denkyira, Akwamu and Asante were the main gold-producing states and they acted as commercial middlemen between the savannah and the coastal regions. By expanding northwards and southwards these states would gain control of the major trade routes. In addition, the presence of the Europeans on the coast provided a strong motivation, since trade with the Europeans had become much more lucrative than trade with the savannah. It is thus in no way surprising that so many should have tried to fight their way to the coast.

The states that made up metropolitan Asante also had a political motivation. They were eager to rid themselves of their tyrannical Denkyira conquerors and were only waiting for the right chiefs to lead them. They found them in Osei Tutu and Opoku Ware, the founders of the Asante empire.

A further reason for the rise of these empires is that, when they embarked on their expansion, they were free from interference in their internal affairs. The Akyem states, though not lacking either the means or the motivation, were unable to develop into great empires because they did not have that freedom. Sandwiched between expanding Denkyira, and, later, Asante and Akwamu, they were constantly on the defensive. Similarly, the coastal states were hampered by constant interference by rival European nations. The inland states of Aowin, Denkyira, Akwamu and Asante were at the outset free from such interference and could sufficiently consolidate their power before coming into contact with the Europeans.

There are two other factors which should be taken into account in explaining the rise of these empires: the adoption of a new technology and the high quality of their leadership. The rulers of these states had the means to buy weapons and ammunition from the Europeans, and that gave them a decisive edge over those who did not have them. The old way of fighting was replaced by the organization of the army into fighting units and this new military formation was superimposed on the traditional political structure. The rulers' ability to adapt to change thus became of vital importance.

At this stage little is known about the Aowin kings, but both oral and European documentary sources acclaim the courage and ability of the rulers of Denkyira, Akwamu and Asante. The Denkyira kings included Werempe Ampem, Boadu Akafu Brempon and the most illustrious, Boa Amponsem; Akwamu's included Ansa Sasraku, Basua and Akwono and Asante's Osei Tutu and Opoku Ware. Many historians believe that these empires were products of the slave trade. What may be true of other parts of West Africa is not for this area. On the coast of Ghana the slave trade only became significant economically from 1700–10, while expansionist activities had begun in the 1670s and 1680s. On the Gold Coast the slave trade was the

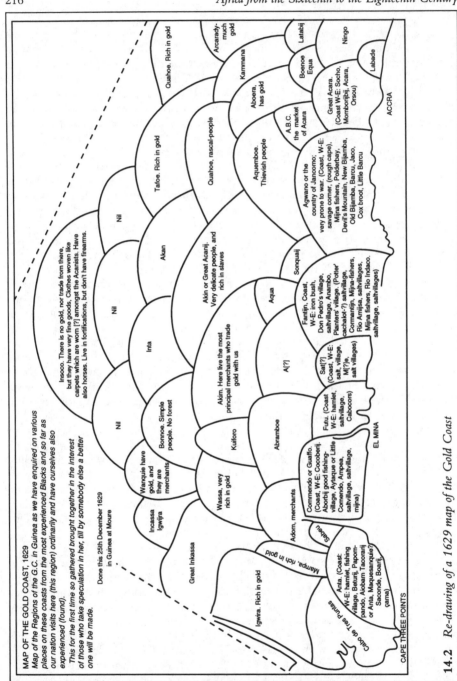

14.2   *Re-drawing of a 1629 map of the Gold Coast*

consequence, not the cause, of the state-building process.

In the Akan areas west of the River Tano and the Ewe areas east of the River Volta, ancestral home of the Lagunaires, the Anyi and the Baule, no such dramatic political change took place at this time. In 1800 they were organized much as they had been 150 years earlier, with small kingdoms or chiefdoms, each made up of loosely united family groups from clans of common ancestry.

In 1800, Ewe territory was still split into many independent territorial units or *dukowo* of varying sizes. Each *dukowo* was ruled by a *fia* (king) elected patri-lineally from one or two lineages of the founding families and assisted by a Council of Elders.

There are several reasons why the Western Akan of the Tano-Bandama basin and the Ewe of the Volta-Mono basin did not undergo political change. First, migrations into the two areas continued throughout the seventeenth and eighteenth centuries. Consequently, by 1800, the Ewe and Western Akan were not sufficiently settled to embark on wars of expansion. Second, as these migrants were themselves escaping the centralizing activities and tyrannical behaviour of their former rulers, they had no desire to recreate the same socio-political structures in their new homes. Third, in the case of the Ewe, the economic motivation for state-building was lacking. Without gold, ivory or kola nuts, the Ewe could not participate in the lucrative north–south Atlantic trade. During the seventeenth and eighteenth centuries the region's main export was slaves, an activity which jeopardized peace and stability and thus did not stimulate political expansion.

The Western Akan did have gold, ivory and kola nuts, but because they were not in control of the trade routes to the north, they did not really have the means to embark on a large-scale expansionist venture.

For the Western Akan, as for the Ewe, there was also an ecological con-sideration in the shape of the lagoons which formed a barrier between the coast and the hinterland and discouraged commercial exchanges.

Finally, their more powerful northern neighbours' constant interference kept them constantly on the defensive and concerned above all with maintaining their own independence.

Social and cultural changes in Lower Guinea

The most obvious socio-cultural change in Lower Guinea between 1500 and 1800 was demographic. With the introduction of so many food crops from the New World and Asia, the population greatly increased. During the eighteenth century, however, largely as a result of the slave trade, the population remained stagnant or even decreased.

Second, society had become more sophisticated. In 1500 it had been com-posed of a ruling aristocracy consisting of a religious élite and a political élite, ordinary subjects and domestic slaves. By 1800, the political élite had super-seded the religious, except among the Ga-Adangbe and the Ewe. The tremendous increase in economic activities and the wars of expansion had led to an increase in the number of domestic slaves. By 1800 most slaves had become integrated into the society in which they lived and it had become a sacred law, especially among the Akan, not to divulge their origins.

Moreover, as a result of trading activities and the European presence, three new classes unknown to traditional society had emerged – a wage-earning class, an independent class of wealthy traders and merchant princes and a mulatto group. The first class consisted of people employed by the Europeans as masons, carpenters, interpreters, writers or secretaries, gold brokers, civil servants, ambassadors and public-relations officers.

The second class consisted of Africans who, through their own efforts in farming or trade, became exceedingly wealthy and more powerful than the traditional rulers. On the coast of present-day Côte d'Ivoire, for example, the Kosehirange had become extremely powerful and were playing a key role in the choice of lineage heads.

The mulatto group was the product of unions between European traders and African women. Such people could be found all along the Lower Guinea coast. Some, such as the descendants of Richard Brew, played important roles in the commercial and political life of the region.

Another important change was the introduction of Christianity and Western education by the Europeans, and of Islam by the Manden and Hausa traders. The Dutch and the English established elementary schools at Cape Coast, El Mina and Accra, and in the 1750s the Society for the Propagation of the Gospel sent missionaries to Cape Coast. Moreover, some children of mulattos and traditional rulers were sent abroad to be educated, returning home as teachers and missionaries. Thus, by 1800 a small educated élite and a few Christian converts could be found in some coastal towns.

Even earlier than Christianity, Islam and Muslim culture spread along the northern trade routes, first into northern Ghana by the fourteenth century and then into Asante and Baule areas by the mid-eighteenth century. By 1800, Kumasi had a thriving Muslim quarter with a Ḳur'ānic school. However, neither Christianity nor Islam had much impact on the peoples of Lower Guinea, although reading and writing in both European languages and Arabic had been firmly established.

As regards arts and crafts, the peoples of the Guinea coast had, by 1800, become highly skilled in pottery-making, were already making pottery, carving, weaving, metalworking and casting brass and gold objects.

Pottery-making in Ghana goes back to the Later Stone Age (after 3000 before the Christian era) and had greatly developed by the early eighteenth century, particularly among the Adangbe. According to J. Anquandah, the Asante produced some of the best-quality polymorphic pottery, such as the *abusua kuruwa*, clan pot, and the *mogyemogye*, a wine jar used for pouring libations on the Golden Stool.

Carving and sculpting in wood, ivory and clay was also developed during this period, particularly among the Akan. Seventeenth- and eighteenth-century European visitors to the coast of Ghana, such as W. Bosman, were impressed

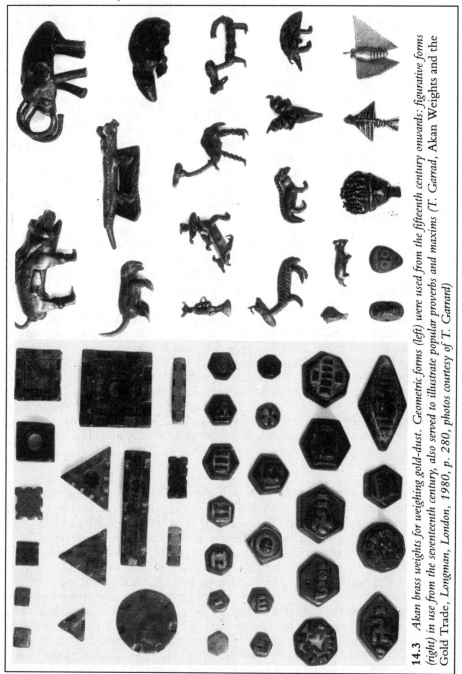

14.3 *Akan brass weights for weighing gold-dust. Geometric forms (left) were used from the fifteenth century onwards; figurative forms (right) in use from the seventeenth century, also served to illustrate popular proverbs and maxims (T. Garrad, Akan Weights and the Gold Trade, Longman, London, 1980, p. 280, photos courtesy of T. Garrad)*

by the beauty of the ivory side-blown trumpets. Among typical objects of this art, the best-known are the *akuaba* (fertility dolls) in wood and clay and the sculptured clay portraits of deceased kings and queens.

Weaving became widespread throughout the region in the sixteenth and seventeenth centuries and, according to the 1629 map, Nsoko (Insoco), present-day Begho, was an important weaving centre. But it was in the eighteenth century that weaving among the Akan and the Ewe attained its maturity, as demonstrated by the famous colourful *kente* cloths of the Akan and the rich *adanudo* cloths of the Ewe. *Adinkra* cloth, with Akan traditional motifs and symbols stamped on it, became famous in the Brong region and was later copied by the Asante.

However, it was in metalworking and casting, especially in gold and brass, that the peoples of Lower Guinea and the Akan in particular excelled. Using mainly the *cire-perdue* (lost-wax) process, the smiths produced exquisite gold and silver objects, including sword handles, rings, bangles, chains and headgear. The Akan smiths also produced thousands of geometric and figurative gold or brass weights, now found in all the world's great art museums.

With the rise of the Asante empire in the eighteenth century, the arts and crafts of Lower Guinea reached their peak. The Asante kings did everything in their power to promote them. After the defeat of Denkyira, Tekyiman and Akyem, they collected the best craftsmen and goldsmiths of those states and sent them to Kumasi. A number of specialized centres was established in the neighbourhood of the capital. The *asantehene* established the *Apagyafie*, a group of goldsmiths and other craftsmen brought from Denkyira whose duty was to make the king's regalia. He also introduced the golden stool (*asomfo*), whose first occupant, Nana Tabiri, was the son of a Denkyira chief.

This blending of different artistic experiences, expertise and traditions enabled the Asante kings in the eighteenth century to raise the cultural development of the Akan people to its highest peak of excellence and to ensure that their power was reflected in works of art of the highest quality.

Conclusion

The period between 1500 and 1800 was indeed a period of radical change for the states and peoples of Lower Guinea. Politically, the process towards centralization was completed. Economically, the trade in gold and ivory was eclipsed by the slave trade; the commercial and economic centres moved from inland to the coast; strong commercial links were forged with the Americas and Europe, thereby integrating the region's economy with the world economy. Above all, this was a period of social change, marked by the emergence of new social classes although on a limited scale and confined mainly to the coast, the beginnings of literacy, the introduction of Western education and Christianity, the spread of Islam and the flowering of indigenous cultures, expressed especially in weaving and metalwork. These were indeed dynamic centuries for the peoples of the Lower Guinea Coast, all the more so because at the end of the period they were still in full control of their destiny.

15

Fon and Yoruba: the Niger delta and Cameroon

This chapter covers the region extending from the valley of the River Volta in the west to the River Cameroon in the east. Most of the area is tropical forest bordered by savannah with shrub forest to the north. The western part, from the border of Nigeria to the River Volta, is also savannah. The peoples living within this part of the Guinea forest and the surrounding savannah comprise the Fon or Aja of the modern Republic of Benin, the Yoruba, the Ijo of the Niger delta, the Igbo to the north-east of the delta, the Ibibio and various peoples in southern Cameroon.

All the languages of the area belong to the Niger-Congo family, the majority of them being within the Kwa sub-family. The Efik/Ibibio and the other languages of the Nigeria–Cameroon border area of Nigeria and the languages of Cameroon itself are closely related to the Bantu languages of central, eastern and southern Africa. The peoples and cultures in this border region form a unifying link between West Africa and Bantu Africa. Among the Kwa language groups, the Yoruba and the Igbo are the largest in terms of the numbers of speakers (between 8 and 12 million) and geographical spread. The Edo group is also large, with a spread of related peoples such as the Isoko and the Urhobo, the Ishan (Esan) and others. Among the Kwa languages, Ijo in the Niger delta is the most divergent from its neighbours, Igbo, Edo and Yoruba.

The long continuities in this region's history should be borne in mind when evaluating the changes supposedly induced by the arrival of Europeans on the coast at the end of the fifteenth century. The Portuguese reached Benin in 1486 and established relations with the *oba* of Benin. They established commercial relations at various points along the coast which became the major origin of stimuli to change.

The slave trade was obviously the focus of European activity between the sixteenth and the eighteenth centuries. The region covered in this study was one of the main markets for slaves on the West African coast. Some states, such as the kingdom of Dahomey, derived great impetus for their formation and growth from the trade. The development of others, from the Niger delta to Cameroon, was influenced by the profits to be derived from it. Other communities, especially those organized in non-state forms, tended to be the victims of the overseas slave trade.

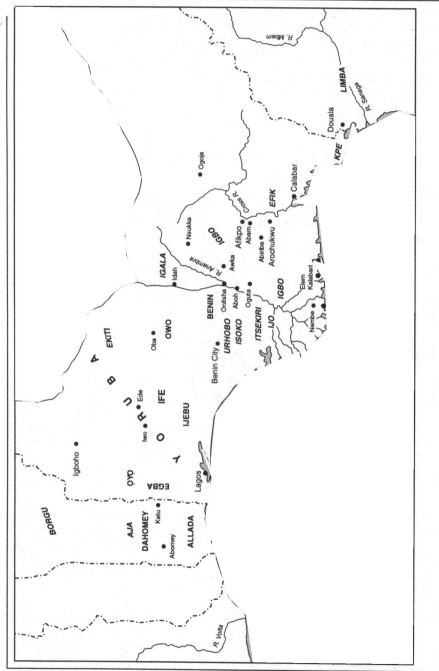

15.1 *The Niger delta area and Cameroon from the sixteenth to the eighteenth century*

The increase in the local slave trade also led to social and political changes within the communities. Oral traditions show the effects of the trade on the fortunes of lineages, groups or dynasties.

The Fon kingdom of Dahomey

The political development of the kingdom of Dahomey and of the neighbouring states of Allada, Whydah, Popo and Jakin was largely related to the activities of the European slave-traders on the coast and to the influence of the Yoruba kingdom of Ọyọ to the north-east.

The traditional institutions of the small communities and states of the area were weakened by the introduction of the slave trade and, by the end of the seventeenth century, a political vacuum had been created. It was at this point that the founders of the kingdom of Dahomey re-established order by fashioning a new form of political organization out of various groups of Aja peoples comprising the Gun, Fon, Arada and other peoples from the southern part of the modern Republic of Benin. By 1700, Dahomey had become a major power in the area. Between 1724 and 1727, its ruler, Agaja, embarked on the conquest of the small but older states surrounding Abomey. This provoked intervention by Ọyọ, but not to establish a system of its own. After 1730 Dahomey accepted the political authority of Ọyọ and agreed to live within the economy of the slave trade.

The crisis that began about 1767 culminated in the fall of the Agaja dynasty in 1818 and the rise of the new dynasty of Gezo. The new dynasty adapted fully to the slave-trade economy and made it the basis of its strength. It thereby benefited from the breakdown of the Ọyọ kingdom and the Yoruba wars in the nineteenth century.

The inter-relationship between the Aja communities and the Yoruba to the east and north-east was deep and long-standing. There are indeed states of Yoruba origin and culture within this area, notably the Ketu, a migrant community of Yoruba from Ile-Ife.

The states in the area were largely organized in systems similar to the Yoruba pattern, the 'father' kingdom being Allada, which had been founded about 1575. Ọyọ intervention, by restricting Dahomey as a military power, enabled the young state to strengthen its internal administration. Some aspects of Ọyọ organization were taken over, such as the *ilari* system introduced by Tegbesu, the last ruler of the founding dynasty.

The effects of the slave trade were so significant because at the point when the trade started in the sixteenth century, the states were still weak. Economic activity was undermined and the rules of society destroyed. Moreover, the rivalries arising out of the competition for trading posts destroyed the traditional relationships among states. Early in the seventeenth century, the Dutch established agents at Assim, the capital of Allada. The French set up a rival trading station at Whydah in 1671. That destroyed the already weakened ties between the two states. It was in this atmosphere of political and commercial competition that migrants from Allada created the kingdom of Dahomey.

They settled in Abomey, out of reach of the Europeans, in about 1625, and tried to set up a new political system. They likened the state to a perforated pot, symbolized by the king. For the perforated pot to hold water, each citizen had to place a finger over a hole, thus sinking his identity in an absolute state. It was the dogged development of this idea of a strong centralized state with a king demanding total loyalty that marked out Dahomey from other states. It was thus that it was able gradually to bring all the neighbouring states under its control.

The predominant role attributed to the Atlantic slave trade in the history of Dahomey is currently being revised by recent research. W. Peukert directly challenges two central concepts: that the history of Dahomey was determined by the slave trade and that its economy was archaic. The historianís new hypotheses call for a revision of old ideas and further research.

The Yoruba kingdoms

The history of the Yoruba communities of south-western Nigeria can be summarized around three points. The first concerns the traditions which make Ile-Ife the centre of origin of the Yoruba kingdoms, an assertion which needs to be reconciled with the archaeological evidence. The second is the rise of the military and political power of Oyo, thought by some to have coexisted with the spiritual authority of the *oni* of Ife over the whole of Yoruba country. The third point is the nature of the political, cultural and social development in other Yoruba communities and kingdoms.

The primacy of Ife in Yoruba history is based on many factors. According to tradition, its founder, Oduduwa, was supposed to have come from heaven or Mecca and his sons or grandsons to have founded all the other Yoruba states. Recent interpretations of these traditions suggest that Oduduwa, or a group of migrants, came to the area about 1,000 years ago but that the land was already occupied, possibly by the Igbo of Ife tradition.

The famous Ife bronzes have played a part in confirming the traditions of the relationship between Ife or Yorubaland and the Edo kingdom of Benin. But the bronzes also relate Ife to Nupe and Benin and regions around the Niger as clear similarities have been found between the large bronzes found in Nupe and those of Ife. Likewise, it has become clear that the 'Mecca' of oral traditions did not refer to any place in the Middle East, Egypt or Meroe but to regions just across the River Niger to the north of present-day Yoruba territory. In addition, the art of Ife has been compared to the Nok terracotta art in central Nigeria, despite the time gap between the two cultures.

Oyo not only became pre-eminent among the Yoruba kingdoms, but it also developed special features. Some of these derived from its location close to Nupe and Borgu. For example, Oyo relied more heavily on officials of slave origin in its military and social organization than did other Yoruba states. In the armed forces, Oyo's supremacy was probably the result of its use of cavalry and archers, derived from its early contact with the trans-Saharan trade and the

15.2 *Fifteenth- or sixteenth-century commemorative head from Benin, Nigeria, cast in bronze and inlaid with iron. Height 22 cm (National Museum of African Art, Eliot Elisofon Archives, Smithsonian Institution, Washington DC, photo: B. Fleischer)*

nɔ. ɪern states. These external contacts as well as its location in the savannah enabled Ọyọ to make innovations in the Yoruba concepts it shared with the other kingdoms.

The foundation of Ọyọ is related to Ife and Benin through its legendary founder, Oranyan (*Oranmiyan*), who is stated to have reigned at both Ife and Benin before moving to Ọyọ. But other states already existed in this area, and Ọyọ made several of them vassal states, including Owu in the south and Ede in the south-east. The expansion of Ọyọ was finally stopped by the Ijesha, as the Ọyọ cavalry could not operate in wooded regions. The Ijebu and the hill country of the Ekiti also escaped direct Ọyọ control. The kingdom of Benin to the east proved another barrier to Ọyọ expansion. Ọyọ opened up a trade route to the coast through the territory of the Egba and Egbado and it was through this route that Ọyọ power expanded to Dahomey.

Ọyọ power developed out of adversity. In the fifteenth century its rulers had been driven out of Old Ọyọ (Ọyọ Ile or Katunga) and had taken refuge in Kusu among the Borgu and later at Igboho. Undaunted, Ọyọ had reorganized its army and adopted a new policy of militarism. By the beginning of the sixteenth century Ọyọ had reconquered its territory and pushed the Nupe back.

Ọyọ remained outside the area of direct European influence until the nineteenth century, developing its major institutions and starting its expansion independently. Its adventure into Dahomey may have been connected with participation in the coastal trade but other oral traditions say that Ọyọ kept out of the slave trade and avoided any contact with the Europeans.

The areas of Yoruba country beyond Ọyọ expansion, to the east and north, consisted of small states in the Ekiti area and others, such as the Igala state, that were more oriented towards the Niger-Benue valley. Other states, such as Owo and Ijebu, appear to have had much more to do with the Edo kingdom of Benin than with Ọyọ. Works of art recovered from excavations at Owo show that by the fifteenth century the sculptural forms of this region were already related to both Ife and Benin styles.

The Niger delta

The history of the Niger delta is linked with the history of parts of the coastal region east to Cameroon and west to the lagoons of Lagos and beyond. Until the nineteenth century, trade routes crossed the region from east to west and north to south. Cloth made in the Ijebu area of Yorubaland was sold in the western delta and appears to have been resold as far east as Nembe in the eastern delta. The Itsekiri (western delta) were related to the Ijebu, as shown by the similarity of language, but they had derived some of their cultural values from the Ijo and traded in pottery, salt and cloth with the states of the eastern delta, especially Nembe.

In the western Niger delta, Ode Itsekiri, the capital of the kingdom, was the focus of political power. When the Portuguese came to this area, the Itsekiri became their major delta contacts. In the eighteenth century some Itsekiri left the capital to establish settlements in the estuary of the Benin river at points of vantage for the trans-Atlantic trade. It was mainly from these new centres that the Itsekiri served as the agents of the Benin kingdom and as middlemen on their own account for the export of the produce of the hinterland peoples.

The Ijo of the western Niger delta were mostly organized in loose stateless communities and tended to participate in the overseas trade by preying on it as pirates. The bronzes found among these Ijo groups, and also among the Mein and Kabowei, may be indications of affluence derived from participation in internal and external trade, and also from contact with Benin and other hinterland centres.

The Ijo of the central delta formed the heartland of the group. Oral traditions suggest migrations from this area to the eastern and western delta and on to the delta peripheries. The present communities in the eastern delta are estimated to have settled there a thousand years ago. Radio-carbon dating of finds from sites at Ke and Saikiripogu (Ewoama) confirms that people were living there before the ninth century.

Excavations in the eastern Niger delta have opened new vistas for Niger delta history. They show that the earliest settlers knew how to exploit the shell-fish of the delta and also kept some animals. The abundance of pottery at such sites as Onyoma suggests a complex economy, based partly on agriculture, partly on trade. The excavations have also revealed evidence of iron-working. This suggests contacts with the hinterland for raw materials and finished goods.

Art in the Niger delta consists principally of sculptures in wood depicting water spirits, ancestors or masks for dancing. Excavations have recovered a small number of masks in terracotta from Ke and human figures from Onyoma, which are unique among Nigerian terracotta but reminiscent of Nok and Ife terracotta.

The Atlantic slave trade and, prior to it, internal long-distance trade, played a large part in the formation of the states of the eastern Niger delta – Bonny, Elem Kalabari (New Calabar), Okrika and Nembe. From the oral traditions it would appear that their founders came from the fresh-water central delta and adapted to life in the salt-water eastern delta. Social and political adaptations were made and kingship institutions were set up from about the thirteenth century. The Atlantic slave trade accelerated the pace of change and the form of state established by the seventeenth century has been named the city-state or trading state. The slave trade provided wealth as a base of power for the *amanyamabo* (king) and ruling élite.

Igboland

A number of Stone Age sites in the Igbo heartland suggest a long history of human habitation. A rock shelter at Afikpo produced stone tools and pottery 5,000 years old, and sites with similar evidence have been found in the Nsukka area. It seems clear that people farmed there at least 3,000 years ago, with yams as their main crop. Other crops of local origin include oil palms, *okro*, *egusi* and

15.3 *Yoruba female statuette, dedicated to the worship of the* orisha *of creativity, Obatala. She is usually clothed with a white cloth like the priests and devotees of that god, an iron bracelet and, here, a necklace of white pearls with a pendant. The bowl that she is holding is intended to receive an offering of the white blood of the snail, a symbol of peace and calm. It is the female element of the* orisha, *the male element being represented by a statuette holding a fan and a fly-whisk. This bowl-bearer should not be confused with the* olumeye, *or vessel for kola nuts, represented by a much larger kneeling maternal figure holding a bowl which often has a lid. Height: 49 cm (H. Dubois, Brussels)*

some varieties of kola nut. Cassava, rice, bananas, plantain and other crops were imported from the Americas.

Iron-working was established early and the bronze art of this area has become world-famous through the excavations at Igbo-Ukwu. The bronzes from this area derive from a different tradition from those of Ife and Benin but equal them in beauty and quality. They are associated with the Nri divine kingship and ritual centre. The Nri priests exercised authority over wide areas of Igboland with power to install *ozo* and *eze* title-holders and wash away abomination. It could have been the income brought back by travelling Nri priests which provided the wealth that sustained this bronze art.

The Nri priesthood performed a vital role in Igboland where communities were organized on the basis of the title system. But some Igbo groups west of the Niger and on its east bank adopted the kingship institutions of the communities with which they came into contact. Thus the Aboh, Onitsha and Oguta kingdoms apparently derived their *obi* from the *oba* (king) of Benin. These states were created by migrants from areas under Benin influence in the sixteenth and seventeenth centuries.

Other states on the River Niger, such as Osomari, claim ancestors from the Igala kingdom of Idah to the north. But Igala influence was probably more pronounced among the northern Igbo in the Anambra valley and in the Nsukka region. The Igbo states along the Niger became the first participants in the overseas slave trade and later in the palm-oil trade of the nineteenth century in collaboration with the Niger delta states.

The Igbo political and social system had mechanisms for wider control than the village or town. One was religious sanction by an oracle. Oracles have operated in Igboland at different times and places, but the best known were Agbala of Akwa and Ibini Okpube (Long Juju) of Arochukwu. Thus, the Awka blacksmiths, who worked at markets and settled all over Igboland and the Niger delta, spread the influence of the Agbala oracle. But the Aro Chukwu oracle became even more successful thanks to the Aro traders, slave–dealers who spread word of him far and wide. The Aro trade network developed in the port of Calabar and later also came to deal with the delta states. The Aro traders used the utterances of the oracle to procure slaves but were also willing to use violence and enlisted the help of the warriors of Abam, Edda, Ohafia, Abiriba and others with whom they shared their loot.

The areas of Igboland without strong centralized government probably suffered most from the effects of slave-raiding. In the eighteenth century, the eastern Niger delta ports were the main centres for the export of slaves from West Africa, and most of them came from the Igbo hinterland.

The Cross river valley and Cameroon

The peoples in this region show affinities of language and also of historical origins. Most of the languages belong to the family of Bantu languages. The largest ethnic group in the Cross river valley, the Ibibio, has long been established in the region. In the northern parts of the valley, the Ogoja area is occupied by a wide variety of peoples with oral traditions of migration from the Benue valley, further north, or from Cameroon. Some communities in the Ibibio group or closely related to them, such as the Andoni and the Ibeno, also claim that they came from Cameroon. Likewise, some communities in Cameroon, such as the Isangele, are of Ibibio origin.

The communities in this region were largely organized in non-centralized societies of great complexity. Age organizations as well as secret societies such as the *Ekpo* and the *Mgbe* (leopard society) provided effective social and political control.

The Efik are closely related to the Ibibio, their proximate home having been Uruan Ibibio on the west bank of the Cross river. Some oral traditions state that they had previously lived at Ibom, near Arochukwu in Igboland. Their final settlement at Ikot Etunko (Creek Town), Obutong (Old Town) and Atakpa (Duke Town) by the beginning of the seventeenth century made these places the major centres for the overseas slave trade in the region. The state the Efik founded on the lower Cross river – now known as Calabar – exported slaves from the Igbo hinterland from the centre at Arochukwu.

The slave trade was partly responsible for the reshaping of the Ibibio *Ekpo* and the Ekoi *Mgbe* secret societies into the *Ekpe* at Calabar. The *Ekpe* became a class-structured society uniting the free aristocratic elements and keeping in control the slaves and the poor. It also enforced political and social rules, collected debts and kept order. Because of the common influences of the slave trade and trans-Atlantic contacts, Calabar developed lineage-based organizations similar to the Houses of the eastern delta states.

The most important groups on the Cameroon coast were the north-west Bantu groups of the Kpe-Mboko, the Duala, the Limba and the Tanga-Yasa. There were numerous groups of fisherfolk, farmers and hunters. Most were organized in small village units but by the eighteenth century the Bubi, the Duala and the Isubu had organized larger political units. They were either connected with the slave trade or took advantage of it. The *Jengu* secret society, a major focus of social and political control, became the most prestigious one in the coastal region of Cameroon.

Conclusion

The major external influence in the history of this region of coastal swamp and rainforest from the fifteenth to the eighteenth century was the slave trade. It had an enormous impact on the peoples of the area but it is hard to assess its exact role in relation to internal factors for change that were at work long before the advent of that trade.

In many oral traditions, the slave trade features as an activity that enriched people and increased the population. This was the case for the coastal communities which took part as middlemen, not themselves engaging in hunting for slaves but buying them to re-sell to the slave traders. The Niger delta states and the Efik state fall into this category.

The Fon kingdom of Dahomey exemplifies a second type of participation in the slave trade — by active procurement of slaves for the slave traders. In Igboland the Aro and their mercenary allies played a similar role as slave hunters.

The third category of community affected by the trade were the victims. These were the communities from whom most slaves were taken for sale on the coast and included parts of Yorubaland, Igboland and Ibibioland. Raids, kidnapping, wars and the general cheapening of human life precipitated the collapse of the economic and social systems of these communities. Villages were destroyed or dispersed, farms were abandoned and people lived in terror.

It is sometimes argued that the slave trade brought these tropical regions of Africa out of isolation and integrated them into the international economy. In addition, the introduction of food crops such as maize, cassava and rice could be seen as redressing the demographic balance by encouraging population growth. These are speculative hypotheses. For the African peoples of the region, the slave-trade era is seen as a bad dream best cast into the dark recesses of their memory.

The Hausa states

The region discussed in this chapter is readily associated with the idea of wealth. This wealth arises from the complementarity between neighbouring regions and Hausaland as a producer and a consumer and from the integrated aspect of the West African economy, with the Wangara, Hausa and Kanuri in the savannah, and the Fante, Bini, Ijaw and Arochukwu in the forest.

The documentation available on the region's development between 1500 and 1800 is of very uneven quality. Source materials on the Hausa states are extremely varied. They include eye-witness reports, surveys and reference works, which are all easily obtainable publications, theses – mainly written by researchers from the region – and the proceedings of seminars covering history and archaeology. Lastly, the point of view of the peoples directly concerned is set out in a number of documents published in English or Hausa, such as the *Kano Chronicle*.

The uneven pattern of research means that the various political entities cannot all be treated with the same degree of thoroughness. The relatively peripheral position of Borgu, Kwararafa and Nupe during the period under consideration is also partly responsible for this situation.

The Hausa states

Political development

Whenever post-1500 central Sudan is being considered, it has become customary to point to the specific influence of western Sudan – Mali and Songhay – and Kānem-Borno. The century opened with the *askiya* Muḥammad's campaign in Azbin. There was also a feeling of nostalgia for the *sarakunan noma* (masters of the crops) emperors, the *mai* (king) of Kānem and the *mansa* (emperor) of Mali. Since western and eastern Sudan were better known, little attention had been paid until that time to the changes taking place in central Sudan. However, it was soon to be integrated into the commercial and ideological system uniting the societies of western Sudan with the Muslim world. Its political development came to be viewed in terms of its relationships

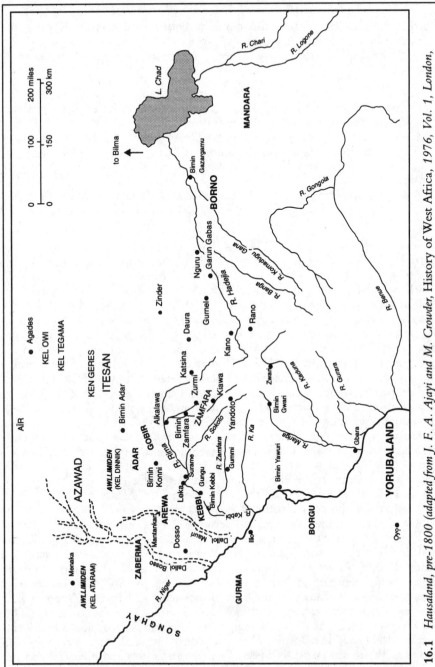

16.1 *Hausaland, pre-1800 (adapted from J. F. A. Ajayi and M. Crowder, History of West Africa, 1976, Vol. 1, London, Longman, p. 555. Adapted by kind permission of Longman Group UK Ltd)*

with the neighbouring states, the conflicts between Kano and Katsina and interludes involving Kebbi, Zamfara and Gobir.

The chronological framework adopted here distinguishes between three periods:

(1) 1500–1620, when the states gained in strength but there were bitter conflicts between Kano and Katsina, and Kebbi remained the dominant power in the western part of Hausaland.
(2) 1620–1730, when Kano was on its way to becoming a caliphate, at a time when Zamfara and Gobir were consolidating their positions following the decline of Kebbi and Kwararafa was further increasing its capacity for attack.
(3) 1730–1808, a period marked by the collapse of Zamfara and Gobir's rise to the peak of its power.

Relations with the neighbouring regions

Although Hausaland's relations with its neighbours are being studied in increasing depth, there still remain some areas of controversy.

With Songhay, undue importance has been attached to the authority of *askiya* Muḥammad. The main outcome of his campaign in Azbin was the emergence of Kebbi as an independent state in 1516. Songhay was subsequently to attempt to regain control of Kebbi. *Askiya* Muḥammad II Benkan Kiriai (1531–7) led an expedition in about 1533 but was defeated. Another expedition was organized in 1552 in the reign of *askiya* Dāwūd, the conflict being brought to an end by the conclusion of a peace treaty in 1553.

Azbin provided the pretext for the clash between Kebbi and Borno. As Kebbi continued its repeated forays, Azbin sought the help of Borno in 1561. After initially winning the day at Surame, the 100,000 man Borno army was defeated at Nguru by the Kanta. Then, at the end of the century, a dynastic crisis flared up in Azbin. Yūsuf, after being deposed by Muḥammad ben al-Mubārak (*c.* 1601) appealed to Kanta Dāwūd for support. The latter, who wished to maintain his influence, helped him defeat his rival, who was backed by Borno. This success checked the *mai*'s designs on Azbin, which was at its peak under the reign of Muḥammad al-Mubārak (*c.* 1653–87). In 1674, taking advantage of the continual conflicts between Gobir and the eastern part of Hausaland and between Zamfara and Kebbi, Muḥammad dispatched an expedition, led by his son Agabba, who conquered Adar and thereby hastened Kebbi's decline. From then onwards, it was left to Zamfara and Gobir to temper the influence of Azbin in the Kwanni regions. In 1675, the conflict between Azbin and Zamfara gave rise to massacres and battles. Gobir, which was pillaging the same area, was attacked and defeated by Azbin in about 1689. Finally, Agabba, who had become sultan, marched on Surame and killed Kanta Aḥmadu. In 1722, the Kebbi court withdrew towards the western areas. However, Azbin was entering a period of dynastic crises and disasters, and this left Zamfara and Gobir to occupy the leading role.

Before 1561, Borno was in a position of strength. *Sarkin* Kano ʿAbdullāhī (1499–1509) was attacked by the *mai* and adopted a subservient attitude which prompted the aggressor to depart. However, his successor, Muḥammad Kisoki (1509–65), made for the city of Nguru in Borno, where he gave orders that only horses and clothing were to be seized. Caught by surprise, the *mai* took the initiative the following year and attacked Kano, but was again forced to withdraw. The humiliation inflicted by Kisoki on the *mai* was a sign of the might of Kano at a time when Borno was suffering from internal strife and several years of famine.

It was not long before Kano was subjected to repeated attacks from Kwararafa: between 1582 and 1618, its population was forced to seek refuge at Daura. The sovereign of Kano was again driven out in 1653, and its inhabitants once more sought refuge in Daura in 1671. According to C. A. Palmer, the peace treaty signed between Kano and Katsina (*c.* 1649–51) was inspired by fear of Kwararafa, which was eventually to be defeated by Borno in 1680.

These conflicts point to an unstable equilibrium between powerful neighbours.

The struggle for hegemony

The Gwanja–Kano–Borno route had been opened up between 1438 and 1452. Moreover, in the fifteenth century, Agades had replaced Takedda as a caravan centre, thereby making Katsina a terminus of the trans-Saharan caravan route, and a trading centre for all Hausaland. The military conflicts between Kano and Katsina may have been due to competition between the two states for control of the trans-Saharan terminus, but nothing is known of the nature and scale of these wars.

The first conflict broke out during the reign of Rumfa (*c.* 1463–99), an extremely wealthy ruler who was the first to be escorted by fully accoutred horses in the war against Katsina. That war lasted eleven years, with no decisive outcome.

The second conflict took place at the time of Abū Bakr Kado (*c.*1565–73), when Ibrāhīm Badankarī was reigning in Katsina. The Katsinawa advanced to the very gates of Kano, were victorious and returned home.

To avenge this defeat, Muḥammad Shashīrī (*c.*1573–82) organized an expedition against Katsina, where Muḥammad Wari (*c.* 1575–87) was ruling. The battle took place at Kankiya, Kano was defeated and its sovereign was deposed.

The next conflict broke out during the reign of Muḥammad Zakī (*c.* 1582–1618) of Kano. In Katsina Muḥammad Wari was succeeded by Sulaymān (*c.* 1587–1600) and ʿUthmān Nayinawa (*c.* 1600–18). There is some confusion as to what happened next, and there may have been a change of dynasty. Katsina was so powerful that Kano was afraid it might be attacked. However, Kwararafa invaded Kano, defeating it and sapping its strength. Shortly afterwards, Muḥammad Zakī of Kano consulted the ʿulamā ʾ and obtained a talisman at a very high price. Suitably protected, Kano then attacked Katsina's military encampments and emerged victorious.

As soon as he assumed power in Kano, Muḥammad Nazaki (*c.* 1618–23) made peace proposals which were rebuffed by Katsina, which was again defeated. In the reign of Kutumbi (c. 1623–48) Kano kept up the pressure on Katsina and there was a series of incidents. In one expedition, Kutumbi's army was routed and he himself killed. One of his successors, S͟hekarau (c. 1649–51), managed to make peace after negotiations conducted by the 'ulamā'. Katsina's power was further consolidated without the peace treaty with Kano being broken.

There was accordingly a long political struggle for control of eastern Hausa-land.

Interludes

Until the end of the sixteenth century, Kebbi feared none of its enemies, not even Morocco. Among the specific factors instrumental in consolidating this state, one author has suggested the mixed origins of the population, the polariza-tion of protests against Songhay domination and the determination of its military leaders to maintain the country's independence. After clashes with Zamfara, Kebbi defeated Borno in 1561 and rose to occupy the leading place in the political life of Hausaland.

The capital of Gobir had been transferred from Azbin to Hausaland, at Birnin Lalle, in the centre of the densely populated and well-watered region of Gulbin Tarka in about 1450. The rulers remained there until about 1600, when the Tuareg launched an attack. The Gobirawa were forced to take up their wanderings again and set out southward. They then struck out towards the north-west and founded the new Gwaran Rama in about 1685–90. From this city, Uban Doro launched attacks against Kebbi and even against Yorubaland and Gurma; his successor, Soba, attacked Adar, Kebbi and Maradi. However, he established friendly relations with Zamfara, which opened up Alkalawa to the farmers and traders of Gobir. The old military aristocracy was gradually eclipsed by a new aristocracy based on money. The decline of Gobir began just as Zamfara was clearly gaining strength.

In the mid-seventeenth century Zamfara was governed by strong sovereigns who drew their support from Islam. Aliyu, the first Muslim ruler of Zamfara, established good relations with Katsina and built mosques there. Zamfara stopped making its sporadic raids and instead concentrated its attacks on Kebbi's major towns. In 1674, Sulaymān put the army of Kebbi to flight. In the same year, Kebbi lost Adar, which was wrested from it by prince Agabba. It was a series of separate defeats rather than a concerted action by Azbin, Gobir and Zamfara. After this victory, Zamfara became the leading power in the area, as was revealed by its victory over the army of Kano during the reign of Muḥammad S͟hārīf (c. 1703–31).

Zamfara had thus recovered from the defeat it suffered at the hands of Azbin, but the military strength of Gobir was also growing: In the reign of Kumbari (c. 1731–43), there was a fierce war between Kano and Gobir, whose *sarkin*'s name was Soba. Defeats and acts of revenge followed one another year in year out, and the massacres only came to an end at the death of Kabi. Gobir was soon to feel the weight of various restrictions imposed upon it by the *sarkin* Zamfara, who was worried by his restive neighbour. At the outset, Gobir was content with harassing its enemy, but then, taking advantage of a dynastic crisis, it destroyed Birnin Zamfara in about 1762.

This development had repercussions on the political situation in the peripheral areas. In the east, the sultanate of Damagaram was founded towards the beginning of the eighteenth century, while the Tsotsebaki states were consolidating their position before subsequently splitting up. This area, which marked the transition between Borno and Hausaland, was extremely sensitive to political and cultural movements.

In the north-west, the history of Adar is better known, but it is not clear what its links were with Kurfay, which is sometimes associated with Adar, sometimes with Borno.

Zarma, the easternmost part of the Songhay empire, first established links with Hausaland when Gobir was part of Azbin. At that time Kebbi, Zamfara and Gobir were all fighting over the area. Before it was eliminated in 1722, Kebbi played a decisive political role in Zarmatarey, where its name was associated with cavalry protected by *lifidi* (quilted armour) which spread terror.

Finally, in the west, on the *gurma* (right) bank of the river Niger, certain Gulmanceba dynasties claimed to originate from central Sudan, Borno or Hausaland – a claim seemingly substantiated by archaeological excavations, at least for the areas along the *hausa* or left bank.

The situation, however, stabilized considerably after Zamfara's defeat in 1762. Katsina, despite a domestic crisis, was able to defeat Gobir, while in Kano, Babba Zaki (*c.* 1768–76) terrorized his collaborators.

Political and administrative organization

Thus, despite the military conflicts, this host of states remained in existence. After their severe defeats, the sovereigns of Kebbi and Zamfara retreated to a smaller territory to safeguard their power. The explanation for this development may lie in the process whereby the *sarauta* (kingship) system was introduced into and developed in central Sudan.

The *sarki*

At the head of the state, which was first and foremost a *kasa* (territory), there was the *sarki*, whose ancestor had seized political power. In Kano, Katsina and Zamfara, it had been wrested from the hands of a high priest, while in Kebbi it was a *magaji* (warrior) who rose to the rank of *sarki*.

The appointment of the successor to the throne was the responsibility of an electoral college. In Katsina, this consisted of four members. It is difficult to say whether such a college existed in Kebbi at this time, but it certainly appeared there at a later stage. In Zamfara, Gobir and Kano, it bore the name *tara* (the nine), followed by the name of the state. The titles and functions of the various electoral colleges differ, but one incumbent can be identified as holding an ancient office, the *basase*, in Zamfara, and there were, besides, governors of cities and important regions and high-ranking public servants. They also included representatives of ousted and reigning dynasties.

The successor had to be chosen unanimously by the grand electors. Once he had been appointed, the enthronement and installation ritual took place. The electoral college also formed the council of the *sarki*, and it was not uncommon for the council to clash with the *sarki* or for the latter to debar one of the council members.

The government

The *sarki* exercised his authority through three groups of officials: members of the dynasty, public servants, governors of the towns and regions.

The members of the dynasty were assigned important duties. The sovereign's sister played a leading political role, although she did so through the traditional form of worship. The history of Kano is studded with the names of famous princesses. If the *madaki* (the queen mother) Auwa had not intervened, 'Abdullāhī (1499–1509) would most certainly have been driven out by a rebellion. His son, Kisoki, governed the city with the support of the same *madaki* Auwa, his grandmother, Iya Lamis, his mother, and Gulli, Auwa's brother.

In what might be called the central government, there were several categories of officials:

(1) The court dignitaries managed the affairs of the palace and the city. They were in a position to act as middlemen between the *sarki* and the regional governments.
(2) The representatives of the guilds were appointed from among the skilled craftworkers, such as blacksmiths, weavers, dyers, tanners, masons, butchers and hunters. They were responsible for relations with the different trades and occupations and, in particular, for collecting the state dues.
(3) The autochthonous groups had their own representatives. The village of Sarkin Naya and the region of Sarkin Mazum, for example, kept their titles even after Gobir had established its capital at Hisatau.
(4) The numerous immigrants were also allowed to have their own representatives. In Gobir, the *sarkin* Azbin handled relations with the Tuareg living in the territory, and the *sarkin* Fullani did likewise for the Fulbe.
(5) The Islamic community was present everywhere with its *mallamai* (scholars).

In terms of regional government or, more specifically, territorial control, a distinction has to be made between several categories:

(1) The authority of the governors of certain cities was independent of the dynasty. Their relations with the sovereign could be difficult, as they were eventually reduced to the status of vassals.
(2) The governors of other cities or regions were either nobles whose ancestors

had become allies of the dynasty while preserving the
public servants. Zamfara provides an illustration of th
danau, who owed his title to the town in which he
commercial centre from where he kept watch over th
and west of Kebbi. In Kebbi, the *innamme* kept wa......
frontier. In Katsina, the *marisa* (destroyer) resided in Gwiwa from where he
supervised the eastern frontier, while the *gatari* (axe) of Ruma kept an eye
on the north-western frontier.

(3) The other governors became mere cogs in the governmental machinery.
The immigrants retained a local hierarchy.

(4) Finally, certain titles were the outcome of historical developments. In
Kebbi, the *kokani* was responsible for relations with the population after the
conquest of Kwanni; the office of *saburu* was created in about 1650 to
provide security on the roads that led to Kwanni and Azbin.

All these dignitaries, nobles, commoners or slaves performed duties of a non-
military nature except that, when the occasion demanded, they became valiant
warriors with their own armed groups.

Military organization

The foundation of Kebbi signified the increasingly important role played by
military leaders in the affairs of the state. The *kanta's* first companions were
from the country's leading families but, subsequently, the elements that had
participated in the struggle for independence were granted two representatives,
one of whom, the *kunduda*, was to be Kebbi's military leader.

Given the need to seek protection against its neighbours and to provide for
security on the borders and the roads, the number of military leaders increased,
and a ranking order was instituted. The highest-ranking title varied from state
to state: it was *kunduda* in Kebbi, *kaura* in Katsina, *ubandawaki* in Zamfara and
Gobir, while in Kano it appears to have been the *galadima*.

As weapons improved, so strategies and tactics changed. In the event of
mobilization, the services of different trades, such as hunters and blacksmiths,
were called upon. The army consisted of two main corps – the infantry,
subdivided into archers and lancers, and the cavalry. Kebbi also had a river
flotilla.

The horses mainly originated from Azbin and Borno and were treated with
special care. The sovereign imported them and set up stables: the *kanta* of
Kebbi, for example, had stables in three places. The role played by the horse
can be explained by such innovations as the acquisition of *sulke* (coats of mail)
and the manufacture of *lifidi* (quilted armour). The *sarkin lifidi* (general in the
heavy cavalry division) and the *lifidi* (commander-in-chief of the heavy cavalry
division) were among the highest-ranking officers.

Muskets had been introduced to Kano by a Borno prince in the reign of
Dauda (1421–38), but it was not until three centuries later that they were
imported from Nupe. Babba Zaki (*c.* 1768–76) was the first sovereign to set up

s of fusiliers to serve as his personal bodyguard. Songhay, which had been
to gauge their deadly effectiveness at its own cost, did not bother to
trieve those abandoned by the Moroccan soldiers half a century later
(between 1591 and 1640). Hausaland seems to have deliberately neglected a
weapon that it could have procured for itself with its wealth.

The war tactics used consisted of surprise attacks, ambushes, pitched battles
and sieges. The stepped-up construction of fortifications around the cities was
justified by the frequent sieges and conflagrations. In this region, in which the
pace of economic development had increased, improvements in the art of war
led to the growth of pillaging. It is not easy to distinguish between wars waged
for purposes of conquest or consolidation, the repression of rebellions, wars of
intimidation and simple raids. Gobir was continually obliged to fight for its
survival as a state. The political, administrative and military aristocracy indulged
in pillaging, as the *Kano Chronicle* clearly shows: it grew rich and presented gifts
to the sovereigns and scholars. In Kano, in the space of two centuries –
between 1573 and 1768 – it became so powerful that it urged the state to wage
war, participated in plots and gave the sovereign cause for concern. The total
number of dignitaries varied from one state to another. Gobir had 22 (13
nobles and 9 commoners) and Katsina 46 (16 nobles and 30 commoners).

Resources

The Hausa state developed an ingenious system for controlling the territory and
levying taxes. Three major sources may be singled out.

Taxes and duties

Taxes and duties were the most regular sources. They included the following:

kudin kasa (land tax), paid by farmers. The unit taken into account seems to
have been the *gandum gida* (family field).
kudin sana'a (professional tax), paid by craftsmen and traders.
kudin hito (customs duty), payable on certain products entering the territory. In
addition, salt shipped to Zarmaterey and Arewa was subject to tax.
jangali (livestock tax), paid by the stock-breeders, particularly the Fulbe. In
Kano, it was levied for the first time by Kutumbi (*c.* 1623–48). In Kebbi,
the nomadic Fulbe paid *kudin haki* (grazing duty) while a dignitary, called
the *nono*, collected the milk and butter intended for the sovereign.

Gifts

Governors, dignitaries and other figures sent the sovereign a *gaisuwa* (gift made
to a superior). This was a political act whereby the interested party paid tribute
to the *sarki*, hoping in return to enjoy his favours. Those who were appointed
to high office also presented gifts to the *sarki*. One common method of obtaining
the wherewithal to send a *gaisuwa* was, in fact, pillaging.

Spoils
Pillaging supplied slaves, horses, cattle and a variety of goods. The *Kano Chronicle* stresses the value attached to horses between 1582 and 1623. The slaves were sold or divided among the great royal properties.

Other resources
There were countless measures whereby the *sarki* could fill the coffers of the state. For example, when the sovereign pardoned an offender, the latter had to pay *kudin laifi* (forgiveness tax). Thanks to the *Kano Chronicle*, it is possible to follow the process whereby the taxes and other duties were created for the benefit of the state. Sharif (*c.* 1703–31) instituted seven taxes that were regarded as oppressive, including a duty payable by girls on marriage. His successor, Kumbari (*c.* 1731–43), made the scholars pay a duty, as a result of which the Arabs left and went to Katsina.

Overview

The development of the *sarauta* system evolved in such a way that commoners and slaves could occupy the highest offices if they were considered highly trustworthy. Thus it was that royal slaves, particularly eunuchs, came to constitute an essential cog in the state machinery throughout the region.

This resulted in opposition between the *mai sarauta* (the ruler) and the *talakawa* (the ruled). To a lesser degree, the governors of the cities and regions were potential opponents. The frequent uprisings fomented by the governors of Gaya and Dutse illustrate the recurring friction between sovereign and vassals in Kano's history.

The political, administrative and military aristocracy represented a uniform group which grew rich by various methods of exploitation. It adopted a way of life commensurate with its resources, and decked itself out splendidly to show its prestige, while at the same time becoming difficult to keep under control because of the bribery and corruption in which it indulged.

Economic relations

Agriculture and stock-raising
From 1500 to 1800, Hausaland remained primarily a region of farmers. The *manoma* (peasant) made judicious use of the agricultural potential through a variety of techniques, including fertilizers and crop rotation and association. Their tools were as numerous as elsewhere in Africa, with a wide range of hoes adapted to the nature of the soil. The bulk of the labour force came from the *gida* (extended family) and the *gayya* (mutual aid system).

Besides millet, sorghum, rice, maize, peanuts and beans, farmers grew cotton, indigo, henna, tobacco and onions. Shea, tamarind and *nere* were also cultivated and honey was collected. They also engaged in fishing and hunting. *Jibda* (musk) was removed from the civet-cat and used for making perfume.

There was a substantial amount of stock-raising for domestic purposes. Goats were sacrificed by having their throats cut for certain ceremonies, while donkeys were used as a means of transport, particularly by traders. The Fulbe, with their sheep and cattle, settled in several areas of Katsina, Kebbi and Zamfara. Agriculture and stock-raising became closely associated and pockets of economic life developed based on a combination of the two, such as in the region of Ingawa in Katsina.

Crafts

The diversity and high technical standards attained by craftworkers were already remarkable at the time of Leo Africanus: people worked with iron, wood and leather, and also engaged in basket-making and pottery, while there was spectacular growth in weaving and dyeing. In addition, big demand stimulated high-quality crafts.

A trend towards group specialization can also be observed. In Kebbi, weaving and dyeing were in the hands of the Kebbawa; Zamfara attracted weavers and dyers from Kano. In both Kebbi and Zamfara, the Zoromawa specialized in silver jewellery and pottery; in Kano, pottery was made by the Bambadawa.

A variety of articles was manufactured. Leather, sandals, harnesses and saddles were exported. Jewellery was purchased by the wealthy. Clothes, such as tunics and cloths, were famed for their quality. Hausaland was also among the areas producing excellent-quality woven and dyed goods.

Trade

The stereotype of the *bahaushe* (trader) became widely recognized and it is impossible to overstress his integration into the trading networks of western Africa and the international trader class in the savannah.

The area of influence of the markets differed considerably. Some were important locally and retained their social and economic character: goods were traded, but social life on market day was considerably enlivened. At a higher level, the regional market was a centre to which local products were brought and where imported articles in daily use were distributed. In Zamfara itself, the northern and north-eastern markets supplied cotton, indigo, tobacco, onions and cattle, while the southern ones received abundant supplies of cereals. Upper Kebbi sent yarn, fabrics and slaves to Lower Kebbi, which supplied nets, harpoons, hides and *abara* (large dugout canoes).

Foreign trade remained in the hands of the Hausa, although some Azbinawa, Arabs, Kanuri and Wangara also took part. Caravans linked Kawar to Gao, Azbin to Hausaland and Kano to Gwanja. Each sovereign took security precautions to protect the caravans in his own territory as they paid taxes to the states through which they passed.

There were several international markets within the region and on its periphery. In the north, Agades and Bilma served as links with northern Africa; in the centre, Katsina and Kano were staging-posts in north-south and east-west relations; in the south, Zaria, Birnin Gwari and Birnin Yawuri enabled the networks to be extended towards Yoruba, Nupe, Borgu and Gwanja. A considerable volume of merchandise circulated in Hausaland.

The Sahara and Azbin sent Arab and European goods to these markets, including mirrors and paper, but particularly horses, camels, dates, henna, salt, swords and other articles. A certain proportion of the salt and swords was in transit to the south. In return, Hausaland supplied them with slaves, clothes, fabrics, millet, hides, iron, gold dust and kola nuts from Gwanja.

Borno had horses, natron and salt to offer and in exchange received metal articles, gold dust and kola nuts. Hausaland exported salt, swords, condiments, hides, clothes and fabrics, slaves and horses to Gwanja, Borgu, Nupe and Yoruba and received in return various European goods, local iron, antimony, slaves and eunuchs, muskets from Nupe (for Kano) and kola nuts from Gwanja for domestic consumption.

Social relations

Three basic groups in society can be distinguished.

Producers of material goods

Farmers formed the largest category. The more intensive use of the land and the improvements in farming practices were to bring about far-reaching changes. Until that time, the main source of labour had been the extended family. It is clear that some population groups had been reduced to a state of bondage: the Mazumawa, for example, lost their independence as soon as Gobir reached the Birnin Lalle area. The Maguzawa of Fanfui were subordinate as a group and thus tributaries. The last source of labour was slave labour.

Among craftworkers there was intense specialization, and many slaves engaged in craft activities at their master's behest and for his benefit, at least to begin with. A large number of herders adopted a sedentary life-style. They employed slaves, who rapidly became integrated into the political community.

Whether the producers were free men, tributaries or slaves, they were members of a political community and their relations with the state were codified. Distinctions based on wealth and on proximity to the machinery of state were gradually introduced.

Traders

Traders were divided into several categories, ranging from wholesalers engaging in *fatauci* (trade over medium and long distances) to retailers who organized the *kasuwanci* (retail trade). A group of *attajirai* (rich traders) was formed which included merchants dealing in slaves, horses, kola nuts and clothing. Traders and scholars seem always to have been closely linked. The traders were united by common interests and they did not hesitate to emigrate when they felt they were being taxed excessively,

Between 1500 and 1800, the various Wangara and Hausa sub-groups succeeded in uniting the trade networks throughout western Africa and constituted the middle class in the main towns. They continued to consolidate their position as a class and spread the Islamic faith to their advantage.

The aristocracy

The ruling class included the *masu sarauta* (all those with any political authority). It was subdivided into several levels.

The *sarki* was at the head of the nobility, which was composed of the princely families, families governing the semi-autonomous cities and vassal provinces, and representatives of the various nationalities, particularly the Azbinawa, the S̲h̲uwa Arabs and the Fulbe. The nobility performed various duties within the machinery of state, and tended to become a homogeneous group whose cohesion was strengthened by marriage ties.

All the dignitaries appointed by the *sarki* to run the state formed the second level. They were of commoner or serf origin but their position gave them access to wealth and esteem through the gifts they received, but particularly through pillaging. In some instances, they held key military office. It was they who urged Muhammad Nazaki to reject Katsina's authority and opposed the attack against Katsina planned by Zaudai. Kebbi's decline began when the dignitaries holding military office had grown so rich that they lost interest in affairs of state.

The aristocracy, primarily the princes and royal slaves, confiscated the property of the *talakawa* particularly when the sovereign showed signs of weakness.

The question of social relations seems to have been dominated by two factors: the sale of Africans by certain sovereigns and the participation of Kawar and Zawila in the slave trade. In Kānem, the first indicators of the export of slaves and their use within it appear as early as the eleventh century. In the mid-fifteenth century *galadima* Dawuda went and waged war and sent *sarkin* Kano a thousand slaves every two months. By the end of the campaign, he had accumulated 21,000 slaves scattered among 21 villages and all named Indabo. The term *indabo* (village of slaves) is reminiscent of the Soninke *debe*, the Fulfulde *debeere* and the Songhay *dabey*. In these villages, the productive activities were crafts and particularly agriculture. In Katsina, the city of Tsagero was a royal property where large numbers of slaves were kept, and where even princes were sent. In the estates in the Gozaki area, cotton-growing eventually came to depend on slaves imported from Zazzau, and part of the crop was exported to Kano.

Whether the slave was a commodity, a servant, a high-ranking official or an independent producer in a subordinate position, he had a role to play in the development of the economy and the state. However, the export of slaves has to be examined in relation to the sources of supply in Europe and the Orient, even before the Atlantic trade began to claim its share. The contribution of slavery to the prosperity of the region will become clearer when it has been singled out from all other forms of subordination.

The *masu sarauta* (aristocrats) can be regarded as opposing the *talakawa*, who were free producers but had no political power. As the aristocracy, the scholars and the traders grew rich, the distinction shifted to an economic level between the *attajirai*, the wealthy, and the *talakawa*, the poor. The *bawan sarki* (royal slave) ceased to be a *talaka*, from both the political and the economic stand-points. The situation was thereby clarified, because the ethnic and religious differences had been relegated to the background, and this left those in power and the second-class citizens confronting one another.

Culture and religion

Political and economic developments gave rise to many cultural changes. On a material level, for instance, architecture was improved and, even today, the cities still compete with one another in their styles. In music, some instruments, such as the *kakaki* and the *algaita*, became widespread and orchestras were brought into the royal ceremonial. The main feature of Hausaland in this respect was its richness and cultural unity – the outcome of a homogenizing process that made Guber a *lingua franca* in Africa under the name *Hausa*.

Islamization at the beginning of the sixteenth century was confined to traders and the political élite. However, the end of the period was to be marked by an intensification of the open struggle between the aristocracy and the scholars. The *Kano Chronicle* and the *Wangara Chronicle* show the development of their relations from the inside.

Kano witnessed a massive and regular influx of scholars. In Kisoki's reign (1500–65), several scholars arrived. The first, Shaihu Ba-Tunashe, brought with him the *ashafa* book; the second, Dan Gwarandume, was to read this book; and the third, Shaihu Abdussalami, introduced three books. Then a group of three brothers from Borno arrived, one of whom accepted the post of *kāḍī*. In the reign of Abū Bakr Kado (*c.* 1565–73), a second group of scholars, from Bagirmi, immigrated to Kano. They had stayed some time in Katsina, and Muḥammad Zakī (*c.* 1582–1618) married one of the daughters of Tama, their leader. It was on account of the scholars that the Katsinawa did not sack Kano, and it was the scholars who negotiated peace between Kano and Katsina in the period between 1648 and 1651.

In Birnin Katsina, a distinction could be made between several groups descending from Wālī Abū ʿAbdullāhī b. Masani, Malam Buhārī and Malam ʿUthmān. Many cultivated people from differing backgrounds, ethnic groups and places of origin lived in other cities. This intelligentsia, which was scattered over a territory whose population and leaders considered themselves Islamized, kept their distance from the ruling class.

Zamfara differed in that Islam did not take root there until a late stage, probably because most of its urban centres were far from the caravan routes of central Sudan. Nevertheless, Kanuri scholars may have participated in converting the sovereign to Islam. The *imām* of Anka had nothing short of a fief, and his residence was a place of refuge for all those who incurred the wrath of the rulers. Some posts were reserved for scholars: the *limanin ciki* was responsible for the education of the royal family, while the *dan kodo* and the *dan dubal* were advisors on religious affairs, custodians of the history of Zamfara and responsible for praying for the army's victory.

For their income, the scholars relied on the generosity of the aristocracy.

However, it is difficult to fault the objectivity of the scholars, even when, as in Kano, they were granted fiefs and estates. Their critical attitude was reflected in the *Kano Chronicle*.

The regular travelling of the scholars and the introduction of books partly explain the area's intellectual awakening. However, there must be added to that the existence of centres of learning and, in particular, the use of the *ajami* script (transcription in Arabic) in Kano and Katsina in the sixteenth century. The scholars wrote in Arabic, Fulfulde and Hausa.

Praying for victory in war and consulted on legal matters, the scholars had a decisive influence on social life, particularly through the *wa'azi* (sermons). In Zamfara, among the most celebrated, mention has been made of Ramaḍān b. Aḥmadu (from Fezzan), Haṣhimu Bazanfane, Maman Tukur dan Binta and al-Mustafa Gwani, a Kanuri who confronted 'Uthmān while he was touring Zamfara on the simultaneous presence of men and women during the sermons.

Two names stand out in Katsina: Abū 'Abullāhī b. Masanī b. Muḥammad al-Barnāwī al-Kaṣhinawī (c. 1595–1667) and Muḥammad al-Sabbāgh al-Kaṣhinawī, better known as Dan Marina, who flourished in about 1650 and composed a poem in praise of the *mai* 'Alī, who defeated Kwararafa in about 1680.

However, there can be no doubt that it was Malam Ḍjibrīl dan 'Umaru who stood out most strikingly from the group. This scholar, with his encyclopaedic knowledge, was born in Adar and died there, after having been on several pilgrimages. His main subject of preoccupation lay in the reform of Islam in Sudan. After his failure among the Tuareg in Adar, he approached the Hausa princes, whose hostility he aroused. 'Uthmān was his disciple. The second half of the eighteenth century was marked by a wealth of intellectual activity and lively debate among scholars, a simple form of opposition to the established order represented by the *masu sarauta*.

Conclusion

Just before the *djihād*, there was a marked decline in the turbulent character of the relations between states. Kebbi and Zamfara had been defeated, but the others were faced with difficult problems. In Kano, peace and stability were punctuated by two serious disagreements between the *sarki* and the dignitaries. In Gobir, Bawa (c. 1777–89) for the first time introduced a tax on a certain variety of maize, and stock-raisers had to pay the *jangali* on several occasions during the same year. Two dynastic crises shook Katsina in 1767 and 1796. The risk of instability was noted almost throughout the region, due to resistance on the part of the dignitaries, the increased weight of tyranny and the latent opposition of the *talakawa*. The political authorities had attained a threshold of oppression which no longer spared the scholars, but they were the only ones who ventured to combat the established order openly.

Economically the apparent opposition to progress that seemed to characterize the years between 1600 and 1790 has been overstressed. It is true that neither the wheel nor the windmill was used, and even the musket was scorned. However, despite a host of natural calamities, the area developed in a remarkable manner, owing not only to the growth of trade, thanks to state intervention in various forms, but also to progress in production and processing.

Politically, despite the armed conflicts, none of the states disappeared during the period under consideration. Elsewhere, Ghana, Mali and Songhay disintegrated, while Kānem-Borno enjoyed remarkable longevity. The economic success of Hausaland has overshadowed the great stability of the state as an institution. Its bureaucratic and oppressive nature was highlighted by the measures introduced by Sharīf in Kano. In fact, the machinery of state was efficient and few alterations were made to it by the regimes that followed.

17

Kānem-Borno: its relations with the Mediterranean Sea, Bagirmi and other states in the Chad basin

In the thirteenth century the Muslim state of Kānem was one of the most extensive in the *Bilād al-Sūdān*. The Sēfuwa *mais* (kings) controlled the vast area from the eastern shores of Lake Chad in the south to the oases of Fezzān in the north, but their expansion had not been accompanied by appropriate political and economic development. The emergence of various more or less autonomous ethnic groups distinct from the Sēfuwa ruling dynasty had prevented the development of a centralized political system. In addition, Kānem, mostly desert and semi-desert, lacked the primary resources needed to make such a large system viable.

A serious crisis finally led to the collapse of the Kānem state in the latter part of the fourteenth century. The mai 'Umar b. Idrīs (1382–87), at the head of the Magumi group and its supporters, left for Borno to the west of Lake Chad, where the necessary resources existed and where the Sēfuwa had already settled their vassals. A large number of other immigrants from Kānem had also already settled there.

The Sēfuwa's main objective on their arrival in Borno appears to have been the building of a strong regional economy to support a well-organized, Sēfuwa-dominated political structure. However, during their first century there, they faced many problems which at times posed threats to their very survival: constant civil strife, dynastic crises, periodic attacks from Bulala and overmighty title-holders.

Mai 'Alī Gaji and the foundation of the Borno califate c. 1465–97

'Alī b. 'Dunāma, commonly known as 'Alī Gaji, was able to consolidate power in his own branch of the ruling dynasty. When, in about 1471, the Bulala launched new incursions into Borno, he defeated them but did not pursue them further. In about 1472, he built the fortress of Birnin Gazargamu which eventually developed into the capital of the Sēfuwa and remained so throughout their rule in Borno.

'Alī Gaji is remembered as a reviver of Islam. He attempted to found a proper Islamic government, surrounding himself with *'ulamā'* whose advice he sought. Many of the overmighty title-holders had their powers reduced, especially the *kaigama* and the *yerima* (governors of the northern provinces).

During his pilgrimage to Mecca in about 1484, 'Alī Gaji was said to have been invested as the *khalīfa* of Takrur. From this time onwards the rulers of Borno regarded themselves as *khalīfas*, a claim that came to be accepted by many scholars and rulers in the *Bilād al-Sūdān*.

Problems and opportunities in expanding the Borno califate: c.1497–1564

'Alī Gaji's policies were continued by his son and successor Idrīs b. 'Alī, surnamed Katakarmabe (*c.* 1497–1519), who consolidated his gains and tried to expand the state. But for the next 50 years or more Katakarmabe and his successors faced many challenges which diverted their attention from their goals.

The Sēfuwa's first problem was the resumption of Bulala attacks. Katakarmabe had to face a Bulala attack as soon as he became *mai*. Not only did he defeat them but he victoriously re-entered Ndjīmī, the former Sēfuwa capital which, however, was never reoccupied. After concluding a treaty with the Bulala, Idrīs returned to Borno, but the truce was short-lived and intermittent hostilities continued into the reign of Idrīs Alawoma (1564–96).

Another problem for the Sēfuwa kings was the emergence of many states in the Chad basin and elsewhere in the Sudan, which forced the Sēfuwa to settle their problems with each state.

By the early 1500s numerous petty kingdoms had emerged along the southern border of Borno. These included Bagirmi, Mandara, the Kotoko states, Northern Bolewa of Daniski, Yamta and Margi. Some of these states were forced to recognize some form of Sēfuwa hegemony. But more often the Sēfuwa tried to enter into peaceful relations with these nascent states, encouraging them to develop their own economies and establish regular trade with Borno. Through this association the emerging states absorbed much of Borno culture, which may have contributed to their rapid growth.

In the same period, many states were also emerging in Hausaland. Katsina and Kano soon developed as the termini of the trans-Saharan route as well as entrepôts of the east–west route by which Akan gold and kola were taken to Borno. Further north, there was a slight shift of the trans-Saharan route when Agades supplanted Takedda as the main entrepôt.

Borno had to react to these developments. The new trade route between Borno and Hausaland soon became unsafe and efforts must have been made to protect it. The problems concerning this trade route and the struggle for control of the settlements that developed along it may have contributed to the conflicts between the *mai* Idris Katakarmabe and two kings of Kano, 'Abdullāhī (*c.*1499–1509) and Muḥammad Kisoki (*c.* 1509–65).

Borno must also have wanted to control the new entrepôt of Agades which the then very powerful Songhay sought in 1501 and 1515 to bring within its sphere of influence. However, the emergence of Kebbi in the reign of Muḥammadu Kanta (*c.* 1516–54) frustrated the efforts of both Songhay and Borno. The problems of Agades continued to bedevil the Sēfuwa kings almost throughout their rule.

The period from about 1480 to 1520 was a time of active Islamization in the *Bilād al-Sūdān*. In the east, the Fundj sultanate, which was founded in about 1504, soon adopted Islam. In the west, many scholars from Mali, North Africa, Egypt and the Saharan oases visited Hausaland and contributed to its Islamization. Further west, the Songhay empire reached its zenith with the *askiya* Muḥammad (*c.* 1493–1528), whose reign coincided with a burst of Islamic fervour. During his pilgrimage to Mecca (*c.* 1496–8), this ruler was invested with the title of *khalifa* of Takrūr, as the *mai* ʿAlī Gaji had been ten years earlier.

The Sēfuwa *mais* had been Muslims since the eleventh century and they traditionally surrounded themselves with *ʿulamāʾ*, which gave them an edge over other rulers. The decline and fall of the Songhay empire in the late sixteenth century finally ensured their hegemony.

Borno became a great intellectual centre visited by scholars from the *Bilād al-Sūdān* and other parts of the Muslim world and its cultural influence was felt in many states.

From the reign of Idrīs Katakarmabe, records exist of diplomatic and commercial relations between the Sēfuwa and the various authorities controlling the North African coast. In about 1512 Katakarmabe sent a diplomatic and trade mission to the Spaniards, who had recently occupied Tripoli, to renew commercial ties with the area. When the Ottomans were established in the Maghrib, Dunāma b. Muḥammad in about 1555 sent an embassy which established with Tighūrt Pasha a treaty of 'friendship and trade' which was renewed by their respective successors. Strong ties were probably also established with Egypt.

Katakarmabe's descendants continued his policy in dealing with the Bulala incursions and the emergence of new states. In about 1561 there was a war between Kebbi and Borno over control of Agades, which Borno seems to have lost.

Establishment of a strong regional economy and a centralized political system and the emergence of the Kanuri, c. 1564–77

Most scholars agree that Borno reached its apogee during the rule of Idrīs b. ʿAlī, posthumously surnamed Alawoma (1564–96). He was seen as a military and administrative innovator as well as an Islamizer and a skilled diplomat.

His main objective on his accession was to equip his country with a strong economic and political system. He was the first *mai* to attempt to bring the whole metropolitan province firmly under control. The cavalry was reorganized. There was also a corps of Turkish gunmen which had been developing under his predecessors. Larger boats were built for easier crossing of rivers. It was with such a force that Alawoma launched his conquests.

Most of the hostile groups which refused to be persuaded or coerced into submission by the *mai* were continually attacked. These included the Ngafata, the Talata, the Dugurti, the Maya, the Ngizim and the Bedde. Some, such as the Mukhulum, were allowed to retain their homes in return for a promise of tribute in wheat. Others, considered implacable, were ejected from the metropolitan province.

In place of these groups expelled from their country, others, mostly from Kānem, came and settled in Borno. These large-scale demographic changes, together with extensive intermarriage with female slaves captured during the conflicts or exchanged with satellite states, contributed to the development of the Kanuri group within the metropolitan province.

In southern Borno *ribāṭs* (frontier fortresses) were built to contain dissident groups such as the Gamergu, and agreements were entered into with satellite-state rulers for joint military expeditions against the dissidents.

The final solution to the problems of Kānem

After the pacification and integration of most of the metropolitan province, Idrīs Alawoma turned his attention to Kānem to put an end once and for all to the threat it posed to Borno. He had three objectives: to destroy completely the military strength and power base of the Bulala; to destroy the economic base of the Kānem state; and to transfer as many groups as possible to Borno.

Alawoma undertook several expeditions against the Bulala and other groups who supported them. Three of the most fertile valleys of Kānem were ravaged and some of the most important towns, such as Ikima, Aghafi and Ago, were destroyed and their population removed to Borno. The groups forced to settle in Borno included the Tubu, the Koyam, the Kulu and the Shuwa Arabs. The last two groups, who were cattle-owners, were settled along the southern shores of Lake Chad and to the west of the metropolitan province. The Tubu were settled on the desert margin, both for strategic reasons and to participate in the production of salt.

By the 1580s, Alawoma had achieved most of his objectives and Kānem state was, by common agreement, partitioned between Borno and the Bulala, the latter accepting some loose form of control by Borno.

Internal reforms

Alawoma seems to have made a pilgrimage to Mecca in about 1571. On his return he attempted to introduce a number of reforms to bring the country into line with other Islamic states. He tried, apparently without success, to separate the functions of the judiciary from those of the executive. He did, however, succeed in establishing a court of appeal where 'The learned men and *Imams* held disputations before the Amīr 'Alī concerning doubtful points of law and dogma' (H. R. Palmer, 1936, pp. 33–6). The court attracted numerous North African and other scholars, which gave it a cosmopolitan character.

The rise of a strong regional economy

The conquests of and demographic changes under Idrīs Alawoma, as well as his other reforms, led to the emergence of a strong regional economy based on the metropolitan province, an area of some 20,000 square kilometres.

In the east there was large-scale fishing along the shores of Lake Chad by the Buduma and Kānembu, while the good grazing lands attracted a large number of Kānembu, Shuwa and Fulbe cattle-raising nomads. Natron and salt were produced by the sedentary Kānembu and Buduma. Important urban centres sprang up, including Mungono, Kauwa, Burwa and Ngurno.

In the west of the country there were also big natron deposits, which were worked by the Manga and the Tubu. In the south was a large concentration of farming peoples including the Ngizim and the Bedde. This area received a great variety of immigrants and the many urban centres which developed there, including Nguru Ngilewa, Mashina Kabshari and Maja Kawuri, were more cosmopolitan than their eastern counterparts.

Birnin Gazargamu and its environs formed the third economic centre. Situated on the trade route that crossed the country from east to west, Birnin Gazargamu was also the terminus for the Borno–Kawār–Tripoli caravan route as well as for the main route connecting the area with Hausaland. Thus the city was the nerve-centre of the country's economy and its large market attracted many foreign merchants. In the fertile, irrigated Yobe valley there was a heavy concentration of the emerging Kanuri group which had settled in many urban centres in addition to Birnin Gazargamu.

The development of basic industries led to the establishment of supporting ones such as pottery, weaving, leather work, dyeing and transportation.

The natron and salt trade extended to the Atlantic coast, Hausaland, the Volta basin and northwards to Azbin and Adrār. Dried fish was traded within the country and with Mandara, Hausaland and the Saharan oases. Slaves, eunuchs, hides, ivory, perfumes, leather goods and gold were sent across the Sahara to North Africa and Egypt. In exchange, horses, horse-trappings, armour, copper, bronze and other goods came from Europe and North Africa to be distributed in Borno and other parts of the *Bilād al-Sudān*.

From the reign of Alawoma, various peoples around the Chad basin were apparently encouraged by the Sēfuwa to engage in commercial activities. These peoples were all referred to as Bornoans and must have helped to spread the emerging Bornoan culture in Hausaland and other areas. It was through its regional economy, its control of trade and its primacy in Islam that Borno came to dominate the affairs of the *Bilād al-Sudān* during this period.

The *mais* interfered little with the trade itself, limiting their role to protecting the trade routes and entering into agreements with Saharan and North African governments to ensure the free flow of trade. On the other hand, they were active in the organization of markets – to encourage traders and to obtain revenue. In the capital and the other major centres, the *wasili* (North African traders) were recognized as guests of the government. A quarter was assigned to them and a titled official, the *zanna arjinama*, looked after their affairs. In the markets, the *mala kasuube* supervised sales and took pains to ensure honesty in major commercial transactions.

The diplomatic relations of Idrīs Alawoma with the sultans of Turkey and Morocco

Ottoman–Borno relations started with the arrival of the former in the Maghrib. From about 1549 – when the Ottomans took control of Fezzān – to about 1570, these appear to have been cordial. Things changed in about 1571, when the Ottoman authorities suddenly raised the annual tribute of Fezzān. This decision coincided with a period of famine, and many people were forced to migrate to Hausaland and Borno. The Ottoman officials in Fezzān forced those who remained, many of them old people, to make up the difference. Even the pilgrims from Hausaland and Borno were stopped and forced to pay taxes.

Alawoma was able to obtain first-hand information about the situation when he went on a pilgrimage to Mecca in about 1571. In about 1574, anxious to ensure the security of the route both for pilgrimage and for trade, Alawoma dispatched an embassy to Istanbul with three specific requests: a guarantee of safe passage and security of property for all travellers from Borno crossing Ottoman territory; proper management or, failing that, the ceding to Borno of all the recently acquired fortresses south of Fezzān, including Guran; and co-operation between the two powers in dealing with the troublesome Tuareg and any other people disturbing the peace in the area. There appears to have been no mention or solicitation of arms.

In May 1577, Sultan Murad III agreed to all these requests except the ceding of the Guran fortress, which he promised would henceforth be properly managed. From then on, cordial commercial and diplomatic relations continued between the two powers.

The Moroccan victory at Ḳaṣr al-Kabīr in 1578 was generally hailed as an ideological victory for Islam over Christendom. Borno, like the leading Muslim powers, sent a delegation to congratulate the sultan of Morocco. However, Alawoma was fearful of proposed joint Ottoman-Saʿādī expeditions against the Saharan oases and even the Sudan and sought to frustrate the possibility by suggesting a joint Borno–Moroccan expedition to the Saharan oases, once again in a state of some insecurity. The outcome of this embassy, according to Moroccan sources, was the acceptance of Borno's suggestions on condition that Alawoma acknowledge al-Manṣūr as the *khalif* of the time. For Morocco, securing recognition of his califate by one of the leading powers in the Sudan would constitute an ideological victory and strengthen his position in relation to Songhay. For Alawoma, the price was worth paying if it forestalled the threat of joint Moroccan–Ottoman action against Borno or any other area where its interests lay.

Towards the end of his reign, Alawoma was probably preoccupied by the rapid development of the Mandara and Bagirmi states. Alawoma was forced to lead several expeditions against Mandara, most of them unsuccessful. In Bagirmi, 'Abdullāh b. Lubetko (*c.* 1561–1602), despite having probably gained the throne with Bornoan assistance, started making trouble. It was on a campaign against 'Abdullāh that Alawoma is said to have been assassinated by a Gamergu.

The death of Idrīs Alawoma, contrary to the views of some writers, did not lead to the collapse of the Borno empire. It was in fact during the reigns of his four immediate successors (*c.* 1596–1677) that his conquests were consolidated and the administrative machinery assumed its final form. It was also at this time that the Kanuri finally emerged as an ethnic group with a distinct culture.

The social and material culture of the Kanuri

The term Kanuri probably came into use in the early seventeenth century. It refers to the dominant ethnic group of Borno upon whom the power of the Sēfuwa *mais* was based. The Kanuri were the product of intermarriage of the Magumi from Kānem and the indigenous Chadian speakers of Borno, a development accelerated by the population policy of Idrīs Alawoma.

Most Kanuri lived in villages in compounds containing several round huts with conical grass roofs. Many compounds were surrounded by *sugedi* (grass matting). In the larger towns, most huts and mosques were mud-built, and the houses of the rich were protected by high mud walls. Most towns and villages were in the shape of a U, in the middle of which the *dandal* (main street), running east–west, led to the palace of the local governor, next to the main mosque.

At Birnin Gazargamu and in some of the larger towns, the houses were usually rectangular with thick mud walls and flat roofs. Royal palaces at Birnin and Gambaru, their main mosques and the residences of important dignitaries were surrounded by impressive walls of fired bricks, one of the distinguishing traits of Kanuri culture from the mid-sixteenth to the early eighteenth century.

A typical Kanuri was distinguished by language and physical appearance. Both men and women had distinguishing vertical marks on each cheek. An unmarried girl wore her hair in a *kela yasku* (a special style) while a married woman wore her hair in a *jurungul* (crown). Women ate kola nuts and stained their teeth with tobacco flowers. They usually wore *gimaje* (long dyed cotton dresses) and women of distinction wore a *kalaram* (turban). Men wore *tobe* (large open cotton gowns either plain or dyed blue). Men of the upper class wore a multiplicity of gowns of expensive imported cloth, and in the late-eighteenth century they wore outsize turbans, a custom that appears to have been borrowed from seventeenth-century Ottoman practice.

Marriage in Kanuri culture had certain distinctive characteristics involving a mixture of Islamic rites and Magumi and other pre-Islamic practices.

Kanuri society was highly stratified. It was broadly divided into two classes, the *kontuowa* (ruling class or nobility) and the *tala'a* (commoners), and both of these had several subdivisions. Differences of speech, dress and housing distinguished the classes and their subdivisions. Upward mobility was achieved through amassing more wealth, associating with the ruling class or obtaining a high-ranking office.

Kanuri socio-political culture laid especial stress on inferior–superior relations. A social inferior was always required to show his social superior respect in public. In addition, he was also required to pay respectful visits to the house of his 'social father', who could ask him to do any favour. In return, the superior took care of his inferior's basic needs and advanced his interests in society.

Borno by this time was a centre of learning which attracted large numbers of students and visiting scholars from the *Bilād al-Sūdān*, North Africa and the Middle East. Borno specialized in *tafsir* (commentary on the Ḳur'ān) in the Kanembu language, and the custom of writing the Borno language in Arabic letters seems to have developed in the seventeenth century.

There were two types of scholar. The first held official religious offices. The *imāms*, the *kādīs*, the *mainin kinendi* (Islamic and legal adviser to the *mai*), the *talba* (head of the police and the magistrates), the *khazin* (treasurer) and the *wazir* were the great *'ulamā'* who helped the *mai* govern according to Islamic precepts. Their positions were hereditary and restricted to a few leading scholarly families. The institutionalized character of the offices they held associated them with the temporal power and increasingly alienated them from the non-court scholars.

The more austere scholars lived in the rural areas and propagated their religion. During the time of the Sēfuwa, most of them enjoyed the protection of the kings, who granted them *maḥrams* (privileges). However, it was also they who produced the first intensive criticism of Sēfuwa rule.

Political organization

The *mai* was the head of the royal family, the supreme head of state and the *larde kangema* (nominal owner of the land). He was the symbol of the unity and continuity of the state. As the *amīr al-mu'minīm* (commander of the faithful) he was the leader of all the Muslims and the final arbiter in both public and private matters of justice.

Many of the sacred attributes of the pre-Islamic kings seem to have survived into the Islamic period. The *mai* was still largely secluded, appearing in public only in a *fanadir* (cage), and people could not speak to him directly. Muslim scholars appear to have enhanced the sacred attributes of the king.

The *mai* was selected from among the *maina* (eligible princes), but the succession was not always smooth. From the time of the *mai* Idris b. Ali (c. 1677–96), or earlier, the kings seem to have resorted to eliminating rival candidates – a habit they probably learnt from the Ottomans.

The other members of the royal family consisted of the king's four titled wives, the concubines, the princes and princesses, the *magira* (queen-mother) and the *magram* (the king's official sister). The *gumsu* (the king's head wife) was responsible for administering the palace; the *magira* was the holder of the largest number of fiefs in the kingdom and had the right to grant sanctuary; the *magram* usually supervised the cooking of the king's food.

Most princes resided outside the palace and their activities were strictly controlled, although some were given fiefs. The most important of these were the *chiroma* (heir apparent) and the *yerima* (governor of the northern provinces) who was always a *maidugu* (grandson of a previous king) which meant he could have no claim to the throne.

The highest council of state was the *majlis*, which was normally presided over by the king and was composed of military and religious notables. Most of the Muslim advisers already mentioned as well as military commanders were members. It also included powerful slaves of the *mai*, some of whom were eunuchs. The *majlis* examined all great affairs of state. The *noguna* (*mai's* court), which consisted of all the notables in the capital, met daily.

The towns, villages and ethnic units were grouped into *chidi* (fiefs) and all major officials of state were *chima* (fief-holders). The *chima* were responsible for the maintenance of order in their fiefs, for the collection of taxes and for the raising of troops for the army. The *mai* could confiscate, reduce or redistribute fiefs entirely as he saw fit. At the local level, the people were ruled by *mbarma* or *bulala*.

The Sēfuwa's income included the *zakat* (compulsory alms), *dibalram* (road tolls), *kultingo* (tribute) and war booty.

The golden age in Borno

The seventeenth century – not the sixteenth as traditionally claimed – should be regarded as Borno's golden age.

It was during the rule of 'Umar b. Idrīs (*c.* 1619–39) that the offices of the *galadima* of Nguru and the *alifa* of Mao in Kānem were established as semi-autonomous vassals to take care of the western and eastern marches of the state respectively. Buffer states were established along the desert fringe at Muniyo and Mashina as barriers to Tuareg attacks on the metropolitan province. This was the period when 'Abd al-Karīm ben Jame (*c.* 1611–55) founded Wadai – no doubt with Borno's blessing, since Wadai checked for some time the expansionism of Bagirmi. As with the other neighbouring states, Wadai fell within the political, cultural and commercial orbit of Borno.

Diplomatic and commercial relations with the Mediterranean littoral entered one of their briskest periods. Relations with Egypt must also have been good, through trade and because Egypt lay on the pilgrimage route to Mecca.

By the seventeenth century, particularly by the reign of Ali b. 'Umar (*c.* 1639–77), Borno had become the dominant power in the *Bilād al-Sudān*. Not only was it a centre of learning and culture but it also controlled all the easily accessible sources of mineral salts – at Muniyo, Bilma and around Lake Chad. Its close trade connections with the Mediterranean coast led to its domination of the redistribution of imported goods to the states of central Sudan. The *mai*s were recognized as the undisputed leaders of the Islamic states of the region. Most of these states appear to have placed themselves voluntarily under the protection of the <u>khalif</u> in order to benefit from his *baraka* (blessing) and to obtain the goods they needed. It was the general erosion of this system that led to the decline and final collapse of the Sēfuwa.

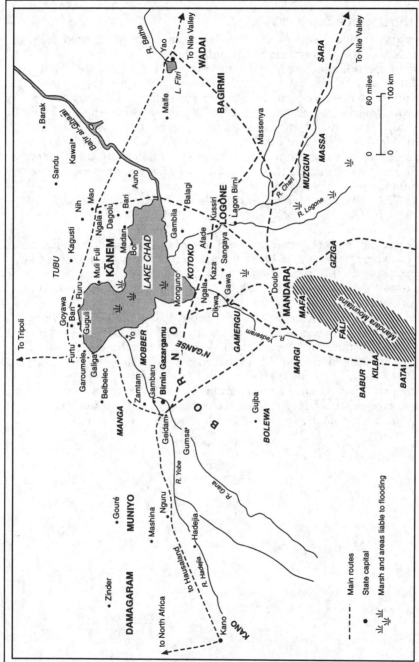

17.1 *Borno, Kānem and their immediate neighbours in the eighteenth century (adapted from map drawn by John F. Antwi, Geography Department, Bayero University, Kano, after B. M. Barkindo)*

Crises of the late eighteenth century

With the reign of ʿAli b. Dunāma (*c.* 1742–92), Borno entered a period of crisis which climaxed in the *djihād* of the nineteenth century.

In western Borno, the Bedde were intensifying their raids on the trade routes to Hausaland, while in the north the Tuareg of Agades were stepping up their incursions. All this precipitated the southward shift of the Manga groups.

In Bagirmi, Muḥammad al-Amīn (*c.* 1751–85) threw off Borno's overlordship and launched a series of attacks on Borno's eastern frontiers, while Wadai under Jawda (*c.* 1747–95) continued its expansionist policy towards Baḥr al-Ghazāl. These attacks set in motion the migrations of the Tubu, the Kānembu and the Shuwa Arabs into Kānem and the metropolitan province, thereby causing conflicts over grazing lands.

In about 1791, Mandara revolted, soon followed by the Sosebalki states and, in about 1785, by Gobir.

Faced with insecurity, famines and impoverished grazing lands, many Fulbe nomads abandoned metropolitan Borno and moved to Hausaland, Mandara and Fombina. Nowhere, however, did they find the security they were looking for, and this may partly explain their dominant role in the *djihād*.

The non-court scholars and the ordinary Muslims blamed the crisis on the increasing corruption of the Sēfuwa rulers and the inability of the *mais* to prevent the growing syncretism among the people. When the *djihād* broke out, the client – rulers in Hausaland called upon the *mai* to fulfil his obligations as *khalif* and come to their aid. That he could not and that he could not even prevent his own expulsion from his capital meant that the *khalif* had lost his primacy.

However, although the *djihād* did contribute to the loss of the vassal states and to the end of the Sēfuwa rule, the system that the *mais* had built, particularly in metropolitan Borno, survived, though modified, well into the twentieth century.

From the Cameroon grasslands to the Upper Nile

In this part of Africa, historical information for the period 1500–1800 is less plentiful, coherent and reliable than for other regions. In areas where political organizations took the form of states, these were mostly formed very late, in the eighteenth and nineteenth centuries. Oral traditions appear uninformative and rarely go back more than a few generations. Those which do exist often record the individual history of a particular lineage and raise the usual problems of interpretation. Other sources are very sparse. A few travellers' accounts exist from the sixteenth century onwards for the areas in contact with foreigners. Finally, archaeology, historical linguistics and ethnolinguistics are only just beginning in the area.

There is, moreover, no single factor uniting the different parts of this region. The forest is certainly its dominant physical feature, but many parts of the region have long been savannah. The low population density appears to be another common characteristic, but there were areas of relatively high density, notably in the savannah and along the waterways. As for the peoples, their languages, ways of life and forms of organization were extremely diverse. This diversity and the inevitable uneven distribution of information necessitate a regional approach to the area.

The northern border area

The northern part of this region, from the central Cameroon highlands in the west to the River Nile in the east, is the area for which historical information is most lacking. Moreover, the tendency of ethnological and historical works to restrict themselves to the limits of ethnic groups and, more recently, to the limits of contemporary states, makes any regional synthesis difficult. It seems wiser therefore, to try to define micro-regions which have some degree of cultural homogeneity or, at least, some degree of common destiny.

The central Cameroon highlands

These relatively fertile grasslands were probably settled very early. There are at least two indications of this early settlement. The first is vegetation, which is today wooded savannah but was once dense forest. This savannahization (the chronology of which is not yet established) might equally well be attributed to the slow and gradual action of compact human communities, to the sudden and brutal action of a small number of immigrants, or to climatic influences. Second, the presence of numerous stone tools testifies to settled human occupation which probably occurred in the second half of the first millennium. But it remains impossible to identify these first inhabitants. They may have been pygmy hunters, a few of whose descendants still survive on the banks of the Mbam, or proto-Bantu language speakers who had not yet discovered metal-working; or a fluid mixture of several distinct peoples.

It is only from the sixteenth century onwards that facts begin to crystallize. The population movements recorded in the traditions involved many different sorts of people. All the evidence suggests that the number of migrants was small for, although they dominated the peoples they found already *in situ*, every-where they abandoned their own language and adopted that of the country where they settled. The traditions also reveal the countless reasons for these movements, which included internal disputes, the search for iron ore and wood to work it, the quest for new land, the salt trade and the pressure of invaders from the north. The northern factor, particularly the Fulbe raids, which is well known for the nineteenth century, was relevant much earlier, from the mid-eighteenth century or even before. The vocabulary and syntax of the Mbum language, spoken in the central Cameroon highlands, include many borrowings from Fulfulde. It thus seems that the Fulbe drove the Mbum southwards and that they in turn forced the Voute to move southwards, and that this led to the migration of the Fang and Beti.

This constant intermingling of populations, spread over several centuries, is a main factor in the striking cultural homogeneity of the peoples of central Cameroon. The peoples there all speak Bantu or semi-Bantu languages. There are numerous similarities in the way in which power is distributed in their political and social institutions. Males belonged to countless associations with ritual or police functions. Technologies were often comparable, too, especially in the working of iron and copper. In all these societies the smith was believed to have magical powers and is prominent in myths and historical traditions. This homogeneity, well established by about 1800, had been gradually formed during the previous centuries.

Three of these numerous peoples deserve special attention. The first are the Tikar, who are important because many other peoples in the Cameroon highlands either claim to derive from them or have been strongly influenced by them. The Tikar are said to descend from a trader from Borno who settled and had offspring among the Mbum. Their various traditions locate their origin in north-east Cameroon. *Tikar* was initially the nickname of the first group of Mbum to leave their homeland for the highlands, but in time it came to be applied to all Mbum emigrants and the peoples they had conquered. The major part of this migration probably took place in the seventeenth century. When they reached the Bamenda region, the Tikar met the Tumu whom they first allied with and then dominated. But the price of victory was their adoption of the language of the conquered and their institutions, particularly the political titles and secret societies.

The foundation of the Bamum kingdom was the work of a group of emigrants related to the royal dynasty of the Tikar of Nsaw. In the *History and Customs of the Bamum*, ten kings are listed between the founder, Nchare, and Kuotu, the ruler immediately before Mbuembue, whose reign is dated to the first half of the nineteenth century. Nchare was a conqueror who crushed some 18 rulers. He founded the capital of the Bamum, Foumban, then called Mfomben. Nchare endowed the kingdom with political institutions mostly taken from those of the Tikar. He set up a body of numerous title-holders, including the *kom ngu* (counsellors of the kingdom) with whom he divided up the available lands; he formed two secret societies, one of which, *ngiri*, was for princes only and the other, *mitngu*, was open to the rest of the population irrespective of social status. However, the Mbum gave up Tikar and adopted Mben, the language of the conquered. The nine kings who followed Nchare get short shrift from tradition. They were not conquerors, for territorial expansion began only at the beginning of the nineteenth century during the reign of Mbuembue. The kingdom even faced the serious threat of Chamba and Fulbe invaders from the north, particularly during the eighteenth century. However, some significant developments can be detected during this period. The growth in large-scale royal polygamy led to a vast increase in the number of princely lineages and the palace nobility also grew substantially. The king recruited most of his retainers from twins and the sons of princesses. Material and social developments remain little known. At the end of the eighteenth century, the kingdom had perhaps 10,000–12,000 inhabitants, among whom there was a small number of slaves. The economy, heavily agricultural, was open to external trade. The Bamum were importing salt, iron, beads, cotton goods and copper objects from a very early date.

As for the Bamileke, their ancient history is closely linked to that of the two previous groups. All came from the north, from the region today occupied by the Tikar. Their migration probably began in the seventeenth century and took place in successive waves. The migrants occupied present-day Bamum country, where they founded several villages before being driven out of most by the Bamum: those who remained were assimilated. Among the various Bamileke groups, the Baleng were the first to cross the river Nun, almost certainly at the beginning of the eighteenth century, and were soon followed by the Bandeng, Bapi and Bafusam. The various chiefdoms had features common to the political societies of the Cameroon highlands. The peoples were highly mobile, a characteristic which appears to be linked to their fairly high population growth and the inheritance system that transferred an estate to a single heir, thus obliging the other sons to secure land from the chief or settle elsewhere.

The areas around the Uele and the Ubangi rivers

Knowledge of the areas around the Uele and the Ubangi rivers has made little progress since the works of the first anthropologists. The most vexed question is that of the settlement of these lands. All the research recognizes three types of population: neolithic, Bantu and Sudanic. The difficulties appear in detailing the vagaries and patterns of settlement and the successive forms of relations among these peoples.

Traditionally, two sub-regions were distinguished, the Uele and the Ubangi. The Ubangi area, today inhabited mostly by Sudanic peoples, was probably occupied until the seventeenth century by Bantu, who themselves had taken possession of the region from little-known populations whose neolithic implements have survived. The Sudanic peoples probably began to move into the region from Dārfūr and Kordofān in the seventeenth or early eighteenth century. Those who were to form the Ngbandi group probably arrived first, followed by the Banda and the Ngbaka.

The succession of groups in the Uele area, today dominated by the Zande, Zande-ized people and Mangbetu, seems to have been different. Until the sixteenth or early seventeenth century the Uele, Mbomu and Aruwimi basins were probably occupied by neolithic populations, the present-day survivors of whom are said to be the Momvu, the Logo and the Makere. Two population groups, traditionally portrayed as invaders, grafted themselves on to this underlying population. There were first the Sudanic peoples, from whom came the Mangbetu, Ngbandi and Zande peoples and then the Bantu, who followed the rivers northwards. It was during this period – the seventeenth and early eighteenth centuries – that the ethno-political groups were formed.

Some researchers have proposed a synthesis covering all Ubangi and Uele areas. Their argument rests on linguistic and ethnolinguistic data and distinguishes three broad stages of settlement. First, in the first millennium before the Christian era, there was a large-scale west–east movement bringing the proto-Ubangians to the River Nile. In the eleventh century there was a Nilotic drive which broke up the Ngbaka-Sere-Ngbandi group and drove the Ngbandi southwards into the area between the Ubangi and Zaire rivers where they met the pygmies and the Bantu. This Nilotic drive also pushed the Zande-Nzakara populations westward into the lands watered by the Uele and Mbomu rivers. The third stage, which began in the eighteenth century, corresponds to the drive by the Bantu from the south, fleeing the effects of the slave trade.

This synthesis is attractive, but calls for two basic reservations. First, it seems difficult to speak of migrations when, in best-known cases, those of the Zande and the Mangbetu, the invaders were élites, content to divide the local populations into chiefdoms and kingdoms. Second, all the traditions, particularly the genealogies of the major clans, show that it was only during the seventeenth century that 'conglomerations of peoples' (E. de Dampierre) came into being as a result of various waves of migration. Later developments, probably dating to the eighteenth century, enabled two clans, the Vungara and the Bandia, to assert their dominance at the expense of the others. The Vungara went on to conquer, assimilate or make allies of the most diverse populations. It was above all their skill in politically organizing these populations that cemented Zande society. As for the Bandia, the high point of their expansion came during the eighteenth century thanks to Ngubenge who carried through the conquest of Nzakara country and helped to drive the Vungara eastward.

Little is known of the material civilization of these peoples. It seems likely, however, that the conquering aristocracies had long engaged in hunting, which remained a highly valued activity. The Zande learned their farming skills from the conquered populations. Iron-working was held in high esteem and among some groups, such as the Ngbandi, smiths were grouped in strictly closed professional associations. The major river network formed by the Ubangi, the Uele, the Mbomu, the Aruwimi and their numerous tributaries was the basis for a busy trade. In the markets, craft products, foodstuffs and animals, together with slaves, were the main items traded. This trade grew rapidly as the trade carried on by Europeans on the Atlantic coast penetrated inland.

The coastal societies and the Atlantic trade

For the forest lands of central Africa, the period from 1500 to 1800 also saw the establishment and development of the coastal trade, soon to be reduced to the slave trade. The coastal fringe was the last link of a long trading chain which reached ever deeper into the interior. By 1800, this chain had reached the upper Mungo, the grasslands of Cameroon, the upper Ogowe and, through the River Congo (Zaire) the River Ubangi.

Peoples

The state in 1500 of the populations and societies in the coastal zone remains obscure. The writings of European navigators and traders show that the whole region was occupied, but we do not know by whom.

For the coast itself, O. Dapper's *Description de l'Afrique*, which contains a list of numbers used by the peoples on the coast, makes it possible to assert that in about 1660 they were definitely Bantu-speaking. These same written sources make it possible to date the reigns of several rulers named in oral traditions. Thus, the height of the reign of Mulobe, the third historical king of the Duala, can be put at about 1650. That makes it possible to date to the sixteenth century the exploits of his grandfather Mbedi, and to beyond the sixteenth century those of the legendary Mbongo, to whom the Duala and related peoples refer.

While it is thus possible to accept a Bantu peopling of the coast by the beginning of the sixteenth century, one is still reduced to conjecture for the neighbouring regions of the interior. For the Minlaaba region and Beti country, six levels of populations have been established with no chronological data, the oldest of which was that of the pygmies, followed by hunter-gatherers, then various Bantu groups whose migrations continued into the nineteenth century. Further south, in modern Gabon, the picture is clearer. At the end of the fifteenth century, the Portuguese found Mpongwe populations in the estuary region. The lands along the lower Ogowe (Cape López and Fernán-Vaz) did

ive any Bantu populations; the peoples there were probably pre-
ly Negrillo. The only organized state was in the Gabon estuary.
Accoi. .g to the later description left by Dapper in the seventeenth century,
the king bore the title of *mani pongo*.

In the far south, the kingdom of Loango was well established by about 1500,
since all the voyagers' accounts of the early sixteenth century refer to Mani
Loango and Mbanza Loango by name. Some traditions make Loango a state
derived from the kingdom of Kongo; for others the foundation of the kingdom
of Loango resulted from processes internal to Vili society. It is possible that
Loango may have maintained close, perhaps vassalage, relations with Kongo
until the late fifteenth century. As in many states in Central Africa, the king's
main functions were ritual ones. The institution of royalty, founded by a family
of smiths, was linked to the fire cult. During the coronation ceremony, each
maloango lit the *ntufia* (sacred fire) which was to burn until his death. Another
ritual concerned rain, for which the king was responsible. The most striking
feature of this society was its complex economy. A dynamic food-crop
agriculture blended with diversified craft production which included the
making of palm-cloth for weaving, the working of ivory, copper and redwood
and salt-making. These products were sold on the local markets, notably the
one in Buali, the capital, and also reached markets outside the kingdom. The
Atlantic trade thus did not create trade in this region: it merely gave it a new
intensity and a new dimension.

The Atlantic trade

The local history of the Atlantic trade in this part of Africa is still little known.
The account books of European traders, many of which have not survived, are
often fragmentary. But some facts have been established.

The trade was initially the monopoly of Portugal, whose navigators Fernão
do Po and Lope Gonçalves reached the island of Formosa and the Gabon in
1472 and 1473 respectively. Trade only began to increase after 1500 when
Portuguese settled on the island of São Tomé, which needed slaves for its own
sugar-cane plantations while also serving as an entrepôt for cargoes destined for
the Americas. At the end of the sixteenth century, slave rebellions, the most
important of which took place on São Tomé in 1574 and 1586, ruined
Portuguese trade in the region. The Dutch arrived after 1598 and developed
the new trading centres of Douala and Cape López, and eliminated the
Portuguese from Loango. After 1660, the slave trade underwent a massive
expansion which continued until about 1850. France and Great Britain became
the main trading powers in the region, but the activity of the Portuguese,
Dutch and Danes succeeded in maintaining a competitive situation.

The exact scale of this trade, which varied from place to place along the
coast, is hard to determine. The position of these lands at the bottom of the
Gulf of Guinea constituted a hindrance. The slaving vessels often followed the
'small route', stopping at the various slaving stations along the coast from
Senegambia to Calabar, and by the time they reached Cameroon, Gabon and

Loango, they had already placed much of their cargo. The 'great route' allowed boats to avoid these intermediate stops and arrive directly south of Cape López and begin trading at Loango or in neighbouring ports.

On the Cameroon coast, trade entered its busiest phase in about 1750, with the Wouri estuary and, more precisely, Douala, as its main centres, especially for Dutch ships. Douala got most of its supplies of slaves from the north and north-east. On the River Gabon, the main trading centre was the estuary region. Cape López only began to take an active part in the Atlantic trade in the reign of Reombi-Mpolo (*c.* 1790–1810). Any estimate of the numbers involved would be risky, but the slave trade was quite extensive, to judge from the seriousness of the conflict between the Portuguese and the Dutch over possession of Gabon at the beginning of the eighteenth century and from the number of ships sent to this region by the French port of Honfleur. In addition to slaves, there were large quantities of ivory, wax and sandalwood supplied by the Kele and Fang hunters and gatherers of the neighbouring region.

The Loango trade is the best known. Its trade in slaves lasted a short time compared with that of the Slave Coast or Angola. It began on a large scale in about 1670 but by 1780 was almost over. Until the mid-seventeenth century Loango supplied mainly ivory, dyewoods and palm-cloth which was widely sought after in Central Africa as a currency. The number of slaves exported by the Loango coast – 100 a year in about 1639 – rose to 12,500 a year in the period 1762–78 and to 13,000–14,000 a year between 1780 and 1790. Slaving captains' account books have left valuable indications of the ethnic origins of slaves bought by Europeans at Loango. The presence of Quibangues (Bubangi and 'river people' from the Congo and Ubangi rivers) shows that, at its peak, the Atlantic trade had reached the heart of the continent.

Complex dynamics

Over such a small region, an analysis of the effects of this system of intense and prolonged trade must be conducted with rigour and care. We shall not enter into the debate over the destructive or positive effects of the Atlantic trade, a debate which remains open. We shall confine ourselves here to stressing, in relation to those exchanges, the dynamic processes of all sorts that were occurring, bringing long-term changes that affected social organization, political structures, population and attitudes.

One of the first changes was the introduction, at the beginning of the seventeenth century, of food crops from the Americas: maize, cassava, groundnuts, beans and tobacco. The spread of these crops did not take place only in the coastal region: they moved rapidly inland, sometimes along trade routes. Cassava had great success, as its yield was distinctly higher than that of yams. It had many uses: its leaves could be eaten, while the root lent itself to several techniques of processing and preserving. Doubtless more slowly, maize, whose presence on the coast is recorded before 1600, replaced sorghum. The other crops were gradually incorporated into the various systems of crop rotation. These changes testify to the great capacity for technological innovation of the peasant communities of Central Africa. Did they contribute, through a more secure and more diversified food supply, to a greater physical resistance among the populations and a higher rate of population growth? Nothing could be less certain, for the nutritional value of cassava is limited. Socially, this agricultural revolution contributed, along with the trade itself, to the establishment of a new division of labour. Numerous agricultural tasks were gradually abandoned by men, who preferred to devote themselves to trade, which was more lucrative, and entrusted to women and slaves. The development of domestic slavery and other forms of dependence was a direct consequence of these agricultural changes.

In the regions nearest the coast, in direct touch with overseas trade, the transformations were highly complex. In the seventeenth and eighteenth centuries, the population stabilized and a process of redistribution began which was to be completed in the nineteenth century. The seventeenth century saw the occupation of the Gabon estuary by new Mpongwe clans and the eighteenth century the arrival of the Orungu at Cape López and the Nkomi at Fernán-Vaz. As regards political structures, the coastal trade had contradictory effects. In only one case, among the Orungu of Cape López, did it lead to the formation of a strong, centralized state, whose royal clan – Abolia or Alombe – held the exclusive monopoly over trade with the Europeans, at the time when the slave trade was at its height. Everywhere else on the coast, the opposite mechanism was at work – a breakdown of centres of authority and a splintering of political power. In this case, the organization of trade, on the African side, was not a state monopoly. Competition benefited a few individuals, princes, commoners and even some ex-slaves, who formed a new aristocracy keen to secure political power. In Douala, rivalry crystallized between the Bela family ('King Bell') and the Ngando family ('King Akwa') and ended in a final break in the nineteenth century. At Loango it was the new men – brokers, traders, caravan leaders and other middlemen – who came out best as they had the means to purchase land from the king and build up an entourage of many free or servile dependants. The *maloango* was reduced to selling senior positions to these *nouveaux riches*.

Meanwhile the condition of the ordinary people was deteriorating. The eighteenth century saw the appearance or development of new magical practices and new conceptions of sickness centred on the individual instead of on the family group, with the main aim being to ensure protection against attacks from all sides. This development is no doubt related to a greater degree of insecurity.

The Congo river axis and large-scale Congolese trade

Until colonization, the River Congo (Zaire) acted as a powerful factor bringing together the various peoples of the vast Congo basin. This role did not only involve the river itself along its navigable portion above Malebo Pool, but also its many tributaries, particularly the Alima, the Likwala, the Sangha and the

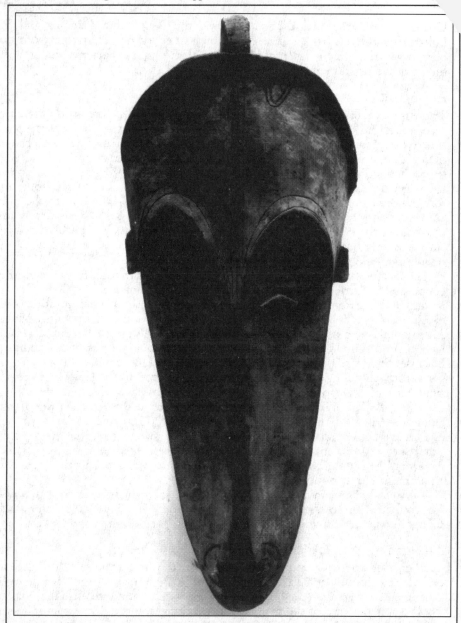

18.1 *Fang mask worn by a member of the Ngil society, an association of men organized on the basis of specific initiations, whose members maintain order in the community and protect it from evil spells. Height: 70 cm (© Collection Musée de l'Homme, Paris, photo: D. Destable)*

... the right bank and the Kwa, the Ruka, the Ikelemba and the ܝ_ulonga on the left bank. Since early times a remarkable trading network had been organized which had moulded most of the human societies living along the river and its affluents.

An ancient exchange economy

There is much evidence of these ancient trading networks. It remains difficult to reconstruct the chronological stages and the precise lines of the settlement of this region, but two main movements can be distinguished. The first brought these Bantu-speaking peoples into this region from their original home. The strong similarities between these languages and certain Nigero-Cameroonian languages suggests a direct migration from the Nigero-Cameroonian homeland towards their present location, following the waterways, which form the most convenient routes in this marshy and heavily forested area. Besides this first movement, there were also smaller-scale movements which probably occurred later and were in an east–west direction, and which gradually led to the stabilization and separating out of some groups.

These latter movements helped to create the conditions for an exchange economy by distributing the population over complementary ecological zones including waterfronts, flood lands and dry lands. Fishing communities could easily trade their fish, which was highly valued, for foodstuffs or craft products. All known layers of Zairean–Congolese archaeology are to be found around Malebo Pool, thus bearing witness to a highly unusual degree of continuity in both density of settlement and the variety of human activities. Two sites are particularly revealing on the subject of trade. In the first, at Kingabwa, on the right bank of Malebo Pool, several types of pottery have been uncovered, one of which has also been found at other minor sites in the Kinshasa region and along the river. This pottery, dated 1450–1640, is evidence of very old-established commercial relations along the Congo and its tributaries. At the other site, at Mafamba, many clay pipes have been discovered, most of which have not been used, which suggests that Mafamba was a production centre or an entrepôt redistributing the pipes in the region.

Two products seem to have dominated the long-distance trade: camwood, for cosmetic purposes, and copper mined from the deposits on the lower Congo. Local trade involved products such as salt, cloth, mats and baskets.

The grafting of the Atlantic trade and its consequences

This grafting took place in several stages. In the first, from the late fifteenth century to about 1560, the kingdom of Kongo played the leading role. Documents of Portuguese origin dating from 1529 indicate that the Malebo Pool region was one of the main suppliers of slaves, through the routes linking it to Mbanza Kongo (São Salvador) and Mpinda. The period 1560–1750 witnessed a decline in Kongo's trade, due to the growing competition of Angola and internal problems caused particularly by the Jaga. During the third stage, from about 1750 to about 1850, the basin of the Congo and its tributaries became the principal suppliers of slaves to the Americas. A dense network of caravan routes linked it to a long chain of ports on both sides of its mouth, Loango, Cabinda, Boma, Ambrizette, Ambriz and Luanda.

Throughout these three stages, Malebo Pool was the meeting-point between long-distance Congolese trade and the Atlantic trade. The latter's galvanizing effect on the regional economy was based on mechanisms that are easy to understand. The export trade involved high-value goods and this made long-distance transport on the Congo and its tributaries profitable. Trade in locally used goods, therefore, even if transported over long distances, also became profitable, and this in turn stimulated regional specialization.

The geographical area encompassed by these various levels of trade grew continuously from about 1500. By about 1690, Malebo Pool was in permanent trading relations with the lower Kasai and the lands around the River Alima. A century later, the River Ubangi was fully a part of this trading pattern, as were all the rivers in between, together with their tributaries. Only in the nineteenth century does the trade frontier appear to have reached the confluence of the Ubangi and the Uele. Numerous markets existed along these waterways, the largest being naturally at the biggest junction, Malebo Pool. Each of the four markets, at Ntamo and Kinshasa on the left bank and Mpila and Mfwa on the right bank, had 3,000–5,000 permanent residents to whom must be added people passing through, who were especially numerous during the trading season, which coincided with the dry season, from April or May to September.

The trading system directed towards the outside world rested essentially on two items – slaves and ivory. Slaves, trade in whom really boomed after 1750, came mainly from four regions: the Lulonga basin; the lands around the River Alima; Boma country between the confluence of the Congo and the Kwa and Lake Mai-Ndombe; and the Ubangi basin. Around the main market, Basankusu, in the Lulonga valley, there were numerous villages where the slaves cultivated the fields until they could be sold. Some of the slaves sold followed the course of the river to be exported; others went up the River Ubangi to be sold to the Loi in exchange for ivory destined for the markets at the Pool and on the Atlantic coast.

Among the Tio, domestic slavery was so developed that the word *mboma* (man of the Boma ethnic group) came to mean a stupid person or anyone in a lowly occupation. With the development of the slave trade, the number of mechanisms of enslavement grew. Among the Bobangi, the main trading people in the Congo basin, a distinction was made between a *montonge* (captured slave) and a *montamba* (slave sold by his kin), which indicates how far social values had been overturned by the slave trade.

The second export stem, ivory, appears in sixteenth-century Portuguese texts as one of the most profitable lines. Ivory had long been used locally for bracelets and hair-pins, but its trade value in the region seems to have remained low. There were numerous herds of elephants in the forest zone, and the pygmies almost monopolized elephant-hunting, but the network of rights over slaughtered animals was so complex that, once the chiefs had taken their share, little profit was left for the hunter. Until the late 1700s, ivory took the same routes and went through the same hands as the slaves who, by value, provided the bulk of the trade. The relationship between the two items of trade was reversed only after 1830.

The range of goods received in exchange from the coast, at first limited to salt, *nzimbu* (shellfish) from Luanda, cloth and beads, was widened in the mid-1600s by the introduction of metal objects, particularly knives, and mirrors. The eighteenth century saw a dramatic increase in muskets and gunpowder, copper and tin products and alcoholic beverages. How these items circulated in the Congo basin is poorly understood and their speed of circulation has been the subject of speculation since Stanley estimated, in about 1880, that it took an average of five years for a European article to move from the coast to the Ubangi.

The trade in locally-used goods covered the same area, perhaps slightly larger, as that in export goods. People often engaged in both trades at once. This local trade involved mainly foodstuffs and salt. Foodstuffs had the advantage of an enormous market because, from the eighteenth century onwards, an ever-rising level of demand had to be met. Cassava, cultivated and processed by women, was one of the most sought-after items. The oil-palm provided oil for domestic use and palm wine. Salt was another vitally important item, whether rock salt from Mbosi country or vegetable salt produced mostly by peoples along waterways. These peoples supplied many species of fish, fresh or smoked according to well-developed techniques. Tobacco and local alcohols were also sold.

Handicrafts also contributed to trade. These were the work of specialists: among agriculturalists, the women farmed, leaving handicrafts to men; among fishing communities, however, catching fish was the men's job and handicrafts the women's. The most sought-after products were: mats; camwood powder, produced by women; palm-cloth, for which the Tio were famous; iron implements; pottery; and finally, canoes of all sizes, 3–20 metres long, or even longer.

There were thus considerable differences between the two types of trade. The export trade was based on an economy of destruction and profited only a tiny minority. The trade in local goods was based on an economy of production and the beneficiaries were the ordinary people, men and women, each according to how much he produced.

Diverse societies

This internal trade promoted the progressive unification of the various peoples of the Congo basin, despite the obstacles that encouraged variety. Among these was the way trade was organized. It was a segmented trade and remained so until the nineteenth century. The river and its tributaries were divided into spheres of influence, each of which was controlled by one ethnic group. It was only in the mid-eighteenth century that the Bobangi began to control the whole Congo–Ubangi axis. Mistrust long ruled relations among the various partners and pillaging was not uncommon. Conflicts of interest often led to full-scale wars, such as that between the Bobangi and the Tio, who reached a lasting agreement only in the early 1800s.

Among the many factors making for unification, most important were the trading techniques themselves. Thus, from the eighteenth century, the whole region began to adopt the same currencies for transactions – palm-cloth, *nzimbu*, cowries and copper rods. The widespread practice of credit created long chains of solidarity throughout the trading area. The profitable conduct of trade also led to strategies of extended alliances through marriage and, above all, blood brotherhoods that created numerous obligations between partners. The river trade thus served as a crucible, bringing different peoples into contact, spreading the same customs and beliefs and facilitating the hegemony of Bobangi as a trade language. This shared civilization, the formation of which speeded up in the eighteenth century, reached its apogee between 1850 and 1880.

However, this growing unity went hand in hand with a degree of diversity, linked partly to the variety of ways in which peoples adapted themselves to large-scale Congolese trade. Not all engaged in trade. In this region, where water was plentiful, fishing, one of the oldest occupations of the Bantu peoples of the Congo basin, remained the main activity of many groups. Fishing communities were characterized by high mobility, which was determined by variations in the water level and the regular movements of fishing banks. Depending on the season, people would live in fixed villages or in fishing camps built during low water and abandoned as the level of the river rose. Socially and politically there was a distinct lack of congruence between political and economic units. The basic political unit was still the village: the chief's authority, essentially ritual and religious, operated solely within this limited framework. The activities of teams of fishermen thus escaped his control. But the basic economic unit was precisely the loosely structured fishing team based on the initiative of a renowned fisherman and including some of his kin and other volunteers. In this way, the family cells on which the villages were based were dislocated to meet the requirements of fishing.

Those who specialized in trading activities evolved differently, as is shown by the contrasting evolution of the Bobangi and the Tio. The details of the Bobangi's long migration from the middle or lower Ubangi to Malebo Pool are hard to reconstruct. What is certain is that what was originally a society of fishermen rapidly switched to trade, which became the sole foundation of all social life. Henceforth, there was complete convergence between the political and the economic unit. Bobangi society was based on trading firms belonging to wealthy traders. It was an open society, with much social mobility: anyone active and successful in trade could acquire wealth, which was the means to increase the numbers of his dependants, to gain power and to lay claim to political titles.

The Tio had the good fortune to live at the biggest crossroads and main break-of-bulk point in the Congolese trading network. Trade had not, apparently, upset the political structures of the kingdom. It was widely decentralized.

The underlying structure consisted of relatively autonomous chiefdoms. The chief had major ritual prerogatives but limited political power. The same situation occurred at the higher level. The king, *ôkoo* (deformed by the Europeans into *makoko*), had above all a spiritual role. Temporal power belonged to a few high notables such as the *ngaailiino*, responsible for collecting tribute and heading the administration, and the *muidzu*, the country's chief justice. Unlike the chiefship, the dignity of *ôkoo* was not hereditary: the king was elected from among the leading chiefs in the kingdom by his peers. This old structure retained its essential features until the advent of colonization. It was at the social level that the most lasting changes occurred. There was first an increasing dissociation between the riverine peoples, who monopolized trading activities, and the Tio in the interior, who specialized in agricultural production (cassava and tobacco) for the river market. Among the riverine peoples, those who profited most from trade were the chiefs, who exploited to the limit their right to sell human beings and ivory. Conversely, the chiefs and title holders established away from the Pool, such as the king who resided at Mbe, participated only fitfully in trade by sending their dependants there. They held political power but their economic power was less than that of the riverine peoples.

These Bobangi and Tio trading economies did not become capitalist, despite the large profits made. It was impossible to buy land or a labour force, except in the form of slaves. Money, accepted in some dealings, was not a universal equivalent which could purchase all goods. Some goods and some social and religious services, such as fines and dowry payments, never came within the money economy.

The picture thus drawn of the peoples and societies of Central Africa clearly demonstrates their diversity as well as their aptitude for innovation, even in constraining situations. It also shows, through the gaps in knowledge, the directions in which researchers should move: large-scale research with ample resources, directed principally towards collecting new materials through archaeology and oral traditions, and detailed theoretical modelling in the study of social structures, cultural evolution and the history of mentalities.

19

The Kongo kingdom and its neighbours

The western part of Central Africa, to the south of the equatorial forests, is inhabited by peoples who speak dialects of the Kongo language and of other closely related languages. That unity is strengthened by a profound cultural unity. This ethnolinguistic group occupies a territory stretching from southern Gabon to the Benguela plateau and from the Atlantic Ocean to well beyond the River Kwango.

The history of this region is well documented from 1500 onwards. Over the past hundred years, texts and guidebooks have been published in many editions, and a historiographical school has been developing since the seventeenth century.

The historical tendency in these areas in the sixteenth and seventeenth centuries was very different from that of later times. Territories of great size were organized, using political structures, to form states. After about 1665, however, these territories were reorganized on an even greater scale, the organizing principle now being derived from the imperatives of an economic structure which was the product of an intensive slave trade. In our approach to the early centuries, therefore, we shall give priority to the history of the kingdoms; and then, as the dynamics of trade brought the kingdoms low, trade will be the focus of attention.

The landscape of these regions is determined by the relief and the rainfall. The mountainous nature of the terrain explains why a population in search of better habitats was unevenly distributed. The most favourable region lay to the north of the Zaire/Congo river, from the coast to the area called Mayombe. Here there were also worthwhile mineral deposits. This was where the two largest states of the coast, the kingdoms of Kongo and Loango, came into being.

Since 400 years before the Christian era at least, farmers speaking western Bantu languages had been settled to the north and south of the lower Zaire, where they produced yams, vegetables and oil palms. From the second to the fifth century, this population was augmented by the arrival from the east of people speaking eastern Bantu languages. These people grew grain and, where the tsetse fly allowed, kept herds of cattle. Lastly, perhaps during the sixth century, banana-growing was introduced to round out the production pattern.

Thereafter, the socio-political organizations became more complex, and chiefdoms were formed between the ocean and the Zaire river upstream from Malebo Pool. It was in the region called Mayombe that the regional division of labour developed most effectively. By about 1500, the coastal dwellers were supplying salt and fish and had transformed the coastal plain of Loango, towards the estuary of the Zaire, into a vast palm-grove producing palm-oil. Further north, near the edges of the great forest, raffia palm was cultivated and used to make fabric. Lastly, in the same area and further into the forest, red dyewood was exchanged for products of the savannah. This was the birthplace of the Kongo civilization.

The Kongo kingdom began in the Vungu chiefdom north of the Zaire river. Nimi Lukeni, the founder of the kingdom of Kongo, founded the town of Mbanza Kongo where São Salvador now stands. His kingdom was constituted partly by alliance with the local chief, the *kabunga*, and with a king who ruled the Mbata in the Inkisi valley, and partly by the conquest of other lands towards the sea and the lower Inkisi valley. The date of the kingdom's founding is unknown, but it was possibly some time between 1300 and 1400.

The Tio kingdom was probably founded earlier. The kingdom of Loango, which developed not far from Vungu to the north of the river, is thought by some scholars to have reached its zenith in the sixteenth century, but this hypothesis is disputed. To the south of Kongo, the state of Ndongo, whose king bore the title *ngola*, which was deformed into Angola, was taking shape about 1500.

A hegemony: Kongo

In the fifteenth and sixteenth centuries a single state, Kongo, held sway over the entire region between the Benguela plateau and the Bateke plateaux and from the sea to beyond the River Kwango. Around 1500, the borders of the state proper followed the River Zaire from its mouth upstream to the confluence with the Inkisi, in places extending northward beyond the river. It included the Inkisi basin and all the lands to the south as far as the Loje. It had a population of between 2 million and 5 million – we do not know the precise figure. The areas in Kongo's sphere of influence at least equalled the kingdom in population. The population of the Tio kingdom must have been very sparse except around Malebo Pool.

The kingdom was divided between a large town, the capital Mbanza Kongo, and the countryside. Three well-defined social strata co-existed: the nobility, the villagers and the slaves. The nobility formed the structural framework of the kingdom, and lived in towns except when required to serve as provincial governors. The upper nobility was composed of relatives of the king or one of his predecessors. In relation to the villages, the nobility made up a group. Matrilineality determined access to the land, residence and succession to the headship of the village. The king appointed his close relatives to key posts. Royalty was elective; the royal council was made up of 12 members, including four women

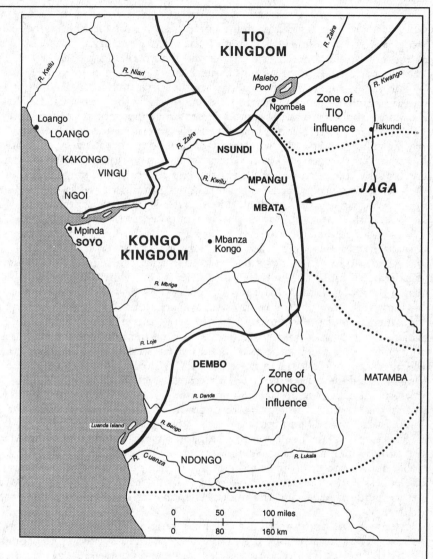

19.1 *Kongo and its neighbours in the sixteenth century (after J. Vansina)*

who, according to A. Hilton, represented the clans of the king's grandparents. Struggles for succession were commonplace. After a struggle between the lords of the north and those of the capital and south, Nzinga Mbemba, otherwise known as Afonso I, succeeded his father Nzinga Nkuwu in 1506.

The kings, much given to polygamy, had many children, and their house quickly reached huge proportions. Kongo was highly centralized. The king appointed the territorial governors except the governor of Mbata and, after 1491, the governor of Soyo. He dismissed governors and other officials as he saw fit. The nobility had no hereditary functions and at every generation its hierarchy was redefined in relation to the new king. Centralization was favoured by the existence of a currency controlled by the king. It consisted of shells called *nzimbu*, taken from the fishing-grounds of the island of Luanda, which was part of the kingdom. There was also military centralization. In the late sixteenth century, the royal guard, composed of slaves, was 16,000–20,000 strong and was the sole standing armed force of the kingdom. In time of war abroad, the peasants were called up in territorial units.

The ideology of royalty, called *nkisi*, derived from religious conceptions in which three important cults played a role. These were ancestor worship, for which the holy place was the royal cemetery grove, the worship of the spirits of the land and the worship of royal charms. The *nkisi* concept was fundamental, and the Christians were to adopt the term, using it to mean 'that which is sacred', for example calling the church the house of the *nkisi*. Diseases and misfortunes were attributed to the *ndoki* (sorcerer) whom *nganga ngombo* (diviners) were able to identify, sometimes by ordeal. Royalty was sacred. The king was addressed as *Nzambi mpungu* (Supreme Creator). By his *tumba* (blessing) the king expressed his protection of royal officials and, in general, guaranteed fertility, principally through his control over rainfall. The king himself was, in a real and profound sense, the *nkisi* of the country.

Structures in the neighbouring kingdoms were different, but the ideology was almost identical. These kingdoms were less centralized. In Loango, the noble houses had not supplanted matrilineal groupings, and this class was much less cohesive than in Kongo. Ndongo had no territorial structure above the petty chiefdom level, and the military system was intended to make good the deficiency.

Afonso I's victory ushered in the longest reign in Kongo's history, from 1506 to 1543. The role played by this king was crucial. He opened up the country to Portugal, thus setting in train a vast economic and political reorganization and a deliberate assimilation of features of Christianity which was to prove permanent. On becoming king, this factional chief rapidly made the Catholic Church the state religion under the leadership, from 1518 to 1536, of his son Henrique, who was consecrated bishop in Rome. The bishopric was later to fall under the control of Portugal. The slave trade developed from 1514 onwards. The king first tried to control it by establishing royal monopolies and then, in 1526, to abolish it. This attempt failed, and even the royal monopolies were constantly breached by the Afro-Portuguese of São Tomé, by the kingdom's neighbours and even in Luanda, which was an integral part of the kingdom. The king used his revenue from the slave trade, the ivory trade and the trade in raffia fabric to attract Portuguese technicians and, above all, missionaries. In his reign, social and political life was transformed. The gulf between the nobility and the ordinary people widened: the former became literate, espoused Christianity and took part in the slave trade, while the ordinary people were harshly exploited.

All subsequent kings were descendants of Afonso through one or other of his three principal daughters. The ever-increasing number of claimants to the throne led to a scission of the royal house into enemy factions and, after 1665, to a civil war. The presence of the Portuguese in the town introduced a new political dimension. Connected by marriage to various noble houses, they were split up into Afro-Portuguese and people from the mother country, and they led the opposing parties at court until 1665 and took part in all the struggles for succession.

International trade, which had been very minor before 1506, developed after it started dealing in slaves. Exports totalled some 4,000–5,000 slaves yearly until about 1540, and 6,000–7,000 thereafter. Imports from Malebo Pool must have been considerable, for many slaves were recruited at Mbanza Kongo not only for the royal guard but also for the food plantations which fed the capital, and other slaves were assigned to the port of Mpinda and the retinue of royal nobles. In addition to this supervised trade, a clandestine slave trade carried on by the inhabitants of São Tomé developed on the northern and southern borders of the kingdom, especially after 1526, when exports from the kingdom of Benin came to an end.

Portugal took a keen interest in the mineral products of the country and wanted to control them. The king of Kongo, however, was determined to keep the mining of Bembe copper and the working of Mbanza Kongo iron under tight control. The Portuguese sovereign, for his part, never allowed the sale of ships to Kongo and opposed its attempts to lay on its own transport to São Tomé or Europe. The Portuguese kept control of trade and made it an unequal exchange. The Kongo court used a substantial part of the revenue to import fabrics, wine and luxury items which quickly became an ostentatious necessity.

Under Afonso I's successors, Kongo's relative power diminished, especially in relation to Ndongo, which was gaining strength mainly through the clandestine traffic with São Tomé. In 1561, Kongo cut itself off from Portugal almost completely, but the successive deaths of two kings during a war with the Tio of Malebo Pool in 1566 and 1567 led to a disarray which, with the invasion of warriors called Jaga from the east, turned into a catastrophe.

Three states: 1575–1640

The Jaga routed the royal forces and the court had to take refuge on an island in the lower Zaire. Numerous refugees were sold as slaves by the Jaga to the people of São Tomé. The king had to appeal to Portugal, which sent an expeditionary force, and the country was reconquered between 1571 and 1573, although the troops were not withdrawn before 1575 or 1576. The hegemony of Kongo over the region was destroyed, for the colony of Angola was founded in 1575 and the Portuguese, in large numbers, came to Loango to trade from that year onwards.

The identity of those who invaded Kongo has never been established. The name Jaga is used in the sources as a synonym for barbarian. The invasion must be associated with the Kongo–Tio wars and probably with the cessation of the slave trade in 1561. It is thought that the ranks of the invaders were swollen by a great many villagers who were weary of being exploited by the nobility.

Paulo Dias de Novaes, after a stay at the court of Ndongo, worked to such purpose that he obtained a contract for conquest and colonization from the Portuguese court. The colony was to be named Angola, from the title of the king of Ndongo. Dias founded Luanda in 1576 and began trading in slaves, endeavouring to supplant a community of Afro-Portuguese from São Tomé who were plying the trade there. This community yielded the market to him and moved to the *ngola*'s court. In 1579, however, pressure from the mother country forced Dias to terminate his contract. When the king of Ndongo was told of this, he had all the Portuguese at his court massacred as a preventive measure, thus furnishing the pretext for a war which was to last for almost a century, until 1671. At first, the fortunes of war fluctuated, and the Portuguese managed – with difficulty – to erect a few fortifications inland. In 1612, however, the Portuguese entered into an alliance with some Mbangala (called Jaga) and, with their aid, and especially that of the Jaga Kasanje, they occupied a large part of the kingdom from 1617 to 1621. The king fled to the east of the country and the allies sacked the region. A peace treaty was drawn up in 1622–23, the *ngola* being represented by his sister Nzinga Mbande, who was baptized and named Anna at Luanda. Nzinga became the leader of an anti-Portuguese party; at the beginning of 1624 the king died and Nzinga became regent, then queen in 1626. War broke out again against her, but also against Kasanje who was still occupying the best part of Ndongo. In the course of operations, Kasanje found a base in the Kwango valley, where he built the Imbangala state during the 1630s, while Nzinga conquered the kingdom of Matamba, where she established a formidable base of opposition to the Portuguese regime. When the Dutch occupied Luanda, she was still campaigning and she formed an alliance with them.

The colony of Angola, ruled by a governor appointed by Lisbon, was divided into the town of Luanda and a few *presidios*. The administrative structure was feudal, its legal basis being contracts of vassalage which linked the *soba* (petty chiefs) to the Portuguese court. The revenues of the state and of its representatives were derived from feudal tributes, all of which, whether due in goods or in labour, were payable in slaves. This system was not replaced until the eighteenth century, with the introduction of a poll-tax and the reduction of the ties of vassalage to a legal instrument justifying the sovereign rights of Portugal.

19.2 *Court of the King of Loango, 1668 (O. Dapper,* Description de l'Afrique, *Wolfgang, Waesberge, Boom and van Someren, Amsterdam, 1686, © and photo: Dapper Foundation, Paris)*

Meanwhile Kongo had recovered. Despite its loss of hegemony and the gradual changes taking place in the structure of the nobility, the kingdom remained sound and even spread eastwards. Kongo successfully resisted other Portuguese attempts at control by forming a diplomatic alliance with the Vatican and by pitting Portugal against Spain and even both against the Netherlands. The most serious loss was that of the maritime province of Soyo, with the port of Mpinda. After 1636, this province became independent.

Loango had become a great power even before 1600. Its territory extended from the Fernán Vaz lagoon to the south of Pointe-Noire. Its cultural influence, spread by trade, extended even further afield; but we know almost nothing of its political development before 1700.

Loango traded in ivory, hides, red dyewood and raffia fabrics, but exported relatively few slaves. From 1600 onwards, the Dutch frequented Loango and Soyo. Dutch ships had better goods to offer at lower prices. They bought copper and, above all, had guns and gunpowder for sale. The upshot was that the traders on the Loango coast, the Vili, who organized the caravan traffic to the interior, extended their networks at an astonishing rate.

At this period, the Vili network was in competition with the existing networks, not only for the sale of ivory or fabrics but also for the slave trade. The Kongo and Angola network was disrupted by the founding of Luanda, which, from the start, exported more slaves than Mpinda; the first exports varied between 12,000 and 13,000 slaves a year, mainly prisoners of war. After the first few years, more and more slaves came from purchases inland, either in Malebo Pool or in the market of Ocanga on the River Kwango. In the 1630s, slaves began arriving in Luanda from Matamba and Cassange, the capital of Kasanje.

These developments affected Kongo adversely, for its capital was no longer the mandatory entrepôt for goods and slaves. Furthermore, its currency greatly depreciated, the Portuguese having imported other shells. By 1619 the *nzimbu* had lost two-thirds of its value – and the king two-thirds of his revenue. The king, however, managed to redress the situation and the currency gradually regained its former value. The revenues of the king and the nobility must, in fact, have suffered from the diversion of trade to Luanda and Loango.

This period saw the introduction first of maize cultivation (between 1548 and 1583) and, soon after 1600, that of manioc, tobacco and probably beans, groundnuts and other New World plants. Pigs are mentioned from 1583 onwards, and these were probably imported animals. They were to spread mainly in Kongo and central Angola. The new crops transformed agriculture in the seventeenth century, especially after 1650, increasing yields and providing, with manioc, a diet better suited to occasional drought and war conditions. Nutritional standards generally improved. As early as 1560, however, reference is made to smallpox, an epidemic introduced from Europe, which was to become a recurrent scourge.

The first half of the seventeenth century thus witnessed changes in nutrition and health conditions – and the introduction of the slave trade. All this inevitably set up new population trends, the details of which are unknown. In Angola in particular, however, the population must have declined.

Towards a new order: 1641–1700

In 1641, the Dutch captured Luanda and occupied a vast part of the colony of Angola before a fleet fitted out in Brazil drove them out in 1648. From then on, the Brazilians dominated Angola's trade, totally until 1730, and partially thereafter. Also in 1641, Garcia II became king of Kongo and, like Nzinga, formed an alliance with the Dutch. The Restoration left them face-to-face with a great Portuguese army with which they had to come to terms. Kasanje, which had stayed out of the wars, signed a treaty of friendship and became an ally of Portugal for more than a century. Disagreements over the treaty ultimately led the Angolans to invade Kongo. Antonio I of Kongo assembled all his nobles and was defeated in 1665 at the battle of Mbwila. He perished in the battle together with many nobles. But a second Portuguese army was so disastrously beaten at Soyo in 1670 that Angola gave up its attempts to conquer

Kongo. In 1671, the last vestige of Ndongo was conquered, and by about 1680, peace had been imposed on Matamba (Nzinga), Kasanje and the chiefs to the south of the middle Cuanza. The conquest was complete.

The kingdom of Kongo did not recover from Mbwila. A disputed royal succession led to a civil war between noble houses, which resulted in Mbanza Kongo being destroyed in 1666 and totally abandoned in 1678. Since the town was the pivot of the political system, everything collapsed. When a single king at last returned to Mbanza Kongo in 1709, his kingdom was no more than a collection of principalities often still rent by internal struggles between claimants. Everything had fallen apart except Soyo, and even Soyo had the greatest difficulty in remaining united. The nobility, having deserted Mbanza Kongo, had to adapt itself to life in the countryside and contended there for the posts of command. A sizeable number of nobles crossed the river northward to found small principalities in Mayombe and between the rivers Zaire and Niari.

The upheaval was total and demolished the very foundations of society, so much so that prophetesses began to appear. In 1704, Dona Beatrice Kimpa Vita began preaching a refurbished Christianity called Antonianism. She rejected the missionaries and the whites, but above all she exhorted rival claimants to the throne to give up the struggle, restore a king and repopulate Mbanza Kongo. She had a large popular following and persuaded a claimant to settle in Mbanza Kongo, where she crowned him with the black Antonian crown. But in 1706, she was captured and burnt as a heretic. Pedro II restored the kingdom and repopulated Mbanza Kongo, but a 40-year tide of political evolution could not be turned back.

With Kongo, the organization of a vast area disappeared. The structural framework of this area, like that of Angola, was henceforth to be economic, with a framework of trade routes articulated by places of transshipment. Angola, which had expanded towards 1680, was also weakened. Neither the governors nor the *Camara* of Luanda could maintain their ascendancy over the *quimbares* and *ovimbali* (the Afro-Portuguese), or over Brazilian traders.

In Loango, the state still appeared to be strong, but when the king died in 1701, it took more than a year to elect a new king. Royalty, for all its religious prestige, would begin to be redefined with regard to its authority over trade.

On the periphery of the slave-trading areas, states strengthened themselves through a growing trade which they controlled, or at least remained sound for such time as they controlled it. Kasanje had become a great power on the Kwango river because it controlled an ever-increasing flow of slaves after 1648. In the north, the Tio kingdom held its ground, apparently without great changes.

The Dutch conquest and the Restoration had substantial economic consequences. Currencies – raffia cloth and *nzimbu* – depreciated. In Angola, the slave trade was reorganized by the Brazilians, who supplied capital, ships and European goods and acted in concert with the organizers of caravans and the Afro-Portuguese slavers.

On the Loango coast, the French and English, with an insatiable demand for slaves making itself felt in their West Indian colonies, entered into hard-driving competition with the Dutch after 1660–65. Here, companies financed in Europe carried on the triangular trade. So began the large-scale slave trade which was to reach its full development in the eighteenth century.

Social and cultural transformations: the sixteenth and seventeenth centuries

We are best informed about Kongo. The division of society into three social strata, the *mwisikongo* (nobles), the *babuta* (sing. *mubata*) (rustics) and the *babika* (sing. *mubika*) (slaves) was to persist until some time between 1666 and 1678, the shift occurring first among the nobility and then in the countryside.

The term *ekanda* (root: *kanda*) today means 'matri-clan' or 'matrilineage'. At that time it meant family – matrilineal, to be sure but also any community. The people of a village made up an *ekanda*, as did the Christian community. The village was thought of as belonging to a matrilineal kinship group, descended from its founder, who was represented by the village leader, the *nkuluntu* (the old one). In fact, since women followed their husbands and their sons did not always go to live in their uncle's village, the village group was bound together by a territorial tie. The village held the rights to the land, and the spirit that dwelt in that land was perpetuated by the village *kitomi* (former lord of the land). Ideologically, these rights belonged to the matrilineage of the founder, but in practice the village acted as a body. This can be seen in particular in the existence of associations such as *khimba*, *nzo longo* or *kimpasi*, all of which were initiation cults for boys or healing cults which differed from one area to the next.

In the course of time, the power of the matrilineage and the village diminished. The villagers were already being harshly exploited by 1525. They may have revolted with the Jaga in 1568, and rebellions took place during the reign of Garcia II. At that time the *kimpasi*, a cult whose aim was to banish *mpasi* (suffering, poverty, calamity or affliction) was very active during periods of oppression or natural disasters. The villagers' lot became more and more precarious as the nobles increasingly intervened to demand concubines and set the sons they bore them to keep the villages under surveillance.

The noble houses, taking the royal house as their model, grew in size and importance. They absorbed a great many slaves. Their heads had large harems of wives from other noble or rural families. They paid high bride-prices for their principal wives, thus securing for themselves the ownership of the future children. The bride-price went to the wife; in this way the noble ladies grew in economic and political importance. The senior woman of a house by bilateral descent was its standard-bearer. Yet the position of patrilineal descendants – sons – grew in importance. Moveable property acquired by trade belonged to the sons, who, after about 1550, no longer took their father's name but a Portuguese surname symbolizing their house. The inheritances, however, were less substantial than might be thought, as everything acquired through the performance of public functions reverted to the king after the death or dismissal of the incumbent.

After 1666, the houses underwent two different series of changes. In Soyo the reigning house became increasingly patrilineal, neglecting nephews in favour of sons – even sons by female slaves. Eventually, in the nineteenth century, the whole of Soyo adopted the patrilineal ideology. In Kongo, on the other hand, the nobles, having lost their town, had to make a new place for themselves in the countryside. The great houses melted away like snow in summer, to be replaced around 1700 by the formation of large matrilineal groups, the *mvila* (clans). Government had been decentralized and ruralized.

Slaves – initially war captives – did not remain a single stratum for long. A distinction came into being between saleable slaves and domestic slaves who could no longer be sold. The latter were attached to noble houses, and some groups – such as the royal slaves and mission-station slaves – became independent, locally powerful groups, and so remained up to the nineteenth century. Since the saleable slaves were exported, they never formed cohesive groups. In time, Kongo's three strata thus became compressed into two – the nobility and their exploited subjects.

In Angola, the indigenous social structure comprised the same social strata as in Kongo, with a Portuguese stratum at the top. But the situation was complicated by the emergence of an Afro-Portuguese stratum made up of mulatto traders, who were, culturally speaking, as much Angolan or Kongolese as Portuguese. This group first formed in São Tomé through miscegenation with Kongo nobles, then hived off to the Kongo capital and to Luanda. By about 1680, there were two large groups in existence, one around the fortress of Ambaka, the other founding Cacunda Velha. In the eighteenth century, the Afro-Portuguese were to spread most widely on the Benguela plateau. They represented a floating population of caravaneers and traders, who worked in concert with African chiefs and married into the local nobility.

The history of religions and ideologies is marked on the surface by conversion to Catholicism, which, in Kongo, spread first among the urban nobility and in the chief towns of the provinces. The ecclesiastical structure remained chiefly Portuguese until 1645, when the Italian Capuchin missionaries began an intense campaign of conversion to Christianity which continued in Kongo until about 1700. In Angola, the Catholicism imposed by the conquerors did not progress beyond the colony except in Matamba. It did not spread in Loango, despite the conversion of a king in 1663.

The development of religious ideas and practices in Kongo shows that the Christian doctrine influenced the old religion and coexisted with it. The Christian terminology stems from the domain of the *nkisi*, the *ndoki* and the *nganga*, the *nkisi* becoming 'that which is sacred' or 'grace'. The missionaries fought against the rites of the *kitomi* and of witchcraft, ancestor worship and healing associations, but tolerated the medicine practised by the *nganga*. The Capuchins used processions and prayers to replace fertility rites, and practised exorcism.

From the sixteenth century onwards there can be said to have been a single religion in which, at least among the nobles, features of Christianity and features of the old religion had merged. The main spread of this religion took place in the seventeenth century. Garcia II was the defender of both Catholicism and the *kitomi*. He was even nicknamed 'the sorcerer'. This new religion was the source of Haitian voodoo.

Various religious movements have been recorded since the 1630s, when the first attempt was made to establish an indigenous church. In 1704, Dona Beatrice preached a far-reaching reform which cannot be explained solely in terms of the political situation. She claimed to be in direct contact with heaven and was regarded as a *munaki* (prophetess). She called for thorough Africanization. The Holy Family was black and hailed from Mbanza Kongo, and the symbols she used were evocative local symbols associated with water, the soil and vegetation. But she recognized the Pope, despite her desire to drive out the white missionaries who falsified revelation. In short, her vision was even more syncretic than the religion practised in her time.

It has been said that after 1700 Kongo lost its Catholicism. This is false, but the Christian missionaries of the late nineteenth century, steeped in the atmosphere of colonialism, failed to recognize the indigenous Catholicism which had become an integral part of Kongo religion.

The arts express culture. While nothing survives in Kongo of the performing arts, such as music, dance and oral art, visual art objects have survived, together with many texts on the subject. These objects, created to symbolize class differences (the art of costume for example), political concepts (emblems and ceremonial objects) and religious concepts (Christian art, objects used in divination, statues of ancestors and spirits and masks) were commissioned by the court, the Catholic Church, the leaders of villages and of village cults and even heads of household.

What is striking in Kongo art is the continuity of stylistic elements, allied to a dynamism of form that assimilates the many European influences. Examples include geometrical decorations criss-crossing at acute angles on a royal emblem (an ivory horn) from before 1533, fabrics from about 1650 to 1800 and basketwork, tattoos and mats from the nineteenth and even the twentieth century. European influence was strong and was reflected in the importation of European stone architecture (churches and palaces), symbols of authority (swords, crowns, flags and vestments) and, above all, religious objects. Almost all characteristics of Kongo art, especially statuary and the graphic arts, have been attributed to Christian influence. But the manifestations of ancient graphic art – rock drawings surviving from different periods – have hitherto been ignored. In the seventeenth century, we find alongside stylized drawings a series of pictograms which are clearly derived from writing and an expression of popular culture. This use of pictograms was to continue and merge with the production of geometrical decoration. Alongside these drawings, a more varied figurative tradition was still practised: witness the narrative bas-reliefs and wall paintings of the eighteenth and nineteenth centuries.

Sculpture is represented first by many Christian objects. They contain elements of the European canon of proportions but the stylization allied to Kongo realism was there from the beginning.

Artists used the most varied materials – copper, ivory, wood, stone, ceramics, fibres and fabrics – and worked on the most diverse objects, including even cooking utensils. The very first chronicles extol the merits of Kongo raffia fabrics, embroidered or worked in velvet. Even the clergy used them to make priestly robes to supplement those which they imported, from Italy in particular. The sculpting of cult objects used in the old religion was forbidden and works were destroyed at various times, especially under Afonso I and Garcia II, and by Kimpa Vita. However, the demand for these objects was constantly renewed.

The influence of Kongo art extended north and east during the whole of this period. The spread of the so-called 'white' masks from Gabon derives from northern Kongo masks and probably accompanied the expansion of Loango, especially in the seventeenth century. The technique of making raffia velvet spread along the Okango route to the east and was the forerunner of the velvets of Kasai, and especially of Kuba.

The eighteenth century: the northern areas

In the eighteenth century, the whole of Central Africa was reorganized. Trading networks – not states – became the dominant factor. A merchant class replaced or complemented the old ruling classes. There were two slaving networks: one, Portuguese, traded from Angola to Brazil and the other, in the north, was tied in with the other European powers; but the overland trade remained firmly in African hands.

This trade in the northern areas, that of the Loango coast, was fuelled by companies which financed the entire triangle of trade. Competition among the different European firms was an even greater factor in driving up prices than the increased demand for slaves in the West Indies and North America. Demand increased steadily from about 1665 to 1755, attaining its peak between 1755 and about 1797, when the great European wars brought it to a temporary halt.

The ports used were first Loango and then Malemba, Cabinda and, after 1800, Boma. The European traders rented warehouse buildings in the ports, where they exchanged their merchandise for slaves through the agency of brokers, the *mercadores*. Brokers were indispensable, for monetary systems were different and it was necessary to agree on exchange values. To that end, a unit of goods – the parcel – was established, corresponding to a unit value of slaves. The parcel was made up of three components: guns and gunpowder, fabrics and miscellaneous goods, especially metal goods. In addition to the purchase price, the European merchant had to pay trade duties and make gifts to the local king and the notable in charge of European trade. The broker, for his part, earned a large commission on the selling price of the slaves.

About 1 million slaves and small quantities of ivory, copper and wax were exported during the eighteenth century. Imports consisted mainly of fabrics and weapons. It is estimated that 50,000 guns a year were imported during the second half of the century.

The caravans were led by guides who were skilled in negotiating rights of passage and had an expert knowledge of the big inland markets. They sometimes travelled very long distances, taking with them not only European products but also salt, salted and dried fish and locally manufactured items, especially jewellery from Loango. On the way they were able to buy other local products which they sold elsewhere.

The principal route linked the ports to Malebo Pool, where the slaves shipped along the river and its tributaries arrived in large numbers. The Bobangi gave up fishing for that commerce, and their trade network stretched from the Ubangi river to the Kwa. These waterborne carriers also conducted an extensive trade in other products – pottery, fish, mats, food, beer, red dyewood and other commodities bought in one place and sold in another; this encouraged different areas to specialize in different goods. The slave-trading zone had reached the Ubangi, the lower Tshuapa and the areas around Lake Mayi Ndombe well before 1800 and continued to expand as the demand for slaves grew. Other caravan routes traversed Kongo, reaching Matamba and Cassange. After about 1750, the capital of the new Yaka state of the Kwango river became a slave-trading centre into which thronged the slaves taken in the constant military campaigns waged by the Yaka beyond the Kwango.

The northern slave trade was so lucrative compared with that of Angola that it pushed the latter's field of operations towards Luanda and Cassange. This led to Portuguese military action against the port of Mosul (later Ambriz) and to the occupation of Encoje in central Kongo in 1759 and subsequently, in 1783, of Cabinda. The Portuguese were driven out by a French squadron supported by local forces.

The demographic effects of the slave trade are still largely unknown. The population fell in Kongo and Mayombe, although we do not know by how much. Elsewhere, the main result was to slow down population growth.

We know more about the economic effects. To the north of the Zaire river a vast area organized itself into an aggregate of regions, each with its own speciality: raffia, tobacco, cane-sugar wine, ivory, foodstuffs, ironware, pottery, boats and so on. This led to technological impoverishment in each individual region, as some activities were given up, but the economic vitality of the aggregate increased steadily, owing mainly to the development of waterborne transport.

The social and political effects were far-reaching. The brokers and notables in charge of the slave trade steadily gained in importance at the courts of Loango, Ngoyo and Kakongo, at the expense of the old nobility linked to the royal house. Royal authority suffered accordingly. In Loango, the royal council witnessed the replacement of territorial nobles of the royal house by these new nobles, the titles being sold by the king to the highest bidder. In or before

1750, the royal line became extinct and six factions contended for the throne, but the royal *kitomi* eventually succeeded in imposing a neutral king at the cost of gravely weakening his power. Moreover, distant provinces such as Mayumba began seceding from Loango from 1750 on.

The Tio kingdom was also in difficulties. The regional great lords trading on their own account had grown rich and adopted a new ideology legitimizing their secession. This power was spiritual, centred upon a talisman, the *nkobi*, and could dispense with the support of territorial spirits. From about 1780 onwards the Tio state was in the grip of civil war and did not recover until about 1830.

In the middle Zaire basin, the expansion of the slave trade led to renewed small-scale population movements and hostilities, both in the Mayi Ndombe area and further north, while large centres of population began to take shape beside the river at points where it could be crossed. These centres became market towns in the nineteenth century.

In Kongo itself, Christian ideology, and especially the Order of Christ to which the rulers belonged, remained the basis of the ruling ideology. Its centres were the king, who was now no more than a supreme *nkisi*, and the former mission stations, run by former mission slaves. Territorial units broke up again and again, sometimes even at village level. At the same time, however, large *mvila* (clans) appeared, structured in lineages that had put down deep roots in the land. This network of clans became the cement that bound the independent villages together.

These transformations were accompanied by significant cultural changes. The role of the great ancestors, linked with the clans, increased. Cemeteries and churches, particularly those of Mbanza Kongo, grew bigger. The notion of *zombi*, a kind of corpse-slave, took hold, as did the confusion of saints with great ancestors. After about 1700 prominent people began to be buried with ever greater ostentation. The fabric wrapping around the corpse was now replaced by an enormous funerary bundle. The wooden heads or busts which were positioned on the bundles in the eighteenth century became wooden or stone statues or ceramic monuments to adorn the tombs on which an increasing number of broken objects were laid. The Boma area and Mayombe were at the centre of these developments.

The group-healing cults prospered everywhere. The *lemba*, an already old example of these *nkisi* in Loango, changed in character and became a *nkisi* of protection for members of the élites who could pay the high enrolment fees. When an important man fell ill, the *lemba* priest came to treat him.

Christianity held its ground but evolved. The scarcity of foreign or local priests left the initiative to the missionaries' former helpers, and at court, to the king's entourage. The reliefs of Ambriz show crucifixion scenes in which the spear has become a python, reminiscent of Mbumba or Bomba, associated with the slave trade and wealth, while the scene is accompanied by drummers. Crucifixes were retained as emblems of authority and, in what was essentially a judicial role, as emblems of *nkangi* (the saviour). Other crosses developed, such as *santu*, or charms associated with divination by hunting and used to discover the cause of collective misfortunes. They were the two sides of the same official religion.

Angola in the eighteenth century

The Angolan slave trade was conducted on a significant scale long before that of the north developed. The system, which was focused mainly on Brazil, was highly fragmented by comparison with that of the north. Before 1730, it had the following components: the export merchant in Portugal; brokers in Brazil; shippers; slave-dealers in Luanda or Benguela; Afro-Portuguese caravaneers; and African lords and traders offering slaves for sale at the markets. A single firm could supply several components but rarely all of them together. Everyone tried to avoid risks and to maximize profits. The greatest risk was that slaves would die of malnutrition, untreated diseases and ill-treatment. J. C. Miller quotes an estimate to the effect that half the slaves bought died between the market of purchase and the port of embarkation and another 40 per cent at Luanda while awaiting embarkation. Losses at sea varied according to the state of health of the slaves shipped and the degree of overcrowding on board. They worked out at 10 per cent of the total number embarked.

The parcel, called *hanzo* in Angola, was supplied on credit to the caravaneer, binding him to his sleeping partner. The parcel consisted mainly of fabrics from Goa or Europe, brandy from Brazil, local salt, beads and sometimes a few weapons. The caravaneers' expenses were high, as were their risks, and they would soon fall into debt and become completely dependent on their creditor. But from about 1760 onwards, the caravaneers began selling their slaves to any trader in Luanda or Benguela in an effort to redress their situation. The sleeping partner was left with a write-off.

After 1730, metropolitan Portuguese firms came back to Luanda to supply European goods, and the Brazilians withdrew to Benguela. The ships also brought numbers of poor immigrants, common convicts and adventurers seeking to grow rich on the slave trade, especially as caravaneers. An unrelenting struggle began between the *quimbares* and the new arrivals. The latter, as traders, had the full support of the high authorities of Luanda, but the *quimbares* enjoyed the backing of the provincial authorities and, in general, of the African chiefs in the inland markets. The Brazilians and *quimbares* not only succeeded in maintaining their position in Benguela but also increased their exports of slaves. But the Portuguese firms, by virtue of their capital and the administrative backing they enjoyed, succeeded in shifting the slave risk. They bought, not slaves, but ivory or bills to be collected in Brazil.

At the turn of the century, the governors supported the Brazilians. Later, they tended to favour the big Lisbon firms. The Jesuits, the allies of the Brazilians, were expelled in 1660. Francisco Innocencio de Sousa Coutinho (1664–72) made a vigorous effort to re-establish the mother country's control in Angola, but neither he nor his successors achieved this. The Afro-Portuguese emigrated once again, moving mainly to the Benguela plateau where a new bridgehead for trade with the interior developed. The slaves were taken to Benguela, avoiding Luanda. But Luanda continued to attract the slave trade through the kingdom of Kasanje. The caravans took the route from Cassange to Mussumba, the capital of the Lunda empire.

The Lunda empire took shape during the eighteenth century. Constant military campaigns yielded large numbers of slaves, while tributes in slaves flowed into the capital from the subject regions. After 1750, the empire succeeded in founding the kingdom of Kazembe on the Luapula river and in establishing communications with Tete and Zumbo in Mozambique. Before then, westward expansion had reached the River Kwango. The Yaka kingdom, founded between 1740 and 1760, occupied a large part of the Kwango valley downstream of Kasanje and extended its conquests eastward in the direction of the Kwilu. Large numbers of captives were brought back from there to be sold to the Zombo, Soso and Vili, but also to the Imbangala and to caravans passing through Nkoje.

In Angola, the slave trade had such an ascendancy that, despite the efforts of de Sousa Coutinho and others, the country failed to develop a diversified economy. The colony remained economically dependent on Brazil; around 1800, 88 per cent of its revenues still came from the slave trade with Brazil and a little less than 5 per cent from the ivory sent to Portugal.

The political system of the Luba and Lunda: its emergence and expansion

The history of the Luba is the story of the development of a political system which first emerged in Shaba, in the present-day Republic of Zaire, and subsequently spread into a large part of the southern grasslands, an area stretching almost from the River Kwango to the River Zambezi.

The connections and the differences between the Luba and Lunda states are implicit in their two names, which reflect not so much ethnic distinctions as two political and cultural systems within which a whole range of separate ethnic referents sprang up. The history of the Luba covers matters affecting the present-day Luba of both Shaba and Kasai as well as matters relating to the Songye, Kanyok, Kete, Sala Mpasu, Bindji and Lulua. The history of the Lunda deals both with the Rund groups (the Lunda in the narrow sense) and the Lozi, Ndembo, Lwena, Imbangala and other groups (the Lunda in the broad sense). The linguistic classification given to the Luba and Lunda languages is indicative of this intertwined relationship.

There is general agreement that the archaeological finds of the Upemba Depression at Sanga and elsewhere are to be attributed to the ancestors of the Luba. Emblems of rule, later common among the Luba, appear by the thirteenth century at the latest, along with evidence at Katota and Sanga of the formation of two chiefdoms. Yet Katota and Sanga were not the direct forerunners of the Luba kingdom. All we know is that the main Luba kingdom came into being and began to expand before the Rund state, fountainhead of the Lunda, was developed. Oral tradition mentions the Rund state by 1680 but does not allow us to date its founding.

The emergence of the Luba and Lunda states

Shaba and the adjoining parts of Zambia and Angola are covered by woodlands, the soils are poor and the dry season is very long. The best lands lie mostly in the river valleys and the worst in eastern Angola. But the southern, half-barren country, especially the south-east, contains mineral treasure – copper, iron and salt.

It is not surprising, therefore, that the population lived in pockets of fertile

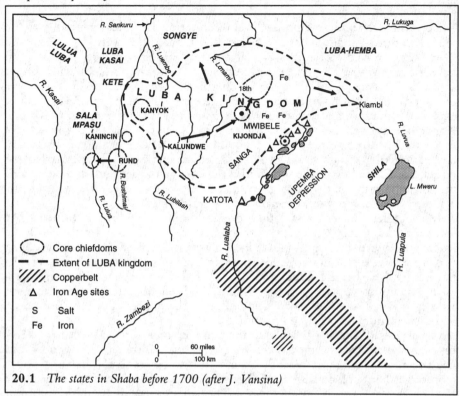

20.1 *The states in Shaba before 1700 (after J. Vansina)*

land, with vast expanses of almost uninhabited areas in between, used mainly for hunting. This population distribution explains the location of the earliest territorial organizations, which were small chiefdoms, each corresponding to one settlement. Thus the Sanga string of settlements becomes the later chiefdom of Kikondja, while Katoka upstream, at the other end of the Lualaba lake system, formed another. In both these areas, people were fishermen and farmers. There were many other chiefdoms, all located in major river valleys.

These population clusters were linked by trade and, presumably, intermarriage. From the north came raffia and palm oil, from the Lualaba fish, from the south copper and salt, and from the central southern area *mbafu* oil. The trade was important enough for currencies to develop from at least 1000 onwards. In the Upemba Depression around 1300, the copper cross became the currency. After 1700 crosses disappeared and, by the nineteenth century, imported beads were becoming the new currency.

In this context developed the political ideology that later would be central to the main Luba kingdom. This consisted of two interlocked principles, that of the sacred character of kingship (*bulopwe*) and that of rule through a closed association.

According to some traditions, the forerunner of the Luba kingdom was the small Kalundwe kingdom. Its capital was at Cifinda. One of its kings, Kongolo (Rainbow), moved to found a capital on the plains at Mwibele, not far from Lake Boya, in what would be the heartland of the future Luba state. Other accounts, however, have Kongolo coming from elsewhere. The epic narrative of foundation tells how Kongolo was defeated and slain by Kalala Ilunga (Ilunga the hunter), a foreigner from the east who moved the capital to Munza. Kongolo may well not be an authentic figure, but Kalala, as *mwine Munza* (master of Munza), represents a founding-father figure that depicts what an ideal Luba king should be. The Luba kingdom dominated, perhaps from the outset, the Kalundwe to the west and the Kikondja to the south and controlled the major north–south trading routes. Nonetheless, until the eve of the eighteenth century it would remain a fairly small kingdom.

Meanwhile, further west, other political units were being formed. The foremost among them, Nkalany, developed in the Mbuji Mayi valley from the fusion of several small areas headed by *tubung* (masters of the land). Nothing really predestined the Rund lands to become an empire. Yet at one point the northern *tubung* were united under one of the Rund lands. The northern *tubung* traditions explain why an Nkond chief left his office to his daughter, Rweej or Rueji, who married Cibinda Ilunga, the hunter from the Luba court, and then abandoned office in his favour.

According to Carvalho Dias, after the conquest stage, power went to Rweej's first son, Yav, who became *mwant yav* (lord Yav). However, the versions that have been collected more recently claim that Rweej was sterile. In order not to jeopardize the succession, she gave her husband a second wife, Kamonga, who became the mother of his successors. This situation accounts for the institutionalized existence of two female dignitaries at the court of the *mwant yav*: the *swan murund* or *swana mulunda*, the symbolic mother of the society, who symbolized the perpetuation of the role played by Rweej, and the *rukonkesh* or *lukonkeshia*, the queen mother, who occupied the role played by Kamonga.

This testimony explains the different institutions that evolved after the appearance of the Luba hunter: first, the two female aristocracies, one symbolizing social fertility and the other biological fertility; and second, the royal title based on the chiefly title *mwant*, to which the name of the first king was added.

The Luba: internal organization and development to 1800

With Kalala as *mwine Munza*, a state appeared on the plains incorporating the Kikondja kingdom to the south and the Kalundwe kingdom to the west. It further expanded to the south-east as far as the lower reaches of the Luvua river.

The foundation and first consolidation of the kingdom led to some disturbances in the region and a number of emigrants left the lower Luvua to found the Shila state on the western shore of Lake Mweru and along the lower Luapula. The most important emigration was towards the north. Groups of Luba Kasai left Shaba and spread northwards along the Lubilash river, where

20.2 *Hemba, Zaire: monoxyloid caryatid seat, the bottom of which is worn away. Note the prominent scarifications and the quality of the bracelets. Height: 35 cm (G. Berjonneau, ART 135, Boulogne-Billancourt, © and photo)*

20.3 *Luba, Southern Zaire: the knob of a ceremonial cane, in the form of a human head decorated with a very tall headdress surmounted by two figures holding each other by the waist. Overall length: 164 cm (G. Berjonneau, ART 135, Boulogne-Billancourt, © and photo)*

they found better watered lands. Famine is given as a major motive for movement in many traditions of related groups in Kasai.

Although, to the south, in Shila and Kanyok country, a variant of the
Shaban Luba political system was set up, in Kasai this did not occur. Here, the
political organization was either limited to the village and its land, or higher
office was given for life – or for a limited period – to the highest bidder, a
system also found among some Songye. The Luba Kasai also adopted some
emblems and some political practices from the Kanyok. Most Songye were,
however, ruled differently. By the 1880s, and probably some centuries earlier,
the Songye were living in huge farming settlements which were virtually
towns, ruled by the Bukishi association and dominated by chiefs with a few
titled notables.

The organization of the Luba state corresponded to a pyramid of pyramids.
At village level, households were linked by patrilineage. Relations between
villages were also thought of as relations between lineages, although each
district had a titled chief. Above this, the kingdom itself was ruled from the
capital, whose very lay-out reflected this structure with royal quarters at its
centre and quarters for titled officials of both sexes, separated according to their
military or civilian function. A closed association, the *bambudye*, helped the king
to rule. The king was not supposed to have a lineage or clan, although the office
was normally handed down from father to brother or son. The king was at the
same time above the political fray and yet linked by kinship to many of the
district heads. He stood at the apex of the pyramid of pyramids of kinship. The
title *mulopwe* signifies the indivisibility of power that could not be shared.

The *mulopwe* was surrounded by a household and titled officials. There was
first his harem, reflecting the real political alliances that bound the kingdom
together. His officials saw to it that tribute was paid in *mingilu* (unpaid labour),
in *milambu* (taxes payable in food and local produce) and in gifts offered at the
investiture of dignitaries. The territorial administration was in the hands of the
bilolo (sing. *kilolo*), each responsible for a region. The central administration
supervised the collection of tribute, organized the army and advised the king
through the *tshidie* (general council) and the *tshihangu* (king's court).

We do not know exactly how the *bambudye* association functioned, as its
secrets have not been revealed. But it had numerous lodges and exerted both
ritual and secular control over the country and even the king.

Local courts were patterned after the organization of the capital and local
chiefs had some sacred paraphernalia and links to local territorial spirit cults,
often for their own ancestors. The coercive power of the king's warriors was
the practical force that kept the country together. But there was no standing
army, so that the ideological force constituted by the *bambudye* was of great
importance. Heavy tribute could only be enforced when central districts were
willing to back the king against internal or external forces. It is not surprising,
therefore, that the kingdom did not expand rapidly.

There is little information about territorial history until about 1700 and the
reign of the king Kadilo. He embarked on unsuccessful campaigns to the north

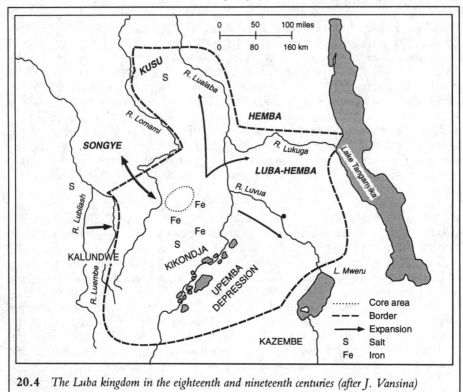

20.4   *The Luba kingdom in the eighteenth and nineteenth centuries (after J. Vansina)*

against the adjacent Songye towns, but the real expansion of the kingdom occurred in the valley of the Lualaba, along the Luvua (Kiambi) and south of the Upemba Depression. Such expansion faltered as a major succession crisis developed from about 1780 to 1810. During this crisis, the Kanyok freed themselves from Luba rule, and Songye political and cultural influence reached a high point. Later, expansion continued towards the east, with the conquest of the lands between the River Lualaba and Lake Tanganyika and a push towards the north along the Lualaba river as far as Buli.

The Lunda: internal organization and development to 1800

The Rund kingdom became the Lunda empire in the eighteenth century. Its earlier organization is not fully known, except that its military character was much more developed than in the Luba kingdom. A little is known, however, about the principles of social and political organization.

The succession of the *tubung* had been matrilineal, but succession to the royal title and at court was bilateral. The matrix of society was based on positional succession and perpetual kinship. This meant that every incumbent of a position or title was supposed to become his predecessor. The incumbent took the name of his predecessor, and his wives, children and other relatives. As a consequence, kinship was perpetual. If, for example, the first holder of a title was the king's grandson, five generations later the holder of the title was still the king's grandson.

It was possible, therefore, to conceive of the state as an organization run by a single family, headed by the *mwant yav* (emperor). New chiefs could be incorporated by giving them a kinship link (as son-in-law, for instance, after a marriage alliance) and providing them with a stable position in the empire. The organization of the empire on a family model automatically regulated relations between officials, based on a strict notion of generation.

So, to the Rund, the state was a family writ large – very large indeed as the empire came to stretch from the River Kwango to beyond the River Luapula. But it was a family of warriors and a family that would thrive on slavery. By about 1700, Lunda warriors had subdued the populations on the empire's periphery, incorporated them and then moved further afield. From 1750 to 1760, strong subsidiary kingdoms took shape from Yaka country on the Kwango river to Kazembe on the River Luapula, along an east–west axis that encompassed the mineral resources of Shaba and access to the Portuguese emporia on the River Zambezi as well as the trading routes from the Rund country to Imbangala territory on the Kwango.

The imperial administration was loose. The empire consisted of a core, plus peripheral kingdoms whose rulers merely paid occasional tribute to the court. The king had created special officials who roamed the countryside with a military detachment to force the *bilolo* to pay tribute. Apart from these forces, there was a major military organization headed by a *kazembe* (general). The *kazembe* wielded all power in his operational area, but once the area was incorporated, he either lost his status or became a ruler in his own right, a *kilolo* of the emperor.

The capital was laid out like an army camp, with a front and a vanguard, wings and centre. Its hub was the royal palace, where the emperor, the *swan murund*, the *rukonkesh* and dignitaries resided. Power was vested in the emperor; his title, *mvant yav* (lord of the viper), referred to the distance between the king and other mortals, but also to his ambiguity, as he stood for both peace and war, prosperity and destruction.

Research has shown that the expansion of the Lunda empire started before 1700. The conquest was towards the south-east, towards the salt-pans of the Lualaba river, near present-day Kolwezi. From there, in about 1700, a break-away group went south into present-day Zambia and set up a state in the Ndembu area after partly assimilating the indigenous Mbwela and pushing others southwards.

From the salt-pans of the Lualaba river, Lunda generals moved eastwards on a new campaign and reached the rich Luapula valley. The Lunda army beat off a Luba attack against them and subjugated the chiefs of Shaba and the Shila state of Luapula. This state grew and by the second half of the eighteenth century Kazembe of the Luapula was lord of a large tightly-knit kingdom. Soon after their settlement, the Lunda of Kazembe made contact with the Portuguese of Sena and Tete. A mission led by F. de Lacerda e Almeida visited the new kingdom from 1798 to 1799. It was impressed by the military power of Kazembe and with the severity of measures used against the inhabitants. This Portuguese visit inaugurated a period of intense trade relations between Kazembe and the lower Zambezi. This was to strengthen the autonomy of Kazembe from the capital, so that the regular tribute payments of the 1790s had become more an equal exchange of gifts by the 1830s.

Towards the north and west, other Lunda expansion was closely linked to the development of the slave trade in Angola. Contacts with the Angolan slave-trading system date from the 1670s at the latest and developed subsequently. The Imbangala developed a system of trading by caravans which brought European goods, such as cloth, beads and crockery, to the Lunda capital, where they served as luxury goods for the local aristocracy. The Lunda would not accept guns, preferring to remain faithful to their sword, the *mpok*. In return, they exported slaves captured initially in the areas north and east of the Rund core. Later, Mbwela captives from northern Zambia and eastern Angola were also added to those exports. At the same time, demand for slaves grew within the Lunda empire itself. They were used to cultivate large fields to grow cassava; they also worked as ferrymen and porters in the caravans.

Shortly after 1700, military expeditions were sent westwards, and by about 1750 Lunda chiefs had reached the Kwango. Eastern Angola, the land of the Lwena, was their first goal. The Lunda leaders superimposed themselves on fairly large-scale societies organized around matrilineages of great depth. West of the Lwena country various chiefdoms were also created by the Lunda by superimposing themselves on existing societies. Among these peoples, the Chokwe were later to prove the most important. Even in the eighteenth century, they were valuable to the empire as metallurgists, carvers and hunters.

In the Kwango valley, the Lunda invaders found Yaka, Suku and perhaps at Okango yet other chiefdoms structured after the Kongo pattern. These they overran. Many inhabitants fled, but the structures were not destroyed. As a result, a complex system came into being in which even the ideology of the state acknowledged the existence of indigenous people and Lunda invaders. But the leader of the Yaka, the *kiamfu*, could not control all his own men. In the north, a semi-independent state, Pelende, arose, whilst a group called the Sonde-Luwa emigrated east of the middle Kwango and founded chiefdoms of their own.

Once established, the Yaka kings started raiding the lands towards the Kwilu to gather slaves for sale to Angolan, Kongo and Vili traders. This provoked major upheavals in the region. The Suku kingdom put up a successful resistance, but elsewhere people fled north-eastwards, provoking high population densities.

The final expedition went from west of the Kasai river northwards, probably along the valley of the Tshikapa. The Lunda founded two small states: one at the main falls of the Kasai with its capital at Mai Munene, which soon became a major market for caravans from the River Kwango, and the other, called Mwaka Kumbana, on the River Loange. In both areas the Lunda mixed with other recent immigrants, the Pende. The resulting political systems were marked by Pende influence.

Conclusion

By 1800, Luba and Lunda expansion had structured all the grassland area of central Africa east of the River Kwango. The peoples of this area shared a common culture, with common rituals and common emblems and symbols. The spread of this culture was facilitated by the existence of the trade routes and even by raids. Population mobility, especially through marriage alliances, was astonishingly high, as evidenced by the spread of clan names inherited through the mother. The same names are found from the Kwango to the Kasai and from the Kasai to the Luapula rivers.

Lunda expansion, however, also led to enormous devastation. The militaristic nature of the Lunda states should not be underestimated, nor the scale of their slave-raiding with its consequences for the populations. This, and the presence of a common political culture from the Kwango to the Luapula, still constitutes for the inhabitants of this huge area the legacy of those centuries.

The Northern Zambezia–
Lake Malawi region

The region discussed in this chapter is bounded on the south by the Zambezi, on the north by the Songwe and Ruvuma rivers, on the west by the Luangwa, and on the east by the Indian Ocean. The southern part of this region was dominated by the Chewa-speakers with their sub-groups. To the west of the Chewa were the Nsenga and to the east the Lolo-Makua-Lomwe speakers and the Yao. The northern zone stretched on the western side of Lake Malawi from the Chewa-Tumbuka marginal zone in the south to the Songwe river in the north. Three language families occupy this zone: the Tumbuka, the Ngonde-Nyakyusa and the Sukwa-Lambya-Nyiha. In 1500, all the people of the southern zone and the Tumbuka of the north belonged to the 'matrilineal cluster of Central Bantu speakers' which stretched from southern Zaire in the west to the Indian Ocean in the east. In the centuries that followed, however, the Tumbuka changed to patrilineal descent. The Ngonde-Nyakyusa and Sukwa-Lambya-Nyiha had always been patrilineal since the dawn of their historical tradition. The region today comprises eastern Zambia, all of Malawi, and northern Mozambique.

In the period under discussion, the southern zone was dominated in the fifteenth century by the arrival of the Maravi and the rise of their states, whose expansion continued in the sixteenth and seventeenth centuries. In the north, in the sixteenth century, the people were organized in clusters of autonomous clans. Late in the same century, however, an immigrant group – the Ngulube – founded the states of Lambya, Ngonde, Chifungwe, Sukwa and a number of Nyakyusa chiefdoms. In the same period, the expansion of the Maravi into the Tumbuka-Chewa marginal zone led to the establishment of new Chewa chiefdoms which imposed their sway over the Tumbuka peoples, creating in the main the Tonga people and language. In both zones the trade in ivory was a major factor in the eighteenth century. The southern zone was then characterized by the decline of the Maravi state system, the rise of successor states and the outward spread of the Yao, initially as traders and latterly as state founders. A group of immigrants from Nyamwezi country – the Balowoka – settled among the Tumbuka and created economic spheres of influence which eventually emerged as political entities. The older established states south of the

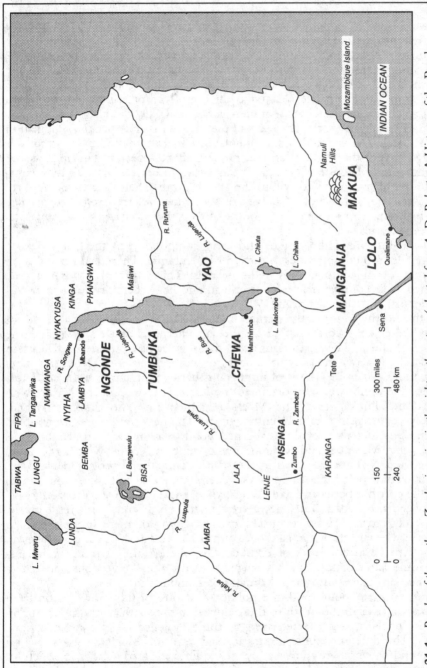

21.1 Peoples of the northern Zambezia region in the eighteenth century (adapted from A. D. Roberts, *A History of the Bemba Before 1900*, London, Longman, 1973, p. xxv. Map adapted by the kind permission of Longman Group UK Ltd)

Songwe, however, remained aloof from these new commercial developments until well into the nineteenth century.

Prior to the sixteenth century, the region experienced a succession of Iron-Age immigrations, including those which brought the first ancestors of the modern Bantu-speaking inhabitants. These new immigrants appear to have arrived from the north after 1200 and they displaced or assimilated the Bantu and pre-Bantu agriculturists and hunter-gatherers already there.

In northern Malawi, the ancestors of the modern Bantu-speaking population were a stateless and pre-dynastic population. In eastern Zambia, east of the Luangwa river, the earliest of the modern Bantu-speaking inhabitants are thought to have been the Katanga. Further east, in central Malawi, they comprised a number of clans to whom the term 'proto-Chewa' has been applied. In oral tradition, the proto-Chewa are sometimes referred to as *Kalimanjira* (path-makers), who cleared the country of its earlier nomadic inhabitants, the Batwa and Kafula.

Little is known of the origins and early composition of the Lolo-Makua-Lomwe and Yao communities of eastern Mozambique. There is no tradition of how they occupied their present homelands. This is probably because they occupied their country many centuries ago and have therefore long since lost the memory of their exact origins.

In the northern zone, the earliest modern Bantu-speaking inhabitants for whom there are records settled in the area between the Songwe and the southern Rukuru. Their traditions claim that they came from the north-eastern side of Lake Malawi and may have been related to the *abilema*. Not long afterwards, more powerful groups of immigrants began to infiltrate the area. These included the Simbowe, who occupied the Karonga plain, and the Mbale, who invaded the Phoka area. The Mbale migration into the Phoka highlands probably occurred in the fourteenth century. The new immigrants were noted iron-smelters and they easily established good relations with the indigenous people, the Mzembe and Chiluba, who supplied them with agricultural produce and coal and received in return iron agricultural tools and weapons. Thus it would appear that there was a general migration of peoples southwards using the corridor between Lakes Tanganyika and Malawi as a main passage.

Between the Phoka and Chewa areas in the north and south respectively, there lived various Tumbuka-speaking clans. Some of these groups seem to have spread as far east as the lakeshore and as far west as the Luangwa valley in the modern Lundazi district of Zambia. The Nsenga, the present-day inhabitants of the latter region, speak a language that is akin to Tumbuka and share the same clan-names with the inhabitants of Tumbukaland.

Thus, prior to about 1500, the political structure of the entire region from the Songwe river in the north to the Zambezi in the south, with the exception of a few pockets, was characterized by the prevalence of stateless small-scale polities. The different ethnic groups formed territorial chieftaincies. The local chief presided over a group of closely related lineage-based villages of which his own was the most senior genealogically. To the community of villages surrounding him he rendered religious, judicial and military services, and was in turn entitled to the allegiance of all his followers.

Though politically and sometimes physically divided into ethnic and clan spheres of influence, the Lake Malawi region enjoyed a certain degree of social and religious cohesion. Over the greater part of this region, religious action was expressed at two levels. At a local level, religion fulfilled the function of ensuring the moral and material well-being of the population, while at the territorial level it also fostered cultural and ecological co-operation. Religious practice for most people involved ancestor veneration, spirit possession, rain-making and control of witchcraft. The chief manifestation of a territorial religious experience were the rain cults, dedicated to a god or spirit acknowledged over a wide area.

It has been shown that at least within the matrilineal belt extending from the Tumbuka-Chewa marginal zone in the north to the Zambezi valley in the south, there was a considerable degree of interaction among the various territorial religious cults. The deity was represented in the same way throughout. Among the Tumbuka and Chewa, for example, he took the physical form of a snake, was thought to be a male force, and had several spirit wives devoted to his service. The functionaries dedicated to the deity were possessed and set apart for their special role. Thus religion provided an important means of communication among peoples who were otherwise divided politically.

Among the Chewa and related peoples of the southern zone, the loose political structure which prevailed before 1500 was greatly transformed by the emergence of the Maravi state system at the beginning of the sixteenth century and its later expansion. The Maravi thus dominate the sixteenth- and seventeenth-century political history of the northern Zambezia region just as the builders of the Mutapa state dominate that of southern Zambezia in the fifteenth and sixteenth centuries.

It is now generally agreed that the Maravi were immigrants who originated in the Luba area of south-eastern Zaire, and that they entered central Malawi from the west. On reaching the southern end of Lake Malawi, they rapidly established themselves as rulers over the earlier proto-Chewa inhabitants, consolidated their rule, and then embarked on a campaign of territorial expansion which took them beyond central and southern Malawi. By the early seventeenth century, their confederation of states encompassed the greater part of eastern Zambia, central and southern Malawi, and northern Mozambique. In this way, the Maravi state system came to have a political, military and economic impact over a vast area.

However, the process which led to the emergence of the Maravi state system is not yet clearly understood by historians. Some historians hold that the Maravi arrived in the country fully equipped with the symbols of chiefly power, with whose help they established themselves as a ruling class over what must have been a stateless indigenous population. Others would stress the role of demographic factors and argue that a growing population engaged in surplus production, albeit modest, would have served as a suitable basis for the accumulation of dynastic power. Another hypothesis takes into account the trade factor,

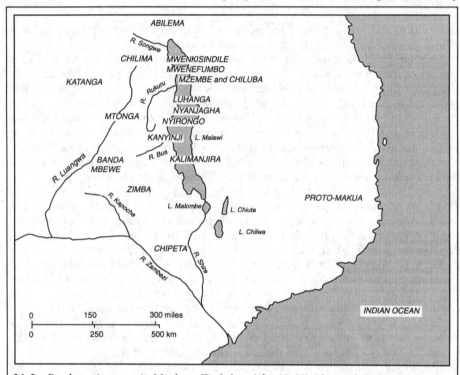

21.2 *Pre-dynastic groups in Northern Zimbabwe (after K. W. Phiri and O.J.M. Kalinga)*

maintaining that the formation of a state at the southern end of Lake Malawi in the fifteenth or sixteenth century arose from the need for an authority to control the development of the trade in ivory between the southern shores of the lake and the east coast of Africa via the Shire-Zambezi water system.

Oral tradition records little of the early history of the area or exactly how the Maravi state was founded. It simply maintains that under the leadership of the *kalonga* (the title of the ruler) Chidzonzi, who headed the most senior Phiri royal lineage, the Maravi established their first kingdom around Mankhamba and Manthimba on the south-western side of Lake Malawi. According to Portuguese written sources, by 1624, Manthimba was an important commercial and political centre, and its inhabitants were trading with Portuguese traders from Tete on the Zambezi.

Oral tradition, however, provides the only indication of the institutional mechanisms through which the *kalonga*'s state was held together. One of these was the *mlira* cult. Once every year, the heads of the different Phiri royal lineages were invited to Manthimba for the ritual veneration of Mlira, the spirit of the great *kalonga* Chinkhole, who had led their ancestors into the country at the time of the migration. This ritual, we believe, was a surface manifestation of a royal cult which had a significant integrative function within the Maravi state. Equally important to the integration of the kingdom was the manner in which appointive offices of state were allocated. The kalonga is said to have appointed some heads of proto-Chewa clans to important leadership positions in his state. The Banda were caretakers of the *kalonga*'s shrine at Mankhamba while the Mwale led the *kalonga*'s warriors. Traditions clearly underscore the extent to which non-Phiri or non-Maravi clan leaders were involved in the making of decisions pertaining to land tenure, the distribution of wealth and the making of war.

The extent to which the *kalonga* was able personally to direct the affairs of his kingdom may have begun to decline towards the last quarter of the sixteenth century when the state began to expand. The heads of the junior Phiri lineages left the Manthimba–Mankhamba zone to occupy adjacent territories. Taken together, the territories controlled by the *kalonga* and these subordinate chiefs formed the heartland of the Maravi state system as it evolved in the seventeenth century.

Another dimension of the Maravi expansion involved the migration of the *kalonga*'s senior kinsfolk into distant lands to the south and south-west of the heartland. This may have been a calculated move on the part of the early *kalongas* as they sought to distance possible pretenders to the throne at Manthimba. Kaphwiti and Lundu migrated into and colonized the lower Shire valley. Kaphwiti initially controlled the whole valley before he lost much of his authority to the *Lundu* who, after imposing his ascendancy in the lower Shire valley, spearheaded Maravi expansion eastward into Lolo and Makua country. The process of Maravi expansion in this part of northern Zambezia started in the mid-sixteenth century.

The Maravi invasion and conquest of Lolo-Makua country first owed much to the fanaticism of the *lundu*'s warriors, whom some historians of eastern Africa have identified with the notorious Zimba marauders of the late sixteenth century whom the *lundu* subsequently employed. The success of this conquest was also due to the statelessness of the Lolo and Makua societies. The Lolo political system was segmentary; the functions of government were performed by village headmen assisted by councils of elders. The Makua also had a segmentary political system, but among them lineages belonging to the same clan sometimes, in moments of crisis, combined under the leadership of the most powerful lineage. Thus, as a result of pressure from the Portuguese, strong chieftaincies emerged among the coastal Makua in the late sixteenth century.

The Lolo and Makua conquered by warriors of the *lundu* were incorporated into a tributary state which the Portuguese residents of the lower Zambezi termed 'Bororo'. As a result, by the beginning of the seventeenth century, the *lundu* controlled a vast territory north of the Zambezi, from the lower Shire in the west almost to the Indian Ocean in the east. Not only was he recognized as 'the second most powerful person in the empire of Maravi (the first being Kalonga)' but his warriors periodically descended on the Makua part of the coast to raid Portuguese settlements.

The *lundu* held his vast kingdom together with the help of loyal military generals and vassals drawn from junior lineages within his clan. Furthermore, his state had an economic underpinning in that the different peoples whom it encompassed depended on the salt, iron and *machila* cotton cloths that were produced by the the *lundu*'s Manganja subjects in the lower Shire valley. Manganja religion was another unifying factor in the state. Centred on the Mbona cult, whose central shrine was at Khulubvi in the lower Shire valley, the theology of Manganja religion encompassed many elements of commoner protest against the misuse of royal power and prerogative. Consequently, the official cult of the *lundu* paramountcy found many adherents over a large territory, stretching from the seat of the *lundu* in the lower Shire valley to the Zambezi delta on the east coast.

The immense prestige enjoyed by the *lundu* in the eastern part of the Maravi confederation did not go unchallenged. The *kalonga,* who himself controlled a vast territory on the western and eastern sides of Lake Malawi as well as along the upper Shire, became extremely anxious about the *lundu*'s growing power. In the 1620s and 1630s, therefore, Maravi expansion eastward was stalled by the vicious internal rivalry which developed between the *kalonga* and the *lundu.* Thereafter, Maravi expansion shifted from the east to the south-west. In this latter direction, the *undi* then established his own kingdom which he later expanded.

According to one version of the traditions relating to the establishment of the *undi*'s kingdom, the founder was sent out by the *kalonga* to occupy the sandy plains near Nsengaland. Another, more reliable version, however, suggests that the *undi*'s departure for the south-west was occasioned by a conflict within the ruling Phiri clan at Manthimba.

In the west, the *undi* and his followers successfully colonized the Kapoche river area, a tributary of the Zambezi. Thereafter, they extended the boundaries of their nascent kingdom toward the confluence of the Zambezi with the Luangwa. There, the *undi*'s warriors came into conflict with the Tawara along the Zambezi and the Nsenga along the eastern bank of the lower Luangwa. But historians differ on the extent to which the Maravi then came to dominate the Nsenga. However, what can be concluded from this debate is that during its expansive phases, the *undi*'s state encompassed a number of Nsenga chieftaincies, but not all. The south-western Nsenga near Feira in Zambia, for example, have no traditions of having been a part of the *undi*'s 'empire'.

There is still the question of how the *undi* may have established a certain degree of political control over the Nsenga. The traditional argument is that the *undi* and his subordinates used force and created perpetual kinship relationships according to which the conquered Nsenga chiefs were recognized as 'sons' or 'nephews' of the Maravi chiefs. Of late, however, a stronger argument has been presented. This is that trade and famine may have played a crucial role in the expansion of the *undi*'s influence over neighbouring peoples. The Nsenga chiefdoms along the Luangwa valley suffered from endemic famine, and their inhabitants often sought relief in the *undi*'s territory, which was more fertile than their own. The *undi* also enjoyed immense influence with Portuguese traders at Tete, and this fact enabled him to exercise some control over traders from neighbouring communities. There is also every indication that the *undi* and his kinsmen allowed the Nsenga chieftains who came under their influence to continue to administer the affairs of their clans and areas, as long as they sent tribute in ivory and slaves to the *undi*'s headquarters.

The Maravi and the Chewa also expanded northwards into Tumbuka country. Among the princely leaders of Maravi origin who migrated in that direction were Chulu, Kaluluma, Kanyenda and Kabunduli.

Chulu and Kaluluma moved into the southern Tumbuka area known as Chimaliro and the surrounding plains. Here, they encountered a Tumbuka people who were self-sufficient economically but loosely organized politically. The manner in which Chulu and Kaluluma took power is subject to conflicting interpretations in Chewa and Tumbuka oral traditions. It would seem, however, that after a period of peaceful cohabitation, the Tumbuka tried to resist and were crushed by force.

Kanyenda and Kabunduli migrated into what later became Tongaland. Both originally came from the heartland of the Maravi empire and their migration northward brought them to Khota Khota, where Kabunduli split from Kanyenda and migrated further north into Tongaland. There Kabunduli soon earned a reputation for reorganizing the once scattered Tonga groups whom he apparently defeated and brought under his own control. As his reputation increased, he was followed by a number of commoner families from the Chewa heartland.

This intermingling of the Maravi with the original inhabitants of Tongaland accounts for the peculiarities of Tonga society as we know it today. Chitonga, the language of the area, is a bridge between the Tumbuka and Chewa languages. The Tonga are also the only group in northern Malawi to have remained matrilineal in descent and inheritance customs to this day.

For the Chewa-Maravi peoples, the seventeenth century was a golden age, when, as a result of their territorial expansion, they emerged as the most renowned power-brokers north of the Zambezi. Even the Portuguese, ensconced in their settlements along the Zambezi, were forced to co-operate with them. This was because the Maravi did not confine their interest to the area north of the Zambezi. From the 1590s through to the 1630s, they actively interfered in what was the Portuguese sphere of influence south of the Zambezi. For two generations at the beginning of the seventeenth century, the Portuguese, from Angoche on the east coast to Tete on the Zambezi, sought to contain the Maravi by collaborating with them. They recruited large numbers of Maravi warriors to help them in their campaigns against the Karanga or Shona south of the Zambezi as well as against enemies in the immediate vicinity of their Zambezi settlements.

The Maravi expansion had several effects. For example, the creation of the *lundu*'s state east of the lower Shire valley made it possible for the Mbona cult among the Manganja to spread its influence more widely. The economic and cultural effects were perhaps as significant. Within territory encompassed by the Maravi confederation in the seventeenth century, trade in ivory flourished. As a result, northern Zambezia had considerable interaction with the mercantile capitalist economy. The Maravi 'empire' may also have fostered cultural uniformity among the different matrilineal peoples of the region, since they share the same clan names and have a common descent system.

While the Maravi were expanding over the southern zone in the sixteenth and seventeenth centuries, the north was being penetrated by the Ngulube immigrants from the north-east, a major event in the history of this zone.

In the vanguard of the Ngulube migration, the *mwaulambya* crossed the Songwe river south of the Misuku hills into what came to be called Ulambya. There he found the Sikwese and Chilima clans. The *mwaulambya* ensured political control through more peaceful means than the *kyungu* who was shortly to invade the Karonga plain. This was partly because the numbers accompanying the former were smaller than those accompanying the latter. The major officials of the *mwaulambya* were drawn from local families, who shared prestige and political power with the new rulers. Similarly, the Msukwa assumed political power over the Simwayi and Silumbu clans without the use of excessive force. Both Ulambya and Misuku were founded on compromise.

The *kyungu*, Kameme and party migrated to the Karonga plain via Unyiha, Uiwa, Unamwanga and then Ulambya and Misuku in the west. Within a short time of their arrival in Karonga, Kameme returned and settled in the area immediately west of Ulambya. Here he established political authority over a people who were mainly of Nyiha stock, although in later years many Mambwe and Namwanga migrated into the Kameme chiefdom. How Kameme established his state is not clear. It was clearly a smaller polity than that of his brother, the *kyungu*, who founded his kingdom on an already established state ruled by the Simbowe clan.

The Simbowe clan came from Unyiha in modern Tanzania and had established itself at Mbande hill. The basis of Simbowe's power is not clear but it would appear that he was a trader and part of a trading network extending to the east coast. Simbowe's relations with the indigenous people do not appear to have been easy; after his arrival, the *kyungu* formed an alliance with the Mwenekisindile who were the custodians of an important religious shrine associated with a snake cult, and it seems that the Mwenekisindile assisted him in launching an attack upon Simbowe. The *kyungu* assumed power at Mbande by force and gradually was able to establish a new order. Once settled, the *kyungu*s maintained their supremacy over their new subjects by establishing a ritual centre devoted to the cult of their royal ancestors. The *kyungu* and his officials further established themselves in the area by marrying into local families.

Before the arrival of the *kyungu* clan, the people seem to have worshipped the high god through intermediary spirits such as the divine snake. The *kyungu*s employed the ancestors as mediums for the worship of their own high god, Ngulube. As the people slowly came to accept ancestor worship and abandoned the snake cult, they also accepted the divinity of the *kyungu*. He became priest-king and communicator with the royal ancestors. To the Ngonde, the *kyungu* became the living representative of god. His health determined their welfare and prosperity and to safeguard this he was restricted to his residence. Should the *kyungu* show even minor signs of illness he was immediately smothered by his councillors, the *makambala*.

These developments occurred during the reigns of the first four *kyungus*, roughly between 1600 and 1720. Soon after the death of the third *kyungu*, Mwakalosi, his son and successor, renounced the throne because he feared that, should he fall ill, the *makambala* would kill him. He also refused to have all but one of his children killed, a practice designed to avoid competition over the succession. The crisis caused by the refusal of Mwakalosi to accede to the throne ended when the *makambala* installed his brother Magemo as *kyungu*.

The Kameme, Mwaulambya and Msukwa chiefdoms also promoted royal ancestral veneration. Yet they became more Nyiha in their philosophy as in their language, and smothering the monarch, restricting his movements and killing royal children never featured in their history. However, all these chiefdoms represent the introduction into the area of a new form of political organization which brought together religion and politics under prestigious leaders and where relations among the citizenry were based more upon political than upon kinship ties.

A new succession crisis occurred in the Ngonde kingdom upon the death of the *kyungu* Magemo, whose son, Mwangonde, was too young to succeed him. His sister's son, Kasyombe, became *kyungu*. With his accession to power the *makambala* began to lose some of their powers to the *kyungu*. Kasyombe, whose father was a Ndali, had been brought up at Ngana in the northern part of the kingdom. He ended the practice of killing the male children of the *kyungu*, and the number of princes began to rise, leading to a further increase in the powers of the monarch, especially after some of his successors had assigned portions of land to some princes, thereby ensuring that the *kyungu*'s influence was felt throughout the region. There can be no doubt, however, that by 1800, the Ngonde kingdom was confident enough to begin asserting itself in the politics of the wider region south of the Songwe.

Thus between the mid-thirteenth and mid-eighteenth centuries the area south of the Songwe river had developed through a number of stages, from an early network of religious shrines associated with a snake cult, to a system of dominant clans and, finally, to the foundation of a number of states: in the north Ulambya, Kameme, Mikusu, Ungonde and Mwaphoka Mwambele, and in the south Kanyenda, Kabunduli, Kaluluma and Chulu. In the north, Kyangonde had been introduced as a new language by the Ngonde and Nyakyusa founders, while in the south Chitonga was evolving out of a fusion of the Tumbuka and Chewa peoples and languages. The central part of the region was dominated by the Tumbuka, who had no centralized government and whose early history is extremely difficult to chart.

The kinds of religious change which occurred following the establishment of the Ngonde state were also discernible in the Maravi zone of influence. The

Maravi state system encompassed a network of pre-Maravi or proto-Chewa rain-shrines centred on Msinja in what is western Lilongwe today. Each of the Maravi state-builders tried to exercise control over the shrine that fell within his jurisdiction. He would offer assistance and protection, and usually make annual pilgrimages to the shrine. Both the *kalonga* and the *undi* tried to gain control of the Msinja shrine, while in the lower Shire valley the *lundu* managed to establish a considerable degree of control over the Mbona shrine at Nsanje. With this level of dynastic participation in the affairs of the rain-cults, their theology gradually became syncretic. It began to accommodate the veneration of the royal ancestral spirits, while purely Chewa creation myths were suppressed. However, the most notable religious change of the period occurred where the dynasts failed to gain control over the rain-cults. They then tended to establish their own cults, and one of their functions was to deify the royal family.

Towards the middle of the eighteenth century, the Maravi state system began to decline. This decline took the form of secessions from or revolts against the *kalonga*, *lundu* and *undi* paramountcies. However, the factors accounting for the decline of these Maravi states are not clear. In the case of the *undi*, the Portuguese who invaded his kingdom during the gold rush of the 1740s and 1750s played only a minor role in undermining his authority. It has also been argued that the authority of both the *undi* and the *kalonga* was weakened by the growing reluctance of Makewana, who controlled the central Chewa religious shrine at Msinja, to use her ritual power in the interest of the ruling dynasties. The early Makewanas had been key links in the religious unity of the *kalonga* and *undi* kingdoms but the Makewanas of the eighteenth century developed secular ambitions and carved out their own sphere of influence. Their resistance to the the *kalonga* and the *undi* was probably indicative of an attempt by the proto-Chewa clans, to which they belonged, to reassert their autonomy.

Finally, a factor which proved crucial to the decline of the *lundu*'s influence east of the Shire river was the emergence of Makua-Lolo nationalism in the eighteenth century. Their nationalism was primarily directed against the Portuguese and their African allies, against whom they waged a bitter war of attrition from 1749 to the end of the century. The challenge which the coastal Makua posed for Portuguese imperialism on the Mozambique coast must have inspired the Makua and Lolo further inland to launch similar campaigns against foreign domination. In the inland areas, it was the Maravi rather than the Portuguese who became the object of Makua-Lolo hostility. Maravi supremacy then began to be shaken from Quelimane in the east to Mount Murambala on the Shire in the west.

The peoples of northern Zambezia in the period under consideration were also greatly affected by their growing economic contacts with the outside world. Such contacts go back to the period of Arab-Swahili commercial dominance on the east coast and along the Zambezi before 1500, but were then rather limited. However, after the settlement of the Portuguese along the Zambezi in the mid-sixteenth century, Portuguese traders regularly sailed up the Shire river from Sena to purchase ironware, *machila* cloth, salt and ivory from the Manganja, with imported cloth, beads and brassware. Further up the Zambezi, the Portuguese settled at Tete established trading connections with the *undi*'s kingdom and the heartland of the Maravi state system as far as the upper Shire and the southern shore of Lake Malawi. With the founding of a *feira* at Zumbo in 1716, the Portuguese gained access to the ivory market in several societies as far west as southern and central Zambia. But it was the rise and spread of the Zambezia *prazos* which played a decisive role in the expansion of Portuguese commercial influence north of the Zambezi.

Prazos came into existence when a number of Portuguese or Goanese colonists assumed the status of political chiefs over land that initially belonged to the indigenous African peoples. The process began around Sena at the close of the sixteenth century and gradually spread to other parts of the lower Zambezi valley in the seventeenth. The crown in Lisbon saw the granting of *prazos* to Portuguese settlers as a way of encouraging private initiative in the colonization of the Zambezi valley, and also hoped that the prospect of acquiring land would attract immigrants to settle the region.

In the eighteenth century, *prazos* dominated the whole lower Zambezi region from the Luabo or Zambezi delta in the east to Chicoa in the west. The big *prazos* were more than private estates. They amounted to areas of jurisdiction in which the estate-owners, known as *prazeros*, 'had absolute power of justice, waged war, imposed tribute, and were often guilty of great barbarities'. Of the many issues about these *prazos* which are of interest to the historian, two stand out. One is that of the complex relationships which they maintained with neighbouring African states; the other is that of the economic impact which they had on the rest of the northern Zambezia region.

Most of the *prazeros* entered into diplomatic and military relations with the surrounding African states with the explicit aim of exploiting their human resources. For example, the Chikunda, who served the *prazeros* as retainers, had access to labour among the Makua, Manganja, Sena, Kalanga, Tonga, Tawara, Nsenga, Tumbuka and others. Through their interest in the gold and ivory trades, the *prazeros* played an important role in the development of commerce north of the Zambezi. Using some of their Chikunda retainers as middlemen, they established a network of trade links with different African peoples in the region: Manganja, Chewa, Nsenga, Lenje and Southern Lunda. These inland peoples supplied copper, ivory, wax and slaves in exchange for imported cloth, beads, brassware, alcoholic beverages and salt. From about 1740, the *prazeros* were also involved in the mining and exchange of gold north of the Zambezi, particularly in the *undi*'s kingdom. Approximately 100 kilograms of gold were extracted annually before the supply began to dwindle in the 1780s.

This gold rush led to the loss of the ivory trade by the *prazeros* and the Portuguese community on the Zambezi; that trade fell increasingly into the hands of other competitors, particularly the Yao.

The Yao emerged as a dominant trading nation in the late seventeenth and early eighteenth centuries and they participated in long-distance trade throughout East-Central Africa. According to Yao oral tradition, it was the Chisi iron-smiths who pioneered trade to the coast. The Chisi depended on their iron-working skills and local trade in ironware for their livelihood. It is thus possible that once Yaoland was adequately supplied with iron goods, the Chisi took their merchandise further afield and established contact with the coast. The further development of Yao commercial activities was facilitated by the creation of a stable market for ivory at Kilwa between 1635 and 1698. When the Kilwa market for ivory fell after 1698 as a result of Omani-Portuguese conflicts, the Yao found an alternative market at Mossuril opposite Mozambique Island. Trade, it would seem, had by that point become indispensable to the Yao way of life. The Yao would carry their ivory to either Mozambique or Kilwa, as dictated by circumstances. To the west of their own homeland, the Yao had a rich source of ivory in Maravi country. Furthermore, from about 1750, they began to receive more ivory from the Bisa of north-eastern Zambia for onward transmission to Kilwa.

For the Bisa, trade probably offered compensation for their political impotence at home. They were trapped between the expansionist forces of the Lunda and Bemba kingdoms, and trade and travel were important avenues to opportunities further afield. The Bisa opened many new routes between the Luapula region in north-eastern Zambia and the east coast. Between 1790 and 1830, they also tried to develop commerce between the Lunda kingdom and the Portuguese on the Zambezi. They procured ivory, copper and slaves from different places in the interior of Central Africa and took them to the settlements on the coast or along the Zambezi to be exchanged for cloth, beads, guns and gunpowder.

One consequence of their trade with the coast was that their own settlements began to drift eastward into the Luangwa valley and beyond. Several Bisa villages were established in the valley by the 1760s, and by the end of the eighteenth century there were Bisa villages in the western part of central Malawi.

For the Portuguese, the failure of the gold-diggings and the loss of the ivory trade to the Yao and Bisa were factors in their active participation in the slave trade. In the late eighteenth century there was a complete change in the nature of trade among the various regions north of the Zambezi. Slaves became the main trade commodity that could be sold to the outside world. This change was pronounced enough to warrant the identification of the eighteenth century with the ivory trade and the nineteenth with the slave trade. Portuguese participation in the slave trade was remarkable enough in the 1780s when slaves from northern Zambezia were exported to the French island colonies of the Mascarene Islands in the Indian Ocean.

As the slave trade became more lucrative than the trade in ivory, the Portuguese were joined by the Yao and Bisa. The Kilwa market began to be dominated by the slave trade from the 1770s onwards and the Yao probably then began to replace ivory with slaves in their caravans from the interior.

The entire northern zone was also drawn into the long-distance trading network. Until the early eighteenth century, no part of the region had been involved in the long-distance trade, although a vigorous local trade had existed near the shores of Lake Malawi and from Tumbuka country into Nsengaland and the northern Chewa area. During the first four decades of the eighteenth century the Tumbuka region was linked to a trading network which stretched from Katanga in the north-west to Kilwa in the east. The people responsible for this change were heads of families known as *balowoka* (those who crossed the lake).

The most famous of these new men was Kakalala Musawila Gondwe, a Nyamwezi who for some time had been involved in the trade to the east coast. Searching for ivory, Gondwe crossed the lake at Chilumba and settled in the Nkamanga plain near the Luangwa valley, which at that time was heavily populated with elephants. He established contact with the head of the Luhanga clan and later married into the Luhanga and other influential families, thereby firmly establishing himself in Tumbuka society.

Katumbi Mulindafwa Chabinga also came from Nyamwezi territory but after crossing the lake at Chilumba he went into the mountainous area which adjoins the Misuku hills and the Nyika plateau and settled at Chigoma in Nthalire. From Chigoma, Katumbi extended his trading contacts westwards to Malambo in the ivory-rich Luangwa valley.

Another trader, Katong'ongo Mhenga, whose original home was in the Ubena-Uhehe region, crossed the lake shortly after Gondwe and Katumbi had settled. Katong'ongo was looking for land where he and his family could settle, and this he found in the Henga valley. A man of many skills, he knew how to produce salt, which enabled him to control the high-quality salt-pans at Kanembe. He also married into local families and gradually became influential. He came to be known as Mwahenga, owner of the Henga area.

The three immigrants began to dominate the trade of most of the area south of the Songwe and east of the Luangwa valley, and they ended up clashing with one another. Gondwe felt it was important for him to have free use of – if not control of – the Chilumba ferry in order to transport his ivory to the east coast. Thus he became involved in the succession crisis following the death of Katumbi and succeeded in getting a weak candidate accepted for the chieftaincy. He then worked out an arrangement with Mwahenga whereby the latter agreed not to impede his trade. Gondwe made similar arrangements with the rulers east of the Henga valley. Thus by 1800 Gondwe was able to claim a trade monopoly of the area between the Luangwa and the western shore of Lake Malawi. In the Nkamanga plain he had achieved political authority and was thus able to extend his trading empire.

There were smaller polities established in the eighteenth century by families from the eastern side of the lake, and many of their founders were, like Gondwe and Katumbi, ivory-traders. Just south of Ungonde, the Mwafulirwa family founded the Fulirwa state in the area that had been dominated by the Mkandawire clan. A relation of the Mwafulirwa later went west and finally settled at Zibang'ombe, where they began to forge the Wenya state, which by the end of the eighteenth century had extended northward to the southern borders of Ulambya. At about the same time the area south-west of Wenya fell under the rule of a Mlowoka family, the Mughogho. This area, Uyombe, was rich in elephants and, a few decades later, attracted many hunters.

Families of hunters crossed the lake further south and settled not far from the present Nkhata-Bay *boma*. They displaced the Phiri rulers and after a generation became the dominant families in the area.

In the eighteenth century, therefore, the Tumbuka area was dominated first by ivory-hunters, then by traders whose control of wealth led to the assumption of political authority. Political decentralization gave way to the power of trader-chiefs. Such political influence was not possible in the northern states, which remained outside the network of long-distance trade for almost a century after the arrival of the Tumbuka. In the eighteenth century the Maravi empire was disintegrating and the states of the Tumbuka-Chewa marginal zone in the south were being left in total control of their own affairs. After 1800, all states and peoples would become deeply involved in the commercial age of ivory and later of slaves, with the well-known disastrous results.

The beginning date for this volume does not coincide with historical periodization in this region. An historical age opens in the southern zone *c.* 1400 with the coming of the Maravi, and in the northern zone *c.* 1600 with the migration of the Ngulube. However, the closing date is apt because new themes dominate the nineteenth century: the changeover in trade from ivory to slaves, the involvement of all parts of the region in externally manipulated commerce, the development of Yao chiefdoms in areas formerly under the Maravi and, finally, the arrival of new peoples – the Nguni, Swahili, Kololo and Europeans – who would ultimately seek to wield political authority, regardless of their disparate motives for coming.

Southern Zambezia

22

The period between 1500 and 1800 is characterized in southern Zambezia by a scarcity of records. We have to rely largely on the accounts of the Portuguese travellers and traders who penetrated the region during the first decade of the sixteenth century. This chapter will therefore concentrate on three polities: the Mutapa and Rozvi empires and the eastern Shona states. The Mutapa and Rozvi polities evolved from the Great Zimbabwe culture (1200–1450, see *Unesco General History of Africa*, Volume IV, Chapter 21).

Great Zimbabwe gradually declined from the mid-fifteenth century onwards, as gold production decreased. Great Zimbabwe's decline gave rise first to an obscure state known as Torwa or 'Butwa', according to Portuguese sources. Its first capital, situated at Khami and probably founded in the mid-1400s, was destroyed by fire during the second half of the seventeenth century. The second capital, at Danangombe, was much smaller than the first. The archaeological remains suggest that almost all the prestige stone buildings in the Torwa state were constructed before 1650.

The second important political development after the fall of Great Zimbabwe was the emergence of the Mutapa empire at the beginning of the sixteenth century. The empire comprised heterogeneous Karanga-speaking populations. In theory it extended from the southern margins of the Zambezi to the Indian Ocean, but in practice the Mutapa rulers exercised a much more limited authority outside the plateau country. There is evidence that the kingdoms of Manyika, Uteve, Barwe and Danda hived away from the empire during the sixteenth century, although they continued to perform their ritual and tributary obligations until the rise of Dombo *Changamire* in the late seventeenth century. It has been suggested that the *Changamires* themselves occasionally paid tribute to the Mutapa emperors during the eighteenth century. Similar developments occurred on the lower Zambezi, where the Tonga and Sena rulers successfully resisted all efforts by the Mutapa rulers to impose their political hegemony over them. These developments reduced the empire to its core, the region spanned by the Dande and Chidima territories.

The practice of prestige stone-building in the Mutapa empire probably continued until the sixteenth century. Some of the earliest ruins, particularly

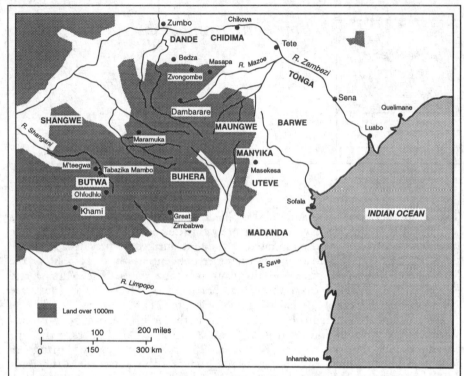

22.1 *Central and south-eastern Africa during the period of the Mustapa and Torwa states (adapted from S. I. Mudenge,* A Political History of Munhumutapa *c. 1400-1902, Zimbabwe Publishing House, Harare, 1988; and* Zimbabwe Epic, *published by the National Archives of Zimbabwe, Harare, p. 47)*

the Zvongombe complex, represented the early capitals of the Mutapa rulers. Later capitals were in the form of stockades several metres high.

In the first half of the eighteenth century, the mutapas lost direct control of the plateau, and the core of the empire shifted to the southern lowlands of the Zambezi bounded by Zumbo and Tete. This loss of political control was the culmination of a long process of fragmentation which began in 1629, when the Portuguese defeated Mamvura mutapa, and ended in 1917, when the Mutapa polity finally disappeared.

Administratively, the empire was controlled at three levels: the capital, the province and the village. The mutapas delegated authority to chiefs at village and provincial levels. In the empire's early days, only relatives of the mutapas were entrusted with these positions. For example, it was customary for a prince or heir presumptive to govern the Dande lands. Those who, though not related to the Mutapas, had aided in the process of conquest, were also appointed to positions of authority. As the Mutapas came to feel more confident, in the seventeenth century, they allowed the villages and provinces to elect their own leaders. In the capital the Mutapas were assisted by high-ranking officials who, in exchange for their services, were granted land.

Beliefs and methods of administrative control

The Mutapas manipulated several mechanisms to control the empire. A typical example was the practice whereby the territorial chiefs had to come and rekindle their fires annually from the original royal fire, thereby reaffirming their loyalty to the central authority. This ritual of fidelity was repeated at the enthronement of a new Mutapa ruler. Failure to perform this ritual was regarded as an act of rebellion and severely punished.

This was done through an efficient army which has been estimated at 30,000 regulars during the sixteenth century and 3,000 men during the eighteenth century. These figures suggest that, before the decline of the empire, the Mutapa rulers were in a position to mobilize many peasants to join the army, but were much less able to do so when the empire fell into decay during the eighteenth century.

The Mutapas also manipulated religion to control their subjects through the close relationship between the monarchy and the spirit world – either the spirits of the ancestors of the emperors themselves or mediums representing the original owners of the land. The emperor was expected to maintain a close contact with the powerful dead on behalf of the nation. The system of observing the cult of royal graves also enhanced the emperor's prestige and strengthened his control over his people.

The owners of the soil, like Dzivaguru, were rain-makers and ritual officers at the Mutapa royal court. The participation of the emperor in rain-making rituals was seen as crucial to the economic prosperity of the empire. Religion was an important mechanism of social control, in an economy dominated by agriculture.

The most common method of political control was the tribute levied by the Mutapa emperors in the form of agricultural produce, lion and leopard skins, ostrich feathers, small and large stock, the breast of every animal killed and, for an elephant, the tusk on which it fell when it died.

Tribute also took the form of labour rent. According to João de Barros, all the officers and servants of the king's court and the captains of the soldiers, each with his men, had to help him cultivate his fields or do other work seven days in every 30. The practice of labour rent was also adopted by vassal rulers.

When opening a new mine, the Mutapa rulers usually sent their trusted agents to collect the tribute. The gold-miners erected a shelter to house the tribute-collectors as well as the tribute itself. The nature of the tribute system does not seem to have changed until the demise of the Mutapa empire in the early twentieth century.

These various mechanisms of control partially succeeded in maintaining a centralized empire at a time when vast distances rendered close supervision of the territorial chiefs impossible. The army's inability to deal effectively with rebellions in the far-flung parts of the empire, internal political intrigue exploited by Portuguese traders and civil wars all account for the gradual decline and fall of the Mutapa empire.

The Portuguese factor

Although the Portuguese arrived at Sofala in 1506, it was only from 1550 to 1630 that they made serious attempts to gain control of the Mutapa empire. Until 1540, trade between the Portuguese and the Shona was conducted on a non-official basis. In 1540, commercial relations were regularized through the establishment of a diplomatic-cum-trade mission at the Mutapa royal court, headed by an officer called the 'captain of the gates'. His main duties were to transmit presents, requests or complaints from the Portuguese traders to the Mutapa emperors and vice versa. The Portuguese paid the Mutapa rulers a tribute, called *curva*.

At the assumption of his office, each new captain of the Portuguese fortress of Mozambique was under an obligation to pay to the *monomotapa* the equivalent of 3,000 cruzados in cloth and beads for the three years of his office. In exchange for this tribute, the Mutapa emperors granted freedom of passage to the traders to travel throughout the empire. If the tribute was not paid within the proper time, the emperor would order the seizure without compensation of all the merchandise in his empire. This actually happened in 1610, when one Mutapa ruler Gatsi Rusere declared a *mupeto* (forcible confiscation) of the Portuguese traders' merchandise, which resulted in the raiding and killing of Portuguese traders.

This system of tributary relations persisted with little change until the second half of the sixteenth century, when the Portuguese began to win control over the Mutapa rulers as a result of the aggressive wars they waged in southern Zambezia between 1569 and 1575, when they succeeded in entrenching themselves in the eastern kingdoms of Uteve and Manyika. In 1575, the Portuguese concluded a treaty with the king of Uteve whereby the captain of Sofala was obliged to pay an annual tribute of 200 pieces of cloth to the Teve rulers. In exchange, the Portuguese traders secured freedom of passage to the kingdom of Manyika where, they believed, there was an abundance of gold. In addition, the inhabitants of the Portuguese fortress at Sofala were allowed freedom of passage into the interior along the Sofala river to buy provisions. A similar treaty was concluded with the king of Manyika in 1573.

This limited success tempted the Portuguese to make further encroachments into the Mutapa empire. The rebellions which broke out there between 1590 and 1607 provided the Portuguese with an opportunity to delve into the complexity of Mutapa politics. Gatsi Rusere, concluded a treaty with them for military assistance, in exchange for which he promised to cede all his gold, copper, iron, lead and tin mines to them. In fact, the Portuguese lacked both the expertise and the manpower to exploit the metals. Moreover, the treaty turned out to be of limited value, because the Portuguese left Gatsi Rusere to deal on his own with the civil wars which continued to rage until he died in 1624. Gatsi Rusere was succeeded by his son Nyambu Kapararidze, the legitimacy of whose claim was challenged by his uncle Mamvura. In the war that ensued between these two pretenders, Mamvura sought and, in 1629, obtained Portuguese military assistance. The treaty which he concluded with the Portuguese after his accession required Mamvura to allow the Portuguese traders freedom of passage throughout the empire, to expel the Swahili–Arab traders and to allow Dominican missionaries to preach their religion. It also required Mamvura to stop the *curva*, and instead to pay tribute to the Portuguese thenceforth. After this treaty, the number of Portuguese traders and adventurers within the Mutapa empire increased. The adventurers seized land, subsequently recognized by the Portuguese crown as *prazos* (crown land). From being the guests of the African rulers, the Portuguese traders now almost became the masters of the land, but their individualism and lawlessness led to a period of chaos and anarchy. Portuguese penetration of the Mutapa empire, therefore, led to its disintegration and gave rise to the *prazo* system, as well as the birth of a new polity, the Rozvi empire.

The *prazo* system

The acquisition of land by individual Portuguese adventurers proceeded almost unchecked, with the result that many *prazos da coroa* were created. They were owned by Portuguese officials, traders, religious orders and frontiersmen.

The *prazo* system was a synthesis of two socio–economic systems. The first was that of the Shona, which consisted of a ruling oligarchy and peasant producers; the second, which was superimposed on the Shona system, consisted of the *prazeros*, ruling as a dominant class over the *achikunda* (armies of slaves). An African chief continued to perform his traditional duties but he 'no longer had absolute authority' (A. F. Isaacman, 1969), as the *prazero* assumed the status of overlord.

The relations of production on the *prazos* were essentially feudal. The African chief paid the *prazero* a tribute in kind: butter, locally woven cloth, honey, tobacco, sugar, large and small stock, ivory and gold dust. In his position as a *de facto* chief, the *prazero* adopted African social and religious practices and married into chiefly families to overcome his major weakness, his lack of legitimacy in African traditional politics.

A. Isaacman has argued that the *prazo* as a Portuguese land-tenure system was so transformed and adapted to the African situation that it became completely African. However, this total Africanization theory is difficult to maintain when it is realized that the *prazo* system was always more or less linked to mercantile capitalism, with the *prazeros* serving as middlemen in the trade between Mozambique and India and, later, Europe. Moreover, the internal organization of the *prazos* had features which could hardly be called African, a notable example being the coexistence of the *colono* (settler) and the *chikunda*. In reality, an opposite process, that of the de-Africanization of the traditional African societies on the *prazos*, was taking place. As the *prazo* system responded to the internal demand for slaves, the *prazeros* enslaved and sold their African neighbours and victimized their *colonos* and slaves alike.

Isaacman has argued that 'in terms of the day-to-day governing of the *colonos*, the *mambo*'s position remained virtually unaltered'. It is true that the *mambo* enjoyed prestige and obedience from his people by virtue of his connection with the founding lineages. But ultimately the *prazero* had the last word in deciding judicial cases or the appointment of an African chief himself. Even the right to distribute land had been usurped by the *prazero*. All that greatly modified the traditional political system. The *prazos* represented the first phase of the Portuguese colonization of Mozambique: they were pockets of political and economic exploitation achieved only through a modification of African political and social institutions.

The geographical spread of the *prazos*

The *prazos* were dotted on both sides of the Zambezi river. There were, however, significant differences between the *prazos* to the south of the river, which were Portuguese crown property, and those to the north, which were not. In theory, the grant of a *terra da coroa* was restricted to three generations, the land could be inherited only through a female, it could not be more than 3 leagues long, and the holder was subject to an annual quit rent. The *prazo*-holders in the north were free from all these conditions and acquired land as a result of a direct arrangement with the local chief.

The *prazo* system was sustained by the work of various categories of slaves. The top slave was the *chuanga*, appointed by the *prazero* because of his loyalty. Every village had its *chuanga*, whose primary function was to spy on the traditional leaders and to collect taxes and ivory. He also had the job of collecting information about the African population on the *prazo* whose size was of crucial importance to the *prazero*. For the enforcement of his authority, the *prazero* depended on a *chikunda*, whose main function was to police the local population, ensure that the laws of the *prazero* were obeyed and deal also with acts of rebellion. A *chikunda* army usually ranged between 20 and 30 men on small *prazos*, while on large ones it could comprise thousands.

In his report of 1766 concerning the coast of Africa, Antonio Pinto de Miranda described the main methods by which slaves were obtained. According to him, slave-hunters stole children and sold them to Portuguese traders, Swahili-Arab traders and African agents. Some people were sold as slaves or pawned in times of famine; and convicted criminals, prisoners of war and credit defaulters suffered the same fate. The picture which emerges from other Portuguese sources is one of voluntary enslavement.

The decline of the *prazo* system

The *prazo* system declined during the second half of the eighteenth century for several reasons. The first was that the *prazero*'s authority was ill-defined compared with that of the traditional African ruler. Often this tempted the *prazero* to abuse his authority by compelling the African peasants to sell their agricultural produce to him exclusively and at artificially low prices. He would also impose heavy taxes on the peasants and commit atrocities with impunity. The colonos reacted by revolting against the *prazeros* and even by migrating. These revolts and migrations led to a decline in agricultural production, drought and famine. The *prazero* and his slave armies relied for their food on what the peasants produced; the *chikunda* used force to get foodstuffs from the peasants, and the *colonos*, again, reacted by migrating from the *prazeros* to look for food and security elsewhere.

The slave trade was another factor that led to the decline of the *prazo* system. The overseas slave trade increased in the 1640s as a result of the Dutch occupation of Angola, which forced Lisbon to turn to south-east Africa as a source. The establishment of a plantation economy in the French Mascarene Islands in the 1730s created an additional demand for slaves. But the numbers of slaves exported from southern Zambezia by 1752 were still relatively small: 300 from Zambezia and 200 from Sofala. Towards the end of the eighteenth century, however, the slave trade gathered such momentum that the *prazeros* in the Zambezi valley saw it as an opportunity for wealth. They organized slave-raids in the Chewa, Nsenga and Manganja territories. They also began to sell the slaves on their estates, thus undermining the very foundation of the *prazo* system. However, beyond the Zambezi valley, the rest of Zambezia was little affected by the slave trade. The decline of the *prazo* system south of the Zambezi was accelerated by the rise of a new polity in the second half of the seventeenth century – the Rozvi Changamire dynasty.

The Rozvi empire

The origins of the Rozvi empire are still obscure. The issue has been further complicated by the name *changamire*, which is associated with the founder of the Rozvi empire in the second half of the seventeenth century, but is already mentioned in the fifteenth century. However, there seems some consensus on four points: first, that the Rozvi were an integral part of the historic Karanga of the Mutapa empire until they broke away in the seventeenth century; second, that 'the designation Rozvi was first applied to a section of those historic Karanga who were associated with the rise to power between 1684 and 1695 of Changamire Dombo I' (S. I. Mudenge, 1974); third, that the creation of the Rozvi empire was the work of Changamire Dombo I; and fourth, that the appellation Rozvi, which was derived from the Shona verb *kurozva* (to destroy), was either assumed by the followers of Dombo out of vanity or was given to them as a nickname by their victims.

Between 1684 and 1695, Dombo Changamire gradually rose to power in the north-east. How he did so is still unclear. He was a herdsman of the Mutapa emperors who rebelled, taking himself and his followers first to the

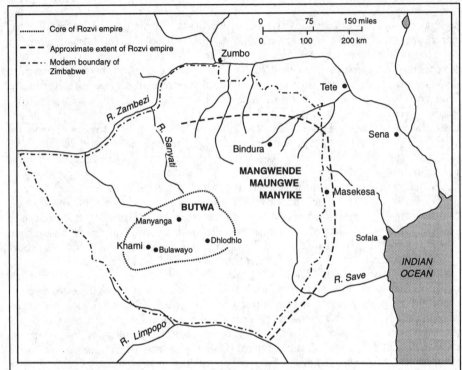

22.2 *The Rozvi empire (adapted from D. N. Beach,* Zimbabwe before 1900, *1984, p. 38, Harare, Mambo Press)*

Torwa state in the south-west, then to the kingdoms of Manyika and Uteve in the east. The Portuguese traders were expelled in 1684 from the kingdom of Maungwe, from the plateau country in 1693 and from the kingdom of Manyika in 1695. They fled to Zumbo, where they established a new settlement in 1710, then returned to their former settlement of Masekasa in Manyika. In every case, however, there was a tacit understanding that they were under the authority of the Rozvi Changamire overlords. In this way, the Rozvi rulers were able to create an empire that stretched as far as Buhera, Bocha, Duma and the south-eastern highlands in the south, to the sodic soils in the north and to the lowveld in the south-west. The core of the empire probably spanned the same area as that of the Ndebele, who succeeded them in the 1840s.

Our idea of the Rozvi capital comes from a nineteenth-century Portuguese description, although it had probably changed little since the 1600s and 1700s. The royal court, according to this account, consisted of three large stone houses, surrounded by walls of elephant tusks. The Rozvi Changamire had many rifles which he obtained from Portuguese traders at Sena.

The Rozvi maintained their identity as a foreign élite amidst people who shared the same *moyo* (heart) totem, having been their allies during the wars of conquest of the Karanga-speaking people as well as those of the Torwa state.

Provincial administration

The Rozvi rulers used methods similar to those of the Mutapas to maintain their empire. The mechanisms involved the allocation of land, the payment of tribute, religion and a well-trained army.

The Rozvi rulers distributed land to newly instated chiefs and levied tribute from them. Their tribute system was organized in a hierarchical pyramid, with the village as the base and the court as the apex. The principal officer and commander of the army supervised the collection of tribute throughout the empire, sending out teams of special tribute-collectors to the various provinces and villages.

The Rozvi developed a religious system altogether different from that of the *mondhoro* prevalent among the northern and eastern Shona. The Rozvi cult of the oracular deity, Mwari, was based on a belief in a high God who expressed himself through natural phenomena such as lightning or earthquakes. The principal officers of the Mwari oracle were the Mouth, the Ear and the Eye, whose main purpose was to collect information. The Mwari cult was manipulated by the Rozvi rulers for political ends.

The proverbial efficiency of the Rozvi army calls for some clarification. Portuguese observers, during the eighteenth century, never ceased to marvel at both the discipline and the efficiency of the Rozvi armies, which were generally well equipped with bows and arrows, daggers, assegais, battle-axes and cudgels. Like most armies in pre-colonial African societies, the Rozvi armies performed certain rituals which instilled military prowess and self-confidence before they went into battle. The Portuguese came to believe that the Rozvi emperor had 'magic oil with which he could kill anyone simply by touching the person with it' (ibid.), and there is no doubt that this belief played an important role in Rozvi military victories, especially Dombo Changamire's victory over the Portuguese at the battle of Maungwe in 1684.

The prowess of the Rozvi armies can also be explained by the thorough training the soldiers underwent. The Rozvi armies were organized and trained much after the fashion of the early nineteenth-century Zulu, Ndebele and Sotho armies.

Another aspect of the Rozvi army that has been exaggerated is its invincibility. The defeat of the Portuguese at the end of the seventeenth century, for example, must be seen in the context of the Portuguese presence in East and Central Africa during this period. The Portuguese were fighting for their survival along the East African coast from the 1650s to 1729, when their fortress at Mombasa was destroyed by the sultan of Oman. In other words, what the *changamires* encountered in southern Zambezia was not the full Portuguese military effort.

The Portuguese military effort in southern Zambezia was in fact based on the *prazeros*, themselves badly disunited by rather conflicting economic interests. If these factors are not taken into account, it is easy to exaggerate the efficiency of the Rozvi military machine.

The economy

The dominant branches of production among the Shona societies were agriculture, animal husbandry, hunting, gathering, fishing and metal-working, along with long-distance and inter-regional trade.

Agriculture

The Shona cultivated three main cereals: finger-millet, drought-resistant bulrush millet and various sorghums. The unit of production was the household, and there is no solid evidence that the division of labour was rigidly based on sex. What little evidence there is suggests that the situation differed from society to society. In some, the men performed the heavier tasks and the women the lighter, more in the spirit of co-operation than in a strict division of labour. In others, however, such as that of the Hlengwe of the lowveld, there was some division of labour, with the adult males devoting most time to trapping and hunting game while the juveniles herded cattle and the women cultivated the fields.

The ploughing season stretched from September to November, with the hoe as the basic implement. Shifting cultivation was practised, whereby the old land was abandoned whenever it became exhausted and new land opened up. The opening of new land involved clearing the bush, burning it and allowing the ash to fertilize it. Shona agriculture, like most pre-colonial agrarian economies, was adapted to local conditions.

The period 1500–1800 witnessed the piecemeal introduction into southern Zambezia of new crops from Europe and Asia, mainly along the coast and in regions where the Portuguese had built their settlements. In Sofala and on the lower Zambezi, the African peasants cultivated rice and yams, although these never became their staple diet. They also cultivated sugar cane to eat rather than to make sugar, as they lacked both the expertise and the appliances. The African peasants also planted many fruit trees from India and Portugal, such as figs, pineapples, guavas, pawpaws and oranges; they also grew melons, cucumbers, sweet potatoes and lemons. The cultivation of exotic fruits was stimulated by demand from foreign traders who exported lemons, in particular, to India.

There is evidence that wheat was being cultivated in the kingdom of Manyika during April and May and that by 1778 peanuts were being cultivated there. Two grain legumes were grown everywhere, bambara groundnuts and cowpeas.

None of the crops introduced from Europe and Asia ever constituted the staple diet of the Shona. The case was different with maize, which was introduced into southern Zambezia during the eighteenth century. This gradually caught up with millet and sorghum to constitute one of the staple foodstuffs of the Shona in the twentieth century, particularly among urban populations.

The Nyanga and the lowveld

The agrarian economy of the Nyanga and lowveld areas was in many ways different from that of the plateau. The Nyanga highlands were characterized by poor soils and steep slopes. The greater part of northern Nyanga was terraced with dry stone walls about 1 metre high. These terraces were made on the hillsides and their purpose was to conserve the soil and dispose neatly of the stones. There is some evidence that a limited amount of irrigation was practised, but only in a supplementary role, as the Nyanga area usually enjoys a fair amount of annual rainfall. It is likely that the dry-season irrigation of vegetable gardens, maize and bananas, which is still being practised in this region, is an agricultural tradition of eighteenth-century origin.

The lowveld economy

The lowveld economy was different. Here a local people, the Hlengwe, practised mainly hunting, gathering and fishing and agriculture only to a limited extent. The lowveld has very low annual rainfall, so that gathering played an important role in the lowveld economy, as it does even at present. The fruits gathered were mainly *nkanyi* and *mahanga*, the sap of which was used to make an intoxicating wine, *kwaka*, and the baobab fruit. These fruits were gathered by women and children while the men hunted big game. The women and children killed mice and gathered large silvery caterpillars and locusts.

The Hlengwe were, as they still are today, excellent hunters and there were many species of game in the lowveld. Fishing was also an important occupation. The lowveld rivers, then as now, were rich in fish. The Nyanga region is especially famous for its trout.

Hunting and fishing were not a monopoly of the Hlengwe of the lowveld. In various parts of the Mutapa empire, men hunted countless species of animals, including lions, tigers, leopards, rhinoceroses, elephants, buffaloes, wild cows, elands and wildebeests, to cite only a few. Guinea-fowl were found in their hundreds in the bush close to the fields. The professional hunters used traps and traditional weapons (spears, clubs, and bows and arrows). With the introduction of firearms by the Portuguese in the early sixteenth century, the hunters' efficiency improved.

The Hlengwe were not solely hunters. That they were able to differentiate between various kinds of soil demonstrates that they paid close attention to agriculture. The Hlengwe differentiated soils mainly on their ability to retain moisture. They called the sandy soils where they built their homesteads *nthlava*. This type of soil was good for growing cucumbers, gourds, cowpeas, bambara beans and groundnuts. They also grew millet and sorghum there, but in or near the valleys. They called the basalt soils *tsovolo*: these were fertile soils that retain moisture for a long period, on which they grew maize and a variety of vegetables. It would seem that the Hlengwe never lacked land and that they were constrained only by the erratic rainfall.

Portuguese observers expressed contradictory views on the efficiency of the agrarian economies of the Shona societies between 1500 and 1800, while historians have tended to over-generalize about famines both in pre-colonial and colonial southern Zambezia. David Beach has characterized Shona pre-colonial agriculture as 'useful but dangerously static'. This, according to him, was because 'no selection of crops and soil and no expertise in predicting *shangwa* (famine) could ward off these disasters, whether caused by climate, locusts or other blights'. But the Shona societies were not 'static'. They had contacts among themselves as well as with other neighbouring African societies – the Swahili-Arabs from the tenth century or earlier and the Portuguese from the beginning of the sixteenth century. For the Shona, these contacts represented efforts to modify their material conditions through barter and exchange. Furthermore, the Shona peasants were adopting new crops throughout the period from 1500 to 1800. All this makes it difficult to describe the pre-colonial agrarian economy as static. The agricultural history in the pre-colonial period is a story of innovation rather than stagnation.

Moreover, the idea that the Shona peasants were helpless victims of droughts and famines has become dated. There were several methods of fighting famine, such as bartering salt, meat, fish, tusks, mats, pots, baskets, spears, arrows and jewels for grain. The Shona also obtained grain during famine through a system called *mukomondera* whereby one borrowed grain on the understanding that it would be refunded without interest in the following good season. Finally, hunting, fishing and gathering did not disappear after the introduction of new crops; they constituted important means of combating famine.

Richard Mutetwa has shown that the problem of storage was not serious, because the three Shona staple crops, millet, bulrush millet and sorghum, could store very well for more than three or four years. The Shona peasants also took precautions to preserve their grain from humidity, carefully plastering their grain bins to make them airtight. These bins were placed on rocks or poles high enough to escape the termites. Parallels with what happened elsewhere in Africa concerning the efficiency of pre-colonial agriculture suggest that there is little justification for suggesting that Shona agriculture was unable to satisfy the needs of the peasants.

Stock-raising

Stock-raising was an important branch of production in both the Mutapa and Rozvi empires. Stock-raising included the raising of sheep, goats and cattle. These animals provided meat, milk and manure, which farmers either used or sold. Possession of cattle also performed a social function in that it bestowed a social status upon an individual. Portuguese documents stress the central role of cattle in the economy of both the Mutapa and Rozvi empires. Large herds of cattle flourished, particularly in the highveld, where they were not threatened by the tsetse fly. There is every likelihood that the Mutapa and Rozvi Changamire rulers practised transhumance, moving cattle from the highveld to the lowveld during the dry season when water and salt were scarce and pasture tended to be poor on the highveld. Transhumance also enabled pastoralists and cultivators to meet and exchange their respective products: animal products for grain. Conflicts occasionally erupted between the pastoralists and the cultivators whenever cattle destroyed the cultivators' crops. This in turn led to a shift in the orbit of transhumance or migrations to entirely new areas – which is how pastoralists became colonists.

Neither archaeology nor the Portuguese documents tell us much about cattle management and their distribution from the sixteenth century to the end of the eighteenth century. Portuguese sources continually point to the fact that southern Zambezia was rich in cattle and other animals. In the early 1500s, Diogo de Alcacova recorded that 4,000 hornless cows were paid as tribute to a Mutapa ruler by a ruler of Butwa in the south-west. In 1569, Father Monclaro likened the large size of cattle in Butwa to the large oxen of France.

Besides cattle, the African peasants reared goats, sheep and chickens for food and exchange.

Mining of metals: iron and copper

A large amount of iron, copper and lead was mined throughout the Mutapa and Rozvi empires, although the available literature leads one to believe that African peasants were interested only in mining gold. The African peasants extracted iron from which they made objects such as hoes, assegais and axes. The Njanja of Wedza acquired a reputation as hoe manufacturers, selling their hoes as far afield as Manyika, Bocha, Burbera and Ndau country. They also mined copper from which they made bangles which both men and women wore round their arms and ankles. A geological survey carried out in 1952 showed that four-fifths of total copper production in Zimbabwe came from Duma. A considerable quantity, however, also came from Urungwe in the north-west.

Salt

The salt industry was very important for the Shona economy between 1500 and 1800, especially in regions that did not enjoy sufficient rainfall to grow crops and raise cattle, such as along the middle Save. This region was also rich in clay, and the local inhabitants took advantage of this resource to specialize in pottery manufacture. Salt and pots were exchanged for grain, particularly during famine years.

Cloth

Textile production was also an important activity among the Shona peasants of southern Zambezia. Cotton-growing and weaving flourished mainly on the eastern bank of the Zambezi river. The Shona wove a cloth from this cotton and also from the bark of the baobab tree. The cotton-growing lowveld area was complemented by the highveld region which abounded in cattle, and this largely determined the pattern of inter-regional trade.

Gold and silver

The existence and extraction of silver from the sixteenth to the eighteenth century was a matter of great speculation among the Portuguese authorities, but throughout the period under review, and even later, no silver mines were located. Silver was in fact obtained as a by-product of gold-mining, and there was plenty of gold on the highveld, in Butwa in the south-west, and in Manyika and Uteve in the east.

The amount of gold present in southern Zambezia was greatly exaggerated by the Portuguese during the sixteenth century. It was claimed, for example, that the whole of 'Mucaranga' was nothing but a vast gold mine and one had only to dig to find gold. Nevertheless, there was indeed plenty of gold in the Mutapa empire and, whatever they said, the Portuguese saw their hopes largely fulfilled until the second half of the seventeenth century.

Historical references suggest that mining was not a year-round activity for the Shona, except in the kingdom of Manyika in the east, where the extraction of gold was carried out year-round because the rivers there are perennial. Shona mining activities were concentrated in the months of August, September and October, the months when land was cleared. Another reason for mining during those months was that miners could sink shafts fairly deep as a result of the seasonal fall in the water-table.

Mining operations followed a pattern prevalent in much of southern Africa. The basic tools used to break out the ore were hammerstones and iron gads as well as a type of crowbar consisting of a piece of iron inserted into the end of a heavy stick. The method for gold-reef mining was fire-setting – as can be deduced from the large quantities of charcoal which Roger Summers found in many of the ancient mines. In one he also came across troughs containing charcoal standing against the face of the reef. According to him, they formed a hearth concentrating the heat against the hard rock face. By cooling the heated rock rapidly with water, the Shona were able to crack the rock face. The pieces thus collected were stacked amongst piles of firewood and roasted, after which the burnt quartz was crushed and the gold washed out of it.

With alluvial gold, the recovery process was village-based. During the mining season, groups of 400 or more miners, with their women and children, assembled in a designated place under the command of the village head. They washed the alluvium in wooden bowls, and the gold that was recovered was packed into hollow reeds or quills ready for exchange. The peasants preferred gold-panning to reef-mining as the workings were shallow and they were not expensive. Nor did they expose miners to the hazards of tunnels through soft soils that regularly caved in.

The Mutapa and Rozvi rulers exercised tight control over the production of gold within their empires. It has been estimated that almost 50 per cent of gold production within the Mutapa empire was appropriated directly by the ruling élite. If a person stumbled upon a gold deposit, he was required to cover it up and report it immediately to the local chief. Failure to comply with this law was punishable by death. The Mutapa and Rozvi rulers did not want the

Portuguese to know the location of the gold mines, as this would tempt them to conquest: moreover, control of the mines enabled them to dictate better terms of trade.

The decline of gold production during the seventeenth century

The dangerous nature of gold-mining explains the low production and also its decline during the seventeenth century. Moreover, once the water-table had been reached, it was not possible to mine deeper without the aid of a new technology capable of pumping out both the water and the mud. Finally, the price the Portuguese traders paid for gold was too low to induce the peasants to risk their lives.

One aspect that has not been examined in detail was the impact of war on gold production. The first half of the seventeenth century witnessed the height of Portuguese aggression against the Mutapa empire. Portuguese intervention in internal Shona politics resulted in wars among the Mutapa rulers themselves and also between the Mutapa rulers and their vassals. These wars resulted in both temporary and permanent migrations and famine, even in areas rich in resources and with favourable weather patterns. The second half of the seventeenth century was characterized by the even more devastating *changamire* wars which resulted in the reorganization of populations into several states. Warfare, therefore, could be blamed for the disruption of gold production in Shonaland during the seventeenth century in the same way that a natural calamity disrupts agriculture by reducing the amount of land available.

In addition, the methods adopted by the Portuguese traders alienated them from the peasants largely responsible for producing gold. In the early 1500s, African peasants used to take their produce directly to the Portuguese *feiras* in the interior. Later in the century, however, the Portuguese sent middlemen into the interior who took merchandise to the peasants' doors. They sold merchandise on credit to the peasants, who often defaulted, with the result that the defaulter became the trader's slave. Relations between the Portuguese and the African peasants deteriorated to the point where they threatened village life. In the mid-1600s, the king of Uteve ordered his people not to extract any more gold but 'to till the land and grow food in order to become rich and have more peace and quiet'. Social factors, therefore, were probably significant in the decline of gold production during the seventeenth century.

Trade

Trade records also provide historical evidence of the diversity of Shona peasant economies. The peasants' main aim was to produce consumables rather than exchange goods. But the production of commodities inevitably resulted in the exchange of products among the peasants themselves and between peasants and craftsmen, and this led to the emergence of regional trade.

The Swahili traders established several bazaars in the Mutapa empire. The first bazaars in Sofala and its immediate neighbourhood were probably established during the tenth century when the Swahili-Arab traders started trading with African peasants in the Mutapa empire. The bazaars were operated on Mondays, with the African peasants exchanging their agricultural produce for beads, cloth and other exotic items. The demand for foodstuffs must have increased when the Portuguese established a fortress at Sofala in 1506, which became an entrepôt where African peasants came to sell their produce to Portuguese traders.

The establishment of this fortress must be seen in the context of Portuguese commercial activities from 1498. Portugal's main aim at this time was to occupy all strategic points along the Indian Ocean. The fortresses of Sofala and Kilwa were built in 1506 to protect the gold trade, while three others were built to control the pepper trade. On arrival at Sofala in 1506, the Portuguese found the Swahili-Arab traders well established, and rivalry between the two groups, characterized by several military encounters, consequently developed. The Portuguese emerged victorious and the Swahili-Arabs fled north to various strategic points on the Zambezi river, from where they continued to undermine Portuguese commercial activities. The Portuguese reacted swiftly by ousting them from most of these places and, in 1531, establishing Sena and Tete as their main trade centres. Portuguese trading activity accordingly shifted northwards, thus reducing the importance of the Sofala region.

The defeat of the Swahili in 1512 and the occupation of Sena and Tete brought to an end the independent trade of the Swahili-Arabs. But as the Portuguese had neither the skill nor the manpower required, and as the Swahili-Arabs were anxious to continue as traders in the region, a natural though uneasy trading alliance developed between them. Throughout the seventeenth century, the Swahili-Arabs were the main agents of Portuguese trade in the interior. African *vashambadzi* (traders) had been acting as middlemen long before the advent of the Portuguese, and their role was formally institutionalized within this alliance.

The defeat of the Swahili-Arabs left the Portuguese traders without major competition along the Zambezi trade route and in the interior. Initially the aim of the Portuguese crown was to monopolize the entire trade in Sofala and the interior, but this proved impossible, as greed drove traders inland to make independent agreements with African rulers.

As with the Swahili-Arab traders, the African peasants exchanged their produce for a variety of exotic items. Peter Garlake's archaeological excavations of the *feiras* of Luanze, Dambarare and Rimuka indicate that beads were the most popular commodity during the early sixteenth century. The most sought-after beads in all kingdoms were the red and black ones known as Cambay beads. There was also a variety of imported beads, including those of 'coral, crystal, pewter, jet, amber and blue Venetian glass' but these were unpopular. Conversely, a locally made variety known as *caracoes* (small stone beads) flooded the market between 1516 and 1518. Cloth was another important trade item, particularly the brightly coloured cloth which was measured by arm-lengths.

In exchange for these articles, the Shona brought to the fortress's market or to the *feiras* sorghum, maize, bambara groundnuts, cowpeas, baskets, mats, pots, chickens, eggs, honey, trapped animals and birds, and a wide range of vegetables and wild fruits. Most smiths, other craft-workers and miners exchanged their goods either among themselves or with the Portuguese traders. The farmers found a ready market for their cattle, goats, sheep and pigs. The Sofala fortress and the *feiras* in the interior struck deep roots into Shona society and became an essential part of its economic and social framework.

Feiras in Shona country

The period 1575-1684 witnessed a change in the pattern of trade between African peasants and Portuguese traders. The Portuguese traders consolidated their commercial and military victory over the Swahili-Arabs by adapting and transforming the bazaars into Portuguese *feiras*. In time, the *feiras* became the main focal points of Afro-Portuguese intercourse. Each feira had a fortress, a garrison of 10–15 soldiers, in theory a church with a priest, and a *capitão-mor*. Some *feiras* were administered by the government of the Rivers of Sena, while others were privately owned. The *capitães-mores* bore some resemblance to the guards of the medieval Portuguese *feiras*. The position of *capitão-mor* in Manyika, Butwa and Karanga country was comparable with that of the *capitão-mor dos Banianes* on the island of Mozambique. Their payment was regarded only as a subsidy and it was the policy of the Portuguese administrators to appoint only wealthy individuals from the Portuguese settlement of Sena to such posts. The duties of the *capitães-mores* involved taxation, price control, arbitrating between Portuguese and African traders, granting licences, protecting caravans, raising soldiers and enforcing laws relating to weights and measures. These powers and duties were greatly modified as *capitães-mores* interacted with various African rulers.

The main feiras

The *feira* of Dambarare was acclaimed the best of all the *feiras* in the Rivers of Sena, where almost all the rich merchants of Sena traded. It was three days' journey from that of Angwa, where there was much gold but few residents, as it was so far from both Sena and Tete.

In Uteve, the Portuguese held an annual *feira* in Bandire to purchase articles from the interior. This *feira* lasted from the sixteenth century to the early eighteenth century, when the Teve authorities stopped it. The methods used by the Teve kings to control Portuguese trade were somewhat different from those of other Shona societies. In Manyika, for example, *feira* trade was controlled personally by both the kings and the prince or princess of the area where the *feira* was held. But in Uteve the *feira* was operated largely by an *inyamasango* (village head) under whose jurisdiction the administration of Bandire fell.

The Portuguese do not seem to have created any *feiras* north of the Zambezi until the early eighteenth century, when Zumbo and Michonga were established. Two reasons may account for the late development of these last two *feiras*: the discovery of *bares* (mines) north of the Zambezi during the eighteenth

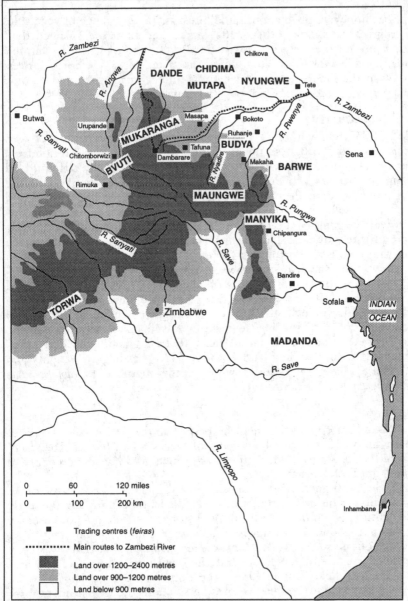

22.3 *The main* feiras *in the sixteenth and seventeenth centuries (adapted from map 3 of H. H. K. Bhila,* Trade and Politics in a Shona Kingdom. The Manyika and their African and Portuguese Neighbours, 1575–1902, *London, Longman. Adapted by kind permission of Longman Group UK Ltd)*

century, and the need for the Portuguese to look elsewhere for trade after their expulsion from Shona country by the Rozvi emperor, Dombo Changamire, between 1693 and 1695.

The expulsion of the Portuguese from their *feiras* by the *changamire* forced the Portuguese to revert to the trading methods they had used during the sixteenth century. They were, however, able to revive the *feira* of Masekesa in Manyika, in 1719, but not the one in Uteve. The system of having one officer to co-ordinate Portuguese relations with African rulers was no longer possible in the case of the Mutapa emperors as there was no longer any effective central authority. It is therefore necessary to examine briefly relations between the Portuguese and some important African rulers during the eighteenth century.

In the east, the king of Uteve did not allow the Portuguese to mine gold in the *bares* in his kingdom. His subjects, however, could buy cloth and beads from the Portuguese settlers at Sena. Even in this trade, the Portuguese traders expended much of their profit in trying to buy safety. Teve policy during the eighteenth century was decidedly anti-Portuguese. In the kingdom of Manyika, Portuguese traders were allowed freedom of passage throughout the land, but their trading activities were strictly controlled by the rulers, to whom the *capitão-mor* and the Portuguese merchants paid a regular tribute.

Similarly, to keep the *feira* of Zumbo and the trade route to Butwa safe, the Portuguese traders paid a regular tribute to the *changamire*. He used to send his envoys to the *feira* of Zumbo, asking for additional gifts over and above the usual tribute. Despite all this expense, the trade route between Zumbo and Butwa was not completely safe. The *changamire's* famous raid of 1756–57, in which he confiscated property worth 1,000 *pastas* (800,000 *cruzados*), was a case in point. The Zumbo trade was also compromised by recurring civil war and famine during the 1760s. Yet the *changamires* valued their trade with the Portuguese. The Rozvi rulers sent expeditionary forces on three occasions – in 1743, 1772 and 1781 – to protect the *feira* of Zumbo from attacks by the neighbouring African rulers.

The nature of relations between the *Mutapa* and the Portuguese appears to have changed little during the eighteenth century. The Portuguese continued to maintain a garrison of 20 soldiers, a *capitão-mor*, a lieutenant, a captain-general and a Dominican friar at the Mutapa royal court. Despite these arrangements, trade between the Portuguese and the Mutapa rulers continued to decline during the eighteenth century. This decline has been explained in the context of developments in southern Zambezia during the eighteenth century. First, there was a gold rush north of the Zambezi with individual Portuguese adventurers discovering *bares* and starting to mine gold themselves. Second, gold production virtually stopped in the eighteenth century. Third, both the African and Portuguese traders on either side of the Zambezi river took to elephant-hunting for ivory.

The ivory trade played an important role in the Mutapa empire. A sixteenth-century Portuguese account tells us that elephants used to 'go about in droves almost like a herd of cows' and that 4,000 or 5,000 of them died every year. Elephant-hunting was less subject than gold to control by African rulers, as the hunting usually took place in remote areas. However, little is known about its organization; there are some indications that much eighteenth-century elephant-hunting took place in Buhera and Rimuka.

Conclusion

Portuguese penetration of southern Zambezia eroded the power of the indigenous ruling class and facilitated direct forms of peasant exploitation by Portuguese mercantile capital and, later, British industrial capital.

The Portuguese merchants were largely concerned with trade in gold and ivory and, consequently, the main commodities of regional trade – iron, salt and copper – were relegated to second position. But long-distance trade and regional trade stimulated each other, and this led to the emergence of an African merchant class, the *vashambadzi*. For long-distance trade to flourish, there had to be gold and ivory and porters, food to feed these carriers, hoes to cultivate the crops and iron to make the hoes. The *vashambadzi* transported not only ivory and gold but also salt and iron hoes, which they exchanged for food on the way. The African cultivators who lived near the trade routes were gradually transformed as they grew more and more surplus agricultural produce for sale to the traders and their porters. Needless to say, the peasants, who were mostly ignorant of the international value of the commodities they sold, were ruthlessly exploited by the Portuguese merchants.

23

Dependence and interdependence: southern Africa, 1500–1800

Between 1500 and 1800, much of southern Africa was transformed. New communities established themselves in the region; many pre-existing communities changed their way of life or their location, and the relationships which grew up within and between communities were radically different from any before. Many of these drastic changes were because of changes in southern Africa's external linkages. When the first European, Vasco da Gama, rounded the Cape of Good Hope in 1497, southern Africa had only the most tenuous links with the rest of the world, but by 1800 the region was firmly enmeshed in worldwide patterns of trade and strategy. It is worth considering the changing international context itself before trying to evaluate its effect on southern Africa.

In 1500, neither sub-Saharan Africa nor the Americas had been drawn into regular relationships with the rest of the world. International trade was particularly concerned with Europe and Asia, and it was conducted almost entirely overland, at very great expense. To the Portuguese, who first developed the sea route round the Cape, and to the Dutch, English and French, who followed them round the Cape, southern Africa was mainly a dangerous navigational hazard. The mapping of its coastline gradually reduced its isolation, but the consistent lack of interest from Arab and European traders is worth looking at.

During the late Iron Age, the temperate regions of the southern hemisphere were not very attractive to international trade. With the low population density and the rudimentary tools in use, it was difficult to produce a regular surplus of food, even in regions which permitted cultivation. The Arabs, who conducted a flourishing trade along the east coast of Africa, were not tempted further south because the gold, ivory and slaves which bulked large in their cargoes were much more readily available on the tropical coasts. Similarly, Europeans travelled round the Cape for 150 years before taking any real interest in southern Africa.

If seaborne contacts were negligible, land contacts were not much more important. Many communities in the south had historical and linguistic ties with the north, but these had little significance in daily life. The Khoi, who herded animals, caught fish and gathered food along the southern coastal belt, had practically no contacts with the north. The same was true of the San, who lived in the hinterland. The speakers of the Nguni languages, mainly east of the mountain chain that divides the region, had little regular contact with their northern neighbours. In the far west (in today's Namibia) the Herero and Ovambo had close linguistic ties with each other and with their northern neighbours, while the Tswana and Sotho, who lived in the centre, traded to the north from time to time. As late as 1500, these societies were effectively independent of the rest of the world: their external links were sporadic and marginal.

When Europeans did begin to interest themselves in the region, they acted vigorously. In the mid-1600s, a wholly new community was planted at the Cape by the Dutch East India Company, which continued to see southern Africa simply as a way-station to the East. The regional consequences of establishing the Cape settlement were much more profound than the company planners intended. The region as a whole was securely linked to Europe and Asia, although it was not yet resolved whether the Dutch (who held the Cape from 1652 to 1795) or the British (who seized the Cape in 1795) would be the main agents. As the new settlement expanded into its hinterland, it established new relationships, marked by dominance and dependence. This marked the advent of capitalist relations of production, together with colonialism and imperialism, which would transform southern Africa more abruptly and more thoroughly than any other part of sub-Saharan Africa.

It is possible to reconstruct the conditions and events of the sixteenth century, but it is difficult to do so objectively. Wherever hunting and gathering communities have come into conflict with cultivators during the past two centuries, they have been destroyed. Cultivators have survived in sufficient numbers to force themselves upon the attention of historians: nomads have been less fortunate.

Some very interesting relationships prevailed in southern Africa in the sixteenth century that defy all notions of historical inevitability. Environmental differences permitted a degree of specialization between communities. Hunters were not evolving into herders, nor herders into cultivators, but rather co-existing, despite the hostilities which sometimes marked their interaction.

The western half of southern Africa, including present-day Botswana and Namibia, enjoys less than 40 centimetres of rainfall each year. The only exception is the hinterland of the Cape peninsula, which enjoys good winter rain quite regularly. In the fifteenth century, without dam-building and food-storage techniques, the inhabitants of this area could not have practised agriculture. Their commitment to hunting and gathering or herding is evidence of sensible adaptation.

The origins and history of the San hunter-gatherer groups are shrouded in myth and misunderstanding. The great diversity of languages they spoke in the sixteenth century is evidence of many centuries of adaptation within the western half of southern Africa. The San had reliable means of subsistence as long as human population density did not outgrow environmental resources. Hunting and gathering made them independent of other societies, but they interacted with other people. Sometimes a group of hunters would attach themselves as clients to herding patrons, obtaining dairy products in exchange for game or

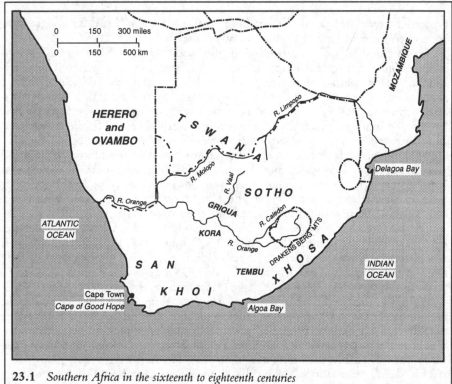

23.1 *Southern Africa in the sixteenth to eighteenth centuries*

advice on animal movements. This form of livelihood relied absolutely on mobility, which imposed restraints on population growth and made it impossible to accumulate property, as it could only hamper the band's speed.

Possession of cattle meant that the Khoi had to cling to well-watered areas rather than roam the arid regions. Since oxen could carry baggage, the Khoi could build tents and transport them whenever they moved. The presence of immobile old or young people was no longer the handicap it had been. Private property could also be accumulated, and within these pastoral societies a measure of stratification developed, differentiating them from the more egalitarian and property-less San. The need for social control did not require the Khoi to develop a formal structure of political authority; but individuals did exercise some authority among their clans.

Herding may have offered a higher level of consumption than hunting during good times, but herds were vulnerable to drought and epidemics, as well as theft and confiscation in war. When such disasters occurred, the Khoi often had to hunt for a living, at least until they could build up fresh herds of stock. Near the Cape peninsula, where hunting opportunities were limited, dispossessed herders took to the seashore, making a living by fishing. Life may have been unstable, but they were not destitute.

There could be no clear ecological boundary between Khoi and Xhosa, as both settled farming and herding were possible in the areas where they met. Indeed, interpenetration seems to have been common. Individual Xhosa abandoned settled farming for herding and sometimes hunting. Whenever a crisis struck the Khoi, they could become clients of established Xhosa nearby, because agricultural production recovers more rapidly from famine conditions than stock-farming. Robert Ross demonstrates how the Gonaqua, Gqunukhwebe and Ntinde were former Khoi who became mixed farmers and were incorporated *en masse* into Xhosa society. It is only with hindsight that Khoi pastoralism seems a transitional and obsolete means of livelihood. For most of the period under review, the Khoi interacted intensively with other specialized societies but without sacrificing their own life-style.

The late Iron Age was well established among the Nguni and Sotho peoples by 1500. Iron was commonly employed and quite widely processed, although not all tools and weapons were of metal. Hunting and herding societies had little need of iron and could rely entirely on stone, bone, wood and fibres. It was also possible for mixed farmers to manage without iron. In southern Africa, some communities practised both agriculture and pastoralism with very few iron tools, for almost 1,000 years. However, the abundance of iron in the late Iron Age must have made existing processes much easier and more productive. Farmers are much more efficient when iron tools are available for clearing, and they have more time available for domestic crafts and for more extensive pastoralism. Archaeological excavations suggest that domesticated animals and pottery became more numerous during the late Iron Age, and that implies a more comfortable standard of living and a heightened division of labour within each community.

Travellers' accounts of the life of Nguni societies east of the mountain range between 1500 and 1800 are uneven, and a reconstruction of those years relies on the study of material remains supplemented by such oral accounts as have survived. The material basis of life was grain and livestock. The traditional reliance upon sorghum was modified in the eighteenth century by the adoption of maize, which gave higher yields. Stock-farming could be conducted best by the use of a combination of fixed pastures and seasonal transhumance to take advantage of the differing qualities of the veld. A general decline in rainfall in the first half of the eighteenth century and a serious drought at the end of the century would have intensified competition for those pastures which were usable even in dry years.

Human population densities appear to have been much lower than we are now accustomed to. J. B. Peires estimates that there were 100,000 Xhosa-speaking people by 1800, despite the integration of ex-Khoi. There cannot have been serious population pressure on land at any time between 1500 and 1800. This is important in any consideration of the political systems recorded for the Nguni. Their essential constituent, and the irreducible unit of viability, was a household of stock-owning and land-using people. The household could behave as an independent unit, trading and exchanging commodities and wives with other households, almost at will. In practice, each household was linked through patrilineal kinship to a lineage, and hence to a clan. The leader of the royal clan, however, had few sanctions with which to enforce his authority over other Xhosa-speakers, except the manipulation of marriage links and gifts. The ability to bestow wives, gifts and land depended ultimately on the royal household's ability to out-produce other households and clans. But there was no particular barrier to a commoner becoming wealthy in stock and wives, so that the margin favouring the chief was not always wide. And against the centralizing ambitions of the chiefs, commoners also had ambitions. The incessant wrangles within dominant Xhosa clans and, presumably, among other Nguni societies were undoubtedly encouraged by thoughtful commoners who sought to paralyse the central authority. These constraints on the evolution of a despotic type of administration were not broken until the end of the 1700s. Until then, daily life seems to have been relaxed and usually comfortable, if we are to believe the reports of the occasional white castaways who found refuge among the Nguni.

Even less is known about the Sotho and Tswana peoples west of the Drakensberg, where lighter rainfall encouraged a greater emphasis on herding. Sotho and Tswana must have interacted with Khoi, San, Nguni and Shona, as there was small-scale trade in all these directions.

Like the San and the Khoi, the southern Bantu communities interacted with other specialized communities but were not transformed by that interaction. The different African groups were, it seems, capable of long-term coexistence without one imposing its mode of production on another.

The historiography of southern Africa is dominated by accounts of the history and expansion of the Dutch settlement at Cape Town. In fact, the Portuguese had been the first Europeans to establish a permanent settlement in the region, and it is easier to grasp the revolutionary quality of the Dutch settlement if it is contrasted with the earlier Portuguese settlement.

Portugal in the sixteenth century was feudal, small and poor. Its overseas expansion was organized by the monarchy as a trading monopoly to India, and was buttressed by the Church, which had a pervasive influence on the administration. By 1510, the centre of overseas rule was Goa, and the sea route was protected by forts commanding the Mozambique channel from Delagoa Bay to present-day Tanzania. With superior ships and firearms, Portugal had no difficulty in conquering the Arab and Swahili ports, but more was required than military superiority to govern the region. This was a maritime empire, tentative in its territorial control. It was also an essentially feudal empire in which important and lucrative offices were sold by the crown for an annual fee. It was populated by Portuguese criminals, non-Portuguese traders and adventurers. Profit was to be had through the gold and ivory trades, and later the slave trade, recognizing the authority of existing African rulers and provoking in them the most anti-social behaviour. By the end of the sixteenth century the Portuguese empire in the Indian Ocean had been disrupted by

23.2 *Khoi Khoi farmers threshing grain (© The Mansell Collection, London)*

competition from rival European trading powers, and the Mozambique channel lost its strategic significance.

The exploitation of Mozambique was inefficient. Instead of introducing new forms of production, the Portuguese and Indian traders strove to become middlemen. The land was parcelled up into *prazos* and leased to *prazeros*, and the estates had the quality of feudal and subsistence-based manors rather than commodity-producing farms. The supply of the export staples – ivory, gold and slaves – depended on indigenous collectors. Merchant capitalism without capital, and colonization without colonists, could certainly disrupt south-eastern Africa: what it could not encompass was a lasting transformation of existing societies.

During the long struggle against the Portuguese trading monopoly, the Dutch East India Company was formed in 1602, with royal support. The company was independent of the reformed churches, and the 'Heren XVII' who made up the governing body could afford to be single-minded in the pursuit of trading profits. The company could afford considerable outlays which would only be recouped in the long term. The garrison settlement at the Cape was precisely such an outlay. It was a strategic point premised upon continuing Asian trade, a place where fresh meat and vegetables could be bought to provision the Dutch fleets sailing to and from Batavia. When neither the Khoi nor company employees could produce victuals on a sufficient scale, the company took refuge in a modified form of capitalist production whereby company employees were released as free burghers to engage in production on their own account, the company itself retaining control over marketing.

Like other European powers which expanded into temperate grasslands with scant populations, the Dutch found that the dynamics of their new settlement were quite different from those of their tropical dependencies. For over a century, until the encounter with settled mixed farmers, their experience was similar to that of the Spaniards in the grasslands of the South American pampa and of the British in the prairies of North America and south-eastern Australia.

Perhaps the fundamental determinant of the Cape settlement was the painfully slow development of agriculture. For the first 40 years of its history, the settlement imported much of its staple food, despite the vast store of agricultural knowledge of the settlers. The second great determinant of the settlement was the absence of a coercible, indigenous labour force. Whereas Indonesians could be directed into commodity production in large numbers by the manipulation of existing social structures, it was impossible to turn Khoi into export producers without the total destruction of Khoi society. The few Khoi who survived and remained within the boundaries of the settlement merged with other elements to form a new community – the Khoi Khoi (Khoisan), later the nucleus of the Cape Coloured. The company could not rely upon the Khoi for labour and had to bring in slaves from other parts of Africa and the East Indies.

The hallmark of the new society was its persistent expansionism. At the Cape, labour was expensive and scarce, while land was cheap and plentiful, so the obvious manner of achieving the expansion of capitalism was not through the more intensive use of land but through territorial expansion. The geographical extension of the settlement replicated the sparse population levels which had characterized Khoi society. Indeed, commercial pastoralism meant little more than grazing much the same cattle and sheep on the same land as before, sometimes with Khoi employed as herdsmen. It was not land usage so much as social relations which were changed by the new regime. On the frontier of the settlement it was particularly difficult for the Dutch settlers to control their labourers, as it was easy for disgruntled workers to flee eastwards or northwards. Slavery constituted only a partial solution, as slaves were costly and they, too, could escape.

During the eighteenth century, the imperatives of extensive commercial pastoralism expressed themselves in a series of social relationships which have more in common with those of the South American pampa and nineteenth-century Australia than with the rest of Africa. Cape Town was the entrepôt, the focus of all trading relationships and meeting point of international cultures and ideas. Company officials not only administered the settlement but also often traded on their own account, consorted with the more prosperous land owners, traders and inn-keepers of the town, and lorded it over the large and strictly disciplined slave population. They felt superior to the pastoralists who came to town occasionally to sell meat, hides and tallow. Speaking a crude form of Dutch, barely literate and wearing unfashionable but functional clothes, the pastoralists obviously lacked urban sophistication. But they were the mainstay of the colonial economy. The slave population was constantly being increased by importation, but the pastoral population increased just as fast, both by immigration and natural increase. One hundred and fifty years after its foundation, the settlement comprised more than 20,000 free burghers and more than 25,000 slaves.

The territorial expansion of the settlement tended to disperse the Khoi and San from the western interior. At the same time, the strict hierarchy and discipline within the new society tended to extrude the more independent-minded of the slaves and the ex-Khoi. An occasional white settler also fled to the frontier, either to escape the law, or in search of quick wealth. These refugees were hardy and violent. They could seek and obtain employment by the state as frontier law-enforcers or try to live a settled life among the white frontiersmen, either as wage-labourers or as independent pastoralists. Although this last was an attractive prospect, it was difficult, especially for the Khoi, to register title to land in their own names. There remained, finally, a third option: to stay one step ahead of the frontier of white pastoral expansion.

The wide, dry region to the north of the company settlement saw the evolution of new societies, such as the Kora, Griqua and Nama societies, which from 1730 to about 1780 were seldom troubled by company authority. To make a living, these little societies captured, bred and sold cattle, relying on firearms acquired through the settlement. Leadership fell on men of the frontier who were able to speak the language of the whites – white outlaws and the descendants of slaves. Many, like the Griqua, remembered their descent from Khoi bands. However, they were not merely refugees from the company settlement but also its cutting edge. They aspired to the status of independent commercial pastoralists, but as they were always obliged to stay ahead of their white rivals, they could not settle anywhere for long. When the frontier was at length 'closed' in the nineteenth century, by a combination of environmental conditions and reinforced colonial administration, the day of the Griqua came to an end.

Similar developments also occurred on the eastern frontier, but there the course of events was swifter, and the climax in the 1790s more dramatic, as it involved not only the white pastoralists, the Cape Town authorities and the refugee communities, but also the southernmost Bantu.

A degree of control over most Xhosa-speakers may have been exercised by the ruler Phalo, but his death in 1775 unleashed the rivalry of his sons, Rharhabe and Gealeka. Gealeka's death divided the forces of his followers, and the death of Rharhabe in 1782 similarly split his followers between the regent, Ndlamba, and the young heir, Ngqika. Each of these factions aspired to dominance over the entire Xhosa-speaking community and the neighbouring Khoi who were enlisted as allies. From the perspectives of both factions, the white pastoralists seemed much like the coloured pastoralists – potential allies and possible clients of wealthy Xhosa. It took a generation for the Xhosa to grasp the unique quality of commercial pastoralism, with its steadily increasing appetite for new grazing land. Meanwhile, they behaved as if the threat was marginal.

The white pastoralists gradually came to provide for their own protection and expansion. The company paid for a resident magistrate – a *landdrost* – at major urban centres, but he alone could not maintain control. In his judicial functions, the *landdrost* was assisted by burghers – *heemraden* – who, in military affairs, took matters more and more into their own hands. Every adult male was, at least potentially, the patriarch of a small community comprising his family, his slaves and his employees; and each patriarchy conducted its affairs largely outside the formal judicial framework. When fighting was imminent, therefore, the patriarchs would elect an *ad hoc* leader, and the unit would be disbanded once the spoils had been divided. As white numbers increased late in the eighteenth century, the burghers became impatient with the company. In 1795, they formally renounced its authority, and declared two independent republics of white patriarchs, the short-lived republics of Swellendam and Graaf Reinet.

Meanwhile, a much more serious rebellion was brewing. A necessary consequence of white pastoral expansion had been the dispossession of Khoi communities. To the whites it seemed quite appropriate that the Khoi should be farm labourers rather than independent farmers and to the Xhosa faction-leaders it seemed appropriate that they should be content to become clients of wealthy Xhosa. But the Khoi rejected this situation and in 1799 many of them rebelled, drawing in reinforcements from the armed Khoi in the service of the new British administration. It was an incipient revolution.

During the French revolutionary wars, the British navy seized a number of garrisons around the world to consolidate their naval supremacy. One of these was the garrison at Cape Town, captured after a short tussle in 1795. The burgher republics were quickly suppressed by the British, but the burghers' control over their land was confirmed. The Khoi revolt, however, could not be put down so easily. With insufficient troops for a protracted frontier campaign, General Dundas was content to calm matters. Some land was granted to individual Khoi; others were encouraged to return to their employment or to rejoin the Hottentot Corps; and the troubles were left to simmer for a few years until they broke out again early in the nineteenth century.

The Cape, which the British acquired at the end of the 1700s, already had many of the characteristics which would distinguish it in the nineteenth century. Cape Town, with a mere 15,000 inhabitants, was still mainly an entrepôt for Asian and European trade; but it had also acquired its role as outlet for an export economy based on the hinterland. In the colony as a whole there were some 22,000 'Christians', most of whom were white, with a few liberated blacks. The Khoi and San were enumerated at about 14,000, and slaves at 25,000. Only 'Christians' could hold land, although the Khoi had not been entirely squeezed out; and only the slaves were entirely without civil rights.

Increasingly, the Khoi were cast in an intermediate situation between the settlement on one side and the Xhosa, Sotho and Tswana on the other. Because it was Khoi – as Khoi Khoi, Griquas, Nama and Kora – who bore the brunt of the pastoral expansion from the western Cape, most of the mixed-farming communities of the whole region were at this point only marginally affected. Among the northern Nguni, the emergence of the strong confederacies which led ultimately to the formation of the Zulu state was entirely independent of events at the Cape. Nevertheless, in the long run it was the transforming force of commercial pastoralism, itself provoked by the capitalist transformation of Europe and Asia, which would prove the most durable social force of the nineteenth century.

The Horn of Africa

The sixteenth and seventeenth centuries are the most dramatic in the history of north-east Africa. The mighty political and military power and the outstanding cultural development of the Christian Ethiopian empire disintegrated. Enemy invasions not only decimated large sections of the Christian population, but also tore whole provinces away from the empire for long periods. For a time the Holy Empire was but a shadow of its former self. The external tribulations were aggravated by religious disorders when emperor Susenyos, who converted to Catholicism in 1630, raised it to the status of the official religion of the state. Violent civil wars swept over the enfeebled empire until eventually the foreign faith and its supporters were finally driven out. There now followed a period of consolidation of empire and cultural revival. Then, from 1700, a period of fragmentation of empire began. The steadily increasing anarchy only came to an end in 1855, when Tewodros (Theodore) II ushered in the age of the great emperors whom the Ethiopian empire had to thank for its restoration and its survival through the colonial era.

North-east Africa, however, does not comprise only the Christian Ethiopian empire. Around 1500, Islamic culture, too, reached its peak in the east and centre of the sub-continent, and warlike Islam was soon to achieve great triumphs. Fired by the spirit of *djihād* (Holy War), Aḥmad ibn Ibrāhīm al-Ghazi, nicknamed *Grañ* (the left-handed) in the Christian Ethiopian chronicles, won victory after victory. Year after year, in the dry season, his hosts overran Amhara and Tigré, forcing whole provinces to embrace Islam. But once the leader had disappeared, the forces he had inspired collapsed. The Christian empire started to counter-attack. Finally the migrations of the great Oromo (Galla) people destroyed the once flourishing communities and cultures of the Islamic peoples in central Ethiopia, leaving hardly a vestige.

The Oromo and the Somali were to play a decisive role in the history of north-eastern Africa. Their evolution followed completely different paths. The Oromo spread out in all directions, in a series of migrations. They advanced into areas depopulated through the religious wars; they subjugated and assimilated other peoples but adapted themselves to their cultures. They did not develop a true national culture of their own.

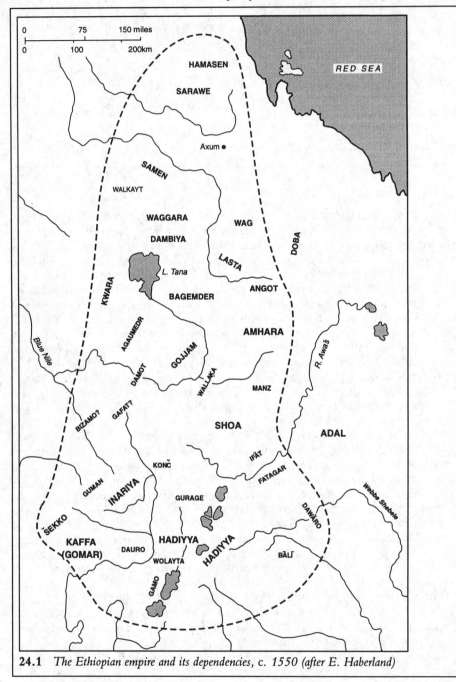

24.1   *The Ethiopian empire and its dependencies, c. 1550 (after E. Haberland)*

Not so the Somali. The participation of large groups in *Grañ*'s Holy War and the influence of Islam were powerful factors in the development of a strong national consciousness. Although divided into many ethnic groups, the Somali considered themselves one people with one culture and one religion.

The political and cultural events in northern, central and eastern north-east Africa were historically fairly well substantiated, but the history of the west and south-west remained rather obscure. We know today that this period saw the beginnings of a very dynamic cultural development. Direct influence from the Christian empire to the north led to the growth of large states and sophisticated cultures extending south to the natural highland boundary. Of particular importance were the foundation of the states of Inariya, Wolayta, Dauro and the small states of the Gamo highlands.

The Christian Ethiopian empire around 1500

By about 1500, the Christian Ethiopian empire had politically and culturally reached heights that it was not to approach again for centuries. It enjoyed undisputed hegemony in north-east Africa. Sudan was not yet Islamic. The Islamic towns along the shores of the Red Sea – in what is now Eritrea – were politically insignificant. Even the coast around Massawa, itself Islamic-Arabic, was part of the Ethiopian empire. The power of the many small Islamic dominions in eastern and central Ethiopia had been cut back by the crushing blows of the Ethiopian emperors of the preceding century, in particular the emperor Zera-Yakob (1434–68).

The influence of the Christian state was even stronger towards the south and south-west. New states with a Christian ruling class emerged; formerly independent peoples and states were made to recognize the political and cultural supremacy of the northern empire. The *Kebra Nagast* (Glory of the Kings), the charter of the Ethiopian empire, provided the moral justification of this imperial expansion.

This work was probably compiled about 1300, shortly after the restoration of the dynasty that from then until 1974 was called the Solomonic dynasty. Folk legends, biblical, Talmudic and Ḳu'rānic traditions were brought together and harmonized with a divine mission of salvation. The *Kebra Nagast* records how the queen of Sheba – here equated with Ethiopia – undertook a journey to Jerusalem to learn the wisdom of Solomon. By him she had a son, Menelik, who was born after her return to Ethiopia and was later to become the first Ethiopian king. Later, on a visit to his father in Jerusalem, Menelik seized the Ark of the Covenant and carried it off to Ethiopia. It was preserved thereafter in the famous cathedral of Axum where the Ethiopian emperors were enthroned. The book ends with the announcement of the spiritual division of the world between the two great Holy Empires of Rome and Ethiopia. The story makes Christian Ethiopians the chosen people of both the Old and the New Testaments for, unlike the Jews, they have accepted the Gospel. The fact that Ethiopia was able to withstand so many storms is due above all to the geographical position of this mountainous land. But the feeling of being the new chosen people must have given spiritual conviction to the empire's determination to extend dominion over most of north-east Africa.

Internally, the empire enjoyed the utmost tranquillity at that time. This is evident from the reports of Francesco Alvares who, from 1520 to 1526, accompanied the Portuguese mission from Massawa to Shoa as chaplain and travelled extensively throughout the country. Order and security reigned; the governor's instructions were obeyed and the emperor's word carried absolute authority throughout an empire that measured at least 1,000 kilometres from north to south. The concept of the Holy Christian Empire, the undisputed claim to power of the House of Solomon and, finally, the Christian faith and common culture of the Amhara and Tigrai who formed the state, constituted strong bonds. The culture and language of these two peoples exerted a powerful assimilating effect on other ethnic groups which came into contact with them. This is particularly true of the different groups of the Agaw, the indigenous inhabitants of central and northern Ethiopia, who were almost all assimilated by the Amhara and Tigrai. In the south, too, in the parts of Shoa province now inhabited mainly by Oromo, not only Christianity but also the Amharic language and culture must have spread at the expense of other ethnic groups living there.

The attempt by the emperor Zera-Yakob to centralize the empire's political organization failed, but the word of the emperor still carried absolute authority, even after 1500. From the chronicles, we can infer that, as regards the autonomy of individual provinces and the question of land law, conditions were very similar to those still obtaining in the nineteenth and twentieth centuries. Most land was the residual property of ethnic and family groups who decided how it should be divided among their members. The Church was also an important land owner. Finally, there were the imperial lands, granted by the emperor on a short- or long-term basis to deserving people or for specific purposes. This feudal land was known as *gult*, a word also used to denote the right conferred by the emperor to the grantee of an office to levy tribute and services.

The extraordinary dynamism of Ethiopian society, with its ideal of the *tellek saw* (great man), who had constantly to prove himself anew and in whom qualities and achievements alone counted, was not conducive to the rise of a nobility. In theory, any free man belonging to a respectable family could be elected to office by his district people's assembly. The emperor could confirm or reject the election. Thus monarchical power and democratic election complemented one another, preventing the formation of a hereditary nobility with political privileges which could have disturbed the unity of the empire. This happened after 1700, with the increasing enfeeblement of imperial power.

Roads were safe. Imperial rest-houses abounded and also great weekly markets. There was general well-being. Taxes in kind flowed from the provinces and the tributary states to the emperor's court, where they were redistributed. Although neither minted coins nor commercial correspondence were known, there was nevertheless extensive trade over long distances and consumer goods were imported from India and the Near East.

Ethiopia was closely linked with lands as far away as Europe. Ethiopian monks – the main purveyors of education, art and science – received their training in Egypt and took part in both Coptic and Islamic cultural life. Although literary production was limited to the fields of religion and history, it flourished until at least 1650. The graphic arts – of which, above all, book illuminations have survived – were stimulated by contact with the Christian east and with Europe. The existence of still little-known ruins of churches and palaces is further proof of the rich complexity and artistic creativity of this period.

Islamic states and cultures: the djihād, the Somali and the Hadiyya

By 1300, if not before, Christianity had developed a vigorous missionary activity in central and southern Ethiopia. As the official religion of the Ethiopian empire, Christianity could always rely on state support – if necessary backed by fire and sword. The spread of Islam in north-east Africa, however, depended on the spread of Arab culture and on trade and communications. Arab and Islamic influences on the north-east African coast are age-old. Trade between the Arabian peninsula, the Ethiopian coast and the Somali coast led to the foundation of a number of towns with mixed populations but with the Arab element predominating. The most important centres, starting from the north, were: Massawa, the Dahlak Islands, Assab, Oboek, Tadjurā, Djibouti, Zaylā', Berberā, Obbia, Mogadishu, Merka and Brava.

The map of the spread of Islam during the fifteenth and sixteenth centuries clearly shows that it was concentrated on both sides of the Rift Valley – along the great trade route into central Ethiopia. From the coast inland, there were a number of states: Adal, the largest, Dara, Dawāro, Bālī, Arababnī (or Ar'en), Sarha and Hadiyya. Islamic influence probably extended westwards across the Rift Valley. To the north of the Rift Valley on the southern slopes of the Shoa highlands lay the twin Islamic states of Ifāt and Fatagar (Fatadjar). Many people in these states must have spoken Semitic languages which spread alongside and overlaid the Kushitic languages originally spoken there. The only ones remaining are the languages of the Harari, East Gurage and Argobba.

These states were all marked by the influence of Arab-Islamic culture from the coast and many elements of that culture still persist today. The most striking example of the town settlements that once dominated the area is Harar, the only genuinely ancient city on Ethiopian soil. The stone-built single-storey or two-storey town dwellings with flat roofs and beautiful interior furnishings betray Arab influences, as do the large number of walled holy sepulchres. Arab influence also left its traces in intensive horticulture, still practised today, and a multitude of food crops unknown in Ethiopia such as oranges, lemons, peaches, vines, bananas and sugar cane. Also traceable to Arab influence is cotton-growing and the consumption of coffee and khat or čat (celastrus). Widespread in central Ethiopia are numerous religious concepts, rites and words that stem from the Arabic, even though the Muslims there later renounced Islam.

The spread of Islam and its culture from east to west brought it into conflict with the Christian empire. This happened mainly in central Ethiopia, in what is now the province of Shoa, and to the east of it. This was also the scene of bloody conflicts between the two powers that went on for several centuries and remained indecisive until the second half of the fifteenth. Although the Christian empire remained the undisputed dominant power in north-east Africa, it was unable to eliminate the Islamic states, although they were insignificant in relation to its own size and population.

We are not certain what changed the war between the Islamic trading states and the Christian empire into a Holy War or *djihād*, nor why the political leadership of the sultans of Adal, the Walasma, was transferred to the religious leaders (*imāms*). Nor do we know what gave the Islamic armies the cohesion and fanaticism to bring the mighty Christian empire to the brink of defeat. One explanation no doubt lies in the brilliant Aḥmad ibn Ibrāhīm al-Ghazi (Aḥmad Grañ) who became the charismatic leader of the *djihād*. There is also no doubt that the rest of the Islamic world, which at that time held northern Somalia tightly in its grip, provided its armies in Ethiopia with a recruiting potential several times the size of the comparatively small population of the Islamic states.

A war with the state of Adal, provoked by the Christians, and initially successful wars in the Chercher area during the reign of the weak emperor Lebna Dengel (1508–40) seemed to herald nothing new in the conflict between the two adversaries. But the fortunes of war suddenly changed. In the decisive battle of Sembera Kure (1529), on the western edge of Chercher, the Ethiopian empire lost not only a whole army but also a considerable part of its ruling élite. The consequences were to be fearful. Until 1543, Islamic armies swept over the Ethiopian Highlands, in the south and the north, each dry season, systematically defeating and subjugating one province after another. In southern and eastern Ethiopia, in Hadiyya and Bālī provinces, the population went over to the Muslims, for they often shared their religion and greeted them as liberators. The same did not happen in the old Christian provinces, especially in the regions inhabited by the Amhara and Tigrai. There, those who did not accept Islam were put to the sword so that whole districts converted – if only nominally – to Islam. Churches and monasteries were plundered and sacked and their treasures given to the Islamic armies. Treasures of Ethiopian literature and painting (miniatures in books or murals on church walls) were destroyed. In 1531, Dawāro and Shoa, two large, densely populated provinces in the south-east and in the heart of the Ethiopian Highlands, were subjugated. Amhara and Lasta, two of the empire's central provinces, followed in 1533. The same year, Ethiopia's most important holy place, Axum, was razed to the ground. (The Tablets of the Law were saved and later brought back to Axum where they are still to be found today.)

But even in the most desperate times, the steadfastness of the Christian people and the strength of the concept of the Holy Ethiopian Empire were apparent. Those forcibly converted to Islam abandoned their new faith the moment the Islamic armies withdrew. The conquered provinces soon rose against their new masters. Even the weak emperor Lebna Dengel, continually on the run, refused to give his daughter in marriage to Aḥmad Grañ, who offered him a pledge of friendship.

Lebna Dengel died a hounded fugitive, in 1540, in the impregnable monastery-citadel of Dabra Damo in Tigré. Within a few years there had been a complete change in the political situation. The accession to the throne of the young emperor Galawdewos (Claudius), one of the most outstanding figures in Ethiopian history, was followed by the rapid restoration of the Ethiopian empire, the arrival of the Portuguese expeditionary corps and the decisive defeat of the Muslims.

By the sixteenth century, Portugal had reached the peak of its imperialist expansion. The Indian Ocean and its inlets had become a Portuguese sea. Portuguese fortresses, which were never completely subjugated, sprang up on the coasts at Hormuz, Oman, Socotra, Mombasa and so on. It was an historical accident that, in 1541, brought a Portuguese fleet into Massawa which, at that time, still belonged to the Ethiopian empire. The year before, a Portuguese fleet had been sent from Goa in India to the Red Sea to combat the expansion of the Turks who, after the conquest of Egypt, were gaining ground in Arabia and even in Sudan. Part of the fleet anchored at Massawa in the spring of 1541. Soon after, the *baḥar nagāš* (sea-king), governor of the northernmost province of the Ethiopian empire, appeared bearing letters requesting support for the Christian empire. By July 1541, a volunteer corps of 400 Portuguese, under the leadership of one of the younger sons of the famous Vasco da Gama, had marched into the Ethiopian Highlands. Their combat tactics and their superior firearms made them formidable opponents for the Muslim occupation troops in northern Ethiopia. A growing number of Ethiopian volunteers accompanied the Portuguese, who inflicted two severe defeats on the invincible army of the *imām* Aḥmad Grañ in two battles. The *imām* succeeded in obtaining assistance in the form of new types of artillery and sharpshooters from the Turkish commanders in Yemen. Before the Portuguese could link up with the emperor's army, they were forced to engage in a third battle and were defeated. Fortune nonetheless favoured the Christians. The imperial army and the remaining Portuguese joined forces and, in February 1543, the Muslim army was destroyed to the east of Lake Tana and the *imām* was killed. Whether it was Portuguese assistance that tipped the balance in this long-drawn-out war is uncertain. In the final battles, their guns had restored a certain strategic equilibrium. What was to be of greater consequence for Ethiopia, however, was the Catholic mission that followed the Portuguese soldiers (see below). The Muslim forces were no doubt strong enough to conquer Ethiopia militarily initially, but too weak to keep the two great peoples, the Tigrai and the Amhara, under control permanently. After 1543, the Christians emerged victorious from the struggle and, during the next few decades, the empire succeeded in winning back lost territory. The might of Islam had been broken for centuries to come.

The Oromo (Galla)

Since the middle of the sixteenth century, members of the great Oromo people
– hitherto known as the Galla – had been penetrating central, eastern and
western Ethiopia in ever increasing numbers. Their arrival, their settlement and
their quarrels with other groups already there had far-reaching effects, both
political and cultural. The Ethiopian empire suffered more and longer through
them than through the Muslims, and lost many provinces forever.

Although it is still not possible to specify the reasons for the great Oromo
migrations, we know that they were not undertaken to escape the pressure of
other peoples. Oromo traditions say nothing about the matter except that they
started out to seek new grazing lands for a growing population.

Notwithstanding the fanciful accounts of Amharic and European authors as
to their origins, the Oromo are a true Ethiopian people. The highlands surrounding what is today the province of Bālī were their home, whence they
moved out in large numbers into the heart of the Ethiopian Highlands and
south, to present-day Kenya and the Indian Ocean. Equally erroneous is all that
was written about their culture. They were described as savages and primitive
cattle-raisers. The Oromo were and are a people with a developed, sophisticated culture admired by their neighbours. Their spread was partly the result of
a sort of chain reaction: in the face of their military superiority, and because of
their much-admired social organization, other ethnic groups joined them. This
was particularly true of the Hadiyya, who lived between Harar and Gurage,
almost all of whom went over to the Oromo.

Oromo culture is marked by several distinctive features, particularly the close
relationship with their cattle. Cattle were not only the basis of their livelihood
but the object of emotional and ritual concern. This cattle complex, with its
moral overtones, permeated their whole culture.

The Oromo consisted of numerous genealogically connected groups and
clans which, as the population increased, tended to break away and form new,
politically independent groups. Borana and Barentu (or Baraytu) were two
mythical ancestors and founders of the two halves of the original stock that
bore their names. After the migrations began, these groups split. The Barentu
made their home mainly in the east, while the Borana settled in the south,
centre and west. Towards the end of the last century, when the Oromo were
defeated by the emperor Menelik and incorporated into the Ethiopian empire,
they split into more than 80 groups of various sizes.

The *gada* system, classification by age groups based on an abstract numerical
principle, was the basis of Oromo social and political organization. It was an
institution that ruled their whole life. Nothing was not subject to its rules:
birth, baptism, marriage, circumcision, emancipation from paternal authority,
permission to bear and bring up children, conscription for war and for hunting,
obligation to make sacrifices, civil death by exclusion from the system, burial
rites and a thousand details of everyday life. It represented the sum total of the
laws by which the life of the Oromo was governed. Forty years after his father

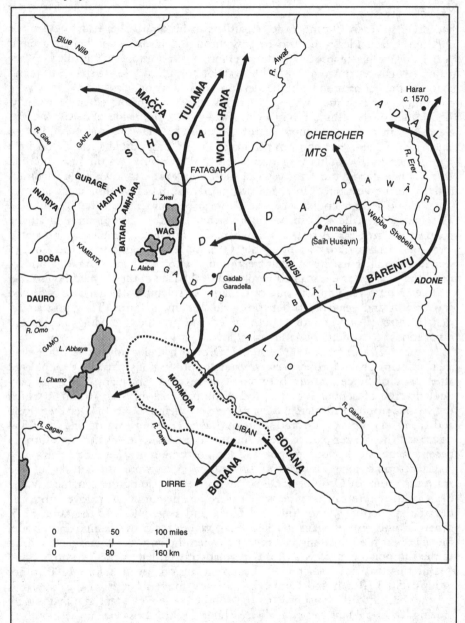

24.2 Oromo migrations in the sixteenth century (after E. Haberland)

had done so, each Oromo male, regardless of his actual age, had to enter the children's class. Ideally he had to pass through ten classes, each lasting eight years, during his lifetime. All those entering a class together formed a *gada* group, which remained an insoluble warrior community for life. The fifth and sixth classes constituted the leadership and warrior classes. As it was a community of free men with equal rights, there was no hereditary hierarchy. The leader of the ethnic group, who usually took the name of *abba gada*, was elected from among the members of the fifth class. He was supported by the *hayu* (judges), also elected from this class, and by other dignitaries. Of decisive significance for the military aggressiveness of the Oromo was the *gada* rule that at least once during the eight years of the ruling *gada* class a warlike expedition had to be undertaken. Only one who had distinguished himself as a brave warrior and hunter could occupy a position of eminence in the community. The ideal of the hero as successful killer and hunter was common to all the peoples of north-east Africa, but nowhere was the killer complex so integrated into the social system as among the Oromo. Every eight years the Oromo warriors would burst upon their neighbours who, until they came to understand the *gada* system, remained perplexed in the face of these cyclical episodes.

The Oromo religion was one of remarkable solemnity. Belief in a god who was creator and heavenly father took Old Testament forms. They possessed a rich treasure of oral literature, both sacred and profane, including prayers and invocations to the deity but also lyrical love poetry.

In their early migrations at least, the Oromo had one advantage other than their military prowess: they were advancing into regions virtually depopulated after years of fierce warfare between Muslims and Christians. This was particularly true of central Ethiopia, today the province of Shoa, through which the Islamic armies had marched every year on their way north. Between 1530 and 1554, groups of Oromo warriors advanced northward, and in 1554 destroyed the greater part of the Islamic state of Adal. At this time the Oromo became acquainted with the horse and soon became renowned horsemen.

Catastrophic for Christians and Muslims alike were the attacks of the Harmufa group of Oromo (1560–70), who were invading the provinces at the heart of the Ethiopian empire, which were just beginning to recover from the devastation of the *djihād*: Angot, Amhara and Bagemder. At the same time, other Oromo groups again attacked Adal, where there was famine and plague, the *amīr* Nūr himself falling victim to it. When the emperor Minas died, a third of the Ethiopian empire was already permanently settled by the Oromo.

But this was not the end of Oromo expansion. Even before 1500, other groups (Gugi, Boran and Orma) had already moved out from the highlands around Bālī into the savannah to the south in their constant search for new grazing lands for their cattle, finally reaching the Indian Ocean at the mouth of the River Tana. In the centre the Arusi established themselves in the vicinity of the former state of Bālī and pushed their borders further and further westwards. The Barentu spread over the area of the old Islamic states of Fatagar, Dawāro and Adal. The fortified city of Harar and the famous pilgrimage centre of Sek

Hussen survived as Islamic islands. Only in the hot, easily defended lowlands, in the gorges of the great rivers and on a few tablelands did pockets of Amhara hold out. The Wollo and Yeğğu Oromo spread over the fertile provinces of Angot and Amhara, once inhabited by Christians. Although they soon adopted the local Amharic language, because of their conversion to Islam the Oromo remained sworn enemies of the Christians. Other Oromo occupied the fertile lowlands to the east of the Ethiopian highlands as cattle-raisers.

At the beginning of the seventeenth century, a last wave of Oromo, consisting of several groups belonging to the large Mačča family, pushed westwards into what are today the provinces of Wallaga and Ilubabor, stopping only when they reached the western slopes of the Ethiopian Highlands. In the east and south of the region they came upon well-organized, densely populated kingdoms in close contact with the Ethiopian empire to the north and whose populations were partly Christianized. Despite the resistance of these kingdoms, Oromo expansion continued ever more vigorously, especially as communications between the empire and its dependencies in the south-west weakened in parallel with the decline in the strength of the empire. Thus Boša and Guman disappeared from the political map and became the Oromo dominions of Gimma and Gumma. However, the indigenous substratum remained so strong here that the Oromo took over much of the culture of the conquered country, in particular the political organization and the monarchy, while the *gada* system gradually disappeared. Inariya, famous for its treasures, was the last of these states to fall, defeated by the Limmu Oromo. After 1700, its king fled to the south, where the other Gonga kingdoms and the many Ometo kingdoms held their ground against the Oromo, thanks to the natural strongholds provided by their terrain.

The Somali

During the same period, if not earlier, another great people – the Somali – began an expansion which had considerable significance for large sectors of the eastern part of the Horn of Africa.

The Somali country of origin is thought to be the area north of where they live today. From there they spread – probably from the eleventh century onwards – south and west. As early as the thirteenth century, Arab geographers tell of Somali settlements in the area of Merka, to the south of the city known today as Mogadishu. As cattle-rearing nomads, the Somali were driven by the pressure of increasing population to seek new grazing lands in the direction of the Ethiopian Highlands, and they probably reached the eastern edge of the Harar plateau in about 1500, coming into contact with the Islamic states there. Names and genealogical data left by the chronicler Sihāb al-Dīn suggest that the Somali played an important role as supporters of the *imām* Ahmad Grañ's *djihād*.

The stimulating and unifying effect of the Arab-Islamic influence was greater on the Somali than on any other north-east African people. Islam became an integral part of Somali culture, and their faith was constantly strengthened by the missionaries who came from Arabia. These holy men were the founding fathers of the Somali people, such as the famous Ismā'īl Gabarti from whom many Somali are descended. This Arab-Islamic cultural influence also gave the Somali a sense of cultural superiority and strengthened their capacity to assimi- liate other related groups in the huge area between Ogaden and Lake Turkana. It is extraordinarily difficult to pinpoint individual stages in the expansion of the Somali because many groups which attached themselves to the Somali nation deliberately suppressed all reference to a different origin and assumed a common Somali genealogy.

Under the influence of Islam, the Somali culture changed, especially in the south. The Somali thus differentiated themselves more than any other group from the large family of north-east African peoples, linked by many common historical, cultural and geographical factors. The influence exerted by the geographical environment is by no means to be underestimated, since, apart from the Afar who live in the desolate wastes of their homeland, the Somali are the only inhabitants of north-east Africa whose territory consists exclusively of dry savannah and semi-desert. This ecological environment caused them to develop a completely different type of culture from that of other north-east African peoples, who are mostly highland-dwellers.

The Ethiopian empire's struggle for survival, 1529–1632: the Portuguese episode and the restoration of the empire after 1632

Between 1529 (the start of the *djihād*) and 1632 (the beginning of the Restora- tion) the Ethiopian empire was struggling for survival. It was not only a dramatic period politically and militarily but it was also a time of intense intellectual and cultural conflict, in which Ethiopia was assailed by ideas from another continent.

The Christian empire showed astonishing strength and capacity for survival in the face of pressure from external and internal enemies. It was during the time of the emperor Sartsa Dengel (1563–97), when the empire was more a fiction than a political reality, that the spiritual strength of the concept of the Holy Empire was forcefully demonstrated. The Turks were consolidating their power on the shores of the Red Sea, seizing all Ethiopian ports and penetrating deep into the Highlands to Tigré; in the central provinces of Bagemder and Samen, a bitter civil war was being waged against the Ethiopians of Jewish faith; and the Oromo invasion had assumed worrying proportions. Real state power may have been reduced to the area the emperor occupied with his troops, but the immortality of the 'evangelical empire' was apparently never in doubt.

The empire did, of course, suffer considerable losses of territory and popula- tion in this struggle for survival. From the Restoration of 1632, the great southward thrust, which had been the whole imperial policy of the preceding centuries, was scarcely pursued. As the imperial power steadily declined, efforts were concentrated on maintaining stability at the centre. The transfer of the emperor's residence to Gondar in 1636 is a sign of this withdrawal. Before this the emperors – in a country where towns were unknown – had moved their

24.3 *The castle at Gondar, the Ethiopian capital built by Emperor Fasiladas (© Werner Forman Archive, London)*

encampments to a different place every year or half year. This had been a hard-and-fast rule, followed even when there was no political or military necessity for undertaking a journey or change of residence. It was therefore not just a break with tradition but also a symbolic renunciation of the dynamic imperial policy of his predecessors when Fasiladas built a fixed residence in Gondar in 1636 after the last great civil wars of religion had ended. Gondar was to remain the centre of what was left of Christian Ethiopia until 1855.

Thus between 1529, the start of the *djihād*, and 1597, the death of the emperor Sartsa Dengel and the beginning of the civil wars, imperial policy was concentrated on defence. Emperor Galawdewos carried on the struggle against the Muslims, in particular those in the state of Adal-Harar, with great success. Former contacts with the south-west were renewed, the influence of Christian-Amharic culture was restored there and the Oromo were driven back, at least temporarily. Under the leadership of the *amīr* Nūr ibn Mugahid, the brave and politically gifted successor to Ahmād Grañ, the Adal-Harar Muslims once more attempted to confront the Christian empire. Although the poorly prepared Ethiopian army was beaten back in an attack on Adal in 1559 and the emperor Galawdewos fell on the field of battle, this marked the end of Islamic power. Within a few decades, the Islamic states and Islamic culture had disappeared from this region. There remained only the fortified town of Harar and the small sultanate of Awsa, in the Hawas river-delta oasis. Emperor Minas (1559–63) had mostly to fight the Turks who, from their bases in the Red Sea ports, tried repeatedly to establish a foothold in the Ethiopian Highlands. Sartsa Dengel (1563–97), Minas's son, who acceded to the throne while still a child, had to wage uninterrupted campaigns in all directions, as the Oromo allowed the empire no respite.

Wars of frightful violence were waged to annihilate the Ethiopians of Jewish faith in the northern Highlands, mainly in Samen, Waggara, Dambiya, Belasa, Sallamt and Sagade, where formerly they had enjoyed a certain autonomy. Their forebears had probably been converted to Judaism by Jewish missionaries in pre-Christian times. Unlike Jews in other parts of the world, they were completely integrated into the culture in which they lived, so much so that their holy books were not written in Hebrew but in Ge'ez, the Ethiopian literary and liturgical language.

It is not known why this religious war broke out at the very time when the empire was already hard-pressed by external enemies. As with the extirpation of the Christians by the Muslim armies of the *djihād* a generation earlier, this war is one of the darkest chapters in Ethiopian history. The Jews were faced with the choice of embracing Christianity or being exterminated. The Jewish population was practically wiped out, as the majority refused to be converted. The few survivors, stripped of their civil rights and dispossessed of their land, were forced to become artisans, and the word Falasha, used to describe Ethiopians of Jewish faith, came to be synonymous with smith, potter, carpenter or weaver, indeed with any type of skilled labourer. Despite the importance of these occupations, a stigma was attached to them in a society whose ideal was the free and independent man who never worked for a wage. Thus social degradation went hand-in-hand with religious persecution.

It is astonishing how the Ethiopian empire found the strength, despite almost three generations of unrelenting struggle, not only to confront the Turks in the north, the Adal Muslims in the east and the Oromo in the south and centre but also, in massive campaigns in the south-west, to force the large states of Inariya, Boša and Kaffa (Gomar) to become once more closely linked to the Ethiopian church and northern Ethiopian culture. The compiler of the *History of the Galla* reports how the emperor Sartsa Dengel offered to halve the Inariya tribute on condition that all became Christians. Under pressure from the emperor, but also mindful of the support to be expected against the Oromo, the king Badanco of Inariya decided to be baptized. The ceremony was performed with great solemnity for the king and all his people together. Shortly thereafter, the king of the Boša, neighbours of the Inariya, was in turn baptized. These events, which took place shortly before 1600, represent the swan-song of imperial expansion. We can conclude from oral traditions still surviving among south-west Ethiopian peoples that the contacts thus made during the time of Sartsa Dengel had a lasting and stimulating effect on southern Ethiopia and its cultural development.

Of far greater consequence for the empire, however, was the almost century-long ideological conflict with the Catholic Church from 1542 to 1632.

With the creation of the Society of Jesus (the Jesuits) in 1540, the Catholic Church acquired a very effective instrument not only for carrying on the Counter-Reformation in Europe, but also for converting the 'heathen' and restoring the 'heretical' Christian churches to the authority of Rome. Even before 1540, letters had been exchanged between the Portuguese kings and the Ethiopian emperors and these contacts were now seized upon. The decisive factor was, of course, the presence in Ethiopia of members of the Portuguese expeditionary force who had remained behind and their families. In 1557, Andrea da Oviedo was consecrated bishop and sent to Ethiopia with some other Portuguese Jesuits to prepare the work of reinstatement – that is, the union of the Orthodox Church with Rome. His discussions with the emperor Galawdewos provoked a brilliant exposé of the Ethiopian religion through the mouth of the emperor, which has gone down in history as Galawdewos' profession of faith.

Here a voice is raised for the first time in Africa pointing out that Christianity is a religion without limitations of time or place, about which no people can claim that its own interpretation is the only true one. Galawdewos shows that certain customs and practices of the Ethiopian Church are neither 'heathen' nor 'Jewish', but have their origins in Ethiopian folk culture, just as European culture has found expression in European Christendom.

Under emperor Sartsa Dengel the Jesuits were given Fremona, near Adwa in Tigré, as their centre. There they were allowed to live in complete freedom and to engage in missionary work. In 1603, Pedro Paez, a Spaniard, took over as head of the mission. He was undoubtedly the most outstanding missionary of the time, and also an unusually tolerant human being. Hence the Ethiopians engaged in the most stimulating theological discussions. To reach the people, the Church went so far as to conduct and record the religious discussions in Amharic. This innovation ceased after the Restoration of 1632 with the re-introduction of the official Church language, Ge'ez, which was as little under-stood by the mass of the Ethiopian population as was Latin by the European peasants of the time. The fruitful effect of this contact, however, was short-lived and the constructive debate soon turned into open enmity between Orthodox and Catholic factions.

Literary production in Ethiopia experienced a remarkable upsurge at this time, and the works written, mainly theological and historical, are among the most important in Ethiopian literature. Theological works that may be men-tioned are the *Fekkare Malakot* (Explanation of the Divinity), the *Mazgaba Haymanots* (Treasury of Faith) and the all-embracing *Haymanota Abaw* (Faith of the Fathers), translated from Coptic Arabic. For the reinstatement of those Christians who had temporarily embraced Islam, the *Mashafa Keder* (Book of Impurity) was written in connection with the atonement rites. Enbakom (Habakuk), an Arab Muslim converted to Christianity who rose to be leader of the Ethiopian clergy, wrote the remarkable book *Ankasa Amin* (Gates of the Faith), a defence of Christianity against Islam. Furthermore, with the translation of *Barla'am* and *Josaphat*, Enbakom made an important work of Eastern literature accessible to the Ethiopian people.

The three works or annals concerning the reigns of the emperors Galawde-wos, Sartsa Dengel and Susenyos and the short *History of the Galla* by the monk Bahrey are also numbered among the important literary productions of this period.

The accession of Susenyos (1607) marks the beginning of the decisive phase of the confrontation between the Ethiopian Orthodox Church and the Catholic Missionary Church. The head of the Jesuit Mission, Pedro Paez, theologian, preacher, teacher and architect, had had access to the imperial court and, under the influence of his strong personality, the emperor began to incline increasingly towards Catholicism. His influential brother, Ras Se'ela Krestos, officially turned Catholic in 1612 and set up a Catholic mission in his province of Gojjam. Despite the remonstrances of the *abuna* (the metropolitan of the Ethiopian Church), in 1632 the emperor himself also embraced the Catholic faith. Pedro Paez died shortly afterwards.

The confrontation between the two doctrines and civilizations, hitherto carried on with intellectual weapons and mutual respect, now turned into open war. Unlike his predecessor, Alphonso Mendez, the new Spanish bishop sent by the Pope, was bigoted and arrogant. Under the emperor's protection, Mendez began to set the Ethiopian Church on what he saw as the right path. All Ethiopian priests had to be re-ordained and all churches re-consecrated. The calendar was Europeanized; circumcision was forbidden; and all Ethiopians had to be re-baptized.

Revolt after revolt broke out against the hated new Church, being particularly

24.4 *Eighteenth-century Coptic painting on cloth of the Virgin and Child, Gondar (© Werner Forman Archive, Addis Ababa Museum)*

fierce in the central provinces of Bagemder, Lasta and Waǧ. The emperor, once so loved, who had brought peace to the land, now had to subdue his subjects in bloody wars during which the fanatical zealotry of the Jesuits increased tension still further. In 1632, there was a great battle from which the emperor emerged victorious, but the emperor was a broken man. He abdicated, restoring his subjects to the faith of their ancestors and asking the former clergy to return to their own liturgy.

Susenyos died shortly afterwards, and the Catholic mission came to an end. The people, insofar as they had adopted the new religion, returned in a body to the traditional faith. The new emperor, Fasiladas, had the Jesuits deported. The gradually dwindling number of Ethiopians who persisted in the Catholic faith were persecuted and their most prominent leaders, amongst them Ras Se'ela Krestos, were executed. Fasiladas went so far as to conclude an agreement with the Turkish governor of Massawa in which the governor undertook to kill any European missionaries landing at Massawa in exchange for head money. Thus ended, through the fault of the Europeans, a contact between Africa and Europe that had lasted almost a hundred years, at first rewarding, but later only negative.

The Ethiopian empire now began a period of deliberate isolation from the rest of the world and pursued a policy of stabilization that, by the end of century, turned into stagnation. The establishment of a permanent imperial residence at Gondar, in the militarily secure centre of the empire, was part of this process. It was no longer possible to pursue an aggressive and dynamic policy from Gondar. There is therefore little political activity to report in Christian Ethiopia during the second half of the seventeenth century. Under the emperor Yohannes (1667–82), the few remaining Catholic Ethiopians were given the choice of accepting the Orthodox faith or leaving the country. The Muslims still in Christian Ethiopia – mainly traders – were allowed to practise their religion freely but made to live in separate settlements.

Iyasu I (1682–1706) was the last of the great emperors. He undertook one last, unsuccessful attempt to re-establish contact with south-western Ethiopia and even visited Inariya. There were no internal or external enemies to endanger the empire. The important port of Massawa, although nominally belonging to the Turkish empire and under the control of a Bēdja governor, remained open for trade with Ethiopia. Shortly after Iyasu's death, however, the disintegration of the empire began, degenerating into complete anarchy after about 1755.

During this period, cultural life flourished for the last time under the patronage of the imperial court at Gondar. To a greater extent than ever, art and science proved to be the sphere of a small élite. It is not possible here to give a complete account of the different aspects of the intellectual life of the period. We shall therefore restrict our remarks to literature, architecture and painting.

In contrast to the previous century, literature lacked originality and took on an edifying and courtly character, with translations from Coptic Arabic predominating. Worthy of mention are *Faws Manfasawi* (Spiritual Medicine), a devotional book of penance, and the *Fetha Nagast* (Jurisdiction of the Monarchs), a collection of laws and instructions intended for the use of Coptic communities in Egypt. This period also saw the creation of a great many sacred hymns.

The graphic arts are marked by this relationship with court life. The famous rock churches, which are among the most original creations of Christian Ethiopian civilization, were still being hewn out of the rock at the end of the fifteenth century, but this type of construction ceased completely after 1500, presumably because of the religious wars. What appeared later, in Gondar and a few other places, was something completely different – huge castles, libraries, chapels and annexes to the palaces of the emperors and members of the imperial family. The form of these structures often indicates foreign models. Most were probably erected by Indo-Portuguese masons who came from Goa with the Portuguese mission. The gradual decline of the empire, the destruction of the city of Gondar by Tewodros and the dervishes, and centuries of neglect have completely robbed these buildings of their architectonic finery and their costly interior decoration. All that remains today is ruins or walls which give little idea of the level of civilization at the time.

Ethiopian painting expressed itself mainly in two media: church wall paintings and illuminations of religious books. While only little remains of the church murals before the seventeenth century, many manuscripts date back to the fourteenth century and clearly show the development of this sort of painting.

In about 1500, book illumination reached a peak that corresponded to the peak of Ethiopian Christian civilization. Independently of the text they illustrated, these paintings were intended to move onlookers through the force of their representation and strengthen them in their belief. The paintings of the second half of the sixteenth century and the early seventeenth are quite different in character. They reflect the multiplicity of foreign influences now penetrating Ethiopia. An illuminating example is the form of the crucifixion adopted by several Ethiopian painters – a copy of the famous woodcut, from the *Small Passion* by the German painter and illustrator Albrecht Dürer. All these pictures bear witness to the remarkable capacity of the Ethiopians for integrating foreign models into their own culture. They are also an expression of a turbulent age, characterized by conflict with foreign forms that did not easily fit the style of traditional Ethiopian art.

The pictures of the Restoration, the Gondar Period, finally stand out above all the others for their courtly elegance and graceful form. They reflect the slowly vanishing splendour of the empire and are painted for a society of courtiers who found delight in their elegant and increasingly conventional forms. In the so-called Second Gondar Period, from about 1700, the thrust of the artistic creation steadily diminishes and finally degenerates into a canon of repetitive forms.

South-western Ethiopia: the emergence of a new culture and new states

We are reasonably informed about contacts between south-west Ethiopia and the Christian empire to the north between 1500 and 1700 from Christian and Islamic written sources, but they do not enable us to determine the influence Christian Ethiopia actually had beyond political domination and exaction of tribute.

The oral traditions surviving in the Ethiopian south today provide a wealth of historical information which has unfortunately still not been fully recorded. Family trees, analyses of cultures and archaeological findings also give valuable clues and prove that northern influence on the south was so far-reaching as to cause the emergence of a new culture.

The cultural situation in southern Ethiopia before the fifteenth century, when influence began to be exerted by the north, can only be deduced today from the study of the contemporary culture of ethnic groups who remained untouched by this influence until recently. Such groups are to be found among the Gimira, Are or Dizi peoples, who still today lack state structures and sophisticated political institutions.

Before the steadily growing stimulus provided by the Christian empire to the north was able to bring about decisive changes, a great number of small clan groups must have lived side-by-side in the south, held together by nothing more than the sharing of a common language and culture, recognition of a common lineage and, perhaps, veneration of a high priest or elder, who embodied the religious affinities of the group. He was surrounded by a certain religious aura by virtue of his descent from the founder of the group and he was credited with supernatural powers, particularly over rain, crops and harvests. Compared with their overriding religious significance, the political functions of these dignitaries seem to have been almost non-existent. The real holders of political power were the clans and their leaders as autonomous, originally self-contained units.

The conquerors from the north with their rigid concepts of state and kingship swooped down upon this unsophisticated world of simple peasants. Conquest and assimilation often proceeded comparatively peacefully, the people of the south recognizing the cultural superiority of the north. Thus the conquest of what was later to become the important state of Wolayta is supposed to have been due to the political shrewdness of the invaders. In the battles, which involved small groups, instead of throwing spears at their opponents, the northerners threw fabrics, strings of beads or pieces of meat. 'If you are so rich and powerful that you can throw away such treasures', the Wolayta cried, 'then shall you also rule over us!' Thus the invaders took possession of a country, which under their influence, soon changed into a dynamic, aggressive state.

It was often accepted without question that monarchically-led states, which were better armed and possessed cavalry, originally unknown in the south, were superior to the democratically organized communities. There are therefore reports of groups voluntarily surrendering to the invaders and accepting the leaders as their new rulers.

In this way a whole series of new states came into being, states that were never to forget their links with the north, whose ruling classes faithfully preserved and developed the traditions and institutions of the north.

In addition to the purely external, formal structure of state organization and court life, the myth of the Ethiopian empire also made its mark. It claimed that they were the chosen people and theirs the true kingdom, and intended to subjugate and assimilate all neighbouring peoples. The history of southern

Ethiopia, as it is known from 400 years of oral tradition, is the story of the expansion of these newly created states which widened their spheres of domination at the expense of independent smaller groups and often contributed to the founding of new dynasties among their neighbours. This process worked in a chain reaction. Thus, according to oral tradition, the first Gonga state, Inariya, was founded before 1500 by an immigrant from Tigré. In the sixteenth and seventeenth centuries, members of the Busaso dynasty of Inariya founded further dominions: Boša, which was absorbed into the Oromo kingdom of Gimma in the nineteenth century, Kaffa, which is reputed to have been the most powerful state in all south-eastern Ethiopia for generations, and Šekko (Močča) in the virgin forest on the western edge of the Ethiopian Highlands.

Oral tradition has it that the kingdom of Gangero was originally founded by Islamic migrants from Arabia. Later an originally Christian dynasty from Gondar assumed rule. Similar accounts survive concerning the area occupied by the Ometo: in Dawāro another group of migrants priding themselves on their Gondar origin succeeded, after years of struggle, in uniting many small groups of indigenous inhabitants into a powerful state. In about 1600, Wolayta was conquered by the descendants of one Sum Tamben from Tigré. Other states, both large and small, have similar traditions. Members of the Gošanaa dynasty, probably also of northern Ethiopian origin, founded a total of ten dominions.

In southern Ethiopia, the social structure was originally characterized by the coexistence and mutual acceptance of free and equal people. Only religious leaders and warrior heroes enjoyed a few privileges. But in the newly-created states under the influence of the hierarchical concepts of the Christian north, things were quite different. Equality was replaced by a complicated hierarchical system of ranks. At the summit stood the sacred king, inaccessible and often invisible to his subjects. His hallowed family enjoyed special privileges, often occupying the most important state offices. The exaggerated pomp and ceremony of the royal households was often in flagrant disproportion to the small size of the country and population. As the kingdoms expanded, so did the royal households, developing into independent, powerful institutions with hundreds of members. They were in sharp contrast to the former high priests or clan leaders who had lived by their own labour and that of their families and voluntary gifts from others.

The scale a royal court could attain is illustrated by Wolayta to the north of Lake Abbaya. Here, the royal court was not only the centre of political life but also a sacral district, protected by a multitude of ritual and ceremonial laws. If the king appeared in public, it was only at a proper distance from the crowd or surrounded by his followers. The royal court was protected by three ramparts and three gates, each one triply secured. Only the king could slaughter animals on the soil of his hallowed residence, or indeed exercise any kind of sexual activity. Therefore the pages who took direct care of the king's person were sexually innocent, forbidden just as strictly as the pages of the Christian Ethiopian emperor to leave the royal court and come into contact with other people. The ground covered by the royal court was so hallowed that sexual intercourse between a man – other than the king – and a woman would have resulted in the death of the offenders and the transfer of the palace to a new site.

Under northern influence, the royal insignia were transformed. These had formerly been symbolic objects, simple in material and form, such as sacred spears, two-pronged forks or grass rope. Their place was now taken by rings, mostly finger or arm rings, fashioned in the two precious metals, gold and silver, which were the mark of royalty in High Ethiopia.

This High Ethiopian influence also had far-reaching effects on the whole social structure. Although most southern Ethiopians were members of a single homogeneous class, a sophisticated system of ranks developed after the High Ethiopian pattern, which found its most marked expression in the worth complex that extended over all Ethiopia. Worth was not inheritable like riches or a respected name, but had to be earned anew by every man so that he could find his publicly recognized place in society. The central criteria were success in war and big-game hunting, and the warrior's obligation to kill. Only a person who earned worth could aspire to one of the innumerable elected offices, the holding of which was the decisive criterion for a man's status. Name and rank were often designated by the same word, and to lack a name was synonymous with social failure. Here again the influence of the north is obvious, for the names of the ranks are borrowings from the Amharic or Tigrai languages.

The free peasants were followed in the hierarchy by the artisans, who were members of specific castes and who occupied a comparatively lowly position. Despite their great economic importance, they were nevertheless looked down upon. They could not own land, and were subjected to demeaning regulations, and physical contact with them was considered to be defiling for people of higher birth.

In the lowest position came the slaves, who, in many countries, made up more than a third of the total population. Most lived as serfs on their masters' fields, but could own property. It was their labour and their productivity that made possible the formation of a rich dominant class which, in Wolayta for example, was the driving force in the great wars of conquest.

All these states had well-educated administrators, elected by the people and confirmed in their positions by the king. The states were divided into communities, districts and provinces. They had public markets, supervised by the state, and a good road infrastructure. They were protected against external enemies by great ramparts and walls with carefully guarded gates.

The material advances brought from the north to the south since the fourteenth century are many. Curiously enough, the plough, the most important agricultural implement in the north, never gained acceptance in the south. Agriculture is, however, indebted to the north for a considerable number of imported crops. It was probably not until after the fourteenth or fifteenth century that peas, broad beans, chickpeas, onions and garlic reached the south. Later came lentils and various oilseeds, including linseed, sesame, safflower and nogo, all from the Near East. Later came the plants of the New World brought from America to Africa in post-Columbian times, probably by the Portuguese.

Of these, red pepper, maize and tobacco are of such significance today that it is hard to imagine life in southern Ethiopia without them. Pumpkin, sweet potato, potato and tomato spread to a lesser extent.

Even today, the techniques used by the descendants of the artisans from the north still bear witness to the impetus they gave this sector: treadle-loom weaving, goldsmithing and silversmithing with sophisticated tools, leatherwork with needles and fine woodwork for the production of door panels, wooden platters and large bowls. Finally, the introduction to the south of the horse should be mentioned, although it was without economic significance, being used only in battle and as a prestige symbol.

Let us now turn to the influence of Christianity: was it strong enough to have a permanent effect on the south and provide a lasting drive? Even today it is clear that the cultural influence was very strong, its vestiges still being visible as far as the borders of Kenya and Sudan. It is more difficult to assess the impact of Christianity on the moral system of individual folk cultures, on customs and usage and spiritual life in general.

The most striking Christian monuments in this area, by no means rich in durable man-made works, are the many sacred groves, mainly on hills and mountain tops, marking the sites of former Christian churches as their names indicate: *Kitosa* (Christ), *Mairamo* (Mary), or *Gergisa* (George). The materials used to build them were perishable and all have disappeared. However, their sites are still regarded as sacred and the descendants of the former Christian priests, who have become members of non-Christian clans, still perform ceremonies that are variants on the sacrifice of the Mass.

How strongly Christianity as a religious entity, not just as a collection of rites, influenced the essence of southern Ethiopian religious ethics has not yet been thoroughly investigated. The exceptionally important role of Mary, a role that relegates Jesus Christ to the background, also needs investigation. The function of Mary as a helpful and forgiving deity, particularly well disposed towards women, can be seen in both north and south Ethiopia.

As regards external forms, an astonishing number of Christian laws and ceremonies survived in the south until recently, when the Ethiopian Orthodox Church resumed missionary activity. Fasting on specific days survived, as did observance of the Sabbath, when all work in the fields was prohibited, at least for the successors of former Christian priests. The seven-day Christian week, regulating the frequency of markets, continued to be observed. Christian Sundays have now become public holidays on which the *kesigas* (successors of the Christian priests) gather their congregations together and in truncated ritual invoke God, Christ and Mary, make the sign of the cross and burn grain instead of incense. Among the great Christian holidays, the Feast of the Holy Cross (27 September) became the New Year feast, with the exorcising of devils and a great folk festival. Christmas and Epiphany – of such importance in the north – were celebrated only by a few groups in the south, while Easter became the day of the great ritual hunt.

East Africa: the coast

The sixteenth, seventeenth and eighteenth centuries opened with the arrival of the Portuguese in East African waters and closed with the attempts by the Omani Arabs to establish some kind of overlordship on the littoral. In those three centuries, the coastal towns and peoples experienced important economic, social and political changes.

The coast at the beginning of the sixteenth century

In 1500, the coast was still enjoying its golden age. The surviving ruins and material culture of the fifteenth and sixteenth centuries conjure up a general picture of prosperity. A closer look reveals differing degrees of economic and material well-being.

Kilwa, which was growing in the fifteenth century thanks to the control of the Sofalan gold trade which it had held since the early fourteenth century, was experiencing the first signs of decline on the eve of Portuguese intervention. By the end of the fifteenth century, Kilwa had lost control over Sofala, and its political influence was declining on the coast to the north, an area of commercial importance to it. Internally, the rapid succession of rulers – 13 between 1442 and 1498 – was symptomatic of a political malaise that sapped its vitality, whilst its bad relations with Zanzibar reflected a recurrent weakness of Swahili towns – internal dissension encouraging intervention by outside forces.

By 1454, Zanzibar was attempting to impose its nominee on the throne of Kilwa. At this time, Zanzibar was not, however, a leading coastal town politically or economically. It was itself divided into at least five settlements, each with its own ruler. Mombasa, however, ranked with Kilwa and Malindi as a leading city-state. Its merchants played an important role in the commerce of the southern coast as far as Angoche. The island town had also established trade links with its hinterland in honey, wax and ivory, which may explain Mombasa's sudden rise until, by the time the Portuguese came, it had become 'the most powerful city-state on the coast' (E. A. Alpers, 1975).

Malindi, Mombasa's arch-rival, was also prosperous by 1500. Its trade was based largely on the export of ivory and, secondarily, of such goods as beeswax,

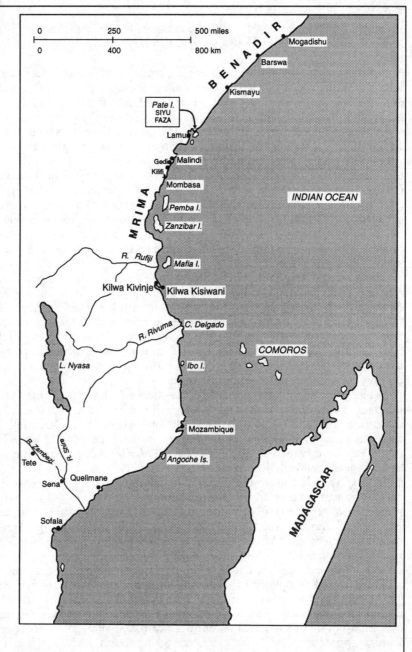

25.1 *The East African coast (after A. I. Salim)*

ambergris and gum copal. Unlike most other settlements in the region, Malindi, even in the sixteenth century, had large plantations of millet and rice worked by slaves.

Further north, petty sultanates were to be found in the Lamu archipelago which were in a state of virtually permanent conflict and so unable to present a united front against the Portuguese invaders. Lamu town existed on its present site by the mid-1300s, but it was to flourish only after 1650.

In between these major commercial settlements were numerous smaller ones which often fell within the sphere of influence of one or other of the big city-states. The larger towns looked more towards international maritime trade than the smaller ones, which depended on agriculture and fishing. The number of settlements proliferated between 1200 and 1500, the coast's golden age.

It is difficult to estimate the size of these settlements in terms of area and population. Malindi is said to have had a population of approximately 3,500 in 1498, based on the occupation of some 1,000 stone houses, but this figure obviously does not include the plantation labourers or the poor, who probably lived in mud-and-thatch huts.

The political fragmentation of the coast was much compensated for by religious and cultural homogeneity, which was well-established by 1500. African, Arab and Shīrāzī ethnic groups intermingled to varying degrees to form a new cultural group known later as the Swahili (people of the coast). Swahili is a generic term which the coastal people applied to themselves only later. In the 1500s, they merely formed urban groups whose élite and ruling families, for reasons of prestige, often claimed dubious, Arabian or Shīrāzī origins, even if they were ethnically mixed.

While the coast was politically fragmented and its people came from different groups, a number of features brought them together. The most important were the common African denominator and the Kiswahili language that was soon to evolve into the *lingua franca* of the coast. Other important influences were Islam and, to a lesser degree, Arab influence, although the latter became dominant only in the nineteenth century.

In fact, Swahili culture is a regional example of Islamic culture. It is regional because it was influenced by the indigenous East African culture which, to a significant degree, was incorporated into it. Although Kiswahili adopted a large number of Arabic words over the years, it is the most important single manifestation of the African contribution to Swahili culture. Others, by no means insignificant, include rituals related to birth and marriage, funerary and investiture ceremonies for chiefs, a belief in spirits and traditional dances.

The material prosperity of some coastal towns in 1500 was very impressive. The rulers lived in palaces and the élite in stone dwellings, with elaborately carved wooden doors. The townspeople's high standard of living is reflected in the importation of such luxury items as damasks, silks, satins, copper objects, Chinese porcelain and Middle Eastern glass vessels and glass beads. Only a minority lived in luxury, however, while the poor and enslaved majority lived in mud-and-thatch huts.

The populations of these settlements were predominantly African, with a minority of Arabs whose numbers increased substantially in the eighteenth and nineteenth centuries. Rulers may have carried legitimate Arab dynastic names, but they were invariably of mixed descent and often black. Colour was of no social or political consequence: it was the *ukoo* (lineage) that distinguished someone and indicated his place in society and his degree of belonging.

The Portuguese intrusion

The Portuguese, like their Spanish neighbours in the Iberian peninsula, embarked upon their voyages of exploration with the din of battle against the Muslims still ringing in their ears. The motives behind the Portuguese expeditions were to outflank Islam commercially, politically, militarily and religiously – to break the Mamluk (later Ottoman) monopoly of the trade routes to Asia and China and to link up with other Christians to eradicate Muslim rule wherever it was found.

Prince Henry, Grand Master of the Order of Christ, was the man behind Portuguese strategy, and a series of expeditions was embarked upon to put his plan into effect. In January 1498, Vasco da Gama's fleet reached the southernmost fringes of the Swahili coast at the mouth of the Quelimane river, where the Portuguese found an Afro-Arab settlement that was in touch with the sought-after lands of the East, namely, the island and town of Mozambique, which had fallen under the influence of Kilwa. The *shaykh* there welcomed them until he discovered they were not Muslims, after which mutual suspicion led to the first skirmishes between coastal Muslims and Portuguese. Vasco da Gama's reception in Mombasa was hostile because news of the Mozambique skirmishes had preceded him. In contrast, the *shaykh* of Malindi greeted him warmly. The two sides formed an alliance and the *shaykh* of Malindi acquired Mombasa with Portuguese assistance at the close of the sixteenth century.

Vasco da Gama's first voyage was successful in its objective of reaching India. It had also yielded valuable intelligence concerning Muslim trade on the Swahili coast, and the wealth of Swahili towns like Mozambique, Mombasa and Malindi had impressed the Portuguese. This largely exploratory voyage was followed by others. One, in 1501, gave the Portuguese a glimpse of Kilwa's size but its *shaykh*, Ibrāhīm, would not be persuaded to co-operate with them in establishing a trading agency in Sofala.

They therefore decided to use force, and the following year, to the accompaniment of the sound of guns, Vasco da Gama's vessels sailed into Kilwa harbour and, under the threat of the destruction of his town, Ibrāhīm agreed to the payment of an annual tribute and to become a vassal of the Portuguese king. In 1503, Ruy Lourenço Ravasco indulged in plunder and piracy around Zanzibar, before landing there and using force to impose tribute. In 1505, on the pretext that the town was behind in the payment of tribute and had not hoisted the Portuguese flag as a sign of allegiance, Kilwa was attacked by Dom Francesco de Almeida, later viceroy of India. Exploiting the factional rivalries, he installed a pro-Portuguese elder, Muḥammad Ankoni, as ruler and, at Kilwa's expense, work was started on building Portugal's first fort on the Swahili coast.

Mombasa had shown hostility towards Vasco da Gama in 1498, and in August 1505 greeted de Almeida's fleet with fire from a cannon recovered from a sunken Portuguese ship. The king of Mombasa and his people put up a determined resistance to the Portuguese, but eventually the king was forced to surrender. The town was looted and burnt before the fleet departed. It seems that the Portuguese aim was to break the power of Mombasa in order to enhance that of Kilwa, which was to be their stronghold.

As an indication that Portuguese actions were blatantly punitive, in 1528 Mombasa was attacked again and occupied for some four months. This short occupation, which ended in the town being razed, gained the Portuguese nothing but the loss of many lives through fighting and disease.

Sixteen years earlier, in 1512, the Portuguese had been compelled to vacate their fort in Kilwa. By then the Portuguese had been made to realize that there were limits to how much tribute the town could pay and that that sum barely covered the cost of maintaining a garrison. They had hoped to monopolize the Sofalan gold trade, but had only succeeded in disrupting it with their ill-considered interventions and commercial controls. By 1506, the garrison in Sofala, stricken by disease, was no longer functioning, and in 1512, the Kilwa garrison was transferred to India.

With the departure of the Portuguese, Kilwa's trade improved significantly, although the ruler remained nominally a vassal of the Portuguese crown. The town's commercial pattern underwent an interesting change. Its traders now avoided Portuguese-controlled Sofala and sought greater contacts with the Angoche coast south of Mozambique which had long-established commercial ties with the Zambezi hinterland. Their aim was to undermine Portuguese control of Sofala, and it was to forestall this that the Portuguese ventured inland and established themselves at Sena and Tete.

Kilwa had been heavily dependent on the trade in gold and ivory that its traders brought from Zimbabwe, as it had little to export itself. Once Sofala was lost, Kilwa had to develop trade links with the interior, and ivory became its most important export. This reorientation of Kilwa trade coincided with the expansion of the Maravi and the Yao.

In conclusion, then, the Portuguese failed to devise a clear-cut policy of occupation or administration on the Swahili coast. They had only a mercenary desire to monopolize all commercial traffic. Even in this they were only partially successful. Because Portuguese occupation was so brief, the Swahili towns managed to continue their commercial activities.

Many say that, from the outset, Portuguese interests really lay beyond in the East, the Swahili coast being considered as only an appendage of the *Estado da India* (state of India), headquartered at Goa where the Portuguese viceroy resided. However, the Portuguese appointed a 'Captain of the Sea of Malindi' with a few small ships at his disposal to patrol the East African coast, and he also had the job of issuing passes to vessels and running the Portuguese trading factory at Malindi. This factory imported cotton and beads from India which it exchanged for local goods such as gum-copal, ambergris, ivory and coir: it is proof of Portuguese interest in the African trade both on the coast and inland.

Until the advent of the Turkish expeditions in the later 1500s, sources give only the scantiest information about the Swahili coast. It seems that a politico-economic compromise had been imposed by circumstances: Swahili towns remained independent so long as no conflict of interest arose with the Portuguese. Some towns suffered more than others. Mombasa recovered well from the destruction wrought by the Portuguese in the guise of reprisals, and in 1569 was described by Father Monclaro as 'large and populous'; but he found Kilwa almost deserted, though still trading in ivory with the Comoros and the interior. By this time, a factor whose impact is even harder to gauge than that of the Portuguese had entered the picture: population movements in the hinterland and their effect on the Swahili towns.

From the moment they had entered the Indian Ocean, the Portuguese had aroused the hostility of not only the local Muslim rulers but also the Mamluks of Egypt. With the defeat of the Mamluks by the Ottomans in 1517, leadership in the struggle against the Portuguese intruder passed to the Turkish sultan in Constantinople. Several battles took place on the west coast of India and in the Persian Gulf. Then, in 1570–71, an insurrection broke out in the Portuguese stronghold of Hormuz, whose inhabitants had called for Ottoman help. The uprising was suppressed, but its example was followed by other towns.

The king of Portugal had advised the viceroy at Goa to put an end to the misconduct of Portuguese officials on the Swahili coast about which the Swahili *shaykhs* had sent complaints. The king had feared that these leaders would seek Turkish help to free themselves from the Portuguese yoke. Events were to demonstrate that these fears were well-founded. When Mir 'Alī Bey appeared in 1585, with a single galley, he was warmly welcomed by all Swahili towns between Mogadishu and Kilwa except Malindi. He left with a promise to return with a stronger force, after collecting booty and taking prisoner some 50 Portuguese soldiers in Lamu. The Portuguese responded with a punitive expedition directed particularly at Faza and Mombasa. True to his promise, in 1588 Mir 'Alī Bey returned with five ships and, once again, won the support of most towns, except Malindi, which put up only token resistance. When 'Alī Bey began to implement his plan to make Mombasa a Turkish base, the Portuguese responded by sending a bigger fleet in January 1589.

The threat of Portuguese retribution coincided with the arrival of the cannibalistic Zimba from the interior, who threatened Mombasa. The towns-people and their Turkish deliverers found themselves caught between two enemies. The destruction of the Turkish fleet by the Portuguese allowed the Zimba access to the island, where they went on a rampage of destruction. The Zimba then proceeded northwards and it was only the fact that the Segeju stemmed their advance that saved Malindi from a similar fate. Meanwhile, the Portuguese expedition sailed north and wreaked vengeance on Lamu, which paid dearly for supporting the Turks. The *shaykh* and several other notables were taken to Pate and beheaded in the presence of the sultans of Pate, Faza and Siyu.

To what extent the destruction wreaked by the Zimba, like that of the Oromo later, contributed to the depopulation and decline of some Swahili towns is difficult to gauge. Mombasa seems to have been sufficiently weakened for her erstwhile enemy, Malindi, to take the town with the help of the Segeju. Thus ended the reign of the Mombasa Shīrāzī dynasty that had put up continued resistance to Portuguese overlordship. It was replaced by the sultan Aḥmad, the ruler of Malindi, who was thus rewarded for his loyalty to the Portuguese. But the long-term effect of the transfer to Mombasa of the captain of the Portuguese garrison, together with Malindi's royal residence, was the gradual decline of Malindi itself, which continued until the second half of the nineteenth century.

Kilifi, a town between Mombasa and Malindi, also played a role at this time. The rulers of Mombasa and Kilifi are said to have been related. Soon after the Zimba onslaught, Kilifi seems to have fought Malindi for Mombasa, possibly on the basis of the dynastic links between the two dynasties, possibly through mere ambition. Malindi complained of Kilifi's raids and decided to put an end both to Kilifi's provocations and also to its claims to Mombasa. After this defeat, Kilifi seems to have suffered an irreversible decline.

The two Turkish expeditions had revealed the fragility of the Portuguese hold on the Swahili coast. To strengthen it, the Portuguese decided to erect a fortress in Mombasa and place a garrison there. Fort Jesus was built in 1593–4 and a garrison of 100 men was placed there under a captain whose jurisdiction stretched from Brava in the north to Cape Delgado in the south. But the strengthening of the Portuguese presence in Mombasa does not appear to have led to any significant change in the administration of the rest of the Swahili coast. Elsewhere, their presence remained minimal and payment of tribute was all they expected from the town rulers. The Mombasa garrison made it easier for the Portuguese to react quickly to any attempts at resistance and revolts which might arise. In 1603, the ruler of Pate rose up in arms for which he was condemned and executed. But this punishment did not prevent subsequent uprisings by Pate and other towns.

Human dispersal and resettlement along the coast

Several important developments took place during the seventeenth century. One was the entry of the Dutch and British into the Indian Ocean to challenge the Portuguese. Another was the deterioration of relations between the Portuguese and the new rulers of Mombasa, their traditional allies. A third was the human dispersal and resettlement along the coast, which led to the emergence of new groups.

Increased insecurity, arising largely from the pressure of the Oromo, led to the movement of Swahili groups from the north to the southern towns. Pemba and Mombasa both acquired immigrants, and it was during this period that the ancestors of the nine nations (Miji-Kenda) of Mombasa settled on the island.

Vumba Kuu developed further and became an independent state in the seventeenth century.

Equally important was the dispersal south from Shungwaya (or Singwaya) of groups which later developed into the Miji-Kenda peoples and the Pokomo. According to T. T. Spear, different groups moved south from Shungwaya and settled in fortified villages (*makaya*; sing. *kaya*) on the hills overlooking the Swahili towns between Malindi and just south of Mombasa. In time, the *makaya* became more than mere havens of security from the Oromo and, later, the Maasai. They came to occupy a major place in the socio-religious life of the Miji-Kenda which outlasted the days of the fortified villages.

The conflict between Portugal and Mombasa

The amicable relations between the Portuguese and Sultan Aḥmad lasted only three or so years after the transfer of the seat of government to Mombasa. The captain of Mombasa was not honouring the administrative and fiscal agreements made with his ally. The sultan complained of obstacles placed on Mombasa's commerce and shipping. He also asked for recognition as ruler of Pemba, which he seems to have conquered with his own forces. Finally, Sultan Aḥmad was given Pemba, but only on lease, his annual payment being 300-500 sacks of rice.

After Sultan Aḥmad had died in 1609, his son, al-Ḥasan, found himself at loggerheads with the new Portuguese captain, Manuel de Mello Pereira. Relations between them became so bad that the sultan sought refuge in Arabaja, rather than submit to a decision to be tried at Goa. At first the Musungolos (mainland Africans) gave him refuge, but later treacherously killed him in return for pieces of cloth offered by the Portuguese.

Lisbon was not party to this treachery and, to make amends, insisted that al-Ḥasan's son Yūsuf be made ruler after a period of education in Goa. There, Yūsuf was converted to Christianity and given a Portuguese-Asian wife. When he returned to Mombasa in 1630, neither the Mombasans nor the Portuguese would accept him. In August 1631, the Portuguese captain, Pedro Leitão de Gamboa, decided that Yūsuf's habit of praying at his murdered father's tomb in the Muslim fashion amounted to renunciation of the Christian faith verging on treason, and planned to ship him back to Goa for trial. Yūsuf decided to fight.

On 15 August 1631, during the Portuguese celebration of the Feast of the Assumption, he made a surprise entry into Fort Jesus with his followers, and all but a handful of the Portuguese were massacred. Yūsuf saw his dramatic return to Islam as the beginning of a *djihād* to oust the Portuguese from the whole coast. But his call was not heeded and no other town would support him. Disheartened by his isolation, he left for Arabia – probably to enlist Turkish help.

When this was not forthcoming, Yūsuf returned to the coast, where he provoked minor uprisings until his death in 1637. The most rebellious region was the Lamu archipelago, and the Portuguese had to undertake a punitive expedition in 1636–7 to subdue Faza, Lamu, Manda and Pate.

Anglo-Dutch intruders

The appearance of the Dutch and English in the area had already contributed to the decline of Portuguese supremacy by the time of Yūsuf's revolt. The Dutch had long been involved in the Eastern trade as agents, shipping to other parts of Europe colonial goods brought to Lisbon. But when Spain and Portugal were united in 1580, the Spanish king sought to cut out the Dutch, who had been fighting since 1566 to liberate themselves from Spanish over-lordship. This determined the Dutch to reach the East independently and, by the end of the sixteenth century, their ships were challenging the Portuguese in the Indian Ocean.

The English, meanwhile, had embarked upon piratical raids on Spanish ships since 1580, when unity between the two Iberian powers made Portuguese interests in the Indian Ocean legitimate targets. Before the turn of the century, English ships had rounded the Cape of Good Hope. In 1591, one landed in Zanzibar before proceeding to India, and in 1608, another dropped anchor at Pemba. Thenceforth, the Portuguese had to fight these European invaders in the Persian Gulf, along the Malabar coast of India and around Sri Lanka. Neither the Dutch nor the English sought to replace the Portuguese by permanently occupying any East African town. Stop-overs in Zanzibar and Pemba were for provisions and water supplies only. Nevertheless, Anglo-Dutch harassment stretched Portuguese resources, and when the English took to helping the local inhabitants against their overlords, the situation deteriorated.

Although officially at peace with Spain and Portugal, in 1622 several English ships helped the Shah of Persia drive the Portuguese from their strategic entrepôt of Hormuz. The Portuguese fell back on Muscat, one of the Omani coastal towns they had dominated since the early sixteenth century. As at Mombasa, soon after the Turkish raids in 1588, the Portuguese had built a fort there as an entrepôt for the Indian–Persian Gulf trade.

The end of Portuguese rule in East Africa

Soon after the fall of Hormuz to the Persians, a new dynasty, the Ya'rubi dynasty, came to power in Oman, determined to liberate the country from the Portuguese yoke. Between 1640 and 1650, the Portuguese were forced by military defeats to demolish their fortresses and evacuate Muscat. With control over their own coastline, the rulers of Oman used their seasoned seafaring inhabitants to build a strong naval force that started challenging the Portuguese beyond the Gulf.

With the recapture of Mombasa after Yūsuf's revolt, the Portuguese decided to stay and rule the town directly. Pate seems to have entered a period of prosperity during this time which led the Portuguese to establish a custom-house there in 1633. But the town's trade was making Pate too powerful; the Portuguese decided to intervene, and relations between the two deteriorated. Meanwhile, complaints against the Portuguese from other towns, such as Siyu,

Pemba and Otondo, reached not only Lisbon but also the new rulers of Oman who were asked for help.

What followed was a prolonged period of struggle during the second half of the seventeenth century between the Portuguese and the Omani Arabs in East African waters. In 1652, an Omani expedition attacked the Portuguese in Zanzibar. The Portuguese retaliated by driving away the queen of Zanzibar and her son, the ruler of Otondo, for encouraging the Omani Arabs. In 1660, a combined fleet from Oman and Pate landed in Mombasa and sacked the Portuguese quarter seemingly without any serious opposition. Other Omani raids were made as far south as Mozambique (1669). In August 1678, the viceroy himself led a major expedition against 'Pate the swaggering'. He was joined by the ruler of neighbouring Faza, which was involved in its local squabbles with Pate. The expedition was forced to withdraw on the appearance of Omani ships in January 1679, but the allies had had the time to seize the rulers of Pate, Siyu, Lamu and Manda, who were then beheaded, together with several other notables. Pate seems not to have admitted defeat, as other expeditions were sent against it, in 1687 for example.

An attempt was made to reach a compromise agreement whereby the s̲h̲aykh of Pate would retain his throne in return for accepting Portuguese overlordship. But this provisional agreement reached in Goa was repudiated by Lisbon. By then, Pate had fallen to the Omanis and, on Christmas Day, the captive ruler and his councillors were killed in an attempt to escape from captivity in Panjim.

For some years, civil strife at home interrupted the Omani raids on Portuguese positions in East Africa. When they were resumed, their target was Pemba, which had revolted against the Portuguese. In 1694, however, the Portuguese managed to suppress the revolt and expel the Omani Arabs. But the following year came the greatest challenge from Oman. In March 1696, seven Omani ships, carrying 3,000 men and the s̲h̲aykh of Lamu, landed in Mombasa. They easily occupied the town and the island before laying siege to Fort Jesus until December 1698, when the fortress surrendered. When the Portuguese expedition from Goa arrived in Mombasa in November 1698, with orders to engage the enemy, the red flag of Oman was already flying over the fort.

From 1728 to 1729 the Portuguese managed a brief return to Mombasa, taking advantage of the scanty Omani presence on the coast and of Swahili disillusionment in some towns with the Arabs. There is no doubt that the ruler of Pate was at odds with the Arab garrison in his town. When a faction rose against him, supported by the Omanis, the ruler finally sought support from Goa late in 1727. From Pate the Portuguese expedition moved against Mombasa, where the Omani garrison in the fort had called for help from the king of Pate against other Arab garrisons guarding smaller forts on the island. Mombasa and its fort surrendered to the joint Portuguese-Patean forces.

But the return of the Portuguese and the Portuguese-Patean alliance was short-lived. The ruler of Pate had been so anxious for help against his rivals and their Arab supporters that he had promised Portugal more than he could deliver, such as the payment of tribute and the monopoly of the ivory trade. Within six months, he was in conflict with them. In June 1729, an armed clash finally convinced the Portuguese that they should withdraw from Pate.

By then, trouble was brewing for the Portuguese in Mombasa. A combined force of Mombasans and Musungulos attacked Portuguese positions in the town and laid siege to the small garrison in the fort. In November 1729, the garrison surrendered and was allowed to sail to Mozambique. Other towns, including Zanzibar, Pemba and Mafia, had followed Mombasa's lead, murdering or driving out the Portuguese.

The Swahili towns themselves, therefore, were responsible for the final expulsion of the Portuguese. But soon after they had left, Pate and Mombasa were once again occupied by the Omanis, and the Swahili coast entered a new era in its history.

The Portuguese defeat has been credited to a variety of factors: their weak, confused colonial system; the ineptitude and greed of officials; the harsh vagaries of the climate and disease among an already small Portuguese population; and the local factional struggles, now working for the Portugese now against them. Towards the end of the period, Portuguese resources were overstretched and an expeditionary force hard to muster.

These military activities took place amidst significant political, economic and cultural developments on the littoral. In the southern part of the coast there developed an important trade between the Yao and Kilwa, which by the end of the seventeenth century was dominated by a thriving trade in ivory. This trade suffered a temporary setback in the early 1700s when the Portuguese lost Mombasa to the Omanis. As a result, the Yao diverted their ivory from Kilwa to Mozambique. But the advent of the Būsaʿidi dynasty in Oman in the mid-1700s ushered in another period of revival for Kilwa.

Further north, Vumba Kuu had consolidated its position and its ruler had taken the title of *diwani*. Its Sharīfite ruling family, the Bā-ʿAlawī, had adopted a number of local Bantu customs which it combined with Islamic rites. The Segeju and one of the Miji-Kenda groups, the Digo, who had settled nearby, entered into close relations with Vumba Kuu. The religious influence of the Sharīfite families who ruled Vumba Kuu helped convert them to Islam, but they retained aspects of their religious beliefs, including the rain-making ceremonies.

In the Lamu archipelago, Pate was at its zenith in the seventeenth century and into the eighteenth. Its prosperity was based on maritime trade, which it exploited at a time when other towns such as Malindi, Mombasa and Kilwa had recently suffered attacks by inland peoples such as the Zimba. Pate established profitable relations with the Oromo, who provided the town with hides for export, and it also traded in ivory from the mainland. The historical sources do not adequately explain its seemingly rapid decline during the second half of the eighteenth century.

The Omani factor in East Africa

The decline of Pate forms the subject of one of the greatest *tenzi* (epic poems) in Kiswahili, *Al-Inkishafi*. Its author, Sayyid ʿAbdallah bin ʿAli bin Nāzir, was a member of the Shārīfite élite of Pate. The *sharīfs* who had settled in Pate became indigenized, and with the *sharīfs* of Lamu came to play a key role in the development of Swahili literary and religious tradition. The methods of teaching Islam, the manuals used, the cult of the saints, the veneration of *sharīfs* and the form and content of poetic verse constitute the cultural legacy of these descendants of the Prophet Muḥammad, who settled not only in the Lamu archipelago but also elsewhere on the coast and formed the main part of its religious intelligentsia.

The Omanis contributed significantly towards the economic resurgence of Kilwa, as did the slave trade. Together with the ivory trade, the slave trade was to dominate the economic history of the east coast for much of the nineteenth century. The trade developed initially to supply the French with the slaves they needed, after 1735, for their plantations in the Mascarene Islands: Ile-de-France (Mauritius) and Ile Bourbon (Réunion). Initially, the French purchased their slaves at Portuguese-controlled Mozambique and Kerimba Islands. But Mozambique's domination began to decline in the mid-1700s, partly because of the challenge from Swahili and Arab merchants who had increased their activities along the coast after the Būsaʿidi dynasty had strengthened its grip on the throne of Oman. Kilwa once again became a major trading centre to which mainland African slave and ivory traders were drawn.

By 1785, Mozambique's domination of the ivory trade in Central and East Africa had almost ended, although it continued to thrive on the slave trade, owing to the increasing demand of the French Indian Ocean colonies. Yao traders sold more and more slaves and ivory to Kilwa, which became a great emporium for sought-after Omani or Indian imported goods, such as Surat cloth. By the 1780s, Swahili or Swahilized traders were making pioneering trading ventures into the interior beyond Lake Malawi.

Politics and trade were often two separate things: the Omani Arabs traded with Kilwa, although its sultan jealously guarded his independence from Oman. From 1784, however, the new *imām* of Oman, Saʿīd bin Aḥmad, embarked upon a military campaign to impose his will on a number of coastal towns, including Kilwa. The ageing sultan of Kilwa, Hasan Ibrāhīm, could put up only token resistance. He was forced to acknowledge the *imām*'s overlordship and accept the presence of an Omani governor and garrison in Kilwa. But these political developments only helped to promote the commercial revival of the Kilwa coast by creating greater stability and encouraging more Indian investment. No doubt Muscat gained even more from this arrangement.

By the turn of the century, the economic value of the few points at which they were represented was becoming evident to the Būsaʿidi. This and other political and strategic considerations led Sayyid Saʿīd bin Sultan (1804–56) to extend his dynastic authority on the coast and, eventually, to establish his capital at Zanzibar.

Conclusion

Between 1500 and 1800, there were important changes on the east coast of Africa. Hitherto independent Swahili towns endured Portuguese invasion, sometimes facilitated by their own intrigues and rivalries.

The Portuguese occupation was ruthless. The Portuguese were determined to strike at Muslims everywhere, take over their lands and trade and even convert them and the followers of traditional African religion to Christianity. But the Muslims were impervious to Christianity, and by the end of the Portuguese occupation no trace of Christianity remained.

As for trade and commercial traffic in the Indian Ocean, the Portuguese only half-succeeded. The Swahili towns were able to retain a significant degree of commercial activity despite the regulations introduced by the Portuguese. Greed and incompetence amongst local officials were responsible for such developments as the decline of the Sofalan gold trade. However, the coast enriched Portuguese officials, if not the Portuguese crown.

Swahili towns experienced varying fortunes. Mombasa's resilience enabled it to recover several times from Portuguese reprisals. Kilwa took the blows less well, although towards the end of the eighteenth century it recovered, thanks to the slave trade. Other coastal towns disappeared or reverted to villages. Their decline was not the work of the Portuguese; the activities of the Oromo and the Zimba, combined with environmental changes, are more likely explanations. Pate is an exception, and it enjoyed its greatest prosperity ever in the seventeenth and eighteenth centuries; its decline began only at the end of the eighteenth century. More research is needed to answer many remaining questions about the Swahili towns, the factors responsible for their growth and development and their eventual decline.

26

The Great Lakes region, 1500–1800

This period can be divided into three parts. The first stretches from approximately 1500 to 1580; the second, from 1580 to 1680, is the era of droughts and famines; the third, from around 1680 to 1800, is the age of state formation and expansion. Before 1580, the main preoccupation of the southern and central regions was the consolidation of the states which had succeeded the Bachwezi empire, while in the north, the first intrusion occurred of Eastern Nilotic-speaking peoples, with all its attendant linguistic consequences.

The second period was dominated by droughts and famines. It also saw the region's greatest movement of populations for the past thousand years. There were large-scale migrations out of Baar, the Luo people scattered, while massive invasions of Banyoro reached areas as far away as Rwanda and Usukuma. In the east, this drought was associated with the appearance of the Central Eastern Nilotes who joined up with the local people, as well as a substantial population drift southward.

The third period was concerned with the proliferation and expansion of state structures. It began with a dynastic crisis in Bunyoro which heralded the decline of that empire and brought about the creation of numerous states. The Mporo state was founded then fragmented. The period drew to a close with the rise and expansion of Buganda in the central area and Rwanda in the south, as the two super-powers of the Great Lakes region, and in the north with the broad outlines of the modern configurations of Central Eastern Nilotic ethnic groups such as the Iteso, the Jie, the Eastern Luo, the Lango Omiro and the Kumam.

The Northern and Central areas

Formation of new groups and societies

Before 1000 of the Christian era, the Central Sudanese were probably the predominant peoples over the entire Great Lakes region. 'Muru' was the Luo term for all these indigenous peoples, and will be used when the ethnic identity of a Central Sudanese people is not known and particularly to distinguish the early peoples of the region from the later Madi immigrants, who were also from Central Sudan. Most of the Central Sudanese peoples were organized along segmentary and gerontocratic lines. They were farmers. They worshipped an earth god and used rain stones or a mixture of oil and water to bring on the rain. They had a complex totemic system and buried their dead in recessed graves. They were known by later immigrants as experts in ironwork. By 1500 they had been assimilated into Bantu culture, south of the Nile–Kyoga divide, but still dominated the north from the Alur Highlands to the mountains of Karamoja.

Around 1000 the Nilotic birthplace of Dog Nam broke up. One group moved to Tekidi and a splinter group from Tekidi migrated to and settled in Pakwac-Pawir. From Dog Nam another group settled in Wipac (Rumbek). In all three Luo enclaves a form of hereditary command associated with the bushbuck totem had been established well before 1400.

The period from 1400 to 1580 was devoted to the internal consolidation of the states which succeeded the empire and the diplomatic manoeuvring of the two great powers, the Bahinda and the Babito. The new rulers recognized certain indigenous chiefs, notably those of Bwera and Buyaga, and there were few arguments over succession.

North of the Nile–Kyoga divide, the year 1500 is important because it possibly coincides with the first major appearance of the northern section of Eastern Nilotes or their Bari cluster. It has been argued that this group left its homeland in three waves occurring some time between 1490 and 1571. Each group in turn attacked Tekidi until this Luo settlement was broken up by the third invasion, that of the Lotuho.

Available data suggest that the Nilotes introduced to the peoples of Central Sudan their organization by age group, their fire ceremony, a sky god, the spear and shield, the sacred spear for bringing on rain, the long straight hoe and elaborate headdresses. In many areas their interaction with the Sudanese peoples probably developed chieftaincies and their language became a new *lingua franca*.

The second Eastern Nilotic invasions may have been affected by the Oromo, who left their homeland north of Lake Turkana between 1517 and 1544 and attacked Tekidi around the same time as they began their invasions of southern Ethiopia. Ancestors of the modern Kakwa possibly took part in this migration.

The land of Baar became an area of intense racial intermixing between the Eastern Nilotes and the Madi people. It appeared that new societies of the Pajulu, Kakwa and Kuku peoples adopted an Eastern–Nilotic language and combined the Nilotic sky god and spear with the Sudanese earth god and bow and arrow. They apparently abandoned the Nilotic organization by age group and adopted Madi dress, burial customs and rain stones. The secular chiefs were generally Eastern Nilotes whereas the ritual experts were Madi. The Pajulu, Kakwa and Kuku were culturally Sudanic and linguistically Eastern Nilotic.

The Bari fusion was very similar, with a somewhat more marked Nilotic influence. One of the main features of Bari and Kuku society was that the *dupi* (servile class) were sometimes physically distinct from the freeborn. In Kakwa and Pajulu societies the *dupi* were clients rather than serfs. Since they were often used as assistants in rain-making rituals and were renowned miners and ironworkers, they may well have been of Muru rather than Madi origin.

The final invasion of the northern group of Eastern Nilotes was associated, in the oral Luo Tekidi tradition, with the Lotuho. The Lotuho overcame the Luo settlement of Tekidi, whose king, Owiny Rac Koma (*c.* 1544–71) fled with his subjects to the Luo settlement in Pakwac-Pawir. It would appear that a Central Sudanese group, the Okarowok, adopted the Eastern Nilotic language due to the influence of the Lotuho.

Apparently the Lotuho assimilated the small Okarowok clans into their own four larger clans and adopted the Okarowok totemic prohibitions. They introduced the fire-making ceremony, organization by age group, and, probably because of their unsettled situation, built tightly-packed, well-populated villages in an area previously distinguished by its scattered settlements. This was the furthest eastward spread of the totemic clans and rain stones indicating, possibly, the eastern limit of Central Sudanese peoples.

While a group of proto-Luo was forced by the incursions of the Eastern Nilotes to move to the Tekidi area, another group moved northward to Wipaco Dwong' in Rumbek. This group subsequently broke up between 1382 and 1418 and went westward, towards the Nile, to settle on the river banks. Later, this cluster re-divided, with one group – the proto-Shilluk and its allies – going north and settling somewhere between 1490 and 1517. The Luo forays into Baar apparently drove the Madi-led Panyimur, Atyak and Koc-Pagak to migrate south to the Mount Kilak area. There ensued a Madi-Luo struggle for power in Pakwac-Pawir. In the chiefdom of Atyak it was prophesied that the sons of Princess Nyilak (*c.* 1517–62) would assassinate her father, the king, and seize the throne. Consequently, the king locked up his daughter, but a Luo traveller gave Nyilak a son, who, as prophesied, killed the Madi king. Out of this, two states probably emerged; Attyak (later known as Okoro) led by the Luo, and Acholi, by the Madi. The story of Nyilak is an allegory (whose characters vary according to the version) intended to explain the overthrow of Sudanese rule by either Luo in the north or Bantu in the south.

Around 1560 the Lotuho overran Tekidi causing most of its inhabitants, along with their king, to flee to Pakwac-Pawir. The main chiefdom to emerge from the Lotuho was Puranga. This Luo group, much influenced by Eastern Nilotes, can be called the Eastern Luo. They formed a predominant element of the population in East Acholi, Labwor, Nyakwai and Lango and along with the Eastern Nilotes had a decisive influence on the dialects spoken in these areas.

The period of droughts and famines

No area of the Great Lakes region, nor indeed of east-central Africa, escaped the effects of the climatic disaster of droughts and their resulting famines which occurred in the late sixteenth century and beginning of the seventeenth

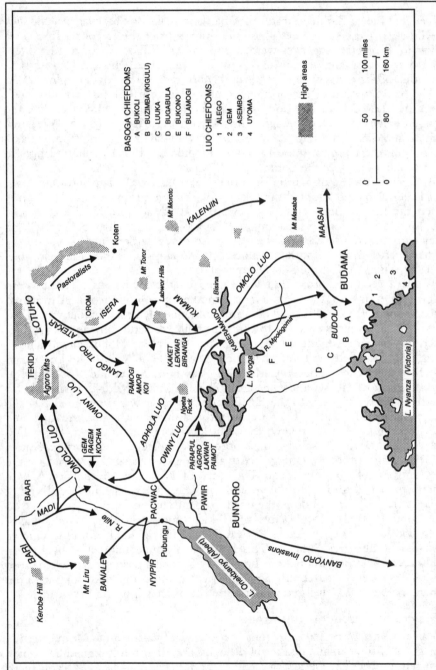

26.1   *The Nyarubanga and the fragmentation of the Luo, c. 1570–1720 (after J. B. Webster)*

century. During this period, rainfall in the northern and central areas was only average for two years. The worst years of drought were probably 1588–90, 1601–02, 1613 and 1617–21. In 1621 the summer Nile reached its lowest level since 622 when records were first kept.

In northern Uganda the entire period is known as *Nyarubanga*, a Luo term meaning 'sent by god'. It came to an end with the Great Famine of 1617–21, which was accompanied by a disease which wiped out cattle herds. The spectre of mass famine is conjured up in all the traditions. In Egypt, accounts that were handed down are appalling. Cannibalism became commonplace and almost half the population died of starvation. What was true of Egypt was probably also true of the Great Lakes region, especially the northern part.

If half the population died, most of the survivors were forced to migrate and flee, gathering near rivers, lakes, along the banks of the Nile, of Lake Nyanza (Victoria) and the chain of lakes stretching southward into central Africa. Twelve major accounts of migration in this period have been collected.

The *Nyarubanga* reshaped the ethnic and political geography of much of the Great Lakes region and perhaps well beyond. It probably dealt a tremendous blow to leadership built on the concept of control over supernatural forces and especially to those who claimed rain-making powers. It bred a new type of leader, based on those who headed the migrations and whose skills as commanders, warriors and hunters assured the survival of large groups of people. Once the shock had passed, the leaders of the survivors created new political units in new regions which were probably sparsely populated and had no political structures of their own.

It is not therefore surprising that traditional sources give the impression that from around 1600 there was a new beginning. In the majority of areas, there was, once again, ethnic intermixing, new habitats and new rulers. If accounts prior to 1600 are skeletal and vague it is because the *Nyarubanga* destroyed oral traditions, wiping out their means of transmission along with most of the elders who were their carriers.

The migrations out of Baar greatly accelerated during the *Nyarubanga*. Pakwac-Pawir became a place of refuge for huge crowds of starving and desperate peoples of different languages and cultures. The influx of these people apparently destroyed the position of the Paluo north of the Nile, and made the question of who would control the Luo and other groups there even more pressing. This led to a conflict between Cwa Nyabongo and Nyipir. This dispute is recounted within the spear-and-bead tradition. Nyipir and Tifool, whose followers were largely Owiny and Omolo Luo, moved west of the Nile out of the land of Cwa. According to tradition, Nyipir drove an axe into the Nile's dry river-bed as a sign of eternal separation. As leader of Attyak, Nyipir founded the Alur kingdom of Okoro whilst Tifool created a state which broke up into two parts, Nyiganda and Angal. The main body of the Owiny apparently headed south-eastwards, passing north of Lake Kyoga and joined up with the Budola encampments in eastern Busoga. According to Jonam traditions, the remaining Luo, led by Daca, overthrew Abok and the Koc state split into three; Koc Ragem to the west of the Nile, Koc Labongo to the east and Koc Paluo led by the Madi.

The Luo founder of the Terego chiefdom of the Lugbara may have emerged out of the dispersal from Pakwac-Pawir. Banale and his nephew Raoule reached Madi country in a state of total destitution. Banale was accompanied by a leprous Madi woman. When their clandestine relationship was discovered, a council of Madi elders decided to accept him as chief. He founded Terego, the biggest chiefdom among the Lugbara or southern Madi. At the same time, Jaki and his ambitious sons were extending their rule over the neighbouring Madi country and it is possible that the council of elders preferred to have Banale as their leader rather than be absorbed into the Eastern-Nilotic speaking Jaki group. It was this decision which allowed them to preserve their language and remain essentially Madi in culture.

The *Nyarubanga* triggered three Luo migrations to the south-eastern bank of Lake Nyanza. A significant body of the Adhola clans left Pakwac-Pawir and joined up with the Owiny in Kaberamaido. One of their leaders was Amor, and the Amor clan later appeared at Padhola with their drum, sacred spear and bushbuck totem. The Adhola and Owiny groups rapidly moved south to settle in camps at Budola in eastern Busoga. Another group of clans who were part of the Omolo cluster, originally of Luo-Sudanese origin, left Pakwac-Pawir to go north to Tekidi and south towards Mount Elgon. Thus there was a gradual build-up of Luo settlers in eastern Uganda, who then combined, probably with the arrival of *Nyarubanga* refugees, to form two separate bodies.

By 1600, the original settlers had joined together with the immigrant clans to form at least four groups: the Omolo group in the Banda camps, the Owiny-Adhola in the Budola camps, two future Adhola clans (the Ramogi and the Lakwar) in the forests of west Budama and a group of future Busoga north of the Mpologoma river. Between around 1598 and 1650, both the Budola and Banda camps broke up, probably because of the terrible drought in the 1620s which marked the end of the *Nyarubanga*. The Owiny headed off towards the Alego region in the Siaya District in western Kenya. A section of the Omolo followed and both groups came into conflict. The Adhola clans were the last to leave their encampments and join their brothers in west Budama.

Among those who retained their Luo language in west Kenya, some created chiefdoms. The majority, however, were like the Padhola, who settled in an unoccupied area and were content with an acephalous political system (i.e. one with no head) which maintained peace between the 31 clans. Ethnic unity was furthered by the myth that all clans were descended from the sons and descendants of Adhola, the chief who had led the great migration out of Kaberamaido to west Budama. The Padhola gradually gained land to the south and east of their original settlement. After about 1650 they also fought the Maasai in the Tororo area.

Eight clans belonging to the Owiny and Omolo clusters moved out of their Budola camps into Busoga. They were all members of the bushbuck totem, with hunting and rearing traditions, although the Owiny group also had a farming tradition. All of the Owiny clans, along with the Wakoli of Omolo origin, became ruling clans in Busoga. The Omolo, who were more pastoral, were reluctant to settle, and only one of their clans became dominant.

Soon after there followed the Pakoyo migrations from Pawir south of Lake Kyoga, culminating in their founding of the chiefdoms of Bagweri and Bugaya. The Luo migrations gathered many retainers along the way through inter-marriages and also because they took over the principal shrines, which then became centres of ritual and royal pilgrimage. Wherever the Luo went, they rapidly accommodated existing local rituals and religious structures; their ability to adapt spiritually was one of their greatest political weapons.

By 1750 nine states had been founded. By the end of the nineteenth century these had fragmented into nearly 30 states, with the Ngobi or bushbuck clan dominant in almost 20 of them. Those states which maintained a father-to-son succession and used administrators who were commoners, experienced no secessions and few civil wars. But those which practised brother-to-brother succession and used royal princes as office-holders suffered repeated disputes over the throne and numerous civil wars. Those dynasties which held on to their original Luo principles were more stable than those which adopted the succession rights of their Bantu subjects.

The *Nyarubanga* and the associated spear-and-bead movement was of great historical importance for the Luo, as it determined their modern geographic distribution. The *Nyarubanga* also set off a massive southern Banyoro invasion, headed by the Bahima-Batutsi, and led to the rural classes' attempt to overthrow the supremacy of the herdsmen. The first stage of the invasion was led by disorganized and ravenous hordes which swept over the whole of the southern region, some ultimately settling in Buzinza, in Burundi and beyond. They in turn sparked off other migrations which followed the chain of lakes into Central Africa.

As the drought persisted, cattle were struck by a disease which wiped out the royal herds of Kitara. This prompted Cwa II into driving his armies southward to replenish the herds and reinforce royal authority. The herdsmen were the obvious target of the Banyoro and the agriculturalist Cwa's natural allies.

The *Nyarubanga* also introduced the central group of Eastern Nilotes on to the scene of the Great Lakes. Historically, this group, made up essentially of the Karimojong-Teso cluster, was divided into two: the Isera, agriculturalists who reared some cattle, and the Koten, cattle-rearers who went in for a little agriculture. While both Isera and cattle-rearing groups are found in all peoples of the central group of the Eastern Nilotes, the ethnic groups to emerge primarily from the former are the Iteso, Toposa and Dodos, and from the latter the Karimojong, Jie and Turkana.

The Okarowok (Ikarebwok) form a major clan among the central group of the Eastern Nilotes. They seem to have first appeared in the Agoro region when the Lotuho imposed their language and customs upon the Lukoya, a Muru population. Agoro was an important centre of Isera-Omiro dispersal.

The major migrations to the south-east of the Luo, linked with the Owiny and Omolo groups, were also very much mixed with the Isera, especially in the case of the Omolo who went southward down the Agoro–Karamoja corridor. The Owiny left behind pockets of Luo speakers in what later became Lango Omiro country in Amac on the northern banks of Lake Kyoga. A significant part of the population eventually identified as Omolo were perhaps originally Eastern Nilotes. Those who reached western Kenya were known to the Luo as Omia, the Lomia being one of the four major Lotuho clans. The last wave of migrants to arrive in Siaya also included groups coming from eastern Uganda, such as the Owila, the Matar and the Bayuma. They were probably all Isera-Omiro descendants of the Bako, who, in turn, were of Ethiopian origin.

In addition to the Central Sudanese peoples and the Northern group of Eastern Nilotes, the Isera included clans of Luo and Ethiopian origin. These groups were reinforced by immigrants undoubtedly from Anywa, or Pari, from Baar and Pakwac-Pawir.

In the course of the seventeenth and eighteenth centuries these migrant groups settled together and formed clusters which were defined by their place of residence and, in some cases, by a certain degree of self-identification. The largest of these bodies were the Bako in central Jie, the Okii (or Miro) in the Mount Moroto-Omanimani River area of central Karamoja, the Abwor in the Labwor Hills, the Kumam in eastern Teso as well as the Iworopo-Iteso (unique because the least coherent of these groups) in central and southern Karamoja. All of these groups included both Luo and Eastern Nilotes in quite differing proportions and bilingualism was common by the eighteenth century.

Pastoralists and farmers

Historians and anthropologists have tended to divide the societies of the Great Lakes region into two watertight compartments; those who cultivate the land and those who raise animals. But in reality the situation is much more complex, dynamic and changing. Population movements and other social upheavals brought together groups whose ideas and customs were often very diverse. Throughout the period with which we are concerned here, linguistically different groups of herdsmen and crop farmers were fusing together to form new and relatively well-integrated societies. Here are a few examples which well illustrate the nature of this social transformation.

Amongst the Central-Eastern Nilotes, a majority of the animal-tending groups settled in the Mount Koten-Magos Hills area of north-eastern Karamoja. These Koten-Magos peoples apparently already had a pastoral orientation before they came south. Hence whilst they arrived in Karamoja with a meagre herd, they quickly developed a mixed economy based on rearing, agriculture, hunting and gathering, which was better adapted to the region's climate than the economies of more agricultural groups. The results of this evolution became evident between 1680 and 1830 when the Koten-Magos groups moved into their present homelands and the agricultural groups either merged with them, adopting their economy, or else retreated to the west.

This process started between 1680 and 1750 with the expansion of the pastoral groups in four directions: the Ngimonia spread along the River Tarash and formed the core of the Turkana; the Korwakol moved west to the Longiro river, and became the most important element of the Jie; a third group, made up of some future Karimojong and Dodos, headed south to the Apule river; and the fourth, the Ngikora, emigrated north and settled in Dodoth.

The situation then stabilized for a time, but the demands put on the land in areas controlled by the pastoralists, along with the droughts of 1780 and 1830 sparked off new migration movements. The majority of the populations that moved into Nyakwai, Labwor, eastern Acholi and Lango were at least bilingual: they spoke a Luo dialect and as they were all joined by Luo-speakers from further west, they adopted the Luo language. Those, however, who went into Teso included few Luo-speakers and thus the Iteso adopted the Eastern Nilotic tongue.

This western flow of agriculturalist refugees was accelerated by a renewed expansion of the pastoralists. In the 1780s the proto-Dodo groups on the Apule went north towards Dodoth, forcing the existing Toposa community to move north to their present territories. Both the Dodo and Toposa herdsmen assimilated a number of Isera groups and thus adopted an economy that was more agriculturally based than that of their southern brethren. Then, in the 1820s, the Korwakol and the Jie Rengen combined to destroy the huge agricultural community of the Poet who lived on the Kapoeta river. Finally, during the same period, the proto-Karimojong on the Apule pushed south into the homelands of the last remaining Okii and Iteso-Iworopom, either absorbing them into their society or forcing them to leave. These developments, along with the 1830s drought, precipitated the last great migrations from this area to the west.

The case of the Bunyoro-Kitara even better illustrates the interrelations between pastoralists and farmers. Between 1760 and 1783 Bunyoro lost valuable grazing land to Buganda. Also, the growing autonomy of the animal-tending Nkore, Buhweju and Buzimba societies further restricted the Bunyoro state to largely agricultural lands. Pastoralists settled amongst agriculturalists and together formed new communities where land, rather than cattle, was the basis for political authority. The different groups, united by wide-scale inter-marrying, provided leaders and land owners who collected tributes from the subjects for the king. Thus a new Nyoro state gradually came into being in the eighteenth century.

Social and political institutions

It was not only language and economy which distinguished the animal-tending groups from the Isera groups, and both from the Luo-speakers. The herdsmen perfected their age-organizations as instruments of gerontocratic control, and these became the key social and political institutions in their societies. Organizations by age-group also existed within the Isera and the societies they influenced, but in a truncated form. The main institutions in these societies were the ritual groupings of several clans, which were used for settling disputes and performing religious ceremonies.

In the ethno-cultural mix north of the Nile–Kyoga–Bisina divide, hereditary chieftaincy was a Luo idea. This type of hereditary leadership was opposed by many Eastern Luo and refused by their elders. Nevertheless it had a certain impact on the political institutions of not only many of the Luo-speaking groups, but also on certain Isera groups. Among the Luo-speakers, those that followed chiefs tended to move into eastern Acholi, where their ideas were reinforced when some Paluo groups came to join them somewhere between 1680 and 1760. In Labwor, Lango, Nyakwac and Kumam, the populations, on the whole, rejected the idea of a hereditary chieftaincy in favour of geronto-cratic ritual rule.

Despite this, these groups sometimes entrusted individual leaders with a good deal of secular authority. The eighteenth and nineteenth centuries witnessed an increase in warfare amongst the Eastern Luo and the Central-Eastern Nilotes. This in turn increased the influence of the military leaders and their councils, as well as of the younger generation, at the expense of the gerontocracy. Thus, in Lango, powerful war leaders formed extensive military confederations in order to conquer their country and raise large mercenary armies which fought in Bunyoro, Toro and Buganda. Similar confederations were formed in northern Teso, Sebei (Mount Elgon), Kumam and Padhola, but in these regions the chiefs were *emuron* (seers). Because of their decisive military role, these men gained considerable political muscle but none was able to secure a chiefly status for his family. The institution of *emuron* created a new centre of power which challenged both the war councils and the gerontocracy but did not combine easily with chieftaincy.

The Iteso who settled in the 'thigh of the cow' (the unusually fertile area in Ngora and Kumi as well as lands colonized from there) closely resembled the original Isera. They had no age-group organizations, no *etem* (ritual clan groupings) and no *emuron*. They were dependent upon three great assimilating clans, the Atekok, the Ikarebwok and Irarak who ensured social cohesion. Being more mixed originally, the Northern Iteso also possessed all the above institutions. Many Iteso filtered into Luo and Bantu territory to the south, as land pioneers or mercenaries. They were made particularly welcome in certain Busoga states where they counterbalanced military and political pressure from Buganda.

In the central area, Buganda contrasted sharply with Bunyoro. Without a royal clan, but with a king who could appoint officials with no regard to custom, tradition or heredity, Buganda had, by the beginning of the nineteenth century, few institutionalized classes, unusual vertical flexibility and a degree of social inequality which was greater than Bunyoro but less than Rwanda.

Politically and socially, Bunyoro-Kitara stood somewhere in the middle. The royal Babito clan was originally made up of agriculturalists who also reared some stock, but the dynasty increasingly acquired a pastoral orientation. However, the non-royal branches of the Bito clan were to be found at all economic levels. Furthermore, representatives of other social classes and allied groups were appointed to various state and court offices, so that a privileged class was created whose fortunes were linked with those of the Bito dynasty.

The *mukama* of Bunyoro had far less wealth and power than the *kabaka* of Buganda, since in Bunyoro the royal court carried out redistribution of wealth and surplus. Power was less concentrated here, with most positions remaining hereditary and the *mukama* merely confirming the chosen candidate; consequently, few peasants ever attained high office. Furthermore, while in Buganda the 30 clans were theoretically equal, in Bunyoro there was a clear distinction between high- and low-status clans.

Among the Nilotic Luo, there were those who were organized in states and those who were non-centralized. State structures were less elaborate than in Bunyoro or Buganda and Luo kings exercised a certain influence but little real power. Although some royal lines go back over several centuries, most of the Luo states only came into existence belatedly. Furthermore, recurrent droughts had forced so many migrations and new regroupings of societies that many states, such as they exist today, date from about 1680 or even later.

None of the Luo states enjoyed the fertile agricultural base of Buganda, Rwanda or the Bahima states. Neither did they possess the rich iron and salt deposits of the Bunyoro or Busongora areas. Prior to the *Nyurabanga*, it seems that the Luo owned substantial herds of cattle but by around 1800 these had been wiped out. Consequently, the Luo state did not exhibit the same disparities of wealth nor the class consciousness which characterized the southwestern states. In all the Luo states, the Eastern Nilotes were very influential, with their presence increasing from west to east and making up the majority of the population of eastern Acholi. They were extremely egalitarian in their political and social concepts and it must have been difficult to convert them to ideas of chieftaincy and hereditary classes. In the eastern regions, the Luo kings appeared increasingly like presidents and spokesmen for the councils of elders.

In the Luo states, theory and practice regarding classes differ. Theoretically, the Luo societies are divided into two classes, the royals and the common people. However, by around 1830 a third distinction, based on Luo or non-Luo origin, became as important. Very often, royal has come to be identified with Luo and non-Luo with commoner. In popular thought, non-Luo commoners are often graded according to how long ago their ancestors integrated into Luo society. Nonetheless, a member of the royal clan separated by ten generations from the chiefly line is treated little differently from an outsider whose ancestors integrated into Luo society ten generations ago. In the Acholi states the royal clan is exogamous and outsiders are quickly assimilated.

The Luo class system can be looked at in a more realistic way. In the course of political compromises made over centuries, many non-Luo clans came to hold office or perform ritual functions which gave the lineages of those officeholders great prestige. If there was a superior class, it was that of the nuclear families of the king, his councillors, the landlords and the ritual experts, including the rain-makers and the *jagos* (territorial sub-heads).

The Luo and the Central-Eastern Nilotes, who had no state structures, had no class system. There were no chiefs and no hereditary offices. The gerontocracies were governed by the elders whose decisions, it was believed, were sanctioned by the ancestors. These gerontocracies often formed huge military confederations in which a warrior chief and his subordinates were recognized and supported by an *emuron*. There was tension between the governing elders and the younger warriors. The elders maintained strict and even oppressive control over the younger men, delaying their possibilities of marriage and independence by monopolizing both women and cattle. Sometimes the young men emigrated to escape such frustrations.

The acephalous Luo and Eastern Nilotic societies often showed great economic disparity, manifested in the number of head of cattle owned. Wealth brought respect and aroused expectations of lavish hospitality but it did not create social inequality. Actually, cattle were widely redistributed through the bridewealth system.

The change in the balance of power; the decline of Bunyoro and the rise and expansion of Buganda

After the *Nyarubanga*, the most significant episodes in the history of the northern and central areas of the Great Lakes region were the crisis in Bunyoro, which led to its decline, and the internal development in Buganda, which led to its rise and expansion. These two factors led to a dramatic change in the balance of power. The Bunyoro crisis began with the death of Cwa at the time of the *Nyarubanga*-led invasion of the south. Cwa's only son, Winyi II, was captured and Kitara was governed by a regent, Cwa's sister, Mashamba. Cwa had no sons by a Luo wife, who could have succeeded him according to the rules of the royal family. Winyi II murdered Mashamba and seized the throne. Thereafter, the old tradition whereby the heir had to be of a Luo or Paluo mother, became the exception rather than the rule. Candidature for the throne was thrown open to all the king's sons and succession disputes became more frequent and more fierce.

Under the first dynasty, the chiefdom of Pawir had held a prestigious position within the imperial structure. A succession of what the Paluo called 'Bantu kings' sought to make use of the unrest at Pawir to encourage separatist tendencies; this they did with such success that the sub-chiefdom of Pawir, which was unified in 1650, had split itself into six small chieflets by 1750. Under the reign of Isana (*c.* 1733–60), these chieflets were placed under the authority of a country chief by which Paluoland lost its semi-autonomous status and was integrated into Bunyoro. The Paluo regularly rejected the Bantu candidates to the throne; some emigrated to the north and east because of the closing of their political horizons, their loss of status and sheer persecution. The frequency of succession disputes, combined with Paluo dissidence, undermined the central power of Kitara.

The most immediate result of the crisis in Bunyoro was the exodus of the Paluo-Pakoyo into Acholi, northern Busoga, Alur and even into Padhola and western Kenya. Whilst the Paluo were spreading their language in the north, the Pakoyo integrated linguistically into Basoga society. In the north, the major form of political organization was gerontocracies or small chiefdoms. The Paluo popularized the royal drum, enhanced the dignity of the chief and incorporated small units into larger states, allowing them to retain their hereditary leadership. They founded new states such as Lira Paluo and Paimol and enlarged and restructured others, such as Padibe, Patongo, Alero and Koc. Puranga and Payera were inspired by Paluo theories and assimilated a number of subordinate units in the process of expansion. Integration into Luo society proceeded either by assimilation or by fragmentation and proliferation of political unities. Lira Paluo is an example of the former, Alur of the latter.

Omukama Isansa played as essential a role in the decline of Bunyoro as did Kabaka Mawanda in the rise of Bugunda. Isansa's rule is noted for its peculiar mix of military success and political failure. The campaign that he led in the south was intended to demonstrate once again Bunyoro's military might. In reality, Isansa was overturning a policy of administering outlying territories which had worked acceptably for three centuries. His biggest political miscalculation was his attack on the palace of Wamara, head of the Cwezi cult in Bwera. Wamara presumably opposed the second Babito dynasty because it had violated the traditional rules of succession. Isansa decided on military intervention. So great was the sacrilege that the trees 'bled' and Wamara cursed Isansa, prophesying that the Bugunda would swallow Bunyoro. The prophecy came true; not only did Buganda take possession of a large part of Bunyoro but the small southern states could no longer remain safe. They became ideal prey for the imperial ambitions of Buganda, Nkore and Mpororo.

The rise of Buganda

While the Bunyoro kings were busy dismantling a political system which had ensured their domination for three centuries, the Buganda monarchs were correcting many of the political evils which had paralysed Buganda ever since its foundation. The first arose from the growing strength of the monarchy and its bureaucracy pitted against the clan heads or Bataka leaders. The second was linked to the multiplicity of ambitious royal princes looking for an opportunity to manipulate clan political factions in order to seize the throne. The third problem concerned the bloody succession disputes which followed the deaths of most kings. These disputes were even more damaging in Buganda than in Kitara. In Kitara the struggle for the throne could be fierce but once a king was chosen and crowned he was rarely assassinated or overthrown, whereas in Buganda a monarch could be murdered or dethroned at any point in his reign.

Buganda was more favourably situated climatically and geographically than the other major Great Lakes states. There is no mention of drought in its lengthy and detailed traditions. It had a secure and diverse agricultural base which freed its male population for war and politics. Furthermore, being located on the banks of Lake Nyanza, it conducted waterborne trade. It produced cloth from bark fibre which was greatly prized by neighbouring peoples. In its expansion, Buganda secured control of iron-ore deposits, a resource it originally lacked. With the possible exception of the southern Basoga states, no other state in the Great Lakes region possessed such a favourable geographical and economic framework.

But unlike the other Great Lakes states, Buganda had no royal clan. Each prince belonged to his mother's clan, whereas the rest of the population followed patrilineal rules. Any clan therefore had a chance to provide the monarch. This system gave all the people a feeling of belonging to the monarchy but, equally, encouraged each clan to give a wife to the *kabaka*, which, of course, led to a proliferation of potential royal heirs.

In the sixteenth and seventeenth centuries, Buganda was merely a tiny state, like so many others in Busoga, which tolerated fraternal succession and relied upon royal administrators. It was unstable and wrecked by interminable civil wars. However, Baganda nationalism was strong enough to prevent secessions and a fragmentation of the state.

The *kabaka* Tebandeke (*c.* 1644–74) strengthened royal power by a successful attack upon the ritual religious officers, whose extortionist practices lay heavy upon the monarchy and the people. The fact that he had succeeded where Isansa had failed has to do with the different religious organization in the two kingdoms. In Kitara the Cwezi cult was a centralized institution whereas in Buganda each ritual officer was apparently independent of the next.

Buganda's territorial expansion is associated with three outstanding kings of the eighteenth century. Mawanda (*c.* 1674–1704) seized Singo, invaded Kyaggwe and took over Bulamogi from Bunyoro. Given the immense gain which this conquest represented, Mawanda wisely abandoned the old system of indirect rule and appointed his favourites to administer the new territories. Mawanda was not only a military genius but also a statesman of imagination and is rightly credited as the father of the modern Kiganda system of government. Both Junju and Kamanya further extended the limits of the kingdom between 1734 and 1794. Junju annexed Buddu and forced Kooki into a tributary relationship. Kamanya seized Buwekula from Bunyoro. By 1800 Buganda had conclusively established its supremacy over Bunyoro.

Semakokiro, in the mid-eighteenth century, turned his attention to the problem of the royal princes. He began the practice of executing unsuccessful rivals, even, if necessary, royal sons. He purged princes from the administration to prevent them from using their positions to plot against the throne. This gave immense power to the king and paved the way for the absolute monarchy which emerged in the nineteenth century. Given the turbulence of the early political years of Buganda, it is tempting to overestimate the great *kabaka* of the eighteenth century, who acted as centralizers. But it is well to recall that despotism could only be achieved at the expense of lengthy rebellions, severe opposition to the *kabaka*, considerable violence and growing numbers of exiles to neighbouring states.

For centuries, Buganda had existed in the shadow of Bunyoro imperialism, but, at the end of the eighteenth century, it was ready to challenge this. Buganda had developed an intense nationalism which allowed its kings to gather power and develop an efficient administrative and military machine. By 1800 it had a highly competitive society which was more upwardly mobile and secular than any other in the Great Lakes region.

The agro-pastoral kingdoms of the South

The term 'interlacustrine culture', employed for almost a century by Africanist ethnologists, was based on observations made in the southern half of the region, in particular in the Rwandan monarchy which has been singled out as an ideal example by several authors. The formation of this cultural complex has been generally dated to a relatively recent period from the sixteenth to the eighteenth century. The work done by historians over the last 20 years or so has demystified this image and set in their true historical dimensions peoples with a past deeply rooted in an ancient Iron Age, going back at least to the beginning of the Christian era. The sixteenth century is a turning point in their history.

A geo-cultural area

The region's natural features and cultural heritage give it a physical and human landscape full of contrasts. In the west, a gigantic fault line scarp, over 2,000 metres high, the Kabira range, extended north by the Virunga volcanoes, dominates the Lake Tanganyika Depression and the Lake Kivu basin. To the east, the high hills of Burundi and Rwanda gradually slope down towards the terraced plateaux leading down to the shores of Lake Victoria. At over 1,000 kilometres from the Indian Ocean, which gives the region its climate, this varied relief gives rise to very marked variations in rainfall. The highlands of the west and the shores of Lake Victoria have an annual rainfall of more than 1,500 mm, while the narrow valley of the Kagera receives less than 1,000 millimetres.

The pattern of language distribution was similarly rather motley. The regions concerned were divided into two zones in which Bantu languages were spoken. People were able to understand each other without much difficulty, from the Virunga volcanoes to lower Malagarazi and from Lake Lutanzige (formerly Lake Albert) to the south of Lake Victoria. In the former area, kings were known as *mwami* and in the latter *mukama* or *mugabe*. These long-established geographical and cultural divides were, however, to become less clear-cut from the sixteenth century onwards, as the kingdoms took shape.

The traces left by Ruhinda and the Bachwezi

The states of the south may have grown out of the disintegration of an ancient monarchy, founded between the sixteenth and eighteenth centuries by a conqueror called Ruhinda; this, at least, was the prevailing belief until the 1950s. The 'empire of Ruhinda' was considered the southern extension of the 'empire of Bachwezi', brought about by a new wave of expansion by Bahima herdsmen. It is now thought that the event, if it actually took place, occurred instead at an earlier period, about the fifteenth century. As for the 'Ruhinda legend', different traditions have handed down widely diverging versions. In Bunyoro and Nkore, the hero Ruhinda is described as the illegitimate son of Wamara, the last Cwezi 'king', and a woman servant, Njunaki, while in Haya and Zinza country, his father is generally said to have been Igaba or Bugaba, one of the local names for the supreme deity. The Hinda dynasties of Nkore, Karagwe, Kyamutwara, Ihaniro and Buzinza took as their respective founders a brother, a son or a grandson of Ruhinda, who is said to have given each of them a country and a drum.

All the evidence suggests that the reference to Ruhinda reflected the meeting of two waves of traditions, connected with two major clan groups, Bahinda and Bayango, which had adopted the same taboo, that of the monkey *nkende*. As for the founding of the Hinda dynasties, the traditions relate that this occurred only one or two generations after that of the legendary conqueror. Probably the most interesting historical fact is the continued existence of the Ruhinda tradition, a source of political legitimacy, well after the sixteenth century. Ruhinda was invoked in the eighteenth century in Kyamutwara against usurpers from the Hima clan of the Bankangos; his name was associated in the nineteenth century with the memory of past greatness (in Karagwe) and of shattered unity (in Buzinza). It was also used in the nineteenth century to rally the Bunyoro and Haya people against the imperialism of the Baganda.

The traditions concerning Ruhinda drew their strength from the existing links between this legendary figure and the exploits of the Bachwezis. Whatever may have been the reality, the extent and the duration of the 'Kitara empire', as a socio-religious model it very clearly had its origins in the plateaux of western Uganda. The south, however, developed its own particular mythology, where the principal roles were played by Wamara, Mugasha and Ryangombe. These deities are merely the most important in a pantheon of 30 or more gods, continually increased according to circumstances. Each god is associated with an area of activity: Wamara with the dead, Mugasha with water, rain and lakes, hence with fishing and agriculture, Irungu with the bush, hence with hunting and travel, Kagoro with lightning and Ryangombe with cattle and hunting.

While Wamara, whose great sanctuary was in Masaka in Bwera (Uganda), is a recurrent name in the traditions of Kitara, Nkore, and Karagwe, the influence of Mugasha seems to have spread out from the Sese Islands, on Lake Victoria. Accounts of Ryangombe are to be found mostly in the west from Rwanda to Lake Tanganyika. Far from being merely monarchical institutions, these religions appear to have very ancient origins which predate the founding of the modern dynasties.

The Cwezi religion (or religion of the *Imandwa*) was independent in terms both of worship and mythology. In the east (in Haya and Zinza country) the same families maintained hereditary functions as mediums and were responsible for the shrines. In the west (Rwanda, Burundi, Buha) initiation to the *kubandwa* was widespread. Symbolism and vocabulary seemed to associate the religion with royalty in Haya country and Nkore, while the acts of worship performed in the shade of the erythrina, the sacred tree of Ryangombe and Kiranga, seemed to be of a more popular nature. But in all cases, these were practices of initiatory divination and healing, offering protection against threats coming from near ancestors or abuses of power.

'Clans' or 'castes'?

Faced with a written tradition which gave great importance to the theory of 'caste' and indeed 'racial' opposition between 'Hima and Tutsi lords' and 'Iru and Hutu serfs', recent historiography has devoted more attention to the 'clan' structure. Despite its universal presence in oral culture, the clan does not have the organic simplicity of a group of kinsfolk, even if it is sometimes experienced as such. Lineages, in the strict sense of the term, are classified in units characterized by a collective name, by one or two taboos, and sometimes by traditions relating to their origins or by the protection of a god of the Cwezi pantheon, but they have no territorial unity. Some clans appear in the long history of several of the kingdoms of the Great Lakes region, examples being the Bayangos of Nkore in Buzinza, the Bakimbiri of Nkore in South Buha and the Basita of Bunyoro in Bukerebe. Taboos sometimes concern even larger groups: the toad is respected in Rwanda by the Bega, the Bakono and the Bahu (three large clans which provided the queen mothers). Amongst instances of the spread of the *nkende* taboo, the most surprising example is that of the Kiziba where the taboo is respected by both the dynastic clan of the Babito and the Bahinda.

The historical background of the clans is clear in Rwanda. The structure here is exceptionally limited to 18 great clans which all comprise Bahutu, Batutsi and Batwa members. Elsewhere, in Burundi, Buha, Karagwe and the lands bordering on Lake Victoria, there were hundreds of clans but each had different forms of association, either exogamic units, or associations based on a joking relationship or the taking of an oath. Identity was often closely linked with the exercise of political or religious duties of greater or lesser standing. The fact of belonging to a given clan defined the individual's social status. The oldest traditions bear witness to the large number of local functions for which one or other of these clans was responsible, without this necessarily implying that each of these principalities comprised a homogenous group.

In Rwanda, there are many pre-Nyiginya political entities and several of these lineages have kept ritual functions in modern Rwanda. In Burundi, the custody of the drums and the religious duties retained by certain clans probably reflect ancient ruling powers. All of these clan principalities were gradually absorbed between the fifteenth and the seventeenth centuries (sometimes later) by the new dynasties, as we shall see. Despite these regional changes and influences, small sub-regional entities retained their individuality right until the twentieth century.

The distinction between pastoralists and farmers is not so clearly obvious in this context as to lend credence to the prevailing hypothesis of invasions and conflicts. It is not only in Rwanda that clans are of mixed composition; this is

26.6 *The southern Great lakes region at the end of the seventeenth century (after J. P. Chrétien)*

also the case for 20 per cent of the clans in Haya country, over 10 per cent of Bahutu, over 50 per cent of Batutsi and 90 per cent of Batwa clans in Burundi. Other clans are in an intermediate or indeterminate situation, described as *bairu* (ennobled) or *bahutu* (from a good family). The Basita are in some cases described as pastoralists (in Rwanda for instance), and in others as farming-blacksmiths.

While the hypotheses concerning a meeting in the distant past between Bantu-speaking groups and groups speaking south Kushitic or central Sudanese languages are interesting, they refer to too remote a period (the first millennium) to throw light on the situation in the sixteenth century, given the cultural fusion of these populations. Ethnic differentiations occurred along regional, clan or political lines which reflected the Hima/Tutsi and Iru/Hutu categories, although it would be risky to attempt to define exactly what these categories represented four centuries ago. One single fact seems to stand out – the extent of pastoral activities of the middle plateaux from Nkore to Buha, passing through Karagwe, Gisaka and Bugesera. The 'Hamitic' conquest, so often mentioned in connection with this period, appears to be no more than another way of presenting the regional and politico-economic pattern of the relations between the predominantly pastoral and predominantly agricultural sectors between the sixteenth and eighteenth centuries.

The formation of the modern kingdoms: a geo-political study

Problems of chronology
The wealth of oral sources contributes to the complex problem of reconstructing the chronology of the region, since dynastic lists and the genealogies of princes present many variants, especially before the seventeenth century. Two solar eclipses often evoked in the traditions provide absolute references but their identification has been questioned. The 'invasions' organized towards the south by the Bito sovereigns of Bunyoro also appear as a binding influence between the different kingdoms, but the traditions compiled in each of them ascribe the event to different periods. In fact, the Bunyoro must have mounted numerous cattle raids. None the less, three large expeditionary waves can be distinguished.

(1) In the first half of the sixteenth century, after the victory in 1520 in Nkore, the Banyoro are said to have twice invaded Rwanda, under the leadership of Prince Cwa, the son of Nyabongo, Olimi's successor.

(2) During the seventeenth century, the small Bito kingdom of Kiziba seems to have been subject to raids by its protector Bunyoro, especially during the reign of Magembe Kitonkire. Karagwe was also affected during this same period.

(3) During the first half of the eighteenth century the most famous raid occurred, which is attributed to a *mukama* known as either Cwa or Kyebambe. After having for years devastated all the Haya lands, this

sovereign is said to have been defeated and killed by the king Nyarubamba Kicumbu in Ihangiro. At the same time another Banyoro group was defeated by a *mugabe* from Nkore, known as Kitabanyoro (Banyoro killer). The kingdoms of the south were thus finally rid of the activities of the Babito, whose influence was undoubtedly significant especially in the military organization of the kingdoms.

The Kagera plateau states

This region of grassy plateau has always represented an important geo-political axis offering an easy route from the valley of the Katonga to that of the Malagarazi. Unfortunately, its political history is the worst recorded in the region, because of the difficulties which have beset its different kingdoms since the nineteenth century, resulting in the rapid erosion of their traditions. Only the northern part, made up of Mpororo, Nkore and Karagwe, is relatively well known.

Despite its prestigious origins (the Sita dynasty), Karagwe began to assert itself chiefly from the seventeenth century onwards, taking advantage of the first wave of Nyoro influence. Little is known about the Ntare and the Ruhinda who came after them, apart from the fact that they were more powerful than their neighbours to the east. They maintained better relationships with Gisaka and Rwanda, even including marriage alliances. The crisis in the eighteenth century, triggered by the Nyoro invasion, led to a fresh, rapid expansion, embodied in the person of Ntare Kitabanyoro, and later consolidated by the establishment of trade relations with Buganda and the Nyamwezi lands.

Mpororo, or Ndorma, inherited a rich tradition of government by clans. The Bakimbiri are said to have been governed by Ryangombe himself, and the Baishekatwa by Queen Kitami. Overall government was taken on by a Hima dynasty from the Bashambo clan who took advantage of the vacuum created by the Banyoro defeat in Rwanda. The Bashambo contracted marriage alliances with the Bahinda of Nkore, who were then less powerful than the Bashambo. In the mid-seventeenth century, King Gahaya, son of Ishemurari, attacked Gisaka and worried Rwanda. The culminating point was reached at the beginning of the eighteenth century, but, 50 years later, when Gahaya Rutindangyesi died, the kingdom split into two rival principalities and the Murorwa drum was hidden near Lake Bwinyoni in the western mountains.

The Gisaka dynasty claimed to have two different clan origins; the Bagesera and the *nkende* totemic group. At the end of the fifteenth century, King Kimenyi threatened to annex the tiny territory of the Rwandan *mwami*, Ruganzu Bwimba. In the mid-sixteenth century, Kimenyi Shumbusho took advantage of the Nyoro attack to occupy the heart of old Rwanda, Buganza and Bwanacyambwe. Rwanda was only to regain this lost territory a century later.

Bugesera could also be seen as a precursor of the political powers which were later to establish themselves in the western mountains. The Bahondogo dynasty was closely linked to that of the Banyiginya of early Rwanda and marriages and military alliances marked the history of the two countries from the sixteenth to the eighteenth centuries. Until the end of the seventeenth century, Bugesera covered a very large territory extending from the Kanyaru to the Ruvubu rivers (the entire northern third of present-day Burundi), and with its watering-places and rituals, represented a typical pastoral habitat. Difficulties arose with the growth of the Baganwa dynasty in Burundi which tended to side with Gisaka. The nineteenth century began with the division of the country.

Further to the south, several kingdoms were established in the Malagarazi basin. From the sixteenth century, a 'north Buha' is said to have consisted of Buyungu, Muhambwe, Ruguru, Buyogoma and even Bushubi. The Bahumbi dynasty remained very powerful until the eighteenth century. Early on, however, to the south of the river, Ruguru became the centre of another state, made up of Heru and Bushingo and governed by the Bakimbiri dynasty, which, with the principality of the Bajiji in Nkarinzi, turned their attention towards the mountains overlooking the eastern shore of Lake Tanganyika. It was only in the mid-nineteenth century that Buha began to break up.

The states bordering Lake Victoria

These countries, which were more populated, extended over grassy highlands, fertile humid plains and valleys with waters teeming with fish. This geographic diversity left its mark on the communities and the states and accounted in part for the splitting up of Kyamutwara and Buzinza in the nineteenth century.

Kiziba, wedged in between Lake Victoria and River Kagera, was torn between its traditional links with Kitara-Bunyoro and the Sese Islands. Furthermore, it was constantly in conflict with its neighbours in the south-west, Kyamutwara and Karagwe, which turned conflicts of succession to their advantage. The Nyoro threat was followed at the end of the eighteenth century by attacks by the Baganda.

In Kyamutwara, Hinda supremacy was apparently established once and for all in the seventeenth century by King Karenara. His insane cruelty is said to have led him to have his son Mukanbya blinded. A new dynasty was founded by Rugomora Mahe who was regarded as a civilizing hero. He and his descendants exploited the weaknesses of Kiziba and Ihangiro, until at least the end of the eighteenth century when Kyamutwara was, in its turn, weakened by internal dissension. Moreover, two Hima lineages of the Bankango clan, originating from Buzinza in the reign of Kahigi Kasita, gained increasing military and political influence in the course of the eighteenth century. At the beginning of the nineteenth century they established an independent government in Bugabo and a small-scale 'Kyamutwara', implanted on the shores of Lake Victoria where in 1890 the Germans were to found Bukoba.

Ihangiro can be clearly divided into the flat lake region and an inland plateau called Mugongo. Succession conflicts at the end of the seventeenth century gave the kings of Kyamutwara, Rugomora and Kahigi the opportunity for intervention in the plateau region. Justification for this intervention could be provided by the dynastic relationship. At the close of the eighteenth century,

Nyarubamba II appealed to the Baganda to help him recover the plateau region from a rebel prince. From then on, all along the western shore of Lake Victoria there developed what could be termed Ganda imperialism.

With Buzinza, we take on another cultural and ethnic region where the influence of the Baha, the Basukuma and even the Tatoga Nilotes inter-mingled. It was also the main home of the Barongo blacksmiths. After the reigns surrounded by the legend of Ntare Muganzara and the first Kabambo, there was a kind of second founding under Kabambo Kinwa. In the eighteenth century the *mugabe* Kakaraza had to fight off attacks from the Baha in the west and the Tatoga in the east. His son, Mwihahabi, was the last sovereign of a unified Buzinza: the war of succession led to the separation of Rusubi under Ntare Muhirc and of all the coastal regions under Ruhinda Mugangakyaro at the start of the nineteenth century.

The history of Bukerebe is one of complex regional influences. From the cultural standpoint, this country, made up of an island and a peninsula, forms part of the Zinza group. In the nineteenth century, however, the Silanga dynasty claimed to be of Ruhindan (even Bunyoro) origin, whereas its founder, Katobaha, is said to have come from Ihangiro in the seventeenth century. The kings (*bakama*) gradually gained the upper hand in the eighteenth century over the Sita and Kula clans, but the Tatoga menace forced them to establish their capital in the island. The important trade in ivory was considerably developed by this principality at the start of the nineteenth century.

The states in the western mountains

Whereas in the east, the dynamics of kingdoms led to fragmentation, in the west we see instead a concentration to the advantage of two powers – Rwanda and Burundi – each of which counted a population of over a million by the end of the nineteenth century.

The tiny Rwandese principality which came into being in the fourteenth century south of Lake Mohazi (in Buganza) succeeded in firmly establishing itself along the River Nyabarongo, thanks to the long reign of Cyirima Rugwe who annexed the lands of the Bongera. But the serious crises of the sixteenth century were to affect the stability of this kingdom. The two Nyoro invasions which made King Kigeri Mukobanya and King Mibambwe Mutabazi flee westwards, culminated in the shifting of the centre of political power to Nduga, while the original territory was captured by Gisaka. After the warlike reign of Yuhi Gahima, the succession conflict between his sons was exploited by the Bashi, the Bahavu and the Bugara people in the west. The king was killed, the drum of the Rwoga dynasty was seized. Despite the tradition which tends to present an unbroken continuity from the country's origins, it is very likely that Ruganzu Ndori founded a new dynasty of the Kalinga drum at the beginning of the seventeenth century. He reoccupied Nduga, and from there, he and his successors extended the kingdom as far as Lake Kivu and the Kanyaru river, recapturing Bwanacyambwe in the east at the same time. The growth of a new dynasty in Burundi held up expansion at the end of the century, but it took off again in the eighteenth century as a result of the exceptional military organization set up by Cyirima Rujugira and Kigeri Ndabarasa. Burundi and Gisaka were forced to retreat, Ndorwa broke up, Mubari was occupied and settlements on the shores of Lake Kivu were extended up to Kinyaga. At the end of the eighteenth century, Bugesera, an old ally, was divided up between Rwanda and Burundi. This expansion continued in the nineteenth century, especially in the north-west and south-east, but the old Hutu and Tutsi powers preserved their independence for a long time under a kind of protectorate of the Banyiginya.

There is far less information concerning the history of Burundi during this period. At the start of the sixteenth century an initial dynasty created by Ntare Karemera seems to have been established in the mountains of the north-west, on the border of the powerful Bugesera. Then, at the end of the seventeenth century, Ntare Rushatsi or Rufuku founded the Baganwa dynasty in Nkoma which unified the south, the centre and the north (the fusion of clan powers of the old kingdom) and rose up against Bugesera, whose king, Nsoro Nyabarega, had to flee to Rwanda. It was not until the long reign of Ntare Rugamba, during the first half of the nineteenth century, that the kingdom extended west to reach the Rusizi river and east as far as the Malagarazi basin.

Further west, around Lake Kivu, the Bashi on the one hand, and the Bafuriru and the Bahavu on the other, refer to a common origin in the Nyindu region (in Lwindi). Traditions also testify to the very long history of relations between these small kingdoms and Burundi and Rwanda.

States, economies and societies

This history of politics and warfare should not overlook the question of population movements, the evolution of landscapes and crop production, and institutional and even ideological changes.

Development of the relationship between herding and farming

Geographical factors determined from the outset two areas, each with their own activity: pastoralism on the Kagera plateaus, and agriculture on the shores of Lake Victoria and the western mountains. During the period considered here, however, both activities were increasingly carried out in conjunction throughout the region. In fact, they had never been in opposition to one another: the association of the earliest cereals, eleusine and sorghum, with cattle-raising, would appear to be a very ancient practice, both in terms of production and consumption (meal and milk). Ancient Karagwe is famous, according to tradition, not only for its cattle but also for its farming and its sorghum beer. Early accounts mention the use of manure, whose importance in intensive farming with two harvests a year in the wettest regions, has been sadly overlooked.

But towards the west in particular, factors such as droughts and famines probably led to the increasing influence of the herdsmen. Such calamities multiplied in the first half of the seventeenth century and the second half of the eighteenth century, forcing farmers to seek the help of the herdsmen, who, through the practice of transhumance, had been able to ensure the survival of their cattle. In the seventeenth century the shifting of the centres of political power from the area of the Kagera and Malagarazi rivers towards the wooded heights of Kiriba overlooking Lakes Kivu and Tanganyika, cannot be explained simply by expeditions or dynastic changes, but was also due to the growth of a system of tribute which was favourable to pastoral groups.

In Rwanda or Burundi, however, it can be seen that those who benefited from the regimes established 300 years ago represented only a part of the herd-owners, the rich Batutsi and the ruling circles linked to royalty. They were, in fact, those who had succeeded, through the actual use or symbolic use of the cow, in acquiring political control over agricultural production. Agriculture was of little interest to ethnologists and yet its importance is evident in the rituals and even the ideology of royalty. In Burundi, for example, the annual *muhanuro* festival, during which royal authority was renewed, celebrated the sowing of sorghum, and determined the most favourable date for this, in a country with a long rainy season. Furthermore, with regard to food crops, the introduction of plants of American origin (sweet potatoes, maize and beans) offered farmers new possibilities of expansion, providing them with the possibility of two harvests a year and supplying plant protein.

The relationship between tillers and herders, then, does not have the immutable and universal character that the socio-biological stereotypes would lead us to believe. The economic, political and territorial changes which took place between the seventeenth and the nineteenth centuries brought about a development of Hima–Iru or Tutsi–Hutu relations from one of local trade to a more comprehensive hierarchical relationship, whose flexibility depended on the states involved or the particular moment in time.

Consolidation of monarchical powers in the seventeenth and eighteenth centuries
Before colonization, each state had a system of tribute which varied according to the ecological situation, the balance between the different forces of production, the clan patterns and the institutional forms in existence. Everywhere, the sovereign directly controlled agricultural areas close to his residences and assigned chiefs elsewhere. They were often princes of royal blood, assisted by delegates who were usually from the most influential local lineages. Tribute was paid to these courts either in the form of labour or in kind. This allowed the ruling aristocracy to extend its influence by redistribution, as luxury was scant. Royal power was consolidated, particularly from the eighteenth century onwards, in the following four ways.

Exploitation of clientship The relationships which were known as *ubugabire* or *ubuhaka* were increasingly removed from their private context and used for political purposes: protection was guaranteed to a family in exchange for increased obligations. In Rwanda, the *buhake* was more especially used to subjugate influential Hutu lineages in the peripheral regions conquered by the Banyiginya, particularly in the last years of the eighteenth century. It was at this same time that the *gikingi* land system became established, which granted exclusive grazing rights to the most important herd-owners, with administrative rights over families living in these areas. This network of privileges, sometimes described as feudal, was accompanied in Rwanda by a remarkable increase in the size of herds resulting from the conquests of the eighteenth century.

Military organization Rwanda developed, especially from the time of the reign of Cyirima Rujugira, a system of hereditary standing armies, consisting of young men of certain lineages stationed in camps located on borders under threat. This militia also looked after herds owned or protected by the king. In the nineteenth century, the role of this institution was mainly reduced to tax-gathering in the service of important chiefs. The importance of the military factor was equally marked in the other kingdoms at the end of the period.

Trade possibilities Until a recent date, institutionalized trade and local barter played a role which was more important in commerce than in specialized trading. None the less, regional products such as salt, articles made of iron, or raffia bracelets were the staple wares of the earliest pedlars. Articles from the coast of the Indian Ocean, including glass beads or ornamental shells, would appear to have spread through the region from the seventeenth century. Copper is thought to have been around from the eighteenth century onwards in Burundi, Karagwe and Buganda. But it was only in the nineteenth century that rulers in Rusubi, Karagwe and Rwanda made attempts, as they had in Buganda, to control this trade in luxury goods.

Ideological control The changes brought about in society as a result of the agrarian crises, the wars of conquest of the seventeenth and eighteenth centuries and the movements of population, furthered the break-up of lineages. The success of the Cwezi religion in the seventeenth century is understandable for it offered a kind of refuge in the face of this instability. To a great extent the legitimacy of the new monarchies was rooted in this religious movement, as testified by myth and ritual. Initiates were, however, also capable of triggering subversive movements among the people or blocking royal action.

Ultimately the monarchies set about controlling this double-edged religion and turning it to their advantage. In Kiziba, the cult of the dead kings counter-balanced the power of Cwezi spirits; in Kyamutwara, the monarchy, from the time of Rugomora Mahe onwards, was based on the cult of Mugasha; in Rwanda, a 'king of the Imandwa' was installed at the court from the reign of Cyirima Rujugira. During the same period the Rwandese monarchy had an official body of panegyric poetry and historical narratives compiled, which was circulated by means of the army.

Rwandese oral sources reflect the exceptional nature of the country's political centralization. In other states, the different strata of society retained a greater degree of independence right up to the eve of colonization.

Conclusion

By the end of the eighteenth century the modern ethnographic and linguistic configurations in the Great Lakes region had taken shape. The major population movements had mostly come to an end and the last ethnic groups to be formed in the region (the Bakiga, the Iteso and the Lango Omiro) were being defined, the process being completed by about 1830. Also, with very few exceptions, the era of state formation came to an end with Rwanda emerging as the most powerful state in the region. In the central area, Bunyoro continued to decline until the secession of Toro and Paluoland in 1830. By the beginning of the nineteenth century, Buganda had emerged as the pre-eminent state in this area. Henceforth, the main concerns of the historian shift from the growth of central power to the efforts of the chiefs to limit the power of the monarch. In the course of the nineteenth century a multiplicity of new themes was to dominate Great Lakes history.

27

The interior of East Africa: the peoples of Kenya and Tanzania, 1500–1800

The period stretching from 1500 to 1800 saw the emergence of societies and social and economic systems that are still characteristic of the interiors of Kenya and Tanzania. The diversity of experience is perhaps the key feature of the history of this region at this time. Centre stage was taken up by the Maasai, Chagga, Pare, Shambala, Gogo and Hehe. On the eastern edge lived the Kikuyu, Kamba, Miji-Kenda, Zigua and Zaramo. To the north-west were the Abaluyia, Kalenjin, Luo, Abagusii and Abakuria, whilst in the south-west the Tanzanian communities such as the Sukuma, Iramba, Nyamwezi, Zinza and Kimbu were to be found.

All these peoples, with the exception of the coastal societies, were still isolated from the coast. There is no documentary evidence of Arab or Swahili penetration of the interior before 1700 and no significant collection of imported objects has yet been found at any interior site north of the Zambezi dating to the period before 1600. From the mid-1600s, however, it is possible to begin to see the emergence of chieftaincies and structured political organizations, as well as changes tending towards a general tributary mode of production. Oral traditions portray this development as one of conquest and assimilation by the migrant populations who were more powerful than the local communities. However, it can also be reasonably supposed that the local communities gradually subdued and stabilized the hitherto nomadic or unsettled populations who infiltrated them.

All history is transition from one stage to another. During the centuries following 1500, the distinct ethnic groups that we know today, with their own peculiar linguistic and cultural characteristics, were evolving within the societies of the interior of Kenya and Tanzania. The predominant economic activity was, by far, agriculture. In all the settled agricultural communities, people endeavoured to find techniques for adapting to their local environment and dealing with it in a rational way. In some areas, advanced methods, such as terracing, crop rotation, green manuring, mixed farming and farming of drained swamp-land were used.

While most East Africans were agriculturalists, the Maasai, Pokot and Turkana were largely herdsmen who drove their cattle to pasture across the

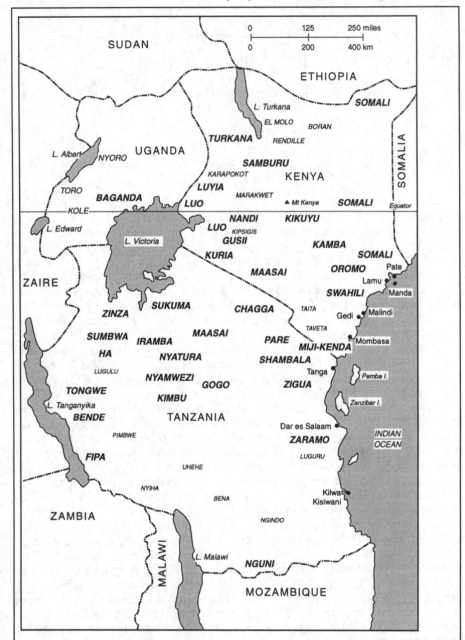

27.1   *Ethnic groups of Kenya and Tanzania (adapted from map drawn by M. Kivuva, Moi University, Kenya, after W.R. Ochieng')*

plains of central Kenya and Tanzania. However, the agriculturalists and the herdsmen at no time sought to pursue an exclusive economic activity. The agriculturalists, like the Luo and the Abagusii, also kept large herds of livestock, while cattlefolk, such as the Samburu and the Arusha Maasai, also practised some agriculture. The Baraguyu, the Kalenjin and the Akamba were half and half.

The Sanye, Okiek, Sandawe and Hazapi remained hunters and gatherers, but even among these peoples a growing spectrum of subsistence patterns could be observed. For example, the Okiek traded honey for agricultural products, and the Dorobi and Athi hunters became involved in the long-distance ivory trade. During most of the seventeenth and eighteenth centuries, both agriculturalists and herdsmen quarrelled over the richer and better-watered grasslands and plateaus. At the same time, they invaded the domains of the hunters and gatherers, which led to the absorption, decimation or isolation of the latter.

Economic evolution

By 1500, the two major economic pursuits in the Kenya-Tanzania interior were agriculture and cattle-rearing. Famine represented, therefore, a veritable distaster. It resulted from poor soils and the unreliable rainfall which affected both crops and pasture. Not even the most favoured regions were spared from the scourge of famine. Banana trees might have thrived in Usambara and yet the traditions speak of a famine at least once every 15 years. When the rains failed, people set off into the bush in search of food, or else they exchanged their cattle for grain from more fortunate groups.

However, the first line of defence against famine was the cultivator's skill. From 1500 there was constant experimentation with the crops introduced much earlier by the Bantu and Nilotes. In forested areas with heavy rainfall, sorghum, eleusine and millet gave way to banana trees and tubers. After 1500, a number of European and American crops, such as maize, groundnuts, sweet potatoes and cassava, were introduced by the Portuguese. Various other foods, including numerous varieties of peas, beans and nuts, were also cultivated and are still grown today.

The East African cultivator experimented with all available crops and adapted to his environment. When the Abagusii, who came from the plains bordering the Winam Gulf, settled in the highlands of south-west Kenya in the mid-1700s, instant crop failure led to famine which decimated their population. They were forced to reduce their production of several varieties of sorghum and other lowland crops and increase production of finger-millet and root crops that flourished in their new environment. By the end of the eighteenth century the interior regions of Kenya and Tanzania had many different agricultural systems. Nevertheless, one common practice over the whole territory was the burning of the bush to clear the ground for cultivation. When, after a few seasons, the soil was exhausted, the farmer would move on to allow the soil time to recover. It appears that all agricultural systems throughout the

Kenya and Tanzania interiors relied on the labour of the homesteads equipped with the same simple tools – axes, hoes, *pangas* (machetes) and digging sticks.

The raising of cattle, poultry, sheep and goats continued to be a vital economic and cultural activity in the interior of East Africa. Animal manure was used in agriculture. Livestock provided clothing and food, weapons and utensils. Among the herdsmen such as the Maasai and Turkana, livestock governed the daily routine and relations of kinship, as family prosperity and individual security were measured in terms of ownership. In many primarily agricultural societies, such as the Kikuyu and Abagusii, the acquisition and ownership of cattle was an important indication of wealth and prestige. Among the Turkana, Luo, Kalenjin and Maasai, it was the custom to freely lend and borrow cattle and to use them for providing bridewealth. In this way, each family herd came to be widely dispersed among friends and relatives often living far away, which was to benefit both individuals and the society as a whole.

Apart from the wealth brought by cattle, the predominantly pastoral people were also rich in land. Groups such as the Oromo, Somali and Maasai expanded their pastoral activity over wide areas of East Africa. Thus, because of its social status, wealth, its range of territory and political and military power, the pastoral way of life was both predominant and envied.

Hunting was a complementary activity to agriculture and cattle-raising, both as a source of food and for protecting crops. Oral accounts, particularly those of the Luo, Shambala, Pare, and Abakuria, frequently explain the movement of people by relating how the pursuit of an animal led them to a location where they decided to settle. The myth of the origin of the Shambala kingdom tells the story of Mbegha, a Ngulu hunter, who killed wild pigs that were destroying their crops, and freely distributed their meat. 'The Shambala, in admiration and gratitude, gave him wives and made him king of all Usambara.' Hunting, therefore, was an important and respectable economic activity.

The importance assigned by tradition to farming, livestock-raising and hunting contrasts with the lack of significance given to fishing, apart from amongst the populations living along the banks of Lakes Turkana, Victoria, Baringo, Eyasi and on the coast of the Indian Ocean. Various types of fish were caught by hook and line, basket-nets and fence traps. Dried fish were, and still are, sold to people far from fishing areas.

The traditions of most of the East African peoples indicate an ancient knowledge of iron-working. Archaeologists and linguists have also established that techniques of iron technology were introduced into East Africa by the Nilo-Saharans and Bantu, probably six centuries before the Christian era. The earliest Iron Age sites are around Lake Victoria. These sites were characterized by tall, cylindrical smelting furnaces and a distinctive style of pottery. Iron-work was usually the exclusive occupation of a few groups and carried much prestige and, occasionally, wealth. Several Ugweno traditions report that towards the beginning of the sixteenth century, certain families specialized in iron-smelting and forging. The major iron-working lineage, the Washana, held political power in the country. They were later overthrown by the Wasuya who transformed what were, hitherto, clan initiation rites into an elaborate state institution with unlimited coercive powers. In western Kenya, the Abagusii claim to have worked iron since the sixteenth century. Among the Luo, to the north of the Winam Gulf, the major blacksmiths were the Walowa of Yimbo. They manufactured hoes, arrowheads, ornaments, needles, axes, spears, knives and razors. Other important regional activities were salt-mining and crafts such as drum-making, canoe-building and pottery. Traditionally, these activities were the guarded specialities of particular clans. Crafts such as basketry and house-building, however, were not specialist activities, but were undertaken by anyone who had time for them.

To sum up, it must be emphasized that, between 1500 and 1800, food production was a crucial factor in the survival and expansion of society. As most of East Africa was put under extensive cultivation and grazing, and as production rose above the level of bare necessity, people could begin to use their time for purposes other than subsistence. It became possible to exempt certain individuals from the task of food production so that they could devote themselves to other objectives such as the distribution of merchandise, war-making, state duty, art, religion, medicine or philosophy and the improvement of technology.

Trade

Until the late 1700s, most societies in the Kenyan and Tanzanian interiors developed independently of external forces. They were independent politically, economically and socially.

Trading, the exchange of goods for mutual benefit, is a universal habit found among even the simplest societies. At no time have all groups and all areas been endowed with similar means and resources, hence the necessity to procure essential commodities from one's neighbours. And so, pastoralists and agriculturalists exchanged their products.

Much has been written about the trading connections that, for centuries, existed between East Africa and the Orient, but it must be emphasized that significant trade relations in East Africa were not limited to trade with the overseas markets; they also included important economic links between different internal regions. Internal African trade had a different purpose and dynamic to that of Arab or European trade. It was, consequently, irregular and sporadic. It was also a means of accumulating wealth in the form of cattle and foodstuffs.

Let us look at several examples of this trade. Traditions from Kikuyuland talk of ancient trading links between the Kikuyu and the neighbouring Akamba and Maasai. The Kikuyu economy was diverse. While they were predominantly farmers, certain sections, such as the Kikuyu of Tetu and Mathira in Nyeri, evolved a semi-pastoral economy and lived almost like their Maasai neighbours. Conversely, the Athi Kikuyu specialized in hunting and the exploitation of forest products, such as beeswax and honey. So, the Kikuyu offered foodstuffs along with manufactured products to the Maasai, who, in turn, paid in livestock, milk, skins, leather cloaks and magic. Kikuyuland also provided the best markets for the Akamba after 1760. From the Kikuyu communities of Muranga and Nyeri, the Akamba traders sought staple crops such as beans, yams, maize and *ndulu*, a green vegetable of which they were particularly fond. The Akamba paid the Kikuyu in animal skins and *uki*, a kind of long-fermented beer. Sometimes, they also traded their labour at harvest-time for an equivalent share of the food crops.

Further west, on the eastern shore of Lake Victoria, there was a widespread trading network linking the various communities. The main trading partners were the Abagusii and the Luo. The Abagusii sold to the Luo agricultural products and iron items such as axes, spears, razors and arrowheads, as well as soapstone and leopard and baboon skins. In return, the Luo offered mainly cattle, but also cattle-salt, skins, ghee, milk, fish, pots and poison.

Further south, in Tanzania, traditions from western Unyamwezi and Uvinza speak of pre-1800 immigrant groups from the north exchanging grain crops for pots with the earlier inhabitants of the region. Among the Nyamwezi, forest products were also traded between villages and were in particular demand in the northern countries where the Iramba, Sumbwa and Sukuma lived. In Unyakyusa, most women made pottery, but those in volcanic areas lacked the necessary clay and so depended on specialists such as the Kisi women of the Nyasa lakeshore, who bartered their pots in Nyakyusa villages, or the people of Ngaseni who traded their huge beer pots along the road which wound its way around the upper slopes of Kilimanjaro.

The two most important items of early trade in central Tanzania were probably iron and salt. The main area of iron-working was in the north, among the Ha and the Zinza. The scarcity of iron stimulated its trade. Throughout Tanzania, iron was used in a great variety of forms: as knife-blades, blades for hoes and for axes, spear lances and arrowheads for hunting, fishing and fighting. Many traders from the north and the south travelled to the land of the Ha and the Zinza to buy these iron items which they would then resell back home. In the north-east, the Chagga and the Maasai obtained iron products from Pare smelters, while in the late 1700s the Mamba chiefdom became the iron-working centre for much of the Kilimanjaro region. In the south, Fipa blacksmiths exchanged their produce for cloth woven in the Rukwa valley, while the Nyakyusa bartered food for the products of the Kinga furnaces. Iron was a scarce and precious commodity: only the wealthy possessed iron hoes. Those used on Kilimanjaro towards the end of the eighteenth century were only a few centimetres broad and the Sandawe used them until they were worn down to the hilt.

Salt was a product of vital necessity to people who lived chiefly on vegetable foods. The major salt-pans were located in Ugogo and at Ivuna, Kanyene, Lake Balangida, Singida and Lake Eyasi, as well as at Bukune, Buha and Uvinza. The most important brine springs were in Buha and Uvinza. The Uvinza springs, in particular, seem to have been exploited since the eleventh century. This Vinza salt industry was later boosted by the foundation of the original Vinza chiefdom in 1800.

Trade between the Miji-Kenda of south-east Kenya and north-eastern Tanzania only really began to develop by the beginning of the eighteenth century. This was the period when most Miji-Kenda, who had previously isolated themselves in fenced-in villages, began to expand outwards. Later, with their population greatly increased, they embarked on secondary migrations settling in the less fertile, lower parts of their hilly country, where they frequently clashed with the Omoro and Maasai.

The Miji-Kenda were largely cultivators of millet, rice and fruits. Throughout the eighteenth century they were staunch allies of the Mazrui, supplying the many coastal settlements with ivory, gum copal, honey, beeswax, tobacco, grain, foodstuffs and timber for building dhows. In return, the Miji-Kenda traders obtained salt, beads, cloth, iron hoes and other goods. In the trade that developed between the coast and the interior, they sent their caravans both northwards, to the countries of the Oromo and Borana, and towards the north-west, to the Akamba and Chagga countries. But their control of the interior trade was short-lived, and by the mid-1700s they had been replaced by the Akamba.

Trade in the interior regions of Kenya and Tanzania may well, by 1700 or before, have involved exchanges over considerable distances; however, it was only from about 1800 that the interior of East Africa began to participate in long-distance trade and thus to be linked to outside economies.

Social and political activity

Social and political institutions and organizations played an important role in the cohesion of society and the protection of property and trade. Between 1500 and 1800, society in the East African interior was far from having taken its definitive shape. There were still significant internal migrations into sparsely settled or uninhabited areas, sometimes bringing together peoples of different languages or dialects, and with different political and economic practices. Internal conflicts multiplied as clans expanded. In some areas, immigrant groups or families imposed their political leadership over established populations. In other areas, the immigrants were absorbed into the local societies. In both cases internal migrations set into motion processes of cultural and political integration which continued into the colonial period.

The period from 1500 to 1800 was, therefore, characterized by a movement towards political centralization and the evolution of larger and larger linguistic and social groups. Thus a variety of societies emerged in the East Africa interior, but the two that contrasted most conspicuously were the pastoralists and the farmers.

Pastoralists, like hunters, depended on herbivores. They lived a wandering life, travelling comparatively large distances in search of pasture for their animals. They followed a more or less regular migrational pattern according to the season. Pastoralists had to protect their herds from predators, whether animal or human. Such a life required organized leadership.

The political history of the Kenya-Tanzania interior was partly linked to population growth which was made possible by, on the one hand, the sedentary life of farmers, and on the other, the disciplined politico-military organization required by pastoralism. The balance tipped in favour of one or other of the protagonists, depending on the fluctuations in social organization and cohesion, and on the development of technology. By 1800, the pastoralists were beginning to lose both economic and military power to the farmers who were rapidly perfecting their political institutions. The pastoral Maasai, in particular, suffered military and economic decline throughout the nineteenth century due to cattle disease, epidemics and civil wars.

By 1700, two main types of socio-political organizations existed in the Kenya-Tanzania interior. On the one hand there were societies such as the Kikuyu, Miji-Kenda, Kamba and Maasai, who lived in scattered, independent settlements with no form of centralized, traditional bureaucracy. Decentralization, however, did not mean disorganization or lack of political and social cohesion. These decentralized societies had family, village and district councils made up of elders. Members of each family, clan and district were united by relationships which defined and governed the actions of individuals and established mutual obligations and rights.

There were also the centralized (or centralizing) societies, such as the Shambala, Pare, Sukuma, Nyamwezi and Wanga, whose chiefs maintained rudimentary administrations that provided a socio-political framework. By the end of the eighteenth century, some of these groups, such as the Shambala and Pare, were ruled by strong despotic kings or supreme chiefs.

Let us look at certain examples of these developments. Among the Pare, the first stage of political development was reached when each clan established itself in its territory and accepted one ritual leader whose descendants could succeed him. Thus the religious needs of the community were at the heart of their political evolution. After settling in an area, each group established its sacred shrine (*mpungi*) which linked it to the founding ancestors and where, periodically, all members gathered to worship. As the population increased, it became necessary to bring together people of different clans. This formative period of unification is shrouded in myth, but, according to Isaria Kimambo, about 'sixteen generations ago', many Ugweno clans recognized as their chief a Washana iron-smith. The Washana were later overthrown by the Wasuya who founded a centralized state. This *coup d'état* was the work of Angovi, but it was his son, Mranga, who consolidated the Ugweno state, transforming what were hitherto clan initiation rites into a complex state institution with unlimited coercive powers. At the peak of its power, the Ugweno state had at its head a *mangi mrwe* (supreme chief) who was assisted by a council of ministers and the *wamagi* (district chiefs).

Another area of Tanzania where chiefly institutions were strong by 1600 was Bukoba, where several ruling lineages had evolved among the agricultural communities. Their political system, which was more centralized than in other Tanzanian states, involved control of land and cattle, in such a way that the tribute system was more exploitative. These states belonged to the Great Lakes region. Further south, many chiefdoms had sprouted, resembling one another in many ways. Each consisted of a small group of villages and neighbourhoods ruled by a single chief whom the villagers appointed from the ruling lineage. He was the holder of special regalia or symbols of power, such as sacred spears. He maintained the royal fire from which all fires of his chiefdom were supposed to be kindled.

Andrew Roberts tells us that numerous Nyamwezi chiefdoms are probably not the result of any single process of migration or diffusion, but originated from the Nyamwezi environment. 'From an early stage', he writes, 'certain men were respected as rainmakers and magicians, as pioneers in opening up woodland and as arbitrators in dispute.' It was from these roots that the Nyamwezi chiefdoms emerged. But unlike in Upare, where development tended towards centralization, the small Nyamwezi chiefdoms tended to increase in number. Only in the nineteenth century was there rapid centralization in Unyamwezi due to the expansion of trade and the emergence of ruthless traders and organisers such as Mirambo.

Among the Fipa of south-western Tanzania the earliest myths of origin are tied up with the origin of the Fipa kingdom (*Milansi*). According to one version, recorded by Roy Willis, 'the first man in the world, who was called Ntatakwa, fell from the sky when the world began and founded the Milansi line of chiefs'. The early settlers of Ufipa were farmers who lived in tightly-packed villages; this encouraged them to organize collective defence and build fortifications. Members of the ruling family seem to have derived their power from their iron-smithing skills.

Later, in the eighteenth century, the Fipa political regime changed, following an invasion by pastoralists from the north who introduced political principles no longer based on relationships between 'father chiefs' and 'son chiefs', but on a personal bond of loyalty between the sovereign and his partisans. They were nominated by the king to ruling posts on the periphery of the kingdom, but had no kinship relation with the king. There was probably a coup which overthrew the traditional Milansi dynasty and brought the Twa dynasty to power. The Twa reign was, however, far from being peaceful, as Ufipa was again invaded towards the end of the eighteenth century, this time by the Nyiha who burnt down Milansi villages. By 1800, civil war between the two rivals for the Twa throne was still raging.

A significant number of chiefdoms of varying sizes and centralization appeared in Tanzania between the sixteenth and the eighteenth centuries, in response to human, political and economic need. They were shaped by the physical and human environment. Centralization and economic expansion was the objective of most Tanzanian states but the process of nation-building often proved difficult.

In western Kenya, the Luo seem to have founded themselves on the kinship system, ancestral cults and hereditary leadership. When they arrived in Nyanza they created socio-political entities that were more centralized and more stratified than the earlier communities. And while the Luo clans and lineages were equal in most respects, the existence of groups of chiefs, priests and commoners indicated a degree of inequality rarely found in Kenyan societies.

The best analysis of the way the Luo socio-political system worked at this time is probably that by Peter C. Oloo Aringo. He agrees with B. A. Ogot that, at the highest level of political organization, the Luo were divided into 12 or 13 *ogendini* (ethnic sub-groups) of varying sizes. Membership of the *ogenda* was through the *gweng'*, a semi-autonomous political and territorial unit. In principle, the *gweng'* was occupied by members of the same clan but often parts were leased to *jodak* (outside clans).

The highest political assembly in any *gweng'* was the council of elders. The *gweng'* council was the custodian of clan territory. It carried out ritual ceremonies and declared war or negociated peace with other *gweng'*. Its decisions had force of law on all subjects. Those who infringed its regulations or defied its decisions could be cursed.

Above the *gweng'* council was the *oganda* council which debated major political, judicial and economic matters, such as murder, cattle theft, boundary disputes, famine, epidemics, invasion, defence, trade and inter-clan and inter-*gweng'* conflicts.

The Kalenjin, who have lived for centuries in the western highlands of Kenya, formed a typically decentralized society. Authority was monopolized by the elders and influential specialists. Eloquence, the ability to voice acceptable views at councils, and a sound knowledge of precedence and custom were considered important qualities for any political leader. But above all, a man had to distinguish himself as happily married with a good social reputation within the community. Among the Nandi, a branch of the Kalenjin, there is evidence to suggest that between the eighteenth and nineteenth centuries, a new dimension was introduced into the governing of society with the adoption of a spiritual leader called the *orkoiyot*. H. A. Mwanzi asserts that while the socio-political structure of Nandi society remained largely unchanged, with the clan and neighbourhood councils maintaining their role, by the end of the nineteenth century, the *orkoiyot* had transformed the Nandi into a theocracy with himself as sovereign.

In time, the *orkoiyot* was able to demand a share of the spoils of war and to impose his authority over councils through having personal representatives as delegates to each council. Thus a special class of officials was created among the Nandi to maintain communication between these councils and the *orkoiyot*. These officials accompanied the war leaders when the *orkoiyot's* permission was sought for a projected raid. They also acted as secret agents for the *orkoiyot*. These arrangements gradually centralized Nandi society in the second half of the nineteenth century.

Conclusion

By 1800, a bewildering number of Nilotic, Kushitic and Bantu-speaking communities were scattered all over Kenya and Tanzania. Only in the Great

Lakes region of East Africa had large states and kingdoms developed. In the Kenya-Tanzania interior, the typical socio-political unity was small and clan-oriented. Most of the Bantu-speakers were farmers, though wherever possible, they kept their own livestock. Herdsmen, like the Turkana, Oromo and Maasai, lived in more aggressive societies and controlled substantial areas of territory between the agricultural Bantu lands. Along the coast were the Swahili city-states, dominated by local Arab oligarchies. The populations of these coastal cities were mixed, the dominant language being Swahili, and the tempo of life considerably different from that of the interior.

The end of the eighteenth century marked the end of independent East African growth. Soon after 1800, the independent people of Kenya and Tanzania were faced with Arab and European invasions. Much of their traditional civilization was seriously damaged or submerged in a rising flood of violence.

East Africa was, at this time, badly placed to withstand this assault from outside forces. Africa as a whole had fallen far behind the enormous powers of the rest of the world in its ability to produce. Whereas Europe, after 1500, had entered a great era of mechanical and scientific discovery and development, the African interior had continued with the steady but slow development of its own civilization. This Iron Age civilization had many achievements. There was much advancement and invention in the arts of community life, the adoption of new crops, the spread of metal-working skills, the growth of trade and, more important, the methods of self-rule and peace-keeping. These were certainly important gains but they did not match up to the growing power of the strong industrial nations of Europe. By 1800, the technical capacity of Europeans far outweighed that of Africans, and by 1900, the gap had become enormous. It is this imbalance which goes a long way to explain the crisis which began around 1800.

28

Madagascar and the islands of the Indian Ocean

Madagascar

The shape of modern Madagascar was fashioned in the course of the nineteenth century when the Merina people of its heartland established their political supremacy, thus becoming virtually the only Malagasy in the eyes of outsiders. Yet, beyond the impact of relatively recent events, there is a different and farther-ranging past in which the period between 1500 and 1800 stands apart in the overall history of Madagascar. It is almost certain that most of the inhabitants of Madagascar came together during these three centuries to form the social, economic, religious, cultural and political groups that make up the Malagasy people today: the Antankara, Antandroy, Antambahoaka, Antanosy, Antemoro, Antesaka, Antefasy, Bara, Betsimisaraka, Betsileo, Bezanozano, Merina, Mahafaly, Sakalava, Sihanaka, Tanala and Tsimihety.

By the mid-sixteenth century, the arrival of immigrants into the country ceased but some of the inhabitants of Madagascar had already come into contact with Europeans, mainly Portuguese, and at least one of the more influential royal families, the *Maroserana*, had started to form. At the beginning of the seventeenth century, Madagascar was a patchwork of small and mainly self-supporting kingdoms. Before the end of the century much of western Madagascar regrouped under a Sakalava empire while several kingdoms emerged in the highlands. In the course of this same century, contacts with Europeans became less confined and more frequent at times as the Dutch, English and French East India companies turned their interests to the great African island. The slave trade, which hitherto had exported to East Africa and Arabia, shifted towards the Cape, the Mascarenes and the New World, embarking from several points along the length of Madagascar's vast coasts. Firearms began to spread not without certain repercussions on the political front. The Sakalava empire and in particular the Iboina kingdom, its northern component, reached its peak in the eighteenth century, while a good part of the eastern coast united for the first time into the Betsimisaraka Confederation. Before the end of the century, the northern Sakalava and the Betsimisaraka saw their power decline irrevocably; in contrast a weak and disunited Imerina

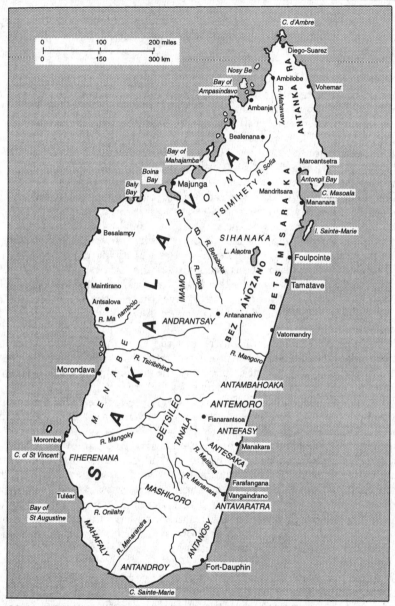

28.1 *Ethnic groups of Madagascar (adapted from map of Madagascar from Raymond K. Kent,* Early Kingdoms *in Madagascar, 1500–1700 (© 1970 by Holt, Reinhard and Winston, Inc.) Map adapted by kind permission of the publisher.)*

succeeded in augmenting its food production and increasing its population, thus undergoing a political rebirth which gave the Merina a solid base for their future expansion.

Newcomers and coalitions

Before the nineteenth century the Antemoro had become famous as the only group able to write in Malagasy (using the Arabic script) and also for their special abilities in the realm of magic and religion. There is no complete agreement on when and where the first ancestors of the Antemoro landed in Madagascar, nor where they came from, the extent of their Islamization and their impact within the island. Gustave Julien was the first scholar to suggest an Eastern African origin, a thesis which has been supported in the past decade. One aspect should remain beyond dispute: the Antemoro arrived on the banks of the Matitana river in the south-east, and it is only after they intermixed with the *tompon-tany* (masters of the soil, original inhabitants of the island) that they formed a society and a state. It is possible, however, to date with some precision their settling on the banks of the Matitana thanks to the reports of three Portuguese sea-captains who visited the area between 1507 and 1514. Only the third who was in the Matitana valley in 1514 speaks of a 'town inhabited by many Moors'. As the ancestors of the Antemoro are the only candidates for the 'Moors', the Matitana colony must have developed between 1509 and 1513.

Written Antemoro traditions record the encounters of the Antemoro with those who inhabited the south-eastern coast before their arrival: they tell us about the conflict of ideas between the newcomers with their patrilineal concepts and the matrilineal concepts of the original peoples, and they describe the many conflicts amongst the newcomers themselves. The Antemoro linked together into four dominant aristocratic clans and four sacerdotal clans. Their internal history well into the 1800s can be viewed as a series of conflicts between the aristocratic Anteoni, Antemahazo, Anteisambo and Zafikasinambo clans. The *andrianoni*, or supreme ruler of all the Antemoro, could come from any of the four clans. The sacerdotal clans vied for supremacy in religious and cultural functions. The Tsimeto, Zafimbolazi, Anakara and Anterotri sought, for example, to be the guardians of the sacred Antemoro manuscripts (*sorabe*), to become the high priests of the realm, or to have the closest proximity to an *andrianoni* and his clan. These divisions would blur in the nineteenth century when the sacerdotal Anakara clans monopolized both religious and political power.

When the Antemoro established themselves on the eastern coast of Madagascar, they found, apart from several *tompon-tany* groups, other communities who had been there before them, like the Zafindraminia, descendants of Raminia. It is generally agreed that Raminia and his companions arrived in Madagascar at least before the fifteenth century, but there is no consensus on their origins. Wherever they came from, Eastern Africa provided an important port of call en route to Madagascar.

By the time the Antemoro arrived, Zafindraminia enjoyed, on the whole, privileged positions among the *tompon-tany*, the custom (*sombili*) being at that time, that only a descendant of Raminia should slaughter domestic animals. The Antemoro ancestors sought to intermarry with Zafindraminia women and there were even rivalries over them. In the end, the conflicts were between the two successive waves of newcomers. This created considerable insecurity which was echoed in certain oral traditions of the *tompon-tany* as a fight of two 'giants'. The peak of this general conflict coincides with the emergence of the aristocratic Zafikasimambo as the new and powerful rulers of the region around 1550. Not without some difficulties, the genealogical Antemoro texts try to demonstrate that the Zafikasimambo descended from the Anteoni, so as to accord them local and aristocratic origins. Nevertheless, it is known from an independent source of the mid-1600s that the Zafikasimambo were the last of the overseas immigrants to settle on the banks of the Matitana and that their name came through a *tompon-tany* wife. They were considered as *ombiasa* (priests) and scribes sent from Mecca to instruct the local inhabitants. The Zafikasimambo influenced the course of Antemoro society in some decisive ways from 1560 onwards. They took over the Zafindraminia ritualistic monopoly of the *sombili* and used it as an economic and political tool. They reduced the freedoms of the common people and made religion the centre of political life. They also settled the conflicts between Antemoro and Zafindraminia by putting to death as many male descendants of Raminia as possible and by putting their women and children into confinement. It could be said that the Zafikasimambo created the first strong Antemoro kingdom at Matitana and gave it two really capable *andrianoni*, namely Rabesirana (*c.* 1580–1615) and Andriapanolaha (*c.* 1630–60).

The turmoil that the Antemoro country experienced had repercussions beyond its own frontiers. It produced, for example, a tendency towards expatriation which became a permanent feature of this society. As the sacerdotal clans fathered more of the specialists than could be absorbed into the subdivisions of the Antemoro kingdom, it became common practice for the *ombiasa* to spread out among other populations and offer their skills to those in need. Concurrently, they worked towards a significant process of political change – the transition from small, isolated and inward-looking chiefdoms to wider political unions. Constant unrest along the banks of the Matitana also led to the exile of occasional members of the aristocracy and the pogrom carried out by the Zafikasimambo against the Zafindraminia must have driven a fair number of involuntary migrants towards the interior of Madagascar.

According to Etienne de Flacourt, the Zafindraminia settled among the Antanosy at the turn of the sixteenth century but they did not manage to impose their authority. They introduced the *sombili* into the area, excelled in the construction of wooden huts, amassed cattle, their main source of wealth, and had a sense of kinship and a will for power. They thus attained a position of privilege in the lands of Antanosy. But their acquisitive impulses, internal rivalries and inability to find symbols that would unite all of the Antanosy militated against the formation of a single state ruled by the Zafindraminia kings. Instead, two parallel societies developed, with the Zafindraminia copying the *tompon-tany* hierarchy. When the French founded Fort-Dauphin in Antanosy in 1643, the two societies had interpenetrated not only as a result of exogamy but also because the upper echelons on both sides were shifting towards political centralization. However, during its 30 years on local soil (1643–74), Fort-Dauphin completely arrested this process and political unity continued to be elusive.

The Zafindraminia were not kingdom-builders and the Antemoro represent a rare instance of newcomers who created their own society and state, but the Maroserana stand out as the most important pan-dynastic family in the political history of Madagascar. They were to give rulers to the Mahafaly, the Sakalava of Menabe and Boina, to a part of the Antandroy and of the Bara. As with other newcomers, their origin and formative period remain matters of controversy. The Mahafaly and Sakalava oral traditions disagree about who the original ancestor was and about where the proto-Maroserana hailed from. Oral texts collected when the Sakalava were still independent simultaneously suggest two very different origins: Andrianalimbe from the interior of Madagascar and Andriamandazoala from overseas.

These contradictions help to explain the claims of certain authors that the Maroserana originated, for example, in south-eastern Madagascar, that they were Indians who had landed near present-day Fort-Dauphin around 1300 and gone north to found the Zarabehava, the royal family of the Antesaka, thence continuing westwards. These hypotheses have been corrected in recent years, on the basis of primary sources. As the Antesaka royal traditions indicate, the Zarabehava rulers were a branch of the west coast Sakalava who crossed Madagascar at some point between 1620 and 1650. Thus there was no movement from east to west of the Maroserana dynasty: they formed in the south-west of Madagascar. Furthermore, there is no evidence to confirm the idea of Indian origin; no Indian linguistic vestiges have ever been found in the vocabulary of the Maroserana rulers.

The two divergent Sakalava traditions are by no means contradictory. Newcomers originating from the interior, represented by Great-Lord-'Alī (Andrianalimbe), and those from overseas, represented by Andriamandazoala, drew closer together by a process of coalitions and conflicts, following a classic pattern for newcomers in Madagascar. It is highly probable that some of the Maroserana ancestors arrived in south-western Madagascar by a sea route. The ruling Maroserana among the Sakalava was known as the Zafivolamena (sons of gold) while the tombs of the Maroserana rulers in Mahafaly are still called *volamena* (red silver, i.e., gold). Given that no gold was found in the entire southern half of Madagascar, traditions which record that it was imported cannot be wrong in substance. Equally, the fact that *volamena* became a sacred metal is a reflection of the pan-dynastic vocation of those who brought it: when one considers the proximity of large Zimbabwean gold mines, with men capable of bringing it to Madagascar in a single crossing, along with the presence of several words and customs common to both Madagascar and Zimbabwe, one can hardly avoid the probability of links between Maroserana and Mwene Mutapa.

Some extremely interesting traditions, collected and published by a Sakalava at the beginning of the twentieth century shed light on the birth of Maroserana history. They point to the initial failures of newcomers to the south-west to become politically established and show that political successes were not possible until links of kinship were established with the families of local chiefs. They also reveal that the capacity for innovation was an important asset to early Maroserana. They had a sense of territorial expansion; began to introduce fortifications and build on elevated sites, used irregular soldiers, settled disputes, knew how to attract followers by redistributing food and cattle and began to consult existing diviners for affairs of state. They followed the same path among the Mahafaly where alliances with the chiefly families, the Andriantsileliky, led to their political supremacy.

It would appear that a combination of the high birth rate among the Maroserana and attempts to apply the principle of primogeniture in royal succession produced endless collateral branches and princes with no right to rule. It was probably in response to this problem that they began to seek new lands in order to give non-ruling members of the royal family villages to rule over. Nonetheless, this problem still existed into the nineteenth century, resulting in the voluntary exile of the collaterals, alliances with opponents of the Maroserana and even to the formation of rival dynasties.

Outsiders and their impact

The accounts of Europeans who visited Madagascar prior to the colonial period have been of inestimable value in their contribution to the study of the island's past. The European presence up to 1800 had, by contrast, much less commendable effects. In a general way, the Portuguese had a negative influence on the Muslim-dominated trade and its outlets in the western Indian Ocean. The north-western trading posts were located on small islets in the Bays of Mahajamba, Boina and Bombetock. They were controlled and inhabited by communities of Swahili-speakers who exported mainly rice and slaves to Eastern Africa and Arabia. The north-eastern trading post, called Iharana, was different in several respects. The Iharanians lived on the mainland; their long-standing culture was of local origin, centred on stone polishing and building crafts. There is little doubt that the decline of Iharana began at the point when Europe interfered with Muslim commerce in the Indian Ocean. From 1700 onwards, Iharana was but a ghost of its former self and its culture disappeared with hardly a tangible trace. In 1506, the Portuguese attacked the main Swahili trading post in the north-west, in the Mahajamba Bay. They attempted to destroy Boina but spared Bombetock as its _shaykh_ proved to be friendly. The Portuguese also came across a dense colony of Africans further north, in the Bay of Anorontsanga. Some 2,000 strong, these Africans prepared for combat, then changed their minds and disappeared inland. Their huts were burned and it was as if 'the whole mountain was ablaze'. Yet this particular colony was not part of the Muslim trade network; the Africans in question were escaped slaves from Malindi, Mombasa and Mogadishu.

After a warlike beginning, however, the Portuguese in Mozambique changed their tune and began to send a ship annually to north-western Madagascar to take back cattle, ambergris, raffia cloth and slaves. In adding to the demand for exports, the Portuguese were a factor in the emergence of several minor political unions in the north-west of the island, not far from the Swahili trading posts. One of these rapidly grew in importance under a ruler whose title was *tingimaro*, who was 'continually at war with his neighbours'. In June 1614, the *tingimaro* was visited in his capital of Cuala by Father Luis Mariano of the Order of Jesus in Mozambique, who hoped to secure a religious foothold in the state, but he refused to sign a treaty with the Portuguese and would not allow any missionary activity within the island.

In the late 1580s, the Moors of Mazalagem refused to trade with the Portuguese and a Dominican priest seeking local converts was killed. Only royal orders from Lisbon prevented war but not before some reprisals against Moors outside Madagascar. In 1590 north-western Madagascar was placed in the trading zone of the Mozambique Island. Between 1614 and 1620 several attempts were made to establish a church in north-western Madagascar.

The Portuguese signed several treaties with rulers along the western coast in 1613 and a Jesuit mission was sent to the Kingdom of Sadia near the Manambolo river in 1616–17. This mission triggered a civil war which had been brewing for some time and which would have important consequences in the foundation of the Sakalava kingdom of Menabe. In 1641, the Portuguese officially annexed western Madagascar in a Luso–Dutch treaty, which had no practical effect. Indeed, around 1700, north-western Madagascar was under Sakalava-Maroserana control and, a century later, the Malagasy would raid not only Portuguese vessels in the Mozambique Channel but also their bases on the Querimba and Ibo islands.

It would appear that in the early 1600s the Portuguese took fewer slaves from Madagascar than their African and Arabian competitors. At the same time, the Comoro Islands became the centre where slaves and merchandise from Madagascar were collected for shipment to Malindi, Mombasa, Mogadishu and Arabia. In 1614, Anjouan was reported to be teeming with male and female slaves from Madagascar waiting to be taken to Arabia and exchanged for Indian cotton and opium. Dhows from <u>Shihir</u> in the Gulf of Aden made direct voyages to Madagascar to buy rice, millet, and young men and women. Clearly, the Portuguese were losing their foothold in Madagascar to traditional buyers and after about 1620 they seem to have lost interest in the island altogether.

As the seventeenth century edged towards its second half, new buyers appeared in Madagascar who would not limit their activities to the north-west of the island. At least eight ships are known to have supplied the Dutch at Mauritius with rice and slaves from Madagascar, especially from the Bay of Antongil, between 1639 and 1647. The Dutch had frequent conflicts with the eastern Malagasy until 1655, when they began to make journeys to the island from the Cape: they also participated in local conflicts. But the eastern coast was disunited and the Dutch presence had no lasting impact. In the eighteenth century, however, the Dutch, along with other Europeans, exerted considerable commercial influence in several parts of Madagascar, and more especially along its western coast.

English vessels came to Madagascar hundreds of times between 1600 and 1800, mostly to its western shores and especially to the Bay of St Augustine. Pidgin English, the language of trade, established itself in the area, and certain local residents adopted English names and titles. In 1645, English Puritans were sent to the Bay of St Augustine to establish a colony, and five years later another colonial venture was started in the north-western islet of Nosy Be. Both attempts failed with considerable loss of life. Unlike the Portuguese and the Dutch, the English did not create any bases around Madagascar but they nonetheless became the most active exporters of Malagasy slaves to the New World, especially to Barbados and Jamaica. A census taken at Barbados at the end of the seventeenth century showed 32,473 slaves, half of whom were from Madagascar. Pirates took part in local wars, and contributed to the constant supply of slaves for export. It was in the course of this period of pirates that two marked changes took place in terms of trade and merchandise. First, as the Europeans started to compete, the coastal rulers took advantage of the situation to raise their prices. Secondly, and perhaps as a consequence, Europeans began to trade discarded and faulty firearms in exchange for the much coveted slaves. These firearms often exploded in the hands of those who used them.

Amongst the European nations seeking to establish a lasting foothold in Madagascar, France was the only one to achieve a modest success with Fort-Dauphin, a fortified settlement in south-eastern Madagascar, which lasted just over three decades, from 1643 to 1674. Many of the men at Fort-Dauphin married local women. Pronis, Fort-Dauphin's first governor, married a Zafindraminia *rohandrian* and the soldier nicknamed 'la Case' married an heiress-apparent in Antanosy land and became a local military hero. The best educated and longest standing of the Fort-Dauphin governors, Etienne de Flacourt (1648–58), author of two fundamental works on Madagascar, became a local potentate, forced to fend for himself as he received little support from France.

The impact of Fort-Dauphin has generally been underestimated: it was locally sensitive but also had a wider dimension. The Antanosy were, for example, about to attain their elusive political union with the Zafindraminia under the leadership of Dian Ramack when Fort-Dauphin became an obstacle. At a time when ships no longer came to it (1650–54), a bloody battle for supremacy broke out with, on one side, the *rohandrian* newcomers and on the other, French soldiers. By 1653, Dian Ramack and many *rohandrian* were dead, and a number of chiefs made allegiances (*mifaly*) to de Flacourt who had no interest in building a local state. The situation worsened after his departure but the second French East India Company, nonetheless, made further colonial attempts in Madagascar.

Outposts were set up at Antongil, on the Matitana and at Sainte-Marie. In 1667, some 2,000 colonists and French soldiers landed at Fort-Dauphin. This prompted a series of *mifaly* as rulers in Antanosy gave up the struggle for good. Outside Antanosy the French presence at Fort-Dauphin accelerated the foundation of Menabe by the Maroserana ruler, Andriandahifotsy, who sought an alliance with Fort-Dauphin. Fort-Dauphin was abandoned in 1674 and its last residents were evacuated to Mozambique, India and the Bourbon Isle (now Réunion).

Plantation economies of the neighbouring Mascarene Islands of Bourbon and Ile-de-France (Mauritius, abandoned by the Dutch in 1710), had a disruptive impact on Madagascar, particularly on its eastern coast, in the course of the eighteenth century. It is generally agreed that the majority of the slaves imported into the Mascarene Islands between 1664 and 1766 came from Madagascar but that the royal French administration, which bought these islands from the French East India Company for over £7.5 million, gradually substituted the Malagasy with slaves from Africa. It should not be forgotten, however, that imports of slaves doubled between 1766 and 1788 and that the Mascarenes, even after 1766, constantly interfered in the north-eastern part of Madagascar.

The northern and western states: Mahafaly, Sakalava, Antankara, Tsimihety

After the early Maroseranas' political success in the south-west, a new society emerged between the Menarandra and Onilahy rivers. Its name, Mahafaly (to make sacred) is linked with social differentiation and rituals of royalty. According to tradition, the first Maroserana went into total seclusion, advised and protected by the ruler's ombiasa. No longer seen, he became sacred (*faly*), and by extension, rendered the land and its inhabitants *maha-faly*. After the Masoserana came to power, Mahafaly society consisted of the privileged (*renilemy*), the common people (*valohazomanga*), and those who came from elsewhere (*folohazomanga*). The descendants of the most powerful chief at the time of Maroserana's formation (Tsileliki, the invincible), his former subjects, all those who arrived with the proto-Maroserana, as well as those who were occasionally rewarded, became the new élite.

Mahafaly history before 1800 is marked by conflicts with its neighbours, by a split into four independent kingdoms and by the annexation of lands belonging to the westernmost branch of the Antandroy. Sometime in the 1650s the first two breakaway kingdoms, the Menarandra and the Sakatovo, were formed. A little later, Menarandra spawned two more kingdoms, the Linta (*c.* 1670) and the Onilahy (*c.* 1750). It was one of the Menarandra kings who conquered the western Karimbola-Antandroy lands in the first half of the eighteenth century. An Antemoro influence can be detected in the Onilahy kingdom, whose first ruler took the Antemoro title of *andrianoni* as his name. There were six rulers in Sakatovo before 1800, seven in Linta, three in

Menarandra and two in Onilahy. These divisions reflect the numerous internal dissensions amongst the Maroserana.

While the Maroserana had their first political success among the *tompon-tany* living south of the Onilahy, the largest waterway of the south-west, their dynasty did not acquire political importance until some of its members went north into the valley of the Fiherenana. This is where the Maroserana-Volamena were born, and from where they crossed the Mangoky to form the dynasty of the Sakalava states, Menabe and Iboina. There is no doubt that Andriandahifotsy founded the Menabe dynasty and probably the Volamena branch as well. The foundings of the Volamena and Menabe dynasties have religious and secular aspects. A royal priest associated with crocodiles, Ndriamboay (noble crocodile) is credited with introducing the cult of the ancestors (*dady*) to the Maroserana, so that the rulers became the *ampagnito-be* (great royal ancestors, fathers of the people). According to other traditions, Ndriamboay sacrificed Andriandahifotsy's wife, from whose blood came both the names Volamena (silver which became red) and Menabe (great red). A more credible tradition holds that Andriandahifotsy's wife managed to bring the first firearms to him during a crucial battle. The ten weapons became part of the royal treasure and her sons became the Volamena.

When the Maroserana came into contact with peoples of Menabe, they were no longer in the lands of the south-western pastoralists. The coastal belt which extends roughly between Majunga and Morondava, for approximately 650 kilometres, was inhabited by fishermen and farmers raising few cattle. With the exception of the densely-populated Sadia, most of the inhabitants lived in small communities, and had no weapons. This stretch of the coast was known as Bambala, and its occupants spoke not Malagasy but Bantu idioms. They were Cafres not Buques. The Sakalava came from Sadia and connected with the Maroserana near the Mangoky river, probably at one of its smaller affluents called the Sakalava. All the traditions agree that the Sakalava were the outstanding warriors of their time. They were the spearhead of the political authority of the Volamena rulers but the *dady* cult gave this authority a religious base which survived the formidable warriors and their direct descendants. The formula which gave the kings posthumous names with the prefix *andria* (lord, noble) and the suffix *arivo* (thousand, thousands) was introduced into Menabe from the outside but probably not directly by the Maroserana. This formula reflects the political idea that a true king must have many subjects.

Southern Menabe was being ruled by Andriandahifotsy in the early 1670s when he was visited by a French cattle-trader from Fort-Dauphin who saw a disciplined army of some 12,000 men and received 50 young bulls as a gift for the fort's governor. Andriandahifotsy died around 1685. Conflicts over the succession left one of his sons, Trimongarivo (who became Andriamanetriarivo) in charge of Menabe, which he expanded and populated with new subjects recruited from the south-western pastoralists. His younger brother, Tsimanatona (by *fitahina* Andrianmandisoarivo), headed north to found Iboina. It is difficult to tell whether Menabe had four or six rulers between 1720 and

1800 but it remained stable during this period apart from one case of regicide reported in the 1730s. In the following decade, an important alliance with the Andrevola rulers of the Fiherenana valley was concluded by a pact of royal blood, which made the southern boundaries of Menabe more secure. In Iboina, protected from the south by its sister-state, Menabe, the Muslim trading posts and traders were forcibly brought under the protection of the Volamena ruler. Majunga grew into the capital of Iboina, while its kings and their court at Marovoay attained a splendour unequalled anywhere in Madagascar. At the time of Andrianinevenarivo (known as Andrianbaga, died in 1752), Iboina was at its height. Migrants from the north, moving south with their cattle herds, gradually absorbed most of the remaining Bambala population. This meant not only the disappearance of the Bantu-speaking *tompon-tany* but also an adverse economic change at a time when the Sakalava states needed more farmers. As it became harder to obtain agricultural labour from other parts of Madagascar, the Sakalava began to raid the Comoro Islands and even South-eastern Africa.

During the last third of the eighteenth century, Queen Ravahiny (*c.* 1767–1808) secured in Iboina a stable government and economic prosperity. Nonetheless, Iboina started to decline during her rule. The Iboina Muslims who had joined with the Sakalava constituted the country's most dynamic element and sought to seize the throne. Another weakness came, this time indirectly, from the east coast, where a Polish-Hungarian noble, Count Benyowsky, had persuaded a number of Betsimisaraka rulers to stop paying tributes to Iboina. Warriors sent in 1776 to punish the former tributaries and eliminate Benyowsky failed in their mission, revealing to the people of the interior that Iboina was no longer omnipotent. Finally, Ravahiny made an error in foreign policy by deciding to support the ruler of central Imerina, Andrianampoinimerina, against neighbouring rivals.

The Sakalava kings were both despotic and lavish. Their daily lives were regulated by the royal *moasy* (priests) and nothing could be undertaken without their advice. There was a Royal Council composed of six elders who lived at court. The first minister, *manantany*, dealt directly with the many royal councillors. His aide, the *fahatelo*, was usually selected for his knowledge of clans and lineages as well as Sakalava customs. Each village had its own royal official who made sure that the people worked four days a week in the royal rice fields, and that the royal herd was constantly renewed through gifts, which were in fact fixed quotas. No monarch could rule without being in possession of the royal *dady* (ancestral Volamena relics), especially since a new king automatically became the sole intermediary between the living and the royal ancestors.

The Tsimihety grew out of groups of leaderless refugees from the east coast, who, had fled the slave wars and settled with their cattle in the great Mandritsara plain. In the far north, in the rocky part of the island, lived the Antankara (rock people). Neither of these peoples had developed their own state and both came to accept rule by Maroserana collaterals, the Volafotsy, who, unable to rule among the Sakalava, had migrated into the northern interior in search of a kingdom. The Tsimihety, however, quickly rejected the Volafotsy (or the Volamena) and deliberately adopted their collective name (*tsimihety*) to indicate their non-submission to Maroserana authority. Since they failed to form a centralized kingdom, their eighteenth-century history remains practically unknown.

The Antankara reactions were quite different. Some came to submit to Iboina's founder and part of them were to be under Sakalava control, at one time or another, well into the nineteenth century. Nonetheless, a royal line going back to a Volafotsy named Kazobe emerged from them. A fully centralized Antankara kingdom did not evolve, however, until the time of his great-nephew, Andriantsirotso, who ruled, according to the texts, either from *c.*1697 to 1710, or from 1710 to *c.* 1750. He built the royal necropolis at Ambatosahana and introduced the unifying symbol of Antankara royalty, the *saina*, the flag with crescent and star. He associated his power with a formidable *moasy* (priest) who made royal amulets. He became advisor to two of his successors and lived to be over 100 years old. His son and successor, Lamboina, had one of the longest rules in Madagascar, noted for its absence of wars. The Antankara borrowed their political organization from the Iboina-Sakalava but did not adopt the *dady* cult.

States of the interior: Betsileo, Merina, Sihanaka, Bezanozano, Tanala and Bara

The Betsileo derive their name from a ruler named Besilau who is known to have opposed the Sakalava expansion of Menabe into the interior highlands during the 1670s. Yet the populations that later became known as the Betsileo only came under a single government through external force in the 1800s. A mixture of *tompon-tany* and diverse newcomers, the Betsileo were subdivided into four main states: Arindrano in the south, merging with Ibara; Isandra in the centre, facing west and the Sakalava; Lalangina in east-central Betsileo with the Tanala as neighbours; and Manandriana in the north. It is unlikely that the Betsileo had developed any kingdoms before the 1650s. Rasahamanarivo, the founder of Lalangina, was forced to abdicate in favour of his brother because he had leprosy, but around 1680 he went to Arindrano and was accepted there by the southern Betsileo as their ruler. Struggles for succession and wars with neighbours arrested the growth of Lalangina which, after a case of regicide, broke up into four provinces. Nonetheless, the usurping branch of Lalangina's royal family produced at least three strong rulers in the eighteenth century; Roanimanalina, who reunited the kingdom and introduced a national militia; Andrianonindranarivo, who carried out economic and social reforms; and Ramaharo, who transformed the militia into an economic adjunct of state intended to increase rice production. Indeed, during the eighteenth century, the Betsileo became Madagascar's principal rice producers.

According to conflicting traditions, the ancestor of Isandra's royal family, the Zafimanarivo, was either an Antemoro female or a Maroserana prince in exile.

Geography certainly favours a Maroserana antecedent. An early Zafimanarivo is associated with the term *volamena*. One could not call Isandra a notable Betsileo state until the 1750s when it came under the reign of a great monarch, Andriamanalina I. Sometimes called the 'jester king' because of his ability to win political arguments through humour, Andriamanalina I was the first Betsileo to conceive of a unified, single state. When diplomacy failed, Andriamanalina I used military force. He expanded his kingdom westward, placing his Betsileo on the Midongy massif and moving southward into Ibara, where he obtained an important vassal, the Bara ruler Andriamanely II. Retaining the traditional structures of each region, Andriamanalina I placed his sons at the head of four new provinces where most of the Betsileo lived. At his death in 1790, the Betsileo were at their political zenith. As for Manandriana, it had only a very short span as an independent state, having formed after 1750, with its second ruler placing himself willingly under the Merina around 1800.

The Merina history begins, strictly speaking, with the reign of Ralambo, variously estimated between 1610 and 1640. Hitherto, Imerina was not an organized state; it consisted of numerous village chiefdoms peopled either by *tompon-tony*, the Vazimba, or by the Hova migrants. The first member of the Andriana dynasty was Andriamanelo, Ralambo's father. It was he who created the first fortifications at Alosava and who started using iron-tipped, rather than clay-tipped, spears in war.

With Ralambo came the first of the twelve *sampy*, amulet-guardians of Imerina, the royal practices of circumcision and incest, the *fandraona* or annual ceremony of the royal bath, divinization of departed monarchs, the noble classes, silversmiths and ironsmiths in the service of the state, head tax, consumption of beef and a small but standing army. His son and successor, Andrianjaka, took certain internal political measures which inspired fear in his subjects but nevertheless he founded Antananarivo and exploited the marshes for rich rice harvests, thus making the Merina the most numerous people among the Malagasy.

The population growth in Merina increased the risk of famine and compelled its rulers to continually expand the irrigated areas. While Andrianjaka's three successors distinguished themselves mainly by lengthening their royal names, his great-grandson, Andriamasinavalona, was, in his turn, a great monarch. He pursued a policy of aggressive expansion and allowed little independence to the many chiefs who came under his authority. He increased the number of noble clans from four to six and rewarded the most deserving nobles with village fiefs and the title of *tompon-menakely* (masters of the fief). Wishing to settle the question of his succession while he was still in power, he divided Imerina into four provinces and placed a son to rule each one. Very soon, he found himself at the head of four independent kingdoms and what is more, he suffered the humiliation of being imprisoned by one of his sons. The old king died around 1750 and Imerina became an arena for internal civil wars in which even outsiders took part. By 1770, Ambohimanga had conquered Ambohitrabiby and appeared strong under its ruler Andrianbelomasina. His nephew, Ramboasalama, who became ruler at Ambohimanga around 1777–8, came to be regarded as the most important of Imerina's kings.

Assuming the name of Andrianampoinimerina, he first managed to secure peace with his royal brothers and rivals, and then fortified the borderlands of his kingdom. Antatanarivo fell under his domination in 1797, Ambohidratrimo shortly afterwards, and several less defined areas of Imerina before 1800. He did not content himself with unifying Imerina and began sending emissaries to rulers in other parts of Madagascar with offers to become his vassal while retaining autonomy, or else, if they refused, to see their territory conquered by the Merina. This form of diplomacy succeeded at times, for example, among the Manandriana Betsileo, the Andrantsay of Betafo, and in western Imamo.

Although neither the Sihanaka nor the Bezanozano developed into powerful state structures, their history remains of considerable interest. The Sihanaka group evolved around Lake Alaotra while the Bezanozano settled in an area between the tropical rainforests of the eastern coast and the slopes of the plateau. Both were ideally situated on the main commercial route linking Imerina with the eastern coast and became suppliers to the Mascarene slave-traders. Indeed, both the Sihanaka and the Bezanozano possessed so many slaves that in 1768 they had to seek help from Europeans to suppress internal slave rebellions. In 1667, when François Martin penetrated into Sihanaka territory he found them inhabiting fortified villages. They had the only bridge seen in Madagascar until that time by Europeans and they were also extremely well armed with bows and arrows. Martin also confirmed the Sihanaka as one of the most important trading groups in the islands, all of which would imply considerable political organization. Yet there is no evidence that they ever had central authority. In fact, the Sihanaka paid tribute to Iboina in the eighteenth century but not without at least one serious attempt to free themselves of it through a major attack which ended in failure. The Bezanozano, whose land was originally called Ankay, were also ruled by local chiefs and lived in fortified villages. Unlike the Sihanaka, however, they had at least one unifying institution, in the form of amulets representing 11 protector-deities said to have come from Sakalava land. Towards the end of the eighteenth century the Bezanozano seem to have accepted the authority of Randrianjomoina, their first king, but he was not to rule for very long as the Merina demanded and secured his submission.

Wedged between the Betsileo highlanders and the coastal Antemoro, the Tanala took their name from their natural surroundings, 'people of the forest'. The Tanala soon developed into a highly mixed population since as many as 23 of their clans have claimed Betsileo descent. They never formed a state. Some of them, however, do stand out in local history, such as the Tanala of Ikongo, a huge rock accessible only by artificial passages. While completely isolated from the Betsileo highlands, the Tanalo-Ikongo area was the natural hinterland of the coastal region, accessible by such waterways as the Sandrananta, the Faraony and the Matitana river of the Antemoro. It is therefore not surprising that the Ikongo-Tanala accepted migrants from the eastern coast and that one

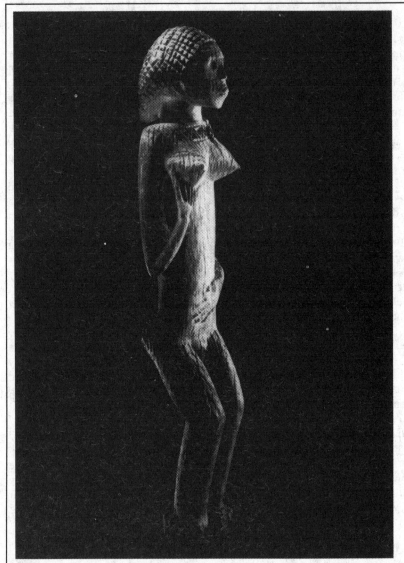

28.2 *Bara ethnic group of Ambusitra, south-eastern Madagascar: memorial statue called*
alualu, *erected when a person dies without male issue or when the corpse does not rest in the*
family grave. The statue was surrounded by an enclosure of posts bearing the horns of zebu
cows sacrificed at the funeral ceremonies. The rule was that it was a female figure that becomes
the replacement for the dead male and symbolizes the element destined to ensure issue. Made
from the hard wood of the camphor treee. Height: 107 cm (G. Berjonneau, ART 135,
Boulogne-Billancourt, © and photo)

of them, Rambo, said to have been an Anteono-Antemoro, fathered the local dynasty of the Zafirambo, first mentioned by outsiders in 1668. According to Tanala traditions, Rambo became king of Ikongo through his knowledge of curative amulets and of *sorabe*. Rambo is also remembered as the 'law-giver'. The greater part of the eighteenth century was marked by conflicts between the Ikongo-Tanala and the Antemoro leading to a devastating Tanala invasion of the lowlands towards the end of the century. At the beginning of the nineteenth century, one of the Zafirambo, Andriamamohotra, allied himself with Andrianampoinimerina.

The Bara, the major pastoralists of Madagascar, who have often been given an African origin, seem to have emerged from somewhere in the southern reaches of Arindrano country, along the Ihosy river. To the three great Bara clans, the Bara-be, the Bara-Ianstsantsa and the Bara-Imamono, were added two smaller clans, the Vinda of south-western Ibara and the Antivondro. There were two distinct dynastic periods in the southern interior regions (of which Ibara is the largest): one which coincides with the proto-Maroserana and is largely unknown, and the more recent one, the period of the Zafimaneli, which started around 1650. A total absence of succession rules and the ease with which dissenters could migrate with their herds to better grazing lands undoubtedly facilitated the disintegration of authority from 1640 onwards, when the Mahafaly ruler, Dian Manhelle, invaded the area and began to instal members of his family as local rulers. After his death in 1653, his descendants, the Zafimanely, gradually assumed positions of authority in Ibara, but not necessarily to its benefit. Between 1650 and 1680, Ibara's history is dominated by competition among Zafimanely kinglets, not so much political as economic in nature. With no system of regular tribute, the Zafimanely could only maintain their power by securing wealth through legal decisions and more especially by raiding their neighbours' cattle. This cycle of tension was broken only after 1800 by Raikitroka, a king who deserves to be studied in greater depth.

The eastern and southern states: Betsimisaraka, Antemoro, Antambahoaka, Antefasy, Antesaka, Antanosy and Antandroy

The Betsimisaraka, often divided into 'Northerners' (Antavaratra) and 'Southerners' (Antatsimo), and the Betanimena, established between the two, lived along the eastern coast of Madagascar, roughly between the Bay of Antongil and Vatomandry. According to numerous sources the *tompon-tany* of this region were strangers to the larger political unions up until the beginning of the eighteenth century and remained under chiefs (*filohany*) who rarely controlled more than one or two villages. The Antavaratra were favoured by nature since they had all the ports, while the Betanimena coast had none. As the Mascarenes came to depend increasingly on eastern Madagascar for their imports, the control of these ports made the *filohany's* fortune. This was also the part of Madagascar which between 1680 and 1720 was most heavily colonized by European, especially English, and American pirates. Many of them intermarried with the Antavaratra, and fathered mixed-race children. From one such union, around 1694, a certain Ratsimilahoe was born and a political change among the Betanimena served as a springboard to launch him on to the political scene. Around 1710, the Betanimena (known at that time as Sicoua) elected the chief of Vatomandry as their supreme ruler, who would lead them into the northern ports. It was by standing firm against an invasion of these ports that Ratsimilahoe managed, despite his youth, to unite most of the Antavaratra.

Ratsimilahoe recaptured Fénérive in 1712 and the hasty retreat of the Sicoua across fields of heavy, red clay earned them the name *Be-tani-mena* (the many of red earth). Ratsimilahoe coined the name Betsimisaraka (the indivisible many) to underline the lasting nature of the political union and in contrast to the Betanimena. He secured peace with them by leaving to their king the port of Tamatave, but eventually he was himself elected king of all the Betsimisaraka and renamed Ramaroumanompou (the lord of many subjects) at his capital of Foulpointe. But this peace lasted only six months and Ratsimilahoe retook Tamatave, forcing the Betanimena king into an inaccessible area further south. He then entered into alliances with the Antatismo and the Bezanozano. Around 1730, Ratsimilahoe was one of the most powerful kings in Madagascar, holding together a confederation of clans and families of rather independent habits. He achieved this by allowing the traditional chiefs to keep their autonomy and pay as much tribute as each saw fit, in slaves, cattle and rice. He compensated the families of *filohany* who had fallen in battles against the Betanimena and he allowed the Betanimena to bail out their relatives taken as prisoners during hostilities. He dealt high justice, permitting any Betsimisaraka to apply directly to him. Keenly aware of the strong centrifugal tendencies which threatened his kingdom, Ratsimilahoe married the king of Iboina's only daughter, in order to bind himself to the Volamena and the Sakalava empire. He died in 1754, after a 40-year reign. Of the three kings who succeeded him between 1755 and 1803, the second, Iavy, achieved fame only as the biggest slave-trader in Madagascar. In the second half of the eighteenth century, Betsimisaraka-land came to resemble Angola at the height of its slaving tragedies in the early part of the seventeenth century.

There is no longer any doubt that both the Antesaka and the Antefasy of south-eastern Madagascar were founded by migrants from the west. The Antesaka, whose name indicates Sakalava origins, had left Menabe and ended up in Nosipandra (later Vangaindrano), which became their capital. It would appear that their migration was over by the 1650s. As for the Antefasy, their traditions hold that the ultimate ancestor, Ndretsileo, came from the African mainland to the River Menarandra and settled in Ibara. Difficulties with the Zafimanely had worsened by the time of his grandson, Ndrembolanony. He married the daughter of the ruler of Antevatobe and one of their three sons, Marofela, coined the name Antefasy (sand people), meaning, by the sand analogy, that his kingdom would be densely populated.

The most important Antefasy ruler prior to the 1800s was undoubtedly Ifara, who resided at Ambaky (the old name for Farafangana). Ifara gained a monopoly of trade with the first European vessels to visit his coast and became so powerful that he was, at one time, regarded as the sole proprietor of the Manampatra river. Another Zarabehava ruler who is particularly remembered is Maseba, who rescued the Antefasy from a brief Antemoro domination. According to Antemoro sources, conflicts between the Antemoro and the Antefasy can be dated to the 1680s. They continued into the 1700s but the wars were not conclusive.

The Antesaka were more inward-looking and they had many difficulties over successions. Tradition recalls that one of their Zarabehava kings, Ratongalaza, 'either killed or expelled all his brothers'. His grandson, Lengoabo, was the last eighteenth-century king and he extended the Antesaka boundaries to their greatest limits. The history of the Antambahoaka and the Antemoro during the eighteenth-century remains unknown, despite the fact that Matitana is cited by European accounts as one of the main exporters of rice and slaves, especially after 1724.

The European presence within Antanosy country was sustained not only by links with Fort-Dauphin but also by the development, after the 1720s, of a plantation economy by the Mascarenes, with an insatiable demand for slaves, rice and cattle. The Count of Modave, governor of the second French establishment at Fort-Dauphin (1767–70), discovered no less than 35 rulers between the Ambolo valley and the Mandrare river. They battled with each other over slaves and cattle, causing frequent migrations of their own subjects. Modave, who opposed the slave trade and came to replace it with legitimate trade, was abandoned by France and ended up becoming a slaver to pay his debts and resupply his own plantations on Ile de France (Mauritius).

It should be recalled that Fort-Dauphin was built at a time when Antanosy-land was already one of the most densely populated in Madagascar, with a surplus agricultural production and serious possibilities of becoming a unified state. Shortly after the collapse of Modave's mission a French traveller described Antanosy-land as 'the poorest and the saddest' in the island, thinly populated and virtually without resources.

Antandroy, the southernmost state of Madagascar, divides into two very distinct sections. In western Antandroy, the Karimbola have no memory of migration. Eastern Antandroy was once occupied mainly by the Mahandrovato, who were later submerged by a great influx of migrants from Ibara and Antanosy seeking refuge in the arid south. It would appear that the ruling dynasty of the Zafimanara emerged from among the Mahandrovato and that their rule was gradually accepted by the Karimbola as well. The collective name, Antandroy, was given by the Zafimanara to all the peoples living between the Menarandra and the Mandare rivers, and it reflects a sense of political unity and implies the existence of a Zafimanara confederation. By the 1790s, the Zafimanara, driven out by floods and unable to cope with the changes in their former domain, had to take refuge on the Manombo plateau. As for many other populations in Madagascar, the end of the eighteenth century did not augur well for the Antandroy.

The Comoro Islands: Grande Comore, Anjouan, Moheli and Mayotte

The Comoro Islands are situated roughly halfway between Madagascar and Africa. The Grande Comore is nearest to the African mainland, Mayotte faces Madagascar, while Anjouan and Moheli are in the middle of the archipelago. There is general agreement that the Comoros were settled by Bantu-speaking mainlanders who had no discernible links with Islam, that this great religion was imported by the Afro-Shīrāzī and that the lasting supremacy of Sunnite Islam among the Comoreans must be attributed to the political successes of more recent Muslim arrivals from Africa. In the traditional accounts collected by Saʿīd Aḥmad ʿAlī, the pre-Islamic and Shirazi periods are associated with the ancient chiefs (*bēdja*) and their *fani* successors, whose daughters (*jumbe*) would come to marry the Sunnite newcomers. A chronology of the *bēdja* and *fani* has not yet been possible in the absence of detailed archaeological, linguistic and historical studies. Such studies could go a long way towards a new under-standing of three monumental events; the migrations of the Bantu-speaking peoples, Indonesian migrations to Africa and Madagascar and the advent of the Swahili culture itself.

Along with the arrival of the last Muslims clearly appeared a political concept. For the first time, the four Comoros were perceived as a single unity where attempts were made to bring them under one monarch (sultan) residing in Anjouan. The sultanic period may have started as late as 1506 or even before 1400. One or more of the Comoros might well have been under the control of traders from Mozambique and Kilwa before the arrival on Grande Comore of 'Muslim Arabs, belonging to the same tribe that founded Malindi'. Whenever Mount Kartala erupted, the Grande Comore could always be seen from the African mainland.

The first Comorean dynasty is said to have originated in Anjouan, despite the fact that the first ancestor migrated into Grande Comore. The second ancestor, Ḥassan/Ḥassani, the real founder of the dynasty, is depicted as a prolific builder of mosques on Anjouan. He is also considered the main propa-gator of the Shāfiʿīte rite and his reign seems firmly linked with the adoption of Sunnite Islam by the people of Anjouan. His sons had two names, one Bantu, the other Arabic, and they extended the Hassanite dynasty to the other Comoros, probably introducing the new religious faith at the same time. But while Sunnite Islam took hold across the Comoros, bringing with it a new system of justice with its *ḳāḍī nāʾib* (village judges) and its *madjelisse* (body of jurists), political rivalry became both a constant and a dynamic feature of Comorean society.

European sources as well as local traditions reveal that Comorean history is dominated not by Grande Comore and Mayotte but by Anjouan and Moheli. Right at the start of the seventeenth century, independent visitors from different parts of Europe confirm that Anjouan did indeed have a monarch – a queen – regarded as the supreme head of all four Comoros. According to the same sources, each island had its own ruler who in turn revered the queen of Anjouan as dynastic head. In 1602, for example, Moheli was ruled by an independent and imposing Muslim king, who stunned European visitors with his astonishing competence in navigational matters, his first-hand knowledge of Africa and Arabia and his command of the Portuguese language. In 1614, English voyagers found that Grande Comore was divided among ten 'lords', that the queen of Anjouan (the 'old Sultana') had 'delegated' power over Moheli to her two sons, and that Moheli's principal port was under Fombony's governor, a man of great influence. In the same year, the old *fani* of M'samudu proclaimed himself an independent sultan and master of northern Anjouan, and the venerable queen no longer controlled her island. By 1626, there were two contenders for the Mohelian Sultanate, a descendant of the *fani* and an 'Arab' who had both married daughters of the 'last Sultan'.

With few exceptions, Comorean rulers sought good relations with the Europeans who came to their islands. Nearly all the English ships bound for Mocha, Persia and Surat, put into port at Anjouan, thus forging a long-lasting Anglo-Anjouan link, a friendship on which the local sultans would call from time to time. The Comorean traders had, for a long time, been middlemen between Madagascar, Africa and Arabia, but this does not mean that the four islands had nothing to export themselves. Wars which raged within an island, such as the one on Grande Comore in 1620, and frequent sea-raids from one island to another, often had as their main objective the capturing of slaves for export. The worst period was that of the pirates in the western Indian Ocean (1680–1720) when the sacking and destruction of Comorean towns became commonplace. It was precisely between 1700 and 1720 that British naval squadrons brought active aid to Anjouan and its sultan. This military assistance reflected the desire to extend Anjouan's effective control over the other Comoros and to obtain, in exchange, the sultan's refusal to shelter the pirates. The pirate supremacy had ended by 1720 but not the British armed interventions on behalf of Anjouan.

In 1736, according to Sa'īd Aḥmad 'Alī, Anjouan had a new monarch, Sultan Aḥmad, who believed that all the Comoros should be under a supreme ruler. His reign was long but marked by an attempted *coup d'état* in 1743, a full-scale political war with Mayotte a few years later, and above all, a major internal revolt. The original inhabitants of Anjouan (the Wamatsaha), led by a charismatic commoner named Tumpa, rose up in 1775 against the ruling Arab element, demanding full equality. The Hassanites, who had taken on a platoon of British marines, had no difficulty in shooting Tumpa down. His death ended a movement that could have had far-reaching consequences for Anjouan and the other Comoros. Yet, as the eighteenth century drew to a close, the real problems were just beginning for the Comoros. Canoe fleets from Madagascar, manned by the Sakalava and the Betsimisaraka, began to raid the four islands for slaves, terrorizing the local inhabitants up to 1825. Moreover, upheavals caused by the Merina expansion in Madagascar had an unexpected consequence.

Following the massive arrivals of Sakalava fleeing from Iboina, Mayotte became Malagasy-speaking and the island acquired Malagasy sultans. Indeed, the situation for the Comoros, halfway between Africa and Madagascar, was not at all easy.

The Mascarene Islands: Réunion and Mauritius

In contrast to Madagascar and the Comoros, the Mascarene Islands east of Madagascar remained uninhabited until the arrival of Europeans in the Indian Ocean. Réunion (Bourbon) and Mauritius (Ile de France) became naval bases controlled by large maritime companies. The development of a plantation economy on these islands affected not only the eastern part of Madagascar but also eastern and south-eastern Africa and even the coast of India. After 1638, the Dutch concentrated their efforts on Mauritius, exploiting its timber and developing a slave-trade with Madagascar, but in 1710 they abandoned the island. Réunion received its first settlers from Fort-Dauphin in 1646 and 1654; they were French and Malagasy rebels against the first French East India Company, which, nonetheless, managed to make Bourbon its preserve from 1664 to 1719. The French had colonized Mauritius from Réunion by 1721 and both islands came under the control of the second East India Company until 1767, when the Mascarenes were turned over to the royal administration. Inspired by the French Revolution in 1790, the planters of Réunion and Mauritius began to demand a form of local nationalism which stood against such metropolitan measures as the abolition of slavery in 1794. At the end of the Napoleonic Wars, Mauritius passed to British control for good, and the supply of slaves was temporarily halted.

Around 1710, Réunion and Mauritius together had some 2,000 inhabitants, a third of whom were slaves. By mid-century the population had increased by 300 per cent but slaves made up more than two-thirds of this increase. Towards the end of the eighteenth century the two islands had 120,000 inhabitants, which included 94,000 slaves. From the beginning of the eighteenth century five social groups could be seen: whites descended from first-generation colonists, white creoles, *mulatto* creoles, resident white foreigners and slaves. There were few emancipated slaves before 1797. Nonetheless, an important change occurred within the slave population when Mascarene buyers gradually turned their interests away from Madagascar and towards Africa and India in search of new labourers. This change can be explained mainly by the belief that the Malagasy were particularly prone to form fugitive slave colonies. In fact, *marronnage* (fugitive slaves) in Réunion and Mauritius was, like everywhere else, a response to slavery, made possible by the environment of mountains and forests.

Although sugar cane had been cultivated on Mauritius since 1639, the first sugar-mill only came into being during the administration of Mahé de Labourdonnais (1735–46). Mauritius did not export sugar until after the advent of the royal French government which discarded the restrictive measures imposed by the French East India Company and opened the islands to all French nationals at the end of the 1760s. Coffee, introduced to Réunion in 1715 to become its main crop, attained its last record harvest in the early 1740s. By 1767, it was in such a state of decline, as a result of competition from the Antilles, that Réunion's planters had to fall back on spices. During the next 30 years, as commercial interest shifted from the Atlantic to the Indian Ocean, the Mascarene Islands became the focal point of a veritable '*route des Iles*'. Mauritius, which, in the Company days used to be visited by some 30 ships a year, saw a tenfold increase in incoming vessels by 1803. Around 1800, the privileged minorities in the Mascarene Islands had a standard of living which equalled, or was superior to, that of all the other colonial territories.

29

The history of African societies, 1500–1800: conclusion

Various labels have been applied to the period stretching from 1500 to 1800 in African history. Many history books present it as the era of the slave trade, overestimating the importance of the phenomenon in the continent's history. They overlook the fact that, in West and Central Africa, the slave trade lasted until about 1850 and in East Africa, it developed during the nineteenth century, if we exclude an earlier slave trade to the Muslim world. The label also takes no account of the fact that some parts of the continent, such as South Africa, knew practically no slave trade at all. Certain historians, particularly the neo-marxists, see the gradual integration of Africa into the world capitalist economy dominated by Europe as the main feature of the period, thereby giving more weight to Africa's external relations than to its internal evolution. They portray the African peoples as hapless victims of world forces which they can neither understand nor control. Other historians single out the movement of populations and the definitive settling of the continent as the distinguishing characteristic of the period. In fact, with the exception of a few cases, one has to note that there were hardly any mass migrations in Africa after 1500. Still other researchers would wish to present the history of these three centuries as a series of ecological catastrophes and consider droughts and famines to be the determining factors of the period.

Each of these labels has some element of truth, but none of them takes sufficient account of the complexity and the dynamism of these three centuries of African history. In this final chapter, we shall endeavour to extract the main themes of the historical evolution of African societies during this period, basing our discussions on the various chapters in this volume.

Let us start by taking the fundamental question of population movements. Most of Africa was already colonized by 1500 and what oral traditions refer to as migrations, were, in effect, population expansion and drift. Only north-east Africa experienced mass movement of population during this period, among the Oromo, the Somali, the Luo, the Karamojong, the Kalenjin, the Turkana and the Maasai (see Chapter 3).

What is of much greater significance than the migrations is the fact that the period from 1500 to 1800 was crucial for the great socio-political formations on the continent. It was during these three centuries that most of the inhabitants of the different regions of Africa coalesced into the wider social, economic, religious, cultural and political units that make up the present-day African peoples.

As African societies evolved into distinct ethnic groups with their own peculiar linguistic and cultural characteristics, much of Africa was changing as a result of developments in its external relations. While in 1500 most African societies were independent of the rest of the world, by 1800 much of Africa had become integrated into the circuits of the world market which securely linked it to Europe, America and Asia. This process of integration was facilitated by the establishment of new communities on the continent, such as the Dutch settlers in southern Africa, the Portuguese in Angola and on the east coast and the Ottomans in Egypt and the Maghrib. Many African societies had, gradually, to change their way of life or move, or both. Soon, radically different relationships grew up within and between societies, characterized by dominance and dependence, both internally and in a world system in which Europe had become the dominant power.

Pathe Diagne has identified the main economic structures which developed during this period (see Chapter 2). The predatory economy of plundering, for example, was the outcome of Spanish and Portuguese expansionism. It completely disrupted the sub-systems of the Mediterranean and the Indian Ocean and impoverished the countryside which was later further plunged into crisis by the slave trade. A military aristocracy that lived by piracy and raiding, using the services of freemen and slaves, emerged.

Like the predatory economy, the trading-post economy concerned itself little with innovation. The new maritime trading posts were fortresses rather than commercial or industrial centres. On the coasts of Guinea and equatorial Africa, in the Kongo, Angola and Senegambia, the Portuguese looted more than they bought. From 1650 to 1800 the trading-post economy relied on the transatlantic slave trade. The societies affected by the trading-post economy were gradually transformed in the seventeenth and eighteenth centuries. This was a complex process involving major reorganizations, the main feature of which, especially in West-Central Africa, was the predominance of the trading networks over the states (see Chapter 18).

As the states declined, so did the old ruling élites, with a merchant class arising to replace or complement them. The Portuguese penetration of Southern Zambezia, for example, seriously weakened the power of the indigenous ruling class and facilitated the institution of direct forms of peasant exploitation by Portuguese capitalists (see Chapter 22). Similar developments brought about the *mestizos* and creoles of Casamance, Guinea and Sierra Leone. The Afro-Portuguese and the Anglo-Africans of Sierra Leone were merchant groups which acted as middlemen between the European ships and the African societies of the interior.

Even in the case of the Fundj and Fūr sultanates, where the sultans appear to have patronized and protected the long-distance trade linking them with Egypt and the Red Sea, the bulk of the trade was in the hands of the Sudanese *djallāba* (traders) who acted as the middlemen and financiers of foreign trade.

Thus from relative isolation in 1500, the various peoples of Africa gradually became integrated into the world economy. In most cases, this integration was accompanied by sharp social and political changes.

Despite the collapse of large states in western Sudan and north-east Africa at the beginning of our period, the total surface area of territories controlled by the states increased over the course of these three centuries: the period is also characterized by numerous examples of political consolidation due to the expansion and centralization of political institutions.

In north-east Africa, for example, although the sixteenth and seventeenth centuries witnessed the collapse of the Christian Ethiopian empire, there was expansion of this empire southwards, which stimulated the growth of new states such as Boša, Kaffa, Sĕkko, Wolayta and Dauro.

In the case of Madagascar, we note the opposite process of centralization. By the beginning of the seventeenth century, Madagascar still consisted essentially of small, self-contained chiefdoms, but by the end of that century, the Sakalava empire had established itself in the western part, and several kingdoms appeared on the island. The Sakalava empire reached its peak in the eighteenth century and the eastern coast became politically united for the first time into the Betsimisaraka confederation. By 1800, these two states were in decline and the state of Imerina, formerly weak and disunited, gained power.

A similar process of unification and centralization occurred on the coast of Lower Guinea. According to a map dated 1629, there were 38 states and kingdoms then in the region, founded by the Ga and Akan peoples. From these states emerged the three large empires of Aowin, Denkyira and Akwamu, which by 1750 had merged to form the Asante empire.

A more common political phenomenon during these three centuries was for a state in decline or collapse to be succeeded by several localized states or by economic systems. Thus, in Central Africa, the Kongo, the Tio, Loango and Ndongo (future Angola) kingdoms, which existed in the sixteenth century, from 1665 began to decline and territories were reorganized on a larger scale on the basis of economic imperatives dictated by the slave trade.

On the Upper Guinea coast, other states succeeded the empires of Songhay and Mali. The Grand Foul empire arose in the seventeenth century on the ruins of Songhay, but gave way to the empire of Kaarta during the second half of the eighteenth century. All along the Atlantic coast, the countries that had grown up as a result of the dismemberment of Mali were unified by the Kaabu (Gabu) in the seventeenth and eighteenth centuries and then by the Futa Jallon in the eighteenth and nineteenth centuries. In the centre, the recovery took place under the aegis of the Bambara of Segu and, in the south, the Jula (Dyula) organized the empire of Kong in the eighteenth century.

A similar process can be seen in Southern Zambezia. The decline of the Great Zimbabwe gave rise first to the Torwa state and later to the Mutapa empire at the beginning of the sixteenth century. The fragmentation and decline of the Mutapa state began in 1629 but the Mutapa political entity did not finally disappear until 1917.

In most of the new states, original systems of government and administration were developed. Dahomey, for example, represented a new idea of the state. The traditional view, which considered the state as a larger version of the family, was succeeded by the notion of a strong centralized state ruled by an absolute monarch demanding unreserved loyalty from all his subjects.

In most of these states, various social classes emerged: aristocrats, military groups, commoners and slaves. Thus, the Kanuri society in Borno was highly layered. In Hausaland, as the aristocrats and traders grew rich, the distinction shifted to an economic level with the *attajirai* (the wealthy) and the *talakawa* (the poor).

The aristocracy (administrative and military) grew rich using various means of exploitation. In Egypt, for instance, as the Ottoman empire declined, internal struggles between different social strata developed. The critical state of the economy was a reflection of a policy of oppression whereby the majority of the people were controlled and exploited by a small élite made up of Mamluk *beys* and their retinues. This oppressive situation led to the rise of popular literature in Arabic, dealing with the exploitation of the peasants.

These oppressive regimes led to peasant revolts in many African regions. There is an urgent need for a thorough study of these peasant uprisings in the seventeenth and eighteenth centuries.

The slave trade

What importance should be given to the slave trade in African history? In other words, what is our interest, as African historians, in the slave trade? All races have been enslaved in the past: the word itself comes from 'Slavs', which means East Europeans. But all other groups have found a way of eliminating the idea from their historical consciousness. The Africans overestimate, to such an extent the importance of slavery in their history that the term 'slave' is almost equated with 'African'. As D.B. Davis has clearly shown in his books slavery is a major phenomenon in the ideology of the modern Western world which we must endeavour to understand.

In Chapter 4, J. E. Inikori attempts to measure the role of black slavery in the economic progress of the Western world. This is another fundamental question which must be studied frankly and in depth. Marx and Engels argued that though slavery is and always has been immoral, it has nevertheless been essential for economic and therefore social progress. Without slavery, they argue, there would have been no Greek or Roman civilization. Inikori argues that African slavery was essential for the development of the Atlantic-oriented economic and geo-political system and the industrialisation of Western Europe. But, Fernand Braudel has presented, in his three-volume *Civilisation and Capitalism*, a different picture of the rise of European capitalism to world power. Starting with the traditional economy of peasant subsistence through the market place, he explains how, finally, a handful of bankers and merchants managed, by monopolizing trade and maximizing profit, to extend the growing power of European capitalism. The role of African slavery in this debate needs a radical reassessment.

In Chapter 5, J.E. Harris raises another important question related to slavery. From all the available evidence, it is clear that the dehumanizing of the Africans intensified between 1500 and 1800 as a result of the increase in slavery from 1619. It is, however, the intercontinental slave trade, more than anything else, which established a black presence all over the world. It led to a major African diaspora especially in the Americas and the Caribbean. This is where the struggle for the liberation of blacks began, which was the foundation of the pan-African Movement of the nineteenth and twentieth centuries.

Introduction of new food crops

The introduction of new food crops from the Americas has been seen by many authors as a positive aspect of transatlantic trade. Some have asserted that these crops, which led to a change in diet, improved the health of Africans, thus contributing to population increase. But, as E. M'Bokolo has observed, the effects of these agricultural changes on the African population are difficult to interpret. He points out, for instance, that cassava has limited nutritional value and the people who relied on it most, such as the Tio and the Mbosi, suffered from serious malnutrition.

Population trends during the seventeenth and eighteenth centuries are difficult to discern because this period, during which the slave trade reached its peak, was also characterized by the introduction into Africa of new diseases, such as smallpox, that were to become recurrent scourges.

What is certain, however, is that the new crops from the Americas and Asia, introduced by Europeans to various African regions between 1500 and 1800, especially maize, cassava, groundnuts, various types of yam, sweet potatoes, citrus fruit, tomatoes, onions and tobacco, diversified the agricultural economy of the continent. The present-day heavy reliance of Africans on maize and cassava as the main staple diet dates back to this period.

Socially, according to M'Bokolo, this agricultural revolution contributed, along with the development of trade, to the establishment of a new division of labour. Men gradually left the many agricultural tasks to the women and slaves, preferring instead to devote themselves to trade, which was much more lucrative. Thus the development of domestic slavery and other forms of dependence was a direct consequence of these agricultural changes (see Chapter 18).

Ecological catastrophes

Attempts have been made to demonstrate a meaningful correlation between periods of aridity, such as the one in question here, and major historical events. These analyses tend to give the physical environment such importance that Africans are reduced to powerless victims of nature. Nowhere do historians discuss measures Africans have taken to counteract the effect of aridity, nor how droughts affect and contribute to changes in systems of production and distribution, the enhanced value of food crops and the development of methods of food preservation.

The question of droughts and famines also relates to the larger issue of the efficiency of African agriculture in the pre-colonial period. The period 1500 to 1800 was characterized, as pointed out by Jan Vansina in Chapter 3, by the emergence of intensive techniques for land use, which in turn allowed higher densities of population. In many areas of Africa, advanced agricultural methods, such as terracing, crop rotation, green manuring, mixed farming and regulated swamp farming were used. These topics deserve more attention from historians than the usual generalizations about famine and drought in Africa.

Christianity and Islam

The period from 1500 to 1800 saw a decline in Christianity in Africa, especially in Ethiopia, on the east coast and, to a lesser extent, in the Kongo. Islam, on the other hand, gained ground in West Africa, Sudan, Ethiopia and on the east coast.

On the Lower Guinea coast, for example, Christianity was introduced into the region by the Dutch and the British. They began by establishing elementary schools in their castles at Cape Coast, El Mina and Accra. Later, in the 1750s, missionaries were sent to Cape Coast by the Society for the Propagation of the Gospel. Also, some of the new converts were sent abroad for further education and many returned home as teachers and missionaries. Thus the foundation for the Christian revolution that was to take place in West Africa in the nineteenth century was laid during this period.

In the Kongo, Christianity was introduced by the Portuguese during the reign of Alfonso I (1506–43). Under the direction of his son Henrique, who was consecrated bishop in Rome, he made the Catholic Church the state religion. It was, to a very large extent, the religion of the urban nobility and the ecclesiastical hierarchy remained chiefly Portuguese. But from 1645 to 1700 the Italian missionaries set out to systematically convert the population, particularly in the rural areas (see Chapter 19).

Both Christianity and Islam, during this period, were syncretic. In the Kongo, for example, Christianity coexisted with traditional religion. However, attempts were made to organize independent churches. In the Kongo, early attempts to establish an indigenous church started in the 1630s and reached a peak in 1704, when Dona Beatrice Kimpa Vita began to preach a reformed Christianity called Antonianism which rejected the missionaries and the whites. Henceforth, indigenous Catholicism prevailed in the Kongo.

Turning now to Islam, it is evident that its expansion in Africa is an important theme of the period from 1500 to 1800. In the Lower Guinea coast, for example, the Manden and Hausa traders introduced Islam. It spread along the northern trade routes, reaching Asante and Baule in the 1750s. By 1800, Kamusi had a thriving Muslim quarter with a Ḳur'ānic school. In the Upper

Guinea coast, the Fulbe and the Manden were responsible for the spread of Islam. They formed a Fulbe–Malinke religious alliance, not only to convert the peoples of the region but also in order to subjugate them. Thus, the spread of Islam was associated with political domination in many regions of Africa, as the case of Senegambia clearly illustrates; here, the opposition between the Muslim theocracies and the *ceddo* (warlord) regimes form the background to the history of the region. In the Sudan, Islamization of the north of the country created an ideological frontier between northern and southern Sudan which is still very marked.

This period saw the establishment and expansion of two Muslim savannah states – the Fundj and Fūr sultanates. In the seventeenth and eighteenth centuries, Islam continued to spread in the Bambara, Mossi, Kong and Gwirika kingdoms, through traders and religious leaders, and even through violence. The same process of Islamic expansion can be seen in Hausaland and in Borno.

Apart from the simple geographical spread of Islam in Africa at this time, Muslim fundamentalism was an important factor in many regions. There was, for example, the Nāṣir-al-Dīn movement, which started in Mauritania and then spread southwards. Its motives were partly economic (to control the trade in grains and slaves) and partly religious (to purify and reform Islam by replacing arbitrary rule with Muslim theocracy). The same reform tendency can be seen among the Muslims in Hausaland, especially during the eighteenth century. A community of Muslim scholars, with similar political, economic and religious backgrounds, developed in various centres and became critical of the established order represented by the aristocracy. As the rule of the aristocrats became increasingly oppressive, the scholars openly attacked the established order. This is the background to the *djihād* of the nineteenth century.

As a result of the oppression of the African peasantry by the rural and urban élites, especially in western Sudan, the Niger–Chad region, Egypt, the Sahara, the Maghrib, Ethiopia and the Kongo, the Muslim leaders and the Christian messianic movements found it easy to enlist the mass support of the peasantry.

Finally, it should be noted that the Africans viewed both Christianity and Islam syncretistically. They accepted Islam while at the same time remaining faithful to their traditional religions. These syncretisms later developed with Christianity in Africa and in Afro-American worship in Brazil, Haiti and Cuba (see Chapter 12).

Selected
bibliography

The publishers wish to point out that, although every effort has been made to ensure that the details in this Bibliography are correct, some errors may occur as a result of the complexity and the international nature of the work.

Abbebe, B. (1971) *Evolution de la propriété foncière au Choa (Ethiopia)* (Paris: Imprimerie National et Librarie Orientaliste, P. Geuthner).

Abdallah, Y. B. (1919) *The Yaos* (arranged, ed. and tr. by M. Sanderson, Zomba; 2nd edn, London: Frank Cass, 1973).

Abitbol, M. (1979) *Tambouctou et les Arma de la conquête marocaine du Soudan nigérien en 1591 à l'hégémonie de l'Empire du Maçina en 1833* (Paris: Maisonneuve & Larose), 297 pp.

Abraham, D. P. (1969) 'The roles of Chaminuka and the Mhondoro cults in Shona political history', in F. Stokes and R. Brown (eds), pp. 28, 46.

Abun-Nasr, J. M. (1975) A History of the Maghrib (2nd edn, Cambridge: CUP), 422 pp.

Adams W. Y. (1977) *Nubia – Corridor to Africa* (London: Allen Lane), 797 pp.

Ajayi, J. F. A. (ed.) (1989) *General History of Africa*, Vol. VI (Paris/Oxford/Berkeley: UNESCO/ Heinemann/University of California Press), 861 pp.

Ajayi, J. F. A. and Crowder, M. (eds) (1971) *History of West Africa* (London: Longman; 2nd edn 1976).

Ajayi, J. F. A. and Espie, J. (eds) (1965) *A Thousand Years of West African History* (Ibadan/London: IUP/Nelson), 543 pp.

Akinjogbin, I. A. (1967) *Dahomey and its Neighbours, 1708–1818* (Cambridge: CUP), 234 pp.

Alexandre, P. and Binet, J. (1958) *Le groupe dit pahouin (Fang-Boulou-Beti)* (London/Paris: IAI/PUF), 152 pp.

Alkali, M. B. (1969) 'A Hausa community in crisis: Kebbi in the nineteenth century' (MA thesis, Ahmadu Bello University, Zaria).

Allan, J. (1965) *The African Husbandsman* (London: Oliver and Boyd).

Alldridge, T. J. (1901) *The Sherbro and its Hinterland* (London: Macmillan), 356 pp.

Alpers, E. A. (1975) *Ivory and Slaves in East Central Africa to the later Nineteenth Century* (London: Heinemann).

Anquandah, J. (1982) *Rediscovering Ghana's Past* (London: Longman), 161 pp.

Anttila, R. (1972) *An Introduction to Historical and Comparative Linguistics* (New York: Macmillan), 438 pp.

Aptheker, H. (1944) *American Negro Slave Revolts* (2nd printing, New York: Columbia University Press), 409 pp.

Arhin, K. (1979) *West African Traders in Ghana in the Nineteenth and Twentieth Centuries* (London: Longman), 146 pp.

Arhin, K. and Goody, J. (1965) *Ashanti and the Northwest* (Legon: Institute of African Studies, University of Ghana).

Atkins, G. (ed.) (1972) *Manding: Focus on an African Civilization* (London: SOAS).

447

Austen, R. A. (1968) *Northwest Tanzania under German and British Rule, 1889–1939* (New Haven: YUP).

Avaro, J. A. (1981) *Un peuple gabonais à l'aube de la colonisation: Le Bas Ogowe au XlXe siècle* (Paris: Karthala/CRA), 290 pp.

Axelson, E. (1940) *South-East Africa, 1488–1530* (London: Longman), 306 pp.

Axelson, E. (1973) *The Portuguese in South-East Africa, 1488–1600* (Johannesburg: WUP), 276 pp.

Barber, W. J. (1964) *The Economy of British Central Africa: a Case Study of Economic Development in a Dualistic Society* (London: OUP), 271 pp.

Barry, B. (1972) *Le royaume du Waalo: Le Sénégal avant la conquête* (Paris: Maspéro), 393 pp.

Bastide, R. (1971) *Les Amériques noires: les civilisations africaines dans le Nouveau Monde* (Paris: Payot), trans. as *African Civilizations in the New World* (London: Hurst), 232 pp.

Bauer, P. T. (1981) *Equality, the Third World and Economic Delusion* (London: George Weidenfeld & Nicolson).

Behrens, C. (1974) *Les Kroumen de la côte occidentale d'Afrique* (Talence: CNRS, Centre d'études de geographie tropicale), 243 pp.

Bernstein, H. (ed.) (1973) *Underdevelopment and Development: The Third World Today* (New York: Penguin Books).

Berque, J. (1982) *Ulemas, fondateurs, insurgés du Maghreb* (Paris: La bibliothèque arabe, Sindbad).

Betoto, C. (ed.) (1950) *Histoire de la royauté sakalava* (Paris: Ecole nationale de la France d'Outre-mer, typescript), pp. 1–32.

Bhila, H. H. K. (1982) *Trade and Politics in a Shona Kingdom. The Manyika and their Portuguese and African Neighbours, 1575–1902* (London: Longman).

Binger, L. G. (1982) *Du Niger au golfe de Guineé par le pays de Kong et le Mossi 1887–1889* (2 vols, Paris: Hachette).

Biobaku, S. O. (ed.) (1973) *Sources of Yoruba History* (Oxford: Clarendon Press).

Birmingham, D. (1981) *Central Africa to 1870: Zambezia, Zaïre and the South Atlantic* (Cambridge: CUP).

Birmingham, D. and Gray, R. (eds) (1970) *Pre-colonial African Trade: Essays on Trade in Central and Eastern Africa before 1900* (London: OUP), 308 pp.

Birmingham, D. and Martin, P. (eds) (1983) *History of Central Africa*, vol. I (London: Institute of Commonwealth Studies), 314 pp.

Blackburn, R. H. (1982) *Kenya's Peoples: Okiek* (London: Evans).

Blake, J. W. (1942) *Europeans in West Africa, 1450–1560* (tr. and ed. by J. W. Blake, London: for the Hakluyt Society, 2nd edn, 2 vols).

Boahen, A. A. (1964) *Britain, the Sahara and the Western Sudan, 1788–1861* (Oxford: Clarendon Press, Oxford Studies in African Affairs) 268 pp.

Boahen, A. A. (1966) *Topics in West African History* (London: Longman).

Bosman, W. (1967) *A New and Accurate Description of the Coast of Guinea* (London: Frank Cass, reprint of 1705 1st edn, with Introduction by J. R. Willis).

Boulègue, J. (1968) 'La Sénégambie du milieu du XVe siècle au début du XVIIe siècle' (PhD thesis, 3rd cycle, University of Paris).

Bouquiaux, L. and Hyman, L. (eds) (1980) *L'expansion bantoue* (3 vols, Paris: SELAF).

Bovill, E. W. (1958) *The Golden Trade of the Moors* (London: OUP, 281 pp; 2nd rev. ed. 1968, 293 pp; London: OUP).

Boxer, C. R. (1963) *Race Relations in the Portuguese Colonial Empire, 1415–1825* (Oxford: Clarendon Press), 136 pp.

Boxer, C. R. (1969) *The Portuguese Seaborne Empire* (London: Hutchinson).

Braudel, F. (1981) *The Structure of Everyday Life: the Limits of the Possible* (trans. and rev. by S.

Reynolds, London).

Braudel, F. (1984) *Civilization and Capitalism* (3 vols, New York: Harper & Row).

Burnham, P. (1980) *Opportunity and Constraint in a Savanna Society* (London: Academic Press), 324 pp.

Bynon, T. (1977) *Historical Linguistics* (Cambridge: CUP), 301 pp.

Cà da Mosto, A da (1937) *The Voyages of Cadamosto and Other Documents on Western Africa in the Second Half of the Fifteenth Century* (trans. and ed. by G. R. Crone, London: Hakluyt Society), 159 pp.

Caillié, R. (1828) *Journal d'un voyage à Tombouctou et à Jenne* (Paris: Imprimerie royale).

Cairns, T. (1971) *Barbarians, Christians and Muslims* (Cambridge: CUP).

Calonne-Beaufaict, A. de (1921) *Azande; introduction à une ethnographie générale des bassins de l'Ubangi-Uele et de l'Aruwimi* (Brussels: M. Lamertin).

Capron, J. (1973) *Communautés villageoises bwa (Mali, Haute-Volta)* (Paris: Institut d'ethnologie, Mémoire No. 9), 379 pp.

Carrette, E. (1844) *Recherches sur la géographie et le commerce de l'Algérie méridionale* (Paris: Sciences historiques et géographiques).

Castries, H. de (1905-36) *Les sources inédites de l'histoire du Maroc de 1530 à 1845* (18 vols, Paris: Paul Geuthner).

Centre de Civilisation burundaise (ed.) (1981) *La Civilisation ancienne des peuples des Grands Lacs* (Paris: Karthala), 495 pp.

Chaunu, H. and Chaunu, P. (1955) *Séville et l'Atlantique, 1504–1650* (11 vols, Paris: Ecole des Hautes études).

Chittick, H. N. and Rotberg, R. I. (eds) (1975) *East Africa and the Orient: Cultural Synthesis in the Pre-Colonial Times* (New York: Africana Publishing Company), 343 pp.

Chrétien, J. P. (1977) 'Les deux visages de Cham: points de vue français du XIXe siècle sur les races africaines d'après l'exemple de l'Afrique orientale', in P. Guiral and E. Temime (eds), *L'idée de race dans la pensée politique française contemporaine* (Paris: Editions du CNRS), pp. 171–99.

Chrétien, J. P. (ed.) (1983) *Histoire rurale de l'Afrique des Grands Lacs* (Paris: AFERA-Karthala), 285 pp.

Cissoko, S. M. (1968) *Histoire de l'Afrique occidentale* (Paris: PA), 233 pp.

Clérici, M. A. (1962) *Histoire de la Côte d'Ivoire* (Abidjan: CEDA).

Cohen, R. (1970) 'Incorporation in Bornu', in R. Cohen and J. Middleton (eds), *From Tribe to Nation in Africa* (Scranton: Chandler Int. Co.), pp. 150–74.

Commissariat, M. S. (1957) *A History of Gujarat* (Calcutta).

Cook, S. F. and Borah, W. (1971–74) *Essays in population history, Mexico and the Caribbean* (2 vols, Berkeley: UCP).

Cornevin, R. (1964) *Note sur l'histoire de Sansanné Mango* (London, Survey on African Chronology).

Coupez, A. and Kamanzi, T. (1962) *Récits historiques du Rwanda* (Tervuren: MRAC), 327 pp.

Courtois, C. (1955) *Les Vandales et l'Afrique* (Algiers: Arts et Métiers Graphiques), 441 pp.

Crosby, C. A. (1980) *Historical Dictionary of Malawi* (New York: Scarecrow Press), 169 pp.

Cruickshank, B. (1853) *Eighteen years on the Gold Coast of Africa* (2 vols, London: Hurst and Blackett).

Cuoq, J. M. (1975) *Recueil des sources arabes concernant l'Afrique occidentale du VIIIe au XVIe siècle (Bilād al-Sūdān)* (Paris: editions du CNRS), 490 pp.

Curtin P. D. (ed.) (1967) *Africa Remembered: Narratives by West Africans From the Era of the Slave Trade* (Madison: UWP), 363 pp.

Curtin, P. D. (1969) *The Atlantic Slave Trade: A Census* (Madison: UWP), 338 pp.

Curtin, P. D., Feierman, S., Thompson, L. and Vansina, J. (1978) *African History* (Boston/ Toronto: Little Brown Company), 612 pp.

Cuvelier, J. and Jadin, L. (1954) *L'ancien royaume du Congo d'après les archives romaines, 1518–1640* (Brussels: ARSOM).

Dampierre, E. de (1968) *Un ancien royaume Bandia du Haut-Oubangui* (Paris: Plon, Recherches en sciences humaines, 24), 601 pp.

Dantzig, A. van (1978) *The Dutch and the Guinea Coast, 1674–1742: A Collection of Documents from the General State Archives at The Hague* (Accra: GASS), 375 pp.

Dapper, O. (1686) *Naukeurige Beschrijvinge der Afrikaensche gewesten van Egypten, Barbaryen, Libyen Biledulgerid...* (Amsterdam: Van Meurs); 1670 Engl. trans. and adaptation, J. Ogilby, *Africa: Being an Accurate Description of the Regions of Aegypt, Barbary, Libya, etc.* (London; 1670 German trans., *Beschreibung von Afrika...* (Amsterdam: Van Meurs); 1686 French trans., *Description de l'Afrique...* (Amsterdam: Wolfgang, Waesberge, et al.).

D'Arianoff, A. (1952) *Histoire des Bagesera, souverains du Gisaka* (Brussels: Institut royal colonial belge), 138 pp.

Davidson, B. (1965) *The Growth of African Civilisation: A History of West Africa, 1000–1800* (London: Longmans), 320 pp.

Davis, D. B. (1984) *Slavery and Human Progress* (New York: OUP), 374 pp.

Debourou, D. M. (1979) *Commerçants et chefs de l'ancien Borgou, des origines à 1936* (Paris: Université de Paris I, CRA).

Debrunner, H. W. (1965) *The Church in Togo: A Church Between Colonial Powers* (London: Lutterworth), 368 pp.

Delafosse, M. (1912) *Le Haut-Sénégal–Niger (Soudan français)* (3 vols, Paris: Larose).

Delcourt, A. (1952) *La France et les établissements français du Sénégal entre 1713 et 1763* (Dakar: Mémoires de l'IFAN No. 17), 432 pp.

Denoon, D. (1983) *Settler Capitalism: The Dynamics of Dependent Development in the Southern Hemisphere* (Oxford).

Deschamps, H. (1949/1972) *Les Pirates à Madagascar aux XVIIe et XVIIIe siècles* (2nd edn, 1972, Paris: Berger-Levrault), 1st edn, 244 pp.

Deschamps, H. (1961/1965) *Histoire de Madagascar* (2nd and 3rd edns, Paris: Berger-Levrault, Monde d'Outre-mer, Série Histoire), 348 pp.

Deschamps. H. and Vianès, S. (1959) *les Malgaches du sud-est* (Paris: PUF), 118 pp.

Diagne, P. (1967) *Pouvoir politique traditionnel en Afrique occidentale: essai sur les institutions politiques précoloniales* (Paris: PA), 249 pp.

Diallo, T. (1972) *Les institutions politiques du Fouta Djalon au XIXe siécle* (Dakar: IFAN, Initiations et études africaines), 276 pp.

Dickson, K. B. (1969) *A Historical Geography of Ghana* (Cambridge: CUP), 379 pp.

Dike, K. O. (1956) *Trade and Politics in the Niger Delta, 1830–1885: An Introduction to the Economic and Political History of Nigeria* (Oxford: Clarendon Press, Oxford Studies in African Affairs), 250 pp.

Diop, A. B. (1981) *La Société wolof, tradition et changement: les systèms d'inégalité et de domination* (Paris: Karthala), 355 pp.

Diouf, M. (1980) 'Le Kajoor au XIXe siècle et la conquète coloniale' (PhD thesis, Paris, University of Paris I).

Dramani-Issifou, Z. (1982) *L'Afrique noire dans les relations internationales au XVIe siècle: analyse de la crise entre le Maroc et le Sonrhai* (Paris: karthala), 257 pp.

Dumestre, G. (1974/1980) *La geste de Ségou* (Paris: A Colin) (2nd edn, 1980); 1st edn, 579 pp.

Dunn, R. S. (1972) *Sugar and Slaves: The Rise of the Planter Class in the English West Indies*

1624–1713 (New York: Chapel Hill, UNCP).

Dupire, M. (1962) *Peuls nomades* (Paris: Institut d'ethnologie), 336 pp.

Dupré, G. (1982) *Un ordre et sa destruction* (Paris: ORSTOM), 446 pp.

Ehret, C. (1971) *Southern Nilotic History: Linguistic Approaches to the Study of the Past* (Evanston: NUP), 200 pp.

Ehret, C. and Posnansky, M. (eds) (1982) *The Archaeological and Linguistic Reconstruction of African History* (Berkeley: UCP), 299 pp.

Evans-Pritchard, E. E. (1940) *The Nuer* (Oxford: OUP), 271 pp.

Evans-Pritchard E. E. (1971) *The Azande: History and Political Institutions* (Oxford: Clarendon Press), 444 pp.

Eyongetah, T. and Brain, R. (1974) *A History of the Cameroon* (London: Longman), 192 pp.

Equiano, Olaudah (1967) *Equiano's Travels*, edited by P. Edwards (London: Heinemann African Writers Series).

Fage, J. D. (1969) *A History of West Africa: An Introductory Survey* (4th edn Cambridge: CUP), 239 pp. (Earlier edn publ. as *An Introduction to the History of West Africa*.)

Fage, J. D. and Oliver, R. A. (eds) (1977) *The Cambridge History of Africa*, vol. 3 (Cambridge: CUP), 803 pp.

Farb, P. (1969) *Man's Rise to Civilisation* (New York: Datton), 332 pp.

Feierman, S. (1974) *The Shambaa Kingdom: A History* (Madison: UWP), 235 pp.

File, N. and Power, C. (1981) *Black Settlers in Britain, 1555–1958* (London: Heinemann Educational Books).

Fisher, A. G. B. and Fisher, H. G. (1970) *Slavery and Muslim Society in Africa* (London: C. Hurst), 182 pp.

al-Fishtālī, 'Abd al-Azīz (1964) *Manahil al-Safia fi Akhbar al-Muluk al-Shurafa* (Rabat: Gunum Allan).

Flint, J. E. (ed.) (1976) *The Cambridge History of Africa*, vol. 5 (Cambridge: CUP).

Forde C. D. and Jones, G. I. (1950/1962) *The Ibo and Ibibio-speaking Peoples of South-Eastern Nigeria* (London: IAI, Ethnographic Survey of Africa, Part III), 94 pp.

Forde, C. D. and Kaberry, P. M. (eds) (1967) *West African Kingdoms in the Nineteenth Century* (London: IAI/OUP), 289 pp.

Forde, D. (ed.) (1956) *Efik Traders of Old Calabar* (London: OUP).

Fortes, M. (1940) 'The political system of the Tallensi of the Northern Territories of the Gold Coast' in M. Fortes and E.E. Evans-Pritchard (eds), *African Political Systems* (London: OUP), pp. 239–71.

Franklin, J. H. (1967) *From Slavery to Freedom: A History of American Negroes* (first published 1956) (New York: Knopf), 686 pp.

Freeman-Grenville, G. S. P. (1962a) *The Medieval History of the Tanganyika Coast* (Oxford: Clarendon Press), 238 pp. (2nd edn 1966, 314 pp.).

Freeman-Grenville, G. S. P. (1962b) *The East African Coast: Select Documents from the First to Earlier Nineteenth Century* (Oxford: Clarendon Press), 314 pp.

Freeman-Grenville, G. S. P. (1963) 'The coast, 1498–1840', in R. Oliver and G. Mathew (eds), pp. 129–68.

Freeman-Grenville, G. S. P. (1965) *The French at Kilwa Island: An Episode in Eighteenth-Century East African History* (Oxford, Clarendon Press), 243 pp.

Freeman-Grenville, G. S. P. (ed.) (1980) *The Mombasa Rising against the Portuguese, 1631, from Sworn Evidence* (London: OUP), 166 pp.

Frobenius, L. (1911–13) *Und Africa Sprach* (3 vols, Berlin, Charlottenburg: Vita, Deutsches Verlagshaus, S. D.).

Fyfe, C. (1964) *Sierra Leone Inheritance* (London: OUP), 352 pp.

Fyfe, C. (1965) 'Peoples of the Windward Coast, A.D. 1000–1800', in J. F. A. Ajayi and J. Espie (eds), pp. 149–65.

Fyfe, C. and McMaster, D. (eds) (1977 and 1981) *African Historical Demography* vol. 1, 1977, 473 pp; vol 2, 1981 (Edinburgh: EUP).

Gado, B. (1972) *Gazetters of the Northern Province of Nigeria*, vol. 1 (London: Frank Cass).

Garlake, P. S. (1973) *Great Zimbabwe* (London: Thames and Hudson), 224 pp.

Garrard, T. F. (1980) *Akan Weights and the Gold Trade* (London: Longman), 393 pp.

Godard, L. (1859) *Le Maroc, notes d'un voyageur* (Algiers).

Goody, J. (1956) *Social Organization of the Lowili* (London: IAI/OUP), 119 pp.

Gorju, J. (1938) *Face au royaume hamite du Ruanda, le royaume frère de l'Urundi* (Brussels: Vromant) 118 pp.

Gourou, P. (1953) *La densité de la population du Ruanda-Urundi: Esquisse d'une étude géographique* (Brussels: Institut royal colonial belge), 239 pp.

Grandidier, G. (1942) *Histoire politique et coloniale (de Madagascar)*, vol. 5 (Paris).

Grandidier, A., Charles-Roux, J., Delherbe, C., Froidevaux, H. and Grandidier, G. (eds) (1903–20) *Collections des ouvrages anciens concernant Madagascar* (9 vols, Paris, Comité de Madagascar).

Grandidier, G. and Decary, R. (1958) *Histoire politique et coloniale (de Madagascar)* vol. 5, part 3 (Antananarivo).

Gray, J. M. (1962) *History of Zanzibar from the Middle Ages to 1856* (London: OUP), 314 pp.

Gray, R. (1961) *A History of the Southern Sudan* (London: OUP), 219 pp.

Gray, R. (ed.) (1975) *The Cambridge History of Africa*, vol. 4 (Cambridge, CUP), 738 pp.

Greenberg, J. H. (1980) 'Classification of African Languages', *General History of Africa*, vol. 1, ch. 12 (Paris/London/Berkeley: UNESCO/Heinemann/University of California Press), pp. 292–308.

Grigg, D. B. (1980) *Population Growth and Agrarian Change: An Historical Perspective* (Cambridge: CUP).

Guillot, B. (1973) *La Terre Enkou* (Paris: Mouton), 126 pp.

Gutman, H. G. (1976) *The Black Family in Slavery and Freedom* (New York: Pantheon Books), 664 pp.

Guy, J. (1979) *The Destruction of the Zulu Kingdom: The Civil War in Zululand, 1879–1884* (London: Longman), 273 pp.

Hacquard, A. (1900) *Monographie de Tombouctou* (Paris: Société des éditions coloniales et maritimes), 119 pp.

Hagenbucher Sacripanti, F. (1973) *Les fondements spirituels du pouvoir au royaume de Loango, R. P. du Congo* (Paris: ORSTOM), 214 pp.

Haig, Sir W. (ed.) (1937) *The Cambridge History of India*, vol. 3 (London: CUP).

Hair, P. E. H. (1974) 'From language to culture: some problems in the systematic analysis of the ethnohistorical records of the Sierra Leone region', in R. P. Moss and R. J. A. R. Rathbone, *The Population Factor in African Studies* (London: ULP), pp. 71–83.

Hama, B. (1967a) *Histoire du Gobir de Sokoto* (Paris: PA), 167 pp.

Hama, B. (1967b) *Histoire traditionnelle d'un peuple: les Zarma-Songhay* (Paris: PA), 273 pp.

Hama, B. (1968) *Contribution à la connaissance de l'histoire des Peuls* (Paris: PA), 362 pp.

Hama, B. (1969) *Histoire traditionnelle des Peuls du Dallol Boboye* (Niamey: CRDTO), 160 pp.

Hamani, D. M. (1989) *Au carrefour du Soudan et de la Berbérie: le sultanat touareg de l'Ayar* (2 vols, Paris: Université de Paris I Panthéon-Sorbonne), 521 pp.

Hanke. L. (ed.) (1969) *History of Latin American Civilization: Sources and Interpretation* (2 vols, London: Methuen).

Harms, R. (1981) *River of Wealth, River of Sorrow: The Central Zaire Basin in the Era of the Slave* *and Ivory Trade, 1500–1891* (New Haven and London: YUP), 277 pp.

Harris, J. E. (1971) *The African Presence in Asia: Consequences of the East African Slave Trade,* (Evanston, Ill.: NUP), 156 pp.

Harris, J. E. (1982) *Global Dimensions of the African Diaspora* (Washington DC: HUP).

Hartwig, G. W. (1976) *The Art of Survival in East Africa: The Kerebe and Long-distance Trade, 1800–1895* (New York/London: Africana Publishing), 253 pp.

Hasan, Y. F. (1967) *The Arabs and the Sudan* (Edinburgh: EUP), 298 pp.

Herskovits, M. J. and Harwitz, M. (eds) (1964) *Economic Transactions in Africa* (London: Routledge and Kegan Paul), 444 pp.

D'Hertefelt, M. (1971) *Les clans du Rwanda ancien: éléments d'ethnosociologie et d'ethnohistoire* (Tervuren: MRAC), 85 pp.

Heusch, L. de (1972) *Le roi ivre ou l'origine de l'Etat* (Paris: Gallimard), 331 pp.

Hill, A. and Kilson, M. (eds) (1969) *Apropos of Africa* (London: Frank Cass), 390 pp.

Hilton, A. (1985) *Family and Kingship* (Oxford: OUP).

Holt, P. M. (ed.) (1968) *Political and Social Change in Modern Egypt: Historical Studies from the Ottoman Conquest to the United Arab Republic* (London: OUP).

Hopkins, A. G. (1973/1975/1983) *An Economic History of West Africa* (London: Longman). (1st edn 1973, 337 pp.)

Hopkins, J. F. P. and Levtzion, N. (1981) *Corpus of Early Arabic Sources for West African History* (Cambridge: CUP), 492 pp.

Ingham. K. (ed.) (1974) *Foreign Relations of African States* (London: Butterworth, Colston Paper, No. 75), 344 pp.

Inikori, J. E. (1979) 'The slave trade and the Atlantic economies, 1451–1870', in *The African Slave Trade from the 15th to the 19th Century: Reports and Papers of the Meetings of Experts Organized by UNESCO,* Port-au-Prince, Haiti, 31 January–4 February 1978, *The General History of Africa – Studies and Documents,* No. 2 (Paris: UNESCO), pp. 56–87.

Inikori, J. E. (ed.) (1982) *Forced Migration: The Impact of the Export Slave Trade on African Societies* (London: Hutchinson University Library for Africa: New York: Africana Publishing Company), 349 pp.

Isaacman, A. F. (1969) 'The prazos da Coroa, 1752–1832: A functional analysis of the Portuguese system', *Studia,* 26, pp. 149–78.

Izard, M. (1981) *Histoire du Yatenga des origines à 1895* (Ouagadougou).

Jackson–Haight, M. V. (1967) *European Powers and South-East Africa, 1796–1856* (London: Routledge and Kegan Paul).

Jadin, L. and Dicorato, M. (1974) *Correspondence de Dom Afonso, roi du Congo, 1506–1543* (Brussels: ARSOM 41-3), 245 pp.

James, C. L. R. (1963) *The Black Jacobins: Toussaint L'Ouverture and the San Domingo Revolution* (New York: Vintage).

Johnston, H. H. (1902) *The Uganda Protectorate* (2 vols, London: Hutchinson).

Jones, A. H. M. and Monroe, E. (1978) *A History of Ethiopia* (Oxford: OUP), 196 pp.

Julien, C. A. (1951–56) *Histoire de l'Afrique du Nord: Tunisie, Algérie, Maroc. De la conquète arabe à 1830,* 2nd edn (2 vols, Paris: Payot).

July, R. W. (1974) *A History of the African People* (London: Faber), 650 pp.

Kagame, A. (1954) *Les organisations socio-familiales de l'ancien Rwanda* (Brussels: Académie royale des sciences coloniales), 355 pp.

Kagame, A. (1963) *Les milices du Rwanda précolonial* (Brussels: Académie royale des sciences coloniales), 196 pp.

Kagame, A. (1972) *Un abrégé de l'ethno-histoire du Rwanda* (Butare: Editions universitaires du Rwanda), 286 pp.

Kaira, O. Y. (1970–71) 'A survey of the history of the Kaira Clan of Northern Malawi' (Student seminar paper, Chancellor College, University of Malawi).

Kalinga, O. J. M. (1985) *A History of the Ngonde Kingdom* (Berlin/New York: Mouton).

Kaniki, M. H. Y. (ed.) (1979) *Tanzania Under Colonial Rule* (London: Longman), 391 pp.

Keen, B. and Wasserman, M. (1980) *A Short History of Latin America* (Boston: Houghton Mifflin), 574 pp.

Kent, R. K. (1970) *Early Kingdoms in Madagascar, 1500–1700* (New York: Holt, Reinhart and Winston).

Kesteloot, L. (1972) *Da Monzon de Ségou, épopée bambara* (4 vols, Paris: F. Nathan).

Kesteloot, L. (1983) *Biton Koulibaly, fondateur de l'empire de Ségou* (Dakar: NEA), 96 pp.

Kietegha, J. B. (1983) *L'or de la Volta Noire* (Paris: Karthala, CREA), 247 pp.

Kimambo, I. N. and Temu, A. (eds) (1969) *A History of Tanzania* (Nairobi: EAPH), 276 pp.

Kimble, D. (1963) *A Political History of Ghana: The Rise of Gold Coast Nationalism, 1850–1928* (Oxford: Clarendon Press), 587 pp.

Kirkman, J. S. (1964) *Men and Monuments on the East African Coast* (London: Lutterworth Press), 224 pp.

Ki-Zerbo, J. (1978) *Histoire de l'Afrique noire* (Paris: Hatier), 702 pp.

Klein, H. S. (1967) *Slavery in the Americas: A Comparative Study of Virginia and Cuba* (Chicago: University of Chicago Press), 270 pp.

Klein, M. A. (1968) *Islam and Imperialism in Senegal Sine-Saloum, 1847–1914* (Edinburgh: EUP), 285 pp.

Kouanda, A. (1984) 'Les Yarse: fonction commerciale, religieuse et légitimité culturelle dans le pays moaga (Evolution historique)' (PhD thesis, University of Paris I).

Kup, A. P. (1961) *A History of Sierra Leone, 1400–1787* (London: CUP), 212 pp.

Labarthe, P. (1803) *Voyage à la Côte de Guinée* (Paris: Bossange, Masson & Besson), 310 pp.

Laburthe-Tolra, P. (1981) *Les seigneurs de la forêt* (Paris: Publications de la Sorbonne), 490 pp.

Lamb, V. (1975) *West African Weaving* (London: Duckworth).

Lamphear, J. E. (1976) *The Traditional History of the Jie of Uganda* (Oxford: Clarendon Press, Oxford Studies in African Affairs), 281 pp.

Lange, D. (1977) *Chronologie et histoire d'un royaume africain* (Wiesbaden: Franz Steiner).

Lara, O. D. (1979) 'Negro resistance to slavery and the Atlantic slave trade from Africa to Black Americas' (working paper, Meeting of Experts organized by UNESCO on *The African Slave Trade from the 15th to the 19th Century*, Port-au-Prince, Haiti, 31 January–4 February 1978, *The General History of Africa – Studies and Documents*, 2 (Paris: UNESCO), pp. 101–14.

Laroui, A. (1970) *L'histoire du Maghreb: un essai de synthèse* (Paris: Maspéro), 390 pp.

Le Barbier, C. (1916–17) 'Notes sur le pays des Bara-Imamono, région d'Ankazoabo', *BAM*, new series, 2, pp. 63–162.

Lee, R. B. (1979) *The Kung San: Men, Women and Work in a Foraging Society* (Cambridge: CUP), 526 pp.

Leo Africanus [Jean Léon l'Africain] (1956) *Description de l'Afrique*, tr. by A. Epaulard, with notes by E. Epaulard, T. Monod, H. Lhote and R. Mauny (2 vols, Paris: Maisonneuve).

Lévi-Provinçial, E. (1922) *Les Historiens des Chorfa* (Paris: Larose).

Levtzion, N. (1968) *Muslims and Chiefs in West Africa: A Study of Islam in the Middle Volta Basin in the Precolonial Period* (Oxford: Clarendon Press, Oxford Studies in African Affairs), 228 pp.

Lewis, I. M. (ed.) (1966) *Islam in Tropical Africa* (London: OUP, for the IAI), 470 pp.

Lewis, I. M. (ed.) (1968) *Islam in Tropical Africa* (London: OUP, for the IAI), 470 pp.

Lewis, W. A. (1978) *The Evolution of the International Economic Order* (Princeton: PUP).

Little, K. (1951) *The Mende of Sierra Leone* (London: Routledge and Kegan Paul), 307 pp.

Lombard, J. (1965) *Structures de type 'féodal' en Afrique noire: étude des dynamismes internes et des* *relations sociales chez les Bariba du Dahomey* (Paris/ The Hague: Mouton), 544 pp.

Lopez, R. S. (1976) *The Commercial Revolution of the Middle Ages, 950–1350* (Cambridge: CUP).

Lougnon, A. and Toussaint, A. (eds) (1937) *Mémoire des Iles de France et de Bourbon* (Paris: Libraire Ernest Leroux), 203 pp.

Lovejoy, P. E. (1983) *Transformations in Slavery: A History of Slavery in Africa* (Cambridge: CUP), 349 pp.

Lovejoy, P. E. (1985) *Salt of the Desert Sun: A History of Salt Production and Trade in Central Sudan* (Cambridge: CUP), 351 pp.

Ly, A. (1958) *La compagnie du Sénégal de 1673 à 1686* (Paris: PA), 316 pp.

MacMichael, H. A. (1922) *A History of the Arabs in the Sudan* (2 vols, Cambridge: CUP).

Madiega, G. Y. (1978) 'Le Nord-Gulma précolonial (Haute-Volta) origine des dynasties, approche de la société' (PhD thesis, University of Paris I).

Madiega, G. Y. (1982) *Contribution à l'histoire précoloniale du Gurma (Haute-Volta)* (Wiesbaden: Franz Steiner).

Mage, E. (1868) *Voyage dans le Soudan occidental (1863–1866)* (Paris: Hachette). (New edn by Karthala, 1980, Frobenius Institute).

Malzac, V. (1921/1930) *Histoire du royaume Hova depuis ses origines jusqu'à sa fin* (Antananarivo: Imprimerie catholique). (Reprinted 1930).

Maquet, J. J. (1954) *Le Système des relations sociales dans le Ruanda ancien* (Tervuren: MRAC), 221 pp.

Marees, P. de (1602/1605/1905) *A Description and Historical Declaration of the Golden Kingdom of Guinea*, abridged English trans. of 1602 Dutch original, published in S. Purchas (1613/1905), vol 6, pp. 247–396; French trans. 1605, *Description et récit historique du riche royaume d'or de Guinée* (Amsterdam: Claessen).

Martin, B. G. (1971) 'Notes on some members of the learned classes of Zanzibar and East Africa in the nineteenth century', *AHS*, 4, 3, pp. 525–45.

Martin, G. (1948) *Histoire de l'esclavage dans les colonies françaises* (Paris: Geuthner).

Martin, P. M. (1972) *The External Trade of the Loango Coast, 1576–1870: The Effects of Changing Commercial Relations on the Vili Kingdom of Loango* (Oxford: Clarendon Press, Oxford Studies in African Affairs), 193 pp.

Marty, P. (1927) *Les Chroniques de Ovalata et de Nema* (Paris: Genthner).

Mauny, R. (1970) 'Les navigations anciennes et les grandes découvertes', in H. Deschamps (ed.), *Histoire générale de l'Afrique noire* (Paris: PUF), vol. 1, Part II, pp. 203–18.

Mauny, R. (1971) *Les siècles obscurs de l'Afrique noire* (Paris: Fayard), 314 pp.

Mauny, R., Thomas, L. V. and Vansina, J. (eds) (1974) *The Historian in Tropical Africa* (London: OUP for the IAI), 428 pp.

Mauro, F. (1960) *Le Portugal et l'Atlantique au XVIIe siècle, 1570–1670* (Paris: SEVPEN).

M'Bokolo, E. (1981) *Noirs et blancs en Afrique équatoriale: les sociétés côtières et la pénétration française* (Paris/The Hague: Mouton, Civilisations et Sociétés, No. 69), 302 pp.

M'Bokolo, E. (1983) 'Histoire des maladies, histoire et maladie: l'Afrique', in M. Augé and S. Herzlich (eds) *Le sens du mal* (Paris: Editions des Archives contemporaines).

McCulloch, M., Littlewood, M. and Dugast, I. (1954) *Peoples of the Central Cameroons* (London: IAI, Ethnographic Survey of Africa, Western Africa, Part IX), 172 pp.

McLeod, M. D. (1981) *The Asante* (London: British Museum Publications).

Meek, R. L. (1976) *Social Science and the Ignoble Savage* (Cambridge: CUP, Cambridge Studies in the History and Theory of Politics), 249 pp.

Meillassoux, C. (ed.) (1975) *L'esclavage en Afrique précoloniale* (Paris: F. Maspéro), 582 pp.

Mellafe, R. (1975) *Negro Slavery in Latin America* (Berkeley, CA: UCP), 172 pp.

Merrick, T. W. and Graham, D. H. (1979) *Population and Economic Development in Brazil,*

1800 to the present (Baltimore: The Johns Hopkins University Press).

Mettas, J. (1978) *Répertoire des expéditions négrières françaises au XVIIIe siècle*, ed. by S. Daget (Nantes).

Miers, S. and Kopytoff, I. (eds) (1977) *Slavery in Africa: Historical and Anthropological Perspectives* (Madison: UWP), 474 pp.

Miller, J. C. (1973) 'Requiem for the Jaga', *CEA*, 49, pp. 121–49. (See also *CEA*, 69 and 70).

Miller, J. C. (ed.) (1980) *The African Past Speaks: Essays on Oral Tradition and History* (London: Hamden, Dawson & Archon), 284 pp.

Minchinton, W. E. (ed.) (1969) *The Growth of English Overseas Trade in the 17th and 18th Centuries* (London: Methuen).

Mokhtar, G. (ed.) (1981) *General History of Africa. Vol. II: Ancient Civilizations of Africa* (Paris/London/Berkeley: UNESCO/Heinemann/University of California Press).

Monteil, C. (1924) *Les Bambara de Ségou et du Kaarta* (Paris: Larose), 404 pp; 2nd edn, 1977 (Paris: Maisonneuve), 441 pp.

Monteil, C. (1932) *Une cité soudanaise, Djenné, métropole du delta central du Niger* (Paris: Société d'études géographiques, maritimes et coloniales); 2nd edn, 1971 (Paris: Anthropos).

Morris, A. (1981) *Latin America: Economic Development and Regional Differentiation* (London: Hutchinson), 256 pp.

Mudenge, S. I. (1974) 'An identification of the Rozvi and its implications for the history of the Karanga', *RH*, 5, pp. 19–31.

Mutumba, M. (1973) *Bulozi under the Luyana Kings. Political Evolution and State-Formation in Pre-Colonial Zambia* (London: Longman), 278 pp.

Mworoha, E. (1977) *Peuples et rois de l'Afrique des lacs* (Dakar: NEA), 352 pp.

Mworoha, E. (1981) 'Redevances et prestations dans les domaines royaux du Burundi précolonial', *Mélanges R. Mauny. Le sol, la parole et l'écrit: 2000 ans d'histoire africaine* (Paris: SFHOM), pp. 751–68.

Nacanabo, D. (1982) 'Le Royaume maagha de Yoko' (PhD thesis, University of Paris I).

Nachtigal, G. (1876) *Le Voyage de Nachtigal au Ouadai: Traduction de Van Vollenhoven* (Paris).

Ndoricimpa, L. (ed.) (1984) *L'arbre mémoire. Traditions orales du Burundi* (Paris/Bujumbura: Editions Karthala/Centre de Civilisation Burundaise).

Niane, D. T. (1975a) *Recherches sur l'empire du Mali au Moyen-Age* (Paris: PA).

Niane, D. T. (1975b) *Le Soudan occidental au temps des grands empires, XIe–XVIe siècles* (Paris: PA).

Niane, D. T. (ed.) (1984) *General History of Africa. Vol. IV: Africa from the Twelfth to the Sixteenth Century* (Paris/London/Berkeley: UNESCO/Heinemann/ University of California Press).

Niane, D. T. and Wondji, C. *Enquêtes orales faites en Côte d'Ivoire (1973–1980) et en Guinée (1966–1970).*

Nicolas, G. (1975) *Dynamique sociale et appréhension du monde au sein d'une société hausa* (Paris: Institut d'ethnologie, Travaux et mémoires de l'Institut d'ethnologie, No. 78), 661 pp.

North, D. C. (1981) *Structure and Change in Economic History* (New York: Norton).

North, D. C. and Thomas, R. P. (1973) *The Rise of the Western World: A New Economic History* (Cambridge: CUP).

Northrup, D. (1978) *Trade Without Rulers: Precolonial Economic Development in South-Eastern Nigeria* (Oxford: Clarendon Press), 269 pp.

Nsanze, A. (1980) *Un domaine royal Burundi: Mbuye (env. 1850–1945)* (Paris: SFHOM), 93 pp.

Nziziwe, I. (1972) *Studies in Ibo Political Systems: Chieftaincy and Politics in Four Niger States* (London: Frank Cass), 287 pp.

Obenga, T. (1976) *La cuvette congolaise: Les hommes et les structures* (Paris: PA).

Ochieng', W. R. (1974a) *A Pre-Colonial History of the Gusii of Western Kenya 1500–1914* (Nairobi: EALB), 257 pp.

Ochieng', W. R. (1975a) *A History of the Kadimo Chiefdom of Yimbo in Western Kenya* (Nairobi: EALB), 78 pp.

Ochieng', W. R. (1975b) 'Undercivilization in Black Africa', in W. R. Ochieng' (ed.) (1975), *The First Word* (Nairobi: EALB), pp. 1–20.

O'Fahey, R. S. (1980) 'State and Society in Dār Fūr' (London: Hurst).

O'Fahey, R. S. and Spaulding, J. L. (1974) *The Kingdoms of the Sudan* (London: Methuen), 235 pp.

Ogot, B. A. (1967) *A History of the Southern Luo, Vol. I: Migration and Settlement 1500–1900* (Nairobi: EAPH), 250 pp.

Ogot B. A. (ed.) (1976a) *History and Social Change in East Africa* (Nairobi: EALB), 235 pp.

Ogot B. A. (ed.) (1976b) *Kenya Before 1900* (Nairobi: EAPH), 291 pp.

Oliver, R. (ed.) (1977) *The Cambridge History of Africa, Vol. 3; From c. 1050 to c. 1600* (Cambridge: CUP), 803 pp.

Oliver, R. and Mathew, G. (eds) (1963) *A History of East Africa,* vol. I (Oxford: Clarendon Press), 500 pp.

Oloo, P. C. (1969) 'History of settlement: the example of Luo clans of Alego: 1500–1918' (undergraduate dissertation, Nairobi University).

Ott, T. O. (1973) *The Haitian Revolution* (Knoxville: UTP), 232 pp.

Pachai, B. (ed.) (1972) *The Early History of Malawi* (London: Longman), 454 pp.

Pageard, R. (1963) *Civilisation mossi et Egypte ancienne* (Geneva: Institut africain).

Pagès, A. (1933) *Au Rwanda sur les bords du lac Kivu: Un royaume hamite au centre de l'Afrique* (Brussels: Institut royal colonial belge), 703 pp.

Palmer C. A. (1976) *Slaves of the White God: Blacks in Mexico 1570–1650* (Cambridge, Mass: HUP) 234 pp.

Palmer, H. R. (1936) *The Bornu, Sahara and Sudan* (New York: Negro University Press), 296 pp.

Palmer, R. and Parsons, N. (eds) (1977) *The Roots of Rural Poverty in Central and Southern Africa* (London: Heinemann).

Patterson, K. D. (1975) *The Northern Gabon Coast to 1875* (Oxford: Clarendon Press), 167 pp.

Pélissier, P. (1966) *Les paysans du Sénégal: les civilisations agraires du Cayor à la Casamance* (Saint-Yrieix, Haute-Vienne: Imprimerie Fabrègue), 941 pp.

Perlman, M. L. (1970) 'The traditional systems of stratification among the Ganda and the Nyoro of Uganda', in A. Tuden and Plotnicov (eds), *Social Stratification in Africa* (London: Macmillan), pp. 125–62.

Perrot, C.H. (1982) *Les Anyi-Ndenye et le pouvoir politique aux XVIIIe et XIXe siècles* (Abidjan/Paris: CEDA).

Person, Y. (1964) 'En quête d'une chronologie ivoirienne', in J. Vansina, R. Mauny and L. V. Thomas (eds), *The Historian in Tropical Africa* (Oxford: OUP), pp. 322–38.

Person, Y. (1970) 'Le Soudan nigérien et la Guinée occidentale', in H. Deschamps (ed.), *Histoire générale de l'Afrique noire,* vol. 1 (Paris: PUF), pp. 271–304.

Person, Y. (1972) *The Dyula and the Manding World* (London: SOAS, Conference on Manding Studies, duplicated).

Phillipson, D. W. (1977) *The Later Prehistory of Eastern and Southern Africa* (London: Heinemann), 323 pp.

Piault, M. H. (1970) Histoire Mawri: introduction à l'étude des processus constitutifs de l'Etat (Paris: Editions du CNRS), 206 pp.

Plancquaert, M. (1971) *Les Yaka: essai d'histoire* (Tervuren: MRAC, Annales sciences humaines, vol. 71).

Pollock, N. C. and Agnew, S. (1963) *A Historical Geography of South Africa* (London: Longman), 242 pp.

Porter, D. H. (1970) *The Abolition of the Slave Trade in England 1784–1807* (New York: Archon).

Price, R. (1976) *The Guiana Maroons: Historical and Bibliographical Introduction* (Baltimore: JHUP) 184 pp.

Priestley, M. A. (1969) *West African Trade and Coast Society* (London: OUP), 207 pp.

Quarles, B. (1961) *The Negro in the American Revolution* (Chapel Hill: UNCP), 231 pp.

Randles, W. G. L. (1968) *L'ancien royaume du Congo des origines à la fin du XIXe siècle* (Paris/The Hague: Mouton), 275 pp.

Ranger, T. O. (ed.) (1968) *Aspects of Central African History* (London/Nairobi: Heinemann/ EAPH), 291 pp.

Ranger, T. O. (1979) *Revolt in Southern Rhodesia 1896–1897: A Study in African Resistance*, 1st paperback edn (London: Heinemann), 403 pp.

Ranger, T. O. and Kimambo, I. N. (eds) (1972) *The Historical Study of African Religion* (London: Heinemann), 307 pp.

Rau, V. (1966) 'Les marchands-banquiers étrangers au Portugal sous le règne de Joao III (1521–1557)', in *Les aspects internationaux de la découverte océanique aux XVe et XVIe siècles* (Paris).

Rinchon, R. F. D. (1964) *Pierre Ignace Liévin van Alstein, capitaine négrier: Gand 1733 – Nantes 1793* (Dakar: IFAN, Mémoire No. 71), 452 pp.

Roberts, A. D. (1976) *A History of Zambia* (London: Heinemann), 288 pp.

Roche, C. (1976) *Conquête et resistance en Casamance* (Dakar: NEA).

Rodney, W. (1970) *A History of the Upper Guinea Coast 1545–1800* (Oxford: Clarendon Press), 283 pp.

Rodney, W. (1972) *How Europe Underdeveloped Africa* (Dar es Salaam/London: TPH and Bogle L'Ouverture), 316 pp.

Rodney, W. (1975) 'Africa in Europe and the Americas', in J. D. Fage and R. Oliver (eds), *The Cambridge History of Africa*, vol. 4 (Cambridge: CUP), pp. 578–651.

Rotberg, R. and Mazrui, A. (eds) *Protest and Power in Black Africa* (New York: OUP), 1274 pp.

Rout, L. B. Jr (1976) *The African Experience in Spanish America, from 1502 to the Present Day* (Cambridge: CUP), 404 pp.

Ryder, A. F. C. (1969) *Benin and the Europeans, 1485–1897* (London: Longmans), 372 pp.

Salim, A. I. (1980) 'Kenya, Muslims' in *Encyclopedia of Islam*, new edn (Leiden/Paris: Brill/Maisonneuve et Larose).

Sautter, G. (1966) *De l'Alantique au fleuve Congo, une géographie du sous-peuplement* (Paris: Imprimerie nationale), 1102 pp.

Schove, D. J. (1973) 'African droughts and the spectrum of time', in D. Dalby and R. J. H. Church (eds) *Droughts in Africa* (London: IAI), pp. 38–53; 2nd edn, 1977.

Séré de Rivières, E. (1965) *Histoire du Niger* (Paris: Berger-Levrault), 311 pp.

Shaw, T. (1978) *Nigeria: Its Archaeology and Early History* (London: Thames & Hudson).

Shepherd, J. F. and Walton, G. M. (1972) *Shipping, Maritime Trade, and the Economic Development of Colonial North America* (Cambridge: CUP).

Shiroya, O. J. E. (unpublished) 'The Lugbara: at the nexus of three worlds', in J. B. Webster (ed.), *Uganda before 1900*, vol. 1.

Skinner, E. P. (1964) *The Mossi of Upper Volta: The Political Development of a Sudanese People* (Stanford: SUP), 236 pp.

Smaldone, J. P. (1977) *Warfare in the Sokoto Caliphate* (Cambridge: CUP), 228 pp.

Southhall, A. W. (1970) 'Rank and stratification among the Alur and other Nilotic peoples', in A. Tuden and Plotnicov (eds), *Social Stratification in Africa* (London: Macmillan), pp. 31–46.

Sow, A. I. (1971) *Le filon du bonheur éternel par Mouhammadou Samba Mambeya* (Paris: Colin).

Steinhart, E. I. (1981) 'Herders and farmers', in C. C. Steward and D. Crummey (eds), *Modes of Production in Africa* (London: Sage Publications), pp. 115–56.

Stokes, E. and Brown, R. (eds) (1966) *The Zambezian Past: Studies in Central African History* (Manchester: MUP), 427 pp.

Suret-Canale, J. (1970) *La République de Guinée* (Paris: Editions sociales), 431 pp.

Swartz, A. (1971) *Tradition et changements dans la société guéré* (Paris: ORSTOM, Mémoires No. 52), 259 pp.

Tamrat, T. (1977) 'Ethiopia, the Red Sea and the Horn', Cambridge *History of Africa*, vol. 3 (Cambridge: CUP), pp. 98–182.

Tardits, C. (1980) *Le royaume bamoum* (Paris: Armand Colin), 1078 pp.

Tardits, C. (ed.) (1981) *Contribution de la recherche ethnologique à l'histoire des civilisations du Cameroun* (2 vols, Paris: Editions du CNRS), 597 pp.

Taylor, J. G. (1979) *From Modernization to Modes of Production: A Critique of the Sociologies of Development and Underdevelopment* (London: Macmillan).

Thomas, J. M. C. (1979) 'Emprunt ou parentés', in S. Bahuchet, *Pygmées de Centrafrique* (Paris), pp. 141–69.

Thompson, R. F. and Cornet, J. (1982) *The Four Moments of the Sun: Kongo Art in Two Worlds* (Washington: National Art Gallery).

Thornton, J. K. (1983) *The Kingdom of Kongo in the Era of the Civil Wars, 1641–1718* (Madison: UWP), 193 pp.

Tosh, J. (1978) *Clan Leaders and Colonial Chiefs in Lango: the Political History of an East African Stateless Society, 1800–1939* (Oxford: Clarendon Press, Oxford Studies in African Affairs), 293 pp.

Toure, M. (1974) *Mande Influences in the Gyaman Kingdom*, Colloquium, Bonduku, January.

Toussaint, A. (1971) *Histoire des l'Ile Maurice* (Paris: PUF), 128 pp.

Toussaint, A. (1972) *Histoire des Iles Mascareignes* (Paris: Berger-Levrault), 351 pp.

Trimingham, J. S. (1970) *A History of Islam in West Africa* (Oxford: OUP), 262 pp.

Turnbull, C. M. (1966) *Wayward Servants: The Two Worlds of the African Pygmies* (London: Eyre and Spottiswood), 390 pp.

UNESCO (1963) *Nomades et nomadisme au Sahara* (Paris), 195 pp.

UNESCO (1979) *The African Slave Trade from the Fifteenth to the Nineteenth Century, General History of Africa, Studies and Documents, No. 2* (Paris: UNESCO), 330 pp.

UNESCO (1980) *Historical Relations across the Indian Ocean, General History of Africa, Studies and Documents No. 3* (Paris: UNESCO), 198 pp.

Valensi, L. (1969) *Le Maghreb avant la prise d'Alger, 1790–1830* (Paris: Flammarion), 141 pp.

Valensi, L. (1977) *Fellahs tunisiens: l'économie rurale et la vie des campagnes aux 18e et 19e siècles* (Paris/The Hague: Mouton), 421 pp.

Vansina, J. (1961) *De la tradition orale; essai de méthode historique* (Tervuren: MRAC, Mémoire No. 36).

Vansina, J. (1966) *Kingdoms of the Savanna: A History of Central African States until the European Occupation*, trans. of *Les anciens royaumes de la savane* (Madison: UWP), 364 pp.

Vansina, J. (1972) *La légende du passé: Traditions orales du Burundi* (Tervuren: MRAC), 257 pp.

Vansina, J. (1973) *The Tio Kingdom of the Middle Congo, 1880–1892* (London: OUP), 586 pp.

Vansina, J. (1978) *The Children of Woot: A History of the Kuba Peoples* (Madison: UWP), 394 pp.

Van Thiel, H. (1911) 'Buzinza unter der Dynastie der Bahinda', *Anthropos*, pp. 497–520.

Vérin, P. (1975) *Les échelles anciennes du commerce sur les côtes nord de Madagascar* (2 vols, Lille: University of Lille).

Wallerstein, I. (1976) 'The three stages of African involvement in the world economy', in P. C.

W. Gutkind and I. Wallerstein (eds), *The Political Economy of Contemporary Africa* (London: Sage Publications), pp. 30–57.

Walvin, J. (1972) *The Blank Presence: A Documentary History of the Negro in England* (New York: Schocken Books).

Walvin, J. (1973) *Black and White: the Negro and English Society, 1555–1945* (London: Allen Lane and Penguin Press), 273 pp.

Warren, R. (1980) *Imperialism: Pioneer of Capitalism* (London: NLB and Verso).

Webster, J. B. (ed.) (1979) *Chronology, Migration and Drought in Interlacustrine Africa* (London: Longman and Dalhousie University Press), 345 pp.

Weiskel, T. C. (1980) *French Colonial Rule and the Baule Peoples, 1889–1911* (Oxford: Clarendon Press) 323 pp.

Wilbur, C. M. (1967) *Slavery in China during the Former Han Dynasty* (New York: Russell and Russell).

Wilks I. G. (1962) *The Tradition of Islamic Learning in Ghana* (Legon).

Wilks, I. G. (1975) *Asante in the Nineteenth Century: The Structure and Evolution of a Political Order* (Cambridge: CUP), 800 pp.

Williams, E. (1970) *From Columbus to Castro: The History of the Caribbean, 1492–1969* (London: André Deutsch), 576 pp.

Williamson, K. (1971) 'The Benue-Congo languages and Ijo', in J. Berry and J. H. Greenberg (eds), *Linguistics in Sub-Saharan Africa* (Mouton), pp. 245–306.

Wilson, M. and Thompson, L. M. (eds) (1969, 1971) *The Oxford History of South Africa* (2 vols, Oxford: Clarendon Press).

Womersley, H. (1984) 'Legends and the history of the Luba', in T. Q. Reefe (ed.), *Legends and History of the Luba* (Los Angeles: Cross Roads Press).

Wright, J. (1977) 'San history and non-San historians', in *The Societies of Southern Africa in the 19th and 20th Centuries*, vol. 8 (London).

Zahan, D. (1960) *Sociétés d'initiation bambara: le N'domo; le Kore* (Paris/The Hague: Mouton), 438 pp.

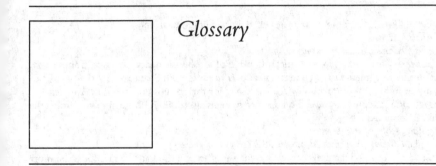

Glossary

abara: the (large) dugout canoes of Hausa, Kebbi and Nupe.

abba gada: in Oromo society (Ethiopia), the leader of an ethnic group, elected from among the members of the *gada*.

'abīd: (sing. *'abd*): is the ordinary word for 'slaves' in Arabic, more particularly for 'male slaves', 'female slaves' being *imā'* (sing. *ama*).

abilema: the earliest inhabitants of Unyakyusa (Lake Malawi region)

Ab Shaykh (title) (Arabic): a rank that was second only to that of the Sultan; a post that commanded great authority.

abuna (title): the Patriarch of the Abyssinian Church; the Metropolitan of the Ethiopian Church.

abusuapanin: head, leader (of a (Akan) family, etc.).

achikunda: in the *prazo* system, armies of slaves, i.e. the lower class, as opposed to the dominant class or *prazeros*.

adamfo ('client state'): in greater Asante, a system of provincial administration in which each of the states composing the confederacy served the *Asantehene* through one of the kings or member-states of the confederacy or one of the wing-chiefs of the Kumasi state, usually resident in Kumasi.

adanudo: a rich Ewe cloth (in Ghana).

adinkra: broad cloth with Akan traditional motifs and symbols stamped on it.

agha (title): commander of the Janissaries (in Egypt).

ahl al-usūl (Arabic): members of the old lineage and rank.

ajami: transcription in Arabic of African languages (e.g. the Hausa *ajami* manuscript).

akuaba: small wooden or terracotta maternity dolls. Still to be found in Ghana.

alfa: title borne by the chiefs of the provinces (*diwe*) in the confederation of Futa Jallon.

alifa: title of an officer (in Kānem).

almadies: boats (in Senegambia).

almamia: land tenure and taxation systems (in Futa Jallon, Futa Toro and the Sokoto caliphate).

almamy: (title in Bundu, Futa Jallon and Futa Toro): a Fulfulde version of the title *imām*.

amenokal (title): The Tuareg equivalent of the Muslim *imām* and *kādī*.

amīr (Arabic): title given to generals, commanders, provincial rulers and sometimes to the sovereigns of small countries (spelt 'emir' in the West).

amīr al-mu'minīn (Arabic): caliphal title meaning 'prince, Commander of the Faithful'.

andrianoni: Antemoro title carried by the first ruler of the Onilahy kingdom in Madagascar.

ant-ankara: 'people of the rocks', i.e. the Antankara of Madagascar's far north.

apagyafie: a group of goldsmiths and craftsmen from Denkyira.

ardo or *rugga*: the Fulbe equivalent of the Muslim *imām* and *kādī*.

'arsh (Arabic): ethnic area; community or group holdings; communal land.

asago: an Akan warrior.

asantehene: title of the paramount king of Asante.

asiento or *assiento* (Spanish *asiento*, seat, meeting place of a tribunal, treaty, contract, from *asentar*, to seat, make an agreement): a contract or convention between Spain and another power or company or individual for furnishing African slaves for the Spanish dominions in America.

askiya: royal title adopted by the Songhay sovereigns to distinguish themselves from the preceding Sonni dynasty.

asomfo: a golden stool of the Asante.

attajirai (or *masu arziki*): rich traders; the wealthy (in Hausa society).

azalai or *azalay*: a term for the great caravans made up of several thousand camels (or to be more precise, dromedaries), which in the spring and autumn carry salt from the salt deposits of the Southern Sahara to the tropical regions of the Sahel and the Sudan. The salt deposits of Taoudéni have replaced those of Taghāza, a source of wealth of the kings of Mali and of Gao (fourteenth–fifteenth centuries).

azel: fiefs.

babika or *bampika* (sing. *mubika*): the slaves, one of the strata in Kongo society.

babuta (sing. *mubata*, from *vata* or *evata*, 'village'): the rustics, one of the strata in Kongo society.

baganwa: title of the princes of royal blood (in Burundi).

bāhar nagāš ('sea-king'): the governor of the northernmost province of the Ethiopian empire.

bahaushe: trader (in Hausaland)

bahutu: see *muhutu*.

bairu: ennobled (clans).

bakama: see *mugaba*.

bakungu: chiefs (in Burundi and Rwanda).

(the) *Bambudye*: the closed association which helped the Luba king to rule.

bami: see *mwami*.

bantamahene (title): one of the wing-chiefs of the Kumasi state, vassals of the *Asantehene*.

baraka (Arabic): 'divine favour', 'gift of working miracles', 'charisma'; a blessing dispensed by *marabouts* and especially by descendants of the Prophet Muhammad (*shurafā'*).

barbariores barbari: savages (Ethiopia).

bares: mines in Northern Zambezia region.

Basace (title in Zamfara, Hausaland): an elder holding an ancient, long-forgotten office, member of a *Tara*.

(the) *bāshiya* (Arabic) or *pashists*: the followers of 'Alī Pasha.

bawa: captive (in Hausaland).

bawan Sarki: royal slave (in Hausaland).

bawdi peyya yiyan: blood drums (in Futa Toro).

Bayt al-māl: the (public) Treasury, in Arabic.

beecio: a title (in Waalo).

bega (Mossi): a great ceremonial cycle which involved the king and all the dignitaries of the land in sacrifices intended to ensure a good harvest.

benangatoobe: in the caste system in Takrūr, the class involving the *sakkeebe*, *wayilbe* and *gawlo*.

bey (gentleman, chief, prince in Turkish): 1) the governor of a district or minor province in the Ottoman Empire; 2) the sovereign vassal of the sultan (e.g. the *bey* of Tunis); 3) a high-ranking official, senior officer, in the Ottoman empire; 4) the bearer of a courtesy title, formerly used in Turkey and Egypt.

beylerbey (pl. *beylerbeyi*): the governor-general of a province, head of a *sandjak-beylik*.

beylik: the term *beylik* denotes both the title and post (or function) of a *bey* and the territory (domain, jurisdiction) under the rule of a *bey*. Later, by extension, it came to mean also 'state, government' and, at the same time, a political and administrative entity sometimes possessing a certain autonomy.

bid'a (Arabic): innovations, i.e. traditional religious practices grafted on to Islam.

bilād al-Makhzen: in the Maghreb, a country under state authority.

Bilād al-Sūdān: literally 'the country of the blacks' in Arabic; this expression is nearly always used by Arab authors in reference to the blacks of West Africa, a very extensive zone comprising not only the Senegal, Niger and Chad basins but also the more southern countries of savanna and forest. The term 'Sudan' now attaches to a state in the Nile valley never so designated in ancient writings.

bilbalse (Mossi): adult servants.

bilolo: see *kilolo*.

birr: silver, in Amharic (Ethiopia).

biton: Bambara title meaning 'the Commander'.

bolo ('arm', in Bambara): a division of the infantry in Samori Ture's army, formed of several *sen*.

boma (Swahili): an enclosure or stockade used for herding beasts and for defensive purposes.

bozales (Spanish): unlike the *ladinos*, the *bozales* were slaves brought directly from Africa and who had had no previous contact with Europe.

brak: title in Waalo.

buch jodong gweng': council of the elders (among the Luo).

buch piny: council of Luo sub-ethnic groups.

bud-kasma: (Mossi) head of a budu.

budu: in the patrilineal and patrilocal Mossi society, this term denotes any descent group, from the broadest and the oldest to the narrowest, that operates as the exogamous reference unit.

bugo (pl. *buguba*): (Mossi) fertility priest.

buhake: a type of clientele link (in Rwanda).

bulopwe: the Luba concept of power (Luba royalty was founded on the principle of *bulopwe* or 'sacredness') .

Burr Jullit ('Great Prayer Masters'): religious leaders, in Senegambia.

capitão-mor (pl. *capitãos-mores* (Portuguese): in Shona country, a representative of merchants in a *feira*, appointed by the Portuguese administration.

caracoes (shells, shellfish, cowries in Portuguese): small stone beads found in the Zambezia region.

ceddo (pl. *sebbe*): warlord, war chief (in Senegambia).

changamire: ruler, member of a dynasty which rose to power in Butua.

chāt: see *kāt*.

chechia: red woollen bonnet.

chidi: fiefs (in Borno).

chikunda: in the *prazo* system, a slave army under the authority of a *sachikunda*.

chikwange: a well-known bread among the Kongo, obtained from the cassava root.

chimas: fief-holders (in Borno).

chiroma (a Borno title): heir apparent.

chuanga: in the *prazo* system, top slave.

cire perdue: lost wax.

colono (Portuguese): colonist, settler (in *prazos*).

comprador (from Portuguese *comprar*, to purchase, buy): 1) Formerly, the name of a native servant employed by Europeans, in India and the Far East, to purchase necessaries and keep the household accounts; a house-steward. 2) Now, in China, the name of the principal native servant, employed in European establishments, and especially in houses of business, both as head of the staff of native employees, and as intermediary between the house and its native customers. 3) One held to be an agent of foreign domination or exploitation.

creole (from Spanish *criollo*, 'native to the locality, country'): a person of European ancestry born in the former colonies (West Indies, Guyana, Réunion); Creole: a language, born of the black slave trade (sixteenth–nineteenth centuries), that has become the mother tongue of those slaves' descendants (in the West Indies, Guyanas, Indian Ocean Islands, etc.). There exist creoles based on French, English, Portuguese, etc.: the creole of Guadeloupe, the English creoles of the Caribbean, etc.

cruzado (or *crusado*) (pl. *cruzados* or *cruzadoes*) (from Portuguese *cruzado*, literally 'marked with a cross'): an old gold coin of Portugal, originally issued by Alfonso V (1438–81) about the year 1457, having a cross on the reverse in commemoration of the king's crusading struggle against the Muslims of North Africa; also: a similar Portuguese coin in silver first issued by John IV (1640-56).

curva: known as 'customs' in lands under Portuguese influence, 'duty' in English; a tribute paid by the Portuguese to the Mutapa rulers.

dabey: in Songhay, a village of slaves.

dadde yiyan: war songs; blood songs (in Futa Toro).

dady: in Sakalava country (Madagascar), the cult of the ancestors; ancestral Volamena relics.

damel: title of a ruler (in Kayor).

damel-teen: title of a ruler (in Kayor).

danau (title in Zamfara, Hausaland): a governor who owed his title to the name of the town in which he resided, an important trading centre from where he kept watch over the roads leading south and west of Kebbi.

dandal ('the opening of the "U" '): the settlement's main street of most Kanuri U-shaped towns and villages .

dan dubal (a title in Hausaland): in Zamfara, an advisor on religious affairs, the custodian of Zamfara's history and responsible for praying for the army's victory.

dan kodo (a title in Hausaland): see *dan dubal*.

(the) *Darb al-'Arba'īn* ('40-Days' Road' in Arabic): the great trans-Saharan route that linked the Darfūr region to Egypt in about 40 days.

debe: a village of slaves (in Soninke).

debeere: a village of slaves (in Fulfulde).

dey (from Turkish *dāyī*, 'maternal uncle') (honorific title): 1) a ruling official of the Ottoman empire in northern Africa, especially the head of the Algiers Regency from 1671 to 1830, i.e. before the French conquest in 1830; 2) also designated a lower rank in the Janissary militia; towards the end of the tenth/sixteenth century in Tunis, the name was born by the heads of the 40 sections of the militia.

al-Dhahabī (from *dhahab*, pure gold in Arabic): 'the Golden': nickname of Aḥmad al-Manṣur, the sixth sovereign of the Moroccan dynasty of the Saʿādī.

diatigui: a title (in Timbuktu).

dimo (pl. *rimbe*): free man (in Futa Jallon).

disi ('chest', in Bambara): the centre of Segu's army when arrayed in battle order.

diwal (pl. *diwe*): a province (in Futa Jallon).

dīwān (Arabic): central state coffers or Treasury; Council of State; military pension roll; collection of poetry; large hall or chamber; ministerial departments; ruler.

diwe: see *diwal*.

djallāb (Arabic): slave merchants, slave traffickers, called 'importers'. They acted as the middlemen and the financiers of the long-distance trade.

Djammā ('the gatherer' in Arabic): the nickname of 'Abdallāh, leader of the 'Abdallābi state.

djihād: literally 'effort' in Arabic; *djihād akbar*: 'supreme effort'; 1) the struggle against one's passions; the greatest effort of which one is capable; an effort to attain a specific goal; 2) personal effort of the believer to serve the Islamic faith, particularly the struggle to defend Islam, its land and the Muslims against the impious enemy, or to enlarge Islamic territory (*Dār al-Islām*), by extension, 'holy war'.

al-Djinn ('the devil' in Arabic): the nickname of the Egyptian *bey* 'Alī Bey.

djuad (Arabic): warrior chiefs.

Dongo (divinity): in Hausaland, a Borgu hunter whose powers were identical to those of Shango in the Yoruba culture.

doomi Buur: see *garmi*.

dukowo: territorial divisions (in Eweland).

dupi: the servile class (in Western Nilotic societies).

dwar: tented camp.

egusi: a local crop (in Igboland).

ekanda: in Kongo society, matriclan, matrilineage, but also ethnic group, republic: in short, any community.

Ekpe: the *Ekpe* society of Calabar was an adaptation of a cult of the leopard (*Mgbe*) present among many forest groups in the Cross river valley and in parts of the Cameroon.

Ekpo: a secret society (among the Ibibio).

emīn (from Arabic *amīn*, faithful, trustworthy): an Ottoman administrative title usually translated 'intendant' or 'commissioner', tax collector. His function or office was called *emānet*.

emuron: a seer (in Teso).

etem (pl. *itemwan*): in Teso and Kumam, multi-clan ritual grouping.

eze (Igbo title): king.

eze Nri (title meaning 'ruler', 'the king of Nri', among the Igbo): priest-king with ritual and mystic, but not military power.

faa (Bambara): father of a biological community.

faama (Bambara title): lord holding supreme power, man of power and authority.

faaya: fathers (in Bambara).

fahatelo: in Iboina (Madagascar), first minister; royal official.

fanadir: cage (in Borno).

fandroana: annual royal-bath ceremony (in Merina, Madagascar).

fani: in the Comoro Islands, the first Islamic chiefs who had originally succeeded the Bēdja of pre Islamic times.

farin or *faren:* rulers of provinces, governors.

farinya (comes from *Fari* and pharaoh): 'ruler' in Soninke, Mande, etc. *Farinya* denotes a monocracy as opposed to the controlled monarchical oligarchy of the original *mansaya*.

fāshir (Arabic): royal residence.

fataući: in Hausaland, trade over medium and long distances; wholesale trade.

fazenda: large estates in Brazil.

feiras: fairs (in Portuguese).

fia: the king of a *dukowo* (in Eweland).

fidda dīwānī (Arabic): fine silver coins.

filohany: chief (in Malagasy).

fitahina: a linguistic taboo (among the Sakalava of Madagascar).

fla-n-ton (or *ton*): peer association; the *fla-n-ton* brought together the members of three successive promotions of those circumcised.

folahazomanga (in Malagasy, 'those who came to Mahafaly from elsewhere'): a component of Mahafaly society, Madagascar.

foroba-dyon ('captives of the big common field') or *furuba-dyon* ('captives of the Great Union'):
crown slaves.

gabar: in Ethiopia, a peasant who worked the lands for the benefit of the landed élite and was,
like the *fallāh*, similar to a serf, or at least a tributary or client obliged to pay the *gabir*,
depending on whether he was a share-cropper or a tenant farmer.

gabir or *siso*: a tax paid by the *gabar*.

gada or *luba*: a classification of the Oromo society of Ethiopia by age groups based on an abstract
numerical principle. It is an egalitarian system which involves rule by rotation age-groups.

gaisuwa or *tsare*: payment of regular gifts to superiors (in Hausaland).

galadima (a Borno title): a kind of prime minister or grand vizier in whom the conduct of all
affairs of state was vested. The title was borrowed from Borno, but there it designated the
governor of the western provinces, that is, those nearest to Hausaland; in Katsina, an
important official who deputized for the *sarki*; in Kano, a military leader; in Sokoto, the
caliph's advisor, acting as the caliph's link with the emirates.

garmi or *doomi Buur*: the ruling class (in Kayor).

gatari ('axe'): in Katsina (Hausaland), title of a governor who watched over the north-western
frontier.

gayya: in Hausaland, mutual aid system; communal work.

gida (pl. *gidaje*): extended family; groups of families (in Hausaland).

gikingi: a land system granting exclusive grazing rights to the owner (in Rwanda).

gimaje: long dyed cotton dresses (in Kanuri).

gobbi: an annual tax on mines.

grumetes: African auxiliaries recruited by the *lançados*.

gulma: title of a high-ranking dignitary among the Songhay.

gumbala: in Futa Toro, the war song of the *sebbe*, which consist of hymns to courage. It is the epic
song of death in which the *ceddo* assumes his destiny as a warrior, his faithfulness to his
ancestors and to the ethic of his caste.

gumsu: the king's head wife (in Borno).

gurma (Hausa): right (e.g. the *gurma* bank of the river, as opposed to *hausa*, the left bank).

gweng' (pl. *gwenge*): a Luo semi-autonomous political and territorial unit.

Ḥabshī: one of the terms used in India to denote those African communities whose ancestors
originally came to the country as slaves, in most cases from the Horn of Africa, although some
doubtless sprang from the slave troops of the neighbouring countries. The majority, at least in
earlier times, may well have been Ethiopian, but the name was applied indiscriminately to all
Africans, and in the days of the Portuguese slave trade with India many such *Ḥabshī* were in
fact of the Nilotic and Bantu peoples.

hacienda: large estates in Latin America.

hakura: tax exemption.

hanzo (from *nso*, 'house' in Kikongo): parcel (in Angola).

hayu: judges (among the Oromo of Ethiopia).

hazne or *hazine*: treasury.

heemraden: burghers (in Southern Africa).

himāye (Arabic): protection charges; caution money protecting the conquered townsfolk from
looting.

hore kosan: grazing land.

iko: power (in Hausaland).

iḳṭāʿ (Arabic): 1) the fiscal allocation of an emir, always strictly monitored and updated, of the revenue of one or more localities, according to status and the number of men in his service; 2) delegation of tax-collecting powers granted by the prince to a military or civilian officer in regard to a fiscal district, as remuneration for a service rendered to the state; this concession was revocable; 3) distribution of fiscal concessions for maintenance of the military class; 4) military fief system.

ʿilm (Arabic): religious knowledge.

iltizam (Arabic): according to the *iltizam* system which superseded the *muḳataʿat* system by about 1658 lands of every village or group of villages were offered for public auction and the highest bidders (the *multazims*) were given the right to collect taxes from the peasants and such lands became their *iltizam*.

imām (Arabic): honorary title awarded to the eminent legal experts who, between the second/eighth and the third/ninth centuries, codified the whole body of Muslim law in various intellectual centres of the Muslim world, particularly Medina and Baghdad; a title given to the founders of law schools and to major theologians; chiefs, supreme leader of the Muslim community; among the Shīʿites, equivalent of a caliph (must be a descendant of ʿAlī).

imāmate: the leadership of the Muslim community; caliphate or inherited power; office or rank of an *imām*; function of the *imām* as head of the Muslim community; the region or country ruled over by an *imām* (e.g. the *imāmate* of Yemen).

indabo: a village of slaves (in Hausaland).

innamme: in Kebbi (Hausaland), title of a governor who kept watch over the western frontier.

insilimen: see *zuwaya*.

inyamasango: a village head in Shona country.

iyāla (*eyālet*, in Turkish) ('management, administration, exercise of power'): in the Ottoman empire the largest administrative division under a *beylerbey* or governor-general. In this sense it was officially used after 1000/1591.

jaggorde: the council of electors (in Futa Toro).

jagos: territorial sub-heads (among the Luo).

jangali: the livestock tax paid by stockbreeders (in Hausaland).

Jengu: the most prestigious secret society among the Duala, Isuwu and other neighbouring groups, based on the veneration of water spirits.

jibda: musk (in Hausaland).

jon: captive (in Mande).

jonya (from the Mande word *jon* meaning 'captive'): black African captive.

jumbe: in the Comoro Islands, this term denoted the daughters of the *fani*, who came to marry the Sunnite newcomers.

jurungul ('crown'): a special coiffure worn by a Kanuri married woman.

kabaka: ruler, king (in Buganda).

ḳabīla (Arabic pl. *ḳabāʾil*) a large agnatic Arab or Berber group the members of which claim to be descended from one common ancestor and who may 'jointly own an area of grazing land'.

kabunga: chief (in Kongo).

ḳāḍī (Arabic): among Muslims, a magistrate concurrently discharging civil, judicial and religious functions in accordance with Muslim law (*sharīʿa*).

ḳafu or *jamana* (in Mande): provinces; small state-like territorial units (among the Malinke and the Bambara).

ḳāʾid (Arabic): commander, army chief; provincial governor; *ḳabīla* chieftain.

kaigama (Borno title): governor of the northern provinces (in Kano).

kakaki: a long trumpet (in Hausaland).

kalaram: turban (in Kanuri).

kalonga: ruler in the Maravi state.

kangam: a provincial chief in Senegambia.

ḳānūn or *lḳānūn* (from the Greek *kanôn,* rule): the corpus of legal regulations (canon law).

Ḳānūn Nāme: a decree which sought to regulate political, military, civil and economic life in Egypt under the Ottoman administration.

kasa: territory (in Hausaland).

ḳaṣaba or *gaṣba* (Arabic) (casbah/kasbah in English): capital; (small) town; citadel, castle or fortress (in North Africa).

ḳāshif (Arabic): head of district (in Egypt) whose task it was to maintain the irrigation system and levy taxes from the farmers; tax collector.

ḳaṣīda: an Arabic or Persian panegyric, elegiac or satirical poem or ode, usually having a tripartite structure. The term is derived from the root *ḳaṣada,* 'to aim at', for the primitive *ḳaṣīda* was intended to eulogize the *ḳabīla* of the poet and denigrate the opposing *ḳabīlas.* Later it was concerned with the eulogy of patrons.

kasuwanci: retail trade (in Hausaland).

ḳāt: (in Arabic) and *chāt* (in Amharic): a shrub (*Catha edulis F.*) native to Arabia, with mildly stimulating properties, grown in Ethiopia and Yemen and exported under the name of *ḳāt* or *chāt;* also the narcotic drug obtained from the leaves of this plant.

kaura (title): a military leader (in Katsina, Hausaland).

kaya (pl. *makaya*): a fortified village; an enclosed or fortified settlement (among the Miji-Kenda people of East Africa).

kazembe: a general (among the Lunda).

kente (also Kente): colourful *kente* clothes (of the Akan); in Ghana, a banded material; also, a long garment made from this material, loosely draped on or worn around the shoulders and waist.

ketema: garrison towns.

khalif or *khalifa* (a title) (Arabic): caliph, successor of the Prophet, sovereign responsible for ensuring observance of Islamic law on earth.

khammāsat (Arabic): fifth share-cropping of the land; tenant farming.

kharādj (Arabic): a land tax, sometimes paid in kind (and in addition to the cash poll tax or *djizya*) on land belonging to the *dhimmī* (non-Muslims living in Muslim territory under the status of 'protégés of Islam'); by extension designates all land taxes (see also *raia*).

khazin (Arabic): treasurer.

khimba (an association in Kongo): an initiation cult for boys.

khuṭba (Arabic): address delivered by the *khaṭib* (preacher), from the top of the *minbar* (mosque chair) of the Great Mosque, during the noontime Friday prayer, in which God's favour was invoked on the recognized caliph in the city and, where applicable, the prince from whom the governor of the town held his delegated power.

kiims'rogo: a Mossi ancestral shrine.

kilolo (pl. *bilolo*): territorial administrators, chiefs (among the Luba/Lunda).

kimpasi (a healing association in Kongo): a cult whose aim was to banish *mpasi.*

kitomi: in Kongo, former lords of the land.

Kokani (a title in Kebbi, Hausaland): the official responsible for relations with the population.

kom ngu: the counsellors of the kingdom (in Bamum).

kubandwa: a practice of initiatory rites in Rwanda, Burundi and Buha.

kudin haki: grazing duty paid by the nomadic Fulbe (in Kebbi, Hausaland).

kudin hito: customs duty (in Hausaland).

kudin kasa: a land tax paid by the farmers (in Hausaland).

kudin laifi: forgiveness tax paid by an offender when pardoned by the sovereign (in Hausaland).

kudin sana'a: a professional tax (in Hausaland).

kultingo: a tribute (in Borno).

Kulughli (from Turkish *kuloghlu*, 'son of slave'): in the period of Turkish domination in Algeria and Tunisia, this word denoted those elements of the population resulting from marriages of Turks with local women.

Kunduda (title in Hausaland): a Kebbi's military leader.

kurita: a Mossi word which means 'reigning dead man', is constructed by analogy with *narita*, 'reigning chief'. The *kurita* is the representative among the living of a dead chief, and is generally chosen from among the sons of the dead chief; he has no power by virtue of his title and is debarred from the succession, but he can become a chief in an area outside his family's command; if a *kurita* becomes a chief, he retains the *nom-de-guerre* (*zab yure*) of *naaba kurita*.

(the) *Kurkwā* corps (spearmen in Fūr): a standing slave-army created by Muḥammad Tayrāb ibn Aḥmad Bukr.

kutama: migration movement (from south-east Africa to Zimbabwe around 1000).

kwaka tree or monkey orange: 1) either of two deciduous African shrubs or small trees (*Strychnos inocua* and *Strychnos spinosa*) having a hard globose fruit with edible pulp; 2) the fruit of a monkey orange.

kwara: a magical symbol (in Mossi).

kyungu: ruler in the Ngonde kingdom.

ladinos (Spanish): the first Africans in America, brought there from Europe by the Conquistadores. They were mainly from Senegambia and had either been previously brought to Europe, or were born there. They were called *ladinos* in America because they knew Spanish or Portuguese, and were at least partly influenced by the civilization of the Iberian countries.

lamana (from the Sereer 'master of the land'): denotes a system of land tenure and a political system in which the masters of the land also exercised power. The *lamana* of the masters of the land developed into the *Mansaya* of purely political chiefs.

lançados (from Portuguese *lançar*, to launch out an adventure) or *tangomãos* ('people who had adopted local customs'): emigrants who had settled on the (African) continent with the agreement of the African sovereigns, intermarried and set themselves up as commercial middlemen. They formed part of the many expatriates who populated the southern rivers and the Atlantic islands (especially Cape Verde). Most of them were Portuguese, with a sprinkling of Greeks, Spaniards and even Indians. They also came to include more and more halfbreed children, the *filhos da terra* (children of the land).

landdrost: a resident magistrate (in southern Africa).

lapto (literally, 'translator'): a native interpreter.

larde kangema: the nominal owner of the land (in Borno).

las li: the descendants of the great *marabout* families who constituted 'the aristocracy of the sword and the lance and the book and the pen' at the top of the *rimbe* (in Futa Jallon).

legha (Arabic): henchmen.

Lenngi: in Futa Toro, the *Lenngi*, sung solely by *sebbe* women at marriages or circumcisions, are heroic songs summoning up contempt for death and the protection of honour.

lifidi (Hausa): a quilted armour; horse trappings; the quilted protection for war-horses.

Lifidi (title in Hausaland): Commander-in-chief of the heavy cavalry division.

Limanin Ciki (title in Hausaland): a Kanuri scholar responsible for the education of the royal family.

Linger: a title (in Kayor).

lizma (Arabic): in the Maghreb, farming out of the provinces, customs, etc.; tax-farming.

lundu: powerful ruler in the Maravi confederation in the seventeenth century.

maccube: slaves, captives (in Fulfulde).

machila: cotton clothes produced by the Lundu's Mang'anja subjects in the Lower Shire valley.

(the) *Madjelisse* (Arabic): a body of jurists.

madrasa (Arabic): a primary and secondary Ḳur'ānic school: *madrasa* designates more particularly an establishment of higher religious education (as a rule attached to a mosque) for the training of the Sunnite clergy, the *'ulamā'*.

magaji: a warrior; a successor (in Hausaland).

magira: the queen-mother (in Kānem-Borno).

magram: the king's official sister (in Kānem-Borno).

(the) Maguzawa: there are non-Muslim groups in both Nigeria and Niger who speak only Hausa and who share the Hausa culture, but who refuse to be called Hausa people. In Nigeria these people call themselves, and are called by other Hausa, Maguzawa (or Bamaguje), whereas in Niger they are known by the name Azna (or Arna), the Hausa word for 'pagan'. Since the name Maguzawa is probably derived from the Arabic *madjūs* (originally 'fire-worshippers', then 'pagans' generally) it is possible that the polarization between Hausa and Maguzawa/Azna began only with the spread of Islam among the common people in Hausaland, after the seventeenth and eighteen centuries.

mah'alla (Arabic): in the Maghrib, an armed expedition; armed camps.

mahanga (ilala palm – *Hyphaene natalenis*): a tree found in the lowveld areas of Southern Zambezia the sap of which was used to make an intoxicating wine called *njemani* or *chemwa* (in Hlengwe).

mahram (Arabic): the granting – by chiefs – of privileges to families or religious notables.

mai: king, ruler (in Kānembu).

maidugu: grandson of a previous king (in Borno).

(the) *mailo* system: the system of land tenure introduced into East Africa under British colonization; it combines chiefdom with ownership and the right to speculate in land.

maina: eligible princes (in Borno).

mainin kinendi (title in Borno): the Islamic and legal advisor to the *mai*.

mai sarauta: ruler (in Hausaland).

majlis: in Kānem, the highest council of state, normally presided over by the *mai* and composed of military and religious notables.

makambala: the councillors of the Kyungu (a priest-king worshipped by the Ngonde).

makaya: see *kaya*.

makhzen (Arabic): privileged peoples from whom Moroccan state officials are recruited.

(the) Makhzen: originally meant 'treasury', but came to be used for the official system of government in Morocco, and more broadly the political and religious élite of the country.

makoko: king, among the Tio of Kongo.

mala kasuube (a title in Borno): the official who supervised sales in the markets and attempted to ensure justice and fair play during major commercial transactions.

malams: Muslim clerics and scholars.

mallamai: scholars (in Hausaland).

maloango: king (in Central Africa: Angola, etc.).

mambo: a title found in south-east/central Africa.

mamlūk: a freed man, a former slave of Christian origin who has been converted and suitably trained to serve at court or in the army.

(the) Mamluks: a dynasty that reigned over Egypt and Syria (1250–1517), whose sultans were chosen from among the militias of slave soldiers (*mamlūks*).

Manantany: the first minister, in Sakalava kingdoms (Madagascar).

mandi-mani ('the Lord of the Manou'): the title of the greatest suzerain in the Sierra Leone-Liberia region.

mandi-mansa: the title of the Emperor of Mali.

mandjil or *mandjuluk*: the title which Fundj monarchs bestowed on their principal vassals.

Mangi Mrwe: the paramount chief of the Ugweno clans of Tanzania.

mani: in the Kongo kingdom, a high-ranking noble; a landlord; a governor.

mani kongo: the ruler of the Kongo.

manoma: farmers in (Hausaland).

mansa (in Maninka): the king, the holder of the most important political power (in Mali).

mansaya (in Maninka): 1) royalty; political territorial groups headed by a *mansa*; 2) a socio-political system, whose dominant ruling class was a polyarchy of an élite of laymen or priests, freemen or slaves, caste or guild members, or noblemen or commoners. It was financed by the taxes which those controlling the machinery of government levied on trade and produce. It was not a landed aristocracy or proprietor class.

mantse: king, among the Ga.

marabout: the word does not have the same meaning in the Maghreb as in black Africa. In the former it applies both to a holy person who has founded a brotherhood and to his tomb; in sub-Saharan Africa it designates any person with some knowledge of the Ḳurʾān and other sacred writings who uses that knowledge to act as interceder between the believer and God, while drawing upon traditional divinatory sources and the use of talismans. In the eyes of the public he is a scholar in the religious sense of the word, a magician, a soothsayer and a healer.

marabtin bilbaraka: in Barḳa, the offspring of pilgrims, usually North Africans.

marisa (title meaning 'the destroyer'): in Katsina (Hausaland), the title of a governor who kept watch over the eastern border.

maroserana ('many paths' in Malagasy): reflects the custom of the first Maroserana kings in Mahafaly of placing their residences in the middle of habitations with paths radiating in all directions to villages around them.

marula or *nkanyi*: the *marulu* (*Sclerocarya caffra*) is a tree of the family Anacardiaceae, found in central and southern Africa, and bearing an oval yellow fruit about 2 inches long that is used locally for making an intoxicating beverage; also *marula* plum: the fruit of this tree.

masu sarauta: in Hausaland, all those with any political authority; aristocrats.

mbafu: red dyewood, in Luba (Zaire).

mbarma or *bulala*: local or ethnic leaders (in Kānem).

mboma (a man of the Boma ethnic group): among the Tio, the word designates a stupid person or anyone in a lowly occupation.

mbua: animal skin (in Kikuyuland).

meen: maternal family (in Kayor).

mercadores (Portuguese): brokers; merchants, tradesmen.

mestizo: a Spanish or Portuguese half-caste (Afro-Portuguese); also applied to other persons of mixed blood, such as Afro-Asians.

(the) *Mfecane* (crushing), in Nguni languages and *Lifaqane/Difaqane* (hammering) in Sotho-Tswana: a social and political revolution that took place in Bantu-speaking southern Africa and beyond, during the first decades of the nineteenth century.

Mgbe: leopard secret society (of the northern Cross river valley and the Cameroon).

mhondoro ('lion'): in the Mutapa empire, spirit mediums whose function was to advise the emperor in all matters of state national ancestor spirits.

mifaly: submission (in Malagasy).

milambu: taxes payable (to the Luba *mulopwe*) in food and local produce.

milk: small family holdings; property; possession, ownership.

mingilu: unpaid labour (a tribute paid to the Luba *mulopwe* by his officials).

mithḳal (of gold, etc.) (Arabic): the Sudanese *mithḳal* weighs approximately 4.25 grams.

mitngu: a secret society opened to the rest of the population irrespective of social status (in Bamum).

mlira (the *mlira* cult): the ritual veneration of Mlira, the spirit of the Great Kalonga Chinkhole, an ancestor of the Phiri royal lineages (see chapter 21).

moasy: a priest (in Madagascar).

mogho-naaba (a title): the Naaba of the Mossi country.

mogyemogye ('ceremonial jaw-bone'): an Asante wine jar used for pouring libations on the Golden Stool.

Monomotapa: see *mwene mutapa*.

montamba: among the Bobangi of the Congo basin, a slave sold by his kin.

montonge: a captured slave (among the Bobangi).

moyo: heart, in the Rozvi empire; soul, spirit in Kikongo.

mpasi (Kikongo): suffering, poverty, need, calamity or affliction.

mphande: shells, among the Tumbuka of northern Zambezia.

mpok: a Lunda broadsword.

m'polio: a catfish (in Bambara).

mpungi: the sacred shrine of the Pare of Tanzania.

mubata: see *babuta*.

mubika: see *babika*.

mugabe ('the milker') or *mukama* (pl. *bakama*): king (in Bunyoro and Buganda).

muhanuro: an annual festival in Burundi, during which royal authority and the drums symbolizing it were renewed, and which celebrated the sowing of sorghum, and determined the most favourable date for this in a country with a long rainy season.

muhutu (pl. *bahutu*): ethnic group in Burundi, Rwanda and several other states in eastern and central Africa.

muidzu: the country's chief justice (in Kongo).

mukama: see *mugabe*.

mukomondera: a cultivation system through which the Shona used to obtain grain during famine.

mulatto (Spanish *mulato*, from *mulo*, mule): one who is the offspring of a European and a black; also used loosely for anyone of mixed race resembling a *mulatto*.

mulopwe: the title of the Luba king which signified the indivisibility of power that could not be shared.

multazims (Arabic): the bidders who collected taxes from the peasants.

munaki: a prophetess (in Kongo).

mupeto: in the Mutapa empire, forcible confiscation.

muteferrikas: the personal guard of the vice-regent of Egypt; the personal guard of a sultan.

muud al-hūrum or *muudul horma*: in the Senegal Futa, an annual tribute payable in grain (grain tax) to the Moors.

mvila: clans (in Kikongo).

mwami (pl. *bami*): the royal title of the former kings of Rwanda and Burundi.

mwant or *mwaant*: the chiefly title to which the name of the first Luba king (Yav or Yaav) was added to become the imperial title.

mwant yav: the highest Luba/Lunda title meaning 'Lord Yav', 'Lord of the Viper', referring to the distance between king and mortals: emperor.

mwene mutapa or *monomatapa* ('lord of metals', 'master of pillage'): a title borne by a line of kings who ruled over a country rich in gold, copper and iron, whence the title 'lord of metals'. This country lay between the Zambezi and Limpopo rivers, in what is now Zimbabwe and Mozambique, from the fourteenth to the seventeenth century. It was often called the empire of the Mwene Mutapa, and is associated with the site known as Great Zimbabwe in south-western Zimbabwe.

mwine Munza: a Luba title meaning 'master of Munza'.

mwisikongo: the nobles, one of the strata in Kongo society.

naaba (a Mossi title): chief.

naabiiga (pl. *naabiise*): Mossi chief's son.

naabiise: see *naabiiga*.

nāʾib (literally 'substitute, delegate, deputy'): the term applied generally to any person appointed as deputy of another in an official position, and more especially, in the Mamluk and Dihli sultanates, to designate: 1) the deputy or lieutenant of the sultan and 2) the governors of the chief provinces. In its most common form, in Persian and Turkish as well as later Arabic, *nāʾib* signified a judge substitute, or delegate of the *ḳāḍī* in the administration of law.

nakombga: see *nakombse*.

nakombse (sing. *nakombga*) (Mossi): princes of the blood; sons or descendants of sons of princes who had not become chiefs, the royal *nakombse* = the royal lineage.

nangatoobe: the upper caste (in Takrūr).

napusum: Mossi ceremonies of greeting the king.

nawab: king.

ndoki (pl. *bandoki*): worker of spells, sorcerer (in Kongo).

ndulu: a Kikuyu green vegetable.

neftenia: landed élite, landed nobility.

nere: an African tree whose roots and seeds are used in traditional medicine.

ngaailiino (Tio): in Kongo, the official responsible for collecting tribute and heading the administration.

nganga: in Bantu languages, healer; sorcerer; medicine man; in Kongo, the recognized term for a religious expert, especially in *nkisi*.

nganga ngombo: diviners (in Kongo).

ngiri: a secret society for princes only (in Bamum).

ngola: a title born by the king of Ndongo, a state to the south of Kongo.

njoldi: symbolic payments attaching to the master of the land; annual ground rent.

nkangi ('the saviour'): in Kongo, a crucifix which was the emblem of the judicial power.

nkende: a grey cercopithecus (a genus of long-tailed African monkeys comprising the guenons and related forms) used as a taboo by the kings of Bujiji.

nkisi: the term, which means 'initiation; magic power; mystic powers; spirit; ancestral force; sacred medicine; idol; fetish', designates, in Kongo, the ideology of royalty derived from religious conceptions in general, in which three important cults played a role: ancestor worship, the worship of territory spirits and the worship of royal charms.

nkobi: a talisman (in Kikongo).

nkoron: deep-mining (in Akan).

nkuluntu ('old one'): the elder; hereditary village chiefs (in Kongo).

noguna: the *mai*'s court (in Borno).

nono (a title): in Kebbi (Hausaland), the dignitary who collected the milk and butter intended for the sovereign.

nthlava: the sandy soils where the Hlengwe used to build their homesteads.

ntufia: the sacred fire lit at his coronation by each king (*maloango*) of Loango, and which was to burn until his death.

nyamankala: the caste system (in Mande).

Nyarubanga (the Luo word for 'sent by god'): in northern Uganda, the period of droughts and famines that ended with the great famine of 1617-21, accompanied by a disease which wiped out the cattle herds.

nzambi mpungu ('supreme creator', 'superior spirit'): the way the king of Kongo was addressed.

nzimbu (shells of *Olivancilaria nana*): shells used as currency in the kingdom of Kongo.

nzo longo (association in Kongo): an initiation cult for boys.

oba (in Edo): the title of the founder of the ancient Kingdom of Benin, holder of religious and political powers.

obeah (or *obi*): an African religion, probably of Asante origin, characterized by the use of sorcery and magic ritual; also: a charm or fetish used in *obeah* and the influence of *obeah* (e.g. put *obeah* on a person).

obi: an Igbo term, of probable Yoruba origin, for king or chief. The *obi* was appointed by the *oba* of Benin.

odjak: a corps of imperial troops introduced in Egypt by Sultan Selim I; also Turkish fortresses and garrisons.

ohene: the king of the Kumasi state.

ôkoo (*makoko*): king (among the Tio).

okro or *okra*: a tall annual plant (*Hibiseus* or *Abelmoschus esculentus*) indigenous to Africa, and its green seed-pods, used for soup, salad and pickles (also called *gumbo*).

omanhene: the king of the Akwamu and Denkyira empires.

ombiasa: often translated as 'sacerdotal person'; priest; medicine man; doctor, etc.; *ombiasa* encompass a number of functions and have a number of categories into which they are subdivided among the Malagasy.

omukama: king.

oni: king (e.g. the *oni* of Ife).

oranmiyan: title of Oranyan, a son of Oduduwa (the founder and first *oni* of Ife) and the legendary founder of the Yoruba kingdom of Ọyọ, who is stated to have reigned at both Ife and Benin before moving to Ọyọ; now the title of a god.

orkoiyot (pl. *orkoik*): a spiritual leader (among the Nandi); also, a traditional leader (in Kenya).

osafohene: war leader in the Akwamu and Denkyira states.

ovimbali or *quimbares*: the Afro-Portuguese (in Kongo).

ozo: a high-ranking person (in the Igbo hierarchy).

panga (Swahili): a large broad-bladed knife used in Africa for heavy cutting (as of brush or bananas) and also as a weapon (machete).

pasha (Turkish): honorary title attaching to senior office, particularly of military commander and provincial governor, in the Ottoman empire.

pastas (Portuguese): 1,000 pastas = 800,000 *cruzados* (c. 1756–57) – see *cruzado*.

piny (pl. *pinje*): the territory of a Luo sub-ethnic group.

(the royal) *pogsyure* (*napogsyure*) system: a system of capitalizing and distributing women (among the Mossi).

pombe (Swahili): in Central and East Africa, a (possibly intoxicating) drink made by fermenting many kinds of grain and some fruits.

pombeiros (in Portuguese): agents from *pombo*; barefoot *mulatto* merchants.

prazeros: in the *prazo* system, a dominant class, holder of the crown lands (*prazos*); estate-owners.

prazos (Portuguese): crown lands; agricultural estates; the *prazo* was also a Portuguese land-tenure system.

prazos da coroa (Portuguese): crown land estates.

presidios (Portuguese): towns.

quimbares: see *ovimbali*.

raia (from Arabic *raʿīyah*, flock, herd, subjects, peasants): a non-Muslim subject of the Sultan of Turkey, subject to payment of such taxes as the *djizya* (poll tax) and the *kharādj* (land tax). (See the *dhimmī* of Vol. III).

raʿīs (or *reis*): a Muslim chief or ruler, a Muslim ship's captain.

rakire: joking relationship (in Mossi).

Ramāḍān: the ninth month of the Muslim lunar calendar, during which Muslims observe a fast (*ṣaum*).

ras (Amharic *rās*, head, chief, from Arabic *ra'īs*) (a title): an Ethiopian king, prince, or feudal lord also, the ruler of an Ethiopian province.

al-Rashīd (Arabic): an honorific title meaning 'the Just'.

(the) *Reconquista*: the process of Christian resistance to Muslim domination and the wars to eliminate Islam from the peninsula, covering the period between 722 (the battle of Covadonga) and 1492 (the fall of Granada).

renilemy: the privileged, in Mahafaly society (Madagascar).

reth: king, in Shillukland.

rima (a Mossi title – from *ri*, 'to absorb or eat food that is not chewed'): king.

rimbe: see *dimo*.

ringu (from *ri* – see above, under *rima*): enthronement.

riyāsa (Arabic): leadership.

rohandrian: the name of the highest Zafindraminia estate in Madagascar.

rukonkesh or *lukonkeshia* (Luba/Lunda title): the queen-mother and head of the logistics for the court.

runde: slave villages (in Futa Jallon).

saburu (a title in Hausaland): the official responsible for security on the roads.

saff (pl. *sufuf*) (Arabic): a confederation formed by alliances between *kabilas*.

sāliyāne (Arabic): annual salaries.

sampy: the royal divinity guaranteeing the well-being of the Imerina state (Madagascar).

sandjak (from Turkish *sanjāk*, literally, flag, standard): in the former Turkish empire, one of the administrative districts into which an *eyalet* or *vilayet* (province) was divided.

sandjak bey (a title, in Egypt): the governor of a *sandjak*; the highest military and administrative personnel of a district.

sandjak-beylik: the most important and fundamental military and administrative unit of the Ottoman empire grouped, regionally, under the authority of a *beylerbey*.

san'dyon: trade slaves (in Bambara).

sango: the thunder cult (in the Ọyọ religious system).

santu (Kikongo): a type of cross; a crucifix, but also a saint.

sarakunan noma: a title meaning 'master of the crops' (in Hausaland).

sarauta: kingship (in Hausaland).

sarki (pl. *sarakuna*) (a title): head of state; chief; king (in Hausaland).

sarkin (a title): chief; king (in Hausaland).

sarkin lifidi (a title in Hausaland): a general in the heavy cavalry division.

satigi (a title in Futa Toro, meaning 'the great ful'): ruler.

sebbe: see *ceddo*.

serdar: the commander of the military operating within or beyond Egypt's borders.

serin jakk (a title in Kayor): the *serin jakk* devoted themselves to religious activities and teaching.

serin lamb: agents of central government (in Kayor) responsible for the defence of the frontiers.

shangwa: famine (in Shona).

sharī'a (literally 'way', 'good road' in Arabic): detailed code of conduct; the *sharī'a* comprises the precepts governing the ritual of worship, standards of behaviour and rules of living. It consists of laws that prescribe, permit and distinguish between true and false. The Ḳur'ānic prescriptions it covers are complemented by prohibitions and explanations contained in the law (*fikh*). The sources of the Islamic *sharī'a* are the Ḳur'ān and the *ḥadīth*.

sharīf (Arabic pl. *shurafā'*): literally 'noble'; an honorary title given to all the descendants of 'Alī and of Fāṭima.

shaykh (Arabic pl. *mashāyikh*): old man; chief of an Arab *kabīla*; spiritual master; title given to the founders of mystical brotherhoods, to great scholars and to teachers.

Shaykh al-Balad (Arabic): an unofficial honorary title, only indicating a senior among the Egyptian *beys* (senior grandee).

sība (Arabic): dissident blocks.

siddi: one of the terms used to denote blacks or African slaves in Asia.

soba: petty chief, leaders (in Angola).

sombili: (ongoing) custom; prerogative (practised by the Zafirambo in Madagascar) of slaughtering domesticated animals.

sonda (sing. *sondre*) (Mossi): collective names or mottoes.

sorabe (or *volan'Onjatsy*) (in Malagasy): Arabic script used to transcribe the Malagasy language; Arabic Malagasy characters; manuscript in the Antemoro language written in Arabic characters. These are *katibo*'s (scribes specializing in the writing and interpretation of the *sorabe*) traditions.

ṣūfī: literally 'dressed in wool', from the Arabic root, *ṣūf*, meaning 'wool', to denote 'the practice of wearing the woollen robe' (*labs a-ṣūf*), hence the act of devoting oneself to the mystic life on becoming what is called in Islam a *ṣūfī*: an adept of Muslim mysticism (*Ṣūfīsm* or *taṣāwwuf*)

ṣūfī tarīkas: see *tarīka*.

Ṣūfīsm (*taṣawwuf* in Arabic): ascetic Islamic mysticism originating in the eighth century and developing especially in Persia into a system of elaborate symbolism of which the goal is communion with the deity through contemplation and ecstasy.

sugedi: grass matting (in Kanuri).

suk: an Arab market or market-place.

sūk: an Arab market or market-place, a souk, a bazaar; shops grouped by corporations.

sulke: coats of mail (in Hausaland).

sultan: the sovereign or chief ruler of a Muslim country; especially (formerly) the sovereign of Turkey; also formerly, a prince or king's son, a high officer.

swan mulopwe: heir-presumptive and commander of the Lunda army.

swan murund or *swana mulunda* (a Luba/Lunda title): the symbolic mother of the society; symbolic queen–mother named Rweej.

tafsīr (Arabic): commentary of the Ḳur'an; exegesis.

talakawa (sing. *talaka*): the ruled; in Hausa society, serfs; free commoners; the poor; poverty-stricken farmers and herdsmen of Hausaland and the Niger-Chad area.

talba: head of police and magistrate (in Borno).

talse: Mossi commoners.

tara (a Hausa title meaning 'the Council of nine'): in Zamfara, Gobir and Kano, designated an electoral college responsible for the appointment of the successor to the throne from among the princes.

tarīka (Arabic pl. *turuk*): literally 'way'; association or brotherhood (each *tarīka* bears the name of its founder); congregation, *Ṣūfī* religious brotherhood; local centre of a religious brotherhood; lodge of brotherhoods.

ta'rīkh (Arabic): history in general, annals, chronicles; usually synonymous with 'historical account'. It is the title of a great many historical works, like *Ta'rīkh al-Sūdān* (the history of the Sūdān, or Negroes of West Africa – see *Bilād al-Sūdān*); *Ta'rīkh al-Andalus* (the history of Andalusia), etc.

tasobnamba ('masters of war' in Mossi): war chiefs.

tata: a fort (in Bambara).

Teen: a title (in Kayor).

tengsoba ('the master of the land' in Mossi): earth priest.

tenzi: epic poems (in Kiswahili).

terras da coroa: in the *prazo* system, a Portuguese crown property.

tingimaro: title of a ruler (in Madagascar).

tobe (Kanuri): large open cotton gowns either plain or dyed blue.

tompon-menakely (a Malagasy title meaning 'masters-of-the-fief'): chiefs of village fiefs.

tompon-tany ('masters of the land'): original inhabitants (in Madagascar).

ton (Bambara): an association of boys circumcised at the same time, political association.

ton-den (Bambara): association members.

ton-dyon ('captives of the *ton*', in Bambara) mostly captives or former captives taken in war.

tonjon: crown slaves (at the *mansa*'s court).

too: millet paste that forms the staple diet among the Bambara.

too-daga: *too* pot (in Bambara).

Torodo: the Torodo revolution of 1776 in Futa Toro was begun by the Torodo *marabout* movement which took much of its inspiration from the success of the *djihād* in Bandu and Futa Jallon at the beginning of the eighteenth century. It was a revolt of the small peasants against both the *muudul horma*, imposed by the Moorish *kabīlas*, and the oppressive eastern Muslim tax system introduced by the Islamized Denyanke aristocracy.

Trek (the Great Trek – 1834–39): an emigration movement of the Cape Boers towards the Vaal and the Orange following the British thrust in South Africa.

trekboer: the *trekboers* were the Boer immigrant farmers who went across the Orange river in search of land before the Great Trek. They settled mostly in the south of what later became the Orange Free State.

tshidie: a general council (at the court of the Luba king). tshihangu: the court of the Luba king.

tsi-mihety: the collective name adopted by the Tsimihety (Madagascar) to indicate, by refusing to cut their hair, non-submission to Maroserana authority.

tsovolo: name given by the Hlengwe to the basalt soils.

tubung ('masters of the land'): heads of small political units (among the Luba/Lunda).

tunka (a Soninke title): king.

turaki: a protocol officer in Katsina (Hausaland).

tweapea: (Akan) chewing-sticks.

ubandawaki (a title): a military leader (in Zamfara and Gobir, Hausaland).

ubuhake: in Rwanda, a type of clientele link (see *buhake*).

ubugabite: a type of clientele link (in Burundi).

uki: a type of beer made by the Akamba; it is fermented for longer than that of neighbouring communities.

ukoo: lineage, descent.

'ulamā' (sing. *'ālim*) (Arabic): Muslim scholars, erudite persons, doctors of law or theologians.

undi: powerful ruler in the Maravi confederation in the eighteenth century.

vaha: a medium.

valohazomanga: the commoners in Mahafaly society (Madagascar).

vashambadzi: traders; African merchant class, in the Zambezi region.

veli: governor of a province (see *wāli*).

vodun: an African religion.

(the) *Volafotsy* ('white silver'): in Madagascar, the collaterals of the ruling Maroserana, descendants of white silver sons of non-Maroserana women and Maroserana royals.

volamena ('red silver', i.e. gold): in Mahafaly (Madagascar), the tombs of the Zafivolamena (sons-of-gold), the ruling Maroserana branch among the Sakalava.

wa'azi: sermons (in Hausaland).

wakf (Arabic pl. *aukāf*): 1) an Islamic endowment of property to be held in trust and used for a charitable or religious purpose; 2) a Muslim religious or charitable foundation created by an endowed trust fund; 3) a juridical-religious measure taken by the owner of land or other real estate to vest its ownership in a religious institution (a mosque) or some public or social facility (a *madrasa*, hospital, etc.) and/or his or her descendants.

wālī (pl. *wulāt*) (from Turkish *vālī*): governor or vice-governor of a province (*wilāya*).

wamagi: district chiefs, in the Ugweno state (Tanzania).

Wambai: a Kano title.

wasili: North African traders (in Borno).

wasiliram: in Borno, a special quarter assigned to *wasili*.

wazir (Arabic) (title of the successors of S͟hayk͟h Muḥammad Abū Likaylik): in the Ottoman empire. Title of high-ranking state officials or ministers and of the highest dignitaries; holders of positions analogous to that of Muslim viziers; vice-regents, viceroys.

woloso ('born in the house', in Mande): the status acquired by a woman purchased by a community as soon as she produced a child. A man could also acquire the same status as soon as his master had sufficient confidence in him; house-born slave.

xaadi: a title (in Kayor).

yav: see *mwant yav*.

Yadega-tenga: the land of Yadega (Yatenga), in Mossi country.

Yatenga-naaba (a Mossi title): the king of Yatenga.

yerima: the governor of the northern provinces (in Borno).

yiiri (pl. *yiiya*): the household, the second level in the Mossi patrilineal and patrilocal society.

zabyuya: a ritual announcement at the ceremonial investiture of Mossi chiefs.

zaka (pl. *zakse*): the smaller unit in the Mossi patrilineal and patrilocal society.

zakāt (Arabic): compulsory alms-giving that, for any Muslim enjoying a certain income, consists of distributing a proportion ranging from 2.5 per cent to 10 per cent – to the poor and to a specific category of the needy. The *zakāt* is the fourth pillar of Islam.

zakse: see *zaka*.

Zanna Arjinama: a titled official (in Borno).

zāwiya (pl. *zawāyā*) (Arabic): religious brotherhood; brotherhood seat (and funerary sanctuary of the founding saint); cultural centre; when fortified and manned by defenders of the faith, it is called *ribāṭ*.

zombi or *zombie* (of Niger-Congo origin; akin to Kongo and Kimbundu and Tshiluba *nzambi*, god, Kongo *zumbi*, good-luck fetish, image): 1) the deity of the python in West African voodoo cults; the snake-deity of the voodoo rite in Haiti and the southern USA; the supernatural power or essence that according to voodoo belief may enter into and reanimate a dead body, a will-less and speechless human in the West Indies capable only of automatic movement held to have died and been reanimated but often believed to have been drugged into a catalepsy for the hours of interment; 2) a person thought to resemble the so-called walking dead; a person markedly strange or abnormal in mentality, appearance, or behaviour.

zuwaya or *insilimen*: Berber or Sudanese *marabout* groups.

Zwayiya (the *Zwayiya marabouts*): a branch of the *marabout* movement.

Index